# Financial Intermediaries: An Introduction

# Financial Intermediaries: An Introduction

## Benton E. Gup

The University of Tulsa

Houghton
Mifflin
Company

Boston

Atlanta
Dallas
Geneva, Illinois
Hopewell, New Jersey
Palo Alto
London

Table 3–1 on page 50 is copyright © by the United States Savings and Loan League 1974 Fact Book. Printed in U.S.A.

Library of Congress Catalogue Card Number 75–31005

ISBN: 0–395–19828–3

To the Tulsa bankers who provide support for The University of Tulsa Chair of Banking and Finance. Without their support, this book would not have been possible.

# Contents

# Figures

Figures

# Tables

Tables

Tables

Tables

Tables

# Preface

*Financial Intermediaries* is the modern term for financial institutions. This book emphasizes change—the perpetual shifting of assets, liabilities, forms of organization, laws and regulations—in response to new economic developments.

The text was designed for courses dealing with financial institutions. It can also be used to supplement courses in money and banking and financial markets.

*Financial Intermediaries* was written for students who want to know what is happening now in the financial world and what changes are likely to occur in the future. This goal is accomplished by going beyond the traditional approach that concentrated mainly on describing assets and liabilities of major financial institutions. It explains the major trends and problems these institutions are facing as they cope with a dynamic economy. In addition, institutions such as stockbrokerage firms, real estate investment trusts, private pension plans, mortgage banking companies, and some government credit agencies are also covered. Finally, current issues such as the bankruptcy of some pension plans, electronic funds transfer, and the recent collapse of hundreds of stockbrokerage firms are examined.

Students with a minimal background in economics or finance should have no difficulty with the text. The emphasis is on concepts rather than quanti-

tative techniques. The few quantitative techniques discussed here are explained in simple terminology; others can be found in the appendixes.

*Financial Intermediaries* was also written with the professor in mind. Professors and interested readers who wish to go beyond the material presented in each chapter are provided with bibliographies, detailed footnotes, end-of-chapter discussion questions, and appendixes. Some of the appendixes consist of speeches on specific topics by experts in those fields. One appendix contains a speech dealing with bank reserves by Arthur Burns, Chairman, Board of Governors of the Federal Reserve System. At the end of the book there is an appendix containing Flow of Funds accounts covering all the financial institutions and credit markets for a several year period. The Flow of Funds can be used to illustrate financial relationships between various sectors of the economy. For example, students tend to get a better understanding of, say, disintermediation if they can trace the flow of funds out of financial institutions and into marketable securities.

Because *Financial Intermediaries* is about what is happening now, periodicals such as *The Wall Street Journal* and the *Federal Reserve Bulletin* are important supplements. Articles and data from these suggested sources keep the text up-to-date and keep the material relevant for the students.

This is the appropriate time and place to thank those who aided in the preparation of this book. I am particularly indebted to former students—G. Robert Harrison, Bill Simms, Jack Brown, Bill Snow, Virginia Estes Goosen and Sarah L. Wilson—who did a lot of the leg work and research for me. In addition, I want to acknowledge the following persons who reviewed or made suggestions on various chapters: Norman Bailey (University of Iowa); S. Lees Booth (National Consumer Finance Association); William Carlson (Duquesne University); Robert H. Cramer (University of Wisconsin, Madison); Robert Crowe (Memphis State University); Kenneth Frantz (Boston College); William F. Ford (American Bankers Association); William C. Freund (New York Stock Exchange); John Hand (Auburn University); Kenneth Holcomb (University of Tulsa); Panos Konstas (Federal Deposit Insurance Corporation); Frank Mastrapasqua (Capital Management, Inc.); Lucille S. Mayne (Case Western Reserve University); Neil B. Murphy (University of Maine); Walter Polner (ASCU); Allen R. Soltow and Stephen Steib (University of Tulsa); John Stowe (Florida Atlantic University); Gary Tallman (Kent State University); Kenneth J. Thugerson (U.S. Savings and Loan League); G. Dale Weight (Syracuse Savings Bank); and Wilbur Widicus (Oregon State University). Particular thanks is due to T. Gregory Morton of the University of Connecticut for preparing the instructor's manual and the

questions at the end of each chapter. Finally, a very special thanks to my wife, Joanne, who edited virtually every page of this manuscript.

Although the above persons and others sought to improve the text, I am responsible for its errors and shortcomings.

Benton E. Gup
The University of Tulsa

# Financial Intermediaries: An Introduction

# 1

# Introduction

Part 1 consists of two chapters that provide an introduction to the economic function of financial institutions and the concepts that can be used to analyze them.

Chapter 1, "The Financial System," defines the economic role of financial intermediaries and discusses the types of securities held by financial intermediaries.

Chapter 2, "Portfolio Theory and Flow of Funds: The Tools of Analysis," introduces two concepts: the first, portfolio theory, helps to explain why some changes occur in financial assets; the second, Flow of Funds, shows the financial interrelationships between different types of economic units in the United States.

# 1

# The financial system

## Introduction

Financial intermediaries are economic units whose principal function is managing the financial assets of other economic units—business concerns and individuals. Thus they bring savers and borrowers together by selling securities to savers for money and lending that money to borrowers. Financial intermediaries have experienced rapid growth in the United States, not only in dollar volume, but in the extent of their role in the social, economic, and political system of the United States. They have an important influence on every business concern or individual who saves or borrows money. Later in this chapter we will consider business concerns and individuals independently, to see how they interact with financial intermediaries and form with them the three components of the financial system of the United States.

The term *financial intermediary* can be applied to a variety of institutions, some of which are listed below.

Commercial banks                    Investment companies
Mutual savings banks                 Stockbrokers and stock dealers
Savings and loan associations        Quasi-governmental agencies
Credit unions                        Finance companies
Insurance companies                  Leasing companies
Pension funds                        Trust companies

3

Although this list is not complete, it gives an indication of some of the types of institution that are classified as financial intermediaries. To keep our study of the inherently complex financial system within manageable limits, the role of government borrowing will not be examined in our initial discussion of financial intermediaries. However, the process of borrowing by business concerns is discussed in detail, and is similar to the process of government borrowing.

Given this definition of financial intermediaries—economic units whose principal business is managing financial assets—some business concerns could be considered quasi-financial intermediaries. For example, the American Express Company is in the international travel service, but it also sells traveler's checks and insurance; the large automobile manufacturers have subsidiary companies to finance their automobile sales; the major oil companies have large credit card departments. Therefore, some of the comments that will be made about the regular types of financial intermediaries can also apply to such quasi-financial intermediaries.

**Intermediation**

Financial intermediaries could not exist without intermediation, the process which takes place when business concerns and individuals invest funds in financial intermediaries such as banks and savings and loan associations. These investors receive claims with stable market values and high *liquidity* (an investor's ability to convert securities to cash on short notice with little or no loss in current value), such as demand deposits (checking accounts) and time and savings accounts. In turn, the financial intermediaries invest the funds in various kinds of primary securities (stocks, bonds, mortgages, etc.) that have unstable or fluctuating market values and low liquidity (see Tables 1–3 and 1–6). In essence, financial intermediaries change risky primary securities (assets) into less risky secondary securities (liabilities). Primary and secondary securities will be discussed in detail later in this chapter.

### Benefits of Intermediation

The intermediation process enables individuals to invest their funds safely and business firms to borrow funds, so that the borrowing-lending process in our economic system functions smoothly. Imagine what would happen if General Motors wanted to borrow $100 million and had to seek out individuals who would lend it that amount. Or, assume that you had $500 in surplus funds to lend. How would you as an individual find a borrower who wanted that exact amount? Fortunately, neither you nor General Motors has to face that problem because financial institutions serve as intermediaries, pooling the funds of individual savers and lending them to borrowers.

There are other benefits of the intermediation process. Pooling of funds provides certain administrative economies of scale, since it is less costly to administer one $10-million loan than it is to administer ten $1-million loans. Equally important, pooling of independent funds reduces an individual's per dollar risk with respect to loan default, and many types of secondary securities are insured, thereby reducing investors' risk in holding secondary deposits (e.g., the Federal Deposit Insurance Corporation insures bank deposits). On the other side of the balance sheet, laws and regulatory authorities frequently set guidelines concerning the type and quality of investments that financial intermediaries can deal in. Since some financial institutions specialize in selected types of financing, they can lower costs to the borrowers. For example, some life insurance companies have particular expertise in large real estate developments. Real estate developers can reasonably expect to borrow at a slightly lower cost from these insurance companies than from institutions that specialize in other types of investments.

On balance, the process of intermediation is carried on in a relatively efficient manner, "relative" because certain laws and regulations, such as usury laws and interest-rate ceilings on time and savings deposits, impede the movement of funds.

## Business Concerns

One of the principal "customers" of financial intermediaries is nonfinancial business concerns, businesses which produce goods and services for profit. Most business concerns can be classified as sole proprietorships, partnerships, or corporations.[1] In order to understand how a business concern is distinguished from a financial intermediary, it is helpful to examine a hypothetical corporate *balance sheet* (a statement of the assets and liabilities of a business at a specified date), as shown in Table 1–1.

Table 1–1

Hypothetical balance sheet for nonfinancial business concerns

| Assets | Liabilities | |
|---|---|---|
| Financial assets (cash, accts. receivable) | Trade debt | |
| Real assets (plant, equipment, inventories) | Bonds & notes | |
| | Mortgages | Primary securities |
| | Bank loans | |
| | Net worth | |
| | Stocks | |
| | Retained earnings | |

[1]For legal purposes, a *sole proprietor* is one who has the legal right or exclusive title to a business; a *partnership* is a voluntary contract between two or more people who agree to carry on a business together on terms of mutual participation in its profits and losses; a *corporation* is an artificial person or legal entity with rights, privileges, and liabilities separate from those of its owners.

## Assets

The assets of business concerns vary according to the type of business. For example, the real assets of wholesale and retail businesses consist largely of inventories, while those of industrial concerns consist mainly of capital goods, such as factories and equipment used in the production process. In addition to real assets, business concerns have financial assets that include cash, short-term securities, and accounts receivable.

## Liabilities

The other side of the balance sheet consists of liabilities and net worth. Liabilities arise when business concerns borrow money. When a business borrows money from a bank, the loan becomes a liability of the business and gives the bank a claim against it.

The data in Table 1–2 show the total liabilities of U.S. corporate nonfinancial business divided into major borrowing categories. They reveal that corporations borrow their largest amount of money by selling corporate bonds and that trade debt (accounts payable), bank loans, and mortgages account for most of the remaining liabilities. It should be noted that large business concerns borrow money by selling claims against themselves: a bond is a claim against the issuing firm for a stated amount of interest, plus the principal amount. While these claims are liabilities of the issuing firm, they are financial assets of the one who holds the claim. If General Motors sells a bond to you, you hold a financial asset (the bond) which is a liability of General Motors.

## Net Worth

Net worth represents the ownership of a business corporation. The stockholders are the owners of the company and are entitled to receive any dividends declared. In addition, they have a limited voice in the company's

Table 1–2

Total liabilities of corporate nonfinancial business (year-end outstandings 1972)

| Liabilities | Billions of dollars | Percentage of total |
|---|---|---|
| Corporate bonds | 198.3 | 24.3 |
| Trade debt (accounts payable) | 183.1 | 22.5 |
| Bank loans[a] | 147.4 | 18.1 |
| Mortgages | 202.1 | 24.8 |
| Other liabilities | 83.5 | 10.3 |
| Total | 814.4 | 100.0 |

[a] Other than mortgages
Source: Board of Governors of the Federal Reserve System, Flow of Funds Accounts

management, generally the right to vote on certain major decisions facing the corporation, such as mergers and stock options.

## Financial Intermediaries

Unlike those of nonfinancial business concerns, the assets of financial intermediaries consist of primary securities and real assets, while their liabilities consist of secondary securities (Table 1–3). Real assets include the land, buildings, and equipment that financial institutions need to carry on their business.

### Primary Securities

Primary securities are all claims (debt and equity securities) against business concerns and individuals. In the case of business concerns, bonds, notes, bank loans, mortgages, and stocks are examples of claims or primary securities. In the case of individuals, they are home mortgages and consumer installment debt. Table 1–4 shows how these liabilities of business concerns and households are held as assets by financial intermediaries.

Some financial intermediaries specialize in dealing in particular types of primary securities. Savings and loan associations specialize in mortgages, while mutual funds specialize in stocks and bonds. In contrast, commercial banks invest in mortgages, commercial and industrial loans, consumer loans, and other types of loans. Primary securities are examined in more detail in Appendix 1A.

Many types of primary securities are considered risky by investors for two reasons. First, the market value of primary securities can change dramatically. For example, in 1973 and 1974 stock prices dropped sharply. Also, in recent years the market values of outstanding bonds and mortgages have varied widely. In the case of bonds and mortgages, the market price varies

---

Table 1–3

Hypothetical balance sheet for financial intermediaries

| Assets | Liabilities | |
| --- | --- | --- |
| Primary securities | Demand deposits | |
| Real assets | Time and savings deposits | |
| | Insurance and pension fund reserves | Secondary securities |
| | Mutual fund shares | |
| | Stocks | |
| | Net worth | |
| | Retained earnings | |

Table 1–4

Primary securities

| Business concerns | | Financial intermediaries | | Individuals | |
|---|---|---|---|---|---|
| Assets | Liabilities | Assets | Liabilities | Assets | Liabilities |
| | Primary securities ⟶ (e.g., bank loans, bonds, stocks) | Primary securities | | | Primary securities (e.g., consumer loans, mortgages) |

inversely with the level of market interest rates: when market interest rates go up, the market price of outstanding bonds and mortgages goes down. A further explanation of this and some of the factors affecting stock prices is found in Appendix 1A. Second, because the market values of primary securities can change dramatically in short periods of time, they may not be considered liquid. For example, one can sell stocks on short notice, but one may not be able to sell a real estate mortgage on short notice without realizing a substantial loss.

## Secondary Securities

Just as business concerns sell primary securities to obtain funds, financial intermediaries sell secondary securities to obtain funds to finance their activities. Secondary securities are claims against financial intermediaries, and may take the form of demand deposits (checking accounts), savings accounts, certificates of deposit, life insurance policies, and, in some cases, bonds and other types of securities. Table 1–5 shows how liabilities of financial intermediaries, such as demand deposits and savings accounts, are held as assets by business concerns and individuals. Table 1–6 illustrates the different primary and secondary securities held by several types of financial intermediaries.

Table 1–5

Secondary securities

| Business concerns | | Financial intermediaries | | Individuals | |
|---|---|---|---|---|---|
| Assets | Liabilities | Assets | Liabilities | Assets | Liabilities |
| Secondary securities (e.g., demand deposits, time deposits) | | | Secondary securities ⟶ (demand deposits, savings accounts, mutual fund shares, etc.) | Secondary securities | |

Table 1-6

Examples of securities at selected financial intermediaries

| Financial intermediary | Primary security | Secondary security |
|---|---|---|
| Savings and loan associations | Mortgages | Savings shares |
| Mutual funds | Stocks<br>Bonds | Mutual fund shares |
| Life insurance companies | Stocks<br>Bonds<br>Mortgages | Life insurance policies<br>or certificates |
| Credit unions | Consumer loans | Credit union shares |
| Commercial banks | Commercial and industrial<br>loans<br>Consumer loans<br>Mortgages | Demand deposits<br>Savings accounts<br>Certificates of<br>deposit |
| Pension funds | Stocks<br>Bonds | Pension fund reserves |

Secondary securities differ from primary securities in their degree of liquidity and degree of change in market values (see Table 1–7 for selected examples). As noted previously, many types of primary securities have low liquidity and large changes in market value. In contrast, short-term secondary securities, such as savings accounts, have high liquidity and do not change in market value, although certain long-term secondary securities, such as mutual fund shares, do experience large changes in market value.

Table 1-7

Selected characteristics of primary and secondary securities

| Primary securities | Degree of liquidity | Changes in market value |
|---|---|---|
| Stocks | High | Large |
| Bonds | Relatively high | Large |
| Mortgages | Low | Large |
| Loans | Low | N.A.[a] |
| Leases | Low | N.A. |

| Secondary securities | Degree of liquidity | Changes in market value |
|---|---|---|
| Short-term | | |
| Demand deposits | High | No change |
| Savings accounts | High | No change |
| Long-term | | |
| Mutual fund shares | High | Large |
| Pension fund shares | Low | No change |
| Life insurance policy reserves | High | No change |

[a] Not applicable

*Regulations*    The degree to which financial intermediaries deal in particular types of primary and secondary securities and hold particular types of assets and liabilities is largely determined by federal and state laws and regulations. Under federal laws and regulations are found such governing bodies as the Board of Governors of the Federal Reserve System and the Federal Deposit Insurance Corporation, which regulate most of the commercial banking system in the United States. Similarly, the Securities and Exchange Commission regulates stockbrokerage firms, stock exchanges, and investment companies.

## Asset Management

The central problem of asset management is that financial intermediaries must maintain a sufficient amount of liquid assets to satisfy potential withdrawals of funds, while investing their remaining assets profitably. Another factor influencing the types of primary securities held by financial intermediaries is the relative stability of the dollar volume of the secondary securities they sell. When individuals want to withdraw their funds, a financial intermediary can satisfy their claims either by reducing its cash reserves or by borrowing. In the latter case the financial intermediary could pay off a claim by selling additional secondary securities. If the dollar volume of the secondary securities is believed to be stable, the financial institution will make long-term loans (buy long-term primary securities). Conversely, instability and short-term loans go together. For instance, the dollar volume of time and savings deposits at commercial banks may change substantially within a short period of time. In response to the potential instability of these deposits, commercial banks invest a substantial portion of their assets in short-term, liquid primary securities. In contrast, since funds deposited with pension funds are not likely to be withdrawn on short notice and the outflow of these funds is highly predictable, pension funds can invest the bulk of their assets in long-term primary securities.

## Individuals

Individuals constitute the third part of the economic system. The term *individual* is used in the broad sense of the word and refers to "persons" in contrast to "business." One difference between individuals and business is that individuals acquire real assets for the services they provide rather than for use as a capital good. Their real assets are houses, automobiles, and other consumer durables (see Table 1–8).

Their financial assets consist mainly of equity shares (stocks) and secondary securities (such as demand deposits, savings accounts, bonds, insurance and pension fund reserves, and mutual fund shares). These assets are held for the liquidity they provide and for investment purposes.

Table 1–8

Hypothetical balance sheet for individuals

| Assets | Liabilities |
|---|---|
| Secondary securities | Home mortgage debt |
| Primary securities | Consumer credit |
|   Stocks | |
|   Bonds | |
| Real assets | |
|   Houses | |
|   Automobiles | |
|   Consumer durables | Net worth |

Individuals' liabilities consist of home mortgage debt and consumer debt. This statement serves to re-emphasize that individuals acquire real assets for the services they provide instead of financing capital goods. Home mortgage debt is used to finance a place for individuals to live. Similarly, consumer credit is used to finance automobiles, television sets, and other consumer goods. In contrast, a business concern uses mortgage debt to finance a factory or warehouse that is used in the production of other goods.

Another difference between individuals and businesses is that, generally speaking, individuals are considered risk averters. An example of a risk averter is someone who buys fire insurance on his house, accepting a certain small loss (the insurance premium) in preference to the small chance of a large loss (the value of the house).[2] Individuals' aversion to risk is relative. They do not borrow large sums for risky capital investments, but they do borrow to finance mortgages, car loans, and other consumer purchases. In contrast, business firms are willing to take more risks than individuals and invest in risky projects. (The Edsel was such a project.) The final point is that since individuals are mortal, and many business concerns are thought of as perpetual, their investment goals are different.

Within the context of the economic system, individuals are net savers and put their surplus funds in secondary securities. If the investment return on primary securities is significantly higher than the return on secondary securities, they may invest some of their funds in primary securities, but more usually they provide funds to financial intermediaries, who in turn acquire primary securities.

## Interest Rates

A major factor governing the relationships between borrowers and savers is interest rates, the charge paid for the use of credit. The disparity of interest rates among different financial intermediaries may be the decisive factor

[2]Milton Friedman and Leonard J. Savage, "Utility Analysis of Choices Involving Risk," *The Journal of Political Economy*, 56, (August 1948), 279–304.

that determines where an individual—or business concern—chooses to allocate his funds. Business concerns pay interest on their primary securities when they borrow funds, and financial intermediaries pay interest on their secondary securities when they borrow.

Because they influence the allocation of funds, interest rates play a strategic role in the financial system. Low interest rates are conducive to borrowing, while high interest rates may discourage it. Another view is that low interest rates may reflect a lack of demand for funds, while high interest rates reflect strong demand. These statements suggest that interest rates influence and, in turn, are influenced by the supply and demand for funds.

## Determinants

The supply and demand for funds are the basic determinants of market interest rates and are influenced by a variety of factors, including economic conditions, monetary policy, and expectations. Although they tend to lag behind, the levels of interest rates generally conform to business activity.[3] An increasing tempo of business activity is usually accompanied by a rise in interest rates. Conversely, a slowdown in economic activity is accompanied by a decline in interest rates in general and short-term interest rates in particular. Many of the wide swings in market interest rates in the last half of the 1960s and in more recent years can be traced to monetary policy actions.[4] Frequently, current levels of interest rates reflect lagged effects of past monetary actions. Thus, the sharp rise in interest rates from 1967 to 1969 can be attributed to the accelerated monetary expansion in 1967, which stimulated demands for credit.[5] On the other hand, the decline in rates during 1970 reflected easing credit demands in response to slower monetary growth in 1969.

## Expectations

Expectations also affect the supply and demand for funds, and, in turn, interest rates. Investors who expect interest rates on long-term bonds to rise may sell long-term bonds. Rationalizing that a rise in market rates means a decline in market value of long-term bonds, they sell bonds *en masse*,

---

[3]Philip Cagan, "The Influence of Interest Rates on the Duration of Business Cycles," in *Essays on Interest Rates*, ed. Jack M. Guttentag and Philip Cagan (New York: National Bureau of Economic Research, 1969), I, pp. 3–28. A "market"-oriented view of cyclical variations in interest rates can be found in Sidney Homer and Richard I. Johannesen, *The Price of Money, 1946–1969* (New Brunswick, N.J.: Rutgers University Press, 1969), Chapter IX.
[4]For the interested student, a more advanced theoretical discussion of monetary aggregates and interest rates can be found in Albert E. Burger, *The Money Supply Process* (Belmont, Calif.: Wadsworth Publishing Company, 1971), Chapter 7. For a review of the role of interest rates in the monetarist and Keynesian schools of thought see Ronald Teigan, "A Critical Look at Monetarist Economics," *Review,* Federal Reserve Bank of St. Louis (January 1972). An analysis of monetary aggregates and interest rates during 1970 can be found in "Capital Markets and Interest Rates in 1970," *Review,* Federal Reserve Bank of St. Louis (March 1971).
[5]Denis S. Karnosky, "The Significance of Recent Interest Rate Movements," *Review,* Federal Reserve Bank of St. Louis (August 1971).

which can depress bond prices. In some cases, actions based on these expectations result in a self-fulfilling prophecy. For a detailed discussion of bond prices and the expectations theory see Appendixes 1A and 1B.

In conclusion, interest rates are considered here as the price paid for the use of credit. At any given time, the level of interest rates is determined by the supply and demand for funds, which reflect complex interactions within the economy. Interest rates are the price mechanism of the financial system, and they reveal the preference for funds of businesses, individuals, and financial intermediaries.[6] An example would be financial intermediaries buying funds at 5 percent from individuals and simultaneously selling these funds to business concerns at 7 percent. The intermediaries' gross profit is the difference between the average cost of funds (5 percent) and the average return on investments (7 percent). Their operating expenses must also come out of this spread. By offering this service the financial intermediaries help businesses to borrow and expand their real assets, while allowing individuals to invest their funds in relatively safe, liquid securities.

## Summary

In this chapter, three types of economic unit (business concerns, financial intermediaries, and individuals) are used to introduce the reader to the financial system in the United States. The two major themes of the chapter are: 1) the role of financial intermediaries, and 2) the characteristics of the primary and secondary securities used by financial intermediaries. Basically, the role of financial intermediaries is to bring the borrowers and savers of funds together. To accomplish this, they sell secondary securities to savers and buy primary securities from borrowers (Table 1–9).

The principal difference between various financial intermediaries concerns the types of securities they hold as assets or sell as liabilities. All financial

Table 1–9

Primary and secondary securities

| Business concerns | | Financial intermediaries | | Individuals | |
|---|---|---|---|---|---|
| Assets | Liabilities | Assets | Liabilities | Assets | Liabilities |
| Secondary securities | Primary ⟶ securities | Primary securities | Secondary ⟶ securities | Secondary securities | Primary securities |

[6]The notion of revealed consumption preference was examined by Paul Samuelson, "Consumption Theory in Terms of Revealed Preference," *Economica* (November 1948), 243–253.

intermediaries hold as assets primary securities, which are relatively risky because their market prices vary and they may not be liquid, and all financial intermediaries issue as liabilities secondary securities, such as demand deposits, which have stable market values and high liquidity. Once this similarity of all financial intermediaries is understood, it is easy to distinguish between different types by noting the particular primary and secondary securities in which they deal. For example, savings and loan associations deal primarily in mortgages, while pension plans deal mostly in corporate securities, and each issues different secondary securities (savings shares versus pension plan contract certificates). Nevertheless, their roles in the overall scheme of the financial system are the same.

## Questions

1 What are the principal differences between primary and secondary securities?
2 Define the term "financial intermediaries." Do you consider a pawnbroker, a gambling casino, or the Sears Roebuck Company to be financial intermediaries?
3 Define the term "liquidity" and explain how it relates to: demand deposits, common stocks, corporate bonds, mortgages.
4 How do the main financial assets and main liabilities of the individual sector and business sector differ? Why?
5 Discuss the strategic role interest rates play in the financial system.
6 What are some of the major determinants of the level of interest rates?
7 Explain the economic benefits of intermediation.
8 Compare the expectations theory with the market segmentation theory of the term structure of interest rates. How do these theories differ?

# Appendix 1A

# Primary Securities

This appendix takes up issues about primary securities that were introduced in Chapter 1. It examines why the market prices of primary debt securities (bonds) and primary equity securities (stocks) change.

## Debt Securities

One feature of primary securities is that they have uncertain capital value: their market prices fluctuate. There is an inverse relationship between the market price of primary debt securities and the level of market interest rates. When market interest rates rise, the market price of a primary debt security varies so that the *yield to maturity* of that security will be equal to the current level of market interest rates for a similar security. (Yield to maturity is the average percentage yield earned annually from the purchase date to the maturity date and includes both capital gains or losses.) The yield to maturity[7] of a bond can be found by solving the following equation for *r*.

$$P = \frac{C/m}{\left(1 + \frac{r}{m}\right)} + \frac{C/m}{\left(1 + \frac{r}{m}\right)^2} + \frac{C/m}{\left(1 + \frac{r}{m}\right)^3} + \cdots + \frac{C/m}{\left(1 + \frac{r}{m}\right)^{mn}} + \frac{V}{\left(1 + \frac{r}{m}\right)^{mn}}$$

where $P$ = current market price
$C$ = annual income ($) from bond
$m$ = number of payments per year[8]
$n$ = number of years to maturity
$V$ = face value of obligation payable at maturity ($)

The interest rate-price adjustment can be shown by examining the effect of an increase in market interest rates on the market price of a bond. In this example, the bond is used to illustrate the price behavior of all types of primary securities. Suppose a $1,000 bond has a fixed coupon interest rate of 6 percent, which means that the bond pays $60 interest per year, and a maturity date of twenty years, when the principal amount or face value of $1,000 comes due. The market interest rate for a similar newly issued bond is 6 percent. Since the yields on the original bond and similar new issues are identical (6 percent), the market value of the existing bond is $1,000.

---

[7]Yields to maturity for bonds can be found in *Expanded Bond Value Tables* (Boston: Financial Publishing Co.).
[8]Interest on most bonds is paid twice a year.

$$P = \frac{60/2}{\left(1 + \frac{.06}{2}\right)} + \frac{60/2}{\left(1 + \frac{.06}{2}\right)^2} + \frac{60/2}{\left(1 + \frac{.06}{2}\right)^3} + \frac{60/2}{\left(1 + \frac{.06}{2}\right)^{40}} + \frac{\$1,000}{\left(1 + \frac{.06}{2}\right)^{40}} = \$1,000$$

If market interest rates for similar newly issued bonds rise to 8 percent, the original bond's yield to maturity will increase to 8 percent, but, in the process, its market price will decline to $802.

$$P = \frac{60/2}{\left(1 + \frac{.08}{2}\right)} + \frac{60/2}{\left(1 + \frac{.08}{2}\right)^2} + \frac{60/2}{\left(1 + \frac{.08}{2}\right)^3} + \frac{60/2}{\left(1 + \frac{.08}{2}\right)^{40}} + \frac{\$1,000}{\left(1 + \frac{.08}{2}\right)^{40}} = \$802$$

Similarly, it can be shown that, if market interest rates decline to 4 percent, the original bond will sell for $1,274. Thus, bond prices (primary debt securities) and the level of market interest rates are inversely related.

Another reason for the price instability of primary debt securities is the *default risk* of the issuing corporation, the possibility that the company that issued a bond may not be able to make the requisite periodic payments. Although default risk is a factor affecting bond values in recent years, bond defaults have been rare.[9] However, in 1970 one of the largest companies in the United States, Lockheed Aircraft Corporation, teetered on the brink of bankruptcy, and Penn Central actually went bankrupt and defaulted on some of its bonds in the same year. Needless to say, the threat of bankruptcy had an unfavorable effect on the price of the bonds of both Lockheed and Penn Central.

The relationship between market interest rates and market bond prices is depicted in graphic form in Figure 1A–1. In addition, the figure demonstrates how the maturity of an obligation affects this relationship. Basically, the longer the maturity of a bond, the greater will be the effect of market interest rates on the market price of that bond. For example, if market interest rates are 8 percent, the market price of a 6-percent $1,000 bond with fifteen years to maturity will be $827, and with five years to maturity the price will be $989. If the market interest rates declined to 4 percent, the market price of the 6-percent bond with fifteen years to maturity would be $1,224, and with five years to maturity the price would be $1,089. In each case, as the bond approaches maturity, the market value of the bond approaches the face value of that obligation. It follows that, when market interest rates vary, primary debt securities with a long term to maturity will have wider price fluctuations than similar securities with a short term to

[9]For information on corporate bond defaults, see W. Braddock Hickman, *Corporate Bond Quality and Investor Experience* (Princeton, N.J.: Princeton Research, 1958), pp. 141–197. Also see Thomas R. Atkinson, *Trends in Corporate Bond Quality* (New York: Columbia University Press for the National Bureau of Economic Research, 1967), p. 43.

**Figure 1A–1**

Relationship between the market price of a 6-percent, twenty-year $1,000 bond and market interest rates of 8 percent and 4 percent

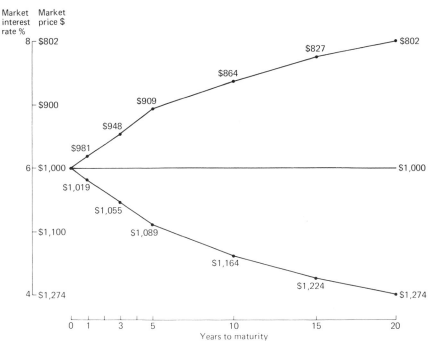

Source: *Expanded Bond Value Tables* (Boston: Financial Publishing Co.)

maturity. Because of this potential fluctuation, investors consider long-term primary debt securities more risky than short-term ones. The extent to which they invest in long-term and short-term securities will be discussed in later chapters.

## Historical Changes

The inverse relationship between primary debt securities and market interest rates is important because wide fluctuations in interest rates are a part of our financial history. As shown in Figure 1A–2, during the 1965–1970 period, market yields of long-term corporate bonds rose irregularly from 4½–5 percent to about 9 percent. After 1970, market interest rates declined somewhat. As a result of the rise in interest rates during the 1965–1970 period, holders of previously issued long-term primary securities saw the value of their securities shrink.

Figure 1A–2

Weekly bond yields[a]

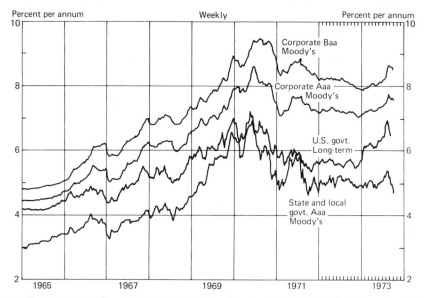

[a] Latest figures plotted: U.S. govt., September 8; state and local govt., September 27; all others, September 28

Source: Board of Governors of the Federal Reserve System

## Equity Securities

So far the discussion has focused on the reasons for the price instability of primary debt securities (bonds). Now we will examine some reasons for the price instability of primary equity securities (stocks). As shown in Figure 1A–3, there have been wide swings in stock prices in recent years. Stock prices are represented by the Standard and Poor's Index of 500 common stocks, which includes 425 industrial issues, 55 public utility stocks, and 20 railroad issues that are also plotted separately.

### Value

Generally speaking, stock prices reflect investors' expectations about future returns, including future dividends. Two examples will serve to illustrate the relationship between stock prices and dividends. Assume that an investor expects a return of 10 percent per annum on his stock investment. We will call this the expected rate of return ($k$) or the *capitalization rate*. If the company pays a $2 dividend ($D$) on its stock and this dividend is not expected to change in the future, the price of the stock will be as follows:

## Figure 1A–3

Stock prices and trading (weekly averages)[a]

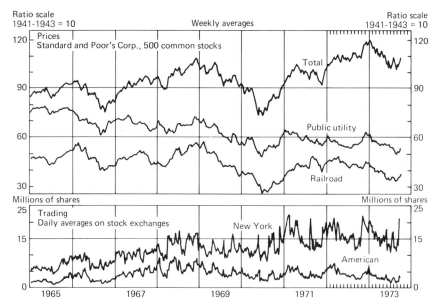

[a] Latest figures plotted: September 28
Source: Board of Governors of the Federal Reserve System

$$\text{Price} = \frac{\text{dividends}}{\text{capitalization rate}}$$

or

$$P = \frac{D}{k}.$$

Hence,

$$\text{Price} = \frac{\$2}{0.10} = \$20.00.$$

If the dividends of the company are expected to grow at a constant rate $(g)$ of 5 percent, this equation can be modified as follows:

$$\text{Price} = \frac{\text{dividends in the following year}}{\text{capitalization rate} - \text{growth rate}}$$

or

$$P = \frac{D_1}{k - g}$$

and the price of the stock will be

$$P = \frac{\$2}{0.10 - 0.05} = \$40.00.$$

In a world of certainty, there would be no doubt about the company's ability to pay the $2 dividend and that the dividend would grow at a constant rate of 5 percent. However, because we do not live in a world where the outcomes of future events are certain, the above method of valuation does not give precise results. Nevertheless, it does provide a basis for discussing some of the factors that affect stock prices.

The major determinants of stock prices are a company's ability to pay dividends in the future $(D_1, g)$ and the capitalization rate $(k)$ used by investors. A company's dividend policies are influenced, among other things, by the general business outlook. If business is going to be bad in the future, corporate profits will decline and dividends may be reduced. Conversely, an upswing in business activity may lead to increased dividends. It follows that factors which affect corporate profits ultimately affect stock prices. The factors that influence the investors' expected rate of return (the capitalization rate) are much more difficult to pin down. The capitalization rate reflects investors' attitudes towards risk associated with the company in question, as well as returns on alternative investments. While the returns on alternative investments can be observed and measured objectively, the concept of risk is at least partially subjective; it is determined by investors' attitudes about a firm's management, financial structure, and other considerations.

## Investor Psychology

The final factors contributing to the volatility of stock prices in the short run are investors' reactions to specific events and their attempts to guess what other investors are going to buy or sell next. Collectively, these factors can be called *investor psychology*. The following statement by John Maynard Keynes describes one aspect of investor psychology:

> *Professional investment may be likened to those newspaper competitions in which the competitors have to pick out the six prettiest faces from 100 photographs, the prize being awarded to the competitor whose choice most nearly corresponds to the average preferences of the competitors as a whole. So, each competitor has to pick, not those faces which he, himself, finds prettiest, but those which he thinks likeliest to catch the fancy of the other competitors, all of whom are looking at the problem from the same point of view. It is not a case of picking those who, to the best of one's judgment, are really the*

*prettiest, or those which average opinion generally thinks the prettiest; we have reached the third degree where we devote our intelligence to anticipation of what average opinion expects the average opinion to be. And there are some, I believe, who are practicing the fourth, fifth and higher degrees.*[10]

## Summary

Business concerns finance a portion of their expansion of assets by issuing primary debt and equity securities. Because business profits are uncertain, there is some business risk associated with all types of primary securities. Since changes in market interest rates, the business outlook, investor psychology, and other exogenous factors affect the market price of primary securities, both primary debt securities and equity securities have uncertain capital value.

---

[10]John Maynard Keynes, *The General Theory of Employment, Interest, and Money* (New York: Harcourt Brace and World, 1936), p. 156.

# Appendix 1B

# Expectations Theory

Economists and others are concerned about the future course of market interest rates. Over a period of years, a body of knowledge concerning the prediction of interest rates has been developed, called *expectations theory*. This theory explains the current relationship between interest rates and the maturity of a security in terms of expectations. The basic elements are summarized below to give the reader some idea of what has evolved, but no attempt is made here to discuss the ramifications and controversies surrounding this theory. However, the market segmentation theory is also presented to provide another point of view. Those who are interested in exploring the matter further should refer to the Bibliography.

## Hypothesis

The expectations theory postulates that the course of short-term market interest rates can be forecast for long periods of time. It follows that market interest rates on long-term debt securities are some function of the current short-term rate and future expected short-term rates. According to this theory, long-term rates are an average of the intervening short-term rates.

The theory is based on the following assumptions:

1 Debt securities are riskless with respect to principal and interest.
2 Future short-term interest rates are predictable.
3 There are no transactions costs or taxes.
4 Investors attempt to maximize profits.
5 Investors are indifferent with respect to investing in long-term or short-term securities as long as the returns are the same. They seek to equalize *holding-period yields* among all possible combinations of maturities. A holding-period yield is the total return on a security (coupon interest received plus capital gains or losses divided by the purchase price) for a given period of time.
6 The average long-term interest rate is calculated in the following manner. If the coupon interest received on the securities is *not* reinvested, the long-term rate $(R_n)$ is equal to the arithmetic average of the short-term rates $(r_n)$:

$$R_n = \frac{(1 + r_1) + (1 + r_2) + \cdots + (1 + r_n)}{n}.$$

If the funds *are* reinvested, the long-term rate is equal to the geometric average of the short-term rates:

$$R_n = \sqrt[n]{(1 + r_1)(1 + r_2) \cdots (1 + r_n)} - 1$$

Figure 1B–1

Illustration of current and expected rates

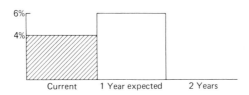

| Current | 1 Year expected | 2 Years |

## Example

The following example illustrates assumption number 5 and shows how holding-period yields are brought into equality. In this example, coupon interest received is not reinvested. In Figure 1B–1, the *current* rate on a one-year security is 4%, and the *expected rate next year* on a one-year security is 6%. Provided the current rate on a two-year security is 5%, the market will be in equilibrium, because an investor with a two-year holding period can either invest in two one-year securities that will provide an average yield of 5% [(4% + 6%)/2 = 5%] or invest in one two-year security at 5%. However, if the two-year security yielded more than 5% (e.g., 5.3%), investors would prefer it to holding two one-year securities. Since investors are assumed to be profit maximizers, they would sell the one-year securities and buy two-year securities until the yields on each were in equality. Thus, because investors can predict future short-term rates accurately, and because long-term rates are an average of short-term rates, holding-period yields for all securities and all holding periods will be equal.

## Term Structure

Now we turn to the *term structure of interest rates* (the relationship between interest rates and the maturity of a security). If current short-term rates and long-term rates are equal, the expectations theory tells us that investors will expect no change in interest rates for a particular holding period (see Figure 1B–2. However, this condition will not last for long. Even in stable

Figure 1B–2

Flat yield curve

Time to maturity

Figure 1B–3

Normal yield curve

market conditions, long-term interest rates command a premium over short-term interest rates, because long-term debt securities have greater market price risk and price level risk than short-term debt securities.[11] (Remember assumption number 1—that the securities are riskless with respect to principal and interest.) Therefore, taking the normal risk premium into account, long-term interest rates are normally somewhat higher than short-term interest rates (Figure 1B–3).

If short-term interest rates are lower than long-term interest rates by more than the normal amount (Figure 1B–4), the theory holds that long-term rates will tend to rise. Investors will sell their long-term securities, thereby forcing long-term rates up (and prices down), and buy short-term securities, forcing the short-term rates down (and prices up). Conversely, if short-term rates are above long-term rates (Figure 1B–5), according to the theory long-term rates will tend to decline. Investors who expect long-term rates to decline will buy long-term securities, forcing long-term rates down (and prices up), and sell short-term securities, forcing short-term rates up (and prices down). The point of the expectations hypothesis is that expectations about future short-term interest rates determine the long-term interest rate.

Figure 1B–4

Upward-sloping yield curve

[11]The concept of risk is discussed in Chapter 2.

Figure 1B–5

Downward-sloping yield curve

## Market Segmentation

Some economists disagree with the expectations hypothesis. They argue that the market for securities is segmented—that there are distinctly different groups of borrowers and lenders participating in the securities market who do not consider short-term and long-term securities perfect substitutes. Investors tend to deal primarily in either short-term or long-term securities, and they do not readily substitute one for the other. For example, commercial banks deal mostly in short-term securities while pension plans deal mostly in long-term securities. Therefore, according to the market segmentation hypothesis, the relative supply of securities at each end of the market is the major determinant of the term structure of interest rates.

# Bibliography

### Financial Intermediaries

Goldsmith, R. W. *Financial Intermediaries in the United States Since 1900.* New York: National Bureau of Economic Research and Princeton University Press, 1958.

Gurley, John G., and E. S. Shaw. *Money in a Theory of Finance.* Washington, D.C.: Brookings Institution, 1960.

———. "Financial Intermediaries and the Savings-Investment Process." *The Journal of Finance,* 11 (May 1956), 257–66.

Moore, Basil J. *An Introduction to the Theory of Finance.* New York: Free Press, 1968.


### Interest Rates

Conard, Joseph. *Introduction to the Theory of Interest.* Berkeley, Calif.: University of California Press, 1959.

Culberton, John M. "The Term Structure of Interest Rates." *Quarterly Journal of Economics,* 71 (1957), 485–517.

Hahn, F. H., and F. P. R. Brechling. *The Theory of Interest Rates,* Proceedings of a Conference held by the International Economic Association. New York: St. Martin's Press, 1966.

Lutz, Friedrich A. *The Theory of Interest.* Chicago: Aldine Publishing Co., 1968.

Malkiel, Burton. *The Term Structure of Interest Rates.* Princeton, N.J.: Princeton University Press, 1966.

———. *The Term Structure of Interest Rates: Theory, Empirical Evidence, and Application.* Morristown, N.J.: General Learning Press, 1970.

Meiselman, David. *The Term Structure of Interest Rates.* Englewood Cliffs, N.J.: Prentice-Hall, 1962.

Modigliani, Franco, and Richard Sutch. "Debt Management and the Term Structure of Interest Rates: An Empirical Analysis of Recent Experience." *Journal of Political Economy,* 75, Nov. 4, Supplement Part 2 (1967), 569–589.

———. "Innovations in Interest Rate Policy." *American Economic Review Papers and Proceedings,* 56 (1966), 178–197.

# 2

# Portfolio theory and flow of funds: the tools of analysis

## Introduction

Portfolio theory and the Flow of Funds Accounts are tools for analyzing the financial behavior of business concerns, financial intermediaries, and individuals. Portfolio theory is a conceptual framework which studies why investors make changes in their financial assets. Although the composition of individuals' assets is determined by personal preferences as well as by the availability of alternative investment opportunities, in recent years individuals' holding of financial assets have shifted markedly (e.g., from savings accounts to marketable securities such as Treasury bills), largely because of changes in market rates of interest. In some years investors shifted their funds from savings accounts with low yields into marketable securities with higher yields, even though in many instances the higher-yielding marketable securities offered more risk to the individual than the lower-yielding savings accounts. It is evident, then, that there is some relationship between risk and reward. That relationship is the basis of portfolio theory.

The second part of the chapter examines the Flow of Funds Accounts, a Federal Reserve Board accounting matrix that shows the interrelationships of the various financial sectors of the economy. Because one type of economic unit cannot make a financial transaction without involving other types of economic units, the Flow of Funds Accounts offer the student an

excellent opportunity to trace the movement of funds through the nation's financial system and thereby examine the dynamics of the system.

## Portfolio Theory

Portfolio theory is concerned with that aspect of decision making where the outcome of future events cannot be predicted with complete certainty.[1] Since this definition is broad enough to apply to a myriad of situations, the discussion here will be largely descriptive and limited to decisions about financial assets. Because most of the literature on portfolio theory is quantitative, some of the features of the theory will not be discussed.

Individuals, business concerns, and financial intermediaries all attempt to maximize the utility derived from owning assets by selecting those expected to yield the highest returns relative to risk, that is, making up a *preferred portfolio*. To simplify our discussion of portfolio theory, we will restrict our comments and illustrations to individuals, but the same principles can be applied equally to all the components of the financial system. The object of portfolio theory, for business concerns and financial intermediaries as well as for individuals, is to determine the most efficient combinations of financial assets for investment purposes, and to analyze why asset shifts occur. Although the theory has many applications, at present it is used primarily in the selection of stocks by large institutions. In his study on portfolio theory, Sharpe termed it "a set of rules for the intelligent selection of investments under conditions of risk."[2]

Although a single individual may have no significant impact on financial markets or institutions, the sum total of the financial activities of all individuals (the Federal Reserve Board considers "individuals" to be households, farms, and nonfarm noncorporate businesses) exerts considerable influence on financial institutions and is to a large extent responsible for changes in market interest rates (see Figure 2–1). Wide fluctuations in interest rates have taken place in recent years against a background of inflation, erratic monetary policy, and recessions. Beginning in late 1965, interest rates advanced so dramatically that within two years their level had doubled. This advance was followed by a sharp decline. Individuals responded to these changes in interest rates by changing their financial assets. When market interest rates exceeded the interest rates paid on some deposits at thrift institutions (banks or savings and loan associations), individuals shifted their funds from low-yielding savings accounts into higher-yielding marketable securities.[3] This process of withdrawing funds

[1]The original work in portfolio theory is that of Harry Markowitz, "Portfolio Selection," *The Journal of Finance*, 7 (March 1952), 77–91. See the Bibliography at the end of the chapter for additional works.
[2]William Sharpe, *Portfolio Theory and Capital Markets* (New York: McGraw Hill, 1970), p. viii.
[3]Figure 2–1 shows the *maximum* interest rate that could have been paid on time and savings deposits as determined by the Board of Governors of the Federal Reserve System. The maximum rates paid on deposits in 1966 varied from 5 to 5½ percent on various types of time deposits. Many investors received less than the 5½ percent maximum rate on their time and savings deposits.

Figure 2-1

Selected interest rates (quarterly)

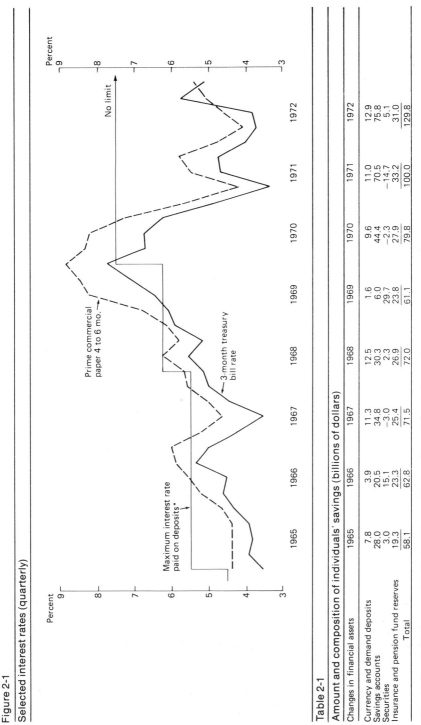

Table 2-1

Amount and composition of individuals' savings (billions of dollars)

| Changes in financial assets | 1965 | 1966 | 1967 | 1968 | 1969 | 1970 | 1971 | 1972 |
|---|---|---|---|---|---|---|---|---|
| Currency and demand deposits | 7.8 | 3.9 | 11.3 | 12.5 | 1.6 | 9.6 | 11.0 | 12.9 |
| Savings accounts | 28.0 | 20.5 | 34.8 | 30.3 | 6.0 | 44.4 | 70.5 | 75.8 |
| Securities | 3.0 | 15.1 | -3.0 | 2.3 | 29.7 | -2.3 | -14.7 | 5.1 |
| Insurance and pension fund reserves | 19.3 | 23.3 | 25.4 | 26.9 | 23.8 | 27.9 | 33.2 | 31.0 |
| Total | 58.1 | 62.8 | 71.5 | 72.0 | 61.1 | 79.8 | 100.0 | 129.8 |

Source: Board of Governors of the Federal Reserve System, Flow of Funds Accounts

*Maximum interest rate paid on deposits.

from financial institutions and investing in marketable securities, i.e., shifting secondary securities into primary securities, is called *disintermediation*. In 1966, because of disintermediation, the amounts of funds invested in currency and demand deposits (checking accounts) and savings accounts was substantially less than in the previous year, but funds invested in marketable securities increased 500 percent (see Table 2–1). In 1967, this process was reversed; because market interest rates were below the interest rates paid on deposits at thrift institutions, individuals liquidated their holdings of securities and increased their holdings of demand deposits and savings accounts. The 1966 scenario was repeated in 1969, when market interest rates again became more attractive to investors than rates at thrift institutions, and disintermediation again resulted. When market interest rates declined during 1970 and 1971, individuals liquidated their holdings of securities and increased their deposits at thrift institutions.

This survey shows some of the interrelationships between individuals, financial markets, and financial institutions, and indicates that individuals attempt to invest their funds where they will receive the highest returns. In order to realize increased returns in 1966 and 1969, they substituted relatively risky marketable securities for less risky demand deposits and savings accounts.

If investors (both individual and institutional) lived in a world of complete certainty, there would be no need for portfolio theory since the optimum portfolio would simply consist of the single asset with the highest return. Investors would maximize their returns by investing in the asset with the highest yield (in the case of equity stocks, capital gains plus dividends). However, since investors do not live in a world of complete certainty and do not have perfect foresight, they must diversify their portfolios to reduce their risk of financial loss. The extent to which an investor diversifies his portfolio is influenced by a variety of factors: his goals, the variability and permanence of his income, his tax status, search costs (the actual costs of investigation), transaction costs, legal restrictions, and the degree to which he accepts risk.

### Risk and Portfolio Theory

In portfolio theory, the term *risk* is applied to the variability of the return on a security. At the core of portfolio theory are investors' attitudes toward risk and return, or how much risk they are willing to assume in order to achieve a certain rate of return. For instance, the owner of a stock has a *market risk* because the price of his stock can go up or down.

The extent to which stock prices change is depicted in Figure 2–2, which gives the percentage changes of common stock prices listed on the New

Figure 2–2

Stock price changes: the New York Stock Exchange profile[a]

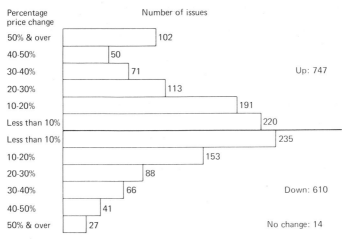

a Percentage price changes of 1,371 common stocks in year ended December 31, 1972

York Stock Exchange (NYSE) in 1972. In 1972 prices of 610 stocks declined and prices of 747 stocks advanced. The market value of all common stocks listed on the NYSE increased by $29.7 million during 1972. Table 2–2 gives figures for stock price changes during the four preceding years (1968–1971) for comparison.

*Systematic and Unsystematic Risk*    Business risk, price-level risk, and other types of risk may affect the return on a security, in addition to the

Table 2–2

Common stock price changes (1968–1971)

| | Number of issues | | | | | | | |
|---|---|---|---|---|---|---|---|---|
| | 1968 | | 1969 | | 1970 | | 1971 | |
| Price change (%) | Up | Down | Up | Down | Up | Down | Up | Down |
| 50 & over | 218 | 1 | 12 | 144 | 31 | 65 | 180 | 3 |
| 40–49.9 | 72 | 1 | 13 | 153 | 21 | 84 | 54 | 18 |
| 30–39.9 | 126 | 14 | 18 | 178 | 43 | 105 | 97 | 33 |
| 20–29.9 | 136 | 26 | 36 | 251 | 80 | 143 | 144 | 62 |
| 10–19.9 | 194 | 91 | 53 | 166 | 128 | 155 | 161 | 132 |
| Under 10.0 | 167 | 111 | 69 | 106 | 210 | 180 | 208 | 187 |
| Totals | 913 | 244 | 201 | 998 | 513 | 732 | 844 | 435 |
| No change | 4 | | 3 | | 8 | | 17 | |
| Total issues | 1,161 | | 1,202 | | 1,253 | | 1,296 | |

Source: New York Stock Exchange

market risk discussed above. Those interested in the concept of risk as used in portfolio theory should be familiar with the terms *systematic risk* and *unsystematic risk.* Systematic risk is that portion of an asset's variability which is attributable to an external source, such as changes in economic conditions. For example, if a recession is expected, many stock prices will decline. Generally, systematic risk affects all stocks in the same manner, and in theory, an investor cannot eliminate systematic risk by diversification. Unsystematic risk is due to unique events which affect an individual stock, such as a labor strike at the XYZ Company, and can be eliminated by diversification. The effect that the unique event has on the price of one company's stock may have no bearing on the behavior of other stock prices. Systematic risk plus unsystematic risk equals *total risk.*

*Business and Price-Level Risk*    Business risk arises from the possibility that a business will not be able to meet all of its obligations when they are due. Failure to fulfill these obligations could result in bankruptcy and a loss to investors. (In 1971, there were 10,326 industrial and commercial bankruptcies in the United States, affecting 0.42 percent of all concerns in business in that year.)

Price-level risk concerns the effect of inflation on the purchasing power and investment values of investors. Suppose you make an investment this year that will return $100 next year. If the price level index is 100 today, and if it increases 4 percent by next year, the purchasing power of the income you will receive, in terms of today's dollar, will be $100/104 = $96.15. As a result of inflation, the "real" value ($96.15) of the income one year after investment, expressed in constant dollar amounts, is less than the "nominal" value ($100) of the income. If inflation were to continue to increase at the same rate, the value of $100 received ten years from now would be only $67.15 in terms of today's dollar.

In periods of inflation it is better to be a debtor than a creditor. Creditors (or those receiving fixed incomes) lose purchasing power during periods of inflation if the return they receive is less than the percentage rate of inflation. In contrast, debtors benefit from inflation because they repay their debts with nominal dollar amounts ($100) that have a diminished real purchasing power ($96.15). However, if creditors correctly anticipate inflation, they will add an *inflation premium* to the interest rate in order to obtain the real rate of return on their original investment. Suppose an investor were to lend $1,000 for one year and wanted to receive a real rate of return of 5 percent ($50/1000: 5 percent). If the price level was expected to increase by 3 percent, the investor would charge a nominal interest rate of 8 percent (5% + 3%), so that his real rate of return would be 5 percent. In summary, the debtor benefits if the actual rate of inflation exceeds the anticipated rate

of inflation. Conversely, creditors benefit if the actual rate of inflation is less than the anticipated rate.

## Risk and Probability

Risk refers to a situation where the possible outcomes of decisions can be estimated, in statistical terms, as by a *probability distribution*. Assume that an investor is asked to predict the value of a particular common stock six months from now. If he has some knowledge about the value of the stock, such as its earnings per share, the probability distribution for the predicted dollar values of the stock may or may not be a normal one. In this context, risk is defined as the dispersion of the expected outcomes around the predicted value and is generally measured by the standard deviation (designated by sigma, $\sigma$). The *standard deviation* is a statistical term that measures the variability of a set of observations from the mean (average or predicted value) of a distribution. For example, if the predicted price of a stock is $60, the likelihood of any deviation from that price is considered risk. If the probability distribution is normal (symmetric) for this same stock, with a standard deviation of $5 per share, the chances are about 68 out of 100 that the future value of the stock will be between $55 and $65 per share (Figure 2–3), and the chances are 32 out of 100 that the future value of the stock will be less than $55 or more than $65 per share. If the standard deviation were $1 instead of $5 per share, the risk associated with the predicted value would be substantially less. A small dispersion (standard deviation) is less risky than a large one.

## Risk Averters

Generally speaking, rational individuals will take on additional risk only if it is accompanied by increased returns. The amount of increased returns

Figure 2–3

Probability of predicted values

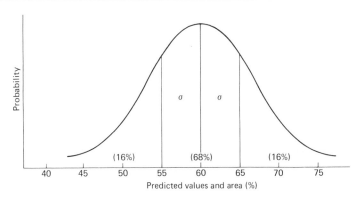

Predicted values and area (%)

required by an individual before he will take on additional risk determines whether he is a risk averter, a risk neutral, or a risk seeker. Risk averters have diminishing marginal utility for money; they believe that the additional return is not worth the risk associated with obtaining it. Risk seekers have increasing marginal utility for money; they believe that the additional return *is* worth the risk associated with obtaining it. Risk neutrals are between the two extremes and have a constant marginal utility for money.

Most individuals are risk averters: they would rather make less money than risk the loss of money. The risk averter would rather place ten bets of $100 on ten flips of a coin than one bet of $1,000 on one flip of a coin. (The outcome of the flip of a coin is either heads or tails; the probability of either outcome is 50 percent.) In both cases the expected value is zero because the chances of winning ($+\$1,000$) or losing ($-\$1,000$) are equal ($+\$1,000 - \$1,000 = 0$). In contrast, a risk seeker would be one who buys a lottery ticket, accepting the large chance of losing a small amount (the price of the lottery ticket) for the small chance of winning a large amount (the prize).[4]

It may be helpful to think of risk averters as having a series of utility schedules (in Figure 2–4, $U_1$, $U_2$, $U_3$) that reflect every value of their decisions with respect to risk and expected returns. These utility schedules are indifference curves; a particular level of utility or satisfaction can be derived from any combination of risk and return on a particular curve ($U$). For example, the same level of utility can be derived at points $M$, $N$, or $O$ on $U_3$, and the risk averters are indifferent about any point on that curve. The utility

**Figure 2–4**

**Utility schedules**

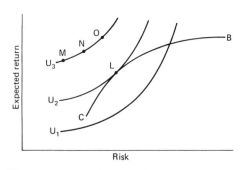

[4]A classic discussion of risk-utility can be found in Milton Friedman and Leonard Savage, "The Utility Analysis of Choice Involving Risk," *The Journal of Political Economy*, 56 (August 1948), 279–304. Another article on the same topic, but more germane to portfolio theory, is James Tobin, "The Theory of Portfolio Selection," in *The Theory of Interest Rates*, ed. F. H. Hahn and F. P. R. Brechling (New York: Macmillan, 1966), pp. 3–5.

curves in Figure 2–4 are concave, upward, and to the right, suggesting that the individuals' aversion to risk is an increasing function of the amount of risk. In theory, individuals select those assets expected to yield the highest return relative to the amount of risk they are willing to assume. Accordingly, they move along the efficient investment frontier curve CB to a position where the utility of ownership of assets is maximized, at point L on $U_2$. This is the highest utility curve attainable with the assets in the portfolio.

By diversifying their assets, investors can reduce the unsystematic risk in their portfolios. Consider a portfolio consisting of two assets, A and B. In Figure 2–5, points A and B represent the combinations of risk and return for assets A and B respectively. The straight line connecting points A and B represents one possible combination of risk and return offered by the assets A and B. If the expected values of A and B are perfectly positively correlated, the efficiency frontier of all combinations of A and B will be represented by the straight line AB. The term *perfectly positively* correlated means that the values of A and B change in precisely the same manner. When the value of A increases, the value of B will increase at the same rate, and, when the value of A decreases, that of B will decrease at the same rate. The *efficiency frontier* is the average of the best risk-return relationships of the various assets; it is the set of efficient risk-return choices.

A portfolio is efficient if it has the highest expected return for a given level of risk *and* the lowest risk for a given expected return. If the expected values of A and B are independent of each other or are not perfectly positively correlated, the risk-return choices assume a curved shape (ACB). All risk-return choices on the positively sloped portion of ACB (from C to B) comprise the efficiency frontier.

Figure 2–5

Two-asset portfolio

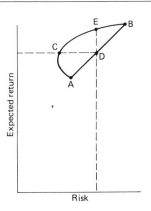

If the area *ACB* represents the portfolios (combinations of risk and return) of many assets, only the *CB* portion of the efficiency frontier is considered efficient. By way of illustration, consider two additional assets D and E, represented by points *D* and *E* on Figure 2–5. Point *C* is more efficient than point *D* because it has the same return as point *D,* but less risk. Similarly, point *E* is more efficient than point *D* because it has a higher return than point *D* for the same degree of risk. In summary, it is less risky for an investor to have his holdings spread among various assets than to have them all concentrated in a single kind of asset.

## Conclusion

In Chapter 1 it was noted that the function of each type of economic unit in the financial system and its respective attitudes toward risk are different; therefore, the composition of each unit's portfolio is different. Portfolio theory is a useful method of viewing the assets of an economic unit as a single portfolio, and it provides an overview of the different relationships that can exist between risk and financial rewards. In the hope of reaping large rewards, some business concerns assume a greater degree of risk than others, according to the nature of the organization's business and various other factors. Financial intermediaries also take risks, limited in part by federal laws and regulations governing their operations. Some intermediaries (commercial banks, for example) invest in certain types of risky primary securities. Although individuals are usually risk averters, they can still attempt to improve their portfolios' performance within the constraints of the degree of risk they are willing to assume.

The portfolios of financial intermediaries are more complex than those of individuals, but the same principles of portfolio theory apply to them. On the surface, all financial intermediaries' portfolios consist mostly of primary securities. However, because the portfolios of different intermediaries are not alike, they diversify their portfolios in different ways. Savings and loan associations, with the bulk of their assets in mortgage loans, diversify by investing in different types of properties in different geographic areas and by offering different types of mortgages. All their assets are real estate-oriented, and one can assume that they are all positively correlated (i.e., they tend to move in the same direction). On the other hand, commercial banks have more opportunities for diversification because they can invest in a wider variety of primary securities, including mortgages and consumer loans, as well as commercial and industrial loans. With these opportunities to diversify, risks on the assets of banks are probably less correlated than those of savings and loan associations. It follows that the portfolios of savings and loan associations are inherently more risky than those of commercial banks.

Portfolio Theory and Flow of Funds 37

## Flow of Funds

### System of Accounts

The next question is how changes in the composition of the portfolio of one type of economic unit affect the portfolios of other types of economic unit. The survey at the beginning of this chapter showed that in recent years individuals shifted their funds from time and savings deposits into marketable securities. These shifts of funds implied a simultaneous change in the portfolios of thrift institutions as well as in the portfolios of those who sold the marketable securities. The exact manner in which the shifting of funds affected the economic system can be traced through the Flow of Funds Accounts. This is a system of national accounts that measures the interactions between financial markets, the market for goods and services, and the amount of savings and investment in the economy. The Flow of Funds can be viewed as an extension of the National Income and Product Accounts. While the National Income and Product Accounts focus on income and output (e.g., Gross National Product, National Income, etc.), the Flow of Funds Accounts concentrate on financial transactions and are published quarterly in the *Federal Reserve Bulletin*. The Flow of Funds Accounts (both year-end levels and changes) for the 1965–1972 period are listed in the Appendix, *Flow of Funds Report*. The following discussion suggests how to use the Flow of Funds as an analytical tool to see how the assets and liabilities of different types of economic units are intertwined.[5]

### Example of Flow of Funds

The Flow of Funds Accounts are presented in the form of a matrix. The columns of the matrix represent sectors of the economy, and the rows represent transaction categories. To illustrate the use of Flow of Funds in tracing transactions from one sector to another, a simple hypothetical matrix is presented in Table 2–3, listing only two sectors of the economy, households and business, and only three transaction categories (lines 1–3), currency, bonds, and plant and equipment. In the Flow of Funds Accounts the household sector is the largest component of "individuals," which also includes farms and nonfarm noncorporate business. The business sector includes nonfinancial nonfarm corporate business such as the machine tool industry and the steel industry. Under each sector in the table are columns for sources and uses of funds. An increase in liabilities or a reduction in assets is a *source* of funds, e.g., an increase in bank loans or a reduction in cash; an increase in assets or a reduction in liabilities is a *use* of funds, such as an increase in cash holdings or a repayment of debt.

---

[5]Readers interested in the theoretical development of the Flow of Funds can find references in the Bibliography at the end of this chapter. The author does not feel that it is necessary to understand the theory underlying the Flow of Funds in order to use it, any more than it is necessary to understand the mechanics of an internal-combustion engine in order to drive an automobile.

Table 2–3

Hypothetical flow of funds (billions of dollars)

| | Sector | | | |
|---|---|---|---|---|
| | Households | | Business | |
| Transaction category | Use | Source | Use | Source |
| 1  Currency | | −10 | | |
| 2  Corporate bonds | +10 | | | +10 |
| 3  Plant and equipment | | | +10 | |

Two key points are to be observed from this matrix. First, the Flow of Funds records *changes* in the portfolios of economic sectors. For example, the household sector reduced its holdings of currency by $10 billion and increased its holdings of corporate bonds by an equivalent amount. The business sector used the funds raised by the sale of these corporate bonds to increase its stock of plant and equipment. The household sector used one asset—cash—as a source of funds to acquire another asset—bonds. Therefore, cash was reduced by −$10 billion while bonds increased by +$10 billion. In contrast, business concerns increased their liabilities (+$10 billion) by selling bonds as a source of funds. These funds were used to buy plant and equipment (+$10 billion), which is an increase in assets. In summary, the matrix in Table 2–3 shows the flow of funds between two sectors of the economy. (In this case the terms *change* and *flow* are synonymous.) The Flow of Funds Accounts also record the stock of assets held by various sectors in the economy. The term *stock* refers to the amount of assets outstanding at some point in time. The two terms can be reconciled by thinking of the balance sheet of a business concern as a stock concept and the income statement as a flow concept. The balance sheet shows a year-end level of assets and liabilities while the income statement reflects changes in income and expenses.

The second point which the matrix illustrates is the distinction between financial and nonfinancial flows. Financial flows are always recorded on two sector statements because financial assets are created by liabilities. By definition, all liabilities are debts owed and their counterparts appear as assets on someone else's balance sheet. Thus, in Table 2–3 corporate bonds appear as an asset on the statement of the household sector and a liability on the statement of the business sector. In contrast, nonfinancial flows represent changes in real assets such as plant and equipment and appear on only one sector statement. Thus, in Table 2–3 plant and equipment appear only on the sector statement of business concerns.

## Uses of Flow of Funds Information

A summary matrix for the entire country can be developed by placing the sectors side by side in columns and listing the transaction categories in

rows. Table 2–4 lists all of the sectors and financial transaction categories used in the Flow of Funds Accounts. This information can be used to examine either particular sectors of the economy or particular transactions.

*Sector*   The first use of the Flow of Funds Accounts is to select a sector of the economy and analyze the transaction categories that affect that sector. To illustrate this use, it is not necessary to examine all the transaction

---

Table 2–4

Flow of Funds sector structure and financial transaction categories

**Sector structure**

| | |
|---|---|
| Households | Mutual savings banks |
| Farm business | Credit unions |
| Nonfarm noncorporate business | Life insurance companies |
| Corporate nonfinancial business | Other insurance companies |
| State and local governments | Private pension funds |
| U.S. government | Finance companies |
| Rest of world | Security brokers and dealers |
| Monetary authorities | Open-end investment companies |
| Commercial banks | Agencies of foreign banks |
| Savings and loan associations | Banks in U.S. territories and possessions |

**Financial transaction categories**

| | |
|---|---|
| Gold | Corporate stocks |
| Official foreign exchange position | One- to four-family mortgages |
|   International Monetary Fund | Other mortgages |
|     gold tranche position | Consumer credit |
|   Convertible foreign exchange at |   Installment |
|     Treasury and Federal Reserve |   Noninstallment |
| Treasury currency | Bank loans not elsewhere classified |
| | Other loans |
| |   Open-market paper |
| Demand deposits and currency |     Dealer-placed paper |
|   Private domestic |     Directly placed finance |
|   U.S. government |       company paper |
|   Foreign |     Bankers' acceptances |
| Time deposits at commercial banks | Security credit |
| Savings accounts at savings institutions |   Owed by brokers and dealers |
| Life insurance reserves |   Owed by others |
| Pension fund reserves | Taxes payable |
| | Trade credit |
| Consolidated banking items | Equity in noncorporate business |
| U.S. government securities | Miscellaneous |
|   Direct and fully guaranteed |   Deposit claims |
|     Short-term |   Equities |
|     Other except savings bonds |   Insurance claims |
|     Savings bonds |   Unallocated claims and bank floats |
|   Nonguaranteed agency issues | |
|   Loan participation certificates | |
| State and local obligations | Sector discrepancies |
| Corporate and foreign bonds | |

categories for a particular sector. Accordingly, the data in Table 2–5 are limited to the financial sources of funds for the corporate nonfinancial business sector for selected years. The transaction categories (lines 1–13) reflect the sources of funds. The interrelationships between corporate business and financial institutions can be seen from the table without going into great detail. Between 1965 and 1972, the dollar volume of funds raised by businesses in the credit markets doubled (line 2). Bonds and mortgages (lines 5 and 6) accounted for an increasing share of the total funds raised. Even though it is not shown in the table, financial institutions were the chief purchasers of bonds and mortgages. In contrast, the share of funds supplied by bank loans (line 7) declined sharply until 1972. This example shows how one sector of the economy, business, interacted with the other economic units that bought the bonds and mortgages and then made the bank loans.

*Transaction Category*    The other use of the Flow of Funds is to select a transaction category and determine how that transaction category affected certain economic sectors. The data in Table 2–6 show that corporate business issued the bulk of the bonds in the years shown (line 2). In recent years the largest dollar volume of bonds was acquired by households (line 7),[6] but state and local governments (line 8) and life insurance companies (line 11) were still the main supporters of the corporate bond market throughout the entire period shown. This example demonstrates that

Table 2–5

Financial sources of funds for corporate business (billions of dollars)

|  | 1965 | 1968 | 1971 | 1972 | 1973 |
|---|---|---|---|---|---|
| 1 Total financial sources (net) | 34.8 | 51.9 | 52.5 | 69.3 | 91.6 |
| 2 Net funds raised in credit markets | 20.4 | 31.5 | 46.8 | 55.3 | 67.2 |
| 3 New share issues | —[a] | -0.2 | 11.4 | 10.9 | 7.4 |
| 4 Debt instruments | 20.5 | 31.7 | 35.4 | 44.4 | 59.7 |
| 5   Bonds | 5.4 | 12.9 | 18.8 | 12.2 | 9.2 |
| 6   Mortgages | 3.9 | 5.7 | 11.4 | 15.6 | 16.1 |
| 7   Bank loans | 10.6 | 9.6 | 4.4 | 13.5 | 30.6 |
| 8   Open-market paper | -0.3 | 1.6 | -1.5 | -0.5 | -0.3 |
| 9   Finance co. loans | 0.6 | 1.7 | 1.9 | 2.8 | 2.0 |
| 10   U.S. govt. loans | 0.3 | 0.2 | 0.2 | 0.2 | 0.3 |
| 11 Profit tax liability | 2.2 | 2.9 | 2.0 | -0.1 | 2.3 |
| 12 Trade debt | 12.1 | 17.2 | 3.8 | 13.7 | 19.6 |
| 13 Miscellaneous | —[a] | 0.3 | -0.1 | 0.4 | 2.5 |

[a] Insignificant amount
Source: Board of Governors of the Federal Reserve System, Flow of Funds Accounts

[6]In 1971, households liquidated $12.7 billion worth of U.S. government securities, but bought $8.1 billion worth of corporate bonds. The reason for selling the short-term government securities and buying the long-term corporate bonds is that short-term market interest rates were relatively low in 1971 (see Figure 2–1) while long-term market rates were still attractive to investors. In 1972, households bought $4.8 billion in corporate bonds.

Table 2–6

Changes in corporate and foreign bonds (billions of dollars)

|  |  | 1965 | 1968 | 1971 | 1972 | 1973 |
|---|---|---|---|---|---|---|
| 1 | Net issues | 8.6 | 15.0 | 24.8 | 20.2 | 12.5 |
| 2 | Corporate business | 5.4 | 12.9 | 18.8 | 12.2 | 9.2 |
| 3 | Finance companies | 1.9 | 0.8 | 3.8 | 5.4 | 1.8 |
| 4 | Commercial banks | 0.8 | 0.3 | 0.9 | 1.1 | a |
| 5 | Rest of world | 0.5 | 1.1 | 0.9 | 1.0 | 1.0 |
| 6 | Net purchases | 8.6 | 15.0 | 24.8 | 20.2 | 12.5 |
| 7 | Households | 1.0 | 5.2 | 9.1 | 4.8 | 1.1 |
| 8 | State and local govts.[b] | 2.3 | 2.1 | 4.4 | 5.7 | 5.9 |
| 9 | Commercial banks | −0.1 | 0.3 | 1.3 | 1.7 | 0.5 |
| 10 | Mutual savings banks | −0.1 | 1.3 | 3.9 | 2.1 | −1.1 |
| 11 | Life insurance cos. | 2.8 | 3.9 | 5.5 | 7.0 | 5.9 |
| 12 | Private pensions funds | 1.5 | 0.6 | −0.7 | −0.8 | 1.6 |
| 13 | Other insurance cos. | 0.6 | 1.2 | 0.3 | −0.7 | −1.0 |
| 14 | Others | 0.6 | 0.4 | 1.1 | 0.4 | −0.4 |

[a] Insignificant amount
[b] Includes retirement funds
Source: Board of Governors of the Federal Reserve System, Flow of Funds Accounts

changes in the portfolio of one economic sector influenced the portfolios of other economic sectors.

*Portfolios of Financial Intermediaries*    A Flow of Funds matrix similar to those just discussed can be used to compare the size and composition of portfolios of different types of financial intermediaries. The matrix in Table 2–7 has financial institutions at the head of columns and their principal financial assets listed by rows. In this case, the Flow of Funds Accounts depicts the *stock* of financial assets held by financial intermediaries. The matrix reveals that in 1972 commercial banks held the largest dollar volume ($655 billion) of financial assets (line 9), followed by savings and loan associations, life insurance companies, and private pension funds. In fact, their financial assets were more than the *combined* assets of savings and loan associations, life insurance companies, and private pension funds. Commercial banks hold the largest dollar volume of their assets in loans (line 8) and U.S. government securities (line 1), but they still have the most diversified portfolios, compared with several other types of financial institution. Savings and loan associations invest the bulk of their assets in home mortgage loans, credit unions extend consumer credit, and open-end investment companies (mutual funds) invest almost exclusively in corporate securities. On the other hand, a mutual fund diversifies by investing in stocks and bonds of many companies.

Basically, all types of financial intermediaries are similar because their portfolios consist of primary securities and their liabilities consist of secon-

Table 2–7

Selected assets of financial institutions (year-end 1972; billions of dollars)

| Financial assets | Deposit-type institutions | | | |
| --- | --- | --- | --- | --- |
| | Commercial banks | Savings and loan assoc. | Mutual savings banks | Credit unions |
| 1 U.S. govt. securities | 90.0 | 21.8 | 5.5 | 2.2 |
| 2 State and local obligations | 89.0 | — | 0.8 | — |
| 3 Corporate bonds | 5.7 | — | 15.4 | — |
| 4 Corporate stock | — | — | 3.6 | — |
| 5 Home mortgages | 57.0 | 167.6 | 41.7 | 0.9 |
| 6 Other mortgages | 42.3 | 38.8 | 25.9 | — |
| 7 Consumer credit | 70.6 | 2.4 | 1.5 | 16.9 |
| 8 Other loans n.e.c.[a] | 203.8 | — | 1.5 | — |
| 9 Total financial assets[b] | 655.0 | 243.6 | 100.6 | 21.7 |

| Financial assets | Insurance and pension funds | | | | Other | |
| --- | --- | --- | --- | --- | --- | --- |
| | Life ins. cos. | Other ins. cos. | Private pension funds | State and local govt. retirement | Fin. cos. | Open-end inv. cos. |
| 1 U.S. govt. securities | 3.8 | 3.5 | 3.7 | 5.1 | — | 0.7 |
| 2 State and local obligations | 3.3 | 25.0 | — | 1.7 | — | — |
| 3 Corporate bonds | 86.8 | 8.8 | 27.4 | 43.4 | — | 5.1 |
| 4 Corporate stock | 26.4 | 20.5 | 111.8 | 14.2 | — | 51.7 |
| 5 Home mortgages | 22.5 | — | 3.0 | — | 11.1 | — |
| 6 Other mortgages | 54.9 | 0.2 | — | 7.0 | — | — |
| 7 Consumer credit | — | — | — | — | 37.5 | — |
| 8 Other loans n.e.c.[a] | 21.2 | 5.0 | — | — | 26.1 | — |
| 9 Total fin. assets[b] | 231.8 | 64.6 | 152.3 | 71.8 | 78.0 | 59.8 |

[a] n.e.c.-not elsewhere classified
[b] Includes assets not listed on table
Source: Board of Governors of the Federal Reserve System, Flow of Funds Accounts

dary securities. The differences among them arise from the laws and regulations which require some of them to invest in particular types of primary securities and which restrict the type of secondary securities they may issue. For example, savings and loan associations and credit unions can have savings accounts, but they cannot have demand deposits. Financial intermediaries as a group can be considered a regulated industry. In spite of this, they are highly competitive among themselves and with other types of economic units. For example, the data in Table 2–7 suggest that commercial banks, savings and loan associations, and life insurance companies all deal in mortgage loans, so it is likely that they may compete for some mortgages. Moreover, these same institutions are in competition to sell secondary securities because individuals who buy life insurance policies will have fewer funds to invest in time and savings deposits.

Finally, as the example at the beginning of this chapter showed, in the years when market interest rates on corporate bonds were substantially higher than interest rates paid on time and savings deposits, thrift institutions had to compete with business firms for funds.

## Summary

Financial institutions compete with business firms and among each other for primary and secondary securities, and each type of economic unit strives to optimize its portfolio. Whenever one type of economic unit alters its portfolio, it affects other types of economic units. The portfolio shifts of all the units in the economy are recorded in the Flow of Funds Accounts.

It is apparent that financial intermediaries exist in an environment that is continuously changing. The environment includes both economic conditions, which are manifested by changes in the supply and demand for primary and secondary securities, and laws that regulate what financial intermediaries can and cannot do. Forthcoming chapters will include some discussion of both factors.

The reader should keep portfolio theory in mind when reading about changes in portfolios and organizations in the next few chapters. Basically, financial intermediaries respond to these changes in such a way as to increase their returns. In portfolio theory terms, they move toward an *efficient frontier*.

## Questions

1 Explain the term *disintermediation*.
2 How do changes in levels of market rates of interest affect the rate of disintermediation? Compare the current market interest rate with the rate paid on deposits at commercial banks.
3 Explain how the optimum portfolio would differ between a world of certainty (no risk) and a world where risk is present.
4 How is the term *risk* used in portfolio theory? Differentiate between systematic risk and unsystematic risk. Differentiate between business risk, price-level risk, and market risk.
5 Define the concept of the efficiency frontier and explain under what circumstances a portfolio is considered efficient.
6 How do the concepts of risk aversion and a diminishing marginal utility for money relate to portfolio theory and affect the selection of preferred portfolios?

7 Discuss how the concepts of "stocks" and "flows" relate to the information provided in the Flow of Funds Accounts.

8 Explain how the Flow of Funds Accounts provide information on how the portfolio changes of one economic unit affect the portfolios of other economic units.

9 Explain how financial intermediaries compete with each other and with nonfinancial business firms for primary and secondary securities.

# Bibliography

## General Financial Institutions

Dougall, Herbert E. and Jack E. Gaumitz. *Capital Markets and Institutions,* 3d ed. Englewood Cliffs, N.J.: Prentice-Hall, 1975.

Farwell, Loring C. *Financial Institutions,* 4th ed. Homewood, Ill.: Richard D. Irwin, 1966.

Fenstermaker, J. Van. *Readings in Financial Markets and Institutions.* New York: Appleton-Century-Crofts, 1969.

Gies, Thomas G., and Vincent P. Apilado. *Banking Markets and Financial Institutions.* Homewood, Ill.: Richard D. Irwin, 1971.

Goldsmith, Raymond W. *Financial Intermediaries in the American Economy Since 1900.* Princeton, N.J.: Princeton University Press, 1958.

————. *Financial Institutions.* New York: Random House, 1968.

Horvitz, Paul M. *Monetary Policy and the Financial System,* 3d ed. Englewood Cliffs, N.J.: Prentice-Hall, 1974.

Krooss, Herman E., and Martin R. Blyn. *A History of Financial Intermediaries.* New York: Random House, 1971.

Ludtke, J. G. *The American Financial System: Markets and Institutions.* Boston: Allyn and Bacon, 1965.

Polakoff, Murray E., *et al. Financial Institutions and Markets.* Boston: Houghton Mifflin, 1970.

Robichek, Alexander A., and Alan B. Coleman. *Management of Financial Institutions.* New York: Holt, Rinehart and Winston, 1967.

Robinson, Roland I., ed. *Financial Institutions.* Homewood, Ill.: Richard D. Irwin, 1960.

Silber, William L. *Portfolio Behavior of Financial Institutions.* New York: Holt, Rinehart and Winston, 1970.

Smith, Paul F. *Economics of Financial Institutions and Markets.* Homewood, Ill.: Richard D. Irwin, 1971.

## Portfolio Theory

Francis, Jack Clark, and Stephen H. Archer. *Portfolio Analysis.* Englewood Cliffs, N.J.: Prentice-Hall, 1971.

Jensen, Michael C. "Capital Markets: Theory and Evidence." *The Bell Journal of Economics and Management Science,* 3 (Autumn 1972), 357–398.

Markowitz, Harry. *Portfolio Selection: Efficient Diversification of Investment.* New York: John Wiley and Sons, 1956.

Sharpe, William F. *Portfolio Theory and Capital Markets.* New York: McGraw-Hill, 1970.

Smith, Keith V. *Portfolio Management.* New York: Holt, Rinehart and Winston, 1971.

## Flow of Funds

Copeland, M. A. *A Study of Moneyflows in the United States.* New York: National Bureau of Economic Research, 1952.

*Flow of Funds Accounts—1945–1967.* Washington, D.C.: Board of Governors of the Federal Reserve System, 1968.

Goldsmith, Raymond W. *Capital Market Analysis and the Financial Accounts of the Nation.* Morristown, N.J.: General Learning Press, 1972.

Ritter, Lawrence S. "The Flow of Funds Accounts: A Framework for Financial Analysis." In *Financial Institutions and Markets,* Murray E. Polakoff, *et al.* Boston: Houghton Mifflin, 1970.

Salomon Brothers. *Supply and Demand For Credit* (New York: Annual).

Taylor, S. P. "Uses of Flow of Funds Accounts in the Federal Reserve System." *Journal of Finance* (May 1963), pp. 249–258.

Part

# 2

# Deposit-type intermediaries

Part 2 consists of four chapters on deposit-type financial intermediaries.

Chapter 3, "Savings and Loan Associations: The Home Mortgage Lenders," highlights the problems of borrowing short-term funds and making long-term loans.

Chapter 4, "Mutual Savings Banks and Credit Unions," deals with the conversion from a mutual form of organization to a stock form. It also shows how the types of services offered by financial institutions are changing.

Chapter 5, "Commercial Banks," shows the interrelationships between the Federal Reserve System and commercial banks, and illustrates how commercial banks have adapted to changing economic and monetary conditions in recent years.

Chapter 6, "The Federal Reserve System," discusses the structure and regulatory functions of the system and its effects on monetary policy and bank supervision.

# 3

# Savings and loan associations: the home mortgage lenders

The economic function of savings and loan associations is to obtain savings from the public and invest the bulk of those funds in home financing. Accordingly, savings and loan associations have a specialized structure, with assets that consist of long-term mortgages and liabilities that consist of short-term deposits.[1] This imbalance between the maturity structure of their assets and liabilities has contributed to the financial instability of savings and loan associations. This chapter examines the savings and loan associations, some of their problems, and some suggested solutions for those problems. In addition, the Federal Home Loan Bank System and three federal credit agencies (the Federal National Mortgage Association, Government National Mortgage Association, and Federal Home Loan Mortgage Association) that deal in mortgages are discussed.

## Industry Structure

### Number of Organizations

At the end of 1973, there were 5,244 savings and loan associations in operation throughout the United States (including Puerto Rico and Guam), with total assets of $272.4 billion. As shown in Table 3–1, six states

---

[1]The use of the term *mortgage* conforms to the definition developed by the U.S. Department of Housing and Urban Development. A mortgage loan denotes indebtedness, for whatever purpose, incurred by private borrowers, which is secured by a mortgage or other lien on real property. For further details see *Mortgage Loan Gross Flows* (Washington, D.C.: U.S. Department of Housing and Urban Development, December 1968), Chapter 5.

Table 3–1

Savings and loan associations and assets, by states (December 31, 1973)

| State | Number of assns. | Total assets (millions) | State | Number of assns. | Total assets (millions) |
|---|---|---|---|---|---|
| Alabama | 58 | $ 2,171 | Montana | 16 | $    442 |
| Alaska | 4 | 153 | Nebraska | 45 | 2,294 |
| Arizona | 14 | 2,534 | Nevada | 6 | 753 |
| Arkansas | 66 | 1,757 | New Hampshire | 18 | 538 |
| California | 176 | 47,138 | New Jersey | 280 | 10,896 |
| Colorado | 48 | 3,922 | New Mexico | 36 | 884 |
| Connecticut | 35 | 2,437 | New York | 171 | 15,794 |
| Delaware | 22 | 171 | North Carolina | 177 | 5,508 |
| District of | | | North Dakota | 11 | 837 |
| Columbia | 17 | 3,352 | Ohio | 450 | 19,496 |
| Florida | 132 | 19,117 | Oklahoma | 57 | 2,404 |
| Georgia | 101 | 5,295 | Oregon | 28 | 2,748 |
| Guam | 2 | 12 | Pennsylvania | 507 | 12,133 |
| Hawaii | 11 | 1,396 | Puerto Rico | 10 | 757 |
| Idaho | 11 | 456 | Rhode Island | 6 | 537 |
| Illinois | 491 | 20,976 | South Carolina | 75 | 2,809 |
| Indiana | 180 | 5,374 | South Dakota | 16 | 406 |
| Iowa | 86 | 3,040 | Tennessee | 72 | 3,152 |
| Kansas | 92 | 3,402 | Texas | 291 | 12,662 |
| Kentucky | 122 | 2,733 | Utah | 13 | 1,399 |
| Louisiana | 105 | 3,480 | Vermont | 7 | 135 |
| Maine | 24 | 347 | Virginia | 70 | 3,479 |
| Maryland | 218 | 5,124 | Washington | 53 | 4,070 |
| Massachusetts | 178 | 5,436 | West Virginia | 32 | 643 |
| Michigan | 65 | 7,692 | Wisconsin | 123 | 5,933 |
| Minnesota | 71 | 5,056 | Wyoming | 13 | 298 |
| Mississippi | 77 | 1,473 | Entire U.S.[a] | 5,244 | $272,358 |
| Missouri | 125 | 7,245 | | | |

[a] Components do not add up to totals because of differences in reporting dates and accounting systems
Source: *United States Savings and Loan League 1974 Fact Book*

(California, Illinois, Ohio, New York, Florida, and Pennsylvania) account for 50 percent of the total assets of all savings and loan associations. The uneven distribution of savings and loan associations among the states reflects many factors: historical entrenchment in some states, competition from other types of financial institutions, population size and income, and the degree of urbanization. Savings and loan associations (S & L's) can be organized under either a state or a federal charter. About 63 percent of the associations are organized under state charters, although more than half of the total asset value is held by the federally chartered associations. All federally chartered associations are mutuals; they are owned by their depositors rather than by stockholders. State-chartered associations can be organized as either mutuals or stock associations, depending on the laws of the state. In addition, all federally chartered associations are members of the Federal Home Loan Bank System, and their deposits must be

insured by the Federal Savings and Loan Insurance Corporation. Ninety-five percent of the 3,400 state-chartered associations are also members of the Federal Home Loan Bank System and have federal deposit insurance.

### The Federal Home Loan Bank System

The Federal Home Loan Bank System (FHLBS), created as an independent federal agency by the Federal Home Loan Bank Act in 1932, is a central credit facility and regulatory agency for such mortgage lending institutions as savings and loan associations, mutual savings banks, and insurance companies. The system charters and regulates federal savings and loan associations; some building and loan associations, cooperative banks, and homestead associations are also eligible for membership in the system. Cooperative banks (Massachusetts) and homestead associations (Louisiana) are basically the same as state-chartered savings and loan associations. At the end of 1972, the FHLBS had 4,412 members: 4,362 savings and loan associations, 48 mutual savings banks, and 2 life insurance companies. There are Federal Home Loan Banks in twelve districts throughout the country. The system is run by a three-man board whose members are appointed by the president and confirmed by the Senate. The FHLBS advances funds to members of the system when they require additional liquidity to support their mortgage-lending activity, and also makes long-term funds available to member savings and loan associations. Finally, the system supervises and administers the Federal Savings and Loan Insurance Corporation, which insures the individual deposits held in its member associations for amounts up to $40,000.

### Assets of Savings and Loan Associations

### Mortgages

As specialists in home mortgage lending, savings and loan associations have portfolios consisting mostly of mortgage loans and a relatively small amount of cash and securities (Table 3–2). The associations prefer conventional mortgages to those insured by the Federal Housing Administration (FHA) or guaranteed by the Veterans Administration (VA), because they make more money on conventional mortgage loans. Although the savings and loan associations assume a greater risk with conventional mortgages, government-backed mortgages (on which the federal government assumes most of the risk) are subject to restrictions such as maximum specified interest rates and limits to the dollar value that can be loaned. Moreover, the homes on which the loans are made must meet certain physical standards. However, government-backed mortgages have one distinct advantage over conventional mortgages in that the secondary market for FHA-insured and VA-guaranteed mortgages is widespread among various

Table 3–2

Balance sheet for all operating savings and loan associations at year-end 1973 (in billions)

| Assets | | |
|---|---:|---:|
| Mortgage loans outstanding | | 232.1 |
| FHA and VA | 29.7 | |
| Conventional | 202.4 | |
| Other assets | | 19.2 |
| Cash and investment securities | | 21.0 |
| Total[a] | | $272.4 |

| Liabilities | | |
|---|---:|---:|
| Savings capital | | 227.3 |
| Borrowings | | 17.0 |
| FHLB advances | 14.9 | |
| Other | 2.1 | |
| Loans in process | | 4.7 |
| Other liabilities | | 6.2 |
| Net worth | | 17.1 |
| Total[a] | | $272.4 |

[a]Totals may not add due to rounding
Source: Federal Home Loan Bank Board

types of financial institutions. The *secondary market* deals in mortgages already in existence that are traded among institutions. It is the equivalent of a used-car market for mortgages. Until recently, the secondary market for conventional mortgages was limited to savings and loan associations. For example, savings and loan associations located in areas where capital is available may purchase loans from savings and loan associations located in areas where the demand for mortgage loans exceeds the available supply of funds.[2] In 1972, net new loans amounted to 16 percent of the total mortgage loans made by savings and loan associations.

*Maturity of Mortgages*    Mortgages written by savings and loan associations have an original maturity of about twenty-seven years.[3] However, most mortgage loans remain on the books of the associations for only seven to ten years.[4] A seven-year average means that the mortgage portfolio will have a 14 percent (100%/7 years = 14%) turnover rate per year. The average maturity of mortgages varies directly with the level of mortgage

---

[2]The term *loan* as used here also includes *participations* (mortgage loans in which more than one association has an interest).
[3]According to the Federal Home Loan Bank Board, in December 1972, the average term to maturity of conventional first-mortgage loans originated by savings and loan associations was 27.7 years for new homes and 26.5 years for existing homes.
[4]The characteristics of conventional mortgage loans are outlined in Leon T. Kendall, *Anatomy of the Residential Mortgage: Loan, Property and Borrower Characteristics,* Occasional Paper no. 2 (Chicago: United States Savings and Loan League, 1964). The average life of thirty-year FHA-insured mortgages is about twelve years.

interest rates. When mortgage interest rates fall, debtors pay off their mortgages by refinancing them at the lower rates. Conversely, when mortgage interest rates rise, debtors are reluctant to prepay their mortgages. Since mortgage portfolios turn over slowly and since some of the turnover is at the mortgagee's option, the mortgage portfolio of the S & L's is adversely affected.

*Problem of Asset Turnover*    The inability to turn over their mortgage portfolios at a faster rate has had serious consequences for savings and loan associations in recent years. For example, one facet of the inflation that began in 1965 was a sharp increase in market interest rates. During the 1965–1970 period, conventional mortgage interest rates on new homes soared from 5.8 percent to a record level of 8.4 percent. At year-end 1973, mortgage interest rates were 8.3 percent. Since the portfolios of most S & L's consist of mortgages issued when interest rates are low, the average return on their assets lags behind a rising level of interest rates.

*Squeeze on Profits*    At the same time, savings and loan associations have had to pay higher interest rates on their savings and deposits in order to compete with other types of thrift institutions and market instruments. Consequently, their profits, which are the difference between the average return on their assets (mortgages) less the average cost of their liabilities (savings deposits) and other expenses, were squeezed.

*Interest Rates and Market Values*    In addition, the rise in interest rates resulted in reduced market values of the mortgage loans held by savings and loan associations. (As discussed in Chapter 1, for primary securities such as bonds and mortgages, market interest rates and market values are inversely related.) For example, the dollar value of a thirty-year, 5¼ percent, FHA-insured mortgage issued in 1965, when interest rates were relatively low, would have declined about 16 percent by 1970, when mortgage interest rates were at their highest level.[5] This suggests that because conventional mortgage interest rates in 1973 were 43 percent (8.3%/5.8% = 143%) above the 1965 level, the market value of mortgages held by all operating savings and loan associations was less than the $232 billion figure listed on their balance sheets. This fact carries the implication that, in a sense, savings and loan associations and insurance companies that hold mortgages were technically insolvent because their assets were worth less than their liabilities. Along this line of reasoning is the following

---

[5]The ceiling on FHA-insured mortgage loans was 5¼% in 1965 and 8–8½% in 1970. Because the maximum interest rates on FHA-insured loans were less than the market yields on conventional loans, lenders charged the sellers *points* (a percentage of the value of the loan) in order to raise its effective yield. The charges ranged from two points in 1965 to eight points in 1969. Government regulations prohibit lenders from charging buyers because that would be equivalent to an increase in the fixed interest rate. Therefore, the points are charged to the sellers. For additional information see Benton E. Gup, "Recent Developments in Housing," *Economic Commentary*, Federal Reserve Bank of Cleveland (July 7, 1969).

interchange that took place between William G. Dewald, professor of economics at Ohio State University, and Charles A. Wellman, then president of the Equitable Savings and Loan Association, Van Nuys, California, at the 1968 Conference on Savings and Residential Financing.[6]

> MR. DEWALD: *I have a few technical questions on savings and loan failures. How does the examining authority appraise assets? Is it on the basis of a market evaluation or a maturity value? . . . I am interested in the technical matters—whether the examiners really adjust the maturity value or whether they consider the depreciation associated with the increase in interest rates.*

> MR. WELLMAN: *I know of no regulatory or supervisory approach that takes into account money market risks—which is really the question you are raising. Whatever appraisal of asset quality has been done is purely in terms of market value approach, of the value of the collateral or the security of the mortgage, and not whether the coupon rate on the note is going to be sufficient to cover the overhead.*

> MR. DEWALD: *Are there not a substantial number of savings and loan associations that are technically insolvent in the sense that their assets have depreciated in terms of the increase in market rates, such that if they had to be liquidated, they could not come up with enough funds to satisfy their shareholders?*

> MR. WELLMAN: *One of the great virtues of the American financial system is that we never sell all of our assets at current market price at the same time. I could probably break every commercial bank in the United States on the basis of its losses in bond and municipal bond portfolios. I suspect I probably could severely impair the net worth of every life insurance company if I were to apply a money market cost to its long-term assets.*

> MR. DEWALD: *That is true. That is why the examiners or regulators play such an important role in the sense that if they have a rule that says if your assets fall to less than your liabilities, you are out of business.*

> MR. WELLMAN: *They don't, though. The only time a life insurance superintendent will go to market value based on money cost is on equities. He does not write down bond portfolios on the basis of market.*

---

[6]*Savings and Residential Financing, 1968 Conference Proceedings* (Chicago: United States Savings and Loan League, September 1968), pp. 149–151.

MR. DEWALD: *How many savings and loan associations are now technically insolvent?*

MR. WELLMAN: [*Response not reported.*]

## Liabilities of Savings and Loan Associations

### Savings Capital

As shown in Table 3–2, the largest part of the liabilities of savings and loan associations is savings capital, which consists of regular passbook savings and a variety of certificate-type accounts. The latter carry higher interest rates than regular passbook savings accounts if federal and state requirements are met as to the minimum denomination of the certificate and the length of time that the funds will remain on deposit (this can range from ninety days to ten years). The Federal Home Loan Bank System regulates the maximum interest rates that member associations can pay on deposits. For example, in 1973, the interest-rate ceiling on regular passbook savings was 5 percent, whereas the interest-rate ceiling on $100,000 minimum denomination certificates with a one- to ten-year maturity was 7.5 percent. Associations that are not members of the FHLBS are regulated by their respective state laws. Regular passbook savings account for over half of the savings capital in savings and loan associations. Certificate accounts with no minimum denomination but with maturities ranging from two to ten years are the next most popular type of savings deposit, making up 23 percent of total deposits, and $100,000 certificates represent less than 1 percent of total deposits.[7] The ability to offer a variety of forms of savings accounts segments the savings market and increases the average maturity of the liabilities of savings and loan associations.

### Deposits of Individuals

The majority of funds deposited in savings and loan associations are owned by individuals; the average size of the nearly fifty-five million accounts is only $3,800. For many years, when interest rates were low by current standards, individuals' savings remained on deposit at savings and loan associations, and the *turnover ratio* (the number of times funds turn over in the entire system in one year) of savings deposits remained virtually unchanged at about 30.9 percent during the 1955–1964 period. Because of this experience, managers of savings and loan associations and the Federal Home Loan Banks may have been lulled into believing that funds of individuals could be counted on to remain on deposit for long periods of

---

[7]Figures are based on data published annually in *Savings and Loan Fact Book* (Chicago: United States Savings and Loan League, 1971, 1972, 1973, 1974.)

time. Therefore, in their view, it was not risky to loan short-term deposits out as long-term mortgages. They were wrong! Table 3–3 shows that the turn-over ratios increased substantially in 1966, 1969–1970, and 1973, indicating the increased volatility of the deposits, although some of this increase may reflect double accounting. When funds withdrawn from passbook accounts were deposited in certificate accounts, both a withdrawal and deposit took place but the amount of money at the savings and loan association remained unchanged.

Federal Home Loan Bank (FHLB) advances are the second largest liability of S & L's. During periods of credit restraint, FHLB advances are an important source of funds for savings and loan associations. In 1970, such advances reached a peak level of $14.9 billion.

## Sources of Funds

Savings and loan associations have four major sources of funds: net savings inflows, borrowing, retained earnings, and mortgage loan repayments. The first three sources of funds are reflected on the balance sheet (savings capital, borrowing, reserves and surplus); of these, net savings and mortgage loan repayments are the two largest. Mortgage loan repayments consist of monthly payments to amortize the loan and prepayments of outstanding loans. Monthly payments are a more stable source of funds than volatile prepayments. Because total mortgage loan repayments tend to be more stable than net savings, they sometimes exceed savings as the largest source of funds. In 1970, for example, mortgage loan repayments amounted to $14.8 billion, while savings amounted to $11.0 billion. Again, in 1973 mortgage loan repayments were the principal source of funds and exceeded savings by $10.4 billion. In addition, savings and loan associations derive funds from selling mortgages and issuing debentures.

Table 3–3

Turnover ratio of savings and loan deposits (percent)

| Year | Ratio |
| --- | --- |
| 1965 | 30.1 |
| 1966 | 37.2 |
| 1967 | 32.7 |
| 1968 | 32.2 |
| 1969 | 36.7 |
| 1970 | 39.1 |
| 1971 | 34.1 |
| 1972 | 36.3 |
| 1973 | 45.0 |

Source: Federal Home Loan Bank Board

## Portfolio Adjustments

### Recent Changes

Table 3–4 shows the effect of market interest rates on the assets and liabilities of savings and loan associations over an extended period of time. In 1966, market interest rates exceeded the average yield (as well as the ceiling rates) on savings accounts. As a result, individuals invested fewer funds in savings than in the previous year and increased their investments in marketable securities.[8] During July 1966, when short-term market interest rates were near their peak levels, withdrawals of funds from savings and loan associations exceeded new savings by 24 percent. To help offset the reduced dollar volume of savings in 1966, the associations increased their borrowing from the FHLB by a small amount, but were still forced to sharply curtail their mortgage lending activity. It is important to recognize that member associations can only borrow as much as the FHLB is willing to lend. Had the FHLB extended more credit, savings and loan associations could have made more mortgage loans.

Again, in 1969 market interest rates exceeded the yield on savings accounts and the dollar volume of savings shares shrank. However, this time the savings and loan associations borrowed heavily from the FHLB, and their mortgage lending activity increased somewhat. When market interest rates declined in 1971, savings inflows increased and the associations repaid the borrowings.

Table 3–4

Selected statistics of savings and loan associations (1965–1973)

| Year | 3-Month treasury bill rate (%) | Yield on savings accounts (%) | Annual changes (billions of dollars) | | |
|------|--------------------------------|-------------------------------|------------------|--------------------|---------------|
| | | | Net savings shares | Net mortgage loans | FHLB advances |
| 1965 | 4.0 | 4.2 | 8.5 | 8.9 | 0.7 |
| 1966 | 4.9 | 4.5 | 3.6 | 3.8 | 0.9 |
| 1967 | 4.3 | 4.7 | 10.6 | 7.5 | −2.5 |
| 1968 | 5.3 | 4.7 | 7.4 | 9.3 | 0.9 |
| 1969 | 6.7 | 4.8 | 3.9 | 9.5 | 4.0 |
| 1970 | 6.5 | 5.1 | 10.9 | 10.2 | 1.3 |
| 1971 | 4.3 | 5.3 | 27.8 | 23.9 | −2.7 |
| 1972 | 4.1 | 5.4 | 32.6 | 32.0 | 0.0 |
| 1973 | 7.0 | 5.6 | 20.5 | 26.9 | 7.2 |

Sources: Board of Governors of the Federal Reserve System, *Flow of Funds Accounts;* U.S. Savings and Loan League

[8]Until the passage of the Stevens Act in September 1966, the maximum interest rates paid on savings and loan association deposits were not federally regulated. For details on individuals' investments during this period, see Table 2–1 and the accompanying discussion.

The 1966 and 1969 experiences highlight the problems facing savings and loan associations. Inflation, monetary restraint, and high interest rates were common to both years. Managers of savings and loan associations (as well as other types of financial institutions) learned that they could not depend on savers to leave their funds on deposit when market interest rates were more attractive than rates paid on deposits. Moreover, the combination of volatile short-term deposits and long-term assets (mortgages) that are not liquid make the associations financially vulnerable.

## Suggested Reforms

Many reforms have been suggested to alleviate the savings and loan associations' inherent problem of financial instability.[9] Generally, they focus on diversifying the associations' assets and lengthening the maturity of their liabilities. The most important recommendations include allowing savings and loan associations to deal more extensively in consumer credit, to invest in corporate bonds and other securities, to issue capital notes, and to have demand deposits (checking accounts). Since 1970, some of these recommendations have become operational on a limited basis. Savings and loan associations can now make loans on consumer durables such as refrigerators, washers, dryers, and televisions, which are included as part of a house being financed by a mortgage loan. They can also make home improvement loans and loans on mobile homes. On the liability side of the balance sheet, savings and loan associations have adopted "third party payments." These are orders from a depositor directing an association to withdraw funds from his savings account in order to pay a third person. Third party payments are similar to checking accounts but are restricted to mortgage payments and payment of real estate taxes and utility bills. Theoretically, such diversification of assets and liabilities will assure the profitability of savings and loan associations because they can obtain low-cost funds (demand deposits) and invest in profitable short-term consumer loans. However, profits are determined by the spread between the rates of return they receive on loans (assets) and the rates they pay for deposits (liabilities). When the maturities of assets and liabilities are not synchronized, unanticipated changes in volatile short-term interest rates can either produce sizable profits or result in losses, even if portfolios are diversified.

## The Mortgage Market

In addition to the above recommendations, the market for government-backed and conventional home mortgages has improved because of the

---

[9]The most comprehensive compendium of recommendations affecting savings and loan associations, along with an analysis of their problems, is in Irwin Friend, ed., *Study of the Savings and Loan Industry*, Vols. I–IV (Washington, D.C.: Federal Home Loan Bank Board, 1969). Also the *Report of the President's Commission on Financial Structure and Regulation* (Washington, D.C.: U.S. Government Printing Office, 1971).

Federal National Mortgage Association (FNMA or Fannie Mae), the Government National Mortgage Association (GNMA or Ginnie Mae), and the Federal Home Loan Mortgage Corporation (FHLMC or Freddie Mac). These financial intermediaries are discussed again in Chapter 12, "Federal Credit Agencies."

### Fannie Mae (FNMA)

Fannie Mae is a government-sponsored, privately owned corporation whose stock is traded on both the New York Stock Exchange and the Pacific Stock Exchange. The organization's primary function is to provide liquidity and stability to the home mortgage market, by buying or by committing to buy government-backed and conventional home mortgages when funds are scarce and by selling mortgages when funds are plentiful. Every other week there is an auction where Fannie Mae determines the dollar volume of mortgages to be bought, and sellers (such as mortgage companies) determine the price. Starting from the lowest price, Fannie Mae accepts offers until the predetermined volume has been reached. Then Fannie Mae gives the sellers a commitment to buy mortgages at the determined price for a period of time such as four months, or longer. However, the sellers deliver mortgages to Fannie Mae only if no better alternative is available to them. If, during the four-month period, a mortgage company can sell mortgages to a life insurance company at a better price than that offered by Fannie Mae, it is free to do so. At year-end 1973, Fannie Mae held $24.2 billion in mortgage loans and had commitments to buy $7.9 billion additional mortgage loans. Fannie Mae finances its activities through the sale of debentures and short-term discount notes that enjoy the status of federal agency securities. These securities amounted to $23.0 billion at the end of 1973.

### Ginnie Mae (GNMA)

At present, the Government National Mortgage Association (Ginnie Mae) performs some functions previously assigned to Fannie Mae, including the management and liquidation of federally owned mortgage portfolios and special assistance in the purchase of mortgages when insufficient funds are available for home financing (if authorized by the president or by Congress). In addition, Ginnie Mae has a program to sell mortgage-backed securities that will attract new funds into the mortgage market and make mortgage loans more liquid. Ginnie Mae securities are of a pool of FHA and VA mortgages guaranteed by Ginnie Mae and carrying the full faith and credit of the U.S. government. The security is a *fully modified pass-through security,* which means that all monthly repayments of principal and interest, as well as prepayments, are made to the security holder whether they are collected from the mortgages or not. It has a stated rate of interest (e.g., 7½ percent) and a thirty-year maturity (although the average life of thirty-year

government-backed mortgages is about twelve years). It is sold in a minimum amount of $50,000, and the minimum size of any issue is $2 million. The pool of securities is obtained from FHA-approved mortgage lenders, who are sanctioned by Ginnie Mae to issue the security. The issuer accumulates qualified mortgages and submits them to a custodian, such as a bank, for certification and safekeeping. When the mortgages have been certified by the custodian, Ginnie Mae issues its guaranty. The important feature of this security for savings and loan associations and other mortgage lenders is that it increases the liquidity of their portfolios.

### Freddie Mac (FHLMC)

The Federal Home Loan Mortgage Corporation (FHLMC or Freddie Mac) is a new and growing participant in the secondary mortgage market. It was created by the Emergency Home Finance Act of 1970 to strengthen the existing secondary markets for government-backed residential mortgages and selected conventional mortgages. The FHLMC is owned by the twelve Federal Home Loan Banks and deals mostly with members of the Federal Home Loan Bank System. It sells participation sale certificates similar in principle to the Ginnie Mae pass-through securities, but with a minimum denomination of $200,000.

### Variable-Rate Mortgages

The Fannie Mae auctions and Ginnie Mae and FHLMC flow-through securities increase the liquidity of mortgage loans, but they do not deal with the problem of keeping the value of existing mortgage loans in line with current market interest rates. Variable-rate mortgages are an attempt to solve that problem.[10] The two most common techniques for varying rates are short-term or demand notes and tied-rates. In the first case, the lender writes the first mortgage note for a three- to five-year period; when this period is up, he converts the mortgage into a demand note or re-extends the term. When the mortgage is converted into a demand note, the interest rate can be adjusted upward or downward depending upon the level of market interest rates at that time. In the second case, the mortgage interest rate is tied to some other interest rate, such as the prime rate, so that both rates will move together.

*Problems of Tied-Rates*    There are a number of problems associated with using tied-rates. The first problem is to select a basic interest rate to which mortgage rates can be tied. Some variable mortgages are tied to the prime rate, but the prime rate is volatile and short-term whereas mortgage rates

---

[10]A comprehensive analysis of variable-rate mortgages can be found in Paul S. Anderson, "Variable Rates on Mortgages: Their Impact and Use." *New England Economic Review* (March/April 1970), pp. 3–20.

are relatively stable and long-term. For example, in 1973 the range of changes in the prime rate was 2.5 percentage points while the change in the mortgage rate was only 0.8 percentage points. Another alternative is to tie mortgage interest rates to a national indicator such as the Federal Home Loan Bank Board or FHA series on mortgages.

The implications of tying mortgage interest rates to a long-term or short-term interest rate can be related to the problems that savings and loan associations and others are trying to resolve by using variable-rate mortgages: their portfolios consist of long-term nonliquid assets (mortgages) and short-term volatile deposits. By definition, mortgages are long-term contracts with fixed interest rates. Accordingly, the lender (mortgagee) assumes the risk when market interest rates change. If market interest rates rise, the market value of the mortgage will decline. The market risk is compounded by the fact that disintermediation is associated mostly with changes in short-term market interest rates. As noted earlier, one way in which financial institutions meet the outflow of funds during disinter-mediation is to sell some of their primary securities such as mortgages. Because disintermediation occurs when interest rates are high and the market value of mortgages that were issued when contract interest rates were lower is reduced, savings and loan associations are in an awkward position. By tying mortgage interest rates to a short-term rate the mortgage lender can transfer some of his risk to the borrower (mortgagor).

In addition to the problem of choosing a basic rate, there are some legal barriers. Federal regulations prohibit the use of variable rates in government-backed mortgages, and usury laws in some states would restrict the upward movements of rates.

Finally, the reason for varying mortgage interest rates is to increase the cash flow to the lender organizations and to increase accounting earnings so they can pay more for savings. This can be accomplished only by increasing the size of the monthly payment. Assume that a 23-year mortgage loan of $30,000 is written at 6 percent, and the monthly payment is $193.30. If after three years the interest rate is raised to 8 percent, the monthly payment will increase to $228.07. Although this method does increase the cash flows to mortgage lenders, such increases in monthly payments could create serious financial problems for borrowers on limited or fixed incomes who may not be able to meet the higher payments.

## Summary

The chapter first examined the structure of the savings and loan industry and the role of the Federal Home Loan Bank System. Then the focus shifted to the assets and liabilities of savings and loan associations and their

problem of lending long-term mortgages and borrowing short-term deposits. Several aspects of this problem were: the turnover rate of mortgage portfolios is slower than the turnover rate of deposits; the market value of existing mortgages declines when market rates of interest increase; and mortgages are not very liquid. Additionally, in recent years savings and loan associations experienced large outflows of funds when market interest rates exceeded the rates paid on savings deposits. These and other factors adversely affected the financial stability of the savings and loan industry. Possible solutions include increasing the variety of assets (primary securities) and liabilities (secondary securities) held by savings and loan associations. The increased participation of federal credit agencies in the mortgage market has also helped the savings and loan associations.

## Questions

1 Savings and loan associations have an inherent imbalance between the maturity structure of their assets and liabilities. Discuss this imbalance and describe how it could weaken their ability to compete with other financial intermediaries in times of rising interest rates.

2 Describe the organizational structure and main functions of the Federal Home Loan Bank System (FHLBS). Explain why state-chartered savings and loan associations might join the FHLBS and the Federal Savings and Loan Insurance Corporation (FDLIC).

3 Savings and loan associations hold both conventional mortgages and mortgages backed by the Veterans Administration (VA) and Federal Housing Administration (FHA). Discuss the relative merits of conventional mortgages versus VA- and FHA-backed mortgages from the viewpoint of savings and loan portfolio holdings.

4 Explain how rising interest rates could cause some savings and loan associations to become technically insolvent.

5 Discuss how the ability to offer a variety of forms of savings accounts (secondary securities) segments the savings market and affects the average maturity of the liabilities of savings and loan associations. To what extent could this variety of savings plans help to reduce the traditional imbalance between the assets and liabilities of savings and loan associations?

6 Explain how rising interest rates and the maturity structure of savings and loan liabilities led to deposit withdrawals from these institutions during the late 1960s and early 1970s.

7 Suggest some changes in the assets and liabilities of savings and loan associations that might strengthen their competitive position in relation to other depository institutions.

8 Briefly explain the primary functions of the Federal National Mortgage

Association (FNMA), the Government National Mortgage Association (GNMA), and the Federal Home Loan Mortgage Association (FHLMA). Discuss the effect of these agencies on the secondary market for mortgages.

9 Explain what variable-rate mortgages are and how they could affect the market value of savings and loan portfolios. Discuss some of the problems associated with them.

## Bibliography

Friend, Irwin, ed. *Study of the Savings and Loan Industry,* Vols. I–IV. Washington, D.C.: Federal Home Loan Bank Board, 1969.

Kendall, L. T. *The Savings and Loan Business,* a Monograph Prepared for the Commission on Money and Credit. Englewood Cliffs, N.J.: Prentice-Hall, 1962.

*Savings and Loan Fact Book.* Chicago: United States Savings and Loan League (annual).

Teck, Alan. *Mutual Savings Banks and Savings and Loan Associations: Aspects of Growth.* New York: Columbia University Press, 1968.

United States Savings and Loan League, *The Savings and Loan Business: Its Purposes, Functions, and Economic Justification.* Prepared for the Commission on Money and Credit. Englewood Cliffs, N.J.: Prentice-Hall, 1962.

# 4

# Mutual
# savings banks
# and credit
# unions

Over the years, both mutual savings banks and credit unions have grown substantially and served their communities well. In order to continue this, some savings banks now want to change from a mutual to a stock form of organization, and some credit unions want to offer services that they are not allowed to offer at present.

This chapter begins with a brief history of mutual savings banks, their geographic location, organizational form, and asset structure. Because savings banks and savings and loan associations have similar organizational forms, the problems of their organization and of conversion from a mutual to a stock form are discussed jointly. This is followed by an examination of the assets and liabilities of savings banks, and some of their allied activities.

The second half of the chapter examines the credit union movement from its inception up to the present and discusses the structure of the industry, the concept of common bond, and the assets and liabilities of credit unions.

## Mutual Savings Banks

### Early Development

Mutual savings banks were originally developed for the advancement of human welfare through the encouragement of thrift. They were to provide a safe place where the poor and working class could keep their funds and at

the same time earn some return on them. The first such institution was organized by the Reverend Henry Duncan in Ruthwell, Scotland, in 1810. Two years later, savings banks were organized in the United States in Philadelphia and Boston.

The introduction of savings banks in the United States virtually coincided with the development of trust companies, investment trusts, building and loan companies, and mutual life insurance companies. These and other financial innovations developed during a period when the country was undergoing a dynamic economic change. The Industrial Revolution was under way, the population was growing and beginning to move westward, and the general level of income was rising. As a result of the economic growth, wage earners along the northeastern seaboard needed a safe place to deposit their funds (since commercial banks would not accept savings deposits); savings banks developed to help satisfy that need. In contrast, west of the Allegheny Mountains the population had few wage earners but many farmers who invested their surplus funds in land and livestock rather than depositing them in a financial institution. At the same time, the industry and commerce along the northeastern seaboard needed funds for expansion, but savings banks were not willing to make these "risky" loans. Savings banks consistently adhered to the policy of being "safe" places to deposit funds, and they limited their investments to relatively safe assets such as railroad bonds, federal, state, and local bonds, bank and utility securities, and loans backed by real estate. Commercial banks, however, were willing to make the relatively risky loans needed to develop industry and commerce, both along the northeastern seaboard and in the West. Thus, by the time the West had developed to the degree that wage earners needed a place to deposit their funds, commercial banks were already established there, and they hindered the development of savings banks in the West.

As a result of these developments, most savings banks are located along the northeastern seaboard. As Table 4–1 shows, the largest number of savings banks are located in Massachusetts, New York, and several other northeastern states; the remainder are scattered throughout the Midwest and along the West Coast. New York is the leading savings bank state with 56 percent of the total deposits of mutual savings banks. The second most important state, Massachusetts, holds about 15 percent of the total deposits. Interestingly, in New York, Massachusetts, Connecticut, New Hampshire, Maine, and Rhode Island, mutual savings banks hold more savings deposits than commercial banks and savings and loan associations combined. Mutual savings banks located in the New York City metropolitan area account for $40 billion of the $54 billion on deposit in the state, and at least fifteen mutual savings banks in the New York City area have deposits

Table 4–1

The distribution of mutual savings banks, and deposits by states (December 31, 1974)

| State | No. of savings banks | Deposits (millions of dollars) |
|---|---|---|
| Massachusetts | 167 | $14,991 |
| New York | 119 | 55,130 |
| Connecticut | 68 | 7,797 |
| Maine | 32 | 1,397 |
| New Hampshire | 29 | 1,478 |
| New Jersey | 20 | 4,777 |
| Washington | 8 | 2,144 |
| Pennsylvania | 8 | 6,615 |
| Rhode Island | 6 | 1,035 |
| Vermont | 6 | 441 |
| Maryland | 3 | 1,006 |
| Indiana | 4 | 167 |
| Wisconsin | 3 | 50 |
| Alaska | 2 | 90 |
| Delaware | 2 | 590 |
| Minnesota | 1 | 812 |
| Oregon | 1 | 173 |
| Puerto Rico | 1 | 8 |
| Total | 480 | $98,701 |

Source: National Association of Mutual Savings Banks

in excess of $1 billion each. The largest, the Bowery Savings Bank, has more than $3.5 billion in deposits.

## Organizational Forms

*Mutual and Stock*    Although there are legal differences between savings banks and savings and loan associations, their organizational forms are similar. Therefore, the following discussion will cover both. One of the most important features of savings banks and of 88 percent of all savings and loan associations is their mutual form of organization (the remaining 12 percent of the savings and loan associations are stock associations). This reflects the founding philosophy of savings banks and of some savings and loan associations: they were developed for the benefit of the working class and the earnings from the organizations were to be returned to the depositors. The mutual form of organization accomplishes this end because the net earnings, after allowance for operating expenses and reserves against losses, are distributed as dividends to depositors.

The principal advantage of the mutual form of organization is that there are no stockholders to share earnings; therefore, depositors may be paid higher dividends. However, regulatory authorities, such as the Board of Governors of the Federal Reserve System, the Federal Home Loan Bank

Board, and the Federal Deposit Insurance Corporation, fix the maximum interest rates that mutual savings banks and savings and loan associations can pay on deposits. Even so, in 1972 both mutual savings banks and savings and loan associations paid up to 5 percent (5¼ percent in Massachusetts) on ordinary savings deposits while commercial banks were limited to paying 4¼ percent on the same type of deposit, because the mutual institutions are granted an interest-rate advantage to allow them to compete with commercial banks. The National Association of Mutual Savings Banks had this to say about the matter:

> In connection with differential deposit interest rate ceilings, the savings bank industry had recognized that such protective devices cannot remain effective indefinitely and that deposit rate ceilings provide no protection against competition with open-market investments. However, the industry has held that so long as the powers of savings banks remain narrowly restricted, the limited protection provided by ceiling differentials will continue to be needed to prevent periodic large-scale shifts of funds from mortgage-oriented institutions.[1]

Another claim for the mutual form of organization is that it results in lower costs to borrowers.[2] Unfortunately, the evidence in this regard is not conclusive. A recent study revealed that, with the exception of California, the operating costs of mutual savings and loan associations were significantly lower than those of stock associations,[3] but in California, where about one-fourth of all stock savings and loan associations are located, the reverse was true. Another study in California found that the average salary of the highest-paid executives of mutual savings and loan associations was significantly larger than the average salary of the highest-paid executives in stock associations of similar size.[4] For example, in 1966 the highest-paid executives received an average salary of $33,200 in stock associations, compared with $43,600 in mutual associations. (To some extent, the differences between the salaries reflect the fact that stock companies can supplement salaries with stock options, thereby raising the total compensation of their executives.) Even if the operating costs of mutual organizations were lower than those of stock organizations, only part of the cost difference would be passed on to borrowers, while some of the remainder would be passed on to depositors in the form of higher dividends. Moreover, the interest rates that mutual savings banks charge for loans reflect the amount of the loan, the value of the collateral, and the credit-worthiness of the

[1]*Annual Report—1972* (New York: National Association of Mutual Savings Banks, May 1972), pp. 27–28.
[2]*Annual Report—1971* (New York: National Association of Mutual Savings Banks, May 1971), p. 20.
[3]George G. Benston, "Savings Banking and the Public Interest," *Journal of Money Credit and Banking*, Vol. IV, No. 1, Part 2 (February 1972), pp. 209–214.
[4]Eugene F. Brigham and R. Richardson Pettit, "Effects of Structure on Performance in the Savings and Loan Industry," in *Study of the Savings and Loan Industry*, ed. Irwin Friend (Washington, D.C.: Federal Home Loan Bank Board, 1969), pp. 1205–1209.

borrower, as well as the cost of funds to the bank. A recent study of annual percentage rates charged on various loans revealed that savings banks charged less than commercial banks on new automobile loans (9.92 percent vs. 10.08 percent), but more on mobile-home loans (11.7 percent vs. 10.9 percent).[5] In another example, mutual savings banks did charge lower contract interest rates on conventional mortgage loans on new homes than other lenders (Table 4–2). However, the lower rates may be due to factors other than organizational form, for example, geographical differences and different standards for making loans. One also has to consider the term to maturity of the mortgage loan, the loan-to-price ratio (the percentage of market value that a lender is willing to lend to a borrower), and the average purchase price. Once all this is done, the differences between the effective interest rates charged by major lenders become blurred.

*Conversion from Mutual to Stock*    There is considerable interest in allowing savings banks and savings and loan associations to change from the mutual form of organization to the stock form.[6] One reason for the proposed change in organizational form is that stock companies can raise funds in the credit markets more easily than mutual companies can. This ties in with the fact that as some mutual institutions have grown in asset size their profit margins have narrowed, thereby contributing to a capital-adequacy problem. *Capital adequacy* is the amount of capital required by law or regulatory agencies to run a financial institution. The capital funds of a mutual savings bank include surplus funds, reserve accounts, and undivided profits, and are analogous to the net worth of a stock company. In New York State, the banking law (Section 244–3) states that a capital funds-to-deposits ratio of 1 to 10 is desirable: there should be $1 of capital

Table 4–2

Selected statistics on conventional first-mortgage loans on new single-family homes by major lenders (December, 1973)

| Type of lender | Contract interest rate, % | Initial fees and charges, % | Term to maturity, years | Loan-to-price ratio, % | Purchase price ($000) |
|---|---|---|---|---|---|
| Mutual savings banks | 8.39 | 0.15 | 24.5 | 71.0 | 40.1 |
| Commercial banks | 8.43 | 0.51 | 18.7 | 65.5 | 35.3 |
| Savings and loan associations | 8.27 | 1.38 | 27.2 | 77.6 | 38.3 |
| Mortgage companies | 8.30 | 1.25 | 27.8 | 83.0 | 36.5 |

Source: Federal Home Loan Bank Board

[5]*Consumer Credit in the United States,* Report of the National Commission on Consumer Finance (Washington, D.C.: U.S. Government Printing Office, December 1972), p. 15.
[6]*The Report of the President's Commission on Financial Structure and Regulation* (Washington, D.C.: U.S. Government Printing Office, 1971); Benston, pp. 209–217. For detailed discussions of conversions from mutual to stock institutions see: U.S., Congress, House Subcommittee on Bank Supervisions and Insurance of the House Banking and Currency Committee, *Conversions (Mutual to Stock Institutions) Hearings,* May 15, 17, and 21, 1973.

for each $10 of deposits. During the 1960–1971 period, the ratio of capital to deposits for mutual savings banks located in New York State declined from 9.4 percent to 7.5 percent. For mutual savings banks located in all states, it was 7.8 percent at the end of 1971.

Because some mutual savings and loan associations have capital-adequacy problems similar to those of mutual savings banks, the Federal Home Loan Bank Board made the following proposal for their conversion into stock organizations.[7] Account holders should be given shares of stock in the savings and loan association based on the amount of their eligible deposits on a particular date. Because it would be too expensive for associations to reconstruct their records for several years back to obtain account holder information, the initial date proposed by the board was July 13, 1972. Thus, if a conversion of a mutual association into a stock association had occurred in 1973, 90 percent of the newly created stock would have been distributed to eligible account holders on the basis of their July 13, 1972 deposits and 10 percent on the basis of their deposits on December 31, 1972. The proposal contains a complex system of forward time-weighting and averaging of accounts to discourage speculation. (Some people might put funds in an association merely for the purpose of obtaining shares of stock upon conversion.) The record date, or the date when account holders must have their funds on deposit to be eligible for shares for plans adopted after 1972, is to be December 31 of each succeeding year. For plans of conversion adopted in 1975, the distribution of securities will be made to account holders having deposits on December 31, 1974, on the following basis: 10 percent of the securities will be allotted on the basis of the account holders' qualifying deposits on December 31, 1974, 15 percent on the basis of the quarterly average of their qualifying deposits during 1973, and 75 percent on the basis of the quarterly average of their qualifying deposits during 1972. In this way account holders who have had deposits for several years benefit the most while those with relatively new deposits benefit less.

The National Association of Mutual Savings Banks has also made a proposal for the conversion of mutual organizations into stock organizations.[8] An independent appraiser would determine the value of the shares of stock, all account holders would be offered the shares at the predetermined price, and those shares that were not taken by account holders would be sold on the open market. The entire proceeds of the sale of the shares would be given to a community trust fund to support worthwhile social projects. Alternately, the proceeds could be given to the state or federal deposit insurance agency because it insures the deposits.

---

[7]"Federal Home Loan Bank Board," *Federal Register*, Part II, Vol. 38, no. 7 (January 11, 1973).
[8]The proposal was reported by Benston, pp. 213–214.

Both the Federal Home Loan Bank Board and the National Association of Mutual Savings Banks proposals highlight some of the issues associated with conversion. One school of thought argues that the reserves and surplus accounts belong to the account holders and should be distributed to them. Another school of thought argues that account holders have no risk capital invested because their funds are insured, and therefore the reserves and surplus funds should go to the insuring agency. Yet others argue that, since no one has a clear moral or legal right to the reserves at the time of conversion, they should be dedicated to beneficial public purposes.[9] Finally, a recent study of the question pointed out that one main purpose of conversion is to permit management to acquire the bulk of the permanent stock with its profit opportunities and risks.[10] However, in some of the proposals now under consideration, the management of mutual institutions would benefit only if they are themselves depositors, and, even so, they would be treated on an equal basis with other account holders. Therefore, it may not be in their interest to convert from a mutual to a stock form of organization. This brings up the question of ownership and responsibility in mutual organizations.

*Trustees*    Because nobody owns mutual savings banks, mutual savings and loan associations, or other types of mutual financial intermediaries, they are governed by a board of trustees or a similar group with a comparable title. The trustees are responsible for overseeing the organization's activities in the best interest of the depositors and for hiring officers who will conduct the day-to-day operations. Those who serve as trustees of savings banks do so mostly for the honor and prestige, because they receive only modest compensation for their efforts. In addition, lawyers, insurance brokers, builders, and realtors who are trustees are compensated for any professional services that they provide to the organization. A survey made by the Federal Home Loan Bank Board reported on the most common occupations of officers and directors of savings and loan associations (as stated earlier, 88 percent of these are mutual organizations). The results of this survey are shown in Table 4–3.[11]

These data suggest that the managements of savings and loan associations have the opportunity to benefit handsomely from their ancillary affiliations. At this point it should be made clear that the management of other types of financial intermediaries and business concerns can also engage in ancillary activities. The motivation of management—regardless of organizational form—is profit. However, it is easier to fire a director or officer of a stock company than it is in a mutual organization. The board of trustees

---

[9]*The Report of the President's Commission on Financial Structure and Regulation*, p. 61.
[10]Edward S. Herman, "Conflict of Interest in the Savings and Loan Industry," in *Study of the Savings and Loan Industry*, ed. Irwin Friend (Washington, D.C.: Federal Home Loan Bank Board, 1969), pp. 774–775.
[11]Herman, pp. 806–808.

Table 4–3

Occupations of officers and directors of savings and loan associations (U.S. average, 1967–1968)

| Activity | Percentage of officers and directors engaged in each activity |
| --- | --- |
| Construction | 11.7 |
| Land ownership and development | 9.6 |
| Building materials and supplies | 17.3 |
| Real estate sales | 26.4 |
| Real estate finance and investment | 12.2 |
| Commercial banking | 28.2 |
| Other financial institutions | 12.9 |
| Casualty and fire insurance | 48.4 |
| Mortgage insurance | 19.7 |
| Title insurance | 8.0 |
| Escrow companies | 5.5 |
| Loan origination and closure | 23.7 |
| Appraisal ˒ | 2.1 |
| Abstract companies | 1.3 |
| Trustee on association loans | 4.8 |
| Other | 3.2 |

Source: Edward S. Herman, "Conflict of Interest in the Savings and Loan Industry," in *Study of the Savings and Loan Industry*, ed. Irwin Friend (Washington, D.C.: Federal Home Loan Bank Board, July 1969).

of a mutual organization tends to be self-perpetuating, since its members are the electorate that vote themselves into power, whereas the directors of a stock organization are elected by the stockholders. In analyzing the savings and loan industry, Edward S. Herman described its management in the following way:

> The vast bulk of the industry is characterized by what amounts to personal or family fiefdoms, or joint venture control by small groups. Personal fiefdoms (or patrimonies) are especially common in the mutual sector of the industry, where they are made possible by a combination of shareholders' lack of interest and limited constraints—traditional, legal and regulatory—on the accretion and use of management power.[12]

This quotation should not be construed as being critical of management or the job that it has done in providing funds and services for over a century. It does, however, raise some questions. The most important one is—Could the organizations have done a better job of providing funds and services if they had been controlled by stockholders? What net public benefits will accrue if mutual institutions convert to a stock form of organization? In the short run, the answer appears to be that conversion to a stock form of

[12]Herman, p. 803.

organization will help to alleviate the capital-adequacy problem referred to earlier. Over a longer time span, most economists would agree that the public benefits most when resources are privately owned and used to produce profits for their owners in a competitive environment.[13]

## Assets of Mutual Savings Banks

Traditionally, mutual savings banks have invested the bulk of their assets in mortgage loans and corporate bonds, because their bankers believe in dealing only in sound investments that will insure their depositors a safe and adequate rate of return. In addition, the mutual savings banks are chartered by states that regulate their freedom to invest by generally confining them to mortgages and high-grade public securities. Today, the investment powers of mutual savings banks have been expanded somewhat, but still 69 percent of their total assets are invested in mortgage loans and 12 percent in corporate bonds (see Table 4–4).

*Mortgages*    Mutual savings banks, like savings and loan associations, are specialists in home mortgage lending. Of the total mortgage loans outstanding at savings banks, 62 percent are for 1- to 4-family homes and another 23 percent are for multifamily properties. Because there are relatively few savings banks and most of them have total assets of less than $100 million, their impact on the mortgage market is limited. At the end of 1973, mutual savings banks accounted for only 11.4 percent of total mort-

Table 4–4

Assets of mutual savings banks (December 31, 1973)

| Type of asset | Amount ($ millions) | Percentage of total assets |
|---|---|---|
| Cash and due from banks | 1,968.4 | 1.9 |
| U.S. government obligations (direct and guaranteed) | 2,957.8 | 2.8 |
| Obligations of federal agencies (not guaranteed) | 2,296.2 | 2.2 |
| Obligations of states and political subdivisions | 926.2 | 0.9 |
| Mortgage-backed securities | 1,861.2 | 1.8 |
| Corporate and other bonds | 13,263.0 | 12.4 |
| Corporate stock | 3,962.3 | 3.7 |
| Mortgage loans | 73,230.8 | 68.7 |
| Other loans | 3,870.7 | 3.6 |
| Bank premises owned | 845.4 | 0.8 |
| Other real estate | 192.8 | 0.2 |
| Other assets | 1,275.7 | 1.2 |
| Total[a] | $106,650.5 | 100.0 |

[a]Totals may not add due to rounding
Source: National Association of Mutual Savings Banks

[13]For further discussion of this point, see Benston, pp. 209–211.

gage debt outstanding. Nevertheless, they are important lenders in their local mortgage markets, and they play a major role in the FHA and VA mortgage markets. By dealing in federal-underwriter mortgages, mutual savings banks can invest in mortgage loans throughout the country. Moreover, conventional mortgage loans are playing an increasingly important role in out-of-state mortgage lending activity. In recent years, both government-backed and conventional out-of-state mortgages have accounted for about 38 percent of the total mortgage holdings of mutual savings banks.

*Corporate Bonds*    At the end of 1973, there were $13 billion in corporate bonds outstanding at mutual savings banks—1.2 percent of their total assets. Eight years earlier, there had been only $3.7 billion in corporate bonds, accounting for 6 percent of total assets. These statistics point out the increasing role of corporate bonds in the portfolios of mutual savings banks. There are two basic reasons for this trend. First, the increased pace of investments in corporate bonds occurred at a time when the maximum interest rates that could be charged for mortgage loans were well below the market yields on corporate bonds. For example, in 1973 the average contract interest rate on conventional mortgage loans on existing homes was 7.8 percent while the yield on Baa-rated corporate bonds was 8.2 percent, so the latter were relatively more attractive investments. Second, deposits increased at a faster pace than the banks could make mortgage loans, because in recent years the demand for home mortgage loans in the northeast part of the country, where most of the mutual savings banks are located, was not as strong as the demand in other parts of the country. This also explains the growing role of out-of-state mortgage lending by mutual savings banks.

### Liabilities of Mutual Savings Banks

As shown in Table 4–5, the liabilities of mutual savings banks consist mainly of ordinary savings deposits, followed by time and other deposits. In addition, mutual savings banks in at least seven states (Delaware, Indiana, Maryland, Massachusetts, New Jersey, Rhode Island, and Vermont) can offer demand deposits or checking accounts to their customers.

*NOW Accounts*    Recently, savings banks in Massachusetts introduced a new type of savings account called a Negotiable Order of Withdrawal or NOW account, which is similar to a checking account except that it pays interest. It is particularly interesting because commercial banks are prohibited by law from paying interest on demand deposits. However, the collection and clearing of checks costs the banks a lot of money, which they normally pass on to their customers in the form of service charges. In certain cases, they are permitted to render "free" services (no charges) to

Table 4–5

Liabilities of mutual savings banks (December 31, 1973)

| Liabilities and general reserve accounts | Amount ($ millions) | Percentage of total liabilities |
|---|---|---|
| Regular deposits | 96,056.4 | 90.1 |
| Ordinary savings | 65,220.6 | 61.2 |
| Time and other | 30,835.8 | 28.9 |
| School and club deposits | 185.3 | 0.2 |
| Other deposits | 254.2 | 0.2 |
| Total deposits | 96,495.9 | 90.5 |
| Borrowing and mortgage warehousing | 403.4 | 0.4 |
| Other liabilities | 2,162.3 | 2.0 |
| Total liabilities | 99,061.6 | 92.9 |
| General reserve accounts | 7,588.9 | 7.0 |
| Total liabilities and general reserve accounts[a] | $106.650.5 | 100.0 |

[a]Totals may not add due to rounding
Source: National Association of Mutual Savings Banks

demand deposit customers, and this is equivalent to paying an implicit interest rate on those deposits.

The significance of the NOW account is that it erodes traditional differences between demand deposits, savings deposits, and time deposits. Demand deposits used to be non-interest-bearing checking accounts and time accounts were a special class of savings accounts that were left on deposit for a specified period of time and recieved a higher rate of interest. Nowadays, some types of time deposit, such as negotiable certificates of deposit in denominations of $100,000 or more, remain on deposit for a shorter period of time than some demand deposits. A business may invest in marketable certificates of deposit for a few days whereas some individuals leave idle funds in their demand deposits for long periods of time.

These developments raise important questions for the banking industry. For example, should the reserve requirements on demand deposits, savings deposits, and time deposits be the same or should they be different? This question is complicated by the fact that mutual savings banks are governed by the laws and regulations of the states in which they are chartered. Consequently, there is considerable variation in the reserve requirements between the states. For example, in 1972, the average ratio of general reserve accounts to deposits ranged from a high of 9.4 percent in New Hampshire to a low of 6.4 percent in New Jersey. The average reserve/deposit ratio for all mutual savings banks was 7.6 percent.

## Allied Activities

Mutual savings banks in some states have established, for their own benefit, insurance companies, mutual funds, trust companies, and a company

that transfers funds electronically. Brief descriptions of several of these allied activities are presented below.

*The Savings Bank Trust Company*    During the Great Depression of the 1930s, mutual savings banks located in New York State formed a commercial bank called the Savings Bank Trust Company, whose purpose was to supply some of the services of a central bank. The services now provided include:

1 A depository for correspondent balances
2 Paying agent for money orders of savings banks
3 Custodian and transfer agent of securities
4 Loans to mutual savings banks against suitable collateral
5 Assistance with investment services
6 Mortgage and real estate information and services

At the end of 1971, the Savings Bank Trust Company had total assets of $366 million. Because of its small size, it primarily serves small and medium-sized mutual savings banks.

*The Savings Bank Life Insurance Company*    In 1938, mutual savings banks in Massachusetts, New York, and Connecticut formed a legal reserve life insurance company to serve mutual savings banks in all states where it was permitted to do so by law. At the end of 1973, the company had about 1.4 million ordinary life insurance policies and group certificates outstanding with a face value of $6.0 billion.

*Drayton Company, Limited*    This is an industry-owned insurance company that insures mutual savings banks' interest in the properties underlying their mortgage loans. Because insurance premiums and deductibles of private all-risk mortgage insurance companies had increased dramatically in recent years, mutual savings banks formed this company in 1971 to cut their insurance costs and provide their industry with better services. Along the same lines, a Bank Group Plan was organized in 1972 to provide the following types of policies:

1 Property and general liability insurance
2 Insurance for automobiles used by bank employees in their business
3 Commercial liability insurance
4 Workman's compensation

*Mutual Savings Central Fund, Inc.*    In 1932, the Mutual Savings Central Fund, Inc., was established by Massachusetts state law to serve as a credit agency from which mutual savings banks could borrow against collateral. Membership in the fund is compulsory for all savings banks in the state. In later years the fund also provided deposit insurance for its members.

*MINTS*   MINTS is an acronym for the Mutual Institutions National Transfer System, which uses computer technology to make possible instantaneous record keeping through direct communication between teller stations and the computer. Participating banks give their customers a plastic money transfer card. If a MINTS cardholder has $300 in his savings account and uses the card to withdraw $100 from an automated teller, the computer will record the transaction on the cardholder's account.

## Credit Unions

In 1864 the first credit society was formed in Flammersfeld, Germany, by Wilhelm Raiffeisen, the former mayor. Credit societies were the forerunners of modern credit unions. Raiffeisen's organization sought to alleviate some of the problems of the poor and working class, by enabling them to pool their savings and then lend them to each other at low interest rates. He believed that the people in such a group should have a *common bond* that would give each member a feeling of responsibility toward the entire group. The original spirit of the credit societies is still embodied in the current motto of the credit union movement: not for profit, not for charity, but for service. Raiffeisen carried his concept to other towns in Germany and formed 245 credit societies before he died in 1888.

The first credit union in the United States was formed in Manchester, New Hampshire, in 1909. Subsequently, the number of credit unions increased at a slow pace until the mid-1930s when the Federal Credit Union Act of 1934 permitted federally chartered credit unions to organize in all states. Prior to that time credit unions were chartered exclusively under state law and not all states had permissive legislation.

According to the Federal Credit Union Act of 1934, a credit union is defined as a cooperative association organized for the purpose of promoting thrift among its members and creating a source of credit for provident or productive purposes. The act limits membership in credit unions to groups having a common bond of occupation or association or to groups within a well-defined neighborhood community or rural district. In addition, each member must own at least one share of stock and pay a membership fee. The basic price (par value) of the shares that members buy is normally $5, and the membership fee is usually a nominal amount such as 25 or 50 cents.

### Organization of Credit Unions

As shown in Table 4–6, at the end of 1972 there were 23,062 credit unions in operation in the United States. Of that total, 12,708 were federal credit

Table 4–6

Selected data on state-chartered and federal credit unions (1972)

| Item | State-chartered | Federal | Total |
|---|---|---|---|
| Number in operation | 10,354 | 12,708 | 23,062 |
| Number of members | 12,118,035 | 13,572,312 | 25,690,347 |
| Average membership per credit union | 1,170 | 1,068 | |
| Average assets per credit union | $ 1,185,520 | $   984,704 | |

Source: National Credit Union Administration

unions and the remainder were state-chartered. Collectively, they served 25.7 million members. Table 4–6 also reveals that, on the average, federal credit unions have fewer members and fewer assets than state-chartered ones. One reason for these differences is that federal credit unions may have access to larger groups of employees (such as the U.S. Navy) than state-chartered credit unions. Many credit unions organize under federal charters because of the services provided by the National Credit Union Administration—share insurance up to an amount of $40,000 per member account, periodic examinations of member credit unions, and advice and guidance on the management of credit unions. State-chartered credit unions are also eligible to obtain federal share insurance for their members if they wish to do so.

It should be pointed out that average statistics are somewhat misleading because of the preponderance of small credit unions. The data in Table 4–7 show that more than half of the credit unions in the United States have assets of less than $250,000. Moreover, only 20 percent have assets in excess of $1 million, and these few institutions account for nearly 70 percent of the total assets of the credit union movement.

Small size is one of the strengths of the credit union movement. Because most credit unions are small, they can operate with voluntary office help,

Table 4–7

Asset size of all credit unions (December 31, 1972)

| Assets ($ thousands) | Number of institutions | Percentage |
|---|---|---|
| Less than 100 | 7,133 | 30.9 |
| 100–249.9 | 4,896 | 21.2 |
| 250–499.9 | 3,647 | 15.8 |
| 500–999.9 | 2,869 | 12.4 |
| 1,000–1,999.9 | 1,980 | 8.6 |
| 2,000–4,999.9 | 1,595 | 6.9 |
| 5,000 and over | 942 | 4.1 |
| Total[a] | 23,062 | 100.0 |

[a]Totals may not add due to rounding
Source: Credit Union National Administration

which holds down their cost of doing business. Many of the volunteers believe that the credit union movement will help members to enjoy a better way of life, and they are willing to devote their time to further the movement. With such beliefs and attitudes, many small credit unions retain the original spirit of the credit union movement: they exist for the service of their members.

At the other end of the spectrum, there are a few large credit unions. Because of their size, these depend more on full-time employees than on volunteers. Nevertheless, they too serve their memberships. Table 4–8 gives the names and asset size of the ten largest credit unions in the United States. The largest had total assets of $284 million and the next two had assets of $108 million each. A perusal of the list shows that the asset sizes of the remaining credit unions declines significantly; even the largest credit unions are small when compared with other types of financial intermediary.

## Common Bond

The notion of a *common bond* is a basic element of the credit movement and one of the features that distinguishes credit unions from other types of financial intermediaries. The most successful credit unions are those that serve well-defined groups of people; the names of several of the largest credit unions (Navy, United Airlines Employees, Los Angeles Teachers) suggest the scope of their respective memberships. However, not all credit unions serve such cohesive groups. For example, the Cincinnati-based Everybody's Credit Union, which was organized to serve the poor in a nineteen-county area, has a common bond of poverty.[14]

Table 4–8

Ten largest credit unions (December 1972)

| Name of credit union | Total assets ($ thousands) |
| --- | --- |
| 1  Navy (federal) | 283,999 |
| 2  Pentagon (federal) | 108,334 |
| 3  United Airlines Employees | 108,044 |
| 4  Los Angeles Teachers | 91,262 |
| 5  Hughes Aircraft Employees (federal) | 71,877 |
| 6  American Airlines Employees | 79,362 |
| 7  Detroit Teachers | 69,857 |
| 8  East Hartford Aircraft (federal) | 68,349 |
| 9  Tinker Air Force Base | 65,396 |
| 10  State Employees (Raleigh, N.C.) | 65,236 |

Source: National Credit Union Administration

[14]"Everybody's Credit Union: A Credit Union for Everybody," *The Credit Union Magazine*, Vol. 37, no. 11 (November 1972), pp. 24–29.

The data presented in Table 4–9 show the common bonds of the membership of credit unions located in the United States, Canada, and elsewhere throughout the world. The bonds are classified as associational, occupational, and residential. In the United States and Canada the largest common bond is occupational and the second largest is associational; residential bonds account for only a small fraction of the total membership. Elsewhere in the world the most important common bond is the residential area where the members live.

## Assets and Liabilities of Credit Unions

At the end of 1972, all credit unions had total assets of $25 billion. That is quite small when compared with commercial banks, which have total assets in excess of $640 billion. In spite of the relatively small size of the total credit union movement, it plays an important role in our financial system by providing a safe depository for savings and making consumer-type loans. As Table 4–10 shows, the liabilities of credit unions consist mainly of members' savings shares and deposits while their assets consist mainly of loans.

## Reasons for Membership in Credit Unions

*Dividends*    Individuals deposit funds in credit unions for numerous reasons. First, credit unions tend to pay higher dividend rates than other thrift institutions. For example, in 1971 the average dividend paid by federal credit unions was 5.48 percent, and almost 70 percent of operating federal credit unions paid dividends of 5 to 6 percent. In contrast, the average annual yield on savings accounts and deposits at savings and loan associations and savings banks was 5.33 percent and 5.13 percent, respectively. Credit unions can afford to pay higher dividend rates because they are not restricted by Regulation Q, which sets the maximum interest rates that can be paid on time and savings deposits; and their costs of doing business are

Table 4–9

Distribution of credit unions by common bonds

| Common bond | U.S.A. | Canada | Elsewhere |
|---|---|---|---|
| Associational (church, co-op labor union, professional and trade associations) | 17.79% | 20.97% | 12.82% |
| Occupational (agriculture, manufacturing, mining, etc.) | 56.88 | 37.84 | 24.20 |
| Educational services | 7.19 | 1.98 | 8.65 |
| Federal, state, and local government | 14.76 | 6.17 | 11.93 |
| Residential | 3.38 | 33.04 | 42.40 |
| | 100.00 | 100.00 | 100.00 |

Source: *International Credit Union Yearbook*, Madison, Wisc., 1970

Table 4–10

Assets and liabilities of all credit unions (1972)

| Assets | Thousands of dollars |
|---|---|
| Cash | 989,974 |
| Loans outstanding | 18,663,273 |
| Total investments | 4,674,674 |
| Other assets | 460,569 |
| Total assets | $24,788,497 |

| Liabilities and capital | |
|---|---|
| Members' savings shares and deposits | 21,577,920 |
| Reserves | 1,412,124 |
| Notes payable | 526,602 |
| Undivided earnings | 966,187 |
| Other liabilities | 305,655 |
| Total liabilities and capital | $24,788,497 |

[a]Totals may not add due to rounding
Source: National Credit Union Administration

lower than those of other financial institutions because of volunteer personnel and the economies of payroll deductions. In addition to paying high
dividends, some credit unions provide their members with either free life
insurance and credit life insurance (to pay off outstanding loans of the
member) or term life insurance. Generally, such life insurance has a face
value of $10,000 or less while the credit life insurance is for the value of the
loan or $10,000, whichever is less.

*Borrowing*    Perhaps the most important reason for membership in a credit union is that only members are entitled to borrow from it. Because credit
unions are specialists in consumer finance, they invest more than three-
fourths of their assets in consumer loans. Tables 4–10 and 4–11 indicate the
amount of loans and the types of consumer purposes to which they were
put. Over one-third of the loans were used to acquire consumer durable
goods such as automobiles, furniture, and boats. Half of the loans were
used for personal expenditures such as vacations, education, and debt
consolidations, and the remainder were used for real estate repair and
acquisition and other purposes.

*Interest Rates*    On average, the interest rates charged on consumer loans
are lower at credit unions than at other lender institutions. By law, federal
credit unions cannot charge more than 1 percent per month (12 percent per
annum) on the outstanding loan made to a member. This includes the cost
of credit insurance that is provided by many credit unions. During 1971, 70
percent of the loans (63 percent of the dollar value) made by federal credit
unions were at the maximum 1 percent per month interest rate. Most of the

Table 4–11

Distribution of loans made by federal credit unions (1972)

| Purpose of loan | Percentage of total | |
|---|---|---|
| Durable goods (total) | 37.4 | |
| New automobiles | | 10.4 |
| Used automobiles | | 12.1 |
| Furniture and home furnishings | | 8.4 |
| Boats, mobile homes | | 2.5 |
| Other | | 4.0 |
| Personal, household, and family expenses (total) | 48.7 | |
| Nondurable goods | | 3.5 |
| Vacations | | 6.6 |
| Education | | 2.0 |
| Medical | | 4.6 |
| Taxes | | 3.0 |
| Insurance | | 1.8 |
| Debt consolidation | | 11.2 |
| Other | | 16.1 |
| Residential repair | 8.9 | 8.9 |
| Real estate | 3.3 | 3.3 |
| Business | 1.8 | 1.18 |
| Total | 100.0 | 100.0 |

Source: National Credit Union Administration

remaining loans were made at rates of ¾ of 1 percent or less. The lower interest rates were generally made on large long-term secured loans to purchase durable goods or modernize residential properties. In addition to charging relatively low interest rates on loans, some credit unions paid year-end interest refunds to their borrowers, ranging from less than 5 percent to 20 percent or more. This system is similar to patronage refunds paid by some consumer cooperatives. The effect of the refunds is to reduce the effective interest cost to the borrowers, which is an additional bonus for credit union members.

## The Future—A Paradox

In recent years, credit unions have sought a wider range of powers in order to offer their members more services. Some of the additional powers sought by the Credit Union National Association (a trade organization) in bills drafted for the House and Senate are listed below:

1 The power to offer third party payments systems
2 The power to perform trust services for members
3 The power to issue credit cards and establish lines of credit for members
4 The removal of restrictions in the Federal Credit Union Act on loan maturities
5 An expanded definition of common bond to include interest groups as well as associations or residence

This indicates how credit unions are seeking to expand beyond their traditional role. Credit unions are caught in the stream of change, but they cannot be all things to all people. If they get too big, they may lose the original spirit of the credit union movement and their concern for people. On the other hand, if they are not big enough to provide their members with the services that they want, they will lose members to other financial institutions. "The crucial question, then, is how to 'keep up' in the business world and yet somehow maintain the original purposes and philosophy behind credit unionism. Unless this is done, credit unions will become just additional financial institutions and will deserve no more loyalty of members than the local bank or the small loan company."[15]

## Summary

For the most part, mutual savings banks are located in the northeastern United States. Like mutual savings and loan associations, they are owned and run by their depositors. In recent years there has been considerable pressure for them to change from a mutual to a stock form of organization, primarily to raise more capital.

The assets of mutual savings banks consist mostly of mortgage loans and corporate bonds and their liabilities mainly of savings deposits. In order to better serve their customers, they participate in a variety of allied activities, which include a life insurance company, a mutual fund, and a commercial bank.

Credit unions are organized to serve particular groups of people having a common bond, rather than the general public as a whole. They specialize in making consumer loans to their members and safekeeping their members' deposits. These institutions frequently pay higher interest on their deposits and charge lower interest rates on loans than other financial institutions. In order to serve their customers, some larger credit unions want to offer new services (trust departments, credit cards, third party payments), which historically were beyond their scope. As they are granted new powers, credit unions are losing their traditional identity and becoming more like other financial institutions such as finance companies.

## Questions

1 Explain the differences between mutual and stock forms of organization for savings banks. Discuss some of the advantages of each.

---

[15]J. Carroll Moody and Gilbert C. Fite, *The Credit Union Movement: Origins and Development, 1850–1970* (Lincoln, Neb.: University of Nebraska Press, 1971), p. 357.

2 Despite the several advantages of the mutual form of organization, there is considerable interest in allowing mutual savings banks (and mutual savings and loan associations) to change to a stock form of organization. What is the primary reason that some mutual institutions might be interested in conversion?

3 Discuss how conversion by savings banks from a mutual to a stock form of organization might be accomplished and what problems might be incurred.

4 Explain the similarities and differences between the portfolio holdings of mutual savings banks and savings and loan associations.

5 Discuss Negotiable Order of Withdrawal (NOW) accounts and explain how these accounts change the traditional differences between time deposits and demand deposits.

6 Discuss some services performed by mutual savings banks in addition to the traditional depository-lender functions.

7 Discuss the major sources and uses of funds by credit unions.

8 Explain the major advantages of credit union membership.

9 Discuss some of the additional services that credit unions are seeking to offer and how the establishment of these services might alter the traditional role of credit unions.

## Bibliography

Moody, J. Carroll, and Gilbert C. Fite. *The Credit Union Movement: Origins and Development, 1850–1970.* Lincoln, Neb.: University of Nebraska Press, 1971.

National Association of Mutual Savings Banks. *Mutual Savings Banking: Basic Characteristics and Role in the National Economy.* Prepared for the Commission on Money and Credit. Englewood Cliffs, N.J.: Prentice-Hall, 1962.

Polner, Walter. *Credit Unions in the 1970's.* Madison, Wisc.: CUNA Supply Cooperative, 1971.

Teck, Alan. *Mutual Savings Banks and Savings and Loan Associations: Aspects of Growth.* New York: Columbia University Press, 1968.

# 5

# Commercial banks

Why are commercial banks different from other types of financial inter-mediaries? We have said earlier that all financial intermediaries are similar because they sell secondary securities and buy primary securities. The differences between them are a function of the kinds of assets in which they invest and the kinds of secondary securities they sell. Commercial banks invest in a wider variety of assets than any other financial intermediary, but they specialize in making loans with maturities of five years or less to business concerns. On the other side of the balance sheet, commercial banks are the principal type of financial intermediary that holds demand deposits—the most liquid of secondary securities. Moreover, commercial banks can create money! Finally, the asset size of the commercial banking system relative to other financial intermediaries is an important distinguish-ing feature. At the end of 1973, the assets of all commercial banks were $835.2 billion, while life insurance companies, the next largest financial intermediary, had total assets of $252.1 billion.

**Features of Commercial Bank Portfolios**

Traditional Role

The traditional role of commercial banks was to make short-term, self-liquidating loans to business concerns and to provide a place for safekeep-ing depositors' funds. This concept is presented in the following excerpts taken from lectures given at Harvard University in the late 1800s.

*The leading wants to be provided for by banks are first, loans upon considerable scale, required by individuals embarking in enterprises beyond their own means; and second, the temporary employment of money which is not required by the owner for immediate use, or at least the means of safely keeping it. . . .*

*Security of the principal and the rate of return are therefore the essential considerations in the selection of investments. . . . Commercial banks must, in addition, endeavor to keep themselves in a highly liquid condition at all times. Most of the conditions of the case are best answered by the "discount" of commercial paper. . . . The time for which such obligations have to run varies . . . but in most cases is short enough to imply early repayment to the bank.*[1]

The lectures went on to say that when commercial loans could not be obtained in sufficient quantity, banks could invest some of their funds in U.S. government bonds and other high-quality bonds. However, bankers were cautioned not to invest in corporate stocks because stock prices were too volatile and not to invest in mortgages because they might be difficult to sell when the banks needed the money. Thus, the traditional view was that banks held liquid deposits and they should invest those funds in short-term liquid assets.

## Assets

### Loans

Some of the tenets of the traditional view of banking are reflected in current banking practices. Over 80 percent of the assets of commercial banks consist of loans and investments. The remainder is cash and other assets. As shown in Table 5–1, commercial banks make their largest dollar volume of loans to business concerns (line 24). In banking terminology, *commercial loans* generally refer to loans with an original maturity of less than one year, and *term loans* refer to loans with an original maturity of more than one year. Over three-fifths of the $150 billion in loans outstanding to business concerns were commercial loans that were self-liquidating within one year. In contrast, and in spite of the admonitions of those adhering to the traditional view, commercial banks made their second largest dollar volume on long-term real estate loans (line 11). Slightly less than one-half of these loans were made on single-family homes and had original maturities in excess of twenty years; the remainder were made on multifamily, commercial, and industrial properties. Commercial banks are second to savings

---

[1]Charles F. Dunbar and Oliver M. W. Sprague, *The Theory and History of Banking*, 3d ed. (New York: G. P. Putnam's Sons, 1922), pp. 2–29.

Table 5–1

Securities, loans, and discounts at all commercial banks (June 30, 1973)

| | | Billions of dollars |
|---|---|---:|
| 1 | Securities (total) | $178.9 |
| 2 | U.S. treasury securities | 57.8 |
| 3 | Securities of other U.S. government agencies and corporations | 24.1 |
| 4 | Obligations of state and subdivisions | 91.3 |
| 5 | Other securities | 5.6 |
| 6 | Federal funds sold and securities purchased under agreement to resell (total) | 27.6 |
| 7 | With domestic commercial banks | 26.0 |
| 8 | With brokers and dealers in securities | 1.3 |
| 9 | With others | 0.3 |
| 10 | Other loans and discounts (total) | 429.6 |
| 11 | Real estate loans (total) | 108.2　108.2 |
| 12 | Secured by farmland | 5.1 |
| | Secured by 1- to 4-family residential properties: | |
| 13 | Insured by FHA | 6.7 |
| 14 | Guaranteed by VA | 3.2 |
| 15 | Not insured or guaranteed by FHA or VA | 51.6 |
| | Secured by multifamily (5 or more) residential properties: | |
| 16 | Insured by FHA | 1.4 |
| 17 | Not insured by FHA | 5.0 |
| 18 | Secured by other properties | 32.0 |
| 19 | Loans to domestic, commercial, and foreign banks | 9.9 |
| 20 | Loans to other financial institutions | 27.7 |
| 21 | Loans to brokers and dealers in securities | 7.4 |
| 22 | Other loans for purchasing or carrying securities | 4.8 |
| 23 | Loans to farmers (excluding loans on real estate) | 16.0 |
| 24 | Commercial and industrial loans (including open-market paper) | 150.3 |
| 25 | Other loans to individuals (total) | 94.4　94.4 |
| 26 | Passenger automobile installment loans | 32.1 |
| | Credit cards and related plans: | |
| 27 | Retail (charge account) credit card plans | 5.0 |
| 28 | Check credit and revolving credit plans | 2.0 |
| | Other retail consumer installment loans: | |
| 29 | Mobile homes, not including travel trailers | 7.3 |
| 30 | Other retail consumer goods | 5.7 |
| 31 | Residential repairs and modernization installment loans | 4.5 |
| 32 | Other installment loans for personal expenditures | 13.1 |
| 33 | Single-payment loans for personal expenditures | 23.4 |
| 34 | All other loans (including overdrafts) | 11.0 |
| 35 | Total loans and securities | $636.1 |

Source: Federal Deposit Insurance Corporation

and loan associations as mortgage investors. Nevertheless, they only hold 40 percent of the amount of mortgages held by savings and loan associations ($223 billion in June 1973). The third largest dollar volume of loans is consumer installment credit, which is called other loans to individuals (line 25). These are loans used to finance automobiles and other consumer goods, and personal loans. They usually mature within three years, although some loans on mobile homes (line 29) can have a maturity of twelve years. In summary, the three major lending categories—commercial and industrial loans, real estate loans, and consumer installment credit—account for the bulk of commercial banks' loans outstanding, but, as Table 5–1 shows commercial banks make other types of loans too. Some loans are made to financial intermediaries, such as securities dealers and finance companies, to finance their activities. Others are made to farm organizations and foreign governments.

## Investments

In addition to making loans, commercial banks also invest in securities. Investments consist of U.S. treasury securities, obligations of state and local governments, and some corporate securities. The data in Table 5–1 show that the total dollar amount of the investments is about one-half that of the loans.

Federal funds are a short-term investment for some banks and a source of funds for others. These funds are immediately available reserves which banks can lend or borrow from other banks on an overnight basis. Thus, banks with a temporary surplus of reserve funds can invest them overnight in banks needing additional funds.

Commercial banks invest in securities because they provide liquidity and income. Should depositors withdraw funds in excess of the cash on hand, a commercial bank could sell some of its investments to provide the necessary funds. Because most of the securities have maturities of less than five years, they can be sold quickly with a minimum loss and a possible gain.

## Income

Investments provide income for commercial banks. For example, assume that the average market yield on a one-year treasury bill is 4.6 percent. The earnings on such a security amount to $126 interest per million dollars of securities held *per day*.[2] As of mid-1973, commercial banks held $57.8 billion in U.S. treasury securities (line 2, Table 5–1). Clearly the return on these securities was substantial. In addition to U.S. treasury securities,

---

[2]The coupon rate equivalent is calculated on a 365-day basis.

commercial banks hold the largest dollar amount of their investments in the obligations of state and political subdivisions (line 4). These include bonds, notes, and tax anticipation bills.

## Municipal Securities

The major attraction of municipal securities for investors is that the interest is exempt from federal income tax. For most commercial banks, which are in the 48 percent marginal tax bracket, a 5.3 percent coupon (the average yield on municipal bonds in 1973) is equivalent to 10.2 percent of taxable interest income.[3] Some municipal securities are exempt from state income taxes, as well as from federal income taxes, if they are held by investors residing in the state where the obligations were issued. Being doubly tax exempt makes municipal bonds particularly attractive because, like other securities, they provide income and some liquidity, and so commercial banks have invested heavily in them; in fact, they are the largest institutional investor in state and local obligations.

## Trading Profits

Some commercial banks buy and sell securities to obtain trading profits. If a banker believes that long-term interest rates are going to decline, which means market prices on exisiting bonds will rise, he may buy long-term bonds in hopes of selling them at a later date at a higher price. Conversely, if long-term interest rates were expected to rise, the banker would sell his long-term bonds and buy shorter-term securities. In either case, potential profit depends on the banker's ability to forecast interest rates correctly.

In review, two features of the loan portfolios of commercial banks distinguish them from other financial intermediaries. First, commercial banks are specialists in making short- and intermediate-term loans to business concerns. Second, in addition to lending funds to businesses, commercial banks have more diversified loan portfolios than any other type of financial intermediary (see Table 5–1). Although they are in the business of making loans, they also invest in obligations of state and local governments and U.S. treasury securities, both of which provide liquidity and some income. In very general terms, modern commercial banks reflect the genes of their ancestors—heavy emphasis on short-term, self-liquidating loans to businesses and high-quality securities.

## The Behavior of Assets

This section deals with changes in selected assets of commercial banks. The assets shown in Table 5–2 should be considered as an entire portfolio.

---

[3]The tax equivalent yield is calculated from the following formula:
$$\text{Tax equivalent yield} = \frac{5.3\% \text{ (coupon rate)}}{1 - 0.48 \text{ (marginal tax rate)}} = 0.1019.$$

Table 5-2

Treasury bill rate and changes in selected assets of commercial banks (1965–1973)

|  | 1965 | 1966 | 1967 | 1968 |
|---|---|---|---|---|
| 1  Treasury bill rate (3-month market, %) | 4.0 | 4.9 | 4.3 | 5.3 |
| Financial assets | Changes in holdings (billions of dollars) | | | |
| 2  U.S. government securities | −2.8 | −3.1 | 9.2 | 3.2 |
| 3  State and local obligations | 5.2 | 2.3 | 9.0 | 8.6 |
| 4  Total mortgage loans | 5.6 | 4.6 | 4.5 | 6.7 |
| 5  Consumer credit | 4.6 | 2.6 | 2.4 | 5.7 |
| 6  Loans to nonfinancial businesses | 16.7 | ' 9.3 | 7.3 | 15.3 |

|  | 1969 | 1970 | 1971 | 1972 | 1973 |
|---|---|---|---|---|---|
| 1  Treasury bill rate (3-month market, %) | 6.6 | 6.4 | 4.3 | 4.1 | 7.0 |
| Financial assets | Changes in holdings (billions of dollars) | | | | |
| 2  U.S. government securities | −10.1 | 10.5 | 7.0 | 6.0 | −1.3 |
| 3  State and local obligations | 0.2 | 10.5 | 12.8 | 7.1 | 5.6 |
| 4  Total mortgage loans | 5.3 | 2.3 | 9.8 | 16.8 | 8.7 |
| 5  Consumer credit | 4.7 | 2.9 | 6.7 | 10.1 | 10.6 |
| 6  Loans to nonfinancial businesses | 12.3 | 4.2 | 11.9 | 27.7 | 46.7 |

Source: Board of Governors of the Federal Reserve System, Flow of Funds Accounts

The changes in the portfolio reflect changes in the liabilities of commercial banks and changes in economic conditions. Thus, in 1966 and 1969 commercial banks liquidated some of their holdings of U.S. government securities (line 2) to help pay off depositors when there was substantial disintermediation. In 1969, since banks were particularly hard-pressed for liquidity, there was virtually no increase in state and local obligations (line 3) besides the liquidation of U.S. government securities. In the following three years, when there were large net savings inflows, commercial banks replenished the liquidity they had lost in the previous period by again buying U.S. government securities and state and local obligations.

## Economic Activity and Portfolio Changes

The amount by which commercial banks increased their liquidity in 1970 was partially in response to economic conditions. From November 1969 to November 1970, the economy experienced a mild recession. The slow pace of economic activity contributed to slack demand for loans (assets) from commercial banks. To illustrate this relationship, compare total expenditures on residential and nonresidential structures to changes in mortgage loans (line 4). In 1970, total expenditures on residential and nonresidential structures amounted to $1 billion, compared with $12 billion in the previous year, and total mortgage loans made by commercial banks in 1970 were less than half the amount made in the previous year. In 1971,

total residential and nonresidential expenditures rose to nearly $17 billion, and the amount of mortgage loans made by commercial banks increased nearly fourfold. A similar relationship existed between the Personal Consumption Expenditures found in the National Income Accounts and consumer credit extended by commercial banks: consumer lending activity was slack in 1969–1970 and strong in 1971 (line 5).

However, the pattern for business loans (line 6) was different; demand was strong in 1969–1970 but declined in the following year. One reason for this pattern of behavior concerns the liquidity of corporate business. A study of the liquidity problem in the 1970 *Annual Report of the Council of Economic Advisors* made the following observations:

> With the sustained period of credit restraint in 1969 and early 1970, some financial imbalances that had accumulated during the long inflation became more apparent. Capital expenditures of businesses were high and large increases were projected for 1970, but it was also clear that financing of these expansion plans had relied heavily on short-term borrowing.[4]

Business concerns made short-term loans from commercial banks because they considered market interest rates on long-term bonds to be too high. During the 1966–1970 period, yields on high-grade corporate bonds soared from 5 percent to over 9 percent. However, when the liquidity squeeze ended in the last half of 1970, corporate treasurers sought to replenish their liquid assets by selling huge volumes of bonds and stocks. As shown in Table 5–3, the dollar value of corporate bonds issued in 1971 was almost double that of bonds issued in 1969. Similarly, the value of equity securities sold increased dramatically. As a result of these heavy stock and bond flotations, the loans that commercial banks made to busi-

Table 5–3

Gross proceeds of new corporate issues (millions of dollars)

| Year | Bonds | Stock | |
|------|-------|-------|--------|
| | | Preferred | Common |
| 1969 | 18,347 | 682 | 7,714 |
| 1970 | 30,315 | 1,390 | 7,240 |
| 1971 | 32,123 | 3,670 | 9,291 |
| 1972 | 28,896 | 3,367 | 9,694 |
| 1973 | 22,268 | 3,372 | 7,750 |

Source: Securities and Exchange Commission

[4]*Economic Report of the President,* transmitted to Congress February 1971, together with *The Annual Report of the Council of Economic Advisors* (Washington, D.C.: U.S. Government Printing Office, 1971), p. 169.

ness concerns in 1970 ($4.2 billion) were about one-third the amount made in the previous year. By 1972 corporations had replenished their liquidity, and once again they borrowed heavily from commercial banks.

## Liabilities

The liabilities of commercial banks consist mainly of demand deposits and time and savings deposits. In mid-1973, the deposits of commercial banks were distributed in the following manner:

| | | |
|---|---|---|
| Demand deposits | $278.4 | billion |
| Time and savings deposits | 351.1 | billion |
| Total | $629.5 | billion |

Time and savings deposits account for the largest share of total deposits, but this was not always so. Before the mid-1960s, the dollar volume of demand deposits exceeded the dollar volume of time and savings deposits. However, when banks sought funds aggressively by offering a wide variety of deposits at relatively attractive interest rates, the volume of time and savings accounts grew at the expense of demand deposits. The information in Table 5–4 can be used to compare the types of accounts and the

Table 5–4

Maximum interest rates payable on time and savings deposits[a] (percent per annum)

| Type of deposit | Nov. 1964 | Type of deposit | July 1, 1973 | Nov. 1, 1973 |
|---|---|---|---|---|
| Savings deposits | 4 | Savings deposits | 5 | 5 |
| Time deposits | | Time deposits | | |
| 12 mos. or more | | Single and | | |
| 6–12 mos. | 4½ | multiple maturity | | |
| 90 days to 6 mos. | | 30–89 days | 5 | 5 |
| Less than 90 days | 4 | 90 days to 1 year | 5½ | 5½ |
| | | 1–2 years | | |
| | | 1–2½ years | 6 | 6 |
| | | 2 years and over | | |
| | | 2½ years and over | 6½ | 6½ |
| | | 4 years or more in | | |
| | | min. denomination | | |
| | | of $1,000 | None | 7¼ |
| | | $100,000 and over | | |
| | | 30–59 days | None | |
| | | 60–89 days | None | |
| | | 90–179 days | None | |
| | | 180 days to 1 year | None | |
| | | 1 year or more | None | |

[a] As determined by the Board of Governors of the Federal Reserve System
Source: Board of Governors of the Federal Reserve System

maximum interest rates payable on time and savings deposits in late 1964 with similar information for 1973. The contrast between the two periods is striking both because of the variety of accounts offered and because of the interest rates paid. In late 1964, the maximum interest rate that could be paid on any type of deposit was 4½ percent. In contrast, by mid-1973 there was no upper limit on the interest rate that could be paid on large denomination certificates of deposit (CD's). These maximum interest rates are established by the Board of Governors of the Federal Reserve System under the provisions of Regulation Q and apply to member banks. Ceiling rates for nonmember insured commercial banks are set by the FDIC and are the same as those in effect for member banks. As will be discussed shortly, the Board of Governors used the ceiling rates as an important tool of monetary policy in the late 1960s.

## The Behavior of Liabilities

### Disintermediation

The response of commercial banks to the changes that occurred in monetary policy and in economic and financial conditions since 1965 is examined next. The data in Table 5–5 show selected liabilities of commercial banks as well as the short-term treasury bill rate that serves as a reference for money market conditions. In 1966 and 1969 when monetary policy was restrictive and short-term market interest rates on treasury bills and other securities exceeded rates paid on deposits at commercial banks, net

Table 5–5

Treasury bill rate and changes in selected liabilities of commercial banks (1965–1973)

|  | 1965 | 1966 | 1967 | 1968 |
|---|---|---|---|---|
| 1  Treasury bill rate (3-month market, %) | 4.0 | 4.9 | 4.3 | 5.3 |
| Selected liabilities | Changes in holdings (billions of dollars) | | | |
| 2  Demand deposits | 5.5 | 1.6 | 11.9 | 13.3 |
| 3  Time deposits | 20.0 | 13.3 | 23.8 | 20.7 |
| 4  Commercial paper | — | — | — | — |
| 5  Eurodollars | 0.3 | 2.7 | 0.2 | 2.3 |

|  | 1969 | 1970 | 1971 | 1972 | 1973 |
|---|---|---|---|---|---|
| 1  Treasury bill rate (3-month market, %) | 6.6 | 6.4 | 4.3 | 4.1 | 7.0 |
| Selected liabilities | Changes in holdings (billions of dollars) | | | | |
| 2  Demand deposits | 4.9 | 11.2 | 13.0 | 16.3 | 12.6 |
| 3  Time deposits | −9.5 | 38.0 | 41.4 | 42.3 | 50.9 |
| 4  Commercial paper | 4.2 | −1.9 | −0.4 | 0.6 | 2.3 |
| 5  Eurodollars | 7.9 | −6.9 | −4.1 | 0.9 | 1.1 |

Source: Board of Governors of the Federal Reserve System, Flow of Funds Accounts

inflows of demand deposits (line 2) and time deposits (line 3) shrank. Because no interest is paid on demand deposits, investors reduced their checking account balances and increased their investments in securities that provided high yields. Similarly, because the interest rates paid on time and savings deposits were below market interest rates, investors disinter-mediated, investing instead in high-yielding marketable securities. One important point is that the regulation of interest-rate ceilings on time and savings deposits became a major tool of monetary policy in the late 1960s. Its major impact was on negotiable time certificates of deposit (CD's) issued in denominations of $100,000 or more. For example, in 1969, when monetary policy was restrictive and short-term market interest rates were sufficiently high, the dollar volume of large negotiable CD's declined by $12.5 billion. In contrast, from 1970 to 1972, as the posture of monetary policy eased and market interest rates subsided, the dollar volume of large negotiable CD's and other deposits increased substantially. These shifts in funds were in part the result of actions taken by the Board of Governors of the Federal Reserve System. The minutes of the Federal Open Market Committee meetings in early 1969, for example, pointed out that "if prevail-ing money market conditions and existing Regulation Q ceilings were maintained, the volume of large-denomination CD's outstanding was likely to decline . . ."[5] and they did decline because the Board of Governors did not change Regulation Q until January 21, 1971. One reason why large-denomination negotiable CD's bore the brunt of monetary policy was that they were generally held by business concerns that were quite sensitive to changes in interest rates and managed their liquid assets carefully. For example, by shifting $1 million for thirty days from a 5½ percent CD to a 5¾ percent treasury bill, investors could increase their return by $208.[6] There-fore, it is not surprising that those with substantial sums to invest moved their funds into securities that yielded the highest rate of return. Disinter-mediation also affected other financial intermediaries, such as savings and loan associations, mutual savings banks, and life insurance companies.

## Nondeposit Sources of Funds

The large outflows of funds that occurred in recent years have put commer-cial banks in an awkward and precarious position, where they found it difficult to honor all of their loan commitments (promises to make loans). It is hard for a banker to tell a customer of long standing that his line of credit is reduced or that he cannot have all the credit he needs. Moreover, large outflows of funds reduced the liquidity of some banks to dangerously low levels. The liquidity ratio (total liquid assets divided by total liabilities less

---

[5]Minutes of the FOMC meeting held on March 4, 1969, appear in the *1969 Annual Report of the Board of Governors of the Federal Reserve System.*
[6]The equivalent bond yield for a 5¾ percent treasury bill for 30 days is 5.78 percent. The total return from the bill would be $4,791.67. The equivalent bond yield for a 5½ percent CD, based on 360 days, is 5.46 percent, and the total return from such a CD would be $4,583.33.

capital accounts and valuation reserves) declined from 12 percent in 1968 to 8 percent in 1969.[7] In the following year, the ratio rebounded to over 13 percent. In order to compensate for the shortages of funds and reduced liquidity, commercial bankers turned to nondeposit sources of funds such as commercial paper and liabilities to foreign branches (Eurodollars, see below). In addition, banks sold loans to other banks and sold capital notes to whoever was willing to buy them.

*Commercial Paper*    The term *commercial paper* describes unsecured promissory notes of major industries, public utilities, finance companies, and banking organizations issued to obtain short-term credit.[8] About two-thirds of commercial paper outstanding is sold directly to investors and is called directly placed paper. The remainder is sold through dealers. During the 1965–1972 period, the amount of commercial paper outstanding increased from $9.3 billion to $32.1 billion. One reason for the increased volume was that business concerns found that selling commercial paper was less costly than alternate sources of funds. For example, in December 1970, the cost of selling 90-day prime commercial paper was 5.6 percent, whereas the cost of a 5-year bank term loan at the prime rate was 7.3 percent and of a 15-year Baa-rated bond was 9.6 percent.[9] Another reason for the increased use of commercial paper is the availability of bank credit. During periods of credit restraint commercial banks tend to restrict the amount of funds that they will make available and business concerns are forced to turn to alternate sources of funds such as commercial paper. However, in the period of tight money or credit restraint in the late 1960s, commercial banks also had difficulty raising funds, so they too turned to the commercial paper market. Commercial banks issue commercial paper through subsidiaries and affiliates, such as bank holding companies, because if they issued the paper directly the proceeds would be subject to reserve requirements and interest-rate ceilings. The bank holding company issues the commercial paper and channels the proceeds to the bank by purchasing loans from the bank's portfolio. The dollar volume of commercial paper acquired by banks during the 1969 period of monetary restraint indicates that they used commercial paper (Table 5–5, line 4) to help offset the outflow of time deposits. Conversely, when there were substantial inflows of time deposits, the dollar volume of commercial paper held by the banking system dwindled. At the end of 1972, the banking system held $2.6 billion of commercial paper.

---

[7]The data are for weekly reporting banks. Liquid assets include federal funds, U.S. government securities maturing within one year, loans to brokers and dealers, loans to commercial banks, bankers' acceptances, tax warrants, and bond anticipation notes.

[8]For a review of the commercial paper market up to the early 1960s see Richard T. Selden, *Trends and Cycles in the Commercial Paper Market,* Occasional Paper no. 85 (New York: National Bureau of Economic Research, 1963). For a review of the commercial paper market during the 1960s see "Commercial Paper," *Money Market Instruments,* Federal Reserve Bank of Cleveland (1970), pp. 66–67.

[9]Henry Kaufman, *The Cost of Money for Corporate Finance: Financing Strategy* (New York: Salomon Brothers, 1970).

*Eurodollars*    Eurodollars, one of the largest nondeposit sources of funds for commercial banks in the late 1960s, are deposits denominated in United States dollars and placed in banks located in countries such as the United Kingdom, Germany, or the Bahamas.[10] Eurodollar deposits work in the following manner. Suppose that a multinational business concern transfers a demand deposit, denominated in United States dollars, from a bank in the United States to a bank in London. After the transfer has taken place, the business concern has a deposit denominated in dollars at the London bank (a Eurodollar deposit), and the London bank holds a claim against the original deposit in the United States. The creation of the Eurodollar deposit does not alter the volume of bank deposits in the United States, but it does result in the ownership of the original deposit being transferred from the business concern to the London bank.

The difference between deposits located in foreign countries and those located in the United States is both geographic and regulatory. For example, banks located in foreign countries are not subject to the interest-rate ceilings on time and savings deposits imposed by the Federal Reserve System. Moreover, until September 1969, when banks located in the United States borrowed Eurodollars from their foreign branch offices, the borrowings were not subject to member bank reserve requirements or to deposit insurance fees.[11]

Some banks used Eurodollars during the period of credit restraint in the late 1960s to obtain funds and at the same time to reduce their required reserves. In 1969, the maximum interest rate that could be paid on a six-month certificate of deposit in the United States was 6¼ percent, while Eurodollar deposits paid as much as 11⅜ percent.[12] Suppose that, in early 1969, an investor held a $100,000 CD that had just matured at a New York bank. Refusing to reinvest the funds in New York because the banks were not allowed to pay more than 6¼ percent, he transferred his funds from the New York bank to its branch office in London where he could obtain the higher interest rate (11 percent). The balance sheet of the New York bank would show that time certificates of deposit declined by $100,000, while liabilities to foreign branches increased by a like amount. The net effect of the transaction was that the New York bank circumvented the 6¼ percent

---

[10]For further information on the Eurodollar market, see "The Eurodollar Market," *Economic Review*, Federal Reserve Bank of Cleveland (March, April, May, 1970); Milton Friedman, "The Eurodollar Market: Some First Principles," *Morgan Guaranty Survey* (October 1969); "Money Creation in the Euro-Dollar Market—A Note on Professor Friedman's Views," *Monthly Review*, Federal Reserve Bank of New York (January 1970); *Euro-Dollar Financing*, 2d ed. (New York: The Chase Manhattan Bank, 1968); Fred H. Klopstock, "*The Euro-Dollar Market: Some Unresolved Issues*, Essays in International Finance no. 65 (Princeton, N.J.: Princeton University Press, 1968).

[11]Effective September 4, 1969, banks that were members of the Federal Reserve System and had foreign branches were required to maintain a 10 percent reserve against foreign branch deposits. For further details see *Federal Reserve Bulletin* (August 1969), p. 657.

[12]In 1969, the range of yields of six-month maturity Eurodollars was 7.13 percent to 11.28 percent. *An Analytical Record of Yields and Yield Spreads* (New York: Salomon Brothers, 1971).

interest-rate ceiling and reduced its required reserves because there were no reserve requirements on liabilities to foreign branches. After reserve requirements were imposed on liabilities to foreign branches, the use of Eurodollars moderated. However, the decline in the use of Eurodollars also paralleled the decline in short-term interest rates. As shown in Table 5–5 (line 5), Eurodollar borrowings reached a peak in 1969 and then declined. In summary, the combination of Eurodollar borrowing and the sale of bank-related commercial paper more than offset the outflow of time deposits. Thus, bankers impeded monetary policy by obtaining funds from nondeposit sources that were not constrained by interest-rate limitations.

*Participations*   In addition to Eurodollars and the sale of bank-related commercial paper, banks utilize two additional nondeposit sources of funds—the sale of loans, or participations in loans, and the sale of notes and debentures. The sale of loans may arise when banks located in areas where the demand for loans is slack make available their ample funds to banks elsewhere, where demand is high. Alternately, a bank may sell a loan, or invite other banks to participate in it, because the loan is too large for it to handle alone. The sale of loans and participations is frequently handled by correspondent banks. The correspondent banking system is a network of large banks providing services for other commercial banks, which, in return, maintain demand deposits with their correspondents. Examples of the services that correspondent banks provide are check clearings, safekeeping of securities, arranging international financial transactions, and making buy-and-sell recommendations for bond portfolios. Correspondents may also assist banks in loan participations. A recent study of correspondent banking indicated that 60 percent of the banks in the Tenth Federal Reserve District (Kansas City District) have placed loan participations with correspondents in recent years.[13] This statistic alone suggests the widespread use of loans and participations.

## Demand Deposits and Money

### Definitions

This section examines significance of demand deposits in our financial system. At the present time, commercial banks are the principal type of financial institution that issue demand deposits as a secondary security. For this reason, they are unique, because they can create money. The term *money* used in this connection refers to demand deposits. For economists, however, the term money, or *money stock*, has several meanings. One

---

[13]Robert E. Knight, "Correspondent Banking. Part I, Balances and Services," *Monthly Review*, Federal Reserve Bank of Kansas City (November 1970); "Correspondent Banking. Part II, Loan Participations and Fund Flows," *Monthly Review*, Federal Reserve Bank of Kansas City (December 1970).

meaning is the narrowly defined money stock ($M_1$) that consists of demand deposits ($D$) and currency ($C$) held by the nonbank public:

$$M_1 = D + C$$

A broader definition of money stock ($M_2$) adds time deposits at commercial banks, other than large certificates of deposit, to $M_1$; another definition ($M_3$) adds deposits at mutual savings banks and savings and loan associations to $M_2$.[14] The data in Table 5–6 give some dimensions to these abstract concepts. As of June 1974, the narrowly defined money stock ($M_1$) amounted to $281 billion (about one-quarter of that total was currency and the rest consisted of demand deposits). The addition of time and savings deposits, other than large denomination CD's, brings $M_2$ up to $597.6 billion. Finally, the addition of deposits at nonbank thrift institutions brings $M_3$ up to $930.6 billion. These examples do not exhaust the definition of money, but they do illustrate three uses of the term. For convenience, this discussion is restricted to $M_1$, the narrowly defined money stock.

## Money Creation

Commercial banks can create money ($M_1$) because they have fractional reserve requirements that allow the banking system to support multiple demand deposits. In some introductory courses in economics or money and banking, the expansion process is summarized in the following manner. Assume that a foreign company has deposited $100 million in U.S. currency in Bank no. 1 in the United States (see Table 5–7). Further assume that all banks in this example are members of the Federal Reserve System and have a 20 percent reserve requirement on demand deposits. Because the required reserves are only $20 million, Bank no. 1 has $80 million in excess reserves that it can lend and it does so. These $80 million dollars are deposited in Bank no. 2. Bank no. 2 must also maintain 20 percent of its

---

Table 5–6

Money stock measures (billions of dollars seasonally adjusted June 1974)[a]

| | |
|---|---|
| Currency | 64.8 |
| + Demand deposits | 216.1 |
| = $M_1$ | 281.0 |
| + Time deposits at commercial banks (other than large CD's) | 316.6 |
| = $M_2$ | 597.6 |
| + Deposits at nonbank thrift institutions | 333.0 |
| = $M_3$ | $930.6 |

[a]Totals may not add due to rounding
Source: Board of Governors of the Federal Reserve System

---

[14]The definitions of $M_1$, $M_2$, and $M_3$ are those used by the Federal Reserve System, and appear in the Federal Reserve Statistical Release Number H.6, *Money Stock Measures*.

Table 5-7

The deposit expansion process[a]

| Transactions | Demand deposits ($ millions) | Loans ($ millions) | Reserves on deposit at Federal Reserve Banks ($ millions) |
|---|---|---|---|
| Bank no. 1 | 100.0 | | |
| Bank no. 1 | | 80.0 | 20.0 |
| Bank no. 2 | 80.0 | 64.0 | 16.0 |
| Bank no. 3 | 64.0 | 51.2 | 12.8 |
| Bank no. 4 | 51.2 | 41.0 | 10.2 |
| ⋮ | ⋮ | ⋮ | ⋮ |
| Total for n banks | 500.0 | 400.0 | 100.0 |

[a] This example assumes that the member bank reserve requirement for demand deposits is 20 percent

deposits (0.20 × $80 = $16) on reserve at a Federal Reserve Bank and it can lend $64 million. The individuals who borrow the $64 million deposit the funds in Bank no. 3, which meets the reserve requirement ($12.8) and lends the remaining funds ($51.2). The process is repeated until the total deposits for all banks in the system amount to $500 million.

There is an easier method for determining the amount of total deposits. The maximum expansion of demand deposits ($D$) is equal to the reciprocal of the reserve requirement ($1/rr$) times the total dollar amount of bank reserves ($R$):

$D = 1/0.20$ ($100 million) = $500 million

The multiplier, or the reciprocal of the reserve requirement, is 5. If the reserve requirement were 10 percent, the bank money multiplier would be 10, and $1 billion in deposits would be created.

This concept of the expansion of demand deposits is misleading because it is based on the following erroneous assumptions: that all bank deposits are subject to the same reserve requirements; that banks loan out all of their funds and hold no excess reserves; and that the public holds only demand deposits and no currency, time, or savings deposits. Because none of these assumptions corresponds to reality, a different explanation of the expansion of deposits is necessary.

## Monetary Base

The following method of computing the money stock corrects some of the shortcomings that were pointed out in the previous explanation of the

expansion process.[15] It examines the relationship between the narrowly defined money stock ($M_1$) and the monetary base. As shown below, $M_1$ is some function ($m_1$) of the monetary base ($B$):

$$M_1 = m_1 B$$

The *monetary base* can be defined as the amount of reserves held by the banking system ($R$) and the amount of currency in public hands ($C$):

$$B = R + C$$

Next, total bank deposits are broken down into private demand deposits ($D$), time deposits ($T$), and government or treasury deposits ($G$). Commercial bank members of the Federal Reserve System are required to maintain reserves against each of these types of deposits. (Specific reserve requirements will be discussed in Chapter 6.) Reserve requirements of non-member banks are determined by state law and are not considered here, but member banks account for nearly four-fifths of all commercial bank deposits. Total member bank reserves ($R$) can be expressed as a function ($r$) of the sum of total demand deposits, time deposits, and government deposits:

$$R = r (D + G + T)$$

Alternately, $r$ is the weighted average reserve ratio of all member bank deposits, and is computed by dividing total reserves by total deposits:

$$r = \frac{R}{D + T + G}$$

The amount of funds that the Treasury is willing to keep on deposit at commercial banks is determined by the financial needs of the federal government. For example, quarterly income tax payments made to the government increase the amounts of treasury deposits held at commercial banks. Conversely, when the government disburses social security payments, treasury balances at commercial banks are reduced. The amount of these government deposits ($G$) can be expressed as a proportion ($g$) of demand deposits ($D$):

$$G = gD$$

---

[15]The discussion of the money creation process was based primarily on Jerry L. Jordan, "Elements of Money Stock Determination," *Review,* Federal Reserve Bank of St. Louis (October 1969); for additional information see Leonal C. Anderson and Jerry L. Jordan, "The Monetary Base, Explanation and Analytical Use," *Review,* Federal Reserve Bank of St. Louis (August 1968); and Albert E. Burger, *The Money Supply Process* (Belmont, Calif.: Wadsworth Publishing Company, 1971).

Similarly, the public determines the amount of funds that it will hold as time deposits $(T)$ or currency $(C)$. Time deposits may also be expressed as a function $(t)$ of demand deposits:

$$T = tD$$

The amount of funds that the public is willing to hold as deposits is influenced by the relative returns on other forms of savings such as corporate securities, pension funds, and some life insurance policies. These and other factors which influence the amount of currency held by the public are outside the banking system. When an individual converts a deposit into currency, this represents a cash drain from the banking system and reduces the system's ability to expand deposits. The amount of currency $(C)$ held by the public can also be expressed as a proportion $(k)$ of demand deposits:

$$C = kD$$

Before continuing with the explanation of the money supply process, the principal definitions are listed below:

| | |
|---|---|
| (1) narrowly defined money stock | $M_1 = D + C$ |
| (2) monetary base | $B = R + C$ |
| (3) bank reserves | $R = r(D + T + G)$ |
| (4) currency | $C = kD$ |
| (5) time deposits | $T = tD$ |
| (6) government deposits | $G = gD$ |

The definitional equations are used to derive the *money multiplier* $(m_1)$, which gives the amount of deposits associated with each dollar of base held by banks.[16] As can be seen from the definition, the money multiplier is

---

[16]The money multiplier is derived by substituting equations (3) and (4) into (2) to obtain:

(7) $B = r(D + T + G) + kD$

Next, substituting (5) and (6) into (7), we get

(8) $B = r(D + tD + gD) + kD$,

which can be simplified as

(8') $B = r(1 + t + g) = k(D)$,

or

(9) $D = \dfrac{1}{r(1 + t + g) + k}(B)$

Equations (9) and (4) are used to derive

(10) $C = \dfrac{1}{r(1 + t + g) + k}$

and substituting (9) and (10) into (1) gives

(11) $M_1 = \dfrac{1 + k}{r(1 + t + g) + k}$,

money stock defined in terms of the monetary base, which can be altered to obtain the money multiplier $m_1$.

influenced by the amount of bank reserves as well as changes in time deposits ($t$), government deposits ($g$), and currency ($k$):

$$m_1 = \frac{1 + k}{r(1 + t + g) + k}.$$

Thus, the amount of money the banking system can create varies. During the 1960s, the money multiplier varied between 2.52 and 2.72. If the money multiplier had remained constant, at say 2.6, then every $1 increase in the monetary base would have resulted in a $2.60 increase in the stock ($M_1$). The money multiplier ($m_1$) in this explanation is similar to the reciprocal of the reserve requirement ($1/rr$) in the first explanation of the money supply process. However, $m_1$ gives a more accurate picture of the intricacies of the expansion process than $1/rr$ because it allows one to examine the component parts of the money supply.

## Summary

The purpose of demonstrating the money expansion process was twofold: it shows the manner in which commercial banks create money, and it serves as an introduction to monetary policy. While this text does not examine monetary policy in depth, it is necessary to understand some of the relationships between monetary policy and commercial banks. The explanation of the money supply process pointed out that the amount of time deposits, government deposits, and currency in the hands of the public are determined by the Treasury and the desires of the public. However, the amount of reserves that the banking system holds is influenced by monetary policy.

## Questions

1 Discuss the major difference between the assets and liabilities of commercial banks and those of other depository-type intermediaries.
2 What is the relationship between demand deposits and "money." Explain how commercial banks can create money.
3 Define the terms "monetary base," "narrowly defined money stock," and "money multiplier," and explain how these terms relate to each other.
4 Describe how a combination of rising interest rates, relatively low Regulation Q ceilings, and a large volume of large-denomination certificates of deposit (CD's) could lead to greatly increased volatility in commercial bank deposits.
5 What are the major nondepository sources of bank funds?

6 Define Eurodollars and discuss how they are created and their significance to American commercial banks.

7 Why might commercial banks be better able to cope with a period of rising interest rates than savings and loan associations?

8 Discuss the traditional view of the role of commercial banks and how some aspects of this view are reflected in current banking practices.

9 Define the term *disintermediation* and explain how commercial banks may be affected by it.

10 Define *loan participation* and give reasons why banks use them.

# Bibliography

American Bankers Association. *The Commercial Banking Industry.* Prepared for the Commission on Money and Credit. Englewood Cliffs, N.J.: Prentice-Hall, 1962.

Crosse, Howard D., and George H. Hempel. *Management Policies for Commercial Banks,* 2d ed. Englewood Cliffs, N.J.: Prentice-Hall, 1973.

Jessup, Paul E. *Innovations in Bank Management.* New York: Holt, Rinehart and Winston, 1969.

Nadler, Paul S. *Commercial Banking in the Economy.* New York: Random House, 1968.

Reed, Edward W. *Commercial Bank Management.* New York: Harper and Row, 1963.

Ritter, Lawrence S., and William L. Silber. *Money.* New York: Basic Books, 1970.

Robinson, Roland I. *The Management of Bank Funds,* 2d ed. New York: McGraw-Hill, 1962.

Chapter

# 6

# The federal reserve system

The influence of the Federal Reserve System is felt by all commercial banks. The major tasks of the Federal Reserve System are described as follows:

*The principal function of the Federal Reserve is to regulate the flow of bank credit and money. Essential to the performance of this main function is the supplemental one of collecting and interpreting information bearing on economic and credit conditions. A further function is to examine and supervise state banks that are members of the system, obtain reports of conditions from them, and cooperate with other supervisory authorities in the development and administration of policies conducive to a system of strong individual banks.*[1]

In short, the conduct of monetary policy and bank supervision and regulation are the primary concerns of the Federal Reserve System. In addition, its other major duties include clearing and collecting checks and acting as the fiscal agent for the Treasury and other government agencies, as well as administering some aspects of the Truth in Lending Act (a law that regulates lenders of consumer credit).

[1]*The Federal Reserve System: Purposes and Functions* (Washington, D.C.: Board of Governors of the Federal Reserve System, 1963), p. 4.

## Organization

### The Board of Governors

The Board of Governors is the principal ruling body of the Federal Reserve System. It consists of seven members appointed by the president of the United States and confirmed by the Senate. Their appointments are for fourteen-year terms and the terms are staggered so that one member is replaced every two years. As shown in Figure 6–1, the Board of Governors exercises general supervision over the Federal Reserve Banks, determines margin requirements, discount rates, and reserve requirements. The general supervision of the Federal Reserve Banks includes the appointment of three of the nine directors of each bank, review or approval of all salaries, approval of the appointment of key officers of the banks, and periodic examinations to assure that the reserve banks are adhering to the board's rules and regulations. Margin requirements stipulate the amount of credit that brokers and dealers in securities can lend to their customers to purchase or carry securities. Discount rates are the rates at which member banks borrow from the Federal Reserve System. (A discussion of reserve requirements appears below.) Finally, the seven members of the Board of Governors serve on the Federal Open Market Committee along with five representatives from the Federal Reserve Banks. This committee directs monetary policy through the open market operations of the system, which are discussed further on in the chapter.

Figure 6–1

The Federal Reserve System: relation to instruments of credit policy

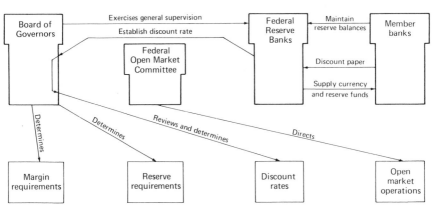

Source: Board of Governors of the Federal Reserve System

## Regional Reserve Banks

Next in the chain of command are the twelve Federal Reserve Banks. The United States is divided into twelve districts, with a Federal Reserve Bank located in each. A list of the districts and the branch offices is given below:

| | |
|---|---|
| Federal Reserve Bank of Boston | District 1 |
| Federal Reserve Bank of New York | District 2 |
| Branch:    Buffalo, New York | |
| Federal Reserve Bank of Philadelphia | District 3 |
| Federal Reserve Bank of Cleveland | District 4 |
| Branches:  Cincinnati, Ohio | |
| Pittsburgh, Pennsylvania | |
| Federal Reserve Bank of Richmond | District 5 |
| Branches:  Baltimore, Maryland | |
| Charlotte, North Carolina | |
| Federal Reserve Bank of Atlanta | District 6 |
| Branches:  Birmingham, Alabama | |
| Jacksonville, Florida | |
| Nashville, Tennessee | |
| New Orleans, Louisiana | |
| Federal Reserve Bank of Chicago | District 7 |
| Branch:    Detroit, Michigan | |
| Federal Reserve Bank of St. Louis | District 8 |
| Branches:  Little Rock, Arkansas | |
| Louisville, Kentucky | |
| Memphis, Tennessee | |
| Federal Reserve Bank of Minneapolis | District 9 |
| Branch:    Helena, Montana | |
| Federal Reserve Bank of Kansas City | District 10 |
| (Missouri) | |
| Branches:  Denver, Colorado | |
| Oklahoma City, Oklahoma | |
| Omaha, Nebraska | |
| Federal Reserve Bank of Dallas | District 11 |
| Branches:  El Paso, Texas | |
| Houston, Texas | |
| San Antonio, Texas | |
| Federal Reserve Bank of San Francisco | District 12 |
| Branches:  Los Angeles, California | |
| Portland, Oregon | |
| Salt Lake City, Utah | |
| Seattle, Washington | |

The regional dispersion of the Federal Reserve Banks and their respective branches is an important feature of the system. Unlike the central banks in England and France that are each located in one place, our central bank(s) consist of twelve reserve banks that are scattered across the country but operate together as a unified system. Consequently, we do not have a central bank, but we do have a central banking *system*. Another feature of the regional decentralization concerns the formulation of monetary policy. The representatives of the Federal Reserve Banks who sit on the Federal Open Market Committee (see p. 112) bring to it their views of business and credit conditions particular to their parts of the country. Such information adds a great deal to the fund of knowledge about the state of the economy, but it does not insure that the Federal Open Market Committee will necessarily make decisions about monetary policy that are agreeable to all.

Each of the twelve Federal Reserve Banks is a corporation whose stockholders are the commercial banks that are members of the Federal Reserve System. Member banks contribute capital and elect six of the nine directors for the Federal Reserve Bank in their district. Three of the elected directors are bankers; three represent commerce, industry, or agriculture and cannot be engaged in banking; the remaining three directors, including the chairman, are appointed by the Board of Governors, and represent the public at large. These last three directors cannot be engaged in any banking activities or even own stock in a bank.

The member bank stockholders of the corporation receive a 6 percent statutory dividend on the paid-in capital stock of the Federal Reserve Bank. Each member bank pays in 3 percent of its capital and surplus and another 3 percent is subject to call. In 1973, the Federal Reserve System earned $5,017 million. Of that amount $4,341 million was paid to the U.S. Treasury as interest on Federal Reserve notes, $51 million was transferred to surplus, and $49 million was paid in dividends to member banks.

The Federal Reserve Banks provide the following services for their member banks: they discount paper (lend money) for short periods of time; they clear checks and transfer funds; they provide currency as needed; and they supervise and examine them.

## Member Banks

Member banks are the third level of organization of the Federal Reserve System. At year-end 1973, there were 5,763 member banks, 42 percent of all commercial banks in the United States, and they held approximately 80 percent of total deposits in all banks. Of the 5,705 banks that were members of the system in 1972, 4,613 were organized under national charters

and 1,092 were organized under state charters. Banks that are chartered by the Comptroller of the Currency are called national banks and have the word National in their names (i.e., the First National Bank of Podunk). National banks are required to join the Federal Reserve System, but membership is voluntary for state-chartered banks. In recent years the number of member banks in the Federal Reserve System has declined, partly owing to mergers and acquisitions, and partly because it was financially advantageous for some banks to drop out of the system, since state-chartered, nonmember banks generally have lower reserve requirements than member banks, and they do not have to tie up funds in the stock of a Federal Reserve Bank. The relatively low reserve requirements, as well as relatively low minimum capital requirements, help to explain why almost 60 percent of all commercial banks in the United States are organized under state charters.

The directors of the Federal Reserve Banks appoint the chief officers of their respective bank, vote on the discount rates their bank will charge, and on other important matters. In addition, the directors of the Federal Reserve Banks select the twelve members of the Federal Advisory Council. The council provides the Board of Governors with information about business conditions, and makes suggestions concerning the operation of the system.

## Federal Deposit Insurance Corporation

All banks that are members of the Federal Reserve System have their deposits insured by the Federal Deposit Insurance Corporation (FDIC). Since most nonmember banks also elect for insurance, about 99 percent of all commercial banks in operation in the United States and about 66 percent of all mutual savings banks are insured by the FDIC. Each depositor is insured by the FDIC for amounts up to $40,000 on all accounts. Because the size of some accounts exceeds that amount, the insured portion of total deposits in all insured banks was only 61 percent in 1973.[2] A survey made by the FDIC revealed that 94 percent of savings deposits in insured commercial banks and 55 percent of demand deposits of individuals and businesses were insured. Since the FDIC was established in 1934, it has paid off depositors, in 502 cases, sums amounting to $903.8 million. Of that total, the FDIC recovered $779.5 million and lost $124.3 million.

### Supervisory Function

Besides its insurance function, the FDIC supervises FDIC-insured banks under its control to insure that they are complying with all appropriate laws

---

[2] *1973 Annual Report, Federal Deposit Insurance Corporation.* (In 1971, accounts were insured only for amounts up to $20,000.)

and regulations, just as the Federal Reserve System examines its member banks. In addition, state banking authorities and the Comptroller of the Currency examine state banks that are not members of the Federal Reserve System and national banks, respectively. All of this adds up to the fact that most banks are subject to multiple levels of supervision. For example, national banks are supervised by the Comptroller of the Currency, the Federal Reserve System, and the FDIC. As a matter of practice, the Comptroller of the Currency examines the national banks and provides the other supervisory agencies with copies of the appropriate reports.

## Reserve Requirements

The historical reason for maintaining bank reserves was to insure that sufficient funds would be available to meet the claims of depositors. Banks had to maintain some degree of liquidity against their deposits, although the amount of liquidity varied with the type of deposit. Because demand deposits are more likely to be withdrawn from a bank than time and savings deposits, reserve requirements on demand deposits are substantially higher than those on time and savings deposits. As shown in Table 6–1, the reserve percentages applicable to demand deposits range from 8 percent to 17½ percent, while the reserve percentages on time deposits are 3 to 6 percent. These reserve percentages on demand deposits only became effective in late 1972 and were modified further in late 1974. They represent a major restructuring of reserve requirements. Under the old system reserve requirements were different for banks located in Federal Reserve Bank cities and for banks located elsewhere.[3] In contrast, the new system

Table 6–1

Membership reserve requirements (November 28, 1974)

| On net demand deposits | Reserve percentages applicable |
|---|---|
| First $2 million or less | 8 |
| $2 million to $10 million | 10½ |
| $10 million to $100 million | 12½ |
| $100 million to $400 million | 13½ |
| Over $400 million | 17½ |

| On time deposits | |
|---|---|
| First $5 million (30–119 days) | 3 |
| Over $5 million (30–119 days) | 6 |
| 120 days and over | 3 |

Source: Board of Governors of the Federal Reserve System

[3]For a synopsis of the history of reserve requirements, see Nicholas A. Lash, "Member Bank Reserve Requirements—Heritage from History," *Business Conditions,* Federal Reserve Bank of Chicago (June 1972). Historical reserve requirements of member banks appear monthly in the *Federal Reserve Bulletin.*

applies the same reserve requirements to member banks of equal size regardless of their geographic location. Besides the change in reserve requirements, the distinction between demand deposits and time deposits has become blurred in recent years. Some time deposits, such as CD's, may turn over faster than some demand deposits. Moreover, in several states mutual savings banks are paying interest on savings accounts that have most of the characteristics of a demand deposit. Thus, the entire concept of reserve requirements is due for a complete overhaul.

Today, the most important justification for reserve requirements is that they limit the maximum amount of loans, investments, and deposits that the banking system can make. The lower the reserve requirement, the more the banking system can expand deposits and in turn make loans to finance industry, commerce, and others.

Once the percentage of reserve requirements is established, the maximum amount of loans and investments can be changed by increasing or decreasing the dollar amount of reserves held by banks. Because of the strategic role of reserves in determining bank credit, the Federal Reserve System uses member bank reserves as an operating target of monetary policy.[4] Operating targets are used for guiding day-to-day open market operations in an effort to achieve certain objectives of the Federal Reserve System.[5] For example, if the objective of monetary policy is to be stimulative, the Federal Reserve System will inject a certain dollar amount of reserves into the banking system through its open market operations.

## Open Market Operations

### Policy Directive

The Federal Open Market Committee (FOMC) is the monetary policy-making body of the Federal Reserve System. Every three or four weeks the FOMC meets in Washington, D.C., to appraise the current state of the economy and to determine the course of monetary policy until the next meeting. Their decisions are presented in an economic policy directive to the manager of the System Open Market Account, who is in charge of buying and selling U.S. government and federal agency securities and bankers' acceptances in order to achieve the objectives of the FOMC. He is

---

[4]On January 11, 1972, the Federal Open Market Committee stated that it would use "reserve available to support private nonbank deposits" as an operating target. For details on this meeting see "Record of Policy Actions," *Federal Reserve Bulletin* (May 1972), p. 459.
[5]The term *operating target* has been the subject of considerable debate in recent years. For a synopsis of the debates see William G. Dewald, "A Review of the Conference on Targets and Indicators of Monetary Policy," in *Targets and Indicators of Monetary Policy*, ed. Karl Brunner (San Francisco: Chandler Publishing Company, 1969), pp. 313–330. Also see Richard G. Davis, "Short-Run Targets for Open Market Operations," in *Open Market Policies and Operating Procedures—Staff Studies* (Washington, D.C.: Board of Governors of the Federal Reserve System, 1971), pp. 39–69.

a senior officer of the Federal Reserve Bank of New York, where all open market operations are carried out. The following is the economic policy directive issued to the Federal Reserve Bank of New York in March, 1972.

> The information reviewed at this meeting suggests that real output of goods and services is increasing in the current quarter at about the stepped-up rate attained in the fourth quarter of 1971. Several measures of business activity have strengthened recently and demands for labor have improved somewhat, but the unemployment rate remains high. Wholesale prices continued to rise rapidly in January and February, in part because of large increases in prices of foods. However, the advance in wage rates slowed markedly after the post-freeze surge in December. Following a period of sluggish growth, the narrowly defined money stock increased sharply in February, partly reflecting a substantial reduction in U.S. government deposits. Inflows of time and savings funds at bank and nonbank thrift institutions continued rapid in February, although below January's extraordinary pace. Short-term interest rates have risen considerably in recent weeks while yields on long-term securities have changed little on balance. Exchange rates for most major foreign currencies against the dollar appreciated further in February and early March, as recurrent speculative outflows of capital added to the foregoing developments. It is the policy of the Federal Open Market Committee to foster financial conditions conducive to sustainable real economic growth and increased employment, abatement of inflationary pressures, and attainment of reasonable equilibrium in the country's balance of payments.

> To implement this policy, while taking account of international developments and possible treasury financing, the committee seeks to achieve bank reserve and money market conditions that will support moderate growth in monetary aggregates over the months ahead.[6]

The first paragraph of the above statement is a review of economic activity. Based on the FOMC's analysis of the economic situation at that time, it states the broad objectives that the committee desires, such as financial conditions conducive to economic growth, abatement of inflationary pressures, and so on. The committee stresses that it deals only with financial conditions and that it does not directly influence economic growth or employment. The second paragraph tells the manager of the System Open Market Account how to implement the policy, specifically, by seeking moderate growth in bank reserves.

---

[6]FOMC meeting on March 21, 1972. Records of FOMC meetings appear monthly in the *Federal Reserve Bulletin* and in the *Annual Reports* of the Board of Governors of the Federal Reserve System.

## Daily Operations

The task of the manager of the System Open Market Account is to translate the directive into day-to-day operations that will achieve the desired effects.[7] In this case the manager will supply reserves to the system by buying securities. Assume that the manager of the System Open Market Account bought $200 million in treasury bills from a nonbank dealer in government securities. The Federal Reserve Bank of New York would pay the government securities dealer by crediting the dealer's clearing bank which handled all the paper work for such transactions. The immediate effect of such an open market purchase would be: 1) treasury securities held by the Federal Reserve Bank of New York increased by $200 million; 2) the Federal Reserve Bank of New York credited the reserve account of the dealer's clearing bank for $200 million in treasury securities; 3) the reserve balances of the member bank increased by a like amount, and 4) the member bank in turn credited the dealer's demand deposit account with $200 million (see Table 6–2). Now the dealer's clearing bank has additional funds that can be loaned and the amount of deposits that can be generated in the banking system has been increased by $200 million. Had the manager of the System Open Market Account sold securities to the dealer the above transactions would have carried minus (−) signs, and the end result would have been a reduction in member bank reserves. In that case, the ability of the banking system to expand deposits would have been reduced rather than increased as in the first example.

## Effect on Interest Rates

In addition to changing the level of member bank reserves, open market purchases and sales of securities by the Federal Reserve System have a pronounced effect on market interest rates. When the Federal Reserve buys securities (injects reserves into the banking system), it bids the price upward in order to induce dealers to sell. It follows that because the market price of debt securities is inversely related to the level of interest rates,

Table 6–2

The accounts of an open market purchase from a nonbank dealer

| Federal Reserve Bank of New York | | Dealer's clearing bank | |
|---|---|---|---|
| Assets | Liabilities | Assets | Liabilities |
| 1 Treasury bills | 2 Reserve account of dealer's clearing bank | 3 Reserve account at Federal Reserve Bank of New York | 3 Dealer's demand deposit account |
| +$200 million | +$200 million | +$200 million | +$200 million |

[7]For details on the day-to-day workings of the open market operations see Paul Meek, *Open Market Operation*, Federal Reserve Bank of New York (July 1969).

market interest rates decline. Conversely, when the Federal Reserve lowers the price on the securities that it has for sale (withdraws reserves from the banking system), the level of market interest rates rises. The relationship between the net reserve position of member banks and short-term interest rates is shown in Figure 6–2. This is the difference between the excess reserves (the difference between total reserves and required reserves) of member banks and the amount that these banks borrow. When excess reserves exceed member bank borrowings, there are *net free reserves* in the banking system. On the other hand, if member bank borrowings exceed excess reserves, there are *net borrowed reserves* in the banking system.

Figure 6–2

Short-term interest rates and borrowing of member banks

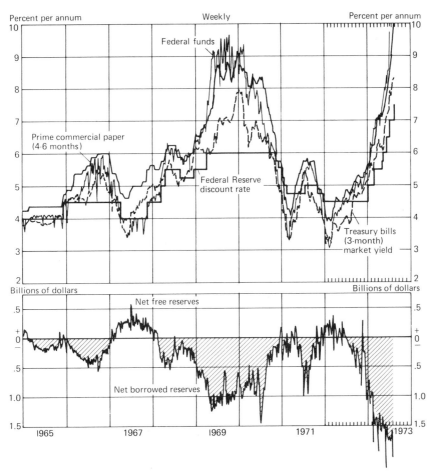

Source: Board of Governors of the Federal Reserve System

For the purpose of this discussion, the net reserve position can be used as a gauge of the posture of monetary policy. Net free reserves are usually associated with a stimulative posture, while net borrowed reserves are associated with monetary restraint. During the period shown in Figure 6–2, there were wide swings between net free reserves and net borrowed reserves. The variability of the net reserve position reflects the vagaries of monetary policy as it shifted between ease and restraint. More important, the figure shows that when monetary ease gave way to monetary restraint in 1966 and again in 1968–1969, 1971, and 1972–1973, the dollar volume of net borrowed reserves increased and short-term interest rates advanced sharply. In the years when monetary policy became less restrictive, the dollar volume of net borrowed reserves diminished and short-term interest rates declined.

In order to keep things in their proper perspective, it should be made clear that monetary policy was only one of many factors influencing the level of interest rates. Another influence was the dollar amount of U.S. government financing in the securities market. For example, in 1971 the U.S. government raised $25.5 billion in the securities market compared with $12.8 billion in the previous year.[8] Heavy U.S. government financings are usually associated with some upward pressure on interest rates. However, in 1971, monetary ease and purchases by foreign investors of U.S. government securities in unprecedented amounts helped to mitigate the upward pressure on short-term interest rates. In addition, the New Economic Program announced by President Nixon in mid-August 1971, expectations by investors of continued inflation, and an international monetary crisis also affected the level of market interest rates. Although the precise degree of influence of these and other factors on the level of short-term market interest rates is not known, it is reasonably certain that monetary policy was the dominant factor. Therefore, monetary policy affects the assets and liabilities of commercial banks by changing the level of member bank reserves and by influencing the level of market interest rates.

## Summary

This chapter stressed the role of the Federal Reserve System on commercial banks. It was shown how changes in Federal Open Market Committee operations influenced member bank reserves, the money supply, and interest rates. The appendix to this chapter is a speech by the chairman of the Board of Governors of the Federal Reserve System about bank reserves, which are important to the Federal Reserve Banks' open market operations and membership requirements.

[8]The dollar amount of funds raised by the U.S. government includes both public debt securities and budget agency securities. For additional details, see the Appendix, "Flow of Funds Accounts."

**Questions**

1 Describe the organizational structure of the Federal Reserve System.
2 What is the principal function of the Federal Reserve System? Discuss how the system uses tools such as the discount rate, reserve requirements, and open market operations to perform this function.
3 Explain the functions of the Federal Deposit Insurance Corporation (FDIC). Discuss how the existence of the FDIC since 1934 may have helped the growth of commercial banks.
4 Describe some of the services that the twelve Federal Reserve Banks provide for their members.
5 Explain how the various national bank regulatory authorities eliminate the necessity of multiple examinations of national banks.
6 Explain how the rationale for having banks maintain reserves has changed in recent years.
7 What are the two major monetary variables that Federal Reserve open market operations affect?
8 Describe the operations of the Federal Open Market Committee.
9 Explain why it can be said that the United States does not have a central bank as some other nations do.
10 Explain the three constituencies represented by the directors of each Federal Reserve Bank.

# Appendix 6A
## The Structure of Reserve Requirements

Address by Arthur F. Burns, Chairman, Board of Governors of the Federal Reserve System, before the Governing Council Spring Meeting of the American Bankers Association in White Sulphur Springs, West Virginia, April 26, 1973.

Let me begin by considering the role and purpose of reserve requirements in the functioning of monetary and credit policies.

Before the Federal Reserve System was founded, reserve requirements were imposed by legislation at the national and state levels as a means of protecting bank liquidity. That philosophy was retained in the original structure of reserve requirements established for Federal Reserve member banks. Higher requirements were set for reserve city banks than for country members, and still higher requirements were imposed on central reserve city banks. Vestiges of that initial structure remain, even today.

Required reserves, however, are not really an important source of bank liquidity. The reserves required to back deposits cannot be withdrawn to finance a rise in loan demand, and they can supply only a small portion of the funds needed to accommodate deposit losses. The true and basic function of reserve requirements is not to provide liquidity, but to permit the Federal Reserve to control the supply of money and credit so that monetary policy can effectively promote our national economic objectives.

To achieve good management over the supply of money and credit, reserve requirements must be met by holding assets whose aggregate volume is under the control of the Federal Reserve. Whatever their role may be in protecting bank liquidity, the reserve requirements set by the various states do not meet this test. This is a serious defect, since the principal reason for reserve requirements is their contribution to effective monetary policy.

Judged by this criterion, the present structure of reserve requirements leaves much to be desired. Reforms are needed to increase the precision and the certainty with which the supply of money and credit can be controlled. Reforms are needed to permit more variation in reserve requirements as an instrument of monetary policy. Reforms are also needed to distribute the burden of monetary controls more equitably among the financial institutions that participate in the payments mechanism.

The Federal Reserve Board has been concerned for some time with inequities in the structure of reserve requirements. Last November, we finally

118

used our authority under Regulation D to carry out substantial improvements in the structure of reserves that are required to be held against the demand deposits of member banks.

As you know, the Federal Reserve Act specifies that the board must distinguish between reserve city banks and other members in the establishment of reserve requirements. Until November 1972, the principal determinant of a bank's reserve status was its geographic location. Banks in principal financial centers were generally classified as reserve city banks; those in other locations fell into the country member category. A bank could, however, have its classification changed by appealing for special treatment based on the nature of its banking business.

With the passage of time, this system of reserve classification became increasingly outmoded and inequitable. Some large banks in cities of substantial size enjoyed the lower reserve requirement on demand deposits applicable to country members. At the same time, there were some small banks in major financial centers that had to carry the higher reserve requirement imposed on reserve city members. Over the years, exceptions had been granted in so many cases—each of them probably justified but different from most others—that the principles underlying the reserve classification of member banks could no longer be readily discerned.

The board moved last year to eliminate these capricious elements in reserve classification by introducing a graduated reserve requirement— that is, by relating the reserve against demand deposits of each bank to the size of the bank. Under the new system, all member banks of a given size, whatever their location, are subject to identical reserve requirements.

This reform was a major step forward in the creation of a more rational and equitable structure of reserve requirements. Yet, much more remains to be done.

One of the principal steps needed is to apply equivalent reserve requirements to member and nonmember banks. At present, nonmember banks are not required to hold reserves in the form of deposits at the Federal Reserve Banks, as member banks do.

In many states, percentage reserve requirements for nonmember banks are comparable to those for Federal Reserve members. However, the reserves required of nonmember banks usually may be carried as correspondent balances, or even in the form of government securities. When reserves are held as correspondent balances at a member bank, that bank is of course required to support these balances with reserves that consist either of vault cash or cash at the Federal Reserve. But in such a case the size of the cash

reserve held by the member bank is quite small relative to the initial deposit at the nonmember bank.

The consequence of these differential reserve requirements is that shifts of deposits between member and nonmember banks alter the quantity of deposits at all commercial banks that can be supported by a given volume of bank reserves. Thus, the links between bank reserves on the one hand, and bank credit and the money supply on the other, are loosened, and the Federal Reserve's control over the monetary aggregates becomes less precise than it can or should be.

The magnitude of this problem is difficult to assess, since nonmember banks submit statistical reports to supervisory authorities infrequently. Annual data, however, suggest a substantial variability in the relative growth rates of member and nonmember banks. Over the past decade, increases in the volume of checking deposits at nonmember banks accounted for around 40 percent of the total rise in checking deposits. But the proportion was as low as one-tenth in 1962 and as high as three-fourths in 1969. Variations of this magnitude add to uncertainty about the effects of open market operations on bank credit and deposits, on the cost and availability of loanable funds, and hence also on the level of aggregate demand for goods and services.

This source of imprecision in monetary control has become more worrisome as the proportion of bank deposits held at member banks has declined. In 1945, 86 percent of total commercial bank deposits was held by member banks. The ratio had fallen to 80 percent by 1970 and to 78 percent by the end of last year.

In part, this trend reflects the relatively rapid growth of population in areas served by nonmember banks, particularly suburban areas. The major causal factor, however, is the competitive disadvantage that is imposed on member banks by requiring them to hold reserves against deposits in the form of vault cash or as deposits at the Federal Reserve. For nonmember banks, required reserves are, in effect, earning assets even when they are held as demand balances with other commercial banks, since these balances normally also serve as a form of payment for services rendered by city correspondents.

One consequence of this inequity is an incentive for member banks to withdraw from the Federal Reserve System, or for newly chartered state banks to avoid Federal Reserve membership. Since 1960, about 700 banks have left the system through withdrawal or mergers. Just over 100 state-chartered banks have elected to join the system since 1960; nearly 1,500 others receiving new charters chose to remain outside the system.

And the trend continues. During 1972, five banks with deposits of $100 million or more withdrew from Federal Reserve membership. Of the 212 new commercial banks receiving state charters last year, only 13 elected Federal Reserve membership.

Over the years, efforts have been made to reduce the competitive disadvantage faced by member banks and thereby make system membership more attractive. Permission to count vault cash in meeting reserve requirements clearly improved matters. The changes made in Regulation D last November were also helpful, because they reduced reserve requirements against demand deposits—particularly for small member banks that compete actively with nonmembers. Recently, a seasonal borrowing privilege at the discount window was established for member banks that have insufficient access to the national money markets. This, too, should make membership more attractive. Nevertheless, there are limits to measures of this kind that can be taken under existing legislation.

The erosion of membership in the Federal Reserve System is therefore a serious problem. It reduces the precision of monetary control, as I have already noted. It may, in time, also weaken public confidence in the nation's central bank and in its ability to maintain a stable currency and a sound banking system. And it has already reduced the potential for using changes in reserve requirements as an effective instrument of monetary policy. When a large and increasing proportion of total bank deposits is left untouched by changes in the reserve requirements prescribed by the board, that alone is a fact of some significance. The greater loss, however, arises because the board must use changes in reserve requirements sparingly as an instrument of monetary policy, since an increase in required reserves would worsen the competitive disadvantage of member banks and thereby threaten a further erosion of membership.

This inhibition has been unfortunate, for there have been times when the prompt and pervasive impact of a higher reserve requirement would have been the best way to signal that monetary policy is moving toward added restraint on the availability of money and credit. In view of the divergence in reserve requirements between member and nonmember banks, the Federal Reserve has sometimes had to turn to other, perhaps less effective, measures to achieve its objectives.

These considerations argue persuasively, I believe, that reserve requirements on demand deposits at nonmember banks should be the same as those faced by Federal Reserve members. Continuation of the present state of affairs is inequitable, and it also weakens monetary control. These difficulties will become more acute in the years to come if corrective legislative action is not forthcoming.

The proposal to treat member and nonmember banks alike for reserve purposes is not new. Its substance was embodied in the recommendations of a congressional committee chaired by Senator Douglas in 1950, repeated in 1952 in the recommendations of a congressional committee chaired by Congressman Patman, endorsed by the Commission on Money and Credit in 1961, reaffirmed by the President's Committee on Financial Institutions in 1963, and restated again in the 1971 report of the President's Commission on Financial Structure and Regulation. Since 1964, the Federal Reserve Board has repeatedly urged the Congress to bring all insured commercial banks under the same reserve requirements, and to provide all these banks with equal access to the discount window.

I am aware that this proposal is not viewed with favor by many segments of the banking community, and that is the major reason why this needed reform has been delayed. The proposal would be more palatable to bankers if some part of the board's reserve requirement against demand deposits could be held in the form of an earning asset, such as U.S. government securities. I do not want to rule out that possibility categorically. Simple honesty, however, compels me to state that, however attractive reserve requirements in that form may be from the standpoint of bank earnings, they cannot serve a useful function in monetary management. As I noted earlier, satisfactory control over the supply of money and credit requires that bank reserves be held in the form of assets whose aggregate volume is directly controlled by the Federal Reserve.

The principle that underlies the board's recommendation is simple and straightforward—namely, that equivalent reserve requirements should apply to all deposits that effectively serve as a part of the public's money balances. Recent efforts of nonbank depositary institutions to evolve new modes of money transfer make adoption of this principle a matter of some urgency. If legislative action is delayed, we may soon find a much larger share of money transfers taking place at institutions outside the reach of the board's reserve requirements.

As you know, participation in third-party transfers by nonbank financial institutions has already commenced. In Massachusetts and New Hampshire, mutual savings banks have begun to offer depositors an interest-bearing account subject to a negotiable order of withdrawal—a "NOW account"—that resembles closely an interest-bearing checking account. In California, savings and loan associations are seeking direct access to an electronic money transfer system operated by California banks. Access to the system would enable these associations to charge and credit the savings accounts of their customers in much the same way that checking deposits are handled at commercial banks. Other forms of third-party transfers are likely to spring up here and there.

The board believes, and has so indicated in testimony to the Congress, that federal regulation should permit developments such as these to flourish, so that the range of services of depositary institutions to American families may be extended. The board believes, however, that present trends could have significant adverse effects on monetary control unless reserve requirements established by the Federal Reserve are applied to all deposit accounts involving money transfer services. Failure to do so would also have damaging effects on competitive relations between commercial banks and nonbank thrift institutions.

Universal application of reserve requirements to all deposits providing money transfer services need not mean a uniform percentage requirement on all these deposits. There may be a reasonable basis for lower reserve requirements on savings accounts with third-party transfer privileges than for deposits that carry full checking account powers. There may also be a reasonable basis for retaining the principle of reserve requirements graduated by size of the depositary institution. Lack of uniformity of reserve requirements on similar deposits does, however, pose potential problems for monetary control.

There are other aspects of present reserve requirements that also deserve careful and continuing review in the light of our evolving financial structure.

The appropriateness of reserve requirements on commercial bank time and savings deposits has been a subject of debate over the years. It has been argued that cash reserves against time deposits are not essential for purposes of monetary control, and therefore should be abolished as an unnecessary impediment to intermediation. Yet, some observers take the position that reserve requirements for commercial bank time deposits should be increased to the same level as the requirements for demand deposits, so that shifts of funds between the two deposit classes would not alter the relation of bank reserves to bank credit and the money supply.

The merits of these conflicting arguments are difficult to evaluate. At present, there is no convincing evidence of frequent, or large-scale, shifts of funds between demand and time deposits of the sort that could be disruptive to financial markets and to the management of aggregate demand. Still, the potential for such shifts may be increasing with the proliferation of new financial services that facilitate transfers from one type of deposit to another.

Removal of reserve requirements against time deposits would, therefore, seem unwise at this time. And in any event, elimination of statutory authority to impose reserve requirements against time and savings deposits would take away a weapon of monetary policy that is potentially useful for contain-

ing increases in bank credit at a time when inflationary pressures are already strong and threaten to become still stronger.

As long as commercial banks are required to hold cash reserves against time and savings deposits, questions will persist about the desirability of similar requirements against savings accounts at nonbank thrift institutions. At present, extension of reserve requirements to savings accounts at nonbank intermediaries does not appear to be needed for reasons of monetary control. There have been times when shifts of funds between banks and nonbank intermediaries have had a disturbing influence on the mortgage market. But those shifts have not produced serious problems for monetary control, and they would not have been prevented by comparable reserve requirements at the two classes of institutions.

From the viewpoint of equity, the case for equal reserve requirements on time and savings deposits at all financial institutions is stronger. Even on this ground, however, it should be kept in mind that the diversified services that commercial banks offer their customers gives them an advantage in bidding for time and savings deposits—an advantage that probably still remains after the costs of holding cash reserves are taken into account.

However, if recent trends continue, the increasing provision of money transfer services by nonbank thrift institutions will blur the distinction between commercial banks and nonbank intermediaries, just as it blurs the distinction between checking and savings accounts. As nonbank depositary institutions become more like commercial banks, the basis for differences in reserve requirements will be weakened and so too will the justification for differences in tax and regulatory treatment.

Public policy must take account of the competitive forces that are altering the structure of our nation's depositary institutions and the character of the services they supply. The need for legislation authorizing identical reserve requirements on demand deposits at member and nonmember banks is of long standing. The time for bringing NOW accounts and any other deposits offering money transfer services under the board's reserve requirements is clearly at hand. And if the distinctions between commercial banks and nonbank financial institutions gradually fade away, regulatory authority to equalize the treatment of time and savings deposits for reserve purposes will also be needed.

Enabling legislation to accomplish these ends should allow flexibility in implementation. The transition to a new and more appropriate system of reserve requirements should be designed so as to minimize the adjustment problems of individual institutions, and also permit the regulatory au-

thorities to monitor the effects of changing reserve requirements on financial markets and on economic activity. Abrupt changes in the structure of reserve requirements are unnecessary and would probably be unwise. The need, as I see it, is for a gradual transition to a reserve structure that will accomplish two objectives: first, ensure adequate control over the supply of money and credit in the years to come, and second, establish an equitable sharing among financial institutions of the costs of monetary control.

# Bibliography

Anderson, Clay J. *A Half-Century of Federal Reserve Policymaking, 1914–1964*. Philadelphia: Federal Reserve Bank of Philadelphia, 1965.

Carson, Deane, ed. *Banking and Monetary Studies*. Homewood, Ill.: Richard D. Irwin, 1963.

Eastburn, David P. *The Federal Reserve on Record*. Philadelphia: Federal Reserve Bank of Philadelphia, 1965.

*Federal Reserve Bulletin*. Washington, D.C.: Board of Governors of the Federal Reserve System (monthly).

*The Federal Reserve System: Purposes and Functions*. Washington, D.C.: Board of Governors of the Federal Reserve System, 1974.

Madden, Carl H. *The Money Side of "The Street."* New York: Federal Reserve Bank of New York, 1959.

*Open Market Operations*. New York: Federal Reserve Bank of New York, 1963.

*Open Market Policies and Operating Procedures—Staff Studies*. Washington, D.C.: Board of Governors of the Federal Reserve System, 1971.

Prochnow, Herbert V., ed. *The Federal Reserve System*. New York: Harper and Row, 1960.

Part

# 3

# Insurance and pension plans

Both life insurance companies and private pension plans deal in long-term contractual obligations and affect the welfare of many people.

Chapter 7, "Life Insurance Companies," focuses on changes in the amount of savings by individuals that take place in life insurance companies.

Chapter 8, "Private Pension Plans," examines the evolution of private pension plans from an unregulated to a regulated industry.

# 7

# Life insurance companies

In order to understand how life insurance companies function as financial intermediaries, it is necessary to be familiar with some of the fundamentals of life insurance. Accordingly, this chapter begins with definitions of the basic types of life insurance policies and then proceeds to the determination of life insurance premiums. The basic theme is that changes in the composition of life insurance in force affect the amount of savings that take place in life insurance companies, since some life insurance policies produce high rates of savings while others yield lower rates. The present trend is toward a diminishing rate of savings through life insurance companies.

## Insurance

Insurance can be thought of as a device to safeguard against economic loss by having the losses of the unfortunate few paid for by the contributions of the many who are exposed to the same risk.[1] The uncertainty of one party (the insured) is reduced by transferring particular risks to another party (the insurer), who offers a restoration of the economic losses suffered by the insured.[2] Thus, if you have health insurance and break your leg, the insurance company will pay a certain amount of money for the medical costs incurred.

[1]S. S. Huebner and Kenneth Black, Jr., *Life Insurance,* 8th ed. (New York: Appleton-Century-Crofts, 1972), p. 3.
[2]Irving Pfeffer, *Insurance and Economic Theory* (Homewood, Ill.: Richard D. Irwin, 1956), p. 53.

## Types of Policies

There are three basic types of life insurance policy: term, whole life, and endowment.

*Term*    Term insurance provides limited protection for a given period of time such as one year, five years, ten years, and so on. The face amount of the policy is payable to a beneficiary at the death of the insured, if it occurs within the specified period. As a rule, term policies do not build cash value. However, some are convertible, which means that they can be exchanged for life insurance that does build cash value.

*Whole Life*    Whole life insurance, or, as it is sometimes called, straight life, ordinary life, or permanent life, gives permanent protection. The face amount of the policy is paid upon the death of the insured regardless of when it occurs. In addition to insurance protection such policies build up cash values. The insured can borrow the cash value built up in the policy—a policy loan—or can stop paying premiums and use the accumulated cash value to buy either extended term insurance or a reduced amount of paid-up insurance. Premiums for ordinary life insurance policies are paid for life or they may be compressed into a shorter time span. Those who choose to compress the time span pay larger premiums than necessary early in the life of the policy and use the accumulated amounts to buy limited-payment policies. In such policies the ten or twenty premiums required by the contract represent a sum which is sufficiently larger than the aggregate amount required during the same period for an ordinary life plan. In this manner the life insurance can be paid up in twenty years (twenty-payment life) or it can be paid up at sixty-five years of age.

*Endowment*    Endowment policies are basically savings plans supplemented by a modest amount of insurance protection. They provide for the payment of the face amount of the policy upon the death of the insured during a specified time period, or the payment of the face amount at the end of that period if the insured is living. Once the endowment matures and the face amount is paid, the insurance coverage expires. Endowment policies are used to accumulate funds to put children through college, for retirement, or for other financial purposes.

*Protection and Savings*    The relationship between protection and savings for the three basic policies is depicted in Figure 7–1. The figure shows that the term policy consists of insurance protection and no savings; the whole life policy consists principally of protection with some savings; and the endowment consists principally of savings with some protection. Both the whole life and endowment policies can be thought of as a combination of decreasing term insurance and increasing investment-cash value. After

Figure 7–1

Comparison of basic policies issued at age 25

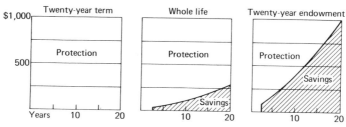

Source: *Decade of Decision* (New York: Institute of Life Insurance, 1974), p. 19.

the first year or two the amount of the protection element in the policy declines and the savings accumulation increases so that they add to the face amount of the policy. For example, in the eleventh year of the particular endowment policy illustrated the savings amount to $500 and the insurance amounts to $500 so the total value is $1,000.

## Life Insurance Premiums

Premiums are the major source of funds for life insurance companies. During the 1960–1969 period, the average size of life insurance premiums per $1,000 of life insurance in force declined from $20.20 to $15.50. Among the reasons for the decline are increased life spans, high rates of return on investments made by insurance companies, and an increased proportion of sales of low-cost insurance.

## Determination of Premiums

Each life insurance company determines the premiums that policyholders must pay. The rates are based on probability of death, compound interest, the cost of doing business, and other considerations (see Table 7–1). Two of the most important factors influencing the size of life insurance premiums are the death rate and the assumed interest rate. Statistics are kept on the number of people who die and the ages at which they die, and the data are compiled into what is called a mortality table. For example, the data in Table 7–2 indicate that the death rate among 20-year-old males is 1.79 per 1,000.

The assumed interest rate is based on the concepts of compound interest and present value. The money paid as premiums in excess of immediate claims or expenses is invested by the insurance companies, thereby earning more money. To illustrate the use of compound interest, assume that an

Table 7–1

What various policies cost (approximate annual premiums for $10,000 of insurance[a])

| Type of policy | Age at which policy is issued | | | | | |
|---|---|---|---|---|---|---|
| | 20 | 21 | 22 | 23 | 24 | 25 |
| Five-year term (renewable and convertible) | $ 49.50 | $ 49.75 | $ 50.00 | $ 50.25 | $ 50.50 | $ 50.75 |
| Straight life | 133.00 | 136.00 | 140.00 | 144.00 | 148.00 | 152.00 |
| Life-paid-up-at-65 | 150.00 | 155.00 | 159.00 | 164.00 | 169.00 | 175.00 |
| Twenty-payment life | 228.00 | 232.00 | 237.00 | 242.00 | 247.00 | 252.00 |
| Retirement income at 65 | 244.00 | 253.00 | 262.00 | 271.00 | 281.00 | 292.00 |
| Twenty-year endowment | 453.00 | 453.50 | 454.00 | 454.50 | 455.00 | 455.50 |

Source: *Decade of Decision* (New York: Institute of Life Insurance, 1974), p. 20
[a] Rates shown are approximate premium rates for $10,000 of life insurance protection for men. Rates of participating policies would be slightly higher, but the cost would be lowered by annual dividends. Nonparticipating policy premium rates would be somewhat lower than those shown and no dividends would be paid. Policies under $10,000 would be a little higher in premium rates and lower for $25,000 and over. Policies for women are at lower rates in recognition of somewhat lower mortality rates.

insurance company invests $100 at 3 percent interest. From Table 7–3, it is clear that at the end of the first year the company will have $103 [$100 + ($100 × 3%)] and at the end of the second year it will have $106 [$100 + ($103 × 3%)]. By the end of the twentieth year, the original $100 invested at 3 percent will amount to $181. Because companies depend on compound interest to add to their income and, thus, to pay a portion of the anticipated benefit payments and expenses, the premiums paid by policyholders are lower than they would be otherwise.

Another aspect of compound interest is *present value,* the value today of $1 received in the future. How much would you have to invest today at 3 percent in order to have exactly $100 at the end of one year? The answer is $97.09 ($97.09 × 3% = $2.91; $2.91 + $97.09 = $100). Similarly, the present value of $100 received twenty years from now is $55.37. Insurance companies use present value to determine how many dollars of premium

Table 7–2

Table of mortality (commissioners 1958 standard ordinary)

| Age (male)[a] | Deaths per 1,000 |
|---|---|
| 15 | 1.46 |
| 20 | 1.79 |
| 25 | 1.93 |
| 30 | 2.13 |
| 35 | 2.51 |
| 40 | 3.53 |
| 50 | 8.32 |
| 60 | 20.34 |

[a] For female lives use age in table 3 years younger than true age
Source: *1973 Life Insurance Fact Book* (New York: Institute of Life Insurance), pp. 110–111

Table 7–3

Compound interest and present value of $1 at various times from now at 3% interest

| Number of years | Compounded interest | Present value |
|---|---|---|
| 1 | $1.0300 | $0.9709 |
| 2 | 1.0609 | 0.9426 |
| 3 | 1.0927 | 0.9151 |
| 4 | 1.1255 | 0.8885 |
| 5 | 1.1593 | 0.8626 |
| 10 | 1.3439 | 0.7441 |
| 20 | 1.8061 | 0.5537 |

income they must collect today and invest at some assumed interest rate (3 percent) in order to pay claims when they come due. The assumed interest rate is used to determine the dollar amount of reserves required to meet policy obligations; overheads and other costs are added to determine the premium paid by policyholders.

### Calculation of Premiums

The information on mortality (Table 7–2) and on compound interest and present value (Table 7–3) can be used to determine life insurance premiums. The following is a hypothetical example and is not intended to reflect premiums charged by actual companies.

Assume that a group of 10,000 males, all age twenty, formed a life insurance company to insure each member of the group for $1,000 for one year (a one-year term policy), with claims paid at the end of the year. If we assume an interest rate of 3 percent, the premium paid by each member can be calculated as follows:

1 From the information given in the mortality table, it is known that the death rate per 1,000 for 20-year-old males is 1.79.
2 Since there are 10,000 members in the group, the amount needed to pay claims is $17,900 (10 × 1.79 × $1,000).
3 Next, the present value of claims must be determined. Given the assumed interest rate of 3 percent, the present value of $17,900 for one year is $17,379 ($17,900 × 0.9709 = $17,379).
4 The final step is to divide the present value of the claims ($17,379) by the number of persons paying premiums (10,000) to arrive at the net premium, which is $1.74.

The above example showed how the premium for a one-year term policy would be determined with no sales charge or operating expenses taken into account. This is the *net premium.* The process for determining the premiums for other types of life insurance policies is more complex but is based on the same fundamental principles. Because term policies do not

accrue cash values, the premium is smaller than in the case of whole life or endowment policies. For example, assume that each member of the group wanted to retain the $1,000 term policy plus an endowment. In this simplified example the endowment consists of $1,000 to be paid at the end of one year. To determine the additional premium for the endowment, the insurance company uses the 3 percent assumed rate to calculate the present value of $1,000 for one year, which is $971 ($1,000 × 0.9709 = $971). Therefore, the insured would have to pay $1.74 for the term policy and $971 for the endowment, a total premium of $972.74. The huge disparity between the two premiums indicates that for policies of the same size, the premium for endowments that contain large savings features is larger than the premiums for whole life policies that contain some savings and term policies that contain no savings. The size of life insurance premiums is directly related to the size of the accrued cash value of the policy.

Before ending the discussion of premiums, it should be noted that most life insurance contracts use level-premium plans, whereby annual premiums remain unchanged during the premium-paying period of the policies. With this method of collecting premiums more funds are accumulated in the early years of the policies than are needed to meet claim expenses. These funds are invested to meet the rising level of death claims as the policies approach maturity.

## Life Insurance in Force

### Amount and Composition

Because premiums are the major source of income for life insurance companies, the amount and composition of the types of life insurance policies they sell are important. The data in Table 7–4 give the amount and composition of life insurance in force in the United States during the 1940–1973 period. During this time span the total amount of life insurance in force increased from $115 million to $1.7 trillion, but the various types of life insurance (ordinary, group, industrial, and credit) increased by different amounts and rates. Although the amount of ordinary life insurance outstanding has increased, as a proportion of the total it has declined from 68 percent in 1940 to 52 percent in 1973. Similarly, the proportion of industrial life insurance declined from 18 percent to 2 percent. Both of these are permanent life insurance: they accrue cash value. In contrast, the proportion of group life insurance in force increased from 13 percent to 40 percent of the total during the same period, and credit life insurance increased to 6 percent of the total in 1973. Virtually all group and credit life insurance is term insurance and accrues no cash value.

Table 7–4

Amount of life insurance in force in the United States[a] ($ millions)

| Year | Ordinary | Group | Industrial | Credit | Total[b] |
|------|----------|-------|------------|--------|----------|
| 1940 | 79,346 | 14,938 | 20,866 | 380 | 115,530 |
| 1950 | 149,116 | 47,793 | 33,415 | 3,844 | 234,168 |
| 1960 | 341,881 | 175,903 | 39,563 | 29,101 | 586,448 |
| 1970 | 734,730 | 551,357 | 38,644 | 77,392 | 1,402,123 |
| 1973 | 928,192 | 708,322 | 40,632 | 101,154 | 1,778,300 |
| | | Percentage of total | | | |
| 1940 | 68 | 13 | 18 | 0 | 100 |
| 1950 | 64 | 20 | 14 | 2 | 100 |
| 1960 | 58 | 30 | 7 | 5 | 100 |
| 1970 | 52 | 39 | 3 | 6 | 100 |
| 1973 | 52 | 40 | 2 | 6 | 100 |

[a] Average amount in force during year
[b] Numbers may not add to totals because of rounding
Source: *1974 Life Insurance Fact Book* (New York: Institute of Life Insurance), p. 23

## Reasons for Changes

*Group Policies*   There are a number of explanations for the changes in the composition of life insurance in force. One explanation is that an increasing number of employers are buying or contributing to group (term) insurance policies for their employees. Today, life and other types of insurance are considered by some to be a part of the basic wage package, an essential fringe benefit. Employer-employee groups account for about 84 percent of the group life insurance in force. Various social, fraternal, and professional organizations also have group insurance programs for their members. Group life insurance policies are becoming increasingly popular because it costs less to provide one policy covering a large number of people than to provide many individual policies. The difference in cost is determined by the size of the group, the type of coverage and benefits included, and the claims experience. Thus, the employers are able to provide (or the employees are able to buy) more life insurance for each dollar of life insurance premium.

Another desirable feature of group policies is that the insured may not be required to take a physical examination to obtain life insurance. Many people have physical disabilities which make it costly and difficult for them to obtain life insurance. Group plans that waive physical examinations enable such persons to obtain low-cost life insurance. In fact, some people join certain organizations just to participate in the group insurance programs offered. Obviously, the insurance companies recognize that a given group will usually include a certain number of high-risk persons and insurance premiums are adjusted accordingly.

Because individuals can obtain group life insurance through their employers and organizations to which they belong, their need for individual policies is reduced, and the type of policy they will buy is different. For example, suppose that Joe Doe decides he wants a $20,000 policy to satisfy his life insurance needs. If his employer provides him with half that amount through a low-cost group plan, then Joe needs to acquire only an additional $10,000 of life insurance. In deciding what type of life insurance to buy, he takes into account that he participates in the company's profit-sharing plan and its pension fund and that he will receive social security when he retires. Because he already has these sources of future income, Joe may decide that he will be better off with a term policy that gives only protection rather than a whole life policy or endowment that gives both protection and income. To some extent, his decision will be based on the relative cost of each type of policy. Table 7–5 shows how the approximate annual premiums for $10,000 of life insurance at ages 20 and 25 differ substantially for various types of life insurance policies. To obtain $10,000 of life insurance, Joe can spend either $53.50, to buy pure protection, or $426.90, for protection plus a savings element. This example suggests that people like Joe who have group insurance, profit sharing, pension funds, and social security are likely to spend a smaller proportion of their incomes in the form of life insurance. The suggestion is supported by the data in Table 7–6 which reflect the diminishing rate of savings through life insurance companies. Between 1945 and 1971, net savings through life insurance companies declined from 2.26 percent to 1.06 percent of disposable personal income (the amount of income left after taxes, etc., that individuals can use for savings or for personal expenditures).

The fact that individuals are saving a smaller share of their incomes through life insurance companies is not a recent development. In 1962, the Life Insurance Association of America prepared a monograph for the Commission on Money and Credit,[3] in which it lamented that the recent growth in life insurance savings had been the lowest experienced in the last 25 years, attributing the trend to the following factors:[4]

1  The increasing importance of term insurance
2  A rise in surrender benefits, i.e., cashing in of existing policies by policyholders
3  A growing reluctance to leave policy proceeds with insurance companies when the supplementary contracts are based solely on interest rates
4  An increased use of policy loans
5  A rise in the general operating expenses of life insurance companies

---

[3]Life Insurance Association of America, *Life Insurance Companies as Financial Institutions* (Englewood Cliffs, N.J.: Prentice-Hall, 1962).
[4]*Ibid.,* p. 33.

Table 7–5

Approximate annual premium for $10,000 of life insurance[a]

| Type of policy | Age at which policy was issued | |
| --- | --- | --- |
| | 20 | 25 |
| Five-year term (renewable and convertible) | $ 52.80 | $ 53.50 |
| Ordinary life | 115.00 | 133.50 |
| 20-payment life | 198.40 | 220.70 |
| 20-year endowment | 425.50 | 426.90 |

[a] Rates are the approximate premiums for males
Source: *Decade of Decision* (New York: Institute of Life Insurance, 1974), p. 14

Inflation and high rates of interest hurt life insurance companies in the late 1950s and these same factors are still present in the early 1970s.

*Portfolio Theory*    The reduction in the rate of savings through life insurance companies can also be thought of in terms of portfolio theory. Individuals want to hold a reduced share of their financial assets in life insurance savings because of substitute forms of savings and higher yields on other types of investment. Nevertheless, accumulated savings through life insurance companies is the largest single form of institutional savings. The point is that the relative importance of the life insurance business in the savings process is declining.

Life insurance companies attempted to retain their share of the savings market by operating pension funds. Noninsured pension funds, trust departments of commercial banks, and independent trustees were also attempting to increase their respective shares of the savings market. According to Goldsmith,[5] life insurance companies were not able to maintain their share of savings by administering private pension funds. Accumulation of funds from that source hardly kept up with the increase in personal income. "There seems, therefore, little doubt that the introduction and expansion of the various retirement and pension fund schemes adversely affected the

Table 7–6

Net savings[a] through U.S. life insurance companies as a percentage of disposable personal income in selected years

| Year | Percentage of disposable personal income |
| --- | --- |
| 1945 | 2.26 |
| 1950 | 1.93 |
| 1960 | 1.54 |
| 1971 | 1.06 |

[a] Net savings is the increase in total annual admitted assets of all U.S. life insurance companies. after adjustments for policy loans and net capital gains and losses.
Sources: Department of Commerce; Life Insurance Association of America

[5]Raymond W. Goldsmith, *Financial Institutions* (New York: Random House, 1968).

position of life insurance companies as users of funds, and hence also their importance as suppliers of funds, although not to a decisive degree."[6]

## Liabilities of Life Insurance Companies

### Policy Reserves

Life insurance policy reserves, which form the basis of saving through life insurance companies, are liabilities held by life insurance companies to meet the obligations of policyholders and their beneficiaries. They constitute the major liability of life insurance companies. Policyholders can borrow (take out policy loans) on part of their accumulated life insurance policy reserves without forfeiting their policies, or they can cancel their policies and recoup a substantial share of the life insurance policy reserves or savings (cash surrender value). Thus, in a limited sense, life insurance policy reserves are a liquid asset. As previously noted, the amount of savings, and thus of life insurance policy reserves, that are built up depends on the type policy involved. The largest amount of savings and life insurance policy reserves takes place with endowment and whole life policies, and the least with term insurance policies. At the end of 1973, the life insurance policy reserves of U.S. life insurance companies amounted to $134.7 billion—$118.3 billion for ordinary policies, $4.0 billion for group certificates, and $12.4 billion for industrial policies. (Industrial life insurance policies are life insurance policies that are issued in small amounts, usually not over $500, with the premiums collected on a weekly or monthly basis by an agent of the company.)

Life insurance policy reserves are one component of the total policy reserves of U.S. life insurance companies. Total policy reserves include reserves for life insurance, health insurance, annuities, and supplemental contracts; they amounted to $203.7 billion at the end of 1973.[7] In the terminology developed earlier in this book, life insurance policy reserves are secondary securities, or liabilities of life insurance companies. As shown in Table 7–7, policy reserves are the largest liability of life insurance companies. The level of these reserves tends to grow steadily over the years because the payments of benefits are predictable and life insurance policies are long-term contracts. This fact should be kept in mind, when the assets of life insurance companies are discussed below.

### Declared Dividends

Declared dividends, another important liability of life insurance companies, are refunds to policyholders of part of the payments they have

---

[6]*Ibid.*, pp. 102–104.
[7]Supplemental contracts are agreements between life insurance policyholders and beneficiaries, by which the company retains the cash sum payable under the insurance policy and makes payments in accordance with the settlement option chosen.

Table 7–7

Liabilities and surplus funds of U.S. life insurance companies (1973; billions of dollars)

| Item | Amount |
|---|---|
| Policy reserves | 203.7 |
| Policy dividend accumulations | 7.6 |
| Funds set aside for policy dividends | 4.4 |
| Other obligations | 16.9 |
| Special surplus funds | 3.3 |
| Unassigned surplus | 14.7 |
| Capital (stock companies) | 1.9 |
| Total[a] | 252.4 |

[a] Numbers do not add to total because of rounding
Source: Institute of Life Insurance

made on policies or annuities sold on a participation basis. In participation, the policyholder receives some of the difference between the premium charged and the actual experience. If the company earns more than the assumed rate, or if the mortality rate or expense experience is lower than provided for in the premium, surplus funds develop, out of which dividends are paid. At the end of 1973, dividend accumulations and funds set aside for dividends amounted to $12 billion.

Life insurance companies that are owned by stockholders usually sell nonparticipating policies (ones that do not provide for dividends), so that the annual cost of the policy is the premium. In contrast, mutual life insurance companies (owned by their policyholders) sell participating policies that do pay dividends, so that the premium rates for their policies are higher. However, when the dividend is taken into account, the net cost may be lower than the net cost of policies issued by stock companies. In a sense, the mutual companies overcharge and then refund part of that amount to the policyholders in the form of dividends.[8]

## Assets of Life Insurance Companies

### Bonds and Mortgages

Since the major liabilities of life insurance companies are contractual and long-term in nature, companies attempt to match the maturity of their assets with the maturity of their liabilities. An examination of the data in Table 7–8 shows that the assets of U.S. life insurance companies consist mostly of long-term securities such as corporate bonds and mortgages. By earning a rate of return on assets that is higher than the interest rate used in calculat-

---

[8]Some stock companies sell participating policies and some mutual companies sell nonparticipating policies. Companies that sell participating policies, regardless of their form of organization, overcharge on their premiums.

Table 7–8

Assets of U.S. life insurance companies (billions of dollars)

| Type of investment | Amount held | | Percentage of total | |
|---|---|---|---|---|
| | 1972 | 1973 | 1972 | 1973 |
| **Government securities** | | | | |
| Short-term (1 year or less) | | | | |
| U.S. Treasury | $    338 | $    262 | | |
| U.S. federal agency | 20 | 36 | | |
| Foreign government and | | | | |
| international agency | 3 | 5 | | |
| Other (over 1 year) | | | | |
| U.S. Treasury | 3,489 | 3,182 | | |
| U.S. federal agency | 715 | 848 | | |
| U.S. state and local | 3,367 | 3,412 | | |
| Foreign government and | | | | |
| international agency | 3,440 | 3,658 | | |
| Total | 11,372 | 11,403 | 4.8 | 4.5 |
| **Corporate securities** | | | | |
| Short-term (1 year or less) | 2,981 | 3,004 | | |
| Other bonds, notes, and debentures | | | | |
| U.S. | 78,478 | 83,974 | | |
| Foreign | 4,681 | 4,818 | | |
| Preferred stocks | 5,052 | 6,313 | | |
| Common stocks | 21,793 | 19,606 | | |
| Total | 112,985 | 117,715 | 47.1 | 46.7 |
| **Mortgages** | | | | |
| Farm | 5,678 | 5,996 | | |
| Nonfarm | | | | |
| FHA | 9,962 | 9,208 | | |
| NHA | 550 | 532 | | |
| VA | 4,660 | 4,402 | | |
| Conventional | 56,098 | 61,231 | | |
| Total | 76,948 | 81,369 | 32.1 | 32.2 |
| Real estate | 7,295 | 7,693 | 3.0 | 3.0 |
| Policy loans | 18,003 | 20,199 | 7.5 | 8.0 |
| Cash | 1,981 | 2,071 | 0.8 | 0.8 |
| Other | 11,146 | 11,986 | 4.6 | 4.8 |
| Total | 239,730 | 252,436 | 100.0 | 100.0 |

Source: 1973 *Life Insurance Fact Book* (New York: Institute of Life Insurance), p. 75
Numbers may not add to total because of rounding.

ing reserves, life insurance companies build surplus funds from which they can pay dividends. (In general, they use a rate of 2½ to 3 percent to calculate their reserves.) In 1973, life insurance companies earned 4.2 percent net on their invested funds after they paid their expenses and taxes.

## Policy Loans

In addition to the major earnings assets—corporate securities and mortgages—policy loans are an important asset. These are loans to policyholders against the cash value of their life insurance policies. In essence, life insurance companies lend policyholders their own funds at relatively low interest rates. They must charge them interest because the premiums are based on an estimated investment return, which can be earned either by investing in bonds and mortgages or by earnings from policy loans. In recent years, when market interest rates exceeded by wide margins the rates that insurance companies charged, the volume of policy loans outstanding increased sharply. For example, policy loans outstanding increased from 4.8 percent of total assets in 1965 to 8.0 percent in 1973. When it was to their advantage, policyholders disintermediated.

## Balance Sheet Trends

The previous discussion focused on the amount of assets and liabilities outstanding in a particular year. Now the focus shifts to trends that have appeared in the balance sheets of insurance companies in recent years. One such trend concerns mortgage-lending activity. As shown in Table 7–9, during the 1968–1973 period, the holdings of home mortgages by life insurance companies declined. In this and subsequent examples the trends cover a longer time span than the number of years shown in the table. While home mortgages have declined, investments in other mortgages have increased. The category "other mortgages" includes large apartment developments and nonresidential commercial properties. One reason that insurance companies have shifted from home mortgages to other mortgages is that home mortgages consist largely of FHA or VA mortgages, with interest rates that may not be competitive with interest rates on conventional mortgage loans. In addition, there are certain economies of scale achieved in making one $2 million mortgage loan rather than fifty small mortgage loans which add up to $2 million.

Another important trend is the increased investment in corporate securities (line 5) which reflects recent changes in the laws of several states permitting life insurance companies and pension funds to invest a certain amount of their assets in corporate securities. In addition, life insurance companies are emphasizing these shareholdings as investments because of their potential returns. Holdings of corporate stock by insurance

Table 7–9

Balance sheet changes in selected years for U.S. life insurance companies (billions of dollars)

|  |  | 1968 | 1969 | 1970 | 1971 | 1972 | 1973 |
|---|---|---|---|---|---|---|---|
| 1 | Current surplus | 0.6 | 0.9 | 0.8 | 1.0 | 1.6 | 1.8 |
| 2 | Physical investment | 0.7 | 0.8 | 1.0 | 1.4 | 1.0 | 1.3 |
| 3 | Net acquisition of financial assets | 9.8 | 9.2 | 9.9 | 12.7 | 15.0 | 16.6 |
| 4 |     Demand deposits + currency | 0.1 | * | 0.1 | * | 0.2 | 0.1 |
| 5 |     Corporate securities | 1.4 | 1.7 | 2.0 | 3.6 | 3.5 | 3.6 |
| 6 |     Credit market instruments | 7.7 | 6.7 | 7.0 | 8.1 | 10.3 | 12.1 |
| 7 |         U.S. government securities | −0.1 | −0.3 | 0.1 | −0.2 | 0.3 | 0.1 |
| 8 |         State and local obligations | 0.2 | * | 0.1 | 0.1 | * | * |
| 9 |         Corporate bonds | 3.9 | 1.5 | 1.5 | 5.5 | 7.0 | 5.9 |
| 10 |         Home mortgages | −0.7 | −1.1 | −1.3 | −2.1 | −2.1 | −0.5 |
| 11 |         Other mortgages | 3.2 | 3.1 | 3.6 | 3.2 | 4.0 | 4.3 |
| 12 |         Policy loans | 1.2 | 2.5 | 2.2 | 1.0 | 0.9 | 2.2 |
| 13 |     Miscellaneous assets | 0.6 | 0.9 | 0.8 | 0.9 | 1.0 | 0.9 |
| 14 |         Open market paper | — | 0.9 | 0.8 | 0.6 | 0.2 | — |
| 15 | Net increase in liabilities | 9.1 | 9.2 | 10.2 | 13.3 | 15.3 | 15.1 |
| 16 |     Life insurance reserves | 4.6 | 4.8 | 5.1 | 6.1 | 6.5 | 7.2 |
| 17 |     Pension fund reserves | 2.9 | 2.9 | 3.3 | 5.2 | 6.0 | 5.2 |
| 18 |     Other liabilities | 1.5 | 1.4 | 1.7 | 2.1 | 2.9 | 2.7 |
| 19 | Discrepancy | −0.8 | 0.1 | 0.1 | 0.3 | 1.0 | −1.0 |

* Less than $500 million
Source: Board of Governors of the Federal Reserve System, Flow of Funds Accounts

companies increased from 5.7 percent of total assets in 1965 to 11.2 percent in 1972. Because stock prices declined significantly in 1973, the proportion of stock held fell to 7 percent.

Life insurance companies have also increased their holdings of corporate bonds (line 9). These include obligations of railroads, public utilities, various industrial, and miscellaneous corporations. There were relatively small increases in corporate bonds in 1969 and 1970, due in part to the write-down by life insurance companies of an estimated $300 million in value of certain issues of the Penn Central Transportation Company that went bankrupt. However, in 1971–1972 there were large increases in holdings of corporate bonds. Life insurance companies are substantial buyers of privately or directly placed bonds. Bonds can be sold to the investing public through an underwriter or they can be sold directly to large institutional investors such as life insurance companies. With directly placed securities, the borrower and the lender negotiate the terms and conditions of the offering, so that the terms of the indenture of the security are designed to meet the specific needs of both the lender and the borrower. Moreover, directly placed securities generally have slightly higher yields than comparable securities that are sold in the open market. In 1973, about one-fourth of all corporate bond issues were privately placed. Finally, life

insurance companies bought $5.9 billion of the $12.7 billion of corporate bonds issued (net, i.e., new issues less retirements) in 1972.

The general rise in the level of interest rates in recent years has made policy loans (line 12) an attractive source of funds for policyholders. As previously noted, policyholders may borrow a portion of their accumulated reserves at low interest cost; this is analogous to depositors disintermediating at deposit-type institutions. When market interest rates were particularly high in 1969 and 1970, the amount of policy loans outstanding increased appreciably.

## Summary

This chapter defined the basic types of life insurance policies (term, whole life, and endowments), and explained how life insurance premiums, the major source of income for life insurance companies, are determined. There is a marked trend for life insurance companies to sell term policies, which provide them with less premium income than other types of policies. This suggests that individuals are saving a smaller share of their funds through life insurance companies.

In order to retain their share of the savings of individuals, life insurance companies manage pension funds.

Finally, there have been substantial changes in the composition of the assets of life insurance companies. The major changes have been reduced holdings of home mortgage loans and increased investments in corporate securities.

## Questions

1 Explain the main features of the three basic types of life insurance policies.
2 Discuss how the three major types of life insurance policies differ in terms of protection and savings.
3 What are some of the advantages of group life insurance policies? How has the increased use of group policies affected the composition of life insurance in force? What other factors could have influenced this?
4 Describe, in terms of portfolio theory, how the increased coverage of government and private pension plans has affected the relative share of savings administered by life insurance companies.
5 How does the maturity structure of life insurance companies' liabilities affect the asset holdings of these companies?

6 There have been significant changes in the composition of asset holdings of life insurance companies in recent years. Discuss these changes and describe what may have caused them.

7 What are the major liabilities of life insurance companies. Discuss these liabilities in detail.

8 Explain the major factors that determine life insurance premiums. Describe the significance of the assured interest rate in the determination of premiums.

## Bibliography

Cohen, Jerome B. *Decade of Decision.* New York: Institute of Life Insurance, 1972.

Huebner, S. S. and Kenneth Black, Jr. *Life Insurance,* 8th ed. New York: Appleton-Century-Crofts, 1972.

Life Insurance Association of America, *Life Insurance Companies as Financial Institutions.* Prepared for the Commission on Money and Credit. Englewood Cliffs, N.J.: Prentice-Hall, 1962.

*Life Insurance Fact Book.* New York: Institute of Life Insurance (annual).

Pfeffer, Irving. *Insurance and Economic Theory.* (Homewood, Ill.: Richard D. Irwin, 1956).

# 8

# Private
# pension
# plans

Pension plans are becoming increasingly important as a financial and social institution because they affect the welfare of so many people. This chapter examines the evolution of private pension plans and deals extensively with current issues. Since pension plans operate under very few regulations, certain common abuses occur, which have received widespread public attention.

The Internal Revenue Service defines a pension plan as a program established and maintained by an employer to provide for the systematic payment of benefits to employees over a period of years, usually for life upon retirement.[1] Typically, employee participation in pension plans is compulsory, and the employee or the beneficiary cannot borrow the reserves that have accumulated for him. When the employee retires, the reserves are paid out in the form of an annuity or some other type of settlement option. At the end of 1973, private insured and noninsured pension plans covered more than 23 million employees, nearly half of all full-time employees in nongovernment employment.

## History

The first pension plan in the United States was established in 1875 by the American Express Company, and the second by the Baltimore and Ohio

---

[1] IRS Code of 1954, Section 401(a).

Railroad five years later. However, it was not until World War II that pension plans gained considerable importance. The upsurgence of pension plans at that time can be attributed to several circumstances. During the war, employers found it difficult to attract and retain employees because of the shortage of labor and the presence of wage controls and excess profits taxes. One method of avoiding wage controls was to offer pension plans, which were not considered part of the monetary wage although they did add to the employee's real income. In addition, employers used contributions for pension plans as deductible expenses to reduce their excess profits taxes. By 1945, private pension plans covered 6.4 million employees, 50 percent more than had been covered five years earlier.

A 1949 Supreme Court decision was another factor contributing to the growth of pension plans. The Supreme Court declined to review an order of the National Labor Relations Board in which the board had ruled (and the Federal Court of Appeals concurred) that the Inland Steel Company must bargain collectively with its employees over wages and other conditions of employment, including pension benefits.[2] This represented a significant departure from the "traditional" concept of pension plans, which employers had generally thought of as gifts to their loyal, retiring employees. Instead, pensions were to be considered as deferred wages, that is, a part of the employee's present wage which was not realized until retirement. Thus, the Supreme Court decision opened the door for labor unions to bargain for pension plans along with wages in a "total" wage package.

Wage controls and excess profits taxes were again imposed during the Korean War from 1950 to 1953, and pension plans, as during World War II, served as a device to raise real wages and lower taxes. By this time, pension plans were gaining wider acceptance as part of an employee's benefits package. Unions representing auto workers and steel workers pioneered negotiations for pension benefits for their respective memberships. The exact extent to which the Inland Steel decision and the Korean War influenced the number and extent of pension plans is, of course, unknown. Nevertheless, the number of persons covered by private pension plans increased from 9.8 million in 1950 to 21.2 million in 1960.

The next milestone in the development of pension plans was the enactment of the Self-Employed Individuals' Tax Retirement Act of 1962, commonly called the Keogh Act after its sponsor in Congress. This legislation permitted self-employed individuals to establish for themselves voluntary retirement plans with certain tax benefits. More than 7 million self-employed persons were eligible to establish retirement plans under this legislation.

---

[2]*Inland Steel Company* v. *National Labor Relations Board,* 170 F. 2d 247 (C.A. 7 1948), cert. den., 336 U.S. 960, 69 Sup. Ct. 887 (1949).

However, by the end of 1972, there were only 270,000 persons covered by 135,480 Keogh plans funded with life insurance companies (comparable data for noninsured Keogh plans are not available). Recent liberalization of tax deductions allowable under the Keogh Act is expected to stimulate growth in the number of Keogh plans.

The latest and most significant development has been the enactment of the Employee Retirement Income Security Act of 1974. The purpose of the act is to protect the interests of participants in employee benefit plans and to improve the equitable character and soundness of pension plans. Specific requirements of the law will be discussed in later sections of this chapter.

## Types of Pension Plans

As Table 8–1 shows, the assets of all pension plans amounted to $338.9 billion at the end of 1973, more than double the amount held a decade earlier. Pension plans are divided into two categories: government-administered, and private. The government-administered plans include state and local as well as federal retirement plans. Private pension plans include both insured and noninsured plans, insured plans being those established with insurance companies. The data reveal that private pen-

Table 8–1

Assets of all private and public pension plans in selected years (book value, end of year; billions of dollars)

| Type of plan | 1962 | 1965 | 1970 | 1972 | 1973 |
|---|---|---|---|---|---|
| Private (total) | 63.5 | 86.5 | 138.2 | 169.8 | 179.0 |
| Insured pension reserves[a] | 21.6 | 27.4 | 41.2 | 52.3 | 54.6 |
| Separate accounts included above[b] | —[c] | 0.3 | 4.9 | 9.8 | 9.8 |
| Noninsured pension plans[d] | 41.9 | 59.2 | 97.0 | 117.5 | 124.4 |
| Public (total) | 61.4 | 72.8 | 123.5 | 148.2 | 160.0 |
| State and local | 24.5 | 33.1 | 58.0 | 72.1 | 80.2 |
| Federal | | | | | |
| Federal old-age and survivors insurance | 18.3 | 18.2 | 32.5 | 35.3 | 36.5 |
| Federal disability insurance | 2.4 | 1.6 | 5.6 | 7.5 | 7.9 |
| Civil service retirement and disability program[e] | 12.5 | 15.9 | 23.1 | 29.2 | 31.5 |
| Railroad retirement | 3.7 | 3.9 | 4.4 | 4.1 | 3.8 |
| Total private and public[f] | 124.9 | 159.3 | 261.7 | 318.0 | 338.9 |

[a] Statement value
[b] Separate accounts of life insurance companies, established for specific pension plans, allow greater latitude than is permissible under state laws for general life insurance assets
[c] Less than $50 million
[d] Includes deferred profit sharing funds and pension funds of corporations, unions, multiemployer groups, and nonprofit organizations
[e] Includes Foreign Service Retirement and Disability Trust Fund
[f] Figures may not add to totals because of rounding
Source: Securities and Exchange Commission

sion plans are larger and have increased at a faster pace than public ones. Additionally, private noninsured pension plans have more than twice the assets of insured pension plans. As shown in Figure 8–1, in 1972 private noninsured pension plans had 4.2 million beneficiaries, triple the number covered by insured plans.[3]

This chapter deals mainly with private *noninsured* pension plans. (Although government-administered pension plans are important, an examination of them is beyond the scope of this text.) Insured pension plans consist mainly of annuities with life insurance companies. Until recently, assets of such plans were considered part of the total assets of life insurance companies, making it difficult to discuss insured pension plans separately from their respective insurance companies. However, life insurance companies in most states can now maintain separate investment accounts for insured private pension plans, resulting in a wider range of investment opportunities for insured pension plans than for insurance companies in general. Although data covering only the investments of insured pension fund reserves are not available, it is known that in 1972 equity investments accounted for nearly 11 percent of the total financial assets of insurance companies.

**Figure 8–1**

**Number of beneficiaries (end of year)**

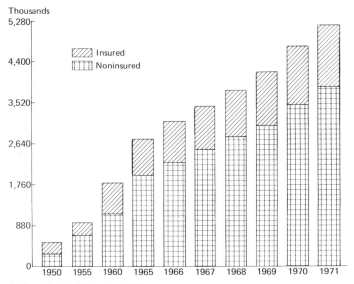

Source: Social Security Administration, 1973

[3]*Social Security Bulletin* (May 1974), p. 21.

## Assets of Private Noninsured Pension Plans

The assets of private noninsured pension plans consist mostly of stocks and bonds. Pension funds invest in such long-term securities because their liabilities are long-term and highly predictable, since it is known how many employees are expected to retire in any given year. However, the composition of these assets has changed markedly over the last two decades. In a search for capital gains, pension plan managers have increased the proportion of funds invested in common stocks and reduced the proportion held in corporate bonds (see Figure 8–2). In 1973, 64 percent of the assets were invested in common stocks, compared with 39 percent a decade earlier. The proportion of the other assets, consisting mostly of liquid securities, also diminished somewhat.

### Reserves

The data in Table 8–2 show the book value and market value of the assets of private noninsured pension plans during the 1967–1973 period. The assets of pension plans are also referred to as pension plan "reserves." At the end of 1973, private noninsured pension plans had a total book value of $124.4 billion and a market value of $129.9 billion. The difference between the two values may be explained by unrealized capital gains and losses in the stock and bond portions of the portfolios.

Figure 8–2

Distribution of assets of private noninsured pension funds (1962–1972) (book value, end of year)

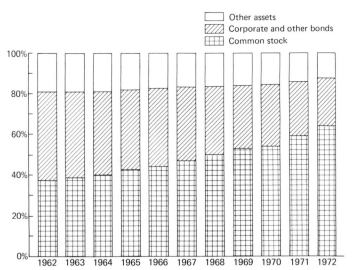

Source: Securities and Exchange Commission, 1973

Table 8–2

Assets of private noninsured pension plans[a]

| | Book value, end of year (millions of dollars) | | | | | | |
|---|---|---|---|---|---|---|---|
| | 1967 | 1968 | 1969 | 1970 | 1971 | 1972 | 1973 |
| Cash and deposits | 1,320 | 1,590 | 1,620 | 1,800 | 1,640 | 1,860 | 2,300 |
| U.S. government securities | 2,320 | 2,760 | 2,790 | 3,030 | 2,730 | 3,690 | 4,330 |
| Corporate and other bonds | 26,360 | 27,000 | 27,610 | 29,670 | 29,010 | 28,210 | 29,810 |
| Preferred stock | 980 | 1,330 | 1,760 | 1,740 | 1,770 | 1,480 | 1,240 |
| Common stock | 34,950 | 41,740 | 47,860 | 51,740 | 62,780 | 74,580 | 79,200 |
| Mortgages | 4,080 | 4,070 | 4,220 | 4,300 | 3,680 | 3,000 | 2,710 |
| Other assets | 4,230 | 4,580 | 4,720 | 4,730 | 4,800 | 4,710 | 4,770 |
| Total assets[b] | 74,240 | 83,070 | 90,580 | 97,010 | 106,420 | 117,530 | 124,360 |
| Change in total assets | 8,070 | 8,830 | 7,510 | 6,430 | 9,410 | 11,110 | 6,730 |

| | Market value, end of year (millions of dollars) | | | | | | |
|---|---|---|---|---|---|---|---|
| | 1967 | 1968 | 1969 | 1970 | 1971 | 1972 | 1973 |
| Cash and deposits | 1,300 | 1,600 | 1,600 | 1,800 | 1,600 | 1,900 | 2,300 |
| U.S. government securities | 2,200 | 2,600 | 2,600 | 3,000 | 2,800 | 3,700 | 4,400 |
| Corporate and other bonds | 22,600 | 22,400 | 21,300 | 24,900 | 26,100 | 26,200 | 27,200 |
| Preferred stock | 1,000 | 1,400 | 1,600 | 1,600 | 2,000 | 1,900 | 1,000 |
| Common stock | 50,100 | 60,100 | 59,800 | 65,500 | 86,600 | 113,400 | 88,000 |
| Mortgages | 4,000 | 3,600 | 3,500 | 3,600 | 3,200 | 2,700 | 2,400 |
| Other assets | 4,200 | 4,300 | 4,300 | 4,300 | 4,500 | 4,600 | 4,700 |
| Total assets[b] | 85,500 | 96,000 | 94,600 | 104,700 | 126,900 | 154,300 | 129,900 |
| Change in total assets | 12,700 | 10,500 | −1,400 | 10,100 | 22,260 | 27,400 | −24,400 |

[a] Includes deferred profit sharing funds and pension funds of corporations, unions, multiemployer groups, and nonprofit organizations
[b] Figures may not add to totals because of rounding
Source: Securities and Exchange Commission

During the period under review (1962–1973),the total market value of assets of private noninsured pension plans increased more than threefold. The largest increases were realized in common stocks where market values increased from $21.2 billion in 1962 to $88 billion in 1973, making these plans one of the largest institutional investors in common stock. This increase reflects the fact that pension plan managers have unrealized capital gains and they are investing an increasing proportion of their assets in common stocks.

## Investment Policies

The increased investments in common stocks were matched by more aggressive investment policies. Such policies are reflected in common stock trading activity rates (see Table 8–3).

Bond market values are affected by changes in long-term market interest rates. When long-term market interest rates rise, the market value of corporate bonds outstanding declines. Since the time period covered by Table

Table 8–3

Common stock activity rates[a] for private noninsured pension plans

| Years[b] | Rates | Years | Rates |
| --- | --- | --- | --- |
| 1964 | 10.6 | 1969 | 21.3 |
| 1965 | 11.4 | 1970 | 20.5 |
| 1966 | 12.6 | 1971 | 22.1 |
| 1967 | 17.2 | 1972 | 19.4 |
| 1968 | 18.7 | 1973 | 14.4 |

[a] Common stock activity rates are defined by the SEC as the average of purchases and sales divided by average market value of stockholdings, stated at annual rates
[b] Data are for third quarter
Source: Securities and Exchange Commission

8–2 was marked by rising market interest rates, one would expect the market value of corporate bonds to be less than the book values shown. Moreover, the disparity between the two numbers is greatest in those years when there was severe monetary restraint and high interest rates. For example, in 1969 there was a $6.7 billion difference between the market value and book value of corporate bonds.

In theory, the investment policy of corporate pension funds is a relatively simple matter, since most enjoy a steady inflow of contributions from employers and employees, and the outflows of funds are highly predictable. Both contributions and disbursements are contractual in nature and cannot be changed in the short run. Therefore, investments can be made with the primary objective of providing sufficient income to cover present and future outlays.

## Disbursements and Contributions

The relationship between disbursements and contributions is important. If disbursements exceed contributions, total assets will decrease by an amount roughly equal to the excess. During the 1962–1972 period, the ratio of disbursements to contributions for noninsured corporate pension funds increased from 42 percent in 1962 to 60.9 percent in 1972 (Table 8–4). At the same time, however, the market value of total assets of these funds tripled, increasing from $46.7 billion in 1962 to $154.3 billion in 1972, as a result of changes in portfolio policies, rising levels of stock prices, and higher market rates of interest.

## Effects on Individuals' Savings

Pension funds affect both the amount and the nature of individuals' savings (the composition of financial assets held by individuals). For many individuals, saving through pension funds is compulsory because company policy requires participation in retirement plans. Such savings are typically contractual, long-term, and not readily accessible.

Table 8–4

Ratio of disbursements to contributions

| Years | Ratio |
|-------|-------|
| 1962 | 42.0 |
| 1963 | 44.2 |
| 1964 | 44.4 |
| 1965 | 45.9 |
| 1966 | 49.2 |
| 1967 | 51.0 |
| 1968 | 53.8 |
| 1969 | 57.2 |
| 1970 | 57.3 |
| 1971 | 58.4 |
| 1972 | 60.9 |

Source: Securities and Exchange Commission; General Economic Research Corporation

Savings accumulated through pension plans, measured by the amount of pension plan reserves (assets), increased from $14.6 billion in 1945 to $317 billion in 1972; this is the equivalent of 13 percent of the total financial assets held by individuals in 1972, an increase of more than 9 percentage points over the 1945 level.

Interestingly, the growth in savings through pension plans does not appear to have reduced certain other forms of savings.[4] In fact, coverage by pension plans seems to stimulate additional savings,[5] because, generally the more savings individuals have, the more they tend to want to accumulate. The results of one study indicate that the amount of additional savings varies with the amount of vested rights and the size of pension contributions,[6] suggesting that some individuals consider only the vested portion of the pension plan as a form of saving. In 1969, 77 percent of all private pension plans had some form of vesting.

## Issues Concerning Pension Plans

### Vesting

Vesting is one of the most important issues related to pension plans. An employee is said to be *vested* the day his benefit credits become the right to future retirement income, even if he leaves the employer before retirement. In essence, vesting means a nonforfeitable right to a retirement income. The following two cases illustrate the importance of vesting to the employee. A large nationwide retail chain had a pension plan with no

[4]Phillip Cagan, *The Effect of Pension Plans on Aggregate Saving: Evidence from a Sample Survey*, Occasional Paper no. 95 (New York; National Bureau of Economic Research, 1965), p. 82.
[5]George Katona, *Private Pensions and Individual Saving*, Monograph no. 40, Survey Research Center, Institute for Social Research (Ann Arbor; The University of Michigan, 1965), p. 90.
[6]Cagan, p. 84.

vesting provisions before qualifying for early retirement at age 55 with 15 years of continuous service (or at age 50 with 20 years of continuous service). Workers who left the company before qualifying for early retirement forfeited all their benefits.[7] A large hardware manufacturer acquired a plant located in Trenton, New Jersey. Previously, the plant had maintained a pension plan with vesting provisions. After the acquisition, the manufacturer negotiated a new contract with the union representing plant workers and the vesting provision was eliminated from the pension plan. Subsequently, he relocated the plant in the Midwest in order to cut production costs. However, none of the 333 plant employees was transferred to the new plant site, and, with the exception of eight employees who were retired because they were sixty-five years or older, all the employees lost both their jobs and their pension benefits. This occurred in spite of the fact that many of them had worked at the plant for more than thirty years.

*Types of Vesting*    There are two basic types of vesting. *Deferred full vesting* takes place as soon as an employee has met certain age and service requirements. *Deferred graded vesting* means that employees are vested for a certain percentage of their benefits when they have satisfied minimum age and service requirements. The percentage of vesting increases as additional service requirements are met. Employees under deferred full vesting plans usually qualify at a later age than employees under deferred graded vesting plans, but the time required for full vesting is usually much longer under deferred graded vesting plans. *Immediate full vesting*—where benefits are vested as soon as they are earned—is still a virtually nonexistent type of plan.

Deferred Full Vesting: A Hypothetical Example

| Years of service | | | | | | | | | | | | | | | |
|---|---|---|---|---|---|---|---|---|---|---|---|---|---|---|---|
| 1 | 2 | 3 | 4 | 5 | 6 | 7 | 8 | 9 | 10 | 11 | 12 | 13 | 14 | 15 | 16 |
| **Percentage of vesting** | | | | | | | | | | | | | | | |
| 0 | 0 | 0 | 0 | 0 | 0 | 0 | 0 | 0 | 100 | 100 | 100 | 100 | 100 | 100 | 100 |

Qualifying date
Full vesting

Deferred Graded Vesting: A Hypothetical Example

| Years of service | | | | | | | | | | | | | | | |
|---|---|---|---|---|---|---|---|---|---|---|---|---|---|---|---|
| 1 | 2 | 3 | 4 | 5 | 6 | 7 | 8 | 9 | 10 | 11 | 12 | 13 | 14 | 15 | 16 |
| **Percentage of vesting** | | | | | | | | | | | | | | | |
| 0 | 0 | 0 | 0 | 20 | 25 | 30 | 35 | 40 | 45 | 50 | 60 | 70 | 80 | 90 | 100 |

Qualifying date

Full vesting

[7]U.S., Congress, Senate, Committee on Labor and Public Welfare, *Interim Report of Activities of the Private Welfare and Pension Plan Study, 1971* (Washington, D.C.: U.S. Government Printing Office, 1972), pp. 87–88.

In these examples pension benefits are based solely on service requirements. In the case of deferred full vesting, the employee receives no vesting for the first nine years of his employment, but at the end of the tenth year, he is 100 percent vested. In the case of deferred graded vesting, the employee receives no vesting for the first four years of his employment. At the end of the fifth year, he or she is 20 percent vested, and the proportion increases until he is 100 percent vested at the end of the sixteenth year.

*Example of Vesting*    In another illustration, the vested amount of accrued pension benefits is determined by the following formula, one of many formulas that can be used to determine benefits:

Vested amount = (stipulated percentage) × (mean monthly salary for last five years) × (number of years in the plan) × (percent vested)

Assume that: the stipulated percentage is 2 percent (this is a factor used in the determination of the benefit formula); the mean monthly salary for the last five years is $600; the employee has been in the plan for nine years; and is 40 percent vested. Then

Vested amount = (stipulated percentage) × (mean monthly salary)
$\qquad$ × (number of years in plan) × (vested percentage)

$\qquad$ = (0.02) × ($600) × (9 years) × (0.40)

$\qquad$ = $43.20/month

If the employee were to leave the plan at this time, he would be entitled to $43.20 per month beginning at the normal retirement age under that plan. Some plans give employees the option of taking reduced benefits at an earlier age.

*Government Involvement*    Part of the vesting controversy concerns government involvement. To prevent loss of benefits due to unreasonable vesting requirements, the Employee Retirement Income Security Act of 1974 established minimum vesting standards for both types of vesting plan. Deferred full vesting plans must be 100 percent vested to any employee who has at least ten years of service. Deferred graded vesting plans must meet a minimum percentage of vested right to pension benefits in accordance with the following table:

| Years of service | 1 | 2 | 3 | 4 | 5 | 6 | 7 | 8 | 9 | 10 | 11 | 12 | 13 | 14 | 15 |
|---|---|---|---|---|---|---|---|---|---|---|---|---|---|---|---|
| Minimum percentage of vesting | 0 | 0 | 0 | 0 | 25 | 30 | 35 | 40 | 45 | 50 | 60 | 70 | 80 | 90 | 100 |
| | | | | Qualifying date | | | | | | | | | | | Full vesting |

An alternate method of computing vesting rights will satisfy the requirements of the act if any employee, after five years of service and for whom the sum of age and years of service equals or exceeds 45, has nonforfeita-

ble rights to vesting percentages of accrued benefits in accordance with the following table:

| Sum of age and years of service | 45 | 47 | 49 | 51 | 53 | 55 |
|---|---|---|---|---|---|---|
| Minimum percentage of vesting | 50 | 60 | 70 | 80 | 90 | 100 |

Some employers view government policies on vesting as an infringement on their rights, since each employer believes that he, and not the government, knows what is best for his company and employees. They argue that they will have a higher employee turnover rate, because employees who change jobs will not lose their pension benefits, and claim that one reason for the substantial rate of growth of private pension plans has been freedom from government regulation. Although this statement is valid, unregulated growth was accompanied by problems concerning vesting, funding, disclosure, and fiduciary standards. The proponents of vesting argue that increased labor mobility is desirable for the economy as a whole.

## Funding

Funding, an issue related to vesting, concerns pension plans that have insufficient assets upon termination, so that all the vested benefits earned under that plan cannot all be paid. The term *funding* refers to the practice by employers, and employees if the plan is contributory, of setting aside funds with a trustee or insurance company for the payment of future benefits. This insures that some pension plan benefits will be paid.

Lack of funding rarely becomes a problem until firms or plants go out of business suddenly. The issue received national attention in 1964, when Studebaker terminated its pension plan because it was no longer going to produce automobiles at South Bend, Indiana. As a consequence, about 8,500 employees were left without pensions or received only a fraction of the benefits to which they were entitled, because the pension plan had been in existence only 14 years and was not fully funded. Only those employees age 60 and over with 10 years or more of service received full benefits. In addition to the Studebaker case, it should be mentioned that some other large pension plans are underfunded. For example, in July 1969, the Western Union Telegraph Company had assets in its pension fund that amounted to only 12 percent of its liabilities, and Uniroyal, Inc., had assets that covered only 35 percent of its liabilities.[8]

When a pension plan is established, the employer makes contributions on behalf of the employees covered by the plan. In the early stages of the plan, only a few participants will retire and current benefits to be paid out will be small when compared to the contributions being paid into the fund. The

[8]*Interim Report of Activities of the Private Welfare and Pension Plan Study, 1971,* p. 81.

contributions not needed for current benefits will accumulate and can be invested. Ultimately, the assets of the plan should grow to a point at which the earnings on these investments will pay for the cost of the current benefits.

*Types of Credits*   One aspect of funding concerns *pension credits*, which are defined as units of service on which benefits are based. There are two types earned in a pension plan, current service credits and past service credits. Current service credits are earned during the life of the plan and are financed as they are earned. Past service credits are granted retroactively whenever a plan is created or its benefit structure liberalized.[9] An employee may be granted immediate credits based on past service with the employer. For example, if the XYZ Company starts a pension plan today, it may grant its employees having 18 years of service credit for 10 of those years. In this case, the plan has incurred a substantial liability for past service credits. According to the IRS Code [Sec. 401(a)], the employer cannot fund more than 10 percent of the past service liabilities per year. Thus, the XYZ Company pension plan is going to be underfunded for at least 10 years.

*Full Funding*   The ideal situation is to have a fully funded plan. A plan is considered fully funded when the employer has no further need to make contributions into the plan. This will be achieved when all past service credits have been financed and the earnings of the investments of the plan are paying the cost of all current service credits. At this time, the assets will be large enough to cover all claims of all participants if the plan is suddenly terminated. However, having all plans fully funded *at all times* is not always practical since amendments to a plan may raise benefits, thereby increasing past service credits. For example, in 1970 the Ford Motor Company pension plan was 86 percent funded before union negotiations. The union bargained for and received increased pension benefits. Had the plan been terminated immediately after the agreement was signed, some Ford employees with fully vested rights would have received only 16 cents per dollar of benefits due them.[10]

A fully funded pension plan can become less than fully funded if the market value of the securities in its portfolio declines significantly. Pension plan portfolios consist mostly of bonds and stocks, and rising interest rates and lower stock prices have an adverse effect on portfolio values. As a result of these factors, pension plans are inevitably exposed to some risks.

*Solutions to Underfunding*   There are two solutions to the problem of underfunding. One legislative solution proposed is to require mandatory

[9]*The Private Pension Controversy* (New York: Bankers Trust Company, 1973), p. 47.
[10]"The Push for Pension Reform," *Business Week* (March 17, 1973), p. 52.

insurance for vested pension rights.[11] Three of the arguments against such insurance are: costs could become excessive if companies promised benefits in excess of their capacity to finance them; pension plans might be induced to invest in excessively risky assets; and the cost of insurance could reduce the amount of benefits that a company can fund.

Another alternative is to have a minimum funding standard. The Internal Revenue Service has issued rulings which have been widely interpreted as imposing a minimum standard of funding as a condition of continued qualification under the tax laws. The minimum requirement for tax benefits appears to be that current service credits, as well as interest on any unfunded accrued liabilities, must be funded. Most companies use actuarial assumptions to determine their funding schedule. Some pay in more than is scheduled when business is good and pay less than is scheduled when business is not so good. Changes in the value of the pension plan's assets can also influence the amount of the contribution the employer must make to meet the funding schedule.

The Employee Retirement Income Security Act of 1974 established minimum funding standards for all private pension plans. The act requires full funding, and sets maximum time limits (ranging from 15 to 40 years) in which underfunding deficiencies must be made up. The act does not require any past service credits, but it does establish procedures for their inclusion in funding and vesting requirements if a particular pension plan provides for them. To guarantee pension benefits in the event of plan termination, the act established the Pension Benefits Guaranty Corporation, a public corporation from which all covered pension plans are required to purchase insurance protection for vested individual retirement benefits to a limit of $750 per month. The corporation would also assume trusteeship of the pension plan funds to supervise termination.

## Portability

The popular notion of portability is that employees ought to be able to take their vested pension benefits with them when they move from job to job and combine those benefits into one pension. Frequently, the issues of portability and vesting are confused. In some cases, employees who are fired or change jobs may forfeit their pension benefits. For example, in 1927 Mr. X started to work at one of his employer's two meat-packing plants located in the same city. During World War II, he was sent to work in the other plant, and remained there until 1965, when that plant closed. He received a lump sum pension payment of $231.55 for his 38 years of service. His employer would not permit him to return to the first plant as a regular employee, but

---

[11]S. 3598, 92nd. Cong.

he did return as a "casual and intermittent laborer." Such employees were not entitled to participate in that plant's pension plan. When Mr. X was dismissed in 1970, because he was over age 65, he received no pension benefits other than the $231.55 in 1965.[12] This is a vesting problem rather than a portability problem.

*Federal Clearinghouse*    The term portability, as used in proposed legislation, refers to a federal clearinghouse for the transfer of the discounted cash value of vested pension credits.[13] An employee changing jobs would be able either to deposit the discounted cash value of his vested pension credits in the central federal clearinghouse until retirement, or have the credits transferred to his new employer and applied to the employee's pension plan there.

Among the numerous unresolved issues concerning the establishment of a federal clearinghouse is the standardization of pension plan benefits. In order for the clearinghouse to function, there must be an equitable way to transfer credits between pension plans, but some pension plans are fully funded, and have early retirement features, disability benefits, and provisions lacking in other pension plans. It is not clear how to equate the credits of pension plans that are structurally different. Moreover, those opposed to the federal clearinghouse argue that standardization of pension plans could be damaging to the vitality of the private pension plan system because it would reduce the incentive to offer new benefits to employees.

The development of a new bureaucracy to manage the federal clearinghouse is another issue. As noted earlier, government bureaucracy per se is not desirable to private business. The federal clearinghouse would be charged with the administration and investment of funds that are deposited with it and would also enforce selected federal pension fund regulations. Although the 1974 act did not establish a clearinghouse, the Pension Benefit Guaranty Corporation can assist individuals in establishing their own retirement plans when they leave an approved plan.

*Liquidity of Assets*    Another issue is the liquidity of pension fund assets. At the present time, the bulk of pension fund assets are invested in long-term securities. If employees could withdraw the discounted cash value of their vested pension credits when they changed jobs, a greater proportion of pension plan assets would have to be invested in short-term liquid securities. Such a shift in assets might reduce the overall rate of return on pension plan assets, resulting in higher pension costs. Moreover, if a large

---

[12]*Interim Report of Activities of the Private Welfare and Pension Plan Study, 1971*, pp. 87–88.
[13]S. 3598, 92d Cong. Also, Testimony of Frank Cummings, in *Hearings before the Subcommittee on Private Pension Plans*, U.S., Senate, Committee on Finance, 93rd Cong. 1st sess. May 31 and June 4, 1973, part 2., pp. 1015–1016.

group of employees were to quit at the same time, the pension plan might have to liquidate assets when market conditions were not favorable, thereby hurting those who remained in the plan.

Finally, employees who deposited their funds (pension credits) with the federal clearinghouse would be guaranteed the payment of future benefits, whereas those who remain with the employer are discriminated against if the plan is not fully funded, because they will not receive their full benefits if the plan should be terminated.

Some multiemployer pension plans are portable, such as the Teachers Insurance Annuity Association (TIAA). At the end of 1972, TIAA covered 2,293 educational institutions throughout the United States. Under TIAA, a professor can change jobs from one participating school to another without losing vested pension benefits: each participant in the plan has immediate full vesting.

## Disclosure

The issue of disclosure concerns employers revealing financial data on the operations of their pension plans as well as an explanation of the provisions of the plans in terms that can be understood by the employees. Prior to 1974, the Welfare and Pension Plans' Disclosure Act (1958) required that pension plans reported annual changes in assets to the Department of Labor. The changes for any group of assets were limited to a single-line entry (all purchases or sales aggregated into one number) and a detailed explanation was not required. Thus, neither the participants in the plan nor the Department of Labor were able to determine if the funds were being managed prudently. One classic case along this line involved the United Mine Workers' Welfare and Retirement Fund. The fund complied with the Pension Plan Disclosure Act. However, the trustees of the fund had deposited 44 percent ($75 million) of its resources in a non-interest-bearing bank account. The union held 74 percent of the bank's stock, which used the retirement fund's money for its own profit. In total, the retirement fund lost an estimated $12 million in foregone earnings.[14] This case also illustrates lack of fiduciary responsibility, a topic which is discussed below.

Another aspect of disclosure is that frequently employees are not able to interpret or understand the provisions of their pension plans. This point was brought out succinctly in the following testimony before the Senate.

*Stephen Duane had worked for the A & P for 32 years when he found at the time of the plant closing that he had no vested rights to his*

---

[14]Ralph Nader and Kate Blackwell, *You and Your Pension* (New York: Grossman Publishers, 1973), pp. 70–71.

*pension. He referred to his knowledge of the plan provisions, and testified, "the average working-man in my class, laborers, and that's all we are, warehousemen, we're not lawyers, we can't sit down and read what they intended it to be."*[15]

In the same hearings, Lester Fox, an official of the defunct Studebaker plant in South Bend, Indiana, alluded to insufficient funding knowledge by the employees. He said:

*The workers really had no way of knowing . . . that the termination of the corporation could, in fact, terminate their rights to a pension or a vested right. They had security built on shifting sands, if I were to summarize it in my own words.*[16]

To rectify some of the problems concerning disclosure, several bills have been introduced into Congress.[17] In general, the proposed legislation calls for annual reports containing all substantial transactions and other pertinent financial data, clear descriptions of pension plans for employees, and annual audits.

With the passage of the 1974 act, annual reports must be filed with the Secretary of Labor by all pension and welfare plans affecting interstate commerce. The annual report for pension plans must include audited financial statements which contain the following: a statement of assets and liabilities aggregated by category; a statement of changes in net assets available for plan benefits; receipts and disbursements; a schedule of assets held for investment purposes aggregated and identified by issuer, borrower, or lesser; and a schedule of each transaction involving a person known to be a "party-at-interest." Furthermore, each administrator of an employee benefit plan must furnish to each participant and beneficiary a summary plan description written in a way that the average participant and beneficiary can understand it.

## Fiduciary Responsibility

The term *fiduciary* can be broadly defined as any person who exercises any power of control over employee benefit plans. The term *fiduciary responsibility* refers to the fact that those controlling employee benefit plans have a responsibility to their plan's membership to manage the assets of that plan in a prudent manner.

There is strong evidence that the managers of some pension plans do not exercise their fiduciary responsibility. The following examples will illustrate this point.

---

[15]*Interim Report of Activities of the Private Welfare and Pension Plan Study, 1971*, pp. 74–75.
[16]*Ibid.*, p. 75.
[17]S. 3598, 92d Cong.; H.R. 1269, 92d Cong.; S. 3024, 92d Cong.

*The Woolworth Company had about 35 percent of the assets of its pension plan invested in its own real estate, mortgages, or property.[18] If the Woolworth Company had failed, the pension plan assets would have been more adversely affected than if the funds were invested more broadly.*

*The Genesco Company had $15 million in their own securities.[19]*

*The Winn Dixie Corporation had 28 percent of their profit sharing plan's assets invested in their own securities.[20]*

While there was no federal law prohibiting the type of activities described above, such investments constitute threats to the inviolability of the plans. Moreover, there is also a presumption of conflicts of fiduciary interests that may not be in the best interest of plan participants. The 1974 act requires that each fiduciary of a plan act with the "care, skill, prudence, and diligence" that a *prudent man* acting in like capacity would use. Moreover, a plan may not invest more than 10 percent of its assets in the employer's securities and real property and no fiduciary may make any transaction for the plan with any party-at-interest or for his own benefit. Finally, a fiduciary who breaches the fiduciary requirements of the act is personally liable for any losses to the plan.

## Summary

Today, private pension plans cover an estimated 23 million full-time employees in private industry. In the future pension plans may cover all employees. Therefore, pension plans are important as a financial as well as a social institution. As a financial institution, private noninsured pension plans had total reserves (assets) of $27.4 billion at the end of 1972. The bulk of these reserves are invested in corporate securities. Thus, investments in common stock are gaining increased importance.

The issues of vesting, funding, portability, disclosure, and fiduciary responsibility have important social ramifications. Every year many employees who believe they will receive retirement benefits from their employers find out that provisions of the plan exclude them from full benefit payments. A recent study[21] also revealed that: the proportion of men covered by private pension plans was 45 percent greater than for women; the

---

[18]*Interim Report of Activities of the Private Welfare and Pension Plan Study, 1971*, p. 85.
[19]*Ibid.*, p. 86.
[20]*Ibid.*, p. 86.
[21]U.S. Department of Health, Education and Welfare, *Coverage and Vesting of Full-time Employees Under Private Pension Plans: Findings from April, 1972*, Survey, SSA 74-11908 (Washington, D.C.: U.S. Government Printing Office, 1973).

proportion of whites covered was 25 percent greater than for persons of all other races; and private plan coverage was highest in high-wage industries (mining and manufacturing, public utilities, and communications) and lowest in low-wage industries (services and retail trade).

## Questions

1 Distinguish between the following categories of pension plans: government-administered and private; insured and noninsured.
2 In recent years private noninsured pension funds have adopted more agressive investment policies. Explain how this change in investment strategy could affect stock market prices.
3 What are the main portfolio holdings of private noninsured pension funds? How have the relative shares of the major components of these portfolios changed in recent years?
4 Explain how the contractual-type liabilities of private pension funds affect the maturity structure of their portfolios.
5 What effect, if any, do pension funds seem to have had on the savings of individuals?
6 Explain the significance of vesting to participants in pension plans. Discuss how lack of vesting can cause employees to lose their retirement benefits.
7 Distinguish between the following types of vesting: immediate full vesting, deferred full vesting, and deferred graded vesting.
8 Explain what full funding of a pension fund is and how this protects employee retirement benefits. Discuss why it may not be practical to have all plans fully funded at all times.
9 What is meant by the "portability" of pension benefits? Would you prefer a portable pension plan or one that has immediate full vesting?
10 How might the existence of a federal pension fund clearinghouse aid employees in protecting their pension benefits?
11 Define the term "fiduciary responsibility" as it applies to pension plans and explain how lack of fiduciary responsibility by those managing a pension plan can lead to abuses.
12 How might complete portability and earlier vesting of pension benefits alter the optimum composition of pension fund portfolios?

# Bibliography

Bernstein, Merton C. *The Future of Private Pensions*. New York: The Free Press, 1964.

Griffin, Frank L., Jr., and Charles L. Trowbridge. *Status of Funding Under Private Pension Plans*. Homewood, Ill.: Richard D. Irwin, 1969.

*Life Insurance Fact Book*. New York: Institute of Life Insurance (annual).

McGill, Dan M. *Fulfilling Pension Expectations*. Homewood, Ill.: Richard D. Irwin, 1962.

————. *Fundamentals of Private Pensions*. Homewood, Ill.: Richard D. Irwin, 1964.

———— ed. *Pensions: Problems and Trends*. Homewood, Ill.: Richard D. Irwin, 1955.

Nader, Ralph, and Kate Blackwell. *You and Your Pension: What Should Be Done About It*. New York: Grossman Publishers, 1973.

Patterson, Edwin W. *Legal Protection of Private Pension Expectations*. Homewood, Ill.: Richard D. Irwin, 1960.

*The Private Pension Controversy*. New York: Bankers Trust Company, 1973.

U.S. Department of Health, Education and Welfare. *Coverage and Vesting of Full-Time Employees Under Private Pension Plans: Findings from the April 1972, Survey*, SSA 74-11908. Washington, D.C.: U.S. Government Printing Office, 1973.

U.S. Department of Health, Education and Welfare. *Social Security Programs Throughout the World, 1971*, Research Report no. 40. Washington, D.C.: U.S. Government Printing Office, 1971.

Part

# 4

# Other types of financial intermediaries

The first two chapters of Part 4, "Transition in the Stock Market" (Chapter 9) and "Investment Companies and Real Estate Investment Trusts" (Chapter 10), highlight changes that have been occurring on Wall Street in recent years.

Chapter 11, "Consumer Credit Institutions," is concerned with the evolution of consumer credit from the colonial period up to the present time, with a look into the future.

Chapter 12, "Federal Credit Agencies," examines how these institutions affect everyone through their influence on mortgage markets and agriculture.

"Mortgage Banking Companies" (Chapter 13) examines a major financial institution that deals in government-backed mortgages.

# 9

# Transition in the stock market

In the late 1960s a financial crisis erupted on Wall Street when some of the largest stockbrokerage firms went bankrupt. Given the economics of the stockbrokerage industry, such failures were predictable. Increasing demand for brokerage services coupled with a rapidly increasing volume of stock trading contributed to rising costs. However, a fixed supply price (commission income) did not cover these increased costs; consequently, many firms failed. The failure of these firms reflects the inability of the Securities and Exchange Commission to regulate the securities market and the unwillingness of the New York Stock Exchange to regulate itself. The first part of this chapter analyzes the causes of the Wall Street crisis of the late 1960s, and examines the responses of the securities industry and Congress to the unusual developments on Wall Street. Finally, there is a discussion of various proposals that are being considered that may affect the direction the securities industry may take in the future.

## Trading Activity

### Volume

In recent years the trading activities of all stock markets in the United States have increased dramatically. The dollar volume of sales on stock exchanges in the United States increased from $45 billion in 1960 to $197

billion in 1968,[1] although by June 1971 it had declined to $101 billion. Another indication of the increased trading activity is given in Table 9–1, which shows the rise in the average daily volume of shares traded on the New York Stock Exchange (NYSE). In 1960 the average daily volume was three million shares; by 1971, this figure had risen to more than fifteen million shares. Because most of this increased trading activity has occurred since 1964, this chapter will focus on the period since then.

## The "Cult of Performance"

Numerous explanations have been given for the increased trading activity on the stock exchanges in the past decade. The principal reason concerns financial institutions such as open-end investment companies, commonly called *mutual funds*. In the mid-1960's, a "cult of performance" developed among some mutual funds and quickly spread to others. Managers of such funds measured success by their ability to turn a quick profit. They traded in and out of stocks searching for instant wealth, which sharply increased their *common stock activity rates* (defined by the Securities and Exchange Commission as the average of purchases and sales divided by the average market value of stockholdings). The activity rates for open-end investment companies soared in the late 1960s (see Table 9–2).

Another indicator of increased institutional participation in the stock market is the rise of large block transactions—transactions of 10,000 shares or more. In 1965 there were 2,171 block transactions amounting to $1.8 billion. By 1971, this had risen to the startling figure of 26,941 block transactions for a total value of $24.2 billion![2]

Table 9–1

Average daily volume on the New York Stock Exchange in selected years

| Year | Millions of shares | Year | Millions of shares |
|------|--------------------|------|--------------------|
| 1950 | 2.0 | 1966 | 7.5 |
| 1955 | 2.8 | 1967 | 10.1 |
| 1960 | 3.0 | 1968 | 13.0 |
| 1961 | 4.1 | 1969 | 11.4 |
| 1962 | 3.8 | 1970 | 11.6 |
| 1963 | 4.6 | 1971 | 15.4 |
| 1964 | 4.9 | 1972 | 16.5 |
| 1965 | 6.2 | | |

Source: New York Stock Exchange

[1]Data are taken from the following stock exchanges: New York Stock Exchange, American Stock Exchange, Midwest Stock Exchange, Pacific Coast Stock Exchange, Philadelphia-Baltimore-Washington Stock Exchange, Boston Stock Exchange, Detroit Stock Exchange, Cincinnati Stock Exchange, and appear in the *37th Annual Report* (1971) of the Securities and Exchange Commission.
[2]New York Stock Exchange, *1972 Fact Book*, p. 12.

Table 9–2

Common stock activity rates

| Year | Private noninsured pension funds | Open-end inv. co.s | Life ins. co.s | Property and liability ins. co.s | Total selected inst.s |
|---|---|---|---|---|---|
| 1964 | 10.6 | 18.2 | 11.8 | 7.8 | 12.9 |
| 1965 | 11.4 | 21.8 | 13.8 | 8.2 | 14.7 |
| 1966 | 12.6 | 34.0 | 16.0 | 8.6 | 19.8 |
| 1967 | 17.2 | 40.7 | 18.2 | 9.7 | 24.7 |
| 1968 | 18.7 | 48.4 | 26.8 | 16.0 | 29.4 |
| 1969 | 21.3 | 51.0 | 29.4 | 26.7 | 32.4 |
| 1970 | 20.5 | 45.6 | 27.8 | 28.1 | 29.8 |
| 1971 | 22.4 | 48.2 | 30.9 | 22.7 | 30.9 |
| 1972 | 19.4 | 45.1 | 29.7 | 23.8 | 29.5 |
| 1973[a] | 14.4 | 34.6 | 17.9 | 16.3 | 19.4 |

[a] Data are for third quarter
Source: Securities and Exchange Commission

## New Stock Issues

The second important factor contributing to the increased trading activity in the stock market was the issuance of new stocks and the retirement of existing ones. Table 9–3 shows that the dollar volume of new issues of equity securities in 1971 amounted to nearly $15 billion, compared with $4.7 billion for similar issues in 1967. During the 1967–1971 period, the dollar volume of retirements fluctuated widely. Retirements reflect issues called by the parent company, conversions by security holders, and mergers. Mergers frequently take place through *tender offers* by the acquiring company, in which stockholders are asked to sell (tender) their shares at a specified price. The fact that a company is acquiring or being acquired frequently increases speculative trading in the security issues of the participating companies. For example, there are those who attempt to arbitrage the securities of the merging companies. An *arbitrage* is the simul-

Table 9–3

Net change in outstanding equity securities (billions of dollars)

| Year | New issues | Common and preferred stocks Retirements | Net change |
|---|---|---|---|
| 1967 | 4.7 | 2.4 | 2.3 |
| 1968 | 6.1 | 7.0 | −0.9 |
| 1969 | 9.3 | 5.1 | 4.3 |
| 1970 | 9.2 | 2.4 | 6.8 |
| 1971 | 14.8 | 1.3 | 13.5 |
| 1972 | 15.2 | 2.2 | 13.0 |
| 1973 | 13.6 | 3.0 | 10.6 |

Source: Securities and Exchange Commission; *Federal Reserve Bulletin*

taneous purchase and sale of the same or equivalent securities to take advantage of a disparity in prices.[3] To illustrate arbitrage, assume that Company A has just offered to buy (tender) the shares of Company B at $25 per share. If the shares of Company B are currently selling at $23 per share, speculators can sell (tender) shares to Company A at $25 per share and buy them in the market at $23 per share, for a $2 profit per share. In summary, the combination of new issues, merger activity, conversions, and speculation contributed importantly to the volume of securities traded.

As a result of the increased volume of trading activity, the existing mechanisms for clearing and transferring stock certificates became clogged. The inadequate clearing and transfer procedures brought unusual financial pressures to bear on stockbrokerage firms, causing some to collapse.

## The Clearing and Transfer Process

### Clearing

*Clearing* is the processing and exchange of information, certificates, and funds after a stock transaction has taken place. The process described here is the one used by the New York and American Stock Exchanges and is called the *balance order* method. At the end of each trading day the details of all trades are compiled and a net trading balance (the amount of each stock owed by one member firm to another) is computed. The Stock Clearing Corporation, a subsidiary of the New York Stock Exchange, directs the selling firms to deliver a specified number of shares to a buying firm.[4] After the firms have sorted out their trades, the stock certificates representing ownership must be transferred from the seller's name into the buyer's name by a transfer agent (generally a commercial bank).

### Transfer

Figure 9–1 shows the *transfer* process for stocks in good delivery in the left panel and the transfer process for stocks that are not in good delivery in the right panel. The term *good delivery* means that a stock certificate is endorsed correctly (the signature of the seller on the back of the certificate is the same name that appears on the face of the certificate) and is for the correct number of shares. Assume that Joe Doe has sold one hundred

---

[3]In some cases arbitrage may involve a short sale—the sale of a security at a high price in anticipation of buying it back at a lower price. In the above example Company B was sold short at $25 per share and simultaneously bought at $23 per share, thereby "covering" the short sale and making a $2 profit per share.
[4]Details of this process can be found in: U.S., Congress, Senate, Committee on Banking, Housing, and Urban Affairs, *Securities Industry Study*, Committee Print (Washington, D.C.: U.S. Government Printing Office, 1972), pp. 12–13.

Figure 9–1

The transfer process of stocks

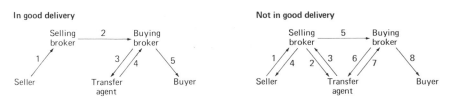

shares of XYZ Corporation through his stockbroker. As shown in the left panel of Figure 9–1, the seller delivers the stock certificate to his broker (step 1). If the certificate is endorsed correctly and is for one hundred shares of XYZ Corporation, Joe Doe's stockbroker delivers the certificate to the buyer's stockbroker (step 2). The buyer's stockbroker sends the certificate to the transfer agent for XYZ Corporation, who will transfer the ownership of the stock from the seller's name into the buyer's name (step 3). A new certificate is then issued by the transfer agent, registered in the buyer's name, and delivered to the buyer's stockbroker (step 4), who delivers the new certificate to the buyer (step 5), and the process is complete.

To complicate the transfer process, suppose the seller delivers a certificate that is *not in good delivery*. If the seller sold fifty shares of XYZ Corporation and delivered a certificate for one hundred shares, the certificate would not be in good delivery. In this case, the seller's stockbroker delivers one hundred shares of XYZ to the transfer agent (step 2, right panel), who issues two certificates (step 3), one for fifty shares in the seller's name and one for fifty shares in the name of the seller's stockbroker. The seller's stockbroker delivers fifty shares to the seller (step 4), and the remaining fifty shares go to the buyer's stockbroker. From this point on, the process is the same as that described above.

## Fails

Before 1968, the Securities and Exchange Commission required the selling stockbroker to deliver the securities to the buying stockbroker within four business days. Since then, the commission has extended the permissible time to five business days. If for some reason the seller's stockbrokerage firm is unable to deliver a certificate in good delivery to the buyer's stockbrokerage firm within five business days, this is called a *failure to deliver*. On the other side of the transaction, the buyer's stockbroker has a *failure to receive*. A "fail" is a liability for both the seller's and the buyer's stockbrokerage firms.

As a result of the increase in the volume of trading activity described earlier, the entire transfer process was swamped by the volume of paper that was circulating. Transfer agents, who in 1966 were able to cancel old certificates and issue new ones in forty-eight hours, took two to eight weeks to perform this same function in 1968.[5] The back offices of most stockbrokerage firms were unable to keep up with the paperwork, and the dollar volume of fails rose from about $2 billion in early 1968 to $4.1 billion in December 1968. The volume of fails subsequently declined, for reasons that will be explained later in this chapter, and by the end of 1971 amounted to only $1.3 billion.[6]

### Net Capital Ratio

Such fails are important because they affect the net capital ratio of stockbrokerage firms. For example, if fails to receive are more than forty days old they are considered to be a debt and must be supported by the firm's net capital. Before August 11, 1971, the New York Stock Exchange required that, for every $20 of debt that a brokerage firm held, it had to have $1 of net capital[7]—the net capital ratio was 20:1. After that date, when the net capital ratio was increased to 15:1, stockbrokers could not have as much debt per dollar of liquidity as they had had previously. As the dollar volume of fails rose in the late 1960s, an increasing number of stockbrokerage firms were unable to maintain even the existing 20:1 net capital ratio. The significance of the net capital ratio is that it is illegal for a firm to continue to do business when it does not meet the minimum capital requirements. Accordingly, some firms in this condition were restricted from particular kinds of business until they could improve their financial position, while other firms were forced to merge or liquidate their business.

It should be noted that the New York Stock Exchange enforced its capital ratio rule selectively. For example, the Exchange allowed several large firms (Dempsey-Tegeler Company, Inc., McDonnell and Company, Blair and Company, and Hayden Stone, Inc.) to operate despite critical capital deficiencies. Unfortunately, the SEC was unable to take action at that time because the Securities and Exchange Act of 1934 exempts organized stock exchanges from the SEC's net capital requirements.

In summary, the crux of the problem in the late 1960s was increased trading activity in the stock market. With it came breakdowns in the clearing and transfer process, logjams in back offices of brokerage firms, increased fails, and inadequate net capital ratios. To improve their financial positions

---

[5]U.S., Congress, Senate, *Securities Industry Study,* p. 17.
[6]New York Stock Exchange, *1972 Fact Book,* p. 19.
[7]The New York Stock Exchange (Rule 325) defines *net capital* as the excess of total assets over total liabilities, after provision for unpaid dividends and less the value of selected assets.

and customer service, stockbrokerage firms and exchanges took the corrective actions that will be discussed next. However, it will be shown that some of these corrective actions had perverse effects and actually contributed to the financial instability of the stockbrokerage industry.

## The Initial Response

### Reduced Trading Hours

The first industry effort to relieve back-office pressures was for the major stock exchanges to stop trading ninety minutes earlier every day. This policy was instituted for about two weeks in August 1967, but it had only a transitory effect on trading volume and was discontinued. The daily average volume on both the New York and American Stock Exchanges continued to rise throughout 1967 (see Figure 9–2). In January 1968, reduced trading hours were reinstated for a period lasting until early March, and the result was a sharp decline in the daily average volume. However, when the restrictions on trading hours were again removed, the daily average volume on the New York Stock Exchange increased dramatically, from 9.2 million shares in March 1968 to 14.8 million shares in the following month. From

Figure 9–2

Stock price indices and trading volume (monthly averages of daily figures)

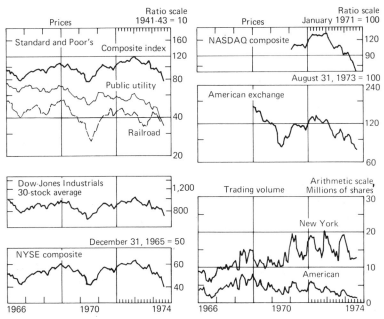

Source: Board of Governors of the Federal Reserve System

June 1968 until mid-December 1968, the major stock exchanges closed on Wednesdays. At the outset this policy, too, contributed to lower trading volume, but as the months passed trading volume started to increase again. A perusal of the average daily volume shown in Figure 9–2 suggests that limiting the number of trading hours or days provided only temporary relief, at best, from the usual high level of trading activity.

While the stock exchanges reduced the number of trading hours and trading days, stockbrokerage firms hired additional clerical personnel and put in many hours of overtime in hopes of solving their seemingly insurmountable problems. Saturday and holiday work schedules, rare before 1967, became commonplace. In addition, many firms purchased computer systems in hopes of eliminating their paperwork problems. Unfortunately, the computers proved inadequate, for two reasons. First, computers are dependent on standardized input, and no such standardized input existed in the late 1960s, as each stockbrokerage firm had its own system of identifying particular companies, transfer agents, and customers, while the exchanges and transfer agents also had their own coding systems. Second, the transfer process can function only as fast as its slowest part. Because some brokerage firms did not use computers and others that had them did

Figure 9–3

Corporate security yields

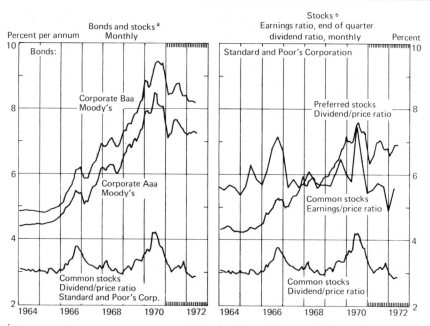

[a] Latest figures plotted: June
[b] Latest figures plotted: common stocks, earnings/price ratio, 1st quarter; all others, June

not use them effectively, the entire process was not speeded up but in many instances slowed down.

## Central Certificate Service

In order to speed up the transfer/clearing process, the New York Stock Exchange initiated a computerized settlement system in 1967. This system, called the Central Certificate Service, operates in the following manner. Some stock certificates that member firms hold for their customers are deposited at the Central Certificate Service and are registered in a common name. These are stock certificates that are registered in the name of the brokerage firm, or, as it is commonly called, *street name*. About 15 percent of all certificates are so held, but because these are certificates for the securities that are traded most often, the New York Stock Exchange estimated that the service cut the handling of securities by 75 percent.[8] At the end of each trading day the net balance of these shares due to (or from) individual firms is computed. By computerized bookkeeping entries, shares are effectively transferred among member firms. The important feature of this system is that stock certificates are stored in one place and the transfer process is accomplished by debits and credits rather than by the old method of physically transferring certificates. However, physical delivery is still necessary for those certificates which are not held in street name.

*CUSIP*    In addition to the efforts of the New York Stock Exchange, a committee of the American Bankers Association called CUSIP (Committee on Uniform Security Identification Procedures) developed a system for the uniform identification of approximately one million issues of securities. After four years of preparation, the CUSIP system was inaugurated in April 1972 on the major stock exchanges.[9]

*Jumbo Certificates*    Another effort to improve the clearing and transfer processes was the creation of large-denomination, or "jumbo," certificates. Stock certificates had formerly been issued in denominations of one hundred shares. Jumbo certificates are denominated for multiples of one hundred shares, thereby reducing the number of certificates to be transferred.

## Sale of Stock

In addition to shortening its trading hours, the New York Stock Exchange changed some of its clearing procedures to expedite the backlog of paperwork. Equally important, they changed their bylaws to impose greater financial and managerial controls on member firms. Meanwhile, some

[8]Carol J. Loomis, "Big Board, Big Volume, Big Trouble," *Fortune*, May 1968, p. 218.
[9]U.S., Congress, Senate, Committee on Banking, Housing and Urban Affairs, *Securities Industry Study*, 15.

Figure 9–4

Stock prices and trading (weekly averages)[a]

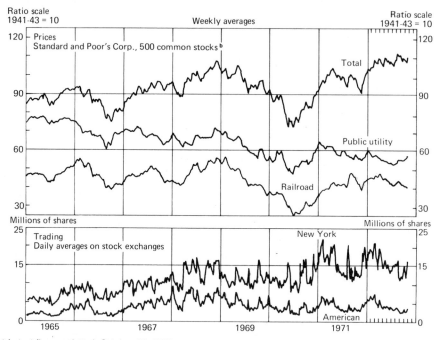

a Latest figures plotted: October 27, 1973
b Industrial stocks not shown separately
Source: Board of Governors of the Federal Reserve System.

stockbrokerage firms were evaluating their own financial positions and turned to the public for capital funds. Among the largest stockbrokerage firms in the country who sold their stock to the public were: Blyth and Company; Eastman Dillon Union Securities; CBWL-Hayden, Stone Inc.; duPont Glore Forgan and Company; Merrill Lynch, Pierce, Fenner and Smith, Inc.; Reynolds Securities Inc.; Bache and Company; Paine, Webber, Jackson and Curtis, Inc.; Halsey, Stuart and Company; A. G. Becker Company; Donaldson, Lufkin and Jenrette Inc. The corrective actions taken by the securities industry contributed to rising costs for stockbrokerage firms. The early closings were most costly to West Coast firms, whose New York Stock Exchange business ended at 10:30 A.M. instead of noon. During the period of early closings, brokers on the West Coast experienced a sharp decline in business activity. East Coast firms with West Coast offices also suffered.

## Rising Costs

*Labor*    Labor expenses rose significantly as stockbrokerage firms added back-office personnel. In 1968, the New York Stock Exchange and

stockbrokerage firms experienced the largest employment gain in history, mostly in clerical and administrative jobs; total personnel rose from 129,200 in 1967 to 163,000 in 1968. Expenses for clerical personnel in 1968 rose to $314 million, 40 percent above the 1967 level. Employment in the stock exchange community peaked in 1969 at 165,000 and subsequently declined to 156,000 in 1971.[10]

*Fixed Costs*    In addition to rising labor costs, stockbrokerage firms added to their fixed costs by purchasing or leasing computers. Moreover, many firms opened new offices in the late 1960s to attract the investing public and to cash in on the rapidly rising volume. These new facilities also added to their fixed costs. During the 1966–1970 period, total occupancy and equipment expenses for member firms of the New York Stock Exchange increased from $140 million to $304 million. During this same period, the break-even point (the minimum volume of shares needed by firms doing business with the public to cover expenses on their commission business) increased from 5.9 million shares to more than 12 million shares. According to estimates made by the New York Stock Exchange, in 1969 56 percent of the exchange's member firms experienced losses on their securities commission business.[11]

The foregoing discussion stressed the fact that during the late 1960s the costs of operating stockbrokerage firms increased. This point is also clear from studying Figure 9–5, which shows that selected expenses for New

Figure 9–5

New York Stock Exchange member firms: commission income and selected expenses [b] (1967–1971)

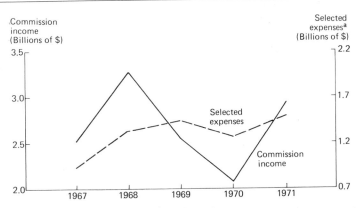

[a] Clerical, administrative, occupancy, and equipment
[b] Includes interim service charge
Sources: New York Stock Exchange, *1970 Fact Book* and *1972 Fact Book*

[10]New York Stock Exchange, *1972 Fact Book*, p. 81.
[11]New York Stock Exchange, *1970 Fact Book*, p. 63.

York Stock Exchange member firms increased until 1969 and then declined slightly. (Selected expenses include clerical, administrative, occupancy, and equipment costs.)

The figure also suggests that the financial position of member firms was squeezed when commission income dropped sharply. The amount of commission income corresponds closely to the volume of trading activity and stock prices, and both of these declined in 1969–1970 and then rebounded in 1971 (see Table 9–1 and Figure 9–2). Commission income followed a similar pattern.

## Commission Rates

### Fixed Rates

In order to be a member of a stock exchange, brokers must abide by the rules of the exchange to which they belong. These rules include the minimum commission rates which any one broker may charge for a stock transaction. Prior to 1968, commission rates were *fixed* and were designed to compensate the broker for his costs of doing business (including research costs). A fixed commission rate means that the commission for each block of 100 shares was specified by the stock exchange. Beginning May I, 1975, fixed commission rates were abandoned in favor of completely competitive rates between brokerage firms on the commissions they charge. The old fixed commission rates were one of the principal factors contributing to lower commission income for the stockbrokerage firms. The problem centered around the fact that the leading institutional investors, such as private noninsured pension funds, open-end investment companies, life insurance, and property and liability insurance companies, want a discount on commissions when trading in blocks of 10,000 or more shares. These institutional investors believe that the fixed commission structure ignores any economies of scale involved in large transactions. On the commission schedule used before April 24, 1972, the commission for executing a 10,000-share transaction would be one hundred times larger than that on a one hundred-share transaction, but the 10,000-share transaction would not receive or necessarily need one hundred times more services (e.g., research). Thus, for institutions that trade mainly in blocks of 10,000 shares or more, the commissions were too high for the amount of service rendered by the broker. Moreover, these institutions reasoned that they should not pay for services that they did not want, receive, or use. The immense amount of money involved in the commissions paid by institutional investors and why they want to save some of this money is illustrated in the following examples. In 1971 the city of New York had more than $445 million invested in common stocks for its various pension funds and paid more than $900,000

in stockbrokerage commissions.[12] Even more impressive is the case of Connecticut General Life Insurance Company, which pays more than $4 million per year in stockbrokerage commissions.[13] A 1971 U.S. Court of Appeals ruling stated that investment managers had a fiduciary responsibility to recapture commission expenses for the benefit of their clients.[14] Along this same line, the Department of Justice stated that:

> *The NYSE is subject to the basic anti-trust rule requiring those who control an essential resource to grant access to it, on equal and non-discriminatory terms, to all those in the trade. . . . The reason for the rule is to prevent those holding a unique monopoly position from using that lawful monopoly to foreclose competition in other related activities which would be competitive. . . . The private club approach to Exchange membership, where the interests of only existing members are taken into account in formulating Exchange policy, was banned by the Securities Exchange Act of 1934.[15]*

## Third Market

Since the New York Stock Exchange was not willing to give a sufficient discount on commissions, institutional investors began to seek other means of reducing their commission costs. Some financial institutions began to trade in the over-the-counter (OTC) or *third market* for stocks listed on the New York and other stock exchanges. Brokers who deal in this market need not be members of the New York Stock Exchange, are not bound by the rules of the Exchange, and do not have to charge minimum fixed commissions. These brokers perform *only* the brokerage function (buying and selling securities) and their commission rates are lower than those charged by firms providing a full array of services. With the attraction of lower commission costs, the trading activity in the third market increased from 2.9 percent of the volume of shares traded on the New York Stock Exchange in 1966 to 9.3 percent in 1971.

In addition to the third market, some financial institutions trade among themselves, bypassing both stockbrokers and stock exchanges. Such dealings are referred to as the *fourth market*. No data presently exist on the size or scope of this market.

The preceding paragraphs suggest the complexity of the issue of commission rates. At one end of the spectrum are the stockbrokerage firms and

---

[12] U.S. Congress, Senate, Committee on Banking, Housing, and Urban Affairs, *Institutional Membership on National Security Exchanges*, Part I (Washington, D.C.: U.S. Government Printing Office, 1972), p. 84.
[13] *Ibid.*, p. 93.
[14] *Moses* v. *Burgin*, 445 F. 369 (1st Cir. 1971).
[15] U.S., Congress, Senate, Committee on Banking, Housing, and Urban Affairs, *Institutional Membership on National Security Exchanges*, Part I (Washington, D.C.: U.S. Government Printing Office, 1972), p. 52.

exchanges, who claim they need the large commissions from institutional trades to remain profitable. Today institutional trading accounts for 75 percent of the trading activity on the New York Stock Exchange, compared with only 30 percent in 1966. At the other end of the spectrum are millions of investors who have entrusted their funds to institutions that seek to maximize the shareholder's rate of return. As part of this service, they attempt to reduce their commission costs. The issue is whether the public is better served by allowing institutions to reduce commission costs (through reciprocal agreements, membership on stock exchanges, or negotiated rates) or by requiring institutions to pay excessive fixed commission fees, thereby in effect subsidizing the stockbrokerage industry.

## Reciprocal Agreements

In spite of the existence of the third and fourth markets, institutions still find it necessary to do frequent trading on organized stock exchanges when buying and selling large blocks of stock. Therefore, they have devised several methods to recapture portions of their commission expenses. Member firms of the New York and American Stock Exchanges have been willing to rebate portions of their commissions to avoid loss of income. Thus, reciprocal agreements have evolved whereby a member firm of the New York or American Stock Exchange gives reciprocal business to the subsidiary of a financial institution. The subsidiary firms may hold seats on regional stock exchanges such as the Pacific Coast Stock Exchange, and institutions can deal with brokers on the New York or American Stock Exchanges who also maintain a seat on one of the regional exchanges. In this way the broker transacting a trade on the New York or American Stock Exchanges can then split commissions with the institutional subsidiary on the regional exchange. Thus, reciprocal arrangements allow member firms of the New York and American Stock Exchanges to retain institutional business to recapture some of their commission expenses by using subsidiary firms.

## Membership

The fact that stockbrokerage firms are willing to rebate portions of their commissions is explicit recognition that commissions on large transactions are excessive or, alternately, it is acknowledgment that half a commission is better than none. Because organized stock exchanges prohibited brokers from rebating commissions to customers, but did allow them to rebate portions of their commissions to other member firms, institutions began to seek membership on stock exchanges in order to obtain the status of member firms.

The New York and American Stock Exchanges do not allow institutional membership, but it is allowed on certain regional stock exchanges. In 1965

the Pacific Coast Stock Exchange was the first to grant an institutional membership, when it admitted Kansas City Securities, an affiliate of Waddell and Reed, Inc., a large mutual fund manager. Within a year the Pacific Coast Stock Exchange admitted three more institutional subsidiaries; similar memberships have also been granted on the Philadelphia-Baltimore-Washington Stock Exchange and the Midwest Stock Exchange.

## Negotiated Rates

An alternative to institutional membership for some institutions is negotiated rates—the amount of commission is negotiated by the institution and stockbroker before a transaction occurs. As noted earlier, many institutions maintain stockbrokerage subsidiaries just to reduce their commission costs. It still costs money to operate such subsidiary firms, and many institutions would be willing to eliminate their affiliates and forego membership on stock exchanges if they could negotiate rates on orders of any size.

In April 1971, the New York Stock Exchange, under the direction of the Securities and Exchange Commission, permitted negotiated rates on that portion of orders in excess of $500,000. A year later, the minimum order size was reduced to $300,000. According to SEC policy, the minimum order size should have been reduced to $100,000 in 1974. However, Donald Baker, Director of Policy Planning of the Anti-Trust Division of the Department of Justice, argued that at least one-third of the transactions made by mutual funds and the average transaction for other types of institutions is substantially below $100,000.[16]

If the minimum order size for negotiated rates were reduced to a zero level (i.e., no minimum order size) there would be little incentive for institutions to become members of stock exchanges in order to reduce commission costs, although some institutions might still retain stockbroker subsidiary firms as part of their diversified operations.

James J. Needham, chairman of the New York Stock Exchange, has stated that the declining profits of stockbrokerage firms are due to rising costs that are not being covered by fixed commission income.[17] Mr. Needham goes on to say that negotiated commission rates would permit firms to base their prices on the cost of the services rendered, thereby assuring them of a reasonable profit. As previously noted, commissions are now made on a negotiated basis.

---

[16]U.S., Congress, Senate, Committee on Banking, Housing, and Urban Affairs, *Fixed Rates and Institutional Membership* (Washington, D.C.: U.S. Government Printing Office, 1972), p. 348.
[17]*Ibid.*, p. 464. Michael G. Tobin, President of the Midwest Stock Exchange, took a similar position favoring abandoning fixed broker fees (*Wall Street Journal*, June 14, 1973, p. 10).

## Why Firms Fail

To recapitulate, the commission income received by New York Stock Exchange member firms declined sharply in the late 1960s, but, because of high fixed costs, brokerage firms could not reduce their expenses sufficiently. While they could lay off some employees, they could not lay off their high-cost computers or shut down their offices on short notice. As a result of these factors, plus a weakened financial structure (due to the large number of *fails* which affected net capital ratios adversely), many stockbrokerage firms failed. From January 1, 1968, to December 31, 1971, 181 member firms (out of a total of 577) of the New York Stock Exchange went out of business, were liquidated, or were acquired by other firms.[18] This number included some of the largest firms on Wall Street, such as Goodbody & Co. and Dempsey-Tegeler & Co. In the case of Goodbody & Co., another member firm—Merrill Lynch, Pierce, Fenner & Smith—agreed to acquire the troubled firm, and the New York Stock Exchange indemnified Merrill Lynch for losses up to $30 million that could have occurred in connection with the merger. In another case, a private investor, H. Ross Perot, helped to bail out duPont Glore Forgan, Inc. Again, the exchange indemnified this transaction for $15 million. Other firms that were not so fortunate were simply liquidated.[19]

### Mismanagement

It would be incorrect to blame all of these failures solely on financial factors; some were due to plain mismanagement. A case in point is McDonnell and Company. In 1967, McDonnell's management recognized that its existing record-keeping system was not adequate to handle its rising volume of paperwork. In 1968 they installed a new computer system and shut down the existing system. The new system was untested, and the programs were written by a software service company that was not familiar with the stockbrokerage industry. (Interestingly, McDonnell and Company was the underwriter for the software company, which had recently gone public, and the contract to do McDonnell's programs was the company's first large-scale job.) By the end of 1968, the new system was a proven failure, and McDonnell was left with no back-up system. Manual processing of transactions was impossible, so McDonnell rented computer time from other stockbrokerage firms. This increased the cost of each transaction significantly, which in turn added to McDonnell's rising fixed costs and weakened its financial position. Because of a strained net capital ratio, McDonnell then sold $2.9 million worth of its own stock to its employees to raise capital. The Securities and Exchange Commission then filed a com-

---

[18]William C. Freund, Vice-President and Economist of the NYSE, personal correspondence, September 21, 1972.
[19]New York Stock Exchange, *Crisis in the Securities Industry* (New York: New York Stock Exchange, 1971), p. 27.

plaint in federal court charging that McDonnell fraudulently omitted material facts regarding its financial condition when it sold the stock, and that the entire sale was illegal because it was not registered properly. The SEC also charged the firm with *churning* (excessive trading to generate commission income) customers' accounts, fraud in the sale of securities, failure to keep current and accurate records, and executing transactions which were not in compliance with the financial requirements of the New York Stock Exchange. As a result of these factors, McDonnell and Company was liquidated.[20]

## Subordinated Debt

Another factor contributing to the demise of some stockbrokerage firms was misuse of subordinated debt. Hayden Stone Inc. is a case in point.[21] In March 1970, a group of businessmen loaned Hayden Stone $17.5 million in marketable securities, receiving a subordinated note for the loan, which was subordinated to Hayden Stone's other liabilities. Hayden Stone used the securities as collateral to borrow $12.4 million from commercial banks. By June 1970, the market value of the securities had dropped sharply and their collateral value was only about $6 million. When the banks asked for additional collateral, Hayden Stone was unable to come up with the money, and consequently, was forced to merge with another firm that had sufficient funds.

Representative John Moss (D., California), Chairman of the House Commerce Subcommittee dealing with securities legislation, summed up the management problems in the following manner:

> *Along with inadequate capital, less than competent management was probably the primary reason for the disappearance of over 200 brokerdealers during the late 1960's.*

> *There were too many executives who didn't know the difference between sales and profits; who thought that internal control was something practiced by the FBI; and that books and records referred only to items sold by the Literary Guild or Columbia House.*[22]

## Congressional Actions

*Securities Investor Protection Corporation*    The failure of both large and small stockbrokerage firms brought widespread public attention to the financial crisis on Wall Street. Congress examined the situation to deter-

---

[20]Hurd Baruch, *Wall Street: Security Risk* (Baltimore: Penguin Books, 1971), pp. 193–196.
[21]*Ibid.*
[22]*Wall Street Journal*, December 5, 1972, p. 12.

mine the role that the federal government should play to restore public confidence in the stock market. On December 31, 1970, the Securities Investor Protection Act of 1970 was signed into law. This act created the Securities Investor Protection Corporation (SIPC), which is designed to protect customers of SIPC member firms against certain losses should the firms liquidate. The act gave the SEC broader powers in regulating stock exchanges. In addition, all broker-dealers registered with the SEC and all members of national stock exchanges are required to be members of SIPC. However, firms engaged exclusively in the distribution of mutual fund shares or variable annuities, the business of insurance, or furnishing investment advice to registered investment companies are excluded from membership in the SIPC. A customer's cash and securities are insured for amounts up to $50,000. Property such as commodity accounts is not insured. It should be noted that SIPC does not protect against losses arising from fluctuations in the market. The corporation is funded by its member firms and receives no direct funding from the government. However, in an emergency, if industry assessments are not adequate, SIPC can borrow up to $1 billion from the U.S. Treasury.

Since the enactment of the Securities Investor Protection Act, Congress has considered amendments to the Securities Exchange Act of 1934 to strengthen the powers of the Securities and Exchange Commission, by giving it a major role in reorganizing the structure of the stock market.

*Proposed Changes*    The SEC, the Securities Subcommittee of the Senate Banking, Housing, and Urban Affairs Committee, and the House Subcommittee on Commerce and Finance of the Committee on Interstate and Foreign Commerce have all published reports dealing with the future structure of the stock market. The reports suggest that there should be a national stock market system and a national clearing and transfer system. The national stock market would be merely a communications system to link market makers from all over the country. Any qualified broker-dealer registered with the SEC would have access to it. Such a system would allow many brokers who are currently excluded from organized exchanges to enjoy the benefits of a broader market. Moreover, the forces of supply and demand would be brought together in a single system rather than being split up into regional submarkets. A nationwide disclosure or information system would make price and volume data available to all interested parties, thereby strengthening competition. Complete details or mechanics have not yet been worked out, but a national stock market system is likely to be the direction in which the markets will eventually evolve.[23]

---

[23]Harrison A. Williams, Jr., "Williams to Resubmit Legislation Designed to Solve Industry's Most Pressing Problems," *The Money Manager*, December 18, 1972, p. 7. See also: Securities and Exchange Commission, *Future Structure of the Securities Markets* (Washington, D.C.: U.S. Government Printing Office, 1972); U.S., Congress, Senate, Committee on Banking, Housing and Urban Affairs, *Securities Industry Study*, p. 33; and U.S., Congress, House, Committee on Interstate and Foreign Commerce, *Securities Industry Study*, House Report (Washington, D.C.: U.S. Government Printing Office, 1972).

A national stock market system would require the support of a national stock clearing and transfer system. Although a national clearing service has many advocates, the New York Stock Exchange has a vested interest in the Central Certificate Service (CCS) now in use. However, the New York State transfer tax makes the CCS undesirable because even computerized bookkeeping entries of the CCS in New York City are taxed no matter where the actual transaction takes place. A trade consummated in California, but recorded by the CCS in New York City, is subject to New York's transfer tax. Moreover, the CCS relies upon the balance order method described above, where some certificates are delivered from buying brokers to selling brokers. This procedure allows for the possibility of fails, if delivering brokers are not able to acquire the needed certificates in the legal time limit. The method used by the Pacific and Midwest Stock Exchanges, known as net settlement, reduces the possibility of fails. In this method, the clearinghouse receives all of the certificates. At the end of a trading day the Midwest Stock Exchange total trades are matched as on the New York Stock Exchange, but instead of directing one broker to deliver to another, the clearinghouse directs the brokers to deliver all of their certificates to the clearinghouse, which then delivers the certificates to the appropriate place. If a firm fails to deliver them, the clearinghouse can borrow certificates from other members of the exchange and charge the borrowed shares to the broker who failed to deliver the certificates. Under the net settlement system, the buying broker is not penalized because the seller fails to deliver, which makes this a more equitable way of transacting business.[24]

A national system of transfer and settlement would require the leadership of the Securities and Exchange Commission. The authority for the SEC to develop, but not to implement, such a plan exists in the Securities Exchange Act of 1934. This act grants the SEC broad powers over settlement practices of national securities exchanges and associations. However, because of some technical quirks in the law, the SEC's ability to regulate stock clearinghouses and depositories is unclear.[25]

To create a national stock-clearing network, the SEC would have to assure a stockbroker located in one geographic region that he would be able to make or receive prompt deliveries from stockbrokers in other regions. As long as stock certificates are necessary, a system of regional depositories linked by a communications system appears to be the logical answer. Securities registered in a common street name could be transferred by computer bookkeeping entries. Other certificates would have to be delivered physically to a depository. To speed up the transfer process, the depository could credit the account of the buyer's firm and then transfer the stock out of the seller's name.

[24]Committee on Banking, Housing and Urban Affairs, *Securities Industry Study*, pp. 16–21.
[25]Committee on Banking, Housing and Urban Affairs, *Securities Industry Study*, p. 22.

If stock certificates were eliminated, the need for regional depositories would disappear. However, some legal problems prevent the elimination of stock certificates at present. For example, certain trusts, estates, and pension funds are required to physically hold stock certificates, and some financial institutions are required to hold stock certificates when they are used as collateral for loans.

## Summary

The purpose of this chapter was to examine the transition that has occurred in the stock market in recent years. An increased volume of trading activity highlighted the inability of the industry and regulatory agencies to cope with change on short notice. The plight of the industry became evident when several large stockbrokerage firms failed and many were unable to perform their normal functions. As a result, the exchange community, regulatory agencies, and Congress stepped into the picture. The recommendations proposed by Congress and others would alter the basic structure of the stock market as we know it today. The most significant changes are likely to result in a national market for stocks consisting of communication links among all market makers (as opposed to a number of regional exchanges) and a national system for clearing and transferring securities.

## Questions

1 The cult of performance that developed among many mutual fund managers during the mid-1960s led to churning of portfolios. How did this have a destabilizing effect on stock prices if there was a buyer for every seller?

2 Define the term "arbitrage." Explain how one might attempt to arbitrage between the securities of merging companies.

3 Discuss the balance order method of clearing and how it simplifies clearing between member firms of the New York Stock Exchange and the American Stock Exchange. Compare the balance order method with the net settlement method used by the Pacific Coast and Midwest Stock Exchanges.

4 Explain what a fail is, how fails can affect the net capital ratio of brokerage houses, and how a reduction in this ratio can force some brokerage houses to merge or liquidate their business.

5 Discuss how increased trading activity in the stock market during the mid-1960s led to severe problems for brokerage houses. What steps did the industry take to remedy these problems?

6 What is a fixed commission rate? How did the existence of fixed commission rates by major stock exchanges lead to the establishment of the third market and the fourth market?

7 Explain how exchange rules concerning partial commission rebates led some institutional investors to seek membership on regional stock exchanges.

8 Do you feel that the existence of rebates and reciprocal agreements indicates that stock commissions are too high?

9 What is the Securities Investor Protection Corporation? Does SIPC protect customers of some brokerage firms against losses from selling stocks that declined in value?

10 Several governmental agencies and congressional committees have recommended the establishment of a national stock market and a national clearing and transfer system. Discuss the advantages and disadvantages of such a system.

## Bibliography

Baruch, Hurd. *Wall Street: Security Risk*. Baltimore: Penguin Books, 1971.

New York Stock Exchange, *Fact Book* (annual).

Securities and Exchange Commission. *Future Structure of the Securities Markets*. Washington, D.C.: U.S. Government Printing Office, 1972.

———. *Institutional Investor Study Report*. Washington, D.C.: U.S. Government Printing Office, 1971.

U.S., Congress, House, Committee on Interstate and Foreign Commerce. *Securities Industry Study*, House Report. Washington, D.C.: U.S. Government Printing Office, 1972.

U.S., Congress, Senate, Committee on Banking, Housing, and Urban Affairs. *Institutional Membership on National Security Exchanges*. Washington, D.C.: U.S. Government Printing Office, 1972.

———. *Securities Industry Study*, Committee Print. Washington, D.C.: U.S. Government Printing Office, 1972.

———. *Fixed Rates and Institutional Membership*. Washington, D.C.: U.S. Government Printing Office, 1972.

# 10

# Investment companies and real estate investment trusts

## Investment Companies

### Benefits for Investors

In 1972, more than 8.5 million mutual fund shareholders received $2.6 billion in investment income dividends and capital gains distributions. Mutual funds offer investors some advantages lacking in other types of investment. Those who do not have the time, inclination, or ability to analyze securities and market trends may obtain a professionally managed, diversified portfolio by acquiring mutual fund shares. Similarly, those who have small sums (e.g., $50) to invest on a periodic basis also benefit from buying mutual fund shares. The only alternative for small investors who want to participate in the stock market is to buy odd lots (less than 100 shares), which have the highest commission charge. Until 1974, the maximum commission charged by member firms of the New York Stock Exchange, on trades of $100 or less, was about $9.24. This charge was considerably higher than the load on mutual funds for small purchases. Moreover, the investor has to pay another commission upon selling the shares. Finally, he owns only one company instead of fractional holding in a portfolio that consists of 25 to 100 or more companies. And although commission rates are now negotiated, they are still relatively high for small trades.

## History

Modern investment companies had their inception in 1822 when King William I of the Netherlands established the "Société Général des Pays-Bas pour favoriser l'industrie nationale." Investors bought shares of the Société Général, which, in turn, invested in coal, iron, textiles, and other industries. Today modern investment companies are corporations that sell their own shares to investors, then take these proceeds and invest them in the securities of other companies.

The concept of investment companies spread from France to Great Britain, where it flourished, because Britain was the leading industrial country and her investors had more funds than they wished to employ domestically. British investments trusts made overseas investments which included American industry, farms, and railroads.[1] The British investment trust companies were the closed-end type; they issue a fixed number of shares to investors. It was not until the 1930s that open-end investment companies, the most common form of mutual funds, were formed. These do not have a fixed number of shares and will sell as many shares as investors are willing to buy.

The first significant appearance of investment companies in the United States occurred after World War I, when hundreds of thousands of people cashed in their liberty bonds that had been used to finance the war and had surplus funds to invest. Their investment in mutual funds was facilitated by the passage of the Edge Act in 1919 by Congress. This was an amendment to the Federal Reserve Act, and its purpose was to aid the flow of capital into foreign investments. To accomplish this end, closed-end investment companies could be established under the control of the Federal Reserve Board. Very few trusts were organized under this act because few investors wanted to be under the control of the Federal Reserve System, or any other government agency. However, in the 1920s and 1930s, shares of domestic investment trusts gained increased popularity as a speculative medium. One result of the speculation was that the Securities and Exchange Commission (SEC) began an investigation that culminated in the Investment Company Act of 1940.

*Investment Company Act of 1940*    The Investment Company Act of 1940 was designed to provide investors with detailed information about the financial condition of investment companies and their operating policies. Some of the key features of the act are listed below:

---

[1]For further historical details see: Stanley D. Ryals and David F. Cox, *Investment Trusts and Funds* (Great Barrington, Mass.: American Institute for Economic Research, 1954); Hugh Bullock, *The Story of Investment Companies* (New York: Columbia University Press, 1960); John F. Fowler, *American Investment Trusts* (London: Harper Brothers Publisher, 1928), p. 4.

1 Registration    All investment companies with one hundred or more shareholders must register with the Securities and Exchange Commission.

2 Diversification    Investment companies must invest at least 75 percent of their assets in cash or securities. Moreover, no more than 5 percent of the assets can be invested in any one company and they cannot hold more than 10 percent of any company's controlling stock.

3 Management    Management must be approved by the shareholders.

4 Tax Exemption    Investment companies are exempt from federal income tax if they distribute 90 percent of their income to the shareholders. This is called a "conduit regulation," because most of the income passes through the investment company to its shareholders.

5 Reports    All financial activities must be reported and filed with the SEC twice a year.

6 Shares    Investors in open-end investment companies must be given a prospectus that provides sufficient information about the company to make an intelligent investment appraisal before buying shares. Each share must represent a proportionate share of ownership and no security may have a prior claim. In addition, the shares may be redeemed at asset value.

7 Categories    The act divides investment companies into three categories:
1 management companies, which are subdivided into open-end (mutual funds) and closed-end
2 unit investment trusts
3 face-amount certificate companies
In a unit investment trust, each investor holds a certificate that represents a unit of securities. For example, a unit may consist of ten shares of stocks of thirty different companies. The units are managed by a trustee who acts on behalf of the investors who are the beneficial owners of the trust property. Face-amount certificates are unsecured obligations to pay either a stated sum to the holder at a specified date if he makes all the payments required by the contract, or a cash surrender value prior to maturity.

## Types of Investment Companies

As shown in Table 10–1, in 1973 there were 1,361 investment companies registered with the SEC. These companies had total assets of $73.1 billion.

Table 10–1

Registered investment companies (June 30, 1973)

|  | Number | Approximate market value of assets ($ millions) |
|---|---|---|
| Management open-end (mutual funds) | 826 | 54,398 |
| Management closed-end | 238 | 9,855 |
| Unit investment trusts | 289 | 7,825 |
| Face-amount certificate companies | 8 | 1,071 |
| Total | 1,361 | 73,149 |

Source: Securities and Exchange Commission

*Mutual Funds*    Mutual funds account for the largest number of companies and the bulk of the assets. Management closed-end companies and unit investment trusts are next in importance in terms of asset size.

Some closed-end investment companies are traded on stock exchanges in the same manner as other listed securities. (An example is Madison Fund, which is traded on the New York Stock Exchange.) Closed-end investment companies can trade at a premium (above) or a discount (below) their net asset value (NAV). This is the market value of assets less liabilities and exclusive of capital stock and surplus, divided by the total number of the fund's shares outstanding:

$$\text{Net asset value} = \frac{\text{Total assets at market value} - \text{liabilities}}{\text{number of shares outstanding}}$$

The offering price of open-end funds is always based on NAV rather than being determined by investors. In the case of closed-end funds, share prices can sell at premiums or discounts that reflect investors' opinion of managements' ability to manage the assets at their disposal.

*Load and No-Load Funds*    Open-end mutual funds can be classified as either load or no-load funds. The term *load* refers to the sales commission that investors pay when they buy investment company shares.Those investment companies that do not require investors to pay a sales charge to buy shares are called *no-load* funds. However, some no-load funds charge a commission when investors liquidate their fund shares. The difference between load and no-load funds is illustrated in Figure 10–1 by a partial list of the mutual funds that appear daily in *The Wall Street Journal*. The list shows the name of the fund, the net asset value, the offering price, and the change in NAV since the previous trading period. Loaded funds have offering prices that are higher than the NAV, while the offering price and NAV are the same for no-load funds. For example, the offering price of Dreyfus Fund (Dreyf fd) is $11.22 while the NAV is $10.24. The sales charge

Figure 10–1

Mutual Funds

# Mutual Funds

Wednesday, April 16, 1975

Price ranges for investment companies, as quoted by the National Association of Securities Dealers. NAV stands for net asset value per share; the offering includes net asset value plus maximum sales charge, if any.


| | NAV | Offer Price | Chg. |
|---|---|---|---|
| Adm Gwth | 3.46 | 3.79+ | .02 |
| Adm Incm | 3.12 | 3.42+ | .01 |
| Adm Insur | 6.10 | 6.68+ | .01 |
| Adviser Fd | 3.40 | 3.72 | .. |
| Aetna Fnd | 6.34 | 6.93+ | .03 |
| Aetna In Sh | 11.32 | 12.37+ | .02 |
| Afuture Fd | 7.23 | N.L.+ | .04 |
| AGE Fund | 4.03 | 4.11+ | .04 |
| Allstate | 9.34 | 10.04+ | .06 |
| Alpha Fnd | 9.36 | 10.23+ | .08 |
| Amcap Fd | 4.39 | 4.80+ | .02 |
| Am Birthrt | 9.90 | 10.88 | .. |
| Am Equity | 4.13 | 4.53+ | .03 |
| **American Express Funds:** | | | |
| Capital | 5.64 | 6.16+ | .05 |
| Income | 7.55 | 8.25 | .. |
| Invest | 6.61 | 7.22+ | .01 |
| Spec Fnd | 5.59 | 6.11+ | .08 |
| Stock Fd | 6.03 | 6.59+ | .02 |
| Am Grwth | 4.41 | 4.82+ | .03 |
| Am Ins Ind | 4.09 | 4.47+ | .01 |
| Am Invest | 4.19 | N.L.+ | .05 |
| Am Mutual | 7.59 | 8.30— | .01 |
| AmNat Gw | 2.17 | 2.37+ | .02 |
| **Anchor Group:** | | | |
| Daily Inc | 1.00 | N.L. | .. |
| Growth | 6.22 | 6.82+ | .04 |
| Income | 6.21 | 6.81+ | .01 |
| Reserv | 10.21 | 11.19+ | .01 |
| Spectm | 4.03 | 4.42+ | .03 |
| Fund Inv | 6.08 | 6.66+ | .02 |
| Wa Natl | 9.29 | 10.18+ | .05 |
| Audax Fnd | 6.43 | 7.03+ | .04 |
| **Axe-Houghton:** | | | |
| Fund A | 4.19 | 4.55 | .. |
| Fund B | 6.30 | 6.85 | .. |
| Stock Fd | 5.39 | 5.89+ | .02 |
| BLC Gwth | 8.62 | 9.42+ | .04 |
| Babson Iv | 9.41 | N.L.— | .03 |
| Bayrock | 4.91 | ..+ | .02 |
| Bayrok Gr | 4.24 | ..+ | .03 |
| Beacon Hill | 7.88 | N.L. | .. |
| Beacon Inv | 8.75 | N.L.+ | .03 |
| Berksh Gw | 2.86 | 3.13 | .. |


| | NAV | Offer Price | Chg. |
|---|---|---|---|
| E &E Mutl | 2.97 | N.L.+ | .04 |
| Eagle Gth | 7.07 | 7.73+ | .10 |
| **Eaton Howard:** | | | |
| Balncd F | 7.72 | 8.44+ | .05 |
| Growth | 8.44 | 9.22+ | .10 |
| Income | 5.19 | 5.67 | .. |
| Spec Fnd | 5.30 | 5.79 | .. |
| Stock Fd | 8.82 | 9.64+ | .14 |
| EDIE SpG | 17.11 | N.L.+ | .11 |
| EGRET F | 9.63 | 10.47+ | .04 |
| Elfun Trst | 12.33 | ..+ | .09 |
| Energy Fd | 11.07 | N.L.+ | .07 |
| Fairfld Fd | 7.25 | 7.92+ | .05 |
| Farm Bru | 7.35 | N.L.+ | .02 |
| **Fidelity Group Funds:** | | | |
| Bond deb | 8.13 | 8.89 | .. |
| Capital | 8.45 | 9.23+ | .08 |
| Contra | 9.64 | ..+ | .18 |
| Cnv SSec | 6.66 | .. | .. |
| Daily Inc | 1.00 | N.L. | .. |
| Destiny | 6.77 | ..+ | .04 |
| Essex | 6.96 | ..+ | .11 |
| Everest | 10.36 | 11.32+ | .09 |
| Fidel Fd | 13.41 | 14.66+ | .08 |
| Puritan | 8.80 | 9.62+ | .03 |
| Salem | 3.51 | 3.84+ | .02 |
| Trend | 18.71 | 20.45+ | .18 |
| **Financial Programs:** | | | |
| Dynam | 3.74 | N.L.+ | .03 |
| Industl | 3.44 | N.L.+ | .01 |
| Income | 5.85 | N.L.+ | .03 |
| Venture | 3.83 | N.L.+ | .03 |
| 1st Fnd Va | 9.51 | 10.39— | .01 |
| **First Investors Fund:** | | | |
| Discovr | 4.00 | 4.38+ | .03 |
| Growth | 5.95 | 6.52+ | .04 |
| Income | 6.77 | 7.42+ | .01 |
| Stock Fd | 6.62 | 7.25+ | .02 |
| 1st MultiA | 7.12 | N.L.+ | .05 |
| **Fleming Berger Funds:** | | | |
| Flmg Br | 7.09 | ..+ | .09 |
| 100 Fund | 6.94 | ..+ | .05 |
| 101 Fund | 6.86 | ..— | .01 |
| Fnd Grwth | 3.63 | 3.97 | .. |


| | NAV | Offer Price | Chg. |
|---|---|---|---|
| Cust K 1 | 6.38 | 7.00+ | .01 |
| Cust K 2 | 4.87 | 5.33+ | .23 |
| Cust S 1 | 17.86 | 19.58+ | .19 |
| Cust S 2 | 8.30 | 9.10+ | .07 |
| Cust S 3 | 7.02 | 7.70+ | .05 |
| Cust S 4 | 2.91 | 3.18+ | .03 |
| Apollo | 3.63 | 3.98+ | .03 |
| Polaris | 2.95 | 3.23+ | .02 |
| Lndmk Gw | 6.22 | 6.79+ | .07 |
| LD EdieCa | 12.94 | 13.84+ | .08 |
| **Lexington Group:** | | | |
| Cp Ledrs | 13.25 | 14.57+ | .12 |
| Growth | 5.78 | 6.32+ | .01 |
| Resrch | 11.92 | 13.03+ | .12 |
| Lifelns Inv | 5.54 | 6.05— | .03 |
| **Lincoln National Funds:** | | | |
| Linc Cap | 5.82 | 6.36+ | .03 |
| Selct Am | 6.15 | N.L.— | .01 |
| Selct Op | 8.01 | N.L.+ | .08 |
| Selct Spl | 12.34 | N.L.+ | .07 |
| **Loomis Sayles Funds:** | | | |
| Cap Dev | 9.83 | N.L.+ | .11 |
| Mutual | x12.20 | N.L.— | .. |
| **Lord Abbett:** | | | |
| Affilatd | 6.53 | 7.04+ | .03 |
| Am Bus | 2.79 | 3.01 | .. |
| Bond deb | 8.93 | 9.76+ | .01 |
| **Lutheran Brotherhd Fds:** | | | |
| Broth Fd | 8.98 | 9.81+ | .01 |
| Broth Inc | 8.15 | 8.91— | .01 |
| Broth US | 9.91 | 10.83 | .. |
| **Mass Company:** | | | |
| Freedm | 6.45 | 7.07+ | .02 |
| Indep Fd | 6.52 | 7.15+ | .03 |
| Mass Fd | 9.22 | 10.10 | .. |
| **Mass Financial Svcs:** | | | |
| MIT | 9.55 | 10.44+ | .03 |
| MIG | 9.58 | 10.47+ | .10 |
| MID | 11.55 | 12.62+ | .10 |
| MFD | 10.62 | 11.61+ | .11 |
| MCD | 11.45 | 12.51+ | .18 |
| Mates Invs | 1.32 | N.L.+ | .01 |
| Mather Fd | 8.80 | N.L.+ | .06 |
| Mid Amer | 4.17 | 4.56+ | .02 |
| Money Mkt | 1.00 | N.L. | .. |
| MONY Fd | 8.79 | 9.61+ | .03 |
| MSB Fund | (z) | (z) | (z) |
| Mutl BnGr | 7.85 | 8.60+ | .02 |
| M I F | 6.96 | 7.52+ | .02 |
| M I F Gro | 3.26 | 3.52+ | .02 |


| | NAV | Offer Price | Chg |
|---|---|---|---|
| Safeco Equ | 6.67 | 7.29+ | .04 |
| Safeco Gth | 5.28 | 5.77+ | .03 |
| **Scudder Funds:** | | | |
| Intl Invst | 12.78 | N.L.+ | .07 |
| Mang Rs | 10.03 | N.L. | .. |
| StvC Bal | 12.66 | N.L.+ | .01 |
| Stv Com | 7.92 | N.L.+ | .02 |
| Specl Fd | 19.96 | N.L.+ | .12 |
| Seabd Lev | 4.46 | 4.89+ | .03 |
| **Security Funds:** | | | |
| Equity | 3.01 | 3.33+ | .04 |
| Invest | 5.47 | 5.99+ | .04 |
| Ultra Fd | 6.14 | 6.73+ | .16 |
| Sentinl Gw | 8.22 | 8.93+ | .11 |
| Sentry Fd | 11.29 | 12.27+ | .01 |
| **Shareholders Group:** | | | |
| Comstk | 4.12 | 4.50+ | .04 |
| Entrprs | 4.92 | 5.38+ | .02 |
| Fletc Fd | 4.16 | 4.55+ | .03 |
| Harbor | 6.99 | 7.64+ | .02 |
| Legal Lt | 5.86 | 6.40+ | .03 |
| Pace Fd | 7.05 | 7.70— | .02 |
| **Shearson Funds:** | | | |
| Apprec | 15.01 | 16.40— | .10 |
| Income | 15.81 | 17.28 | .. |
| Invest | 8.12 | 8.87— | .01 |
| Shrm Dean | 16.75 | N.L.+ | .28 |
| **Sigma Funds:** | | | |
| Capitl Sh | 6.27 | 6.85+ | .09 |
| Invest Sh | 8.50 | 9.29+ | .05 |
| Trust Sh | 6.74 | 7.37+ | .01 |
| Venture | 6.85 | 7.49+ | .02 |
| Sm Barnev | 8.54 | N.L.+ | .06 |
| Sm BrIncG | 8.98 | N.L.— | .01 |
| So GenFnd | 10.61 | 11.11+ | .03 |
| Sowest Inv | 6.18 | 6.68+ | .03 |
| Sowinv gw | 4.40 | 4.76+ | .04 |
| Sovern Inv | 9.82 | 10.75+ | .0 |
| Spectra Fd | 3.50 | N.L.+ | .02 |
| S&P IntDy | 5.03 | N.L.+ | .05 |
| **State Bond Group:** | | | |
| CmSt Fd | 3.84 | 4.20+ | .02 |
| Diversf | 4.04 | 4.42+ | .01 |
| Progrss | 3.70 | 4.04+ | .01 |
| State FrGr | 4.20 | N.L.+ | .02 |
| State Fr In | 7.93 | N.L.+ | .03 |
| StateSt (a) | 36.58 | 37.08+ | .45 |
| **Steadman Funds:** | | | |
| Am Ind | 2.41 | N.L.+ | .02 |

Source: *The Wall Street Journal,* April 16, 1975. Copyright © 1975 by United Press International

for Dreyfus Fund is 8.75 percent of the offering price (9.6 percent of the NAV). The sales charge is reduced on certain large sales, say $10,000 or more. In contrast, the offering price and NAV are the same for the Price Rowe funds. In the list no-load funds are followed by (v).

The reason for the difference in pricing policy is that no-load funds are sold directly to investors while loaded funds are sold through stockbrokers or salesmen, who receive the bulk of the sales charge. In fact, the commissions on trades of the same size are substantially higher for selling mutual funds than for selling listed stocks. The average commission for stocks listed on the New York Stock Exchange is about 1 percent, while the average load on mutual funds is about 8 percent.

In addition to paying a sales charge when buying a mutual fund, investors must also pay a management fee to the fund adviser for managing the fund

securities. Generally speaking, the management fee is ½ of I percent of the average market value of the net assets.

*Other Types of Fund*    Mutual funds can also be classified by their investment objectives, in four broad categories: common stock funds, balanced funds, income funds, and special funds.

*Common stock funds* emphasize capital gains; some of the funds in this group are speculative in nature and are sometimes growth funds. *Income funds* are at the other end of the spectrum in that they emphasize preservation of capital and income. Some funds that hold mostly bonds are included in this group. Between the two extremes are *balanced funds*, which offer a combination of capital gains and income. The *special funds* category consists of a variety of funds that do not fit into the other three categories. For example, there are funds that concentrate their investments in specific industries such as life insurance or chemicals. The Securities and Exchange Commission, in its *Thirty-Eighth Annual Report (1972)*, said that there was continuing interest in the development of funds with specialized objectives. One investment company was created with the purpose of making capital funds available to qualifying minority-owned banks. Another was created to invest primarily in mortgage-backed securities that are guaranteed (by the Government National Mortgage Association) as to their payment of interest and principal. The SEC also reports on offshore funds, investment companies created to trade in the U.S. securities markets, but which are domiciled in foreign countries to avoid U.S. regulations. Other types of specialized funds include *hedge funds*, which buy stocks for capital appreciation and sell short stocks expected to decline in value. *Money funds* invest in short-term marketable securities. They offer investors the opportunity to participate in large-denomination securities through owning shares of the fund.

## Assets of Mutual Funds

At the end of 1972, total financial assets of all mutual funds amounted to $59,831 million. Eighty-six percent of that total was invested in corporate stocks, 9 percent in corporate bonds, and the remainder in cash and other short-term securities. The distribution of assets for individual funds varies widely and reflects the investment objectives of the fund. By way of illustration, in mid-1973, the Dreyfus Special Income Fund, Inc., had invested 72.2 percent of its assets in corporate bonds and 12.2 percent in corporate stocks. In contrast, 98 percent of the assets of Massachusetts Investors Growth Stock Fund were invested in corporate stocks.

Mutual funds are active traders in the stock market. As shown in Table 10–2, their net purchases of corporate stocks vary widely from year to year.

During the 1965–1970 period, net purchases increased when stock prices increased—as noted by the Standard and Poor's Index—and declined when stock prices fell. However, in 1971 net purchases diminished further and there were net liquidations in 1972 and 1973, while stock prices increased. This situation occurred because shareholders of mutual funds redeemed more shares than they purchased. When this happens, the mutual funds have to reduce their holdings of securities to pay off their shareholders. More will be said below about the net redemption of mutual fund shares.

The common stock activity rate is another indicator of trading activity. The Securities and Exchange Commission defines this as the average of purchases and sales divided by the average market value of stockholdings. During the 1965–1969 period, the activity rate increased from 21.8 to 51.0; then, in 1973, it declined to 34.6.

The final indicator of trading activity by mutual funds is the distribution of their common stock portfolios in selected years, as shown in Table 10–3. For example, public utility stocks and financial stocks accounted for 30 percent of total stocks held in 1963 and less than 15 percent in 1973. Other groups of stocks, such as drugs and cosmetics, gained in relative importance during this period.

## Performance of Investment Companies

All of the above indicators of trading activity raise questions regarding the performance of investment companies. What degree of success have mutual funds realized in meeting their investment and portfolio objectives? Do high turnover rates mean superior performance? To answer questions such as these, the Securities and Exchange Commission initiated *A Study*

Table 10–2

Net purchases of corporate stock by mutual funds

| Year | Amount ($ billions) | Standard & Poor's Index Composite* |
|------|---------------------|-------------------------------------|
| 1965 | 1.271 | 88.17 |
| 1966 | 0.953 | 85.26 |
| 1967 | 1.851 | 91.93 |
| 1968 | 2.527 | 98.70 |
| 1969 | 1.722 | 97.84 |
| 1970 | 1.180 | 83.22 |
| 1971 | 0.445 | 98.29 |
| 1972 | −1.821 | 109.20 |
| 1973 | −2.300 | 107.43 |

Source: Board of Governors of the Federal Reserve System, Flow of Funds Accounts; Standard & Poor's Corporation
* 1941–1943 = 10

Table 10–3

Mutual funds' portfolio diversification

| Industry[a] | Percentage of total common stock | | |
|---|---|---|---|
| | 1963 | 1968 | 1973 |
| Agricultural equipment | 0.70 | 0.70 | 0.38 |
| Aircraft mfg. and aerospace | 1.56 | 3.08 | 0.84 |
| Air transport | 1.28 | 2.04 | 1.82 |
| Auto and accessories (excl. tires) | 4.43 | 2.24 | 2.69 |
| Building materials and equipment | 1.42 | 4.01 | 3.21 |
| Chemicals | 7.51 | 6.97 | 6.25 |
| Containers | 0.98 | 1.00 | 0.37 |
| Drugs and cosmetics | 4.56 | 5.60 | 8.32 |
| Electrical equipment and electronics (excl. television and radio) | 5.21 | 7.85 | 5.44 |
| Foods and beverages | 2.63 | 4.03 | 3.51 |
| Financial (incl. banks and insurance) | 14.35 | 8.38 | 8.90 |
| Machinery | 1.46 | 1.72 | 1.81 |
| Metals and mining | 2.97 | 3.09 | 3.53 |
| Motion pictures | 0.16 | 0.68 | 0.00 |
| Office equipment | 4.97 | 9.42 | 8.99 |
| Oil | 13.77 | 12.77 | 14.97 |
| Paper | 1.84 | 1.76 | 3.14 |
| Public utilities (incl. telephone and natural gas) | 14.53 | 6.27 | 5.40 |
| Railroad | 3.23 | 3.17 | 2.56 |
| Railroad equipment | 0.44 | 1.18 | 0.19 |
| Retail trade | 2.96 | 4.02 | 3.59 |
| Rubber (incl. tires) | 1.40 | 1.34 | 0.88 |
| Steel | 2.09 | 1.23 | 1.25 |
| Television and radio | 1.45 | 1.18 | 1.59 |
| Textiles | 0.45 | 0.76 | 0.49 |
| Tobacco | 1.35 | 0.94 | 1.89 |
| Miscellaneous[b] | 2.30 | 4.57 | 7.99 |
| Totals | 100.00 | 100.00 | 100.00 |

[a] Composite industry investments drawn from the portfolios of forty of the largest investment companies, as of the end of calendar year 1973, whose total net assets represented 60.8 percent of total net assets of all Institute member companies.
[b] Includes diversified industrial companies not readily assignable to specific industry categories.
Source: Investment Company Institute

of *Mutual Funds* concerning the investment policies of investment companies during the 1952–1958 period. The report revealed that:

> During the period under study, performance records varied considerably, both within and among types of funds, but on average conformed rather closely to the behavior of securities markets as a whole. For the 5¾ years covered by the study, the Standard and Poor's Composite Common Stock Index was definitely superior to the average performance of the funds, but the disparity can be explained by the portfolio structure of funds; i.e., the division of their portfolios among common stocks, preferred stocks, corporate bonds, govern-

*ment securities, and other assets. When adjustments are made for this composition, the average performance by the funds did not differ appreciably from what would have been achieved by an unmanaged portfolio with the same division among assets.* [2]

*The analysis revealed no strong relationship between turnover rates and performance. . . . Thus, there has been no consistent evidence to indicate that high portfolio turnover rates have worked either to the advantage or disadvantage of the shareholder.* [3]

The *Study of Mutual Funds* challenged investigators to pursue the question of mutual fund performance relative to the stock market as a whole. Another study concluded that:

*Mutual funds were on average not able to predict security prices well enough to outperform a buy-the-market-and-hold policy, but also that there is very little evidence that any individual fund was able to do significantly better than that which we expected from mere random chance.* [4]

Another study compared the performance of sixty large mutual funds with the performance of the twenty largest industrial companies (measured by market values) listed on the New York Stock Exchange for the 1948–1972 period.[5] The study found that only one mutual fund did better than the twenty largest industrials for a ten-year period. These results may shake the confidence of some investors in the ability of fund managers to do better than average performance.

## Industry Problems

In addition to the realization that most mutual funds do not outperform the stock market, investors lost money when stock prices declined sharply in 1969–1970. One consequence of the 1969–1970 bear market was a sharp reduction in the number of new mutual fund shares sold and a sharp rise in the number of redemptions (repurchase of owner shares). As Table 10–4 shows, mutual fund sales peaked in 1968, and then declined. Meanwhile, the number of redemptions rose and eventually exceeded new share sales. In 1973, mutual fund shareholders redeemed more shares than they bought.

[2]U.S., Congress, House, Committee on Interstate and Foreign Commerce, *A Study of Mutual Funds, Report*, 87th Cong., 2d sess., H. Rept. 2274 (Washington, D.C.: U.S. Government Printing Office, 1962), pp. 17–18.
[3]*Ibid.*, pp. 19–20.
[4]Michael C. Jensen, "The Performance of Mutual Funds in the Period 1945–1964," *The Journal of Finance* (May 1968), 415. Burton G. Malkiel, *A Random Walk down Wall Street* (New York: W. W. Norton, 1973), reached the same conclusion with respect to portfolio performance.
[5]R. Minturn Sedgwick, "The Record of Conventional Investment Management," *Financial Analysts Journal*, 29 (July/August 1973), 41–44.

Table 10–4

Mutual funds' capital changes (millions of dollars)

|  | Sale of new shares | Redemptions | Net change |
|---|---|---|---|
| 1967 | 4.7 | 2.7 | 2.0 |
| 1968 | 6.8 | 3.8 | 3.0 |
| 1969 | 6.7 | 3.7 | 3.0 |
| 1970 | 4.6 | 3.0 | 1.6 |
| 1971 | 5.1 | 4.7 | 0.4 |
| 1972 | 4.9 | 6.6 | −1.7 |
| 1973 | 4.6 | 5.7 | −1.3 |

Source: Board of Governors of the Federal Reserve System

Another blow to the mutual fund industry was a change in commission structures. Mutual funds were prohibited by the SEC from paying kickbacks on brokerage commissions to reward stockbrokers who sold their shares. In addition, amendments to the Investment Company Act reduced the profitability of contractual sales of mutual funds, whereby investors sign a contract to buy a certain dollar amount of mutual fund shares over a period of years. Before the amendments, the bulk of the commissions for the entire contract period were paid in the early years of the contract. Those who wanted to get out of the investment plan before they completed the entire contract period had already paid large commissions on shares they had yet to purchase. Such front-end-loaded contracts were great for salesmen, but they were not good for investors. The policy now is to pay commissions on shares as the investor acquires them.

Another problem is that the industry has faced a rise in class-action suits. In one such suit, it was alleged that the management of several mutual funds mismanaged their funds and investment portfolios. The allegations included: excessive management fees, excessive portfolio transactions, failure to take advantage of reduced brokerage commissions available to the fund, failure to use the third market to reduce commissions, and numerous other charges. The fund's management denied any wrongdoing. However, the settlement to the investors in this case was $1,400,000.[6] Such class-action suits are becoming more commonplace in the mutual fund industry.

The mutual fund industry is facing increasing competition from other financial institutions. Since the mid-1960s, all types of financial intermediaries have been competing more vigorously for individuals' savings. Savings and commercial banks offer certificates of deposit, insurance companies offer annuities, and pension funds are growing too. Another competitor is the real estate investment trusts discussed in the second part of this chapter.

[6]"Notice of Settlement Hearings," The Wall Street Journal, November 26, 1973, p. 21.

Table 10–5

Putnam Investors Fund portfolio (December 31, 1972)

Common stocks—88.0% (includes convertible bonds)

| S & P rating[a] | Number of shares or principal amount | | Market value |
|---|---|---|---|
| Consumer products and services (22.8%) | | | |
| A | 83,200 | Black and Decker Manufacturing Company (The) A major manufacturer of portable electrical tools used chiefly in the home and in the construction industry | $  8,985,600 |
| NR | 240,000 | Clorox Company (The) A leading manufacturer of such household products as Clorox, the largest selling household bleach product in the U.S.A. | 11,130,000 |
| A | 90,000 | Disney (Walt) Productions A producer of films for the whole family and the operator of Disneyland and Disney World amusement parks | 21,307,500 |
| A– | 225,000 | Gillette Company A leading razor and blade manufacturer; also makes Toni hair products, Paper Mate pens, and other brand-name toiletries and consumer products | 14,371,875 |
| A | 400,000 | Philip Morris, Inc. A cigarette manufacturer which in recent years has diversified into beer, chewing gum, and razor blades | 47,300,000 |
| A | 100,000 | Simplicity Pattern Co., Inc. A leading manufacturer of paper patterns for women's and children's clothing; accounts for more than half the patterns sold in the U.S.A. and Canada | 5,525,000 |
| A+ | 102,000 | Tampax Incorporated A worldwide manufacturer and distributor of cotton tampons | 11,883,000 |
| | | | 120,502,975 |
| Food and beverage (13.5%) | | | |
| A | 225,000 | Anheuser-Busch, Inc. The oldest and largest brewer in the country | 12,487,500 |
| A+ | 75,000 | Coca-Cola Company (The) The largest company in soft drinks, producing syrups and concentrates under Coca-Cola, Fanta, Fresca, and Tab brand names | 11,137,500 |
| A | 220,000 | Dr. Pepper Company The manufacturer of concentrates for Dr. Pepper soft drinks, with bottling franchises across the country | 5,802,500 |
| NR | 260,000 | McDonald's Corporation[b] One of the foremost operators of fast food restaurants, serving more than four million hamburgers daily | 19,825,000 |

Table 10–5 (cont'd)

| S & P rating[a] | Number of shares or principal amount | Market value |
|---|---|---|
| **Food and beverage (cont'd)** | | |
| B+ | 296,000 Pabst Brewing Company | $22,200,000 |
| | The nation's third largest brewer (with home office located in Milwaukee and plants across the country) | |
| | | 71,452,500 |
| **Insurance and financial services (8.3%)** | | |
| NR | 270,000 American Express Company | 17,516,250 |
| | An international travel and financial service company with subsidiaries in the insurance industry | |
| NR | 30,000 General Reinsurance Corporation | 14,190,000 |
| | The country's leading independent reinsurer providing reinsurance to many insurance companies for all types of property and casualty risks | |
| NR | 161,000 Government Employees Insurance Company | 8,995,875 |
| | A direct writer of auto insurance originally formed to provide auto coverage exclusively to military and civilian government employees | |
| NR | 35,000 MGIC Investment Corporation | 3,351,250 |
| | A major insurer of residential mortgages; provides other financial services as well | |
| | | 44,053,375 |
| **Oil (7.9%)** | | |
| A+ | 100,000 Exxon Corporation | 8,750,000 |
| | The world's largest petroleum company | |
| A− | 60,000 Halliburton Company | 8,415,000 |
| | A supplier of specialized services connected with oil-well drilling and maintenance with growing interests in industrial and marine construction | |
| A+ | 12,600 Louisiana Land and Exploration Company | 544,950 |
| | A holder of oil and gas lands onshore and offshore in the South Louisiana area with additional holdings in several other states | |
| A | 100,000 Mobil Oil Corporation | 7,400,000 |
| | An internationally known oil company, ranking third in world petroleum product sales | |
| A+ | 180,000 Schlumberger Ltd. | 16,290,000 |
| | A provider of worldwide services used in connection with drilling and maintenance of oil wells; also active in the fields of electronics and instrumentation | |
| | | 41,399,950 |

Table 10–5 (cont'd)

| S & P rating[a] | Number of shares or principal amount | Market value |
|---|---|---|
| Retail trade (7.7%) | | |
| A | 515,000 Kresge (S. S.) Company<br>One of the largest retailers of general merchandise in the U.S.A. | $25,170,625 |
| A | 115,000 Penney (J. C.) Company<br>A national chain of department stores with an expanding catalog operation | 10,393,125 |
| B+ | 90,000 Standard Brands Paint Company<br>An operator of a chain of discount paint and home decorating centers in California, Arizona, and Washington | 4,848,750 |
| | | 40,412,500 |
| Business equipment and services (7.0%) | | |
| B+ | 40,000 Burroughs Corporation<br>A major manufacturer of business machines with a line of more than 200 models ranging from simple adding machines to large-scale computer systems | 8,690,000 |
| A+ | 55,000 International Business Machines Corporation<br>The world's foremost manufacturer of computers | 22,110,000 |
| B+ | 100,000 Rank Organisation Limited (The) (ADR Cl. "A" Ord.)<br>A company deriving the major part of its earnings from its interest in Rank-Xerox, the marketer of Xerox equipment in Europe | 2,612,500 |
| A | $2,000,000 Xerox Corporation (cv. sub. deb 6s, 1995)<br>The well-known maker and marketer of products for photocopy reproduction and, more recently, computers | 3,500,000 |
| | | 36,912,500 |
| Utilities (3.5%) | | |
| A+ | 350,000 American Telephone and Telegraph Company<br>The Bell Telephone System, the country's dominant telephone utility company | 18,462,500 |
| Drugs, hospital supplies and medical services (3.3%) | | |
| A− | 150,000 Baxter Laboratories, Inc.<br>A producer of medical supplies including intravenous solutions, artificial organs, and medical electronic products | 8,362,500 |
| A+ | 70,000 Johnson & Johnson<br>An international manufacturer and marketer of health care items, including surgical specialties, Band-Aids, and drugs | 9,135,000 |
| | | 17,497,500 |

Table 10–5 (cont'd)

| S & P rating[a] | Number of shares or principal amount | Market value |
|---|---|---|
| Photography (2.6%) | | |
| A+ | 80,000 Eastman Kodak Company<br>The largest producer of photographic equipment and supplies and an important manufacturer of synthetic fibers, plastics, and chemicals | $ 11,870,000 |
| B+ | 15,000 Polaroid Corporation<br>A well-known producer of cameras whose special Polaroid Land Process develops a photograph within seconds | 1,891,875 |
| | | 13,761,875 |
| Transportation (2.3%) | | |
| B+ | 200,000 Emery Air Freight Corporation<br>The leading domestic air freight forwarder | 11,925,000 |
| Automotive (2.2%) | | |
| A | 100,000 Ford Motor Company<br>The second largest producer of automobiles; also manufactures tractors, Philco appliances, and electronic items | 7,962,500 |
| A– | 107,000 Monroe Auto Equipment Company<br>The leading independent manufacturer of shock absorbers and related ride-control products | 3,517,625 |
| | | 11,480,125 |
| Other products and services (6.9%) | | |
| A– | 300,000 International Telephone and Telegraph Corporation<br>A diversified worldwide company with interests in telecommunications, insurance, and consumer services | 18,075,000 |
| NR | 75,000 National Chemsearch Corporation<br>Supplier of specialty chemical products and cleaners to more than 225,000 commercial customers through a sales force of over 1,600 | 6,525,000 |
| A– | 111,000 Snap-On Tools Corp.<br>A manufacturer of wrenches (with interchangeable sockets and handles) and mechanic's hand tools and related equipment, used primarily for automobile service and maintenance | 5,910,750 |
| | Other investments | 5,518,625 |
| | | 36,029,375 |
| Total common stocks (includes convertible bonds) | | 463,890,175 |

Table 10–5 (cont'd)

| S & P rating[a] | Number of shares or principal amount | Market value |
|---|---|---|
| **U.S. government and agency obligations—3.4%** | | |
| Par value | | Market value |
| $2,000,000 | Federal Home Loan Banks cons. bds. 8.35s, 1973 | $  2,007,500 |
| 5,450,000 | Federal Land Banks 7.95s, 1973 | 5,463,625 |
| 2,000,000 | Federal Land Banks cons. bds. 7.80s, 1973 | 2,027,500 |
| 5,000,000 | Federal National Mortgage Association 7¾s, 1974 | 5,093,750 |
| 1,100,000 | U.S. treasury notes 8⅛s, 1973 | 1,117,875 |
| 2,000,000 | U.S. treasury notes 7¼s, 1974 | 2,037,500 |
| | Total U.S. government and agency obligations | 17,747,750 |
| | Total investments | 481,637,925 |
| **Other assets —8.6%** | | |
| | Other assets and liabilities, net | 45,670,405 |
| | Total net assets | $527,308,330 |

[a] For policy reasons, Standard and Poor's does not rank all stocks including certain categories of financial services. Please note that Standard & Poor's rankings do not purport to measure the relative quality of common stocks, but are designed to indicate relative stability and earnings growth plus relative stability and growth of dividends of certain common stocks. The rankings which range from A+ (the highest) to C (the lowest) do not pretend to reflect an examination of other factors, tangible and intangible, that also bear on a stock's quality. The rankings also state that under no circumstances should they be regarded as a recommendation to buy or sell a security.
[b] Non-income-producing security
Source: Putnam Fund Distributors Inc.

In addition to the continuous management of a portfolio, mutual funds offer investors other services, such as automatic reinvestment of income dividends and capital gains. Frequently, dividends from investment income are reinvested at the public offering price, which includes a sales commission. Many mutual funds also give their shareholders the option of taking their net realized capital gains through the medium of a stock dividend of mutual funds shares, bought at net asset value (without commission), or as cash.

Many mutual funds offer monthly (or quarterly) cash withdrawal plans, which can be used to provide a steady stream of income to the investor or a beneficiary. Most withdrawal plans require an initial investment of $10,000 or more. Dividend income is reinvested or held in cash, and capital gains distributions are accepted in shares. Assume that an investor wants to receive $50 per month. If that amount exceeds income dividends, sufficient shares are redeemed at net asset value (no charge) to make up the withdrawal payment. If the fund prospers and the income dividends exceed withdrawals, investors will not dip into principal. The higher the amount of withdrawals in relation to principal, the greater the risk of depletion.

Exchange privilege is another service offered by some mutual funds. Such funds belong to a group and permit their shareholders to switch from one fund to another for a nominal charge. For example, Massachusetts Investors Trust, Massachusetts Investors Growth Stock Fund, Inc., Massachusetts Capital Development Fund, Inc., and Massachusetts Financial Development Fund, Inc., are members of a group of funds. Shares of any one of the above funds can be exchanged for shares in any other fund in that group. A shareholder who is approaching retirement age may want to switch from Massachusetts Capital Fund, which emphasizes high capital appreciation, to Massachusetts Development Fund, which emphasizes above-average income and some growth.

## Real Estate Investment Trusts (REITs)

Real estate investment trusts (REITs) are analogous to closed-end investment companies for those who wish to invest in real estate. The principal difference between the two is that REITs make extensive use of borrowed funds, while investment companies are not permitted to borrow funds. REITs are organized as business trusts to provide real estate portfolio management for investors who lack funds and experience and who want to maintain the liquidity that real estate investments usually do not offer.

As a general matter, REITs are organized by a management group that serves as its adviser for a fee, usually 1 to 1½ percent of the assets managed. Also, there are fees for servicing mortgages, arranging financing, and managing property. Such management groups and advisers include commercial banks, mortgage companies, and life insurance companies. These organizations can use REITs to extend their mortgage-lending activity, since, in essence, the REIT is a captive buyer.

### Principal Requirements

The real estate investment trust industry began after the passage of the Real Estate Investment Trust Act in September 1960. This act exempted REITs from paying federal corporate income taxes provided they meet certain requirements concerning organization, income, and investments. Several of the principal requirements are listed below:

Organization:
1 There must be at least 100 shareholders. They may be individuals, trusts, estates, and business organizations.
2 The trust cannot be a personal holding company (that is, more than half of the trust should not be owned or controlled by less than five different people).

3 Beneficial ownership must be evidenced by transferable shares or certificates of beneficial interest. Although REITs can be open-end or closed-end, all existing REITs have chosen the closed-end form of organization. This means that shareholders must sell their shares in the stock market to liquidate their investment. Currently, seventy-five REITs are listed for trading on the New York and American Stock Exchanges.

4 Management must be vested in one or more trustees.

Gross income:

1 At least 75 percent of the trust's gross income must be derived from rents, mortgage interest payments, and gains from the sale of real estate.

2 At least 90 percent of the trust's ordinary income must be distributed to its shareholders.

Investments:

1 At least 75 percent of the value of the trust's assets must be invested in real estate, cash and government securities.

## Types of REITs

Although all REITs invest in real estate, some specialize in particular types of real estate and loans, while others have broader investment objectives. They can be classified into four broad categories. The first category of REITs specialize in making short-term construction and development (C&D) loans. They make the development loans to prepare the property for construction (e.g., to clear the land and put in streets) and then make the construction loans. Construction loans are secured by first mortgages and are used to finance single- and multifamily dwellings as well as commercial properties. The duration of construction loans can range from ninety days for a single-family home to more than three years for large office buildings.

The second category consists of REITs that specialize in making long-term investments. These REITs typically hold mortgages on apartment buildings, office buildings, and shopping centers, generally conventional mortgages with maturities of twenty years or more. Interest income from mortgages is their major source of income.

The third category are REITs that own property, which provides them with both rental income and potential gains when the property is sold. These are usually referred to as equity trusts. One advantage of equity trusts is that the money allocated to depreciation of the property owned can be paid out to shareholders as nontaxable return of capital. Alternately, the funds can be returned for property improvements or further investments.

Finally, some REITs have investment objectives that encompass short-term or C&D trusts, long-term trusts, and equity trusts. Such REITs are called combination trusts.

## Assets and Liabilities of REITs

As shown in Table 10–6, at the end of 1973, the total assets of REITs amounted to $20.5 billion. More than four-fifths of these assets were invested in mortgage loans, and the majority of these were on residential property, although commercial property was the largest single category. Equity shares provide the initial capital for REITs, but they raise most of their funds by selling credit market instruments such as commercial paper or by borrowing funds from commercial banks. One consequence of borrowing is that REITs have a high cost of funds, compared with certain other financial intermediaries. A study of REITs by the Federal Reserve Bank of Boston reported that, in 1969, the average cost of funds for commercial banks and savings and loan associations was 3½ percent and 5½ percent, respectively, while the average cost of funds for REITs was about 10 percent.[7] To offset the high costs during the 1969–1970 period, REITs were able to charge high rates of interest, owing to the shortage of funds from commercial banks and other mortgage lenders at that time, and they made good profits as a result. During periods of easy money, REITs held down their cost of funds by increased use of short-term borrowing. They also took on riskier investments (with higher yields) than did other real estate lenders such as commercial banks.

*Leverage*    Another consequence of borrowing is the effect of *leverage* on earnings. Companies that have high debt-to-equity ratios are called highly

Table 10–6

Assets and liabilities of real estate investment trusts (year-end 1973)

|  | | Billions of dollars |
| --- | --- | --- |
| Total assets | | 20.5 |
| Physical | | |
| Multifamily structures | 1.0 | |
| Nonresidential structures | 2.2 | |
| Financial | | 17.3 |
| Home mortgages | 3.9 | |
| Multifamily mortgages | 4.4 | |
| Commercial mortgages | 6.8 | |
| Miscellaneous assets | 2.2 | |
| Total liabilities | | 15.4 |
| Mortgages | 1.5 | |
| Corporate bonds | 2.0 | |
| Bank loans n.e.c.[a] | 7.0 | |
| Commercial paper | 3.9 | |
| Miscellaneous | 1.0 | |
| Net worth | | 5.1 |

[a] n.e.c. = not elsewhere classified
Source: Board of Governors of the Federal Reserve System, Flow of Funds Accounts

[7]Peter A. Schulkin, "Real Estate Investment Trusts: A New Financial Intermediary," *New England Economic Review*, Federal Reserve Bank of Boston (November/December 1970).

leveraged. Because some REITs are highly leveraged, they may experience wide savings in their earnings and share prices. By way of illustration, take three companies, A, B, and C, that are leveraged to different degrees. As shown in Table 10–7,Company A has one hundred shares of stock outstanding and no bonds, Company B has fifty shares and fifty bonds, and Company C has ninety bonds and ten shares. Therefore, Company C is highly leveraged, while Company A has no leverage. Since interest charges on bonds are fixed, assume that each bond costs $1 interest. If each company earned $100, its shareholders would earn $1 per share. However, if earnings were $200, the shares of Company A would earn $2 per share, and those of Company C would earn $11 per share [($200−$90 interest) / 10 shares = $11/share]. If total earnings fell to $50, Company C would be in serious trouble because the earnings are less than the interest payments.

When earnings are good, share prices rise and REITs sell more stock to the public. These funds are used as a base for additional borrowing and more leverage. Everything works well as long as earnings and share prices are rising. However, declining stock prices in 1973, along with materials shortages and other effects of inflation, created problems for some REITs. The major impact was on the mortgage-type REITs because they are more dependent on borrowing and selling new stock to the public than are the equity REITs. As 1973 came to a close, an increasing number of mortgage-type REITs were filing for protection under Chapter 11 of the federal bankruptcy laws.[8] This section of the law provides for court supervision of arrangements between a debtor and the creditors; it means, in effect, that a company has gone bankrupt.

## Summary

Although investment companies have become an increasingly popular mode of investment in the stock market, declining stock market prices combined with poor performance by investment companies have created

Table 10–7

Leverage

|  | Company A | Company B | Company C |
|---|---|---|---|
| Number of bonds | None | 50 | 90 |
| Number of shares of stock | 100 | 50 | 10 |
| Total earnings | Earnings per share | | |
| $100 | $1 | $1 | $1 |
| $200 | $2 | $3 | $11 |

[8]See Priscilla S. Meyer, "Realty-Trust Woes," *The Wall Street Journal,* January 21, 1974, p. 1., for details on particular companies.

problems for the industry—a large number of redemptions, changes in commission structure, and class-action suits. Finally, there is increasing competition from other types of financial institutions. One such institution is real estate investment trusts, which are basically investment companies that specialize in real estate.

## Questions

1 Distinguish between open- and closed-end investment companies, unit investment trusts, and face-amount certificate companies.
2 What is the difference between load and no-load funds? Distinguish between sales charges and management fees. How can you explain the difference between the average sales charge on loaded funds and the average commission on stocks?
3 Discuss the different objectives of common stock funds, balanced funds, income funds, and special funds.
4 Discuss the advantages and disadvantages to investors of mutual funds.
5 Empirical evidence has indicated that mutual funds, on the average, do no better than stock market averages. Does this mean that mutual funds are not rational investments for small investors?
6 Discuss the similarities and differences between real estate investment trusts (REITs) and closed-end investment companies.
7 Explain how the highly leveraged capital structures of some REITs have led to certain financial difficulties and more than a few bankruptcies.
8 What are the major assets and liabilities of REITs?
9 REITs began to be established after the passage of the Real Estate Investment Trust Act of 1960. Discuss the major features of this act relating to the tax status, organization, and gross income of REITs.

# Bibliography

## Investment Companies

*Investment Companies*. New York: Arthur Wiesenberger Services, Division of Nuveen Corporation (annual).

Malkiel, Burton G. *A Random Walk down Wall Street*. New York: W. W. Norton, 1973.

*Vickers Guide to Investment Company Portfolios*. Huntington, N.Y.: Vickers Associates, Inc. (annual).

U.S., Congress, House, Committee on Interstate and Foreign Commerce, *A Study of Mutual Funds, Report*, 87th Cong., 2d sess., H. Rept. 2274. Washington, D.C.: U.S. Government Printing Office, 1962.

## Real Estate Investment Trusts

Campbell, Kenneth. *The Real Estate Trusts: America's Newest Billionaires*. New York: Audit Investment Research, Inc., 1971.

*House Miscellaneous Reports on Public Bills,* vol. 5, 86th Cong., 2d sess. Washington, D.C.: U.S. Government Printing Office, 1960.

Lasser, J. K. *J. K. Lasser's Successful Tax Planning for Real Estate*. New York: J. K. Lasser Tax Institute, 1972.

*Real Estate Investment Planning*, vol. 1. New York: Institute for Business Planning, Inc., 1971.

*Real Estate Investment Planning*, vol. 15, no. 3. New York: Institute for Business Planning, Inc., 1973.

*Real Estate Investment Trusts*. New York: Practicing Law Institute, 1970.

Chapter

# 11

# Consumer credit institutions

Credit has played an important role in the development of America. It has even been said that "if Queen Isabella did hock the Crown Jewels, then it was not she, but some unsung banker of the day, who financed Columbus on her collateral. It is perhaps fitting speculation that America may have been discovered on credit."[1] This chapter examines the development of major types of consumer credit institutions in the United States. A brief history, explaining how different types of finance companies developed in response to particular demands in the economy, is followed by a discussion of the amount of consumer credit outstanding and an examination of sales finance companies and consumer finance companies (included here is an explanation of annual percentage rates and the cost of credit). Bank credit cards and their payments system bring in the use of electronics in consumer credit. The final section concerns consumer credit regulations.

## Developments in Credit

### First Use of Credit

The first extensive use of credit in the United States was to farmers (agricultural credit) on a crop-to-crop basis. In the largely agrarian society of early America, farmers could not pay off their debts until their crops were har-

---

[1]Gabriel Hague, "Some Aspects of Banking in Transition," in *The World Banking Challenge* (Washington, D.C.: The American Bankers Association, 1972), p. 51.

vested and sold. Therefore, they traded their expectations of future income for presently needed goods and services. Consumer credit appeared simultaneously. One noted Philadelphia cabinetmaker of the colonial period, David Evans, sold 90 percent of his goods on credit. In part, the use of both agricultural and consumer credit can be attributed to the shortage of cash in the economy and the widespread use of the barter system.

Merchants who sold goods on credit charged a credit price and a cash price. The difference between the two prices was not considered an interest rate, which would have been subject to usury laws. According to the time-price doctrine established in England in 1774, credit extended by merchants for the sale of goods was exempted from usury laws. This doctrine was used in the colonies in the same manner. In Massachusetts, the usury ceiling (maximum interest rate that could be charged) was 8 percent, but the time-price doctrine permitted merchants to charge more than 8 percent on the sale of goods. Since merchants were exempted from usury laws, they could sell more goods at a profit, while the use of credit permitted consumers to obtain goods that they could not otherwise afford to buy.[2]

## Credit in the Eighteenth and Nineteenth Centuries

During the eighteenth and first half of the nineteenth century, the principal nonbank agencies that extended credit were small merchants, physicians, and pawnbrokers. The Industrial Revolution brought about changes in credit demands and institutions. Industrialization made more goods available to consumers and created a class of wage earners. (The wage-earner class was bolstered by large-scale immigration into the United States as well as by internal migration of workers from rural to urban areas.) The credit needs of these industrial workers differed from the credit needs of farmers, who generally borrowed on "open-book" accounts (without formal credit agreements) and paid off their debts when their crops were sold. In contrast, industrial wage earners received steady incomes and could pay back their debts on a regular basis throughout the year. Accordingly, the concept of installment credit evolved, since many workers were paid low wages and required credit to raise their standard of living above subsistence levels. These credit needs were partially satisfied by a new type of lending institution—small-loan companies that concentrated on making personal loans and used-chattel mortgages on household items, with wage assignments or unsecured promissory notes as security. Those who could not obtain credit from legitimate small-loan companies borrowed from loan sharks, who charged excessive rates of interest. Some loan sharks were known to require the borrower's physical well-being as collateral and

---

[2]For further discussion of early credit see E. A. J. Johnson, *American Economic Thought in the Seventeenth Century* (New York: Russell and Russell, 1961), pp. 213–218.

charged interest rates in excess of 200 percent.[3] Today such extortion and high rates of interest are a violation of federal extortion and credit extension statutes (Title 18, sections 891–896) and are punishable by large fines and up to twenty years in prison.

### Credit in the Twentieth Century

By the turn of the twentieth century, installment credit—and loan sharks—were widespread throughout the United States. The first legislation concerning installment credit and the abuses of loan sharks was enacted in Massachusetts in 1911. This law permitted lenders to make loans of up to $300 and charge an interest rate of 42 percent per year. Other states subsequently enacted similar legislation. A direct result of the effort to curb and regulate loan sharks was the development of consumer finance companies.

After World War I, new types of credit institutions developed. The availability of consumer durables such as automobiles and washing machines expanded the demand for consumer credit. Sales finance companies, which buy consumer installment contracts from retail dealers and provide wholesale financing for those dealers, grew from this demand. Commercial banks were the next institution to enter the consumer loan field. The National City Bank of New York opened the first personal loan department in 1928. Revolving retail credit appeared when John Wanamaker, a large Philadelphia department store, introduced it in 1938. Consumers using revolving retail credit can pay off their debts within thirty days and have no service charge, or they can make regular payments over a period of time and pay interest on the amount of money still owed.

The next major innovation in consumer credit was the development of the credit card. In 1951 the Franklin National Bank (New York) issued the first bank credit card. This plastic money was the forerunner of Bank Americard, Mastercharge, and a host of other credit cards issued by banks, oil companies, retail stores, and others.[4]

### The Amount of Credit

The Board of Governors of the Federal Reserve System defines consumer credit as loans to individuals for household, family, and personal expenditures (except real estate mortgage loans) and further classifies consumer credit as noninstallment or installment credit. *Noninstallment credit* is de-

---

[3]For more information on loan sharks see National Commission on Consumer Finance, *Consumer Credit in the United States* (Washington, D.C.: U.S. Government Printing Office, 1972), p. 181.
[4]For additional discussion on early credit cards see Robert H. Cole, *Consumer and Commercial Credit Management* (Homewood, Ill.: Richard D. Irwin, 1972).

fined as all consumer credit scheduled to be repaid in one lump sum. It includes single-payment loans, nonrevolving charge accounts, and service credit. The payment of a utility bill upon receipt is an example of noninstallment credit. *Installment credit* consists of all consumer credit that is repaid in two or more payments. As shown in Figure 11–1, at the end of 1973 there were $180.5 billion of consumer credit outstanding. Installment credit accounted for $147 billion or 80 percent of the total amount. The four types of installment credit are: automobile paper, other consumer goods paper, repair and modernization loans, and personal loans. Noninstallment credit amounted to $33 billion. Single-payment loans made by commercial banks accounted for the largest share of noninstallment credit; the remainder was equally divided between charge accounts and service credit.[5]

Figure 11–1 also shows the major holders of credit for each of those categories. It is important to recognize that the current holders of credit are not necessarily the originators. For example, one can buy a car and finance it with an automobile dealer, who in turn sells the contract (automobile paper) to a commercial bank or finance company. The major institutions originating and holding consumer credit are commercial banks, credit

Figure 11–1

Short- and intermediate-term consumer credit[a] (December 31, 1973)

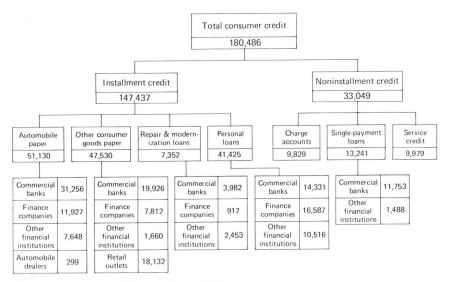

[a] By type of credit and institution, in millions of dollars
Source: *Federal Reserve Bulletin,* September 1974

[5]Charge accounts listed under noninstallment credit include retail outlets, service stations, home heating oil accounts, and miscellaneous credit card accounts. Bank credit card accounts outstanding are included in the installment credit data.

unions, finance companies, and retail outlets. Because other chapters in this book examine commercial banks and credit unions, the remainder of this chapter focuses on finance companies, bank credit cards, and consumer credit regulation.

## Credit Institutions

Before 1971, the Board of Governors of the Federal Reserve System made a distinction between sales finance companies and consumer finance companies. However, in recent years sales finance companies have entered the consumer finance field, and consumer finance companies have entered the sales finance field, thus blurring the distinction between the two types of finance company. The Board of Governors of the Federal Reserve System now includes both types of companies under the classification finance companies, but for analytical purposes the original distinction is useful because each satisfied different credit needs in the economy.

### Sales Finance Companies

Sales finance companies developed in response to the credit needs of the automobile industry.[6] They buy consumer installment contracts from retail dealers and provide these dealers with wholesale financing. For example, a retail automobile dealer originates a sales contract and sells it to a sales finance company. The fact that the buyer purchased a car from an automobile dealer, yet owes the money to a finance company, raises some questions about his rights to withhold payments if the car is not satisfactory.

The use of collateral trust certificates provides an illustration of wholesale financing by sales finance companies. In this case, the sales finance company buys certain goods from a manufacturer and establishes a trust agreement in which the title to the product belongs to the finance company and the retailer has possession of the goods. This method of financing relieves retailers from investing large amounts of money in inventories and enables them to use these funds elsewhere.

There are two types of sales finance companies, captives and independents. Captive sales finance companies are subsidiary companies holding notes receivable which were produced in connection with sales by dealers of their parent corporation's products.[7] They were developed for the fol-

---

[6]For a detailed history of sales finance companies see Clyde W. Phelps, *The Role of Sales Finance Companies in the American Economy* (Baltimore: Commercial Credit Company, 1952).

[7]The discussion of captive finance companies draws heavily on the following works: Victor L. Andrews, "Captive Finance Companies," *Harvard Business Review* (July-August, 1964), 88; Victor L. Andrews, "Captive Finance Companies: Their Growth and Some Speculations on Their Significance," *Industrial Management Review* (Fall 1961), 26.

lowing reasons. First, during the period of credit restraint that occurred in the last half of the 1950s, some independent finance companies were unable to satisfy the credit needs of small trade corporations and unincorporated businesses. Therefore, manufacturers established their own credit outlets to support their sales. By way of illustration, several farm equipment manufacturers—John Deere, Massey Ferguson, and International Harvester—formed captive finance companies. Similarly, Philco and Motorola formed captive finance companies to support their appliance sales.

Second, some manufacturers used their own finance subsidiaries instead of intracompany financing because finance companies can have higher debt-to-equity ratios than manufacturing concerns. Traditionally, finance companies are highly leveraged.

Third, a common feature of captive finance companies is that their parent companies manufacture durable goods which are high-cost items, for example, farm equipment, automobiles, and television sets. If a product line consists of high-cost goods, retailers exert pressure on manufacturers to help finance the purchase of those goods, because the high carrying costs of inventories and seasonal demands make credit extensions to retailers unattractive to some banks.

Fourth, retailers such as Sears, Roebuck and Co., Montgomery Ward, and Macy's experienced a shift from cash sales to installment credit sales and found that their cash flows were reduced in the short run. In searching for new sources of funds to help finance their inventories, they turned to captive finance companies to provide the leverage for additional funds.

Seeing the success of captive finance companies, independent sales finance companies showed an increased interest in providing product-line loans. Thus, today most independent sales finance companies have commercial divisions that provide services similar to those of captive finance companies. On the other hand, some captives discovered that single-line financing is less profitable than diversification. Many have changed their purpose from financing the parent company's products to providing a satisfactory return on the parent's investments, which they accomplish by making consumer loans and providing wholesale financing for a wide range of companies.

Both types of finance company have diversified beyond their traditional roles, entering into the fields of consumer and personal loans, insurance, banking, manufacturing, and retailing.[8] For example, Beneficial Finance

---

[8] A detailed discussion of this diversification is available in S. Hayward Wills, "The Changing Role of Sales Finance Companies," *Industrial Banker* (January 1968), 13–16.

owns Western Auto Supply Stores; General Motors Acceptance Corporation owns a credit life insurance company; C.I.T. Financial Corporation owns the National Bank of North America (assets $2.6 billion), Gibson Greeting Cards, Inc., leasing companies, and two manufacturing firms.

## Consumer Finance Companies

As previously mentioned, consumer finance companies developed at the turn of the century to make cash loans to wage earners. They had a virtual monopoly in the area of making small personal cash loans until 1935, when commercial banks entered the small-loan field.

One unique feature of consumer finance companies is that they are regulated by the law of the states in which they do business. Thus, consumer finance companies in New Jersey are limited to making personal loans of $1,000, while in California they can make personal loans in excess of $10,000. At the other extreme Arkansas has no law permitting small-loan companies to exist.

*Calculation of Interest Rates*   In addition, states regulate the interest rates that can be charged on personal loans; these generally vary from 36 percent per year on the smallest unsecured loans to 12 percent per year on large secured loans.

At this point it is useful to distinguish between forms of rate quotation traditionally in use and the annual percentage rate (APR). For many years, finance companies followed the practice of quoting rates as a rate per month on the unpaid balance. A rate of 3 percent per month would be equal to 36 percent APR (12 × 3). Thus, to borrow $100 at 10 percent APR requires a total repayment of $105.48 in 12 equal monthly installments. The charge may also be expressed as a dollar amount, e.g., $5.48. In more recent years, some state laws have been written in terms similar to banking laws. For example, Connecticut's law permits a charge of $17 per $100 per year to be added to the principal for each $100 up to $300 (for amounts of $300 to $1,800 the rate is $11 per hundred per year). This charge of $17 for $100 repayable in twelve equal monthly payments is the equivalent of 30 percent APR. In a few instances, discount rates have been permitted for finance companies. A discount rate of $17 per $100 per year means that the borrower receives $83 and pays back $100 ($100 minus a discount of $17). The APR on such a loan repayable in twelve equal monthly installments is 35.9 percent.

Federal law requires that the stated APR be calculated according to the actuarial method. Extensive tables have been developed to convert the results obtained in other forms of rate statement to the equivalent APR. A

formula known as the constant ratio method is frequently used to estimate the APR. This formula, however, does not truly reflect the payment flow and overstates the APR as calculated by the actuarial method, which reflects the flow of principal and interest. See below:

$$APR_c = \frac{2Ni}{L(n + 1)},$$

where $APR_c$ = annual percentage rate (constant ratio)

$\qquad N$ = number of payments per year

$\qquad i$ = dollar amount of interest charged

$\qquad L$ = net amount of the loan

$\qquad n$ = total number of payments

$$APR_c = \frac{2(12)(\$17.00)}{\$100(12 + 1)} = 0.314$$

In this example, the 31.4 percent calculated is based on a $17 charge; the APR as calculated on the actuarial basis is 30.0 percent. The higher the rate of interest charged and the longer the maturity of the loan, the greater the error which is introduced by use of the constant ratio formula as an estimating tool.

In most states, finance companies may offer credit life insurance for sale at rates varying from about $0.50 to $1.00 per $100 per year. In some states accident and health insurance is available at rates varying from about $2.00 to $2.50 per $100 per year, and a charge may be added to the finance charge. In rare instances, other charges may be permitted.

While various forms of rate quotation have been used historically, all consumer credit institutions are required by the Truth-in-Lending Act (Federal Reserve Board Regulation Z) to show borrowers the APR on all loans.

In addition to laws concerning the amount of personal loans and permissible interest rate charges, the situation is complicated by the fact that different laws apply to different types of consumer lenders. For example, in Rhode Island a consumer finance company is restricted to making personal loans of not more than $2,500, but commercial banks can make personal loans of $10,000. Moreover, banks can charge 21 percent interest per annum on the principal but retail stores providing revolving credit can charge only 18 percent interest.

Laws that specify the size of loans and interest charges tend to segment the market for consumer loans. Consumer finance companies specialize in

small loans that are relatively costly to process and therefore they charge higher interest rates. Banks charge relatively low interest rates on consumer loans, and the loans they make are less risky than those made by consumer finance companies. Preferred credit risk borrowers are able to borrow from financial institutions that charge low interest rates, whereas borrowers with a high degree of risk do not have this choice. Thus the average interest rate charge on personal loans is one indication of the risk class of the borrower and the cost of making loans. As Table 11–1 shows, in 1972 the average interest rate charged on personal loans ranged from 11.76 percent at credit unions to 25.88 percent at finance companies.

## Bank Credit Cards

While consumer finance companies were originated to provide small loans, consumers in recent years have sought more convenient means of financing their day-to-day credit needs. The development of credit cards has helped to satisfy that demand. During the 1968–1972 period, the amount of credit card credit held by commercial banks increased from $1.3 billion to $5.4 billion.[9]

Bank credit cards are an outgrowth of travel and entertainment cards issued by such companies as American Express and Diners Club. During the early 1960s, the first large-scale use of bank credit cards began in California. In the mid-1960s, The Bank of America (California) instituted the first nationwide credit card system. By the end of the decade the use of bank credit cards was widespread throughout the United States.

All bank credit cards have the following common features:

1  The credit card holder has a prearranged line of credit with a bank that issues credit cards. Credit is extended when the credit card holder buys something and signs a sales draft at a participating retail outlet. The

Table 11–1

Average interest rates charged on personal loans

| Type of lender | Percentage |
| --- | --- |
| Credit unions | 11.76 |
| Mutual savings banks | 12.44 |
| Commercial banks | 13.04 |
| Finance companies | 25.88 |

Source: *Consumer Credit in the United States,* Report of National Commission on Consumer Finance (Washington, D.C., December 1972), p. 128.

[9]For detailed data on credit card plans see: "Credit-Card and Check-Credit Plans," *Federal Reserve Bulletin* (September 1973), 646–653.

retail merchant presents the sales draft to the bank for payment in full, less a service charge discount, which is based on:

a the retail outlet's volume of credit card trade, or
b the average size of each credit card sale, or
c the amount of compensating balances kept at the bank, or
d some combination of all of these factors.

Service charge discounts range from nothing to 6 percent or more. Finally, the bank presents the sales draft to the credit card holder for payment.

2 The credit card holder can pay for the draft in full within a certain period of time (e.g., thirty days), and not be charged any interest on the credit extended, or he can repay a portion of the amount due and pay the remainder on an installment basis. The interest rate charged on the unpaid balance is based on each state's law. Banks depend on the interest from these credit extensions as their primary source of income from credit card operations.

3 The final feature is the plastic credit card itself, which serves a dual purpose. First, it identifies the customer to the merchant. Second, it is used to transfer account information to the sales draft by use of an imprinting machine.

Against this background, there are three basic types of credit card plans. The first type of plan utilizes a single principal bank to issue the credit card, maintain accounts, bill and collect credit, and assume most of the other functions associated with credit cards.

In the second type of plan, one bank acts as a limited agent for the principal bank. The principal bank issues the credit cards, carries the bulk of the credit, and performs the functions described in the first plan. The functions of the agent bank are to establish merchant accounts and accept merchant sales drafts; it receives a commission on the business it generates. This plan is used most often in states with unit or limited branch banking laws in order to provide wider geographic coverage. Of the almost 8,600 banks offering credit card plans, more than 60 percent are agency banks.

In the third type of plan, a bank affiliates with one of the major travel and entertainment card plans. The bank does not set up a credit card system but offers holders of the travel and entertainment card an optional line of credit. The credit card holder can pay his travel and entertainment card bill through the bank and can borrow directly from the bank against a pre-established line of credit. In this plan the bank becomes involved with transactions only if the credit card holder decides to pay the bill in installments or uses the line of credit.

*The Payments System*    As more credit card transactions take place, an increased volume of paper moves back and forth across the country. Assume that you have a Bank Americard issued by a bank in Dallas, Texas, and that you buy a meal at a restaurant in Seattle, Washington, and charge it on your bank credit card. The Seattle restaurant will send the sales draft to the bank that handles its Bank Americard transactions and receive immediate payment. That bank, in turn, mails the sales draft to the Dallas bank for collection. The Seattle bank will be paid by the Dallas bank, and the Dallas bank will present the sales draft to the credit card holder for his meal in Seattle.

Similar paperwork, but on a much larger scale, occurs when bills are paid by check. In January 1971, 21.5 billion checks were written by depositors on the nation's commercial banks.[10] To process these checks required the equivalent of 78,000 full-time employees and equipment worth $213 million. The direct expenses of processing these checks were estimated to be $650 million. In recognition of this problem, the Federal Reserve System has initiated regional check processing centers to speed up the transfer process. In addition, some banks have formed associations to develop uniform standards and procedures for exchanging automatic debits and credits via magnetic tapes or punch cards. The mass of paperwork in both the check system and the bank credit card system suggests that the existing methods of moving paper will give way to electronic recording, transmission, and manipulation of data.

As far as consumer credit is concerned, the electronic funds transfer system may look like this.[11] There will be two major elements in the system. The first is an electronic identifier that will provide positive identification of the user; this could be in the form of a credit card with the holder's photograph on it, or voiceprints, or fingerprints. Second, each merchant and bank in a given area will have an on-line computer terminal. The consumer wishing to make a purchase inserts his identifier in the retailer's remote terminal. The merchant is credited instantly, and the customer is charged with the purchase price. If there are sufficient funds in the customer's account, a green light will flash on the terminal. If there are insufficient funds, the customer can elect to borrow against a preauthorized line of credit. Then a green light flashes on again. If the amount outstanding exceeds the line of credit, a yellow light flashes on the remote terminal. At this point the consumer can ask the bank for more credit or the merchant can extend the credit. Thus, in the future, electronic transfers of funds will come to play an increasingly important role in consumer credit.

---

[10]Allen P. Stults, "The Role of Commercial Banks in Financing Consumption in the United States," in *The World Banking Challenge* (Washington, D.C.: The American Bankers Association, August 1972), pp. 115–136.
[11]The discussion of this system is based on information found in *Consumer Credit in the United States*, p. 205.

## Consumer Credit Regulation

As more people are extended consumer credit by means of loans and credit cards, the need for information concerning credit costs becomes more important. In 1968, Congress passed the Consumer Credit Protection Act (Public Law 90–321) and designated the Board of Governors of the Federal Reserve System to implement the Truth-in-Lending portion of that act (Title I).

*Regulation Z*    The Board of Governors of the Federal Reserve System issues its Truth-in-Lending directives under what is called Regulation Z. According to the Board of Governors, the stated purpose of Regulation Z is to let borrowers and customers know the cost of credit extended to them by any type of lender, so that these costs can be compared with other sources. Regulation Z deals with both consumers and credit lenders. On the consumer side, the regulation encompasses all credit extended to people for personal, family, or agricultural uses not exceeding $25,000, and all real estate transactions by individuals or for agricultural purposes. On the credit lender side, all those who extend credit to individuals for which a finance charge is payable, or which is repayable in more than four installments, are included under Regulation Z.

The two most important disclosures required by Regulation Z are the finance charge and the annual percentage rate (APR) charge on the loan. The finance charge is the sum of all charges payable by the borrower as a condition of the extension of credit; such charges may include interest, finder's fees, transaction or carrying charges, credit report fees, and insurance premiums if required to obtain credit. The annual percentage rate, which was discussed previously, represents the finance charge divided by the unpaid balance to which it applies on an annual basis. Both the finance

---

Figure 11–2

High legal interest rate

---

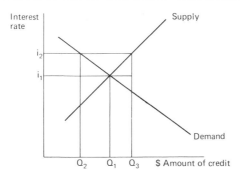

charge and the APR must be presented to the borrower before credit is extended.

Although the intent of Regulation Z is to make borrowers aware of the cost of credit, there is some evidence that the cost of credit makes little difference to individual low-income borrowers.[12] For example, a borrower may be used to making monthly payments of $100 per month on a car loan. If he wants to buy a new car, he will shop around to obtain financing where the monthly payment will remain $100 per month. Thus the level of interest rate charges affects the amount of his purchase but not his monthly payment of $100. The point is that such borrowers are more concerned about the size of the monthly payment than the interest rate being charged on the loan.

In contrast, there is evidence that middle- and upper-income borrowers are more concerned with credit costs,[13] so that the Truth-in-Lending Act seems to benefit them more than the lower-income borrowers who need it the most. Accordingly, the National Foundation for Consumer Credit and other groups have initiated programs to educate low-income and other borrowers about credit costs.

Finally, it should be noted that Regulation Z was designed to provide borrowers with information. It does *not* establish the maximum rates that can be charged. Such ceilings are determined by state law.

***Uniform Consumer Credit Code***　　In an attempt to make the credit law of several states uniform, a Uniform Consumer Credit Code has been adopted by six states (Oklahoma, Utah, Colorado, Idaho, Indiana, and Wyoming).

**Figure 11–3**

**Low legal interest rate**

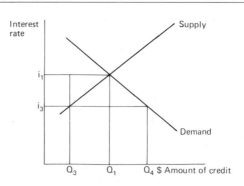

[12]F. Thomas Juster and Robert T. Shey, *Consumer Sensitivity to Finance Rates,* Occasional Paper no. 88 (New York: National Bureau of Economic Research, 1964).
[13]*Consumer Credit in the United States,* p. 177.

This model code sets maximum annual percentage rate ceilings of 24 percent on revolving charge accounts and 36 percent on small loans and sales credit. The designers of the code set the maximum interest rates artificially high in hopes that actual rates charged would be determined by the forces of supply and demand and would be substantially less than the ceiling rates.

The intent of the Uniform Consumer Credit Code can be depicted in graphic terms. As shown in Figure 11–2, $i_2$ represents the artificially high ceiling interest rate. At that rate the amount of credit demanded ($Q_2$) is less than the lenders are willing to supply ($Q_3$), and the interest rate that clears the market is $i_1$. However, there is another situation that should not be overlooked (see Figure 11–3). If the ceiling interest rate ($i_3$) is lower than the market-clearing interest rate, the amount of credit supplied ($Q_3$) will be less than the amount demanded ($Q_4$). This was the case in the late 1960s when market interest rates exceeded the ceilings set by state usury laws and lenders were unwilling to make certain types of loans.

The market interest rate and the amount of credit that lenders are willing to extend are influenced to a significant degree by monetary policy. In a recent study, it was shown that the amount of installment credit extended

---

Figure 11–4

Consumer installment credit held by selected large banks, retailers, and consumer durable goods manufacturers (December 31, 1972[a])

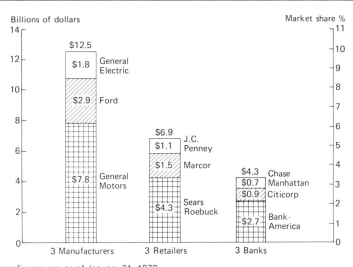

[a] Retail store figures are as of January 31, 1973
Source: Cleveland A. Christophe, *Competition in Financial Services* (New York: First National City Bank, 1974).

was reduced during periods of monetary restraint.[14] One explanation for this phenomenon is that bankers and other lenders allocated less funds to installment credit because they could make more money in other types of loans. Another explanation is that monetary restraint distorts the value of individuals' assets in such a way that they buy fewer goods and services, which in turn leads to a reduced demand for credit.[15] Figure 11–4 shows the amount of consumer installment credit held by several large manufacturers, retailers, and banks.

## Summary

The development of consumer credit institutions closely paralleled the development of the economy in the United States. This chapter traced such institutions from the colonial period up to the present time. Today, consumer credit is issued by a wide variety of financial institutions and business concerns. The latest developments in consumer credit are related to computer technology, and the electronic transfer of funds is likely to revolutionize the consumer credit industry. This chapter also examined the regulation of consumer credit.

## Questions

1  Explain how the advent of many consumer durables during the early part of the twentieth century affected the growth of consumer credit.
2  Discuss some of the major innovations in consumer credit since the year 1900.
3  Distinguish between noninstallment credit and installment credit. Which type accounts for the largest dollar amount of consumer credit?
4  Distinguish between the historical roles of sales finance companies and consumer finance companies and explain how these historical differences have tended to be reduced in recent years.
5  What are the differences between captive and independent sales finance companies? Why might a manufacturer establish a captive sales finance company?
6  Discuss the major features that are common to all bank credit card plans. What are several ways in which credit card plans differ?
7  The Truth-in-Lending Act (Federal Reserve Board Regulation Z) requires all consumer credit institutions to show borrowers the annual percentage

---

[14]Richard T. Selden, "Monetary Restraint and Installment Credit," in *Consumer Spending and Monetary Policy* (Federal Reserve Bank of Boston, 1971), pp. 289–318.
[15]*Ibid.*, p. 292.

rate (APR) on all loans. What rates are charged on consumer loans in your city by different types of lenders? What rates are charged on credit cards that you hold?

8  Does monetary policy affect the supply of consumer credit? Explain your answer.

9  Give your views on whether maximum legal interest rates on consumer credit should be high, low, or completely eliminated.

## Bibliography

Chapman, John M. and Robert P. Shay, eds. *The Consumer Finance Industry: Its Costs and Regulation*, A Report of the Graduate School of Business, Columbia University. New York: Columbia University Press, 1967.

Christophe, Cleveland A. *Competition in Financial Services*. New York: First National City Bank, 1974.

Cole, Robert H. *Consumer and Commercial Credit Management*. Homewood, Ill.: Richard D. Irwin, 1972.

Commission on Money and Credit, Report of The National Consumer Finance Association. *The Consumer Finance Industry*. Englewood Cliffs, N.J.: Prentice-Hall, 1962.

National Commission on Consumer Finance. *Consumer Credit in the United States*. Washington, D.C.: U.S. Government Printing Office, 1972.

# 12
# Federal credit agencies

This chapter examines the major federal credit agencies, which are particularly important in the mortgage market and farm credit system. In addition, current political and economic problems relating to these agencies are discussed. The chapter includes a statistical table showing the outstanding debt of all federal credit agencies, including some not covered in this chapter.

## Categories of Agencies

Federal credit agencies are defined here as those agencies, either of the federal government or closely allied to it, which are active in financial markets in order to obtain a portion of the funds necessary for their operations and to provide credit or stability of credit to some sectors of the economy.

Federal credit agencies are divided into two categories, agencies of the U.S. government and agencies *sponsored* by the U.S. government. There are two types of U.S. government credit agencies: those that continue to borrow in the credit markets and those that have not borrowed in the credit markets since 1969, when there was a change in government policies. Sponsored agencies are former federal government agencies, which have been converted to private ownership but retain ties to the federal government. A list of government and sponsored federal credit agencies is shown in Table 12–1.

Table 12–1

Federal credit agencies

Agencies sponsored by the U.S. government[a]
  Federal National Mortgage Association
  Federal Land Bank System
  Federal Intermediate Credit Bank System
  Banks for Cooperatives
  Federal Home Loan Bank System
  Federal Home Loan Mortgage Corporation
  Student Loan Marketing Association[b]

Agencies of the U.S. government that borrow in the credit markets
  Export-Import Bank of the United States
  Federal Housing Administration
  Rural Electrification Administration
  Environmental Financing Authority

Agencies of the U.S. government that no longer borrow in the credit markets
  Commodity Credit Corporation
  Government National Mortgage Association
  Department of Housing and Urban Development
  Veterans Administration
  Small Business Administration
  Farmers Home Administration
  Department of Health, Education, and Welfare

[a] All sponsored agencies deal in the credit markets
[b] Not in operation as of December 1973

## Mortgage-related Federal Credit Agencies

The federal credit agencies involved in mortgage-lending activity are: the Federal National Mortgage Association, the Federal Home Loan Bank System, the Federal Home Loan Mortgage Corporation, and the Federal Housing Administration. These credit agencies raise funds in the financial markets in order to make or insure mortgage loans. The Veterans Administration and Government National Mortgage Association, which are financed principally through the federal budget, are also involved in mortgage-lending activity.

### Federal National Mortgage Association

The Federal National Mortgage Association (FNMA or Fannie Mae) was chartered in 1938 to create a secondary market for home mortgages. Under the Housing Act of 1954, FNMA was restructured so that its secondary market operation would eventually be privately owned. The secondary market operations were converted to a private corporation on December 1, 1968. This action insured more effective operation of FNMA by removing it from the political and economic constraints which affect the federal budget.

There are currently outstanding 44.9 million shares of FNMA common stock traded on the New York Stock Exchange. The remaining assets that were not converted to a private corporation were turned over to the Government National Mortgage Association, which will be discussed shortly.

The primary purposes of the Federal National Mortgage Association are to improve the liquidity of home mortgages and lessen cyclical disruptions in the housing market. To accomplish this end FNMA makes commitments and buys Federal Housing Administration-insured (FHA), Veterans Administration-guaranteed (VA), and certain Farmers Home Administration-insured mortgages through the Free Market System Auction. Commitments to purchase conventional mortgages are made through a similar auction. Both auctions work in the following manner. FNMA determines the dollar volume of mortgage commitments that it is willing to accept. The commitments are made for four months or longer and are contracts to buy a block of mortgages at specified prices within a given period. Selected mortgage-lending institutions, such as mortgage bankers and insurance companies, pay a fee to bid on the price at which they are willing to sell their mortgages. FNMA accepts the high prices until the quota is filled. Details of several auctions are given in Table 12–2. They show that, throughout the period, the number of offers received was greater than the number accepted by a wide margin and the average yields were increasing. This indicates that mortgage lenders thought that mortgage interest rates were going to rise and funds would become scarce. Therefore, they wanted to be able to sell low-yielding mortgages to FNMA so they could make mortgage loans at higher interest rates in the future.

Mortgage-lending institutions only sell their mortgages to FNMA if they cannot get a better price elsewhere within the commitment period. FNMA also makes purchase commitments outside the auction system on large projects, such as hospitals, apartment complexes, and nursing homes. Generally, FNMA's mortgage purchases are made from institutions in regions where funds for mortgage lending are scarce, thus providing investment funds to capital-deficit areas, and it sells mortgages in regions where there are surplus funds, allowing these funds to be put to work in the mortgage market. In 1973, FNMA purchased $6.l billion in mortgages. At year end it held $24.1 billion in mortgages and had commitments outstanding of $7.7 billion.

FNMA derives the funds to purchase mortgages from commitment fees, from mortgage repayments from its portfolio, and from the sale of secondary securities such as debentures and short-term discount notes. At the end of 1973, FNMA had $23 billion outstanding in bonds, notes, and other debentures.

Table 12–2

Details of recent FHA/VA and conventional mortgage auctions

### FHA/VA

| Date | Offers received/accepted ($ millions) | Average yield/price | Yield/price range |
|------|----------------------------------------|---------------------|-------------------|
| FHA/VA rate at 9.5% effective with 8/26/74 auction | | | |
| 11/18/74 | 25.7–17.6 | 9.805 (97.94) | 9.852–9.759 (97.63) (98.25) |
| FHA/VA rate at 9% effective with 12/2/74 auction | | | |
| 12/2/74 | 52.4–23.3 | 9.608 (95.87) | 9.731–9.589 (95.07) (96.00) |
| 12/16/74 | 49.6–43.3 | 9.520 (96.46) | 9.589–9.485 (96.00) (96.69) |
| 12/30/74 | 35.7–31.8 | 9.471 (96.78) | 9.674–9.405 (95.44) (97.22) |
| 1/13/75 | 25.1–21.2 | 9.372 (97.45) | 9.500–9.305 (96.59) (97.90) |
| FHA/VA rate at 8.5% effective with 1/27/75 auction | | | |
| 1/27/75 | 41.4–28.6 | 9.119 (95.72) | 9.338–9.000 (94.26) (96.52) |

### Conventional

| Date | Offers received/accepted ($ millions) | Average yield | Yield range |
|------|----------------------------------------|---------------|-------------|
| FHA/VA rate at 9.5% effective with 8/26/74 auction | | | |
| 11/18/74 | 20.6–6.8 | 9.920 | 10.109–9.850 |
| FHA/VA rate at 9% effective with 12/2/74 auction | | | |
| 12/2/74 | 24.0–12.0 | 9.802 | 9.900–9.766 |
| 12/16/74 | 20.2–18.6 | 9.716 | 9.759–9.628 |
| 12/30/74 | 17.2–10.1 | 9.592 | 9.750–9.550 |
| 1/13/75 | 17.9–14.9 | 9.500 | 9.514–9.480 |
| FHA/VA rate at 8.5% effective with 1/27/75 auction | | | |
| 1/27/75 | 11.1–10.6 | 9.394 | 9.500–9.250 |

Source: Federal National Mortgage Association

Like any other financial intermediary, FNMA makes its money on the difference between its borrowing costs and its lending costs as well as from the yields on the mortgages that it holds and the commitment fees. When interest rates rise, FNMA buys mortgages with high interest rates and sells high-cost short-term notes to finance those purchases. When interest rates fall, FNMA refinances the short-term notes with lower-cost debentures, thereby locking in a profit. FNMA profits tend to fluctuate according to business activity.

## Federal Home Loan Bank System

The Federal Home Loan Bank (FHLB) System was established in 1932 to provide a central credit system for nonbank mortgage-lending institutions.

In essence, it is the equivalent of the Federal Reserve System for savings and loan associations and other types of mortgage lenders. The system consists of the Federal Home Loan Bank Board located in Washington, D.C., twelve regional Federal Home Loan Banks, and member institutions. All federally chartered savings and loan associations are required by law to be members of the system. Qualified state-chartered savings and loan associations, mutual savings banks, and life insurance companies may also join. At the end of 1972, the Federal Home Loan Bank System had 4,412 members—4,362 savings and loan associations, 48 savings banks, and 2 life insurance companies. These members own the stock of their respective regional home loan banks, and are entitled to borrow funds from these banks, elect some of the banks' directors, and receive dividends.

The regional Federal Home Loan Banks provide member institutions with a facility for depositing their excess funds, which amounted to $1.5 billion at the end of 1972. The regional banks also provide for the safekeeping and purchase and sale of U.S. government securities for their members. However, the most important function of the regional banks is making loans— so-called advances—to their members. The advances are secured by mortgages, U.S. government securities, or liens against the banks' capital stock. Such loans are made to meet unexpected withdrawals of savings and to increase the supply of mortgage funds. The maturity of advances ranges from thirty days to ten years; most have a maturity of about two years. The cost of borrowing is usually determined when the advance is made and depends on money market conditions at that time. Although the Federal Home Loan Bank Board determines general lending policies, regional banks establish the specific terms of credit for their members, taking into account local credit conditions and needs. Thus, the cost to members for borrowing will vary from district to district. At the end of 1972, the weighted average rate on advances ranged from 6.05 percent in the Indianapolis district to 6.71 percent in the San Francisco district.

In recent years, the dollar amount of advances made was closely related to monetary policy and money market conditions. For example, between May 1972 and May 1973, monetary policy became increasingly restrictive and short-term market interest rates increased sharply. During this period, the dollar volume of FHLB advances outstanding at savings and loan associations increased from $5.8 billion to $10.I billion.

The regional banks have three sources of funds which they can use to finance their loans. First, members of the system are required to buy the stock of their regional banks. They can then borrow an amount equal to twelve times the amount of stock that they hold. Second, the banks use member deposits as a source of funds, although only 25 percent of these deposits can be used for advances. Finally, the Federal Home Loan Bank

System sells consolidated obligations through a fiscal agent. These bonds are issued on an unsecured basis, but they are backed by the Federal Home Loan Bank System. Moreover, the Secretary of the Treasury can purchase up to $4 billion of FHLB obligations, and they are legal investments for fiduciary trusts and other financial institutions. As of May 1973, there were $9.6 billion in FHLB obligations outstanding.

The Federal Home Loan Bank Board is an independent agency of the executive branch. It consists of three members appointed by the president and confirmed by the Senate. No more than two of the board members can be from the same political party. The principal function of the board is to supervise the Federal Home Loan Bank System. This includes chartering and regulating all federal savings and loan associations and directing the Federal Savings and Loan Insurance Corporation and the Federal Home Loan Mortgage Corporation.

### Federal Home Loan Mortgage Corporation

The Federal Home Loan Mortgage Corporation (Freddy Mac) was organized under the Emergency Home Finance Act of 1970. All of its capital stock is held by the twelve regional Federal Home Loan Banks. Freddy Mac was created to make a secondary market for government-backed and conventional mortgage loans by buying mortgages and participations and selling securities backed by conventional and government-backed mortgages.

### Federal Housing Administration

The Federal Housing Administration (FHA) is a government agency created by the National Housing Act of 1934 to stimulate residential construction by insuring mortgage loans. Its primary functions are to aid in the expansion of the residential mortgage market and to improve housing standards. These functions are accomplished by the FHA's insurance programs and by the physical standards it sets for the insured properties. By insuring mortgages against default, the FHA has encouraged lenders to make loans they might not otherwise make and borrowers to take advantage of relatively low-interest loans. The FHA also subsidizes interest payments on some single-family and multifamily dwellings. At year-end 1972, the FHA had underwritten about one-fifth of all the nonfarm single-family mortgage debt outstanding and had insured more than $85 billion in mortgage loans.

The FHA insures loans for construction, purchase, improvement, or repair of residential property. The insurance programs are carried out through four major funds, the Mutual Mortgage Insurance Fund (single-family dwellings), the Cooperative Management Housing Insurance Fund (multifamily

dwellings), the General Insurance Fund (multifamily special-purpose dwellings), and the Special Risk Insurance Fund (central city dwellings and experimental housing).

The term *fund* as used in this text has a particular meaning. All federal government agencies are categorized as either corporations or funds. Government-owned corporations are created by enabling legislation, and their initial capital is obtained by issuing preferred stock to the Treasury. The funds considered here differ from corporations only in that the initial capitalization is made by appropriations, with no capital stock being issued. In essence, a fund may be considered a pseudo-corporation.

Since 1965, insurance claims have been paid from fees and premiums collected, income from investments, and by the issuance of debentures. The debentures are obligations of the particular funds against which the claims were made and are fully guaranteed by the federal government. Debentures of $453 million were outstanding as of the end of fiscal year 1973.

## Veterans Administration

The Veterans Administration (VA) is another government agency involved in mortgage credit. While the FHA insures mortgage loans, the VA guarantees mortgage loans. This means that if a borrower defaults on a mortgage loan, the VA purchases the property in question. At the end of 1972, the VA had guaranteed $42 billion in mortgages. Collectively, the FHA-VA government-backed mortgages account for one-fourth of the total nonfarm mortgage debt outstanding.

Prior to 1969, the VA issued debt securities, called participation certificates,[1] and sold property acquired through foreclosure or other means to raise funds. Since that time, it has had to rely primarily on the sale of property for income.

## Government National Mortgage Association

The Government National Mortgage Association (GNMA or Ginnie Mae) was created in 1968 to handle some of the assets of the Federal National Mortgage Association, which was reorganized at that time. Ginnie Mae is a government-owned corporation that operates within the Department of Housing and Urban Development. It deals in the mortgage market through

---

[1] A participation certificate (PC) gives the purchaser a share of the principal and interest payments made on a pool of loans held by the issuing agency. Since 1969, no government agencies (except the Export-Import Bank and the Federal Home Loan Mortgage Corporation) have issued securities called PC's, but they have dealt in similar securities called by other names. For example, the Government National Mortgage Association guarantees pass-through securities.

two funds and several other programs. First, the Management and Liquidation Functions Fund is responsible for the disposal of mortgages acquired from FNMA and other government agencies. Second, the Special Assistance Functions Fund was created to improve the liquidity of mortgages of low- and middle-income housing projects, as well as other types of residential mortgages. Purchases of mortgages by these funds are made on a commitment basis under a tandem program, which consists of a tandem arrangement between GNMA and FNMA for loan purchases. Ginnie Mae issues commitments to buy mortgages, which are then sold to Fannie Mae at the current market price. Any loss is absorbed by Ginnie Mae (except on Section 236 mortgages on multifamily dwellings for lower-income families). At the end of 1972, GNMA had a loan portfolio of $5.1 billion.

In addition to the above funds, there is a program through which Ginnie Mae guarantees the payment of interest and principal on securities backed by pools of FHA and/or VA mortgages. These securities are issued by GNMA-approved financial institutions, such as savings and loan associations, and are fully guaranteed by the U.S. government. Technically, they are called "fully guaranteed pass-through mortgage-backed securities." Ginnie Mae approved the issue of $1.5 billion worth of these securities during the first six months of 1973.

Ginnie Mae finances its operations by borrowing from the Treasury and from mortgage loan repayments and sales. Prior to 1969, participation certificates were also used.

**The Farm Credit System**

The farm credit system consists of three agencies—Federal Land Banks, Federal Intermediate Credit Banks, and Banks for Cooperatives— supervised by the Farm Credit Administration. All three agencies are controlled by farmers to meet their specialized needs.

Structure

The United States is divided into twelve Farm Credit districts. In each district a Federal Land Bank, a Federal Intermediate Credit Bank, and a Bank for Cooperatives are located at the same place. The twelve district cities are: Springfield, Massachusetts; Baltimore, Maryland; Columbia, South Carolina; Louisville, Kentucky; St. Louis, Missouri; New Orleans, Louisiana; St. Paul, Minnesota; Omaha, Nebraska; Wichita, Kansas; Houston, Texas; Berkeley, California; and Spokane, Washington. The central Bank for Cooperatives is located in Washington, D.C. As shown in Figure 12–1, farmers who are stockholders elect the board of directors of local

Figure 12–1

How farmers share in control of the cooperative farm credit system

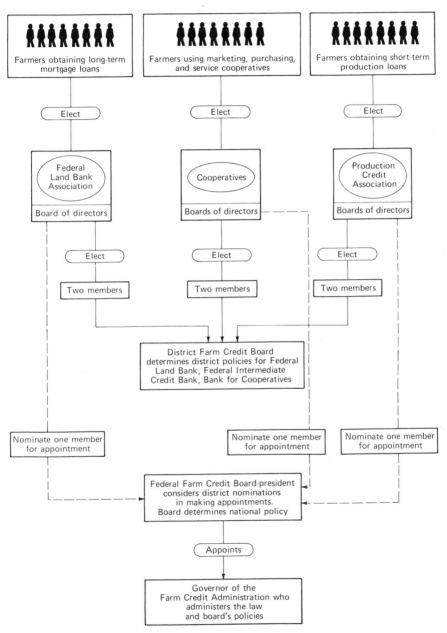

Source: Farm Credit Administration

Federal Land Bank associations, Production Credit Associations, and cooperatives that use Banks for Cooperatives. The directors of the associations and cooperatives in turn elect two members each to the district Farm Credit board. This board consists of seven members, six elected by the farmers and the seventh appointed by the governor of the Farm Credit Administration, and its function is to determine policies for its district. In other words, the three banks in a district have the same board of directors. In addition, the local associations nominate one member for the federal Farm Credit Board. This board determines national farm credit policies and appoints the governor of the Farm Credit Administration, who in turn administers the board's policies and applicable federal law.

## Federal Land Banks

The three farm credit agencies each provide farmers with credit to meet different needs. Federal Land Bank associations make long-term loans to farmers, backed by first mortgages on farm real estate. The Land Banks make loans to farmers through local associations that endorse and service the loans. Those borrowing funds must purchase stock in the association in an amount equal to 5 percent of the loan and pledge that stock as additional collateral against the loan. The association, in turn, buys an equal amount of stock from its district federal land bank. The latter stock serves as collateral for the association's endorsement of the loan to the farmer. Both stock issues are retired when the loan is repaid.

As of June 30, 1972, Federal Land Banks had $7.58 billion in farms loans outstanding. The bulk of the loans were used to purchase real estate, but some loans were also made to purchase livestock and equipment. The Federal Land Banks are authorized to make loans on nonfarm rural homes and to some businesses that provide farm services.

## Federal Intermediate Credit Banks

Federal Intermediate Credit Banks provide credit for Production Credit Associations (PCAs), commercial banks, and livestock loan companies. Production Credit Associations are local farm-credit organizations chartered by the Farm Credit Administration to make secured loans to their members—other than for real estate—and to aid in the production of all kinds of farm products such as grains, cattle, and so on. Borrowers must purchase stock in the PCAs equal to 5 percent of their loans. The PCAs invest these funds in approved securities such as obligations of the federal government. These approved securities and the loans to borrowers (borrower paper) are discounted at the district Federal Intermediate Credit Bank. Commercial banks, agricultural credit corporations, and livestock loan companies may also discount qualified borrower paper at district

Federal Intermediate Credit Banks. As of June 30, 1972, the Federal Intermediate Credit Banks had $5.9 billion in loans outstanding. Of that amount, 88 percent went to PCAs.

## Bank for Cooperatives

The Banks for Cooperatives make secured loans to farmer-owned cooperatives—business concerns that are financed, controlled, and operated by the agricultural producers they serve. Cooperatives provide farmers with equipment and supplies and a marketing outlet for their farm products. There are 7,289 of them in the United States. As of June 30, 1972, about 3,000 cooperatives had borrowed $2 billion from the Banks for Cooperatives. On average, each cooperative borrowed $666,000. These figures indicate that there are some large cooperatives and that the Banks for Cooperatives make large loans. In contrast, the average size of loans made by Federal Land Banks is $18,700.

The Federal Land Bank, the Federal Intermediate Credit Bank, and the Bank for Cooperatives issue their own securities. Each agency's security is the joint obligation of its respective district banks and is backed by the collateral specified for each. The securities consist of notes and debentures. They are legal investments for national banks, federal credit unions, federal savings and loan associations and all trust funds under the jurisdiction of the U.S. government; they can also be used by commercial banks as collateral against advances made by Federal Reserve Banks. The gross income from the debentures is exempt from state and local income taxes.

As shown in Table 12–3, during the 1965–1970 period the amount of debt issued by the farm system almost doubled. By fiscal 1974, the amount of farm system debt was expected to reach $19 billion. Federal Land Banks account for about one-half of the total farm system debt outstanding. Federal Intermediate Credit Banks are the next largest issuer, accounting for nearly 40 percent.

Table 12–3

Farm credit system debt in selected fiscal years (billions of dollars)[a]

| Banks | 1965 | 1970 | 1974 (estimated) |
|---|---|---|---|
| Federal Land Banks | 3.5 | 6.1 | 9.3 |
| Federal Intermediate Credit Banks | 2.5 | 4.9 | 7.6 |
| Banks for Cooperatives | 0.7 | 1.5 | 2.1 |
| Total | 6.7 | 12.5 | 19.0 |

[a] Treasury debt outstanding
Sources: *Treasury Bulletin*, February 1973 (Washington, D.C.: U.S. Government Printing Office), Tables FD–6 and FD–7; *The Budget of the U.S. Government, 1974—Appendix* (Washington, D.C.: U.S. Government Printing Office)

All three banks jointly use a single fiscal agent (located in New York City), who markets their bonds to security dealers and to banks located throughout the United States. He also handles the investment needs of the banks and their respective associations.

## Miscellaneous Credit Agencies

### Export-Import Bank of the United States

The Export-Import Bank of the United States (Eximbank) is a government-owned corporation that aids in the sale of U.S. exports and the purchase of imports.

The bank maintains offices in major cities throughout the world (except Communist nations). Through these offices the bank can make loans to importers for the purchase of U.S. goods. In addition, loans from private sources may be guaranteed or insured by the Eximbank. U.S. importers receive the same services to purchase goods from abroad. As of June 30, 1972, the Eximbank had $5.96 billion of loans outstanding and had guaranteed $2.12 billion worth of loans.

The Eximbank finances its operations through income generated from loans and fees and from the sale of participation certificates (PC's). A PC is a debt instrument that gives the holder a share in the principal and interest payments made on a pool of loans held by the issuing agency. Before 1968, PC's were considered to be sales of assets, thus resulting in the decrease of assets rather than the increase of liabilities. However, in 1967–1968 the Commission on Budget Concepts declared PC's to be basically the same as debt instruments issued by the Treasury and recommended that they be considered as liabilities of the agencies. This recommendation was accepted in 1968. One result of this redefinition was the discontinuance of the sale of PC's by the majority of the agencies involved, because agencies under the federal budget did not want to increase their liabilities for political reasons. Since the Eximbank is not under the federal budget, it continues to issue PC's.

### Rural Electrification Administration

The Rural Electrification Administration was established in 1936 to provide financial aid for the development of electric and telephone service in rural areas. Since then, funds for this purpose have been provided by appropriations from the federal budget. However, in 1971, a new federal credit agency, the Rural Telephone Bank, was created to provide supplemental financing for the telephone program. This new agency was initially capitalized through the sale of stock to the Treasury. Further capitalization

will require borrowers to purchase stock, and, in this manner, the bank will eventually be transferred to complete private ownership. Additional capital for lending purposes will be raised through the issuance of debentures.

## Environmental Financing Authority

The newest of the federal credit agencies, the Environmental Financing Authority (EFA), was created by Congress under the Environmental Financing Act of 1972 and became operational in 1974. The EFA deals in the obligations and participations of state and local agencies which have been issued to finance the construction of waste-treatment works. The purpose is to improve the liquidity of such obligations and to encourage the construction of these facilities. Financing of the EFA will initially come from the Treasury, but the agency has been authorized to issue debt instruments for future financing.

## Current Problems

The federal credit agencies gained increased importance in 1968, when the Federal National Mortgage Association, Federal Intermediate Credit Bank System, and Banks for Cooperatives were transferred from government to private ownership to remove them from the political and economic restraints of the federal budget. When these agencies were included in the budget, borrowing to finance their operations was part of the federal debt and subject to the restrictions and approval of Congress. It was believed by many that such constraints kept the agencies from achieving their full potential. Political considerations were also important. During the late 1960s, the economy was experiencing a period of inflation and large budget deficits. In fiscal 1968, for example, budget deficits ranged from $11.9 billion on a National Income Accounts basis to $25.2 billion on a Unified Budget basis. (In fiscal 1969, however, there were budget surpluses.) Budget deficits were not politically popular, and removal of the agencies reduced the apparent size of the debt. In 1972, the Export-Import Bank was also removed from the budget, although it remains a government corporation.

Many of the agencies were created during the Depression to provide a special function which private enterprise could not or would not provide at the time. In the years since their creation, the agencies have so firmly established themselves that little or no private competition has arisen, and they remain, for the most part, a major source of funds for the sectors of the economy they serve.

In addition, the securities of these agencies, even the private ones, have certain advantages which allow them to raise funds with less cost than

some of the largest corporations. For example, in 1972 the average yield on seasoned five-year agency issues and U.S. government issues was 6.13 and 5.90 percent, respectively. The average yields on new issue five-year utilities, industrials, and rails were 6.65, 6.60, and 6.58 percent, respectively.[2] The securities of government-owned agencies have the characteristics of comparable treasury securities, while the securities of sponsored agencies receive tax advantages, investment approval for financial institutions, and an implied federal guarantee.

Another point is that the federal government has on occasion used the sponsored agencies to aid in the implementation of new credit programs. For example, the Federal National Mortgage Association receives an interest-rate subsidy to improve the return on certain mortgages which it purchases. Housing, agriculture, and the balance of trade have always been major concerns of the federal government, and many programs exist in these areas besides those described here. Continued federal support to these sectors, complementary to a general expansion of the economy, has resulted in increased capital demands from these sectors and the use of the federal credit agencies.

### Impact on Credit Markets

The federal credit agency debt has had an important impact on the credit markets. As shown in Table 12–4, total credit agency debt increased from $15.6 billion in 1965, to an estimated $69.2 billion in 1974. Some idea of its impact on credit markets can be gained by comparing the amount of funds raised by credit agencies with the total amount of funds raised in credit markets: credit agencies accounted for 10 percent of the total funds raised in 1970. In spite of the increased amount of debt issued in recent years, federal credit agencies accounted for only 2 percent of the funds raised in 1972. The increase in the federal credit agency debt outstanding reflects the growing role of government in the economy (see Table 12–5). The federal credit agencies can be classified into three broad categories. In the first category are agencies concerned with mortgage-lending activity: the Federal National Mortgage Association, Federal Home Loan Bank System, and the Federal Housing Administration. In 1974, these three agencies accounted for 59 percent of the total agency debt and the data in Table 12–4 indicate that they are becoming increasingly important. The federal government is increasing its role in the housing market by subsidizing, insuring, guaranteeing, buying, and selling mortgage loans. Through such programs, it "federalized" $37.5 billion of the $64.4 billion mortgage credit raised in 1972. The government is translating social priorities into dollars by channeling more than half of the federal credit agency debt into the housing sector of the economy.

---

[2] *Bond Market Roundup,* Salomon Brothers, Members of the New York Stock Exchange.

Table 12–4

Federal credit agency debt in selected fiscal years (billions of dollars)[a]

| | 1965 | 1968 | 1970 |
|---|---|---|---|
| Federal National Mortgage Association | 1.80 | 5.89 | 13.17 |
| Federal Home Loan Bank System | 4.75 | 4.70 | 9.91 |
| Federal Land Banks | 3.53 | 5.32 | 6.19 |
| Federal Intermediate Credit Banks | 2.53 | 3.78 | 4.94 |
| Export-Import Bank of the United States | 1.02 | 2.57 | 1.89 |
| Federal Home Loan Mortgage Corporation | — | — | — |
| Banks for Cooperatives | 0.71 | 1.23 | 1.53 |
| Federal Housing Administration | 0.57 | 0.55 | 0.52 |
| Environmental Financing Authority | — | — | — |
| Rural Electrification Administration | — | — | — |
| Total federal credit agency debt | 14.92 | 23.34 | 38.15 |
| Other[b] | 0.27 | 8.82 | 7.32 |
| Total agency debt | 15.64 | 32.86 | 45.47 |

| | 1972 | 1974 (estimated) |
|---|---|---|
| Federal National Mortgage Association | 18.56 | 24.66 |
| Federal Home Loan Bank System | 7.08 | 12.28 |
| Federal Land Banks | 7.60 | 9.29 |
| Federal Intermediate Credit Banks | 6.19 | 7.57 |
| Export-Import Bank of the United States | 1.82 | 4.94 |
| Federal Home Loan Mortgage Corporation | 1.62 | 3.59 |
| Banks for Cooperatives | 1.81 | 2.15 |
| Federal Housing Administration | 0.45 | 0.41 |
| Environmental Financing Authority | — | 0.12 |
| Rural Electrification Administration | — | 0.30 |
| Total federal credit agency debt | 45.13 | 64.86 |
| Other[b] | 4.70 | 4.36 |
| Total agency debt | 49.83 | 69.22 |

[a] Treasury debt outstanding
[b] Includes agencies which were classified as federal credit agencies prior to 1966: the Commodity Credit Corporation, Government National Mortgage Association, Department of Housing and Urban Development, Veterans Administration, Small Business Administration, Farmers Home Administration, Department of Health, Education and Welfare
Sources: *Treasury Bulletin*, February 1973 (Washington, D.C.: U.S. Government Printing Office), Tables FD-6, FD-7, and T50-5; *The Budget of the United States Government, 1974—Appendix* (Washington, D.C.: U.S. Government Printing Office)

One side effect of these programs has been to undermine the effectiveness of monetary policy on the economy. Traditionally, restrictive monetary policy had its initial major impact on the housing market. As a result of the agency programs developed in recent years, this impact has been reduced somewhat.

Another social priority of the government is agriculture. The three federal credit agencies concerned with this sector of the economy are the Federal Land Bank System, Federal Intermediate Credit Bank System, and Banks for Cooperatives. Collectively, these farm credit agencies account for 28

Table 12-5

Outstanding debt of federal credit agencies for fiscal years 1964–1974 (millions of dollars)

| | 1964 | 1965 | 1966 | 1967 | 1968 | 1969 |
|---|---|---|---|---|---|---|
| Export-Import Bank | 827 | 1,022 | 1,385 | 2,164 | 2,571 | 2,472 |
| Federal Housing Administration | 793 | 570 | 441 | 492 | 548 | 577 |
| Rural Electrification Administration | — | — | — | — | — | — |
| Environmental Financing Authority | — | — | — | — | — | — |
| Commodity Credit Corporation | 377 | 419 | 855 | 1,021 | 923 | 1,590 |
| GNMA | — | 200 | 785 | 1,475 | 1,891 | 1,897 |
| HUD, Office of Secretary | — | — | — | 680 | 1,820 | 2,433 |
| Veterans Administration | — | 100 | 975 | 1,175 | 1,704 | 1,885 |
| Small Business Administration | — | — | 350 | 800 | 1,160 | 1,007 |
| Farmers Home Administration | — | — | — | 600 | 1,125 | 1,166 |
| HEW | — | — | — | 100 | 200 | 212 |
| Total federal agency debt | 1,997 | 2,311 | 4,791 | 8,507 | 11,942 | 13,239 |
| FNMA | 1,699 | 1,797 | 3,269 | 4,079 | 5,887 | 8,076 |
| Federal Land Banks | 2,974 | 3,532 | 4,106 | 4,612 | 5,319 | 5,720 |
| FICBs | 2,369 | 2,529 | 2,893 | 3,363 | 3,779 | 4,240 |
| Banks for Cooperatives | 525 | 709 | 881 | 1,072 | 1,230 | 1,411 |
| Federal Home Loan Banks | 4,201 | 4,757 | 6,310 | 4,588 | 4,702 | 5,524 |
| FHLMC | — | — | — | — | — | — |
| SLMA | — | — | — | — | — | — |
| Total sponsored debt[a] | 11,768 | 13,325 | 17,459 | 17,714 | 20,917 | 24,971 |
| Total federal credit agency debt | 13,765 | 15,636 | 22,250 | 26,221 | 32,859 | 38,210 |

| | 1970 | 1971 | 1972 | 1973 (est.) | 1974 (est.) |
|---|---|---|---|---|---|
| Export-Import Bank | 1,893 | 2,625 | 1,819 | 2,787 | 4,494 |
| Federal Housing Administration | 517 | 487 | 454 | 383 | 411 |
| Rural Electrification Administration | — | — | — | 30 | 120 |
| Environmental Financing Authority | — | — | — | — | 300 |
| Commodity Credit Corporation | — | — | — | — | — |
| GNMA | 1,707 | 1,626 | 1,433 | 1,353 | 1,304 |
| HUD, Office of Secretary | 2,109 | 1,146 | 741 | 702 | 702 |
| Veterans Administration | 1,749 | 1,650 | 1,543 | 1,295 | 1,234 |
| Small Business Administration | 782 | 691 | 485 | 441 | 441 |
| Farmers Home Administration | 765 | 685 | 517 | 482 | 482 |
| HEW | 209 | 207 | 201 | 197 | 197 |
| Total federal agency debt | 9,731 | 9,117 | 7,198 | 7,670 | 9,685 |
| FNMA | 13,165 | 14,996 | 18,560 | 21,589 | 24,659 |
| Federal Land Banks | 6,192 | 6,652 | 7,603 | 8,434 | 9,290x |
| FICBs | 4,942 | 5,705 | 6,188 | 6,811 | 7,567 |
| Banks for Cooperatives | 1,529 | 1,790 | 1,848 | 1,978 | 2,147 |
| Federal Home Loan Banks | 9,914 | 7,923 | 7,077 | 9,011 | 12,279 |
| FHLMC | — | 615 | 1,615 | 2,090 | 3,590 |
| SLMA | — | — | — | — | n.a. |
| Total sponsored debt[a] | 35,742 | 37,681 | 42,638 | 49,913 | 59,532 |
| Total federal credit agency debt | 45,473 | 46,798 | 49,830 | 57,583 | 69,217 |

[a] Prior to 1969, the Federal National Mortgage Association, Banks for Cooperatives, and Federal Intermediate Credit Banks were U.S. government-owned corporations and are generally included in Federal Agency debt for those years. The data have been rearranged here for easier reading.
Sources: *Treasury Bulletin,* February 1973 (Washington, D.C.: U.S. Government Printing Office), Tables FD-6 and FD-7, and *The Budget of the United States Government, 1974—Appendix* (Washington, D.C.: U.S.

percent of the total agency debt. During the 1965–1974 period, the amount of debt outstanding at these agencies will have tripled.

The final category consists of the remaining agencies—the Export-Import Bank of the United States, Environmental Financing Authority, and Rural Electrification Administration—which have no common area of concern.

### Federal Financing Bank

In December 1971, a bill was introduced before the U.S. Senate to create the Federal Financing Bank. The bank's purpose would be to coordinate the borrowing of federal agencies with that of the Treasury in an effort to reduce competition in the capital markets, and thus reduce the overall cost of federal borrowing. It is not a bank in the conventional sense of the word, as it would actually be a part of the Treasury, functioning like a traffic cop, to insure there were no traffic jams in the government securities market. In addition, it would be able to issue some debt. While the concept is sound, it is doubtful whether the bank could appreciably change current practices for two reasons. First, in the proposed bill sponsored agencies such as FNMA, FHLBs, FLBs, FICBs, and the Bank for Cooperatives would be excluded from participation in it. Second, all federal agencies (Eximbank, Environmental Financing Authority, Rural Electrification Administration, etc.) are currently required by law to coordinate their borrowing with the Treasury. Thus, the major users of funds could not use the bank.[3]

### Summary

Federal credit agencies exert an important influence on the mortgage market and farm credit system, since they reflect social priorities of the government in housing and agriculture. There are also agencies dealing in other sectors of the economy. In recent years, there has been a marked tendency to transfer federal agencies to private ownership. Such action has removed the agencies from the federal budget and has had certain political advantages.

### Questions

1 Distinguish between agencies of the U.S. government and agencies sponsored by the U.S. government. Give examples of agencies in each category.

---

Government Printing Office). Estimates for 1973 and 1974 and all data on the Federal Home Loan Mortgage Corporation were taken from the *Statement of Financial Condition* of each agency.
[3]For further information see U.S., Congress, Senate, Committee on Banking, Housing and Urban Affairs, *Federal Financing Authority: Hearings* (Washington, D.C.: U.S. Government Printing Office, May, 1972) and *Symposium on Government Agency Finance* (Washington, D.C.: Federal Home Loan Bank Board, 1972).

2 Describe the major purposes of the Federal National Mortgage Association (FNMA). Discuss how FNMA pursues these objectives through its operations in the Free Market System Auction.

3 What are the Federal National Mortgage Association's major sources and uses of funds?

4 Describe the organizational structure of the Federal Home Loan Bank System. What are the major purposes of the system?

5 Explain how the Federal National Mortgage Association, the Federal Home Loan Mortgage Corporation, and the Government National Mortgage Association help provide a secondary market for mortgages.

6 Describe the major objective of the Federal Housing Administration and discuss what policies and programs are used to help achieve this objective.

7 What are the three agencies that comprise the farm credit system? In which types of loans do these agencies specialize and how do their loan programs differ?

8 Explain the objectives of the Export-Import bank and describe its main sources and uses of funds.

9 Explain what you feel to be the overall rationale for the establishment of the various federal credit agencies.

10 If the Federal Financing Bank is established, what effect will it have on the securities market operations of most federal agencies?

# Bibliography

*Handbook of Securities of the United States Government and Federal Agencies*. Boston: The First Boston Corporation, 1972.

*Money Market Instruments*. Federal Reserve Bank of Cleveland, 1970.

Robinson, Roland I. *Money and Capital Markets*. New York: McGraw-Hill, 1964.

Robinson, Roland I., and Dwayne Wrightsman. *Financial Markets: The Accumulation and Allocation of Wealth*. New York: McGraw-Hill, 1974.

*The U.S. Government Securities Market*. Harris Trust and Savings Bank, Chicago, 1973.

Van Horne, James C. *The Function and Analysis of Capital Market Rates*. Englewood Cliffs, N.J.: Prentice-Hall, 1970.

Woodworth, G. Walter. *The Money Market and Monetary Management*. New York: Harper and Row, 1965.

# 13

# Mortgage banking companies

Mortgage banking companies play an important role in mortgage-lending activity. They transfer funds to parts of the country where money is needed to make mortgage loans, and then service these mortgages for mortgage lenders. This chapter examines the structure of the industry, the assets and liabilities of mortgage banking companies, and the servicing of mortgage loans. The chapter concludes with a description of some of the major problems facing the industry.

## Mortgage Lenders

Mortgage banking companies are financial intermediaries that specialize in buying and selling government-backed (FHA-VA) mortgages. They make mortgage and construction loans to individuals, developers, and builders, and, in turn, sell these loans to institutional investors such as life insurance companies. Mortgage banking companies help to allocate financial resources by taking funds from areas where there is an abundance of capital and investing them in areas where there is a scarcity of capital. Thus, mortgage bankers located in Florida may sell mortgages to investors located in Oregon.

In recent years, 22 percent of the total residential loans made were originated by mortgage banking companies, making them the second largest mortgage lender after savings and loan associations. In addition, they are

able to service mortgage loans for institutional investors by collecting mortgage loan payments and the principal and taxes on mortgages owned by their institutional investors.

## Structure of Industry

At the end of 1973, 742 mortgage banking companies were members of the Mortgage Bankers Association of America.[1] As shown in Table 13-1, the largest number of the companies service mortgage portfolios of less than $20 million. However, the total amount of mortgages serviced by these small companies is less than 2 percent of the total mortgages serviced by the entire industry. The data also reveal that the number of firms diminishes steadily as the size of the portfolios increases. The 155 firms with portfolios in excess of $200 million account for 72 percent of total mortgage loans serviced.

## Assets of Mortgage Banking Companies

Because of the nature of the mortgage banking business, only a small proportion of the banking companies' assets are held in liquid form. As shown in Table 13-2, cash and marketable securities account for less than 5 percent of total assets. The remaining assets consist mostly of land and buildings owned by the mortgage companies. The reader should keep in mind that the mortgage loans serviced are owned by investors and *not* by the mortgage banking companies. Accordingly, the asset size of mortgage banking companies is usually smaller than the size of the portfolios that they service.

Table 13-1

Size distribution of mortgage banking companies (1973)*

| Size of servicing portfolios ($ millions) | Number of firms | Total mortgages serviced ($ millions) | Percentage of total mortgages serviced |
|---|---|---|---|
| Under 20 | 197 | 1,663 | 1.48 |
| 20–50 | 148 | 4,986 | 4.45 |
| 50–100 | 131 | 9,515 | 8.50 |
| 100–200 | 111 | 15,082 | 13.47 |
| 200–400 | 90 | 25,515 | 22.79 |
| 400–800 | 42 | 24,741 | 22.10 |
| 800 and over | 23 | 30,440 | 27.19 |
| Total | 742 | 111,943 | 100.00 |

* Totals may not add due to rounding.
Source: Mortgage Bankers Association of America, Economics and Research Department, Trends Report no. 15

[1]Data for nonmembers are not available.

Table 13–2

Percent distribution of assets of mortgage banking companies (1973)

| | |
|---|---|
| Cash (except escrows and other fiduciary accounts) | 2.0 |
| Marketable securities at cost | 1.7 |
| Receivables | 2.6 |
| Inventories | 82.7 |
| Other current assets | 1.8 |
| Total current assets | 90.8 |
| Noncurrent assets | 9.2 |
| Total | 100.0 |

Source: Mortgage Bankers Association of America, Economics and Research Department, Trends Report no. 12

As Table 13–2 shows, inventories are mortgage bankers' largest single asset, accounting for 82.7 percent of total assets. The amount of mortgages that they hold in inventory for their own accounts depends in part on the difference between the rates at which they borrow and the rates they receive on mortgage loans. When mortgage banking companies receive higher interest rates from mortgages than from the cost of borrowing, they add to their inventories. For example, in 1972, the average yield on new FHA mortgages was 7½ percent, while the prime rate at commercial banks increased from 4⅜ percent to 6 percent. Thus, the difference or spread between the borrowing and lending rates was large enough to encourage mortgage banking companies to increase their inventories. However, by year-end 1973, the average yield on FHA mortgages was 8.8 percent and the prime rate was 10 percent, which discouraged the building of bankers' inventories.

Another factor that influenced the size of inventories in 1972 was that savings and loan associations were willing to pay premiums for closed mortgage loans that could be delivered immediately. (A mortgage loan is considered closed when the lender consummates the transaction by exchange of a deed for consideration.) At that time, some savings and loan associations were receiving larger savings inflows than they could lend out in mortgage loans in their own geographic areas.

Finally, mortgage companies hold mortgages until they have a sufficiently large amount to sell investors, usually blocks of $1 million or more. Obviously, large amounts of capital are needed to assemble these blocks. To obtain the necessary funds, mortgage banking companies use mortgages they own as collateral to borrow funds from commercial banks for short periods of time. This process is called *warehousing*.

Mortgage bankers handle all the paperwork generally associated with making mortgage loans—obtaining credit reports and appraisals and pre-

paring relevant financial information for investors about the properties and borrowers for a given block of mortgages. For their services, they receive an origination fee from the borrower. These fees range from 1 to 5 percent of the amount of the loan and are an important source of income for mortgage bankers; in 1973, origination fees accounted for 31.4 percent of their gross income.

## Liabilities of Mortgage Banking Companies

The two most important liabilities of mortgage banking firms are notes payable to commercial banks and notes payable to others. Of the two, notes payable to commercial banks are by far the largest liability (see Table 13–3). These notes represent mortgages that are warehoused at commercial banks and lines of credit that are based on the mortgage bankers' financial strength and past history. In addition, some credit is extended on commitments from investors. A *commitment* is a contract stating that a particular financial institution will buy a specified dollar amount of mortgages from a mortgage banker, and specifying the interest rates and dates when the mortgages must be closed. For example, an investor may agree to buy, before a stated date, a $1-million block of mortgages that will yield 8 percent. With this type of arrangement, called an *allocation* commitment, the mortgage banker uses his best effort to obtain the types of mortgages called for in the contract, although there is no penalty if he is unable to do so. There is also a *direct* commitment, which does obligate the mortgage company to produce the full amount of mortgages and at the rates agreed upon in the contract. Direct commitments are considered investments by the investors who negotiate them. Failure on the part of a mortgage banker to fulfill such contracts is a serious matter, because he may lose his reputation and, in turn, income.

The other important liability, notes payable to others, consists largely of commercial paper (unsecured promissory notes) issued by mortgage bank-

Table 13–3

Percent distribution of liabilities and equity of mortgage banking companies (1973)

| | |
|---|---|
| Notes payable to banks | 46.3 |
| Notes payable to others | 36.3 |
| Accounts payable | 1.8 |
| Other current liabilities | 2.0 |
| Total current liabilities | 86.4 |
| Noncurrent liabilities | 4.8 |
| Shareholders' equity | 8.8 |
| Total | 100.0 |

Source: Mortgage Bankers Association of America, Economics and Research Department, Trends Report no. 14

ers to obtain short-term credit. Until January 1973, the 4- to 6-month prime commercial paper rate was lower than the prime rate charged by commercial banks. As a result, mortgage banking companies borrowed heavily in the commercial paper market although, as a general rule, only the large-sized firms issue commercial paper, because it is not economical for small firms to sell small dollar amounts of paper.

## Mortgage Loan Servicing

In addition to buying and selling mortgages, mortgage banking companies service mortgage loans for institutional investors. As previously noted, the term *servicing* refers to collection of payments, principal, escrow for taxes, and insurance, and foreclosure if necessary. Mortgage bankers receive fees based on the outstanding principal balance of the mortgages serviced. Typically, the fees range from ⅜ to 1 percent of the principal amount. In 1972, servicing fees accounted for 31 percent of the total income of mortgage banking firms.

Seventy-five percent of the mortgages that mortgage bankers service are on single-family loans, and of that amount, 69 percent are FHA-VA mortgages; 24 percent are on multifamily and commercial dwellings; only 1 percent are farm and range mortgages.

Servicing may be quite attractive to an investor, particularly if he does not have the facilities to do it himself. Also, because of the mortgage banker's specialization and expertise in the mortgage markets, he is usually able to service mortgages at a lower cost than if the investor serviced his own. Finally, it is costly and inconvenient for investors in one part of the country to service mortgages in another part of the country: it is far easier to let a mortgage banker do it.

In descending order, mortgage bankers sell their largest dollar volume of loans to life insurance companies, savings and loan associations, and the Federal National Mortgage Association. The purchases made by savings and loan associations from mortgage bankers increased from $2.4 billion in 1970 to $4.2 billion in 1973, but mortgage bankers still *service* more mortgages for life insurance companies than for any other type of financial institution. In fact, the proportion of mortgage loans serviced for life insurance companies (30.8 percent) is only slightly less than the combined figures for mutual savings banks (15.9 percent) and the Federal National Mortgage Association (16.4 percent). Savings and loan associations account for only 14.8 percent of the total mortgage loans serviced by mortgage banking companies. Table 13–4 shows the distribution by type of investor of mortgage loans sold and serviced by mortgage bankers.

Table 13–4

Percent distribution by type of investor of mortgage loans sold and serviced by mortgage banking companies (1973)

| Investor | Sold | Serviced |
|---|---|---|
| Life insurance companies | 23.7 | 30.8 |
| Mutual savings banks | 9.0 | 15.9 |
| Savings and loan associations | 20.2 | 14.8 |
| Commercial banks | 4.0 | 4.2 |
| Trusted funds | 1.7 | 2.6 |
| Federal National Mortgage Association | 17.8 | 16.4 |
| Government National Mortgage Association | 5.9 | 1.4 |
| Real estate investment trusts | 2.5 | 1.0 |
| Mortgage pool for GNMA securities | 7.7 | 6.3 |
| Other | 7.5 | 6.6 |
| | 100.0 | 100.0 |

Source: Mortgage Bankers Association of America, Economics and Research Department, Trends Report no. 15

## Problems Concerning the FHA

In September 1972, the Mortgage Bankers Association of America published a revised statement of policy concerning the future of the FHA.[2] The overall thrust of the policy statement was that government-backed mortgage insurance is a major social innovation. Unfortunately, there are indications that some FHA insurance programs may be discontinued. This is important to mortgage bankers because they have originated more than 60 percent of all outstanding FHA loans, and these mortgages have been their major line of business. Obviously, any threat to the future existence of the FHA is a threat to the well-being of mortgage bankers.

The FHA received nationwide attention in the 1950s and 1960s, when scandals arose about certain of its programs. The agency insured some loans for more than the actual cost to certain builders and developers. Because the builders could borrow up to the insured amount, they reaped windfall profits simply by defaulting on loans and allowing the FHA to foreclose.[3] The quality of some insured construction was also suspect, particularly in subsidized low-income, single-family housing projects, and the terms offered on some loans ($50 down and $90 to $100 per month for thirty to thirty-five years) attracted people who did not have the income needed to maintain a house. Many low-income families abandoned their properties when faced with a combination of poor-quality construction and high-cost repairs. This, in turn, led to foreclosures and disillusioned investors in FHA mortgages.

[2]*Statement of Policy on Federal Mortgage Insurance* (Washington, D.C.: Mortgage Bankers Association of America, September 29, 1972).
[3]"Fight on Fraud in FHA Programs," *Business Week*, September 25, 1971, p. 39.

Furthermore, discounting of FHA mortgages discouraged both lenders and borrowers. *Discounting* refers to the fees that lenders charge to make mortgage loans. Because the maximum interest rates on government-backed mortgages frequently fall short of desired yields, lenders have charged the seller *points*, a percentage of the value of the loans. In some cases, sellers have been charged as high as eight points. Government regulations prohibit lenders from charging points to the buyer, because that would be equivalent to an increase in the fixed interest rate. Nevertheless, points do have a real effect on the buyer, and discounting does take place. In brief, high points tend to have an unfavorable influence on housing prices and mortgage-lending activity and may reduce the availability of housing for potential buyers.

In their 1972 policy statement, the mortgage bankers stated that the "FHA's basic programs are now declining in absolute as well as relative importance . . . when conventional mortgage lending is reaching for new records." The statement goes on to say that "Sellers, builders and lenders are no longer willing to cope with FHA programs—their arbitrarily fixed interest rates, red tape, processing delays and a long list of new and impractical laws and regulations."[4] Finally, the FHA has become a drain on the federal budget because income is not covering the increased costs of operating subsidized housing programs.

## Summary

Mortgage banking companies specialize in government-backed (FHA/VA) mortgages. They buy, sell, and service mortgages for institutional investors. The industry is characterized by a relatively small number of firms that account for the bulk of the mortgage loans serviced. At the present time, the industry faces a major problem because the future of certain FHA programs is in jeopardy.

## Questions

1 What is the basic role of mortgage bankers? What tools do they use to perform this role?
2 Explain why the assets of most mortgage banking companies are smaller than the size of the portfolios that they service.
3 What are the major sources of financing for mortgage banking operations?
4 Distinguish between "allocation" and "direct" commitments and explain their significance to mortgage bankers.

---

[4]*Statement of Policy on Federal Mortgage Insurance.*

5 Explain what is meant by servicing mortgage loans. What types of mortgages do mortgage bankers primarily service and for which institutions are most mortgages serviced?

6 What impact would the discontinuation of Federal Housing Administration (FHA) insurance programs have on mortgage banking operations?

7 Describe the problems that have plagued the FHA and which now threaten the existence of some of its insurance programs.

8 Compare the rates and terms charged by mortgage bankers in your city with those charged by other types of mortgage lenders. Be sure to give each type of lender identical information. How do you explain the differences, if any?

# Bibliography

Atteberry, William. *Modern Real Estate Finance,* 3d ed. Columbus, Ohio: Grid, Inc., 1972.

DeHuszar, William I. *Mortgage Loan Administration,* 2d ed. New York: McGraw-Hill Book Company, 1972.

Mortgage Bankers Association of America. *Mortgage Banking 1972, Financial Statements and Operating Ratios.* Economics and Research Committee, Trends Report no. 12. Washington, D.C.: 1972, and Trends Reports nos. 14 and 15 (1973).

————. *Mortgage Banking 1971.* Economics and Research Committee, Trends Report no. 11. Washington, D.C.: 1971.

————. *Statement of Policy on Federal Mortgage Insurance.* Washington, D.C.: April I, 1973.

Pease, Robert H., and Lewis O. Kerwood. *Mortgage Banking,* 2d ed. New York: McGraw-Hill Book Company, 1965.

Part

# 5
# Structure

Financial institutions can respond to change by altering the composition of their assets and claims or by altering their legal form of organization or structure.

Chapter 14, "Bank Holding Companies," examines these organizations that were developed to meet the needs of commercial banks.

Chapter 15, "Branch and Unit Banking," reviews the current state of branch and unit banking and the arguments for and against it.

Chapter 16, "The Hunt Commission," examines the criticisms which have been presented against the recommendations of the Hunt Commission and brings together many of the changes and proposals discussed elsewhere in this book. It suggests what the structure of financial institutions will look like in the future.

# 14

# Bank holding companies

*The growth of diversified bank holding companies is one of the most important forces now at work to unify the nation's capital markets. The bank holding company can overcome, in ways a bank cannot, impediments to flows of capital caused by geographic restrictions, size limitations, and limits on permissible activities. It can help to break down unequal access of various types of business, units of government, and consumers to financial expertise, contacts with specialized investors and professional fund-raising capabilities . . .*[1]

Banking structure in the United States is incorrectly described as having a high degree of decentralization. For example, in 1963, the Supreme Court of the United States stated in *United States* v. *The Philadelphia National Bank* that:

*Commercial banking in this country is primarily unit banking. That is, control of commercial banking is diffused throughout a very large number of independent local banks . . .*

It is true that about 10,000 of the 14,000 banks in this country are unit banks. However, these unit banks hold only one-fourth of all commercial bank deposits while the remaining 4,000 branch banks account for three-fourths

---

[1]Statement by Samuel B. Chase, Jr., Board of Governors of the Federal Reserve System, in *Annual Report, 1973,* Federal Reserve Bank of Minneapolis (1973), p. 5.

of all commercial bank deposits. Of this number, 90 large branch banks hold 40 percent of the total commercial bank deposits in the United States.[2] Obviously, banking structure in the United States is not decentralized. On the contrary, there is a tendency toward increased centralization. In 1965, 548 one-bank holding companies held 4.5 percent of all commercial bank deposits. By mid-1970 about 1,100 one-bank holding companies accounted for one-third of all commercial bank deposits, and of these 1,100, fifteen large banks held 16 percent of all commercial bank deposits.[3] In total, one-bank and multibank holding companies controlled about one-half of the commercial bank deposits in the United States. Equally important, bank holding companies extended their tutelage to such sectors of the economy as insurance, real estate, manufacturing, and data processing. Increasing public concern over these developments was instrumental in the passage of federal legislation late in 1970 that will have a major impact on bank holding companies and the U.S. banking structure.

As shown in Table 14–1, at year-end 1973, 1,607 bank holding companies held 65 percent of the total deposits of all commercial banks. The data in the table, showing the banking structure and number of bank holding

Table 14–1

Bank holding companies by state (year-end 1973)

| State | State banking structure[a] | Holding companies[b] | Banks | Percentage of deposits |
|---|---|---|---|---|
| Alabama | L | 16 | 50 | 54.0 |
| Alaska | S | 2 | 1 | 9.8 |
| Arizona | S | 5 | 6 | 56.1 |
| Arkansas | U | 20 | 21 | 18.5 |
| California | S | 45 | 45 | 93.3 |
| Colorado | U | 72 | 130 | 78.1 |
| Connecticut | S | 8 | 14 | 71.5 |
| Delaware | S | 3 | 3 | 18.7 |
| District of Columbia | S | 5 | 3 | 24.6 |
| Florida | U | 62 | 338 | 78.5 |
| Georgia | L | 26 | 40 | 54.1 |
| Hawaii | S | 1 | 1 | 35.9 |
| Idaho | S | 3 | 3 | 41.9 |
| Illinois | U | 150 | 146 | 59.4 |
| Indiana | L | 26 | 26 | 33.8 |
| Iowa | U | 139 | 168 | 39.7 |
| Kansas | U | 110 | 122 | 32.6 |
| Kentucky | L | 9 | 9 | 9.7 |
| Louisiana | L | 16 | 17 | 35.5 |
| Maine | S | 6 | 25 | 72.0 |
| Maryland | S | 16 | 21 | 61.2 |

[2]Based on FDIC data.
[3]U.S., Congress, Senate, Committee on Banking and Currency, *One-Bank Holding Company Legislation of 1970, Hearings,* part 2, 91st Cong., 2d sess., May, 1970, p. 1034.

Table 14–1 (cont'd)

| State | State banking structure[a] | Holding companies[b] | Banks | Percentage of deposits |
|---|---|---|---|---|
| Massachusetts | L | 22 | 62 | 84.7 |
| Michigan | L | 30 | 71 | 67.8 |
| Minnesota | U | 107 | 227 | 68.3 |
| Mississippi | L | 4 | 4 | 25.6 |
| Missouri | U | 95 | 194 | 63.4 |
| Montana | U | 32 | 65 | 68.2 |
| Nebraska | U | 115 | 127 | 54.1 |
| Nevada | S | 3 | 3 | 66.1 |
| New Hampshire | L | 5 | 14 | 30.0 |
| New Jersey | L | 19 | 61 | 50.4 |
| New Mexico | L | 11 | 28 | 69.2 |
| New York | L | 48 | 117 | 90.3 |
| North Carolina | S | 7 | 10 | 68.2 |
| North Dakota | U | 18 | 46 | 42.7 |
| Ohio | L | 39 | 125 | 48.2 |
| Oklahoma | U | 48 | 53 | 42.8 |
| Oregon | S | 5 | 5 | 81.1 |
| Pennsylvania | L | 23 | 27 | 54.0 |
| Rhode Island | S | 10 | 10 | 95.4 |
| South Carolina | S | 7 | 8 | 53.5 |
| South Dakota | S | 26 | 40 | 60.6 |
| Tennessee | L | 20 | 56 | 62.2 |
| Texas | U | 94 | 188 | 51.9 |
| Utah | S | 9 | 16 | 80.8 |
| Vermont | S | 2 | 2 | 8.9 |
| Virginia | S | 27 | 104 | 77.4 |
| Washington | S | 5 | 9 | 37.2 |
| West Virginia | U | 8 | 9 | 4.5 |
| Wisconsin | L | 54 | 144 | 50.6 |
| Wyoming | U | 19 | 33 | 57.1 |
| Total | | 1,607 | 3,097 | 65.4 |

[a]S = statewide branch banking; L = limited branch banking; U = unit banking
[b]Data are for 1972. In 1973 there were 1,677 holding companies.
Source: Board of Governors of the Federal Reserve System

companies in each state, suggest that states with unit banking laws (U) have more bank holding companies than states with statewide branch banking (S) and limited branch banking (L). It appears that bankers use multibank holding companies as a near substitute for branch banking in states with unit banking laws that do permit multibank holding companies.

This chapter surveys the development of bank holding companies, with particular attention paid to the development of one-bank holding companies. The first section explains the different types of bank holding companies and reviews relevant federal legislation. The remainder of the chapter concentrates on factors that will shape the outlook for the nonbanking activities of holding companies.

## The Development of Bank Holding Companies

### Types of Bank Holding Companies

In a broad sense, any corporation or organization that controls one or more banks may be classified as a bank holding company. Until the 1970 amendments to the Bank Holding Company Act there were important differences between one-bank holding companies (that control one bank) and registered bank holding companies (that control two or more banks). Now both types of holding company are regulated by the Board of Governors of the Federal Reserve System. Nevertheless, it is still meaningful to think in terms of registered bank holding companies and one-bank holding companies because some states do not allow holding companies that control more than two banks.

One-bank holding companies can be divided into three groups: traditional, conglomerate, and congeneric. *Traditional* one-bank holding companies account for the largest number of holding companies. Typically, they are closely held corporations set up to control a small bank, but they may also be engaged in the insurance, finance, and real estate businesses. *Conglomerate* one-bank holding companies are nonfinancial organizations that own a bank. For example, C.I.T. Corporation, Goodyear Tire & Rubber Company, and Hershey Foods, as well as some charitable trusts, labor unions, and nonprofit foundations, own banks. The most important group are the *congeneric* one-bank holding companies. These are one-bank holding companies organized by a large bank to engage in financially related businesses. (Some of these activities, such as managing mutual funds, investment counseling, and underwriting securities, are traditionally closed to banks.[4]) As shown in Table 14-2, the number of one-bank holding companies increased dramatically in recent years. The relationship between the deposits and number of banks indicates that many large banks formed one-bank holding companies (congenerics). The number of registered bank holding companies has also increased in recent years, but at a

Table 14-2

One-bank holding companies (in selected years)

| Year end | Number of banks | Deposits ($ billions) | Deposits as a percentage of all bank deposits |
|---|---|---|---|
| 1954 | 113 | 3.1 | 1.7 |
| 1965 | 548 | 13.9 | 4.5 |
| 1968 | 783 | 108.2 | 27.5 |
| 1970 (April) | 1116 | 140.0 | 33.0 |

Sources: Federal Reserve Bank of Chicago; Board of Governors of the Federal Reserve System

[4]Steven J. Weiss, "Bank Holding Companies and Public Policy," *New England Economic Review*, Federal Reserve Bank of Boston (January/February 1969), p. 26.

more moderate rate. Several reasons for the increase in the number of both one-bank and registered bank holding companies are discussed below.

## Reasons for Development

*Competition and Pressure*    Commercial banks were feeling competitive pressures and increasing customer demand for a wider variety of services. To finance these demands during the period of credit restraint in the late 1960s, they turned to bank holding companies to supplement their funds through the sale of commercial paper. They used this device because commercial paper is not subject to the Federal Reserve System's Regulation Q, which regulates interest rates paid on time and savings deposits.

*Services*    In order to provide an increasing variety of services, some banks wanted to enter product and geographic markets from which they were barred by laws or regulations. One-bank holding companies provided a mechanism to expand their services into nonbanking business and across state lines. A recent study of the activities of one-bank holding companies revealed that they are involved primarily in real estate financing and insurance and, to a lesser extent, in manufacturing, trade, agriculture, service companies, and transportation.[5]

*Computers*    The growing use of computers was another factor that contributed to banks entering related areas. Banks with computers provided an increasing variety of data processing services for their customers. This gave them a new entrée to customer deposits, and it proved sufficiently rewarding that many banks entered the business. Banks also began to offer other services including leasing and travel agencies.

*Tax Laws*    Federal tax laws were an additional incentive for the development of bank holding companies. Bank holding companies can exchange their stock for the stock of a bank they are acquiring. The result is a tax-free exchange. Furthermore, the acquiring holding company, taking advantage of the 85 percent dividend exemption, can use the acquired bank's dividends to pay off loans used to acquire it. If the holding company owns more than 80 percent of the acquired bank's stock, it is entitled to a 100 percent dividend exemption.

*Legal Factors*    An important loophole in the Bank Holding Company Act of 1956 encouraged the development of one-bank holding companies. This was the exemption of one-bank holding companies from federal legislation.

Finally, numerous one-bank holding companies were formed out of fear of forthcoming legislation that might restrict their future activities. Holding

---

[5]"The Changing Structure of Bank Holding Companies," *Economic Review*, Federal Reserve Bank of Cleveland (April 1969).

companies that were formed before restrictive legislation hoped to be exempted from some of the restrictions. To explain the scope, impact, and intent of the new legislation, a detailed review of federal legislation pertaining to bank holding companies is presented next.

## Federal Legislation

### Early Legislation

The Banking Act of 1933 (Glass-Steagal Act) was the first federal law regulating bank holding companies, and was enacted at a time when there was considerable debate over branch banking. It restricted national banks to branching within the same geographic limits given to state-chartered banks, but bank holding companies were not restricted geographically and could acquire banks in areas closed to state-chartered banks.

The act gave the Board of Governors of the Federal Reserve System the power to grant or deny to holding companies owning the majority of the stock of any member bank permission to vote their stock interests in that bank. The permit was issued (or denied) after an examination of the holding company's affiliated banks.[6] In addition, the holding company was required to: maintain certain reserves; publish periodic financial statements; declare dividends only out of new earnings; and disengage from the securities business within a given period of time.

The major accomplishment of the 1933 act was to divorce bank holding companies from the securities business. Beyond that it did little to restrict the formation and expansion of bank holding companies. Holding companies that consisted of nonmember banks were not federally regulated and could invest in virtually any business except the securities industry. In 1935, the Banking Act of 1933 was amended[7] to exclude virtually all one-bank holding companies because owning a bank was usually incidental to the principal business activities of the holding company.[8] For example, R. H. Macy's (the New York retail store), the United Mine Workers, and Cornell University owned banks.

### The Bank Holding Company Act of 1956

In 1948 the Board of Governors of the Federal Reserve System began legal proceedings under the Clayton Act against Transamerica Corporation. This case was instrumental in the development and enactment of the Bank

---

[6]The Board of Governors was authorized to examine both the holding company and its affiliates.
[7]49 Stat. 707 (1935). This statute was repealed by 80 Stat. 242 (1966).
[8]Larry R. Mote, "The One-Bank Holding Company—History, Issues, and Pending Legislation," *Business Conditions,* Federal Reserve Bank of Chicago (July 1970).

Holding Company Act of 1956. In brief, the Board of Governors charged that through bank acquisitions Transamerica Corporation controlled 41 percent of all commercial bank offices, 39 percent of commercial bank deposits, and 50 percent of commercial bank loans in Arizona, California, Nevada, Oregon, and Washington. The court ruled that Transamerica Corporation had to dispose of its Bank of America stock. However, it was allowed to continue ownership of forty-six banks in a five-state area and expand into other states if it wished to do so. With the court ruling in favor of Transamerica Corporation, congressional pressure to regulate bank holding companies mounted.

Between July 1949 and July 1955, fifteen bills to regulate bank holding companies were introduced in Congress. This legislative activity culminated in the Bank Holding Company Act of 1956. The objectives of the 1956 act were twofold: to prevent undue concentration of banks by bank holding companies; and to preserve the historical separation between banks and commerce.

The 1956 act failed to achieve either objective. One reason for the act's failure was that it defined a bank holding company as any corporation, trust, association, or similar organization controlling 25 percent or more of the voting stock or the election of the majority of the directors of each of two or more banks. The definition contained a number of loopholes.[9] Most important, it exempted companies that own one bank or less than 25 percent of the stock of other banks; this provided additional impetus for the development of one-bank holding companies. In addition, there was an exemption that permitted partnerships consisting of the same individuals to control as many banks as they desired. Moreover, trusts and single individuals could control other banks and remain outside the scope of the act. The partnership and trust exemptions were closed by the 1970 amendments.

In addition to defining bank holding companies, the 1956 act required that registered bank holding companies divest themselves, with certain exceptions, of their nonbanking businesses. The exceptions include companies holding bank premises, companies in the safe deposit business, companies providing services exclusively for the holding company, companies which the Federal Reserve System determines are "closely related to the banking business," and shares which do not include more than 5 percent of the voting stock of a company and account for no more than 5 percent of the holding company's assets.

---

[9]The loopholes discussed here are examined in greater depth in: U.S., Congress, House, Committee on Banking and Currency, Staff Report, *The Growth of Unregistered Bank Holding Companies—Problems and Prospects,* 91st Cong., 1st sess. (February 1969). One loophole not covered in this chapter concerns the use of bank loans secured by stock of another bank to gain control of yet other banks.

Finally, holding companies are required to have the Board of Governors' approval before acquiring more than 5 percent of the voting shares of any bank. In general, the Board of Governors is prohibited from approving acquisitions of banks outside the state where the holding company does its principal business.[10] Moreover, board approval of a proposed acquisition is to be based on 1) "banking factors,"[11] 2) the convenience, needs, and welfare of the community, and 3) the degree of economic competition and concentration.

In review, the Bank Holding Company Act of 1956 was designed to control the expansion of bank holding companies. The act defined holding companies in such a way that one-bank holding companies were exempt from the act and could enter into any type of business while multibank holding companies were circumscribed in their activities. In addition, the act required the Board of Governors of the Federal Reserve System to consider particular factors when evaluating proposed bank acquisitions. One factor was the competitive effects of the acquisition (which had not been included in earlier legislation); another factor was that bank acquisitions should be confined geographically.

### Other Pertinent Federal Legislation

Before 1960, federal legislation concerning bank mergers was not stringent. The National Banking Act of 1918 required the Comptroller of the Currency to approve (or deny) proposed mergers of two or more banks under the charter of a national bank. The Federal Deposit Insurance Act of 1950 required banks to obtain permission to merge from the Board of Governors of the Federal Reserve System (for state member banks), the Comptroller of the Currency (for national banks), or the Federal Deposit Insurance Corporation (for nonmember insured banks). Neither law established criteria for the three federal banking agencies to follow when considering merger applications. This situation changed with the enactment of the Bank Merger Act of 1960, which amended the Federal Deposit Insurance Act of 1950. The Bank Merger Act of 1960 required that mergers involving insured banks receive prior approval from one of the three federal banking agencies, and it listed the factors that the agencies must consider when examining merger applications. The criteria were the same as in the Bank Holding Company Act of 1956: banking factors, convenience and need of the community, and competitive effects. Unfortunately, the laws did not indicate which criterion should be given the greatest weight. It is not surprising that the federal banking agencies emphasized banking factors and convenience and needs, while the courts emphasized competitive factors.[12] Part of the con-

---

[10] 80 Stat. 237 (1966).
[11] The *banking factors* include the past, current, and future financial conditions of the banks concerned and the character of their management.
[12] "Federal Laws Regulating Bank Mergers and the Acquisition of Banks by Registered Bank Holding Companies," *Economic Review*, Federal Reserve Bank of Cleveland (January 1971).

fusion was resolved by the Bank Merger Act of 1966, which amended the 1960 act and set new standards; the Bank Holding Company Act of 1956 was also revised in 1966. The emphasis in both new acts was on competitive factors. The federal banking agencies could not approve any merger that would substantially lessen competition or result in a monopoly, unless the anticompetitive effects were clearly outweighed by the needs and convenience of the community. Additionally, the merger cannot take place for thirty days after the federal banking agencies' approval, during which time the Department of Justice can contest it. Following the 1966 amendments, the Department of Justice challenged an increasing number of merger applications. As a result, affected banks were less willing to go to court. A study of twenty-three cases brought to court after 1966 showed that 57 percent of the firms abandoned the mergers, compared with a 13 percent rate before that time.[13] Nevertheless, the volume of merger applications increased significantly.

The importance of the Bank Merger Act of 1966 lies in the increased tendency to incorporate antitrust factors into banking law. This trend will become even more noticeable as the Department of Justice and other regulatory agencies attack nonbanking activities on anticompetitive grounds. An example of such a case is the First National City Bank's attempt to acquire the Carte Blanche credit card business.[14]

### The 1970 Amendments to the Bank Holding Company Act

The key feature of the 1970 amendments to the Bank Holding Company Act is the inclusion of one-bank holding companies under the act. Before December 31, 1970, one-bank holding companies were exempt from federal legislation. Now they are under the purview of the act that defines a holding company as "any company which has control over any Bank . . ."; consequently, they must register with the Federal Reserve System. Of course, there are exceptions to the rule such as banks holding other bank shares in a fiduciary capacity, except where the trustee has sole discretionary authority to vote the stock. Moreover, a firm that acquires bank stock used as collateral for a loan is not considered a bank holding company until that stock has been held for two years.[15]

More important, the term *control* in the definition of a bank holding company was ambiguous. Earlier legislation defined control as ownership of 25 percent of a bank's stock. Under the new amendments a holding company owning less than 5 percent interest is presumed to have no control. Thus,

---

[13]Oscar R. Goodman, "A Survey of Judicial and Regulatory Opinions Affecting Banking Competition Under the Bank Merger Acts of 1960–1966," in *Proceedings of a Conference on Bank Structure and Competition,* Federal Reserve Bank of Chicago (1969).
[14]For discussion of this case see Robert P. Mayo, "The 1970 Amendments of the Bank Holding Company Act: One Year Later," *Business Conditions,* Federal Reserve Bank of Chicago (December 1971), p. 3.
[15]This list of exemptions is not exhaustive.

the Board of Governors defined control as an interest between 5 and 25 percent. Conclusive presumption of control exists where a company has the power to vote 25 percent or more of a bank's stock or a company owns a bank.[16] Presumption of control also exists where a company owns 10 percent of the voting shares of two banks or 5 percent of the voting shares of three or more banks. In addition, certain interlocking directorships and partnerships constitute control.

*Regulatory Authority*    The 1970 amendments charged the Federal Reserve System with regulating bank holding companies. One of the first tasks of the board was to establish for bank holding companies a list of permissible business activities that are "closely related to banking or managing or controlling banks . . ." Accordingly, bank holding companies, with permission from the Board of Governors, can engage in one or more of the activities that appear in Table 14–3. The Board of Governors has stated that it plans to make additions and changes to the list from time to time.[17] Table 14–3 also shows activities denied or under consideration by the board.

There are three more substantive sections to the 1970 amendments. The first section stipulates that if the Board of Governors does not act on an application within ninety days after receipt of all requisite forms, the application is automatically approved. The second section concerns tie-in restrictions. Basically, banks are prohibited from extending services (e.g., credit) on the condition that the customer must obtain some additional services from that bank or its holding company. However, the law does allow banks to impose requirements on its customers that are usually provided in connection with a loan, discount, deposit, or trust service. Finally, there is a "grandfather clause," which provided selected exemptions for nonbanking subsidiaries acquired before June 30, 1968. However, the statutes permit the Board of Governors to review all nonbanking subsidiaries regardless of the date they were acquired. If the board finds undue concentration, anticompetitive effects, or unsound banking practices, the holding company may be asked to divest itself of the subsidiary. It will have ten years from the date of determination to take such action. The amendments also require that nonexempted subsidiaries acquired after June 30, 1968, be divested before year-end 1980.

## The Future of Bank Holding Companies

The 1970 amendments to the Bank Holding Company Act set the stage for a new chapter in banking history. At this point the question is: Where do bank holding companies go next? Although that question cannot be answered

---

[16]The Board of Governors defined control on July 1, 1971.
[17]The first significant change was announced June 15, 1971, when the board broadened the scope of the data processing activities permissible for bank holding companies.

Table 14–3

Activities approved, denied, and under consideration by the Federal Reserve Board under section 4 (c) (8)

Approved
  1 Lending activities such as mortgage banking, finance companies, credit cards, and factoring companies
  2 Operating an industrial bank, Morris Plan bank, or industrial loan company
  3 Servicing loans
  4 Trust company
  5 Investment or financial adviser to real estate investment trusts and to investment companies under the Investment Company Act of 1940
  6 Leasing personal property (with full pay-out)
  7 Investing in community development projects
  8 Data processing services
  9 Underwriting credit life insurance in connection with the extension of credit
  10 Acting as an insurance agent, principally in connection with the extension of credit
  11 Limited courier services
  12 Management consulting for unaffiliated banks
Denied
  1 Equity funding (combined sale of insurance and mutual funds)
  2 Underwriting general life insurance
  3 Real estate brokerage
  4 Land development
  5 Real estate syndication
  6 Property management
  7 Management consulting
Under consideration
  1 Leasing real property
  2 Armored car service
  3 Mortgage guarantee insurance
  4 Savings and loan associations
  5 Underwriting bankers' blanket bond insurance (the deductive portion)

Sources: Regulation Y; *Federal Reserve Bulletin*

with certainty, some observations about the future are appropriate. The following remarks concentrate primarily on nonbanking activities.

## Congress

A study of the past is one key to the future. A review of federal legislation pertaining to bank holding companies revealed that Congress intends to preserve the separation of bank and bank-related activites from commerce. This principle is incorporated in the Banking Act of 1933 (Glass-Steagall Act), the Bank Holding Company Act of 1956, and most recently in the 1970 amendments to the Bank Holding Company Act. Moreover, in the Glass-Steagall Act, Congress separated banking from the securities business.

## The Federal Reserve

One can also review the rulings of the Board of Governors of the Federal Reserve System on nonbanking subsidiaries of registered bank holding

companies. A recent study examined such rulings and disclosed two traits used by the Board of Governors in determining whether activities are closely related to banking.[18] The first trait is *process similarity* to bank lending. Thus, finance companies, "factors" (whereby borrowers sell accounts receivable to lenders), and commercial paper companies extend credit in a manner that allows them to be considered closely related to banking. The second trait is the *operational integration* of the activity into the bank lending process. For example, underwriting credit life insurance is operationally integrated in the lending process but underwriting ordinary life and property insurance is not. However, the agency function of ordinary life and property insurance is closely related to banking.

Another illustration of operational integration is data processing. The electronic automation of banking operations is widespread and banks with excess computer capacity can use their equipment to process other kinds of data. Accordingly, the Board of Governors may permit bank holding companies "to process banking, financial, or related economic data for any type of customer."[19] This is not an open invitation to engage in all types of data processing. There is a caveat that the service can only be furnished "if such data processing service is not otherwise reasonably available in the relevant market area."[20] This may not be an impediment because the data processing service is operationally integrated with other banking functions and there may be no similar service available. For example, a member of the Board of Governors suggested that banks might prepare individuals' income tax returns on the basis of standardized information inputs.[21] They could use their data processing equipment to sort checks according to tax-deductible payments and present the client with appropriate totals at year end. The client would use checks bearing a coding device to indicate a deductible item. In addition, banks could use data processing to offer complete record-keeping and financial management for small businesses and payment for them of their taxes (sales, social security, and income tax withholding).

In summary, the two traits provide a limited frame of reference for assessing whether activities are closely related to banking. They are not the only criteria that the Board of Governors uses to determine appropriate nonbanking businesses. In the first case under the 1970 amendments, the Board of Governors permitted a bank holding company (American Financial Corporation) to acquire a newspaper (the *Cincinnati Enquirer*).[22] It is difficult to

---

[18]Charles D. Salley, "1970 Bank Holding Company Act Amendments: What Is 'Closely Related to Banking'?" *Monthly Review*, Federal Reserve Bank of Atlanta (June 1971).
[19]This is one of the permissible activities listed in the Federal Reserve press release of June 15, 1971.
[20]*Ibid.*
[21]William W. Sherrill, Member, Board of Governors of the Federal Reserve System, "Banking at the Crossroads: The Outlook for Change over the Coming Twenty Years," speech before the National Automation Conference, American Bankers Association, New York (May 3, 1971).
[22]Permission was granted May 6, 1971, pursuant to the settlement of an antitrust case in which the Scripps-Howard Company that owns the *Enquirer* sells its majority interest.

apply either trait in this case. The Board of Governors does favor bank holding companies entering nonbanking businesses on a *de novo* basis. A hypothetical case would be a bank holding company entering the mortgage banking business. The holding company could develop its own mortgage banking company, which might increase competition in the relevant market area, or it could acquire an existing company, which might decrease competition. The Board of Governors would probably approve the first acquisition, particularly if a small company was being acquired and the acquiring company did not already control a large portion of the relevant market. The likelihood of approval of a second similar acquisition is substantially less. In fact, if the acquiring firm or the two mortgage firms would control a substantial share of the relevant market, the Board of Governors probably would not approve the new acquisition.

### The Courts

Until recently congeneric one-bank holding companies had no cause to fear antitrust actions because the U.S. Supreme Court had ruled in 1963 that banking is a "unique line of commerce."[23] Hence, commercial banks compete only with other commercial banks. However, a review of four 1969–1970 court cases on "potential competition" disclosed that the pertinent line of commerce was not limited to commercial banks and that other types of financial institutions were included.[24] The broad line of commerce encompassed savings and loan associations, mutual savings banks, credit unions, consumer lenders, finance companies, Production Credit Associations, the Federal Land Bank, life insurance companies, and mortgage companies. Ultimately, the Supreme Court will determine whether commerce should be defined in a narrow or a broad sense.

In another area of interest, a 1971 Supreme Court ruling refused to allow bank holding companies to operate mutual funds as a permissible nonbanking activity.[25] The Investment Company Institute attacked the Comptroller of the Currency's Regulation 9, which purported to authorize national banks to operate collective investment funds. They argued that the Comptroller gave First National City Bank (New York) permission to operate such a fund in violation of the Banking Act of 1933 (Glass-Steagall Act). Mr. Justice Stewart delivered the opinion of the Court that Regulation 9 was invalid insofar as it authorizes the sale of interests in an investment fund of the type established by First National City Bank. He pointed out that no provision of banking law suggests that it is improper for a national bank to pool trust assets, to act as an agent for the customer, or to purchase stock for the customer. "But the union of these powers gives birth to an investment

---

[23]*United States* v. *Philadelphia National Bank et al.,* 374 U.S. 321 (1963).
[24]Oscar R. Goodman, "Judicial Decisions and Litigation Affecting Competition in Banking," in *Proceedings of a Conference on Bank Structure and Competition,* Federal Reserve Bank of Chicago (1970).
[25]*Investment Company Institute* v. *Camp,* 401 U.S. 617 (1971).

fund whose activities are of a different character. The differences between the investment fund which the comptroller has authorized and a conventional open-end mutual fund are subtle at best . . ."[26] Mr. Justice Blackmun in a dissenting opinion expressed doubts that the three banking operations, each concededly permissible, when combined produced something different from the mere sum of the parts. In addition to the Court decision, the Board of Governors announced that permissible nonbanking activities do not include acting as investment advisers to an open-end investment company.[27] However, a bank holding company can organize a closed-end investment company as long as such a company does not either frequently sell securities or have a name similar to the holding company or its subsidiary banks.

## Management

In addition to federal legislation, the Board of Governors' promulgations, and court rulings, management will set the course for bank holding companies. William Sherrill, a member of the Board of Governors, stated that the chief executive of a bank holding company must decide whether to continue to regard himself as a commercial banker or something significantly different—a bank holding company executive.[28] If he continues to act as a commercial banker, his organization will be an essentially static concern, merely acquiring deposits and lending money. In contrast, if the chief executive regards himself not merely as a *lender* with some new subordinate interests but as a *leader* having new and innovative functions, the organization will develop quite differently.

Along this line management must decide whether to consider its organization a multiproduct firm that seeks profit on each service, or a composite service firm that emphasizes profit on a total package of services rather than on each service. To a large extent the management philosophy of the executive officers will influence the direction and profitability of the bank holding company. This point was brought out in a study of operating policies of bank holding companies.[29] Investigation was undertaken to determine 1) the relationship between organizational characteristics of bank holding companies and the degree of centralization of decision making, and 2) areas of operation where holding company control was greatest. The analysis revealed that the policies of bank holding companies could not be explained by the economic or organizational characteristics of

---

[26]*Investment Company Institute* v. *Camp.*
[27]Federal Reserve press release of January 24, 1972.
[28]William W. Sherrill, Member, Board of Governors of the Federal Reserve System, "Some Reflections on the New Bank Holding Company Legislation," speech before the National Public Affairs Conference, American Bankers Association, Washington, D.C. (March 16, 1971).
[29]Robert J. Lawrence, *Operating Policies of Bank Holding Companies,* Staff Economic Studies (Washington, D.C.: Board of Governors of the Federal Reserve System, March 1971).

the companies. It follows that policies can only be determined by investigating the management philosophy of the executive officers.

Management philosophy must include some statement about profitability. Presumably, management formed bank holding companies because they believed it would increase profits. At the present time there are no profit data available on holding companies' nonbanking activities; however, it is well documented that acquiring more banks does not add to profitability in the short run.[30] Banks that merged had higher returns on their assets than nonmerging banks, but they also incurred increased operating costs that offset the higher revenues. The apparent failure of bankers to increase profitability in their own bailiwick casts some doubt about their ability to increase profitability in nonbanking activities. This strongly suggests that management must view a holding company as a new and different form of business if it is to be successful.

## Financial Soundness and Public Benefits

When determining whether a holding company can acquire control of a bank or engage in a nonbanking activity, the Federal Reserve Board has to be assured of the soundness of its banking practices and whether there are positive public benefits. Unless the banking system is financially sound there will be no public benefits. Therefore, one of the major tasks of a bank holding company is to build a sound organization.

### Improved Operational Efficiencies

*Management*    Small independent banks face a number of management problems that can be alleviated through affiliation with a larger organization. For example, the holding company permits better development and use of management skills because the costs of management are spread out over the individual unit banks affiliated with the holding company. Each individual bank can maintain less depth in management because of the depth in management inherent in the holding company. Additionally, some management skills are complementary: one affiliate bank may have an expert in cattle loans and another an expert in estate taxes. Because both belong to the same organization, there is no need to duplicate their services at each bank.

Management succession is a related problem. As a banker nears the age when a successor must be found, the depth of management of a holding company will produce experienced personnel.

---

[30]Several studies that support this conclusion are: Robert J. Lawrence, *The Performance of Bank Holding Companies* (Washington, D.C.: Board of Governors of the Federal Reserve System, June 1967); Weiss, "Bank Holding Companies and Public Policy;" David L. Smith, "The Performance of Merging Banks," *Journal of Business* (April 1970); Thomas R. Piper, *The Economics of Bank Acquisitions by Registered Bank Holding Companies,* Reserve Report no. 48, Federal Reserve Bank of Boston (March 1971).

Employee benefits can be improved with larger personnel base, and they are one of the factors that will attract high-quality people into banking as a career. Special benefits such as group life insurance, health insurance, and retirement programs are more economical for large organizations than for small ones. In-house training programs for managers and other personnel also become feasible. Such programs are necessary so that personnel can be moved both laterally and vertically in the organization to obtain the maximum potential from their skills.

*Economies*    Large organizations can do some things more efficiently than a number of small organizations doing those same things. Trust services are an example of this. A holding company may find it advantageous to have one trust department serving the entire organization instead of each affiliate having its own department. It is possible to provide other specialized skills, such as leasing, that cannot be justified from an economic standpoint for a small independent bank. Similarly, centralized and computerized bookkeeping serves to reduce the costs of data processing that are common to all banks (advertising, marketing, purchasing, research, and so on).

In addition to reducing costs, larger organizations may be able to take advantage of their size when making loans and borrowing funds. By combining the resources of a number of affiliated banks, the holding company has better access to the capital markets for stocks and bonds than the individual banks it represents. For example, Moody's will not even give a quality rating to the commercial paper of small banking organizations.

Moreover, banks affiliated with holding companies generally have higher loan-to-asset ratios, higher municipal securities-to-asset ratios, and higher installment loans-to-assets ratios than independent banks.[31] These ratios suggest that holding companies manage their funds more aggressively than independent banks.

The fact that bank holding companies tend to have more aggressive portfolio management than independent banks is significant for both the banks and the public. The banks tend to have a higher proportion of earning assets to total assets and the public has more funds to spend in the community. The public also benefits because the holding company may acquire more state and local obligations than could probably be acquired by a local bank.

Finally, through participations the holding company can reduce the risks of making loans and increase the rewards to members of the organization.

---

[31]For a comprehensive review of studies dealing with such ratios see Peter S. Rose and Donald R. Fraser, "The Impact of Holding Company Acquisitions on Bank Performance," *Bankers Magazine,* 156 (Spring 1973).

Related to the problems of risks and rewards is the fact that the banker must know his customers' needs and problems. This is possible in a holding company because each bank retains its own identity. Officers and directors of the affiliated banks include local people who know their communities, thus helping to match the resources of the holding company with the needs of the community.

## Public Benefits

When considering applications from holding companies, the Board of Governors has to determine whether the benefits to the public, such as convenience or increased efficiency, outweigh possible adverse effects such as undue concentration or unsound banking practices.

*Services*   Multibank holding companies can benefit a market area by offering new or improved financial services. For example, a small independent bank may not be able to justify on an economic basis specialized services such as a trust department or an international department even though there may be a demand for them. Through the holding company mechanism the costs of such services can be spread over a number of banks, making them economically feasible. Additionally, there is a geographic expansion of the services offered by the holding company. A trust or leasing department located in one part of the state can serve affiliated banks located throughout the state.

*More Funds Available*   As previously noted, banks affiliated with holding companies tend to have higher ratios of loans to assets than do independent banks. This means that more funds are being infused into their respective communities. The large financial base of the holding company enhances the affiliated banks' ability to support economic growth of the area.

*Competition*   The offering of new or improved financial services and the infusion of funds into an area results in competition that benefits the public. Competitive rates will be paid on time and savings deposits and competitive rates charged on loans. For example, at the present time substantial differences exist between the average interest rates paid on time deposits in urban and rural areas.

*Convenience*   Banking is a convenience business. Holding companies that offer a full array of banking services and increase credit availability through the efficient use of funds are making their affiliate banks a convenient place to do business.

## Selected Issues

There are a number of arguments against multibank holding companies. This section examines the arguments and discusses responses to them.

## Concentration of Resources

One argument holds that multibank holding companies lead to greater concentration of banking resources. A recent study published by the Board of Governors of the Federal Reserve System sheds some light on this issue.[32] It focused on holding company acquisitions made during the 1968–1973 period. One conclusion was that acquisitions had virtually no impact on states that already had a high degree of concentration. Concentration was measured by the percentage of total deposits held by the five largest banking organizations in the state. Highly concentrated states included Utah, Washington, California, Alaska, Hawaii, Delaware, Arizona, Nevada, and Rhode Island; the concentration ratios ranged from 72.2 to 96.5 percent. These are states where there is statewide branch banking, and there was little pressure to expand through the use of holding companies. In addition, the regulatory authorities would resist pressure for additional concentration.

The study did find some increase in concentration ratios in states that permitted expansion of multibank holding companies and that had low or moderate concentration ratios. For example, in Florida, which had the largest increase, the concentration ratio increased from 25.2 percent in 1968 to 31.7 percent in 1973. In Alabama, which had the next largest ratio, it increased from 34.5 to 45.1 percent.

The study was also found that in twenty-seven states (thirteen where holding company expansion was prohibited) acquisitions had no impact on statewide concentration ratios.

## Absentee Ownership

A second view is that absentee ownership is a detriment to the community, the implication being that a business must be owned by local people in order to serve the community. It is widely recognized that large retail chain stores, service stations, insurance companies, and other businesses that are not locally owned serve the communities where they are located. The test is not one of ownership but one of service. As previously noted, banks affiliated with holding companies have higher loan-to-asset ratios than independent banks: they invest more funds in consumer loans and business loans. They may also be able to offer more services at lower costs than small, independent banks.

Another aspect of this issue is that each bank in a holding company organization is an individual entity with its own board of directors. Typi-

---

[32]Samuel H. Talley, "The Impact of Holding Company Acquisitions on Aggregate Concentration in Banking," *Staff Economic Report* (Washington, D.C.: Board of Governors of the Federal Reserve System, 1974).

cally, the directors include local citizens who will guide the operating policies of the bank.

### Investment Policies

Third, bank holding companies drain funds from local communities. The responsibility of any banking organization is to make a reasonable profit for the owners of that organization. To accomplish this end, bankers must invest their funds where they earn the highest returns consistent with safety and liquidity. If demands for funds are strong in their communities, they invest in their communities. If demands are slack in their communities, they invest elsewhere. For example, in Oklahoma, where there are no multibank holding companies, 254 reporting state banks had invested $203,689,000 in federal funds on April 24, 1974. This amounts to 14 percent of the total loans and discounts made by these banks. In other words, independent state banks in Oklahoma invested a substantial portion of their assets outside their respective communities. There is no reason to believe that banks affiliated with holding companies would have behaved differently.

In conclusion, the following statement by an official of the Board of Governors summarizes the benefits of bank holding companies.

> *The growth of diversified bank holding companies is one of the most important forces now at work to unify the nation's capital markets. The bank holding company can overcome, in ways a bank cannot, impediments to flows of capital caused by geographic restrictions, size limitations, and limits on permissible activities. It can help to break down unequal access of various types of business, units of government, and consumers to financial expertise, contacts with specialized investors and professional fund-raising capabilities . . .*[33]

### Summary

Legal, judicial, and regulatory decisions have set the parameters for the development of bank holding companies. Now that one-bank holding companies are regulated by the Federal Reserve System, many will acquire banks and become registered bank holding companies (where permitted to do so by state law). These bank acquisitions will contribute to greater concentration of banking resources, which may, in turn, lead to increased public concern and more vigorous enforcement of antitrust laws. In addition, the Board of Governors of the Federal Reserve System may become less willing to approve bank acquisitions. In terms of nonbanking activities, holding companies will expand into mortgage banking, data processing,

---

[33]Statement by Samuel B. Chase, Jr., Board of Governors of the Federal Reserve System, in *Annual Report, 1973*, Federal Reserve Bank of Minneapolis (1973), p. 5.

leasing, and other permissible businesses. As participation in nonbanking activities grows, banks *should* contribute a diminishing share of earnings to the holding companies. Management will determine the extent to which nonbanking activities contribute to earnings. As previously noted, managing a successful holding company requires a different philosophy from managing a bank.

It is clear that Congress intended to preserve the separation of bank and bank-related activities from commerce. This principle is incorporated in the Banking Act of 1933, the Bank Holding Company Act of 1956, and most recently in the 1970 amendments to the Bank Holding Company Act. Nevertheless, as the Board of Governors enumerates the list of permissible business activities, the distinction between bank-related activities and commerce becomes less clear.

## Questions

1 Discuss the similarities and differences between the main types of one-bank holding companies.
2 What are the major reasons that led to the rapid increase in the number and importance of bank holding companies?
3 There are approximately 14,000 commercial banks in the United States, yet some feel that the banking structure is not decentralized. Express your views on whether American banking structure is centralized or decentralized.
4 What were the primary objectives of the Bank Holding Company Act of 1956? How well did the act achieve those objectives?
5 Explain how the 1970 amendments strengthened the Bank Holding Company Act.
6 The Bank Merger Act of 1960 listed several factors that federal banking authorities must consider when reviewing bank merger applications. List these factors and explain how banking agencies and courts have tended to view them differently.
7 Do you feel that bank holding companies are, as a whole, beneficial or detrimental to the American economy? Cite reasons to support your choice.
8 Do you feel that the same antitrust laws that apply to other businesses should be applied to commercial banks or do you agree that banks are a unique line of commerce and should be governed by other statutes? Support your answer.
9 Explain how management philosophies might be different depending on whether the chief executive of a bank holding company viewed himself primarily as a banker or as a bank holding company executive.
10 What banks in your area are affiliated with holding companies? Are they engaged in any nonbanking activities? What?

# Bibliography

*Conference on Banking and Regulations*. Federal Reserve Bank of Minneapolis, 1973.

Johnson, Richard B. *The Bank Holding Company: 1973*. Dallas, Texas: Southern Methodist University Press. 1973.

*Proceedings of Conference on Bank Structure and Competition*. Federal Reserve Bank of Chicago (annual).

U.S., Congress, House, Committee on Banking and Currency, Staff Report, *The Growth of Unregistered Bank Holding Companies—Problems and Prospects,* 91st Cong. 1st sess. (February 1969).

U.S., Congress, Senate, Committee on Banking and Currency, *One-Bank Holding Company Legislation of 1970, Hearings,* 91st Cong. 2d sess. (May 1970).

Chapter

# 15

# Branch and unit banking

Banking structure is in a state of evolution, one important aspect of which concerns branch banking.[1] Although branch banking in this country dates back to the eighteenth century, this chapter focuses on recent developments. Changes in state banking laws are one development. During the 1960s, four states—New Jersey, New Hampshire, New York, and Virginia—liberalized their branching laws. Further evidence of the development of branch banking is the increased number of additional bank offices. As shown in Figure 15–1, in 1962 the number of banks exceeded the number of their additional bank offices—mainly branches—by a substantial margin. However, by year-end 1964, the number of additional bank offices surpassed the number of banks. Even more startling, by the end of 1973 additional bank offices exceeded banks by nearly 100 percent. Following this chapter is an appendix that examines branching in the savings and loan industry.

## The Structure of Banking

### Definitions

Banking structure in the United States is determined by both federal and state banking law. However, branch and unit banking is determined primarily by state law. Because there are considerable differences in the laws

---

[1] A substantial portion of this chapter appeared as an article by the author, "A Big Debate: Branch Versus Unit Banking," *Bankers Magazine* (Autumn 1972), 89–93, and appears with the permission of the publisher.

Figure 15–1

Number of commercial banks and offices in the United States

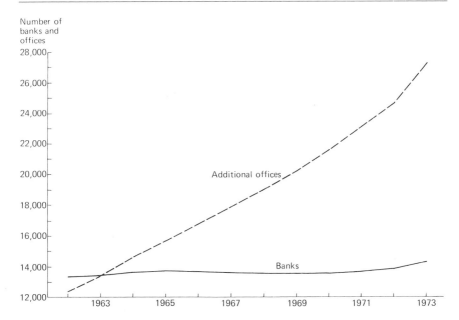

of various states, it is helpful from the outset to define two basic terms, branch banks and auxiliary teller windows. A *branch bank* is a non-mainoffice banking facility that is capable of offering services similar to those of the bank's main office; it can make loans and investments, receive deposits, exchange currency, and carry out other functions of the main bank. An *auxiliary teller's window* is a facility that offers only services similar to those performed by a bank teller and may or may not be physically disconnected from the main banking office; it can accept deposits and exchange currency, but it cannot make loans or investments.

Given this definition of a branch bank, state laws can be divided into three categories: 1) laws that permit branching throughout the state (*statewide* branch banking); 2) laws that permit branching within limited geographic areas (*limited* branch banking); and 3) laws that prohibit branch banking (*unit banking*). Within this framework, a state with a unit banking law cannot have branch banks, but it can have auxiliary teller's windows. States with limited or statewide branching laws can have both branch banks and auxiliary teller's windows.

Although the terms statewide, limited, and unit banking are conventional ways to classify banking structure, they can be misleading. Some states with unit banking laws allow group and chain banking to exist, resulting in a

quasi-branching system.[2] An example of quasi-branching occurred in Florida, a unit banking state, when group and chain banks held 72 percent of total bank deposits.[3] Holding company organizations accounted for over half of the group and chain banks' deposits. Similarly, in states with limited branching laws, the existence of group and chain banking can result in quasi-statewide branching. In spite of this inherent weakness in the classification, it provides a useful framework for analysis and will be used throughout this chapter.

As shown in Table 15–1, at the end of 1973, twenty states permitted statewide branching, fifteen permitted limited branching, and fifteen permitted unit banking. (If the District of Columbia were included in this study, it would be classified as permitting statewide branching because it allows branching throughout the district.) Although New York State is listed as a limited branch banking state, laws have been passed that will change it to a statewide branch banking state in 1976.

Table 15–1

Status of branch banking by state (year-end 1973)

| Statewide branch banking | Limited branch banking | Unit banking |
| --- | --- | --- |
| Alaska | Alabama | Arkansas |
| Arizona | Georgia | Colorado |
| California | Indiana | Florida |
| Connecticut | Kentucky | Illinois |
| Delaware | Louisiana | Iowa |
| Hawaii | Massachusetts | Kansas |
| Idaho | Michigan | Minnesota |
| Maine | Mississippi | Missouri |
| Maryland | New Hampshire | Montana |
| New Jersey | New Mexico | Nebraska |
| Nevada | New York | North Dakota |
| North Carolina | Ohio | Oklahoma |
| Oregon | Pennsylvania | Texas |
| Rhode Island | Tennessee | West Virginia |
| South Carolina | Wisconsin | Wyoming |
| South Dakota | | |
| Utah | | |
| Vermont | | |
| Virginia | | |
| Washington | | |

Source: Various state laws

[2]In *group banking* two or more banks are under the control of a holding company, which may or may not be a commercial bank. In *chain banking* control over several independent banks is exercised through stock ownership of common directors.
[3]Charles D. Salley, "A Decade of Holding Company Regulations in Florida," *Monthly Review*, Federal Reserve Bank of Atlanta (July 1970). In Minnesota, Montana, and Nevada, deposits of banks in holding company groups account for more than half of the deposits in their respective states. For more information on deposits of banks in holding company groups see *Federal Reserve Bulletin* (August 1970), p. A95.

## Geographic Aspects of Banking Structure

*Regional Patterns*    There are marked regional patterns in the U.S. banking structure. As shown in Figure 15–2, statewide branching predominates on the West Coast and exists in more than half of the states along the East Coast. In states between the East Coast and Mississippi River limited branch banking is widespread, and unit banking is found principally in the Midwest.

*Patterns of Assets*    There are substantial differences in dollar volume of commercial bank assets in each of the three banking structure categories. As shown in Table 15–2, at the end of 1973, the assets of insured commercial banks amounted to $155 billion in states with statewide branching laws, $282 billion in states with limited branching laws, and $171 billion in states with unit bank laws. The total dollar volume of assets does not reflect the wide range within each group. Certain states have a much larger dollar volume of assets. California, the most populous state, accounted for 41 percent of the total bank assets in the statewide branch banking category. Most of the other states in this category have relatively small populations and low dollar volume of assets. In the limited branch banking category, New York (the second most populous state) accounted for 37 percent of total bank assets, and Pennsylvania and Ohio make up another fifth of the total. In the category of states with unit banking law, Illinois and Texas

Figure 15–2

States according to status of branch banking (1975)

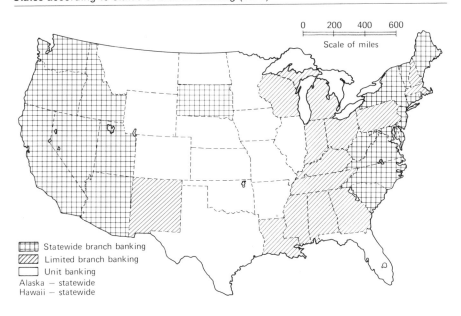

0    200    400    600
Scale of miles

Statewide branch banking
Limited branch banking
Unit banking
Alaska — statewide
Hawaii — statewide

Table 15–2

Insured commercial bank assets by state and by type of branching law (year-end 1973; $ millions)

| Statewide branch banking | Total assets | Limited branch banking | Total assets | Unit banking | Total assets |
|---|---|---|---|---|---|
| Alaska | $    742 | Alabama | $  6,792 | Arkansas | $  4,230 |
| Arizona | 5,248 | Georgia | 9,925 | Colorado | 5,977 |
| California | 64,068 | Indiana | 13,486 | Florida | 19,714 |
| Connecticut | 6,447 | Kentucky | 7,037 | Illinois | 45,432 |
| Delaware | 1,674 | Louisiana | 8,814 | Iowa | 8,369 |
| Hawaii | 2,108 | Massachusetts | 12,783 | Kansas | 6,434 |
| Idaho | 1,867 | Michigan | 25,435 | Minnesota | 11,449 |
| Maine | 1,577 | Mississippi | 4,252 | Missouri | 13,973 |
| Maryland | 6,848 | New Hampshire | 1,288 | Montana | 2,157 |
| New Jersey | 19,299 | New Mexico | 2,201 | Nebraska | 4,657 |
| Nevada | 1,545 | New York | 106,075 | North Dakota | 1,790 |
| North Carolina | 10,076 | Ohio | 26,679 | Oklahoma | 7,408 |
| Oregon | 5,169 | Pennsylvania | 35,792 | Texas | 34,682 |
| Rhode Island | 2,145 | Tennessee | 10,329 | West Virginia | 3,868 |
| South Carolina | 3,208 | Wisconsin | 12,101 | Wyoming | 1,109 |
| South Dakota | 2,017 | | | | |
| Utah | 2,460 | | | | |
| Vermont | 1,129 | | | | |
| Virginia | 10,753 | | | | |
| Washington | 6,998 | | | | |
| Total assets[a] | 155,378 | | 282,989 | | 171,249 |

[a] Totals may not add because of rounding
Source: Federal Deposit Insurance Corporation

accounted for nearly half of the total bank assets. On balance, the data suggest that the largest dollar volume of bank assets is found in heavily populated and industrialized states regardless of their banking structure.

*Number of Offices*    The final facet is the number of banking offices in each of the three categories by state. As shown in Table 15–3, the total number of banking offices in states with limited branching laws exceeds the total number in states with unit banking and statewide branching laws by a wide margin. California and New York each have more banking offices than any other state. Interestingly, the number of banking offices in New York, which permits limited branching, is only 17 percent less than the number in California, which permits statewide branching. The data also show that many states with limited branching laws have more banking offices than some states with statewide branching laws. Finally, the number of banking offices in states with unit banking laws is relatively small, less than 6 percent of the total additional and branch bank offices in the United States. Iowa stands out as having an exceptionally large number of banking offices for a state with unit banking laws. In fact, Iowa has more banking offices than many states with limited and statewide branching laws.

Table 15–3

Commercial bank branches and additional offices by state and type of branching law[a]
(June 30, 1973)

| Statewide branch banking | Branches and offices | Limited branch banking | Branches and offices | Unit banking | Additional banking offices |
|---|---|---|---|---|---|
| Alaska | 71 | Alabama | 350 | Arkansas | 202 |
| Arizona | 387 | Georgia | 519 | Colorado | 38 |
| California | 3,320 | Indiana | 750 | Florida | 65 |
| Connecticut | 504 | Kentucky | 406 | Illinois | 159 |
| Delaware | 115 | Louisiana | 458 | Iowa | 355 |
| Hawaii | 147 | Massachusetts | 834 | Kansas | 79 |
| Idaho | 178 | Michigan | 1,353 | Minnesota | 23 |
| Maine | 257 | Mississippi | 420 | Missouri | 166 |
| Maryland | 613 | New Hampshire | 84 | Montana | 12 |
| New Jersey | 1,216 | New Mexico | 165 | Nebraska | 50 |
| Nevada | 95 | New York | 2,771 | North Dakota | 74 |
| North Carolina | 1,385 | Ohio | 1,484 | Oklahoma | 88 |
| Oregon | 390 | Pennsylvania | 1,992 | Texas | 101 |
| Rhode Island | 204 | Tennessee | 619 | West Virginia | 11 |
| South Carolina | 518 | Wisconsin | 304 | Wyoming | 2 |
| South Dakota | 105 | | | | |
| Utah | 164 | | | | |
| Vermont | 102 | | | | |
| Virginia | 1,009 | | | | |
| Washington | 624 | | | | |
| Total branches and offices | 11,404 | | 12,509 | | 1,425 |

[a] Includes banking facilities at government establishments
Source: Board of Governors of the Federal Reserve System

The differences in the number of banking offices per state cannot be explained by the banking structure of that state. Many of the differences among the states can be explained by size of population, number of population centers, and length of time the branching law has been in existence. Moreover, as previously mentioned, quasi branching through group and chain banking makes the numbers less meaningful.

## State Laws

This section highlights selected legal conditions affecting branch and unit banking. The discussion is based on the law as it is used today in establishing additional banking offices.

*Unit Banking*    By definition, states with unit banking laws do not allow branch banking but may permit auxiliary teller's windows. Currently, Wyoming is the only state that prohibits the establishment of new auxiliary teller's windows. The remaining unit banking states allow teller's windows to be

established under a variety of legal conditions. In general the law specifies the number of auxiliary teller's windows allowed and the distance permitted between them and the main banking office. Florida has the most restrictive code in terms of distance: a bank can have only one auxiliary teller's window on property contiguous to its main office. In contrast, Iowa has the most liberal law in terms of distance between the main bank and its teller's windows, as a bank can have one auxiliary teller's window in a contiguous county and two in the city where the main bank is located. (As noted earlier, Iowa has the largest number of additional banking offices of any unit banking state.) In Arkansas, which has the second largest number of additional banking offices, a bank in a large city can establish one auxiliary teller's window within the city limits for each 25,000 of population.[4] Within the gamut of legal conditions that ranges from those of Florida to those of Iowa and Arkansas there are relatively small differences between the remainder of the states. Most allow banks to establish only one auxiliary teller's window, located 1,000 to 2,600 feet from their main office. Some states even specify that auxiliary teller's windows must be some minimum distance from the bank's main office (i.e., 100 feet from a competing bank), and several states provide for banking facilities on military establishments. The remaining states allow banks to have two or more auxiliary teller's windows, with one window in close proximity to the bank and the other(s) permitted to be quite far away. Finally, Kansas and Nebraska banks are permitted to jointly own an auxiliary teller's window.

*Limited Branch Banking*    Limited branch banking refers to branching that is restricted to a relatively small geographic area. The branches may be established by merger, *de novo*, or both, depending on state law. Several states with limited branch banking laws (and some with statewide branching laws) have head office and branch office protection rules. For example, in New Jersey a bank cannot establish a *de novo* branch in a city having a population of 7,500 or more if another bank's head office is located there. Such laws tend to encourage mergers.

As shown in Table 15–4, fifteen states have limited branch banking laws, which among other things establish the maximum distance between the main bank and its branches. More states allow branching on a countywide basis than allow branching in contiguous counties. New York limits branching to banking districts, which are geographic regions into which the state has been divided. Banks are allowed to branch within these banking districts in the same way branching is allowed in a county or contiguous county. Several states use a definite mileage to establish the maximum distance between the main bank and its branches. Thus, Mississippi and New Mexico specify that the maximum distance between a main bank

---

[4]The term *city limits* refers to the city or town where a bank's main office is located.

Table 15–4

Restrictions on limited branch banking

| State | Maximum geographic limit | Population requirement | Capital requirement | Auxiliary teller's windows | Foreign branching |
|---|---|---|---|---|---|
| Alabama | County | Yes | Yes | | |
| Georgia | City | Yes | | | |
| Indiana | County | Yes | Yes | | |
| Kentucky | County | Yes | Yes | | |
| Louisiana | Parish[a] | | Yes | | Yes |
| Massachusetts | County | | | | Yes |
| Michigan | Contiguous county/ 25 miles | | Yes | Yes | Yes |
| Mississippi | 100 miles | Yes | | Yes | |
| New Hampshire | City + 30 miles | | | | |
| New Mexico | 100 miles | | | | |
| New York | District | | | Yes | Yes | Yes |
| Ohio | County[a] | Yes | Yes | | |
| Pennsylvania | Contiguous county | Yes | Yes | | Yes |
| Tennessee | County | | | | |
| Wisconsin | Contiguous county 25 miles | | | | |

[a] Under special circumstances banks can branch in contiguous counties or parishes
Source: Various state laws

and its branches can be 100 miles, while New Hampshire specifies the maximum distance as 30 miles. Georgia has the smallest geographic limit and restricts branching to the city where the main bank is located.

In addition to geographic constraints seven states restrict branch banking on the basis of population.[5] For example, a bank may have one branch in a city with a population of less than 40,000 and two branches if the city has a population of more than 40,000 but less than 60,000. In several states population is defined so narrowly as to suggest that legislators had particular cities or counties in mind when drafting the law. This appears to be the situation in Alabama, where the law singles out a county with a population of not less than 26,000 and not more than 27,000. A review of state banking law reveals that population covenants tend to be more narrowly defined and, consequently, more restrictive in sparsely populated areas than in densely populated ones.

Finally, as shown in Table 15–4, eight states have laws restricting branch banking on the basis of capital and surplus. Capital requirements for branch banks are less restrictive than population requirements. They are based on: 1) the paid-in capital and surplus of the main bank, 2) the

[5]Population is based on recent census reports.

minimum capital per branch bank, and/or 3) the minimum capital of the main or branch bank for a given population and/or location.

In addition to branch bank offices, five states with limited banking laws allow auxiliary teller's windows, and four have provisions for the establishment of foreign branches.

*Statewide Branch Banking*    The statewide branch banking category includes twenty states (see Table 15–1) and the District of Columbia. Statewide branch banking means that commercial banks can establish branch banks throughout the state either by means of merger or *de novo*. This license does not mean that banks will establish an unlimited number of branch offices. In fact, as noted earlier, the number of banking offices established in states that allow statewide branching is frequently less than the number in states with limited branching laws.

Also, statewide branch banking is not quite as liberal as it may appear because most of the states impose some minimal restraints on branching, such as capital requirements, population restrictions, and limits to the number of branch offices. For example, in some states the amount of capital required to establish a branch is increased when the branch is outside the city or county where the main bank is located. In Maryland and North Carolina capital requirements are based on population. Hawaii, on the other hand, places some limit on the number of branches allowed each bank. In Hawaii banking laws permit statewide branching but limit the number of branches a bank may have in the Honolulu area, which is divided into three banking zones with a bank permitted up to four branches within each zone.

## The Pros and Cons of Branch and Unit Banking

Arguments for and against branch banking have raged in this country since the last half of the eighteenth century.[6] Alexander Hamilton, one of the first to criticize multiple-office banking, feared that weak branches might endanger the whole banking system. (Interestingly, Hamilton's First Bank of the United States had eight branch offices, and the Second Bank of the United States had 27 branches located in almost every state.) History tells us that Hamilton was right. Management, communications, and transportation problems contributed to unprofitable branches, which weakened the banking system.

As time progressed, arguments for and against branch banking became emotional and vitriolic. Those opposed to branch banking argued that it

---

[6]For an interesting survey of banking history see Gerald C. Fischer, *American Banking Structure* (New York: Columbia University Press, 1968), Chapter 2.

leads to monopoly, that local interests are sacrificed, and that branch managers tend to be impersonal.[7] Some argued that the "development toward centralized control is out of harmony with the traditional American principle of local autonomy under which vast national resources have been developed."[8] Small unit banks had furnished the financial services that helped extend the nation westward, and they "became objects of community pride; they were controlled by a local board of directors; and they had intimate personal knowledge of the character, ability, and resources of their customers."[9] Those in favor of branch banking agrued that it strengthens the system, because with greater resources branch banks can achieve economies of scale and the diversification needed for soundness. Furthermore, branch offices generally require less capital than unit banks. In the past it was the small, poorly managed banks—not branch banks—that failed.

Great care must be taken not to confuse arguments about banking structure (i.e., branch versus unit banking) with arguments about size. Large banks can offer a wider variety of services than small banks, and some of the largest commercial bank organizations in the United States are located in unit banking states. The data in Table 15–5 show the twenty-five largest banks in the United States. Three of them are located in unit banking states (Texas and Illinois).

In spite of the comments on size, there are elements of truth in arguments about branch and unit banking. An example would be the number and size of banks that failed during part of the Depression. During the 1921–1933 period the number of banks in the United States declined by more than 16,000 and the number of branches increased by 1,500.[10] Many of the banks that were suspended were small, had capital of less than $25,000, and were located in towns with a population of less than 10,000. Fewer than 10 percent of the suspensions occurred in towns with a population over 10,000.[11]

On the other hand, there is evidence that branch banking results in a more concentrated banking structure in states and metropolitan areas than unit banking.[12] There were more banks, with smaller concentration of deposits, in

[7]These arguments and others can be found in "The New Look in Banking Structure," Monthly Review, Federal Reserve Bank of Richmond (July 1963).
[8]Charles Wallace Collins, The Branch Banking Question (New York: Macmillan, 1926), pp. 8–9.
[9]Ibid.
[10]U.S. Department of Commerce, Bureau of Census, Historical Statistics of the United States, Colonial Times to 1957 (Washington, D.C.: U.S. Government Printing Office, 1960), pp. 624–635.
[11]For a discussion of bank suspensions and their significance during the 1921–1930 period see Gains Thomson Cartinhour, Branch, Group and Chain Banking (New York: Macmillan, 1931), Chapter 11.
[12]Bernard Shull and Paul Horvitz, "Branch Banks and the Structure of Competition," National Bank Review (March 1964); Jack M. Guttentag and Edward Herman, "Banking Structure and Performance," Bulletin, New York University, Institute of Finance, 41/43 (1967), 52–65; "The Structure of Commercial Banking," Federal Reserve Bulletin (March 1970).

Table 15–5

The twenty-five largest banks in the United States (year-end 1973)

| Rank | Structure[a] | Name | Location | Deposits ($ billions) |
|---|---|---|---|---|
| 1 | S | Bank of America, N.T. & S.A. | San Francisco, Cal. | 41.8 |
| 2 | L | First National City Bank | New York, N.Y. | 34.9 |
| 3 | L | Chase Manhattan Bank, N.A. (The) | New York, N.Y. | 29.8 |
| 4 | L | Manufacturers Hanover Trust Co. | New York, N.Y. | 16.9 |
| 5 | L | Morgan Guaranty Trust Co. of N.Y. | New York, N.Y. | 15.3 |
| 6 | L | Chemical Bank | New York, N.Y. | 14.2 |
| 7 | L | Bankers Trust Company | New York, N.Y. | 14.0 |
| 8 | U | Continental Illinois National Bank and Trust Company of Chicago | Chicago, Ill. | 12.3 |
| 9 | U | First National Bank of Chicago (The) | Chicago, Ill. | 12.0 |
| 10 | S | Security Pacific National Bank | Los Angeles, Cal. | 11.4 |
| 11 | S | Wells Fargo Bank, N.A. | San Francisco, Cal. | 9.0 |
| 12 | S | Crocker National Bank | San Francisco, Cal. | 8.0 |
| 13 | L | Mellon Bank, N.A. | Pittsburgh, Pa. | 7.3 |
| 14 | L | Irving Trust Company | New York, N.Y. | 6.9 |
| 15 | S | United California | Los Angeles, Cal. | 6.8 |
| 16 | L | National Bank of Detroit | Detroit, Mich. | 5.2 |
| 17 | L | Marine Midland Bank—New York | New York, N.Y. | 4.8 |
| 18 | L | First National Bank of Boston (The) | Boston, Mass. | 4.6 |
| 19 | S | Union Bank | Los Angeles, Cal. | 3.6 |
| 20 | L | Franklin National Bank | Mineola, N.Y. | 3.5 |
| 21 | L | First Pennsylvania Banking and Trust Company (The) | Philadelphia, Pa. | 3.4 |
| 22 | U | Republic National Bank of Dallas | Dallas, Texas | 2.8 |
| 23 | L | Cleveland Trust Company (The) | Cleveland, Ohio | 2.6 |
| 24 | S | Seattle-First National Bank | Seattle, Wash. | 2.5 |
| 25 | L | Girard Trust Bank | Philadelphia, Pa. | 2.5 |

[a] S = statewide branch banking; L = limited branch banking; U = unit banking
Source: *American Banker* (February 13, 1973)

states with unit banking than in states with branch banking.[13] Nevertheless, studies of banking structure and performance "have not revealed any strong, inherent tendencies toward undue concentration and monopoly."[14]

It is not clear why the concentration of deposits is higher for branch banking than for unit banking. Because banks are multiproduct firms serving different types of customers, the relevant market is not easily defined in geographic terms. Business loans may be made to firms located in regional markets or throughout the United States or worldwide, while real estate and

[13]The term *concentration* refers to the degree to which deposits are held by a few (i.e., three or five) large banks in an area such as a state.
[14]Clay J. Anderson, "Diversification, Supervision, and the Public Interest," *Business Review,* Federal Reserve Bank of Philadelphia (January 1968), p. 10. For a similar conclusion and further discussion see "Recent Changes in Banking Structure in the United States," U.S., Congress, Senate, Select Committee on Small Business, 91st Cong., 2d sess., March 30, 1970. Also "The Structure of Commercial Banking," *Federal Reserve Bulletin* (March 1970).

consumer loans are made locally. Similarly, large negotiable certificates of deposit are held by business concerns and investors who can be located anywhere, while passbook savings generally belong to local depositors. Thus, there is little reason to believe that state boundaries and meaningful banking markets coincide. Consequently, the geographic limits that underlie deposit-concentration ratios are arbitrary, and the ratios themselves are of questionable value.

The arguments for and against branch banking could be debated endlessly, but two facets of the argument deserve additional comment. The first concerns the quantity of services that branch and unit banks offer their customers, and the second concerns competition between branch banks and unit banks.

## Banking Structure and the Quantity of Service

Several studies suggest that there is a significant relationship between banking structure and the quantity of services offered to banking customers. Two studies made by the Federal Reserve System surveyed the number of commercial banking institutions in population centers of various sizes.[15] One finding of the studies was that the number of banks operating in a given area generally increases with the population. Regardless of the type of banking structure, no community with a population of less than 1,000 has more than one bank. However, banking structure is important in larger population centers. In metropolitan areas with populations of more than 50,000, branch banks provide more offices than unit banks. States with branching laws had an average of eighty-nine banking offices per metropolitan area surveyed by the Federal Reserve, compared with thirty-six banking offices per area in states with unit banking. The difference between the number of banking offices was particularly striking in the large metropolitan areas. Another way to illustrate the same point is to examine the average population per bank office. In early 1970, the average population per bank office was 5,924 in states with unit banking and 4,915 in states that allow branching. Thus, states that allow branch banking tend to have more bank offices per capita than states with unit banking.

The number of bank organizations located in a community does not tell us how well the bank serves that community. Obviously, one of the most important functions of a bank is to lend money, and the loan-to-asset ratio is one measure of a bank's lending policy. In general the higher the loan-to-asset ratio, the greater the credit extension to the community. In a recent article, the Federal Reserve Bank of Chicago reviewed seven studies that

---

[15]"Changes in Banking Structure," *Federal Reserve Bulletin* (September 1963), p. 1197, and "The Structure of Commercial Banking," *Federal Reserve Bulletin* (March 1970), p. 206.

examined loan-to-asset ratios.[16] All seven studies found that branch banks have higher loan-to-asset ratios than unit banks.

There are several explanations for branch banks having higher loan-to-asset ratios than unit banks. One explanation is that many branch banks are located in rapidly growing western states where large amounts of capital are required. Further explanations for the differences in loan-to-asset ratios are found in a study prepared for the Pennsylvania Banking Law Commission.[17] According to Guttentag and Herman, the higher ratios of branch banks appear to result from their wider network of offices that place them in closer proximity to their customers. They point out that branch banks are willing to be less liquid than unit banks, and they have an automatic mechanism for channeling funds from offices where loan demand is slack to offices where loan demand is strong.

To some extent unit banks can also transfer funds to areas where loan demand is strong. On the national level the channeling of funds is accomplished quickly through the purchase and sale of federal funds and loan participations. In addition, funds can be transferred through correspondent bank relationships and interbank deposits.

## Competition

Can small unit banks compete effectively with large banks with branches? This question concerns both bank competition in general and competition between small unit banks and large banks with branches.

First, with whom do banks compete? Banks are multiproduct companies that compete for both liabilities and assets. On the liability side of the balance sheet, commercial banks did not fare well in recent years. To illustrate the point, data for 1969 are presented because some of the changes in financial assets in that year were more dramatic than in recent years. In 1969, large negotiable certificates of deposits at commercial banks declined by $12.5 billion. When market interest rates exceeded the maximum rates that banks could pay on deposits, investors withdrew their funds from savings institutions and invested them in marketable securities. In 1969, individuals invested $27 billion in marketable securities, more than seven times the amount invested in the previous year! The bulk of the funds were invested in U.S. Treasury securities and state and local obligations. Investment in U.S. government agency securities was also substantially greater.

---

[16]Larry R. Mote, "Competition in Banking: What Is Known?" *Business Conditions,* Federal Reserve Bank of Chicago (February 1967).
[17]Guttentag and Herman, p. 26.

Banks also compete with other types of savings institutions for the savings dollar. At the end of 1969, time deposits at all commercial banks amounted to $197 billion, $5 billion less than deposits at savings and loan associations and mutual savings banks. In addition, commercial banks compete with insurance companies, pension funds, and credit unions. The extent of the competition between banks and nonbank financial institutions is frequently underestimated. For example, in 1969 savings deposits at commercial banks declined, but the amount of ordinary life insurance (which contains a savings feature) in force in the United States increased almost 8 percent and amounted to $679 billion. It is clear that commercial banks compete not only with local banks for savings, but also with marketable securities and other financial institutions. In a study prepared for the Commission on Money and Credit, the American Bankers Association came to the same conclusion and went one step further. They stated that "statutes in several states that limit a commercial bank to one office constitute an impediment to some commercial banks in their competition with nonbank financial institutions."[18]

Similarly, it can be shown that competition for bank assets such as loans is not confined to local banks, but it is widespread. A few statistics on major loan categories will help to illustrate the point. One major category is mortgage loans, which in 1969 accounted for one-fourth of total loans outstanding at insured commercial banks. In terms of dollar volume, mortgage-lending activity amounted to $4.9 billion at commercial banks and more than $14.6 billion at other savings institutions.[19] Likewise, in 1969 commercial banks accounted for less than half of the $11 billion in consumer credit loans made.[20] The point is that commercial banks compete in many markets. To limit a bank's relevant market, or its sphere of competition, to the bank next door—be it large or small—may be misleading at best and wrong at worst. There is some evidence to support the view that the spread of branch banking increases bank competition.[21] However, there is little or no evidence that this increased competition is harmful.

To turn to the second question concerning competition: Can a small unit bank compete with a large bank with branches? A recent study by Ernest Kohn, sponsored by the New York State Banking Department, sheds some light on that question.[22] Kohn made a comparative analysis of small banks' profitability before and after a large bank entered the community by

---

[18]American Bankers Association, *The Commercial Banking Industry*, prepared for the Commission on Money and Credit (Englewood Cliffs, N.J.: Prentice-Hall, 1962), p. 29.
[19]Savings institutions include savings and loan associations and mutual savings banks.
[20]Total consumer credit loans made in 1969 amounted to $11.1 billion and commercial banks accounted for $4.9 billion.
[21]David C. Motter and Dean Carson, "Bank Entry and the Public Interest: A Case Study," *The National Bank Review* (June 1964). Also, Guttentag and Herman, p. 77.
[22]Ernest Kohn, *The Future of Small Banks*, New York State Banking Department (December 1966).

merger. The results of the study "do not support the contention that the profitability of most small banks is adversely affected by large banks, although their deposit growth rates appear to have been adversely affected."[23]

In addition to the Kohn study, the author concluded from interviews with bankers, regulators, and economists that well-managed small banks could compete with, if not outperform, many large banks. Other studies came to similar conclusions.[24]

## Summary

Branch and unit banking is an emotional issue for some bankers, who view any change from past practices with suspicion. For the public it is a matter of convenience. The crux of the problem is summarized neatly in the following statement by Professor Roy Schotland of Georgetown University.

> *Unless we give fully as high a priority to change as we do to lawfulness and efficiency we will find on the one hand that many strands in our legal, regulatory web are blocking wise and efficient business conduct because of a vanished problem or fear of an earlier generation, while on the other hand we lack protection against new evils. Similarly, one generation's efficiencies will become the plodding antiquities of the next generation . . .*[25]

The following appendix provides a contrasting philosophy of branch and unit banking within the context of one state's savings and loan industry.

## Questions

1  Distinguish between branch banks and auxiliary teller's windows and explain how these terms relate to the branch banking versus unit banking question.
2  Explain how the terms "statewide," "limited," and "unit banking" can be misleading in classifying a state's banking structure. What is the banking structure in your state? Would you be in favor of a change? Why?
3  Discuss the differences in banking structure that may exist among states that are classified as unit banking states.
4  Explain the various factors considered by limited branch banking states in determining the extent of branching that is allowed.

---

[23]*Ibid.*, p. 167.
[24]For a discussion see Fischer, *American Banking Structure*, pp. 168–173.
[25]*Annual Report, 1973*, Federal Reserve Bank of Minneapolis (1974), p. 7.

5 Why may there be more restrictions on branching in states with statewide branching than the statewide classification implies?

6 Do you favor unit banking, branch banking, or a combination of the two? Support your answer with a discussion of the relative merits of branch and unit banking.

7 Throughout Canada there are only nine banks, and there has not been a bank failure in Canada since 1923. In the United States thousands of banks failed during the 1930s, and even now several banks fail almost every year. What implications, if any, does the Canadian example have for banking structures in the United States?

8 Do you feel that the lack of nationwide branching seriously impedes the flow of funds between regions of the United States?

9 It has sometimes been argued that statewide branching can reduce monopolistic tendencies in banking. Is this statement true?

10 Distinguish between arguments about banking structure and bank size.

11 What type of banking structure provides the greatest benefits to the public?

# Appendix 15A

## The Changing Structure of the California Savings and Loan Industry

*Remarks by Dr. Maurice Mann, President, Federal Home Loan Bank of San Francisco, at the Annual Convention, California Savings and Loan League, Los Angeles, September 23, 1974. Dr. Mann acknowledges the assistance of Dr. Mark J. Riedy, Vice President and Chief Economist, and Dr. Thomas R. Harter, Economist, Federal Home Loan Bank of San Francisco.*

Not surprisingly, my natural tendency is to deal with topics involving economic matters. Today is no exception, although I am putting my discussion in a regulatory context. This, it seems to me, is highly appropriate in view of the fact that the structure and regulation of financial institutions have a wide range of economic implications, which is one reason the unique California S & L industry reacts so strongly to national economic events and policies. Moreover, I think it is both fitting and timely for me to discuss some of the basic philosophies, concepts, and approaches that underlie the decision-making process at our bank and the Federal Home Loan Bank Board in matters involving the structure and development of the S & L industry.

Let me lay some groundwork for my remarks by reviewing a few fundamental precepts. For example, it is generally acknowledged that, on average, a typical savings and loan association in California pools the savings of ten individuals and lends those funds to one borrower for the purchase of a home. The relationship between savers and borrowers has an extremely important connection to the structure of the savings and loan industry, in California as well as elsewhere.

The reason for this is that S & L's are financial intermediaries, whose primary function is to be the middle man—or to serve as an agent—between individual savers seeking financial security and interest income, and individual borrowers seeking long-term capital at a reasonable cost, primarily to buy a home. But S & L's perform more than a simple "brokerage" function; they assume certain risks in the process. First, associations accept an interest-rate risk by borrowing short and lending long.

Second, associations are willing to accept a reasonable risk that the mortgage loan will not be repaid. The ability of associations to handle these risks successfully largely determines, and is determined by, growth and profitability. From an industry standpoint, it is obvious, therefore, that the ability of the industry to perform the intermediary function between savers and borrowers will be affected appreciably by the efficiency of the industry itself.

Pursuing this concept further, efficiency—as it applies to savings and loan associations—has at least two major dimensions: operating efficiency and allocative efficiency. In the case of S & L's, operating efficiency concerns the optimal size of an individual association—the size at which the lowest cost per unit of output is achieved. Allocative efficiency relates to the ease and convenience of resource allocation, which—for S & L's—would involve an industry structure that supports the smooth and rapid flow of funds among various submarkets.

Operating and allocative efficiencies, however, are not necessarily achieved by the same means or in the same way. In fact, certain structural decisions may cause or permit a reduction in one area in order to achieve greater efficiency in the other area. For example, a liberal branching policy tends to increase allocative efficiency by improving the flow of funds within or between markets. At the same time, however, rapid expansion of branches may reduce operating efficiency by increasing production costs, at least initially. Likewise, liberal and aggressive merger policies might increase operating efficiency through economies of scale, but may reduce allocative efficiency by eliminating competition. This is not to say, however, that the elimination of competition necessarily inhibits allocative efficiency, nor that greater economies of scale will always result from mergers.

Association management ultimately plays a major role in determining the social benefits and social costs—and the efficiency—of active branching and merger policies. Ideally, these concepts of efficiency guide regulators—either consciously or subconsciously—as they react to changing market conditions and to the multitude of applications received from S & L's, and as they attempt to achieve an industry structure that maximizes social benefits. Obviously, measurement of the operating and allocative efficiency of any application that will affect industry structure reflects, at best, well-informed judgment, not complete and certain knowledge. Moreover, regulators—believe it or not—are human, and, as such, tend to interpret social costs and social benefits in unique and different ways, which may be subject to legitimate debate by all interested parties.

## Branching—A Key to Industry Structure

With these brief conceptual comments as background, let me turn now to a narrower aspect of the structure question—the branching phenomenon—which is, of course, a crucial determinant of overall industry structure. I am well aware, also, that the branching issue probably is of greater concern to many of you than the broader concept of industry structure.

As I recall it, Chairman Thomas R. Bomar "shook up" many of his listeners when he spoke at the annual stockholders meeting of our bank last March.

The passage that seemed to be disquieting to so many was the following, quoted directly from the chairman's remarks:

> We [the FHLB Board] have adopted what would be considered a progressive viewpoint and feel approval of all [branch] applications is in order unless there are compelling reasons to the contrary.

In the question period following his remarks, Chairman Bomar amplified his comments by explaining that the board's philosophy is to consider a branch office application as the end result of good business judgment on the part of S & L management, and to accept that judgment barring regulatory or legislative considerations to the contrary.

A few numbers at this point will help to illustrate the extent to which this philosophy has been applied at the board in recent years. For example, during 1970, approximately one-third of the applications handled by the board's Office of Industry Development were branch applications. During 1973, two-thirds of all applications were for branches, of all types. More to the point of Chairman Bomar's comments, the approval ratio doubled in just four years—from 44 percent of all branch applications in 1969 to 88 percent in 1973. This change, I think, is consistent with the bank board's philosophy. The culmination of a rising tide of branch applications to the board's Office of Industry Development and a doubling in the approval ratio by the bank board is a 550 percent jump in the number of branch office facilities approved in 1973 compared with 1969. In 1969, 154 branch applications were approved, while just four years later, 1,008 approvals were granted.

These numbers leave little doubt that branching activity—for federal S & L's—is vigorous and healthy and is a nationwide phenomenon. However, the numbers tell only one part of the branching story—the overall part of the story that covers federal S & L's across the nation. Clearly, the philosophy and attitude of the Federal Home Loan Bank Board are illustrated by these figures. Moreover, to the extent that the attitude and philosophy of the board are carried through at the twelve district FHL Banks, the data reflect what is happening "in the field."

It almost goes without saying, however, that each of the district banks operates in a slightly different fashion from its eleven counterparts and each applies the board's regulations and policies in terms of the unique character of its indigenous industry—S & L associations, savings and loan markets, and the relationships with other deposit-type financial institutions. Variations among the twelve districts are formally recognized by the board in Washington through special arrangements with state commissioners, as exemplified by the working understanding between the board and the California Savings and Loan Commissioner. In addition, the board infor-

mally recognizes inter-district differences by permitting the banks to emphasize the three major criteria in branch applications—which I will mention later—in slightly varying degrees. Nevertheless, the board, as it should, preserves its right and duty to assure overall consistency in the application process by enforcing its policy guidelines at the district bank level.

## The Economics and Philosophy of Branching

Let me return to my opening comments and elaborate on the concepts of allocative and operating efficiency as they relate specifically to branching. Later, I will turn to the structure of the California savings and loan industry.

To underscore a point suggested earlier, behind all legislative and regulatory decisions on branching is a basic concern for the public good. For this reason, some states are unit banking states, while others allow either limited or full branching powers to banks. Similarly, savings and loan associations are given varying amounts of freedom to branch by state and federal authorities—in some cases according to guidelines applicable to banks, and in other cases, with wholly different guidelines. Federal regulations covering S & L's seem to be leading the way toward statewide branching for S & L's and banks in several states—despite strong resistance by state S & L and bank authorities, in some instances. We are fortunate, perhaps, that the three states comprising the Eleventh FHLB District—Arizona, California, and Nevada—resolved the statewide branching question long ago, both for S & L's and commercial banks.

The question of "To branch, or not to branch" (if I may paraphrase Shakespeare) involves the economic concepts discussed earlier. To be specific, the basic economic criteria that support the concept of branching are, in essence, convenience and need to the saver and borrower (allocative efficiency), and the strength and stability of the savings institution (operating efficiency). I am not ignoring two other criteria—"reasonable probability of usefulness and success, and no undue injury to local thrift and home-financing institutions;" these two criteria reflect regulatory, rather than economic, standards. The economic factors already mentioned are, of course, inextricably intertwined with the broader functions and purposes of the financial system—the mobilization of capital and the allocation of scarce financial resources between and among areas of surplus and areas of need. An S & L with a branch office in Ventura, for example, might use its savings balances from Ventura to lend in San Diego, if the funds are more in demand in San Diego than in Ventura. In so doing, the S & L has fulfilled the valuable function of allocating economic resources, in addition to enhancing its own financial position.

To assess the economics of branching in more concrete terms, an S & L should consider opening a branch office only if the office can add to present and prospective profitability and to the financial stability of the overall operation of the S & L. Although "banking by mail" or "S & L-ing by mail" can bring a financial institution practically into the saver's home, certain financial transactions are more appropriately carried out in an S & L office than through the postal service. Hence, an S & L may choose to establish a branch office network that maximizes the exposure and availability of indigenous services to customers, even though the home office retains most or all of the operating decision-making and many of the physical operations that are most economical and efficient when centralized. A branch network allows an S & L to organize and maintain control over geographically dispersed marketing programs, and at the same time to take advantage of operating economies of scale by centering at the home office certain technical specialists and expert administrators, thereby employing the latest in advanced technology for the entire system. Similarly, the development of a branching network permits an S & L to pool capital on both the asset and liability sides of the balance sheet in order to take advantage of financial economies of scale.

A recently released survey clearly indicates the importance of convenience to the consumer as a determinant of branching among financial institutions, and for savings and loan associations in particular. Unidex Corp., an Indiana-based company specializing in consumer preference studies, surveyed 2,000 households to determine the major factors consumers take into account in selecting a bank and a savings and loan association. Convenience of location was the prime consideration in the bank selection process, followed by the friendliness of employees (only half as many responses as convenience), and services available (a 14 percent response). In fifth, or last place on the list, was consideration of the interest rate paid on savings at a bank. While convenience received a 32 percent response, interest paid rated only 5 percent. In selecting a savings and loan association, consumers also headed their preference list with convenience, a 27.5 percent response rate. In strong second place, however, were the interest rates paid—almost 24 percent of the responses. Services available received just 7.1 percent of the consumer preferences and finished in last place.

In my opinion, findings such as these have an important bearing on the determinants of branching for an S & L and for branching policies among the regulatory authorities involved. Convenience is clearly a critical consideration, but that is not a particularly complex decision. More interesting and more important is the fact that S & L's have only a narrow range of services to offer consumers. In marketing terminology, S & L's have an undifferentiated product—savings accounts. Economics tells us that firms whose products lack identification or differentiation from competitors'

products must resort primarily to price competition to attract customers. Savings and loans price savings accounts higher than bank savings accounts, as befits such a market situation. Regulation Q ceilings formally acknowledge the competitive disadvantages of S & L's vis-à-vis banks by providing a rate differential in favor of S & L's. In this connection, some would argue that lowering the differential to one-quarter of one percent only pays lip service to at least one of the original purposes of Regulation Q. The relevant point to be drawn from this analysis of competition for savers (and savings) is that because S & L's have an undifferentiated product—money—and because all S & L's in a given market are generally forced by competition to pay identical (ceiling) rates for savings, convenience of location for branch offices is of paramount importance to an S & L.

Carried to an extreme, the importance of the convenience factor *may* justify the approval of four S & L offices on four corners of an intersection, if the nature of the intersection offers unusual convenience for savers. I want to emphasize, however, that this is a conclusion derived from economic considerations that could—and undoubtedly would—be overridden by regulatory policies. I am not sure the S & L industry wants to repeat the experience of the four-service-station intersections of the 1960s. There are and were, of course, far more service stations than S & L branch offices, but—to be facetious—this situation could be reversed, if (1) we have another oil crisis and (2) S & L's continue to branch at the present rapid rate.

# Bibliography

American Bankers Association. The Commercial Banking Industry. Prepared for the Commission on Money and Credit. Englewood Cliffs, N.J.: Prentice-Hall, 1962.

Fischer, Gerald C. *American Banking Structure*. New York: Columbia University Press, 1968.

Guttentag, Jack M., and Edward Herman. "Banking Structure and Performance." *Bulletin*, New York University, Institute of Finance, 41/43 (1967).

# 16

# The Hunt Commission: a financial format

In the years 1966 and 1969, there were precipitous declines in the number of private housing starts and wrenching changes in the liabilities of financial institutions. In 1969, the number of new private housing starts declined more than one-third, and the dollar volume of large negotiable certificates of deposit at commercial banks declined $12.5 billion. These related incidents were symptoms of an unhealthy economy. Against this background, President Nixon appointed a commission under the leadership of Reed O. Hunt to study the financial structure of the United States.[1] It was hoped that the recommendations of the commission would improve the health of our financial institutions and help the battered housing industry. In late 1971, the President's Commission on Financial Structure and Regulation, commonly called the Hunt Commission, made public eighty-nine recommendations for federal and state legislation and regulatory changes affecting commercial banks, mutual savings banks, savings and loan associations, credit unions, life insurance companies, and pension funds.[2] It is important to keep in mind that the commission believed its recommendations should be considered as a unified whole rather than individually. "Taken together . . . [the recommendations] produce a structural and regulatory system which

---

[1]Reed O. Hunt is the retired Chairman of the Board, Crown Zellerbach Corporation. For further discussion of the economic climate at the time the report was written see Donald P. Jacobs and Almarin Phillips, "The Commission on Financial Structure and Regulation: Its Organization and Recommendations," *Journal of Finance,* 27 (May 1972), 319–328.
[2]*The Report of the President's Commission on Financial Structure and Regulation* (Washington, D.C.: U.S. Government Printing Office, 1971).

will efficiently and equitably serve the financial needs of the country in the coming decades."[3]

This chapter is a critique and synopsis of the commission's recommendations concerning deposit-type institutions. Specifically, it describes aspects of financial structure that would emerge if particular recommendations of the Hunt Commission were adopted. It does not deal with certain issues that the Hunt Commission avoided: 1) the Vietnam war—a principal cause of the financial pressures in the last half of the 1960s; 2) the pervasiveness of inflation; and 3) specifying social goals and acceptance of the social priority of housing.[4] Following the chapter is an appendix dealing with legislative problems associated with changing the U.S. financial structure.

## Issues and Answers

The basic problem that the Hunt Commission dealt with concerned mortgage-lending institutions, such as savings and loan associations, which had difficulty in coping with the changes in monetary policy, interest rates, and economic conditions during the late 1960s. Savings and loan associations exemplify the problem because they have a greater imbalance in the maturity structure of their assets and liabilities than any other type of financial institution. They borrow short-term savings deposits and lend long-term mortgages. Consequently, their mortgage portfolios turn over at a slower rate than their deposits. The central problem is the fact that the short-term rates they paid on deposits increased relatively more than the long-term rates they received from mortgages, thereby reducing their profits in recent years.[5] In addition, relatively low interest-rate ceilings on their savings deposits resulted in massive disintermediation that kept them from providing funds for new mortgages and in some cases threatened the very existence of some savings and loan associations. Another view that appeared after the commission's report was published is that the differences between the time pattern of cash inflows and outflows as well as consistent underprediction of increases in short-term interest rates was the real problem.[6] In either case, institutional rigidities contributed to credit-affected downturns in new private housing starts, and the near breakdown of our financial system.

---

[3]*Ibid.*, Letter of Transmittal, iii.
[4]These issues and others are discussed in Roland I. Robinson, "The Hunt Commission Report: A Search for Politically Feasible Solutions," *Journal of Finance,* 27 (September 1972), 765–777.
[5]Irwin Friend, ed., *Study of the Savings and Loan Industry* (Washington, D.C.: Federal Home Loan Bank Board, 1969).
[6]George G. Kaufman, "The Thrift Institution Problem Reconsidered," in *Proceedings of a Conference on Bank Structure and Competition,* Federal Reserve Bank of Chicago (1971).

Solutions to these problems generally consist of reducing the average maturity of the assets of mortgage-lending institutions, lengthening the average maturity of their debt, and removing interest-rate ceilings on deposits. The solution for underpredicting short-term interest rates is better economic forecasting and better economic stabilization policies. The Hunt Commission did not address itself to the last solution, but did make recommendations for restructuring the assets and liabilities of selected financial institutions. Many of the same recommendations were made a decade earlier in the report of the Commission on Money and Credit, but were never adopted.[7] The fate of the recommendations of the Hunt Commission is not so bleak.

## Assets

The recommendations of the Hunt Commission concerning assets focused primarily on expanding the range of loan and investment powers of savings and loan associations, mutual savings banks, and credit unions. Savings and loan associations specialize in mortgage lending; mutual savings banks specialize in both mortgages and corporate bonds; credit unions specialize in consumer goods finance. First, the Hunt Commission recommended that the portfolios of these institutions diversify, if it were to their advantage to do so, although they should retain their traditional roles as mortgage and consumer lenders. Mortgage lenders should be given more leeway in the types of mortgage and construction loans they make, and certain geographic restrictions on where they can make mortgage loans should be removed. In addition, they should be allowed to engage more actively in short-term loans to consumers, which would reduce the average maturity of their assets and perhaps add to their profits. Similarly, credit unions should diversify their portfolios by investing in private and public debt securities and mortgage loans, which would work to lengthen the average maturity of their assets.

The collective effect of these recommendations would be that the three types of financial institutions would have portfolios with similar types of securities. Nevertheless, savings and loan associations and mutual savings banks would still concentrate primarily on mortgage loans, while credit unions would continue to specialize in consumer loans. One advantage of a diversified portfolio is that the collective risk of the assets is reduced by increasing the variety of assets held, as long as the flow of returns from those assets is not perfectly positively correlated. However, the two most important benefits from the eased restrictions would be different

---

[7]*The Report of the Commission on Money and Credit; Their Influence on Jobs, Prices, and Growth* (Englewood Cliffs, N.J.: Prentice-Hall, 1961). For a comparison of the Hunt Commission and the Commission on Money and Credit see Robinson.

average maturities for the institutions' portfolios, and an increased number of institutions capable of providing mortgage credit.

Because the institutions would be competing in the same markets on more or less an equal basis, they should be regulated and taxed in the same way. More will be said about this subject shortly.

## Liabilities

The Hunt Commission also recommended that savings and loan associations, mutual savings banks, and credit unions be allowed to lengthen the average maturity of their respective liabilities and offer a full range of secondary securities to their customers. Currently, their liabilities consist mostly of short-term savings accounts and time deposits. The commission recommended that these institutions be permitted to issue long-term debentures, have third-party payments, and in some cases checking accounts. Both third-party payments and checking accounts are considered low-cost funds because no interest is paid on them, and fees are generally collected for their use. Thus, the recommendations have the effect of lowering costs of short-term funds, lengthening the maturity structure of the longer-term liabilities and increasing the variety of services offered. Finally, interest-rate ceilings (Regulation Q) on some deposits should be removed over a period of years. Interestingly, some of these recommendations (e.g., third-party payments) were already operational at the time the report was written. The intended effect of the report was to obtain wider acceptance for these recommendations and to insure that all financial institutions (state and federal) use them on an equal and orderly basis.

The Hunt Commission also made recommendations affecting the assets and liabilities of commercial banks. In general, the recommendations would make it easier for commercial banks to do what they were already doing. For example, restrictions on borrowing from Federal Reserve Banks should be eased and certain regulatory restrictions on real estate loans should be abolished. On the other side of the balance sheet, commercial banks could also issue long-term debentures. It should be noted that these recommendations are by necessity probably attractive only to large commercial banks. Moreover, commercial banks already issue debentures and offer a complete range of deposits.

## Symbiosis Raises Questions

To recapitulate, the Hunt Commission recommended that the average maturity of the respective assets and liabilities of savings and loan associations, mutual savings banks, and credit unions be matched more closely in the future than they are now. To accomplish this end, their portfolios should

become more diversified and they should be permitted to offer savers a wider variety of forms of savings and payments mechanisms. The adoption of such recommendations would make these institutions similar in many respects to commercial banks. The difference between them would be one of degree rather than kind. Each type of financial institution would serve one principal market, but they would compete in other markets. For example, credit unions would continue to specialize in consumer goods finance, but they would also make mortgage loans. Savings and loan associations would still specialize in home mortgage lending, but would make consumer loans as well. Commercial banks would concentrate on business loans, but would also make consumer loans, mortgage loans, and other types of loans and investments. In short, the Hunt Commission's recommendations imply that in time savings and loan associations, mutual savings banks, and credit unions would become quasi-commercial banks. In fact, the commission recommended that the charters under which some financial institutions are organized should be made more flexible so that the institutions could convert from, say, a mutual to a stock form of organization. In addition, the commission proposed the creation of "mutual commercial banks" that would blend together some of the characteristics of existing thrift institutions. It is important to recognize that both the organizational form of the institutions and their functions would change. The new type of financial institution with a diversified portfolio would be less susceptible to economic shocks than institutions with specialized portfolios. Hopefully, mutual commercial banks would have a beneficial effect on the housing market.

*Number of Outlets*  The creation of a financial system consisting of quasi-commercial banks raises several fundamental issues. First, at the end of 1971, commercial banks, savings and loan associations, mutual savings banks, and credit unions operated about 58,600 main offices and branches throughout the United States.[8] This amounts to one quasi-commercial bank office for every 3,500 people! Some observers may consider such a large number of offices per capita all providing similar services excessive. Moreover, the commission favors statewide branch banking, which by itself is a good idea, in the context of the excessive number of facilities now in existence, consolidation rather than proliferation is a better idea, though not politically feasible.

*Effect on Housing*  The second issue is the effect of institutional credit on housing activity. The Hunt Commission did recommend some tax credits and subsidies to affect housing. One study addressed to this question used a large scale econometric model—the Federal Reserve-MIT-Penn

---

[8] In 1971, there were 24,083 commercial and mutual savings bank offices, 10,500 savings and loan association offices, and about 24,000 credit union offices. The population of the United States was 207 million.

Econometric Model—to evaluate some of the commission's recommendations.[9] The investigators were careful to point out the inability of the
model to measure the effects of recommendations when the institutional
structure has changed. Nevertheless, they concluded that the overall impact of the proposals of the Hunt Commission report "would not have
serious repercussions for the mortgage and housing markets . . .the housing market would probably, on net, gain under the Hunt report, while the
mortgage stock may gain or lose depending on the specific assumptions.
In any case, the magnitudes involved are small relative to the current
outstanding stocks of these assets."[10] In addition, a recent study of housing
experience during periods of credit restraint in Belgium, Canada, Germany, Great Britain, Italy, Switzerland, and the United States concluded
that:

> Cyclical declines in private housing production have been recorded
> to some extent in various nations almost regardless of the prevailing
> types of institutional arrangements. This experience implies that there
> is probably no simple solution for eliminating credit-affected housing
> fluctuations altogether. One step in this direction, however, appears to
> lie in efforts to provide greater stability for flows of funds to mortgage
> lending institutions. To this degree, of course, other sectors of the
> economy may be affected by credit restraint more adversely than
> before.[11]

The obvious question raised by the last two sentences is whether the cure
will be worse than the disease. No one knows what the synergetic effects of
the new structure will be, but the study of other nations reveals that the type
of institutional arrangements affects the amplitude of the housing fluctuations. Germany, for example, has achieved greater stability in this sector
than some other countries.[12] This was accomplished by: 1) a good maturity
mix of the liabilities of their savings institutions, 2) tax and interest subsidies on savings deposits, and 3) a heavily subsidized Bausparkassen (a
closed system of savings and mortgage borrowers that is relatively insu-
lated from monetary conditions). The price paid for this system is considerable pressure to extend subsidies to other types of financial assets and,
more important, the reduced effectiveness of monetary policy.

*Taxation and Regulation*    The final issue centers around the fact that
since savings and loan associations, mutual savings banks, and credit

[9]Ray C. Fair and Dwight M. Jaffee, "The Implications of the Proposals of the Hunt Commission for Mortgage
and Housing Markets: An Empirical Study," in *Policies for a More Competitive Financial System*, proceedings of a conference held in June 1972, Federal Reserve Bank of Boston (June 1972), pp. 99–148.
[10]*Ibid.*, p. 144.
[11]Robert Moore Fisher and Charles J. Siegman, "Patterns of Housing Experience During Periods of Credit
Restraint in Industrialized Countries," *Journal of Finance*, 27 (May 1972), 204–205.
[12]Leo Grebler, "Discussion of the Fisher-Siegman Paper," *Journal of Finance*, 27 (May 1972), 225.

unions are going to act like commercial banks, they should be taxed and regulated like commercial banks. Indeed, the commission did recommend that there should be a uniform nondiscriminatory tax treatment for savings and loan associations, mutual savings banks, and commercial banks. Credit unions were excluded from the uniform tax recommendations because they serve particular groups rather than the general public, and they have other special characteristics. However, credit unions should be allowed to convert their charters to a mutual savings and loan association charter or a mutual commercial bank charter if they wish to do so.

In addition to uniform tax treatment, there would be uniform reserve requirements on demand deposits and on some other types of deposits, while reserve requirements on time and savings deposits would be abolished over a period of time.

Finally, there would be a shuffling of regulatory and supervisory functions, and new agencies would replace those already in existence. One new agency would be created to supervise the insurance funds of all types of financial institutions instead of having a different agency for each fund. In addition, two regulatory agencies were recommended to supervise state-chartered banks and federally chartered banks, taking over most of the examination and supervisory functions of the Federal Reserve System.

To facilitate conversions and new charters, the commission stated that:

> "The widest feasible options among chartering and supervisory agencies should be created and maintained. When a particular type of financial institution can be chartered by only one agency—whether state or federal—... the agency may become over-zealous in protecting existing firms, with the result that entry by new firms is foreclosed ... [and] the agency may not be innovative and imaginative. ... Opportunities for dual chartering and supervision mitigate these dangers and improve service to the public ..."[13]

Joseph R. Barr, President, American Security and Trust Company, and former Secretary of the Treasury, took sharp exception to the above statement and argued against the dual banking system.[14] He claimed that diffused power over financial institutions has created more problems than it solved and cited the following historical evidence:

1 The chaotic money conditions that existed in various states under the Articles of Confederation were responsible for the provision in the Con-

---

[13]*The Report of the President's Commission on Financial Structure and Regulation*, p. 60.
[14]Joseph R. Barr, "A Revised Regulatory Framework," in *Policies for a More Competitive Financial System*, proceedings of a conference held June 1972, Federal Reserve Bank of Boston (June 1972), pp. 205–208.

stitution that gave Congress the "power to coin money and regulate the value thereof."

2 When the First Bank of the United States collapsed, the country lacked the financial strength to fight the War of 1812.

3 Wildcat banking after the Civil War helped to foster the National Bank Act.

4 Diffuse chartering and regulatory authorities were a factor that contributed to the failure of thousands of financial institutions in the 1920s and 1930s.

Barr concluded his arguments by pointing out that the commission is in a dilemma because it backs a federal administrator of state banks and requires all banks and some institutions to join the Federal Reserve System. Such recommendations are not consistent with the recommendations for competing regulatory authorities.

Even if all supervisory and regulatory authority for financial institutions were at the federal level of government, this would not assure greater efficiency or stability for our financial system. The relationships between monetary policy, the number of charters, deposit insurance, and bank examinations is far from clear. With respect to the last point, a recent study found that most bank failures were the result of frauds not detected in advance by examiners.[15] Moreover, the study suggested that the principal effects of examination were anticompetitive and anti-innovative. If the correct reason for having examinations is to protect insurance funds, questions are raised whether government or private insurance companies should insure and examine banks. These issues were not discussed in the Hunt Commission report.

## Summary

There are two discernible trends taking place in our financial system. First, many financial institutions have formed holding companies to engage in activities which financial institutions are normally prohibited from entering either by law or regulations. The most important aspect of this trend is the involvement of financial institutions in nonfinancial activities such as data processing, agriculture, manufacturing, and transportation. Since the passage of the 1970 amendments to the Bank Holding Company Act, holding company activities in nonbank-related areas have been constrained.[16] In

---

[15]The study by George Benston was summarized in Allan H. Meltzer, "What the Commission Didn't Recommend," *Journal of Money, Credit, and Banking* (November 1972), 1005–1009.

[16]The Hunt Commission recommended multibank holding companies as an alternative to branch banking. Although a discussion of bank holding companies is beyond the scope of this chapter, it should be pointed out that multibank holding companies are not perfect substitutes for branch banks. Briefly, *each bank* in a holding company has its own charter, officers, capital structure, and portfolio. Only the ownership is common. In contrast, a bank with branches has only one portfolio, capital structure, etc. Moreover, funds can flow more freely between branches than between holding company affiliates. Finally, holding companies are designed to provide bank-related services whereas branch banking offices are designed to provide banking services.

contrast, the second trend is the increasingly congruous nature of financial institutions. Along this line, the essence of the Hunt Commission report is a series of recommendations that would alter savings and loan associations, mutual savings banks, and credit unions, into quasi-commercial banks. These institutions and commercial banks would have similar assets and liabilities and would be uniformly regulated and taxed. Moreover, they would be permitted to convert their charters and become commercial banks.

The new financial structure may solve some problems, but it may also create others. It is reasonable to believe that the portfolios of financial institutions would be more liquid than before, and that the number of sources of mortgage funds would increase. Beyond this, however, the implications of the Hunt Commission's recommendations become less clear. Do we need 58,600 or more financial outlets offering the same services? Why is it that credit-affected housing fluctuations occur in other countries regardless of their financial institutional arrangements? Do we want to eliminate specialized financial institutions? Finally, what are the unintended effects of the new structure? Further research may in time shed some light on these questions.

The basic recommendations of the Hunt Commission report concerned the viability of selected financial institutions and housing activity. By early 1973, neither the viability of financial institutions nor the level of housing activity was a major concern. The amount of savings at thrift institutions and the amount of new private housing starts were near record levels. The major reason for congressional action on the recommendations of the Hunt Commission came from two different quarters. First, there was intense competition for deposits in Massachusetts between mutual savings banks and commercial banks. The mutual savings banks developed a negotiable order of withdrawal (NOW) account, which is equivalent to an interest-bearing checking account. Such accounts were paying 5¼ percent interest. Commercial banks that are not allowed to pay interest on checking accounts are disturbed, to say the least, by NOW accounts. Payment of interest on demand deposits raises a host of questions. Because the distinction between demand deposits and time and savings deposits is blurred, the level of reserves that should be maintained against those deposits is not clear. Moreover, should the Federal Reserve pay interest on the member bank reserves that it holds?

Consumerism is the second factor drawing attention to the Hunt Commission report. Some consumer advocates argue that interest-rate ceilings on time and savings deposits do not benefit consumers. Perhaps, as a result of competitive pressures and consumerism, some of the recommendations of the Hunt Commission will bear fruit.

Finally, Kenneth Boulding, a noted observer of social change, said:

> *As I was driving into Nairobi from the airport a couple of years ago, I looked at the skyline, and I said, "Oh Lord, we've landed in Wichita by mistake." I took my son up the Post Office Tower in London to show him London and we couldn't see St. Paul's through the skyscrapers. And now Tokyo looks like Dallas, Johannesburg looks like Dallas, everything looks like Dallas, if it isn't Wichita. You get the feeling that we travel faster and faster to places that look more like what we left behind. So there really isn't much point in going anywhere . . .*[17]

What does this have to do with financial intermediaries? Well, they, too, are all going to look alike if permissive legislation is passed. The following appendix examines some of the difficulties associated with passing such legislation.

## Questions

1 What economic circumstances led to the creation of the Hunt Commission (The Commission on Financial Structure and Regulation)? What was the major purpose in establishing the commission?
2 What specific problems of savings and loan associations caused them to be studied in such great detail by the Hunt Commission? What general solutions did the commission recommend for these problems?
3 Discuss the recommendations of the Hunt Commission concerning the assets and liabilities of savings and loan associations, savings banks, and credit unions.
4 Explain the differences and similarities between the Hunt Commission recommendations for commercial bank assets and liabilities and the commission recommendations for nonbank depository intermediaries.
5 Explain what "mutual commercial banks" are and what their proposed functions would be.
6 What effects might the Hunt Commission recommendations have on housing activity?
7 Would the Hunt Commission recommendations concerning reserve requirements for depository institutions strengthen or weaken the effectiveness of monetary policy?
8 What changes in regulatory and supervisory agencies were recommended by the Hunt Commission?
9 Discuss the Hunt Commission recommendations concerning branching by depository institutions.

---

[17]*Annual Report, 1973,* Federal Reserve Bank of Minneapolis, p. 9.

10 Discuss the recommendations of the Hunt Commission concerning dual chartering and supervision of banks. Explain why you agree or disagree with these recommendations.

11 Explain how each of the following will affect the structure of the financial system in the future: a) legislation; b) electronic funds transfers; c) financial innovations such as NOW accounts; d) reserve requirements.

# Appendix 16A
## Press Release

*By U.S. Senator Thomas J. McIntyre (D–N.H.), Chairman of the Senate Banking, Housing and Urban Affairs Committee's Financial Institutions Subcommittee, April 18, 1973.*[1]

So the next question is "Senator McIntyre, in what direction are you moving with regard to the Hunt Commission report?" And my response to that question would be "That's a damn good question"—because right now no one that I know in Washington has developed any clearly defined approach to handling the issues and recommendations contained in that report.

As we're well aware, the president's commission strongly urged that all the recommendations contained in the report be considered as a package and warned that piecemeal adoption of the recommendations would raise the danger of creating new and greater imbalance between financial institutions.

Now that position in and of itself creates an almost insurmountable problem for Congress to handle.

Legislative bodies in this country operate through committees with each committee having a separate area of jurisdiction. The Hunt Commission report tied several issues into one bundle and in so doing interposed complicated jurisdictional problems for Congress.

Let me give you an example:

One section of the recommendations deals with taxation of financial institutions, while most of the other sections deal with structure.

So, what's wrong with that?

Well, the problem is that the Senate Banking, Housing and Urban Affairs Committee has clear jurisdiction over the structure of the financial community, housing, and federal banking regulations—but the Senate Finance Committee has exclusive jurisdiction over all tax matters and the same is true in the House with the House Banking and Currency Committee and the Ways and Means Committee.

---

[1]This appendix presents the views of a congressional leader on some legislative problems associated with changing our financial structure.

So, at the beginning of the Hunt Commission report you get as its first recommendation an impossible situation. The structure of the Congress itself makes it nearly impossible to consider this report as a package.

Another problem is the administration's position regarding the Hunt Commission report. This was a presidentially commissioned study instructed to report to the president on its findings—which the commission did on December 22, 1971. It has now been over a year, and Congress has not received one piece of legislation from the president encompassing any or all of the Hunt Commission study.

Whenever anyone asks the officials at the Treasury Department what is happening to the Hunt Commission report, strong assurances are given that they have a hard-working task force engaged in drafting legislation to implement the commission's recommendations.

However, when you read financial institution trade publications, *they* indicate the administration has little or no interest in this report and is not moving with all deliberate speed. My latest contact with the Treasury Department indicates that Treasury thinks some legislation should be ready some time this summer.

So the question boils down to whether the Financial Institutions Subcommittee should begin an examination on its own initiative—without suggested legislation from the president—or to wait for the administration's legislative proposals to finally surface.

The problem is that while we're waiting for the president's proposals, circumstances and events are already forcing us into legislative considerations of several Hunt Commission recommendations.

What I'm saying is that my experience in the Senate tells me that the probability of any examination of the Hunt Commission recommendations as a *package* are very slim.

If I were Jimmy the Greek, I'd say that the odds are better than 100 to 1 against.

But while the Congress has been waiting for the president to send his legislation recommendations to Congress, other events originating primarily in this state and in my own state of New Hampshire have already forced Congress to get involved with *some* of the primary recommendations of the Hunt Commission report, namely, the continuation of the flexible interest rate provisions of Regulation Q and the question of third-party payment systems for thrift institutions.

Regulation Q authority expires on May 30 of this year, and the first question is whether this provision should be extended. As we know, the Hunt Commission report discusses in depth the rationale behind the existence of the authority to impose ceilings on deposit interest rates. And it questions whether such a mechanism does, in fact, provide the desired shelter for deposit thrift institutions from increases in interest rates and sustain the flow of funds into the mortgage markets.

Federal maximums for interest rates on savings accounts have been used since 1966 to protect the liquidity positions of deposit thrift institutions.

There were two basic reasons for limiting interest rates between various financial institutions. One was to hold down deposit rates and insulate deposit institutions from forces in the money markets that might drain funds from them. The other was to maintain a differential between the rates paid by commercial banks and deposit thrift institutions in order to prevent a shifting of funds from the latter to the former.

The Hunt Commission took a very negative position regarding the continuation of Regulation Q, stating that "interest rate regulations have discriminated against small savers." And the commission recommended that rate regulations on time and savings deposits be gradually eliminated.

Other recommendations contained in the report dealt with demand deposits. The commission recommended that prohibition against the payment of interest on demand deposits be retained at this time but reviewed in the future, and it also recommended that savings and loan associations and mutual savings banks be allowed to provide third-party systems, including checking accounts and credit cards to individuals.

As you know, both the Senate and House Banking Committees have completed their inquiries into both the question of the extension of Regulation Q and what to do about NOW accounts. Everyone in this room knows what I am talking about and, in fact, I haven't encountered such intense interest in such a localized issue for several years. What we have at this time is an issue confined to two states, and, in my opinion, the controversy should be settled by the states involved and should not at this time be the subject of federal legislation.

During the hearings not one of the federal regulatory agencies dealing with financial institutions recommended prohibition of NOW accounts and the bills reported out of both the Senate and House Banking Committees took a similar approach. While not outlawing NOW accounts, the reported legislation does provide the FDIC with the authority to regulate these accounts.

The bill reported out of the House Banking Committee repealed the so-called Massachusetts exemption of Regulation Q interest-rate ceiling authority for both mutual savings banks and cooperative banks in the state. The bill reported by the Senate Banking Committee did not go that far, however. In the bill we reported to the Senate floor, we did not completely repeal the Massachusetts exemption on Regulation Q but did change it to provide the FDIC with authority over NOW accounts offered by noninsured banks.

If and when competitive distortions develop because of the existence of NOW accounts, then the FDIC would have clear authority in Massachusetts and all other states to make the necessary competitive adjustments. Both bills are scheduled for floor action in early May, and the issue must be resolved before Regulation Q expires at the end of next month.

The committee's hearings on Regulation Q and NOW accounts did focus on the need to examine the present structure of our financial institutions, and it may well be that in the not too distant future everyone—mutual savings banks, commercial banks, savings and loan associations, and credit unions—will be offering some type of individual interest-bearing account on which third-party instruments could be drawn.

So, I think you can see that Congress is already into an examination of the Hunt Commission report even though at this time we have not received legislative recommendations from the president. It is clear that as the 93rd Congress continues, the subcommittee will get more and more involved with the Hunt Commission study. I would anticipate that either later this year or early next year we would be holding comprehensive hearings and moving toward the implementation of a number of the commission's recommendations.

As I said earlier, however, I doubt that any legislation implementing the Hunt Commission recommendations would emerge as a package. But there are clear indications that the movement within the financial community is toward more competition between commercial banks and thrift institutions. So I am sure one of the central issues that the Financial Institutions Subcommittee will deal with in the near future is the question of third-party payments systems, whether they are in the form of demand deposits, electronic transfer systems, or an expansion of the NOW account concept.

# Flow of Funds, Seasonally Adjusted (Third Quarter, 1974)

Division of Research and Statistics,
Board of Governors of the Federal
Reserve System, Washington, D.C.
20551

# Table List

## Summary Tables

1 Income and product accounts: GNP expenditures and gross saving
2 Total funds raised in credit markets by nonfinancial sectors
3 Direct and indirect sources of funds to credit markets

## Sector Tables

4 Households
5 Total and noncorporate business
6 Corporate business
7 Governments
8 Banking system
9 Subsector statements for component groups in commercial banking
10 Nonbank Financial Institutions
11 Insurance and pension funds
12 Finance not elsewhere classified
13 Rest of the world

## Transaction Tables

14 Gold, official foreign exchange, Treasury currency, and insurance reserves
15 Money stock and time and savings accounts
16 Relation of Flow of Funds money stock data to daily average series
17 U.S. government securities market summary
18 Private securities and mortgages
19 Mortgage markets by type of mortgage
20 Consumer credit and bank loans not elsewhere classified
21 Open market paper and other loans
22 Security credit, trade credit, and taxes payable
23 Miscellaneous financial claims
24 Total financial assets and liabilities
25 Amount and composition of individuals' saving
26 Discrepancies: Summary for sectors and transactions

# Seasonally Adjusted
# Flow of Funds Accounts
# (Third Quarter, 1974)

These tables present first estimates of third quarter Flow of Funds data together with revisions for the first two quarters of 1974. Earlier data are unchanged.

Revisions for the first two quarters of the year reflect the usual source information, listed in the following paragraph, that are not available for first preliminary estimates. In addition, they include sizable revisions of commercial banking data, both assets and liabilities, that reflect June 30 banking totals for bank Call Report tabulations.

Third-quarter figures are based on early indicators and are therefore highly tentative, particularly in the distribution of financial asset holdings among private nonfinancial sectors. The most important information not yet available in these tables are SEC data on net new security issues and current assets and liabilities of corporations. The lack of these data weakens the figures for total credit flows, household investment in securities, and distribution of liquid assets as between households and business. Also missing at the time the accounts were put together were balance of payments statistics, final income-and-product data, end-of-quarter balance sheets for insurance companies, mutual savings banks, pension funds, investment companies, and the Treasury survey of ownership of federal securities.

Requests for unadjusted and for historical annual tables or to be put on the mailing list should be addressed to the Flow of Funds and Savings Section, Room 3222, Division of Research and Statistics, Board of Governors of the Federal Reserve System, Washington, D.C. 20551. Telephone requests for Flow of Funds data may be made to: (202) 452–3483.

Table 1

Income and product accounts: GNP expenditures and gross saving (billions of dollars)

| | 1969 | 1970 | 1971 | 1972 | 1973 | 1973 I | II | III | IV | 1974 I | II | IIIa | |
|---|---|---|---|---|---|---|---|---|---|---|---|---|---|
| 1 | 930.3 | 977.1 | 1,054.9 | 1,158.0 | 1,294.9 | 1,248.9 | 1,277.9 | 1,308.9 | 1,344.0 | 1,358.8 | 1,383.8 | 1,411.6 | Total GNP |
| 2 | 789.4 | 837.2 | 901.4 | 984.7 | 1,081.6 | 1,050.6 | 1,072.3 | 1,093.2 | 1,110.3 | 1,136.9 | 1,173.5 | 1,211.2 | Current outlays |
| 3 | 579.5 | 617.6 | 667.1 | 729.0 | 805.2 | 781.7 | 799.0 | 816.3 | 823.9 | 840.6 | 869.1 | 899.9 | Households |
| 4 | 90.8 | 91.3 | 103.9 | 118.4 | 130.3 | 132.4 | 132.1 | 132.4 | 124.3 | 123.9 | 129.5 | 136.0 | Consumer durables |
| 5 | 111.2 | 123.3 | 136.6 | 150.8 | 169.8 | 162.6 | 167.1 | 171.6 | 177.9 | 184.8 | 190.1 | 194.8 | State and local government |
| 6 | 98.8 | 96.2 | 97.6 | 104.9 | 106.6 | 106.4 | 106.2 | 105.3 | 108.4 | 111.5 | 114.3 | 116.4 | U.S. government |
| 7 | 139.0 | 136.3 | 153.7 | 179.3 | 209.4 | 199.0 | 205.1 | 209.0 | 224.4 | 210.5 | 211.8 | 204.6 | Gross domestic investment |
| 8 | 131.1 | 131.7 | 147.4 | 170.8 | 194.0 | 189.0 | 194.4 | 197.1 | 195.5 | 193.6 | 198.3 | 198.8 | Private fixed investment |
| 9 | 32.6 | 31.2 | 42.8 | 54.0 | 57.2 | 58.5 | 58.7 | 58.1 | 53.6 | 48.4 | 48.8 | 46.3 | Residential construction |
| 10 | 22.1 | 20.5 | 29.9 | 36.3 | 37.0 | 38.4 | 38.7 | 37.3 | 33.5 | 30.8 | 33.6 | 33.2 | 1-4-family structures |
| 11 | 22.0 | 19.6 | 26.9 | 34.3 | 37.5 | 37.3 | 37.9 | 38.0 | 37.0 | 32.8 | 30.6 | 33.2 | Household purchases |
| 12 | 0.6 | 0.5 | 0.6 | 0.6 | 0.5 | 0.5 | 0.4 | 0.5 | 0.6 | 0.7 | 0.8 | 0.8 | Farm |
| 13 | -0.5 | 0.4 | 2.4 | 1.5 | -1.1 | 0.6 | 0.4 | -1.1 | -4.2 | -2.8 | 2.2 | -0.8 | Change in work in process on nonfarm |
| 14 | -0.3 | 0.2 | 1.2 | 0.8 | -0.5 | 0.3 | 0.2 | -0.6 | -2.1 | -1.4 | 1.1 | -0.4 | Noncorporate |
| 15 | -0.3 | 0.2 | 1.2 | 0.8 | -0.5 | 0.3 | 0.2 | -0.6 | -2.1 | -1.4 | 1.1 | -0.4 | Corporate |
| 16 | 10.6 | 10.7 | 13.0 | 17.6 | 20.3 | 20.1 | 20.1 | 20.8 | 20.2 | 17.7 | 15.2 | 13.1 | Multifamily units |
| 17 | 7.3 | 7.5 | 9.1 | 12.3 | 14.2 | 13.9 | 14.1 | 14.5 | 14.3 | 12.4 | 10.6 | 9.2 | Noncorporate business |
| 18 | 3.2 | 3.1 | 3.8 | 4.9 | 5.8 | 5.8 | 5.5 | 6.2 | 5.9 | 4.8 | 4.4 | 3.9 | Corporate business |
| 19 | 0.1 | 0.1 | 0.1 | 0.4 | 0.2 | 0.4 | 0.4 | 0.1 | * | 0.4 | 0.2 | * | REITs |
| 20 | 98.5 | 100.6 | 104.6 | 116.8 | 136.8 | 130.5 | 135.6 | 139.0 | 141.9 | 145.2 | 149.4 | 152.5 | Nonresidential plant and equipment |
| 21 | 5.1 | 5.3 | 5.6 | 6.0 | 6.3 | 6.3 | 6.5 | 6.3 | 6.1 | 6.5 | 6.4 | 6.2 | Nonprofit institution |
| 22 | 5.9 | 6.3 | 6.4 | 7.1 | 9.5 | 8.3 | 9.3 | 9.7 | 10.5 | 10.9 | 12.0 | 12.4 | Farm |
| 23 | 10.6 | 10.6 | 11.5 | 12.2 | 12.9 | 13.0 | 13.0 | 12.9 | 12.8 | 12.8 | 12.9 | 12.9 | Nonfarm noncorporate business |
| 24 | 2.9 | 3.3 | 4.0 | 4.4 | 4.8 | 5.0 | 5.0 | 4.8 | 4.3 | 7.0 | 4.6 | 4.2 | Financial corporations |
| 25 | 74.0 | 75.1 | 77.1 | 87.1 | 103.3 | 97.9 | 101.9 | 105.3 | 108.2 | 108.0 | 113.5 | 116.8 | Corporate business |

| No. | | Values |||||||||||| 
|---|---|---|---|---|---|---|---|---|---|---|---|---|---|
| 26 | Inventories | 7.8 | 4.5 | 6.3 | 8.5 | 15.4 | 10.0 | 10.7 | 11.8 | 28.9 | 16.9 | 13.5 | 5.8 |
| 27 | Farm | 0.1 | 0.2 | 1.4 | 0.7 | 4.0 | 3.5 | 3.0 | 4.4 | 4.9 | 3.8 | 3.1 | 2.7 |
| 28 | Nonfarm | 7.7 | 4.3 | 4.9 | 7.8 | 11.4 | 6.5 | 7.7 | 7.4 | 24.0 | 13.1 | 10.4 | 3.1 |
| 29 | Noncorporate | 1.0 | -1.4 | -0.1 | -1.9 | -1.5 | -2.2 | -2.5 | -2.1 | 0.8 | -4.2 | -2.0 | — |
| 30 | Corporate | 6.7 | 5.7 | 5.1 | 9.7 | 12.9 | 8.7 | 10.1 | 9.5 | 23.2 | 17.4 | 12.4 | 3.1 |
| 31 | Net exports | 1.9 | 3.6 | -0.2 | -6.0 | 3.9 | -0.8 | 0.5 | 6.7 | 9.3 | 11.3 | -1.5 | -4.1 |
| 32 | Exports | 55.5 | 62.9 | 65.5 | 72.4 | 100.4 | 88.8 | 95.4 | 103.7 | 113.6 | 131.2 | 138.5 | 143.9 |
| 33 | Imports | 53.6 | 59.3 | 65.6 | 78.4 | 96.4 | 89.5 | 94.9 | 96.9 | 104.3 | 119.9 | 140.0 | 148.0 |
| 34 | Disposable personal income | 634.4 | 691.7 | 746.4 | 802.5 | 903.7 | 869.5 | 892.1 | 913.9 | 939.4 | 950.6 | 966.5 | 990.8 |
| 35 | Personal savings | 38.2 | 56.2 | 60.5 | 52.6 | 74.3 | 65.3 | 69.6 | 73.2 | 89.3 | 84.4 | 71.5 | 64.6 |
| 36 | Saving rate (percent) | 6.0 | 8.1 | 8.1 | 6.6 | 8.2 | 7.5 | 7.8 | 8.0 | 9.5 | 8.9 | 7.4 | 6.5 |
| 37 | Federal government surplus | 8.1 | -11.9 | -21.9 | -17.5 | -5.6 | -11.1 | -7.4 | -1.7 | -2.3 | -1.5 | -1.3 | 5.3 |
| 38 | State and local government surplus | 0.7 | 1.8 | 3.4 | 12.3 | 9.2 | 13.2 | 10.4 | 8.4 | 4.6 | 3.4 | 2.2 | 2.7 |
| | Corporate profits, taxes, and dividends: | | | | | | | | | | | | |
| | Profits (total) | | | | | | | | | | | | |
| 39 | Profits (total) | 84.9 | 74.0 | 83.6 | 99.2 | 122.7 | 120.4 | 124.9 | 122.7 | 122.7 | 138.7 | 143.5 | 168.4 |
| 40 | Farms | 0.1 | * | 0.1 | 0.3 | 0.6 | 0.4 | 0.5 | 0.6 | 0.8 | 0.7 | 0.7 | 0.7 |
| 41 | Foreign | 4.5 | 4.7 | 4.9 | 5.2 | 7.3 | 7.0 | 7.0 | 7.4 | 8.0 | 13.2 | 7.9 | 8.0 |
| 42 | Financial corporations | 12.4 | 13.6 | 15.6 | 17.6 | 19.6 | 18.7 | 19.4 | 19.8 | 20.4 | 20.8 | 20.7 | 22.6 |
| 43 | Corporate business | 67.9 | 55.7 | 63.1 | 76.0 | 95.2 | 94.2 | 98.1 | 94.9 | 93.5 | 104.1 | 114.1 | 137.1 |
| 44 | Tax accruals (total) | 40.1 | 34.8 | 37.5 | 41.5 | 49.8 | 48.9 | 50.9 | 49.9 | 49.5 | 53.6 | 57.9 | 68.2 |
| 45 | Farms | 0.1 | 0.1 | 0.1 | 0.1 | 0.2 | 0.2 | 0.2 | 0.2 | 0.3 | 0.3 | 0.3 | 0.3 |
| 46 | Financial corporations | 6.4 | 7.2 | 7.8 | 8.2 | 9.0 | 8.4 | 8.9 | 9.3 | 9.7 | 9.9 | 10.1 | 10.9 |
| 47 | Corporate business | 33.6 | 27.5 | 29.7 | 33.3 | 40.5 | 40.3 | 41.9 | 40.3 | 39.6 | 43.5 | 47.6 | 57.0 |
| 48 | Dividends (total) | 24.3 | 24.7 | 25.0 | 27.3 | 29.6 | 28.7 | 29.1 | 29.8 | 30.7 | 31.6 | 32.5 | 33.2 |
| 49 | Farms | 0.1 | * | 0.1 | 0.1 | 0.1 | 0.1 | 0.1 | 0.1 | 0.1 | 0.1 | 0.1 | 0.1 |
| 50 | Net foreign | 2.0 | 2.4 | 2.9 | 3.1 | 3.6 | 4.3 | 3.9 | 3.5 | 2.8 | 1.7 | -2.7 | -2.7 |
| 51 | Financial corporations | 1.6 | 2.3 | 1.9 | 2.0 | 2.2 | 2.1 | 2.2 | 2.2 | 2.4 | 2.5 | 2.8 | 3.0 |
| 52 | Corporate business | 20.7 | 20.0 | 20.2 | 22.1 | 23.6 | 22.3 | 22.9 | 23.9 | 25.4 | 27.3 | 32.4 | 32.8 |
| 53 | Undistributed profits (total) | 20.5 | 14.6 | 21.1 | 30.3 | 43.3 | 42.8 | 44.9 | 43.1 | 42.5 | 53.5 | 53.0 | 67.0 |
| 54 | Farms | * | -0.1 | * | 0.1 | 0.3 | 0.2 | 0.3 | 0.3 | 0.4 | 0.4 | 0.4 | 0.4 |
| 55 | Foreign branch profits | 2.5 | 2.3 | 2.0 | 2.1 | 3.7 | 2.7 | 3.0 | 3.8 | 5.2 | 11.5 | 10.6 | 10.7 |
| 56 | Financial corporations | 4.5 | 4.1 | 5.9 | 7.4 | 8.3 | 8.3 | 8.3 | 8.3 | 8.4 | 8.3 | 7.9 | 8.6 |

Table 1 (cont'd)

| | | 1969 | 1970 | 1971 | 1972 | 1973 | 1973 I | 1973 II | 1973 III | 1973 IV | 1974 I | 1974 II | 1974 III |
|---|---|---|---|---|---|---|---|---|---|---|---|---|---|
| 57 | Corporate business | 13.6 | 8.3 | 13.3 | 20.7 | 31.0 | 31.6 | 33.3 | 30.7 | 28.5 | 33.3 | 34.2 | 47.3 |
| 58 | + Inventory value adjusted | -5.1 | -4.8 | -4.9 | -7.0 | -17.6 | -16.5 | -20.0 | -17.5 | -16.3 | -31.0 | -37.9 | -58.5 |
| 59 | + Branch profits | 2.5 | 2.3 | 2.0 | 2.1 | 3.7 | 2.7 | 3.0 | 3.8 | 5.2 | 11.5 | 10.6 | 10.7 |
| 60 | = Nonfinancial corporations (net) | 10.9 | 5.8 | 10.3 | 15.7 | 17.1 | 17.9 | 16.4 | 17.0 | 17.3 | 13.8 | 6.9 | -0.5 |
| 61 | Total capital consumption | 81.6 | 87.3 | 93.7 | 102.9 | 110.8 | 107.4 | 110.5 | 111.5 | 113.9 | 115.8 | 118.6 | 120.7 |
| 62 | Owner-occupied homes (hh) | 8.7 | 9.0 | 9.3 | 10.0 | 10.4 | 10.2 | 10.5 | 10.3 | 10.4 | 10.5 | 10.8 | 10.6 |
| 63 | Nonprofit institutions (hh) | 1.6 | 1.7 | 1.9 | 2.0 | 2.1 | 2.1 | 2.1 | 2.1 | 2.2 | 2.2 | 2.3 | 2.3 |
| 64 | Farm noncorporate | 6.2 | 6.0 | 6.5 | 6.9 | 7.8 | 7.4 | 7.8 | 7.8 | 8.1 | 8.4 | 8.6 | 8.8 |
| 65 | Nonfarm noncorporate business | 13.1 | 14.6 | 15.7 | 17.7 | 19.3 | 18.3 | 19.2 | 19.6 | 20.3 | 20.6 | 21.2 | 21.5 |
| 66 | Total corporate | 51.9 | 56.0 | 60.4 | 66.3 | 71.2 | 69.4 | 70.9 | 71.6 | 72.9 | 74.1 | 75.7 | 77.6 |
| 67 | Financial business | 1.8 | 2.0 | 2.2 | 2.7 | 3.1 | 3.0 | 3.0 | 3.1 | 3.3 | 3.4 | 3.5 | 3.6 |
| 68 | Corporate farms | 0.3 | 0.4 | 0.5 | 0.6 | 0.6 | 0.6 | 0.6 | 0.6 | 0.6 | 0.7 | 0.7 | 0.7 |
| 69 | Corporate business | 49.8 | 53.6 | 57.7 | 63.0 | 67.5 | 65.8 | 67.2 | 67.8 | 69.0 | 70.1 | 71.6 | 73.3 |
| 70 | Capital consumption on consumer durables not included above | 74.6 | 80.7 | 87.5 | 94.1 | 103.3 | 100.3 | 103.5 | 104.9 | 104.4 | 104.3 | 104.5 | 104.3 |
| 71 | Total capital consumption including durables | 156.1 | 168.0 | 181.2 | 197.0 | 214.1 | 207.7 | 214.0 | 216.3 | 218.3 | 220.1 | 223.1 | 225.0 |
| 72 | Statistical discrepancy | -6.1 | -6.4 | -2.3 | -3.8 | -5.0 | -5.9 | -6.5 | -4.9 | -2.6 | -6.3 | 0.3 | -4.6 |
| 73 | Profit tax rate (%) | 47.2 | 47.0 | 44.9 | 41.9 | 40.6 | 40.6 | 40.8 | 40.6 | 40.4 | 38.7 | 40.4 | 40.5 |
| 74 | Personal tax rate (%) | 15.5 | 14.4 | 13.6 | 15.1 | 14.3 | 14.2 | 14.2 | 14.4 | 14.5 | 14.6 | 14.8 | 15.0 |

[a] In all the tables in the appendix, III/74 figures are tentative estimates based on incomplete information

Table 2

Total funds raised in credit markets by nonfinancial sectors (billions of dollars)

I. Funds raised, by type and sector

| | | 1969 | 1970 | 1971 | 1972 | 1973 | 1973 I | 1973 II | 1973 III | 1973 IV | 1974 I | 1974 II | 1974 III |
|---|---|---|---|---|---|---|---|---|---|---|---|---|---|
| | Total funds raised | | | | | | | | | | | | |
| 1 | By nonfinancial sectors | 91.8 | 98.2 | 147.4 | 169.4 | 187.4 | 218.5 | 181.4 | 177.4 | 172.2 | 177.3 | 206.5 | 199.1 |
| 2 | Excluding equities | 88.0 | 92.5 | 135.9 | 158.9 | 180.1 | 212.1 | 172.9 | 172.3 | 163.3 | 171.1 | 202.0 | 193.7 |
| 3 | U.S. government | −3.6 | 12.8 | 25.5 | 17.3 | 9.7 | 32.8 | 2.9 | −7.1 | 10.3 | 8.7 | 2.1 | 15.1 |
| 4 | Public debt securities | −1.3 | 12.9 | 26.0 | 13.9 | 7.7 | 30.1 | 3.1 | −9.7 | 7.4 | 7.0 | 1.3 | 16.6 |
| 5 | Agency issues and mortgages | −2.4 | −0.1 | −0.5 | 3.4 | 2.0 | 2.6 | −0.2 | 2.6 | 2.9 | 1.7 | 0.8 | −1.5 |
| 6 | All other nonfinancial sectors | 95.5 | 85.4 | 121.9 | 152.1 | 177.7 | 185.7 | 178.5 | 184.5 | 161.9 | 168.7 | 204.5 | 184.0 |
| 7 | Corporate equities | 3.9 | 5.8 | 11.5 | 10.5 | 7.2 | 6.3 | 8.5 | 5.1 | 8.9 | 6.3 | 4.5 | 5.4 |
| 8 | Debt instruments | 91.6 | 79.7 | 110.4 | 141.6 | 170.4 | 179.3 | 169.9 | 179.4 | 153.0 | 162.4 | 200.0 | 178.6 |
| 9 | Debt capital instruments | 50.6 | 57.6 | 84.2 | 94.9 | 97.1 | 88.6 | 104.3 | 106.3 | 89.1 | 92.7 | 110.8 | 87.7 |
| 10 | State and local government sectors | 9.9 | 11.2 | 17.6 | 14.4 | 13.7 | 10.6 | 12.7 | 15.6 | 16.0 | 15.8 | 19.7 | 12.3 |
| 11 | Corporate and foreign bonds | 13.0 | 20.6 | 19.7 | 13.2 | 10.2 | 8.4 | 10.4 | 11.4 | 10.5 | 19.6 | 20.9 | 21.8 |
| 12 | Mortgages | 27.7 | 25.7 | 46.9 | 67.3 | 73.2 | 69.6 | 81.2 | 79.3 | 62.6 | 57.3 | 70.2 | 53.5 |
| 13 | Home mortgages | 15.7 | 12.8 | 26.1 | 39.6 | 43.3 | 42.0 | 47.6 | 46.9 | 37.0 | 33.0 | 41.7 | 31.1 |
| 14 | Other residential | 4.7 | 5.8 | 8.8 | 10.3 | 8.4 | 8.5 | 11.0 | 9.7 | 4.5 | 7.1 | 8.7 | 9.2 |
| 15 | Commercial | 5.3 | 5.3 | 10.0 | 14.8 | 17.0 | 15.3 | 18.2 | 18.1 | 16.6 | 13.4 | 15.1 | 8.8 |
| 16 | Farm | 1.9 | 1.8 | 2.0 | 2.6 | 4.4 | 3.9 | 4.4 | 4.7 | 4.5 | 3.8 | 4.8 | 4.4 |
| 17 | Other private credit | 41.0 | 22.1 | 26.3 | 46.7 | 73.4 | 90.7 | 65.7 | 73.1 | 64.0 | 69.7 | 89.1 | 90.8 |
| 18 | Bank loans n.e.c. | 15.3 | 6.4 | 9.3 | 21.8 | 38.6 | 64.3 | 29.9 | 34.4 | 25.9 | 41.1 | 47.1 | 35.2 |
| 19 | Consumer credit | 10.4 | 6.0 | 11.2 | 19.2 | 22.9 | 25.6 | 24.6 | 22.3 | 19.2 | 8.2 | 17.2 | 15.8 |
| 20 | Open market paper | 3.3 | 3.8 | −0.9 | −1.6 | 1.8 | −10.0 | 5.3 | 3.4 | 8.6 | 11.4 | 18.0 | 22.5 |
| 21 | Other | 12.0 | 5.9 | 6.6 | 7.3 | 10.0 | 10.8 | 5.8 | 13.1 | 10.3 | 8.4 | 6.8 | 17.3 |
| 22 | By borrowing sector | 95.5 | 85.4 | 121.9 | 152.1 | 177.7 | 185.7 | 178.5 | 184.5 | 161.9 | 168.7 | 204.5 | 184.0 |
| 23 | Debt instruments | 91.6 | 79.7 | 110.4 | 141.6 | 170.4 | 179.3 | 169.9 | 179.4 | 153.0 | 162.4 | 200.0 | 178.6 |
| 24 | Foreign | 3.2 | 2.7 | 4.6 | 4.7 | 7.7 | 9.1 | 7.7 | 4.2 | 9.9 | 14.0 | 25.6 | 13.3 |
| 25 | State and local governments | 10.7 | 11.3 | 17.8 | 14.2 | 12.3 | 10.0 | 9.6 | 15.4 | 14.1 | 14.5 | 17.4 | 11.5 |

323

Table 2 (cont'd)

Funds raised, by type and sector (cont'd)

| | | 1969 | 1970 | 1971 | 1972 | 1973 | 1973 | | | | 1974 | | |
|---|---|---|---|---|---|---|---|---|---|---|---|---|---|
| | | | | | | | I | II | III | IV | I | II | III |
| 26 | Households | 31.7 | 23.4 | 39.8 | 63.1 | 72.8 | 74.5 | 72.1 | 80.5 | 64.1 | 51.4 | 53.6 | 57.6 |
| 27 | Nonfinancial business | 46.0 | 42.3 | 48.2 | 59.6 | 77.6 | 85.8 | 80.5 | 79.3 | 64.9 | 82.5 | 103.3 | 96.1 |
| 28 | Farm | 3.2 | 3.2 | 4.1 | 4.9 | 8.6 | 7.4 | 7.7 | 9.6 | 9.8 | 6.3 | 8.5 | 8.7 |
| 29 | Nonfarm noncorporate | 7.4 | 5.3 | 8.7 | 10.4 | 9.3 | 11.5 | 10.8 | 8.8 | 6.0 | 4.4 | 10.2 | 8.3 |
| 30 | Corporate | 35.5 | 33.8 | 35.4 | 44.4 | 59.7 | 66.9 | 62.0 | 60.9 | 49.1 | 71.8 | 84.7 | 79.1 |
| 31 | Corporate equities | 3.9 | 5.8 | 11.5 | 10.5 | 7.2 | 6.3 | 8.5 | 5.1 | 8.9 | 6.3 | 4.5 | 5.4 |
| 32 | Foreign | 0.5 | 0.1 | * | -0.4 | -0.2 | -0.7 | -0.2 | * | * | 0.1 | -0.5 | * |
| 33 | Corporate business | 3.4 | 5.7 | 11.4 | 10.9 | 7.4 | 7.0 | 8.7 | 5.1 | 8.9 | 6.2 | 5.0 | 5.4 |
| | Totals, including equities | | | | | | | | | | | | |
| 34 | Foreign | 3.7 | 2.7 | 4.6 | 4.3 | 7.5 | 8.4 | 7.5 | 4.2 | 10.0 | 14.1 | 25.1 | 13.3 |
| 35 | Nonfinancial business | 49.4 | 48.0 | 59.6 | 70.5 | 85.1 | 92.8 | 89.2 | 84.4 | 73.8 | 88.7 | 108.3 | 101.5 |
| 36 | Corporate | 38.9 | 39.5 | 46.8 | 55.3 | 67.2 | 73.9 | 70.7 | 66.1 | 57.9 | 78.0 | 89.7 | 84.6 |
| 37 | Memo: U.S. government cash balance | 0.4 | 2.8 | 3.2 | -0.3 | -1.7 | 13.8 | -6.2 | -18.4 | 4.2 | 0.2 | -3.8 | 1.6 |
| | Totals net of changes in U.S. government cash balances: | | | | | | | | | | | | |
| 38 | Total funds raised | 91.4 | 95.5 | 144.2 | 169.7 | 189.0 | 204.7 | 187.6 | 195.8 | 168.1 | 177.1 | 210.3 | 197.5 |
| 39 | By U.S. government | -4.0 | 10.0 | 22.3 | 17.6 | 11.4 | 19.0 | 9.2 | 11.3 | 6.1 | 8.4 | 5.9 | 13.5 |

Private domestic net investment and borrowing in credit markets

| | | 1969 | 1970 | 1971 | 1972 | 1973 | 1973 | | | | 1974 | | |
|---|---|---|---|---|---|---|---|---|---|---|---|---|---|
| | | | | | | | I | II | III | IV | I | II | III |
| | Total (households and business) | | | | | | | | | | | | |
| 1 | Total capital outlays[a] | 226.7 | 224.2 | 253.5 | 293.0 | 334.7 | 326.0 | 331.7 | 336.5 | 344.4 | 326.9 | 336.5 | 336.3 |
| 2 | Capital consumption[b] | 154.3 | 166.0 | 178.9 | 194.3 | 211.0 | 204.7 | 211.0 | 213.2 | 215.0 | 216.7 | 219.6 | 221.4 |
| 3 | Net physical investment | 72.4 | 58.2 | 74.6 | 98.7 | 123.7 | 121.3 | 120.8 | 123.3 | 129.4 | 110.2 | 116.8 | 114.9 |
| 4 | Net funds raised | 81.1 | 71.4 | 99.4 | 133.6 | 157.9 | 167.3 | 161.3 | 164.9 | 137.9 | 140.1 | 161.9 | 159.2 |
| 5 | Excess net investment[c] | -8.7 | -13.2 | -24.8 | -34.9 | -34.2 | -46.0 | -40.6 | -41.7 | -8.5 | -29.9 | -45.1 | -44.3 |
| | Total business | | | | | | | | | | | | |
| 6 | Total capital outlays | 108.9 | 108.0 | 117.1 | 134.3 | 160.5 | 150.1 | 155.3 | 159.8 | 177.0 | 163.7 | 169.9 | 161.0 |
| 7 | Capital consumption | 69.5 | 74.6 | 80.3 | 88.2 | 95.2 | 92.1 | 94.8 | 95.9 | 98.1 | 99.7 | 102.0 | 104.3 |
| 8 | Net physical investment | 39.4 | 33.5 | 36.8 | 46.0 | 65.3 | 57.9 | 60.4 | 63.9 | 78.9 | 64.0 | 67.9 | 56.7 |

| | | | | | | | | | | | | |
|---|---|---|---|---|---|---|---|---|---|---|---|---|
| 9 | Net debt funds raised | 46.0 | 42.3 | 48.2 | 59.6 | 77.6 | 85.8 | 80.5 | 79.3 | 64.9 | 82.5 | 103.3 | 96.1 |
| 10 | Corporate equity issues | 3.4 | 5.7 | 11.4 | 10.9 | 7.4 | 7.0 | 8.7 | 5.1 | 8.9 | 6.2 | 5.0 | 5.4 |
| 11 | Excess net investment[c] | −10.0 | −14.5 | −22.8 | −24.5 | −19.8 | −34.9 | −28.7 | −20.5 | 5.1 | −24.8 | −40.4 | −44.8 |
| | **Corporate business** | | | | | | | | | | | | |
| 12 | Total capital outlays | 83.7 | 84.0 | 87.2 | 102.5 | 121.5 | 112.7 | 117.7 | 120.4 | 135.2 | 128.8 | 131.4 | 123.4 |
| 13 | Capital consumption | 49.8 | 53.6 | 57.7 | 63.0 | 67.5 | 65.8 | 67.2 | 67.8 | 69.0 | 70.1 | 71.6 | 73.3 |
| 14 | Net physical investment | 33.9 | 30.4 | 29.5 | 39.4 | 54.0 | 46.9 | 50.5 | 52.6 | 66.2 | 58.7 | 59.8 | 50.1 |
| 15 | Net debt funds raised | 35.5 | 33.8 | 35.4 | 44.4 | 59.7 | 66.9 | 62.0 | 60.9 | 49.1 | 71.8 | 84.7 | 79.1 |
| 16 | Corporate equity issues | 3.4 | 5.7 | 11.4 | 10.9 | 7.4 | 7.0 | 8.7 | 5.1 | 8.9 | 6.2 | 5.0 | 5.4 |
| 17 | Excess net investment[c] | −5.0 | −9.1 | −17.3 | −15.8 | −13.1 | −26.9 | −20.2 | −13.5 | 8.2 | −19.4 | −29.9 | −34.5 |
| | **Households** | | | | | | | | | | | | |
| 18 | Total capital outlays | 117.8 | 116.2 | 136.4 | 158.8 | 174.1 | 175.9 | 176.5 | 176.7 | 167.5 | 163.2 | 166.5 | 175.3 |
| 19 | Capital consumption | 84.8 | 91.4 | 98.6 | 106.1 | 115.7 | 112.6 | 116.1 | 117.3 | 116.9 | 117.0 | 117.6 | 117.2 |
| 20 | Net physical investment | 33.0 | 24.7 | 37.8 | 52.7 | 58.4 | 63.3 | 60.3 | 59.4 | 50.5 | 46.3 | 49.0 | 58.2 |
| 21 | Net funds raised | 31.7 | 23.4 | 39.8 | 63.1 | 72.8 | 74.5 | 72.1 | 80.5 | 64.1 | 51.4 | 53.6 | 57.6 |
| 22 | Excess net investment[c] | 1.3 | 1.4 | −2.1 | −10.4 | −14.4 | −11.2 | −11.8 | −21.2 | −13.5 | −5.1 | −4.7 | 0.5 |
| 23 | Houses less home mortgages | −2.8 | −1.9 | −6.6 | −14.1 | −17.0 | −14.4 | −19.9 | −20.1 | −13.7 | −12.8 | −20.1 | −9.2 |
| 24 | Durables less consumer credit | 5.9 | 4.5 | 5.2 | 5.2 | 4.1 | 6.5 | 4.0 | 5.2 | 0.8 | 11.4 | 7.8 | 15.9 |
| 25 | Nonprofit plant and equipment less mortgages | 2.2 | 2.2 | 2.5 | 2.6 | 2.7 | 2.8 | 2.9 | 2.7 | 2.6 | 2.9 | 2.7 | 2.5 |
| 26 | Less: unallocated debt | 4.0 | 3.5 | 3.2 | 4.1 | 4.3 | 6.0 | −1.1 | 9.0 | 3.1 | 6.7 | −4.8 | 8.8 |

[a]Capital outlays are totals for residential and nonresidential fixed capital, net change in inventories, and consumer durables, except outlays by financial business

[b]Capital consumption includes amounts for consumer durables and excludes financial business capital consumption

[c]Excess of net investment over net funds raised

Table 3

Direct and indirect sources of funds to credit markets (billions of dollars)

| | 1969 | 1970 | 1971 | 1972 | 1973 | 1973 | | | | 1974 | | |
|---|---|---|---|---|---|---|---|---|---|---|---|---|
| | | | | | | I | II | III | IV | I | II | III |
| 1 Total funds advanced in credit markets to nonfinancial sectors | 88.0 | 92.5 | 135.9 | 158.9 | 180.1 | 212.1 | 172.9 | 172.3 | 163.3 | 171.1 | 202.0 | 193.7 |
| By public agencies and foreign | | | | | | | | | | | | |
| 2 Total net advances | 15.7 | 28.1 | 41.7 | 18.3 | 33.2 | 65.0 | 17.1 | 27.3 | 23.5 | 14.1 | 61.6 | 41.5 |
| 3 U.S. government securities | 0.7 | 15.9 | 33.8 | 8.4 | 11.0 | 44.3 | -3.1 | -4.8 | 7.4 | -9.8 | 26.8 | -2.2 |
| 4 Residential mortgages | 4.6 | 5.7 | 5.7 | 5.2 | 7.6 | 4.9 | 5.1 | 12.5 | 8.0 | 9.9 | 13.5 | 15.9 |
| 5 FHLB advances to S & L's | 4.0 | 1.3 | -2.7 | * | 7.2 | 5.4 | 10.7 | 10.2 | 2.4 | 3.3 | 10.4 | 9.8 |
| 6 Other loans and securities | 6.3 | 5.2 | 4.9 | 4.6 | 7.5 | 10.4 | 4.4 | 9.4 | 5.7 | 10.7 | 10.9 | 18.0 |
| By agency: | | | | | | | | | | | | |
| 7 U.S. government | 2.9 | 2.8 | 3.2 | 2.6 | 3.0 | 4.0 | -2.2 | 7.8 | 2.2 | 2.2 | 1.7 | 4.3 |
| 8 Sponsored credit agencies | 8.9 | 10.0 | 3.2 | 7.0 | 20.3 | 13.3 | 23.3 | 27.8 | 16.6 | 13.0 | 27.6 | 25.3 |
| 9 Monetary authorities | 4.2 | 5.0 | 8.9 | 0.3 | 9.2 | 17.2 | 3.1 | 5.7 | 10.9 | -1.0 | 13.1 | 10.6 |
| 10 Foreign | -0.3 | 10.3 | 26.4 | 8.4 | 0.7 | 30.3 | -7.0 | -14.0 | -6.3 | -0.4 | 19.4 | 1.3 |
| 11 Agency borrowing not included in line 1 | 8.8 | 8.2 | 3.8 | 6.2 | 19.6 | 12.6 | 22.1 | 26.7 | 17.0 | 9.3 | 24.3 | 21.2 |
| Private domestic funds advanced | | | | | | | | | | | | |
| 12 Total net advances | 81.1 | 72.6 | 98.1 | 146.7 | 166.5 | 159.7 | 177.9 | 171.6 | 156.9 | 166.2 | 164.7 | 173.4 |
| 13 U.S. government securities | 4.8 | 5.2 | -4.4 | 15.2 | 18.4 | 1.1 | 28.3 | 24.4 | 19.9 | 27.7 | -0.4 | 38.7 |
| 14 State and local obligations | 9.9 | 11.2 | 17.6 | 14.4 | 13.7 | 10.6 | 12.7 | 15.6 | 16.0 | 15.8 | 19.7 | 12.3 |
| 15 Corporate and foreign bonds | 12.5 | 20.0 | 19.5 | 13.2 | 10.1 | 8.2 | 10.0 | 10.8 | 11.2 | 18.5 | 19.6 | 19.1 |
| 16 Residential mortgages | 15.7 | 12.8 | 29.1 | 44.6 | 44.1 | 45.4 | 53.4 | 44.0 | 33.5 | 30.2 | 36.8 | 24.2 |
| 17 Other mortgages and loans | 42.2 | 24.6 | 33.7 | 59.5 | 87.4 | 99.8 | 84.3 | 87.0 | 78.7 | 77.3 | 99.3 | 88.8 |
| 18 Less: FHLB advances | 4.0 | 1.3 | -2.7 | * | 7.2 | 5.4 | 10.7 | 10.2 | 2.4 | 3.3 | 10.4 | 9.8 |
| Private financial intermediation | | | | | | | | | | | | |
| 19 Credit market funds advanced by private financial institutions | 55.3 | 74.9 | 110.7 | 153.4 | 158.8 | 192.7 | 165.3 | 150.6 | 126.9 | 135.0 | 174.4 | 118.1 |
| 20 Commercial banking | 18.2 | 35.1 | 50.6 | 70.5 | 86.6 | 101.2 | 86.1 | 83.7 | 75.3 | 70.4 | 103.2 | 48.6 |
| 21 Savings institutions | 14.5 | 16.9 | 41.4 | 49.3 | 35.1 | 57.6 | 41.1 | 22.7 | 18.9 | 41.9 | 28.8 | 17.2 |
| 22 Insurance and pension funds | 12.7 | 17.3 | 13.3 | 17.7 | 22.1 | 22.8 | 19.9 | 24.8 | 21.1 | 19.7 | 36.1 | 37.1 |
| 23 Other finance | 9.9 | 5.7 | 5.3 | 15.8 | 15.0 | 11.0 | 18.1 | 19.4 | 11.6 | 3.0 | 6.3 | 15.2 |

| # | Item | | | | | | | | | | | | |
|---|---|---|---|---|---|---|---|---|---|---|---|---|---|
| 24 | Sources of funds | 55.3 | 74.9 | 110.7 | 153.4 | 158.8 | 192.7 | 165.3 | 150.6 | 126.9 | 135.0 | 174.4 | 118.1 |
| 25 | Private domestic deposits | 2.6 | 63.2 | 90.3 | 97.5 | 84.9 | 115.9 | 88.7 | 69.0 | 65.9 | 81.3 | 97.3 | 35.6 |
| 26 | Credit market borrowing | 18.8 | -0.3 | 9.3 | 20.3 | 31.6 | 42.0 | 31.1 | 38.9 | 14.4 | 15.4 | 33.7 | 26.1 |
| 27 | Other sources | 34.0 | 12.0 | 11.0 | 35.5 | 42.4 | 34.8 | 45.5 | 42.7 | 46.5 | 38.4 | 43.4 | 56.5 |
| 28 | Foreign funds | 9.3 | -8.5 | -3.2 | 5.2 | 6.5 | 2.8 | 7.7 | 4.7 | 10.7 | 11.1 | 9.5 | 14.2 |
| 29 | Treasury balances | * | 2.9 | 2.2 | 0.7 | -1.0 | 6.1 | -6.8 | -6.4 | 3.1 | 0.8 | -4.4 | -0.9 |
| 30 | Insurance and pension reserves | 10.8 | 13.1 | 9.1 | 13.1 | 16.7 | 16.4 | 15.5 | 22.6 | 12.5 | 16.6 | 30.8 | 29.3 |
| 31 | Other, net | 13.8 | 4.4 | 2.9 | 16.5 | 20.2 | 9.5 | 29.2 | 21.7 | 20.3 | 9.9 | 7.5 | 13.9 |
| | **Private domestic nonfinancial investors** | | | | | | | | | | | | |
| 32 | Direct lending in credit markets | 44.5 | -2.6 | -3.2 | 13.7 | 39.3 | 9.1 | 43.6 | 60.0 | 44.5 | 46.8 | 23.9 | 81.3 |
| 33 | U.S. government securities | 17.0 | -9.0 | -14.0 | 1.6 | 18.8 | 8.6 | 22.8 | 27.8 | 15.8 | 19.0 | 5.3 | 37.4 |
| 34 | State and local obligations | 8.7 | -1.2 | 0.6 | 2.1 | 4.4 | 5.1 | 5.9 | 7.2 | -0.5 | 7.8 | 7.9 | 14.3 |
| 35 | Corporate and foreign bonds | 6.6 | 10.7 | 9.3 | 5.2 | 1.1 | -0.5 | * | -1.4 | 6.1 | 3.4 | 0.3 | 4.9 |
| 36 | Commercial paper | 10.2 | -4.4 | -0.6 | 4.0 | 11.3 | -2.6 | 8.2 | 22.8 | 16.7 | 16.5 | 4.3 | 20.2 |
| 37 | Other | 2.0 | 1.4 | 1.5 | 0.8 | 3.8 | -1.4 | 6.7 | 3.5 | 6.2 | 0.1 | 6.2 | 4.6 |
| 38 | Deposits and currency | 5.4 | 66.6 | 93.7 | 101.9 | 88.8 | 119.0 | 97.0 | 70.0 | 69.3 | 89.7 | 105.9 | 38.7 |
| 39 | Time and savings accounts | -2.3 | 56.1 | 81.0 | 85.2 | 76.3 | 107.7 | 81.1 | 65.4 | 50.8 | 82.6 | 96.5 | 36.3 |
| 40 | Large negotiable CD's | -13.7 | 15.0 | 7.7 | 8.7 | 18.5 | 39.4 | 15.1 | 34.8 | -15.1 | 17.7 | 42.8 | 27.6 |
| 41 | Other at commercial banks | 3.4 | 24.2 | 32.9 | 30.6 | 29.5 | 24.7 | 33.8 | 20.8 | 38.9 | 27.3 | 38.2 | 1.1 |
| 42 | At savings institutions | 8.0 | 16.9 | 40.4 | 45.9 | 28.2 | 43.6 | 32.3 | 9.9 | 27.0 | 37.6 | 15.5 | 7.6 |
| 43 | Money | 7.7 | 10.5 | 12.7 | 16.7 | 12.6 | 11.3 | 15.9 | 4.5 | 18.6 | 7.1 | 9.3 | 2.4 |
| 44 | Demand deposits | 4.8 | 7.1 | 9.3 | 12.3 | 8.6 | 8.2 | 7.6 | 3.5 | 15.2 | -1.4 | 0.7 | -0.7 |
| 45 | Currency | 2.8 | 3.5 | 3.4 | 4.4 | 3.9 | 3.0 | 8.3 | 1.0 | 3.4 | 8.4 | 8.6 | 3.1 |
| 46 | Total of credit market instruments, deposits, and currency | 49.9 | 64.1 | 90.5 | 115.7 | 128.1 | 128.1 | 140.6 | 129.9 | 113.8 | 136.5 | 129.7 | 120.0 |
| 47 | Public support rate (%) | 17.8 | 30.4 | 30.7 | 11.5 | 18.4 | 30.6 | 9.9 | 15.9 | 14.4 | 8.2 | 30.5 | 21.4 |
| 48 | Private financial intermediation (%) | 68.3 | 103.1 | 112.8 | 104.5 | 95.4 | 120.7 | 92.9 | 87.7 | 80.9 | 81.2 | 105.9 | 68.1 |
| 49 | Total foreign funds | 9.1 | 1.8 | 23.2 | 13.6 | 7.2 | 33.1 | 0.7 | -9.3 | 4.4 | 10.7 | 28.9 | 15.5 |

Table 3 (cont'd)

| | 1969 | 1970 | 1971 | 1972 | 1973 | 1973 I | 1973 II | 1973 III | 1973 IV | 1974 I | 1974 II | 1974 III | |
|---|---|---|---|---|---|---|---|---|---|---|---|---|---|
| Corporate equities not included above | | | | | | | | | | | | | |
| 1 | 10.0 | 10.4 | 14.8 | 12.9 | 8.0 | 8.4 | 10.9 | 10.1 | 2.7 | 7.8 | 4.0 | 9.2 | Total net issues |
| 2 | 4.8 | 2.6 | 1.1 | -0.7 | -1.6 | -2.1 | -1.8 | 1.2 | -3.7 | * | -1.6 | 2.3 | Mutual fund shares |
| 3 | 5.2 | 7.7 | 13.6 | 13.6 | 9.6 | 10.5 | 12.7 | 8.9 | 6.3 | 7.8 | 5.6 | 6.9 | Other equities |
| 4 | 12.2 | 11.4 | 19.3 | 16.0 | 13.4 | 12.7 | 13.5 | 7.0 | 20.6 | 9.0 | 8.1 | 5.6 | Acquisitions by financial institutions |
| 5 | -2.2 | -1.0 | -4.5 | -3.1 | -5.4 | -4.3 | -2.6 | 3.2 | -18.0 | -1.2 | -4.1 | 3.6 | Other net purchases |

Table 3

Line
1  Page 327, line 2
2  Sum of lines 3–6 or 7–10
6  Includes farm and commercial mortgages
11  Credit market funds raised by federally sponsored credit agencies. Included below in lines 13 and 33. Includes all GNMA-guaranteed security issues backed by mortgage pools
12  Line 1 less line 2 plus line 11. Also line 19 less line 26 plus line 32. Also sum of lines 27, 32, 39, and 44
17  Includes farm and commercial mortgages
25  Lines 39 + 44
26  Excludes equity issues and investment company shares. Includes line 18
28  Foreign deposits at commercial banks, bank borrowings from foreign branches, and liabilities of foreign banking agencies to foreign affiliates
29  Demand deposits at commercial banks

Table 3

Line
30  Excludes net investment of these reserves in corporate equities
31  Mainly retained earnings and net miscellaneous liabilities
32  Line 12 less line 19 plus line 26
33–37  Lines 13–17 less amounts required by private finance. Line 37 includes mortgages
39 + 44  See line 25
45  Mainly an offset to line 9
46  Lines 32 + 38 or line 12 less line 27 plus line 45
47  Line 2/line 1
48  Line 19/line 12
49  Lines 10 plus 28

Corporate equities
Line
1 and 3  Includes issues by financial institutions

Table 4

Sector statements of saving and investment: Households (billions of dollars)

Households, personal trusts, and nonprofit organizations

|  |  | 1969 | 1970 | 1971 | 1972 | 1973 | 1973 I | 1973 II | 1973 III | 1973 IV | 1974 I | 1974 II | 1974 III |
|---|---|---|---|---|---|---|---|---|---|---|---|---|---|
| 1 | Personal income | 750.9 | 808.3 | 864.0 | 944.9 | 1,055.0 | 1,013.6 | 1,039.2 | 1,068.0 | 1,099.3 | 1,112.5 | 1,134.6 | 1,165.9 |
| 2 | − Personal taxes and nontaxes | 116.5 | 116.6 | 117.6 | 142.4 | 151.3 | 144.1 | 147.2 | 154.2 | 159.9 | 161.9 | 168.1 | 175.1 |
| 3 | = Disposable personal income | 634.4 | 691.7 | 746.4 | 802.5 | 903.7 | 869.5 | 892.1 | 913.9 | 939.4 | 950.6 | 966.5 | 990.8 |
| 4 | − Personal outlays | 596.2 | 635.5 | 685.9 | 749.9 | 829.4 | 804.2 | 822.5 | 840.7 | 850.1 | 866.2 | 894.9 | 926.2 |
| 5 | = Personal saving, NIA basis | 38.2 | 56.2 | 60.5 | 52.6 | 74.3 | 65.3 | 69.6 | 73.2 | 89.3 | 84.4 | 71.5 | 64.6 |
| 6 | + Credits from government insurance | 7.1 | 8.8 | 9.2 | 11.1 | 11.8 | 11.8 | 14.1 | 10.8 | 9.6 | 10.0 | 21.5 | 11.1 |
| 7 | + Capital gains dividends | 2.5 | 0.9 | 0.8 | 1.4 | 0.9 | 1.2 | 1.3 | 1.0 | 0.3 | 0.7 | 0.9 | 0.9 |
| 8 | + Net durables in consumption | 16.2 | 10.6 | 16.5 | 24.4 | 27.1 | 32.1 | 28.6 | 27.5 | 20.0 | 19.6 | 25.0 | 31.7 |
| 9 | = Net saving | 64.1 | 76.4 | 86.9 | 89.4 | 113.9 | 110.4 | 113.6 | 112.4 | 119.1 | 114.7 | 119.0 | 108.3 |
| 10 | + Capital consumption | 84.8 | 91.4 | 98.6 | 106.1 | 115.7 | 112.6 | 116.1 | 117.3 | 116.9 | 117.0 | 117.6 | 117.2 |
| 11 | = Gross saving | 148.9 | 167.9 | 185.5 | 195.5 | 229.6 | 223.0 | 229.8 | 229.7 | 236.1 | 231.7 | 236.6 | 225.4 |
| 12 | Gross investment | 145.4 | 167.7 | 186.1 | 203.8 | 235.6 | 219.2 | 247.8 | 233.7 | 241.9 | 239.9 | 248.5 | 237.3 |
| 13 | Capital expenditure (net of sales) | 117.8 | 116.2 | 136.4 | 158.8 | 174.1 | 175.9 | 176.5 | 176.7 | 167.5 | 163.2 | 166.5 | 175.3 |
| 14 | Residential construction | 22.0 | 19.6 | 26.9 | 34.3 | 37.5 | 37.3 | 37.9 | 38.0 | 37.0 | 32.8 | 30.6 | 33.2 |
| 15 | Consumer durable goods | 90.8 | 91.3 | 103.9 | 118.4 | 130.3 | 132.4 | 132.1 | 132.4 | 124.3 | 123.9 | 129.5 | 136.0 |
| 16 | Nonprofit plant and equipment | 5.1 | 5.3 | 5.6 | 6.0 | 6.3 | 6.3 | 6.5 | 6.3 | 6.1 | 6.5 | 6.4 | 6.2 |
| 17 | Net financial investment | 27.6 | 51.5 | 49.7 | 45.0 | 61.5 | 43.3 | 71.3 | 57.0 | 74.4 | 76.7 | 82.0 | 62.0 |
| 18 | Net acquisition of financial assets | 56.8 | 74.1 | 92.8 | 114.0 | 130.8 | 114.9 | 139.1 | 134.5 | 134.6 | 129.2 | 136.7 | 116.2 |
| 19 | Deposit and credit market instruments[a] | 42.5 | 54.4 | 72.3 | 93.6 | 110.4 | 98.9 | 115.8 | 103.8 | 123.4 | 109.9 | 100.1 | 83.8 |
| 20 | Demand deposits and currency | 1.5 | 11.2 | 11.0 | 11.8 | 13.1 | 10.5 | 10.3 | 5.5 | 26.0 | 4.1 | 0.9 | −4.7 |
| 21 | Time and savings accounts | 6.0 | 44.4 | 70.3 | 75.4 | 67.7 | 83.8 | 74.2 | 50.8 | 61.9 | 74.4 | 73.9 | 22.9 |
| 22 | At commercial banks | −2.0 | 27.5 | 29.8 | 29.5 | 39.5 | 40.2 | 42.0 | 41.0 | 34.9 | 36.9 | 58.4 | 15.3 |
| 23 | At savings institutions | 8.0 | 16.9 | 40.4 | 45.9 | 28.2 | 43.6 | 32.3 | 9.9 | 27.0 | 37.6 | 15.5 | 7.6 |

329

Table 4 (cont'd)

| | 1969 | 1970 | 1971 | 1972 | 1973 | 1973 I | 1973 II | 1973 III | 1973 IV | 1974 I | 1974 II | 1974 III | |
|---|---|---|---|---|---|---|---|---|---|---|---|---|---|
| | | | | | | | | | | | | | Households, personal trusts, and nonprofit organizations (cont'd) |
| 24 | 35.0 | −1.1 | −8.9 | 6.4 | 29.7 | 4.6 | 31.3 | 47.5 | 35.5 | 31.4 | 25.3 | 65.7 | Credit market instruments |
| 25 | 12.8 | −9.7 | −14.4 | 0.6 | 20.4 | 12.1 | 27.8 | 27.1 | 14.4 | 14.3 | 12.3 | 35.8 | U.S. government securities |
| 26 | 9.6 | −0.8 | −0.2 | 1.0 | 4.3 | 3.7 | 2.8 | 8.9 | 2.0 | 5.6 | 7.7 | 13.5 | State and local obligations |
| 27 | 6.6 | 10.7 | 9.3 | 5.2 | 1.1 | −0.5 | * | −1.4 | 6.1 | 3.4 | 0.3 | 4.9 | Corporate and foreign bonds |
| 28 | 4.8 | −1.5 | −3.9 | 1.5 | 3.5 | −7.7 | −1.3 | 11.2 | 11.6 | 7.8 | 3.1 | 10.0 | Commercial paper |
| 29 | 1.1 | 0.1 | 0.2 | −1.8 | 0.5 | −3.0 | 1.9 | 1.6 | 1.4 | 0.3 | 1.9 | 1.4 | Mortgages |
| 30 | 4.8 | 2.6 | 1.1 | −0.7 | −1.6 | −2.1 | −1.8 | 1.2 | −3.7 | * | −1.6 | 2.3 | Investment company shares |
| 31 | −8.6 | −4.4 | −6.5 | −4.7 | −6.6 | −7.2 | −1.3 | −1.5 | −16.3 | −2.7 | −2.5 | 0.9 | Other corporate shares |
| 32 | 5.0 | 5.2 | 6.2 | 6.6 | 7.3 | 7.1 | 7.4 | 7.4 | 7.2 | 7.1 | 7.5 | 7.3 | Life insurance reserves |
| 33 | 16.3 | 19.1 | 21.6 | 23.8 | 24.4 | 24.8 | 24.9 | 25.3 | 22.5 | 20.1 | 39.2 | 27.1 | Pension fund reserves |
| 34 | −3.5 | −4.7 | −4.7 | −7.4 | −4.4 | −7.1 | −6.0 | −4.1 | −0.6 | −6.6 | −7.4 | −7.6 | Net investment in noncorporate business |
| 35 | −1.8 | −0.9 | 0.5 | 0.1 | −0.2 | −0.7 | −1.3 | 0.7 | 0.5 | −0.8 | −0.9 | 0.1 | Security credit |
| 36 | 2.1 | 2.6 | 2.3 | 2.7 | 1.5 | 1.3 | 1.5 | 1.6 | 1.6 | 2.2 | 2.2 | 2.3 | Miscellaneous assets |
| 37 | 29.2 | 22.5 | 43.1 | 68.9 | 69.3 | 71.6 | 67.8 | 77.4 | 60.1 | 52.6 | 54.7 | 54.2 | Net increase in liabilities |
| 38 | 31.7 | 23.4 | 39.8 | 63.1 | 72.8 | 74.5 | 72.1 | 80.5 | 64.1 | 51.4 | 53.6 | 57.6 | Credit market instruments |
| 39 | 16.1 | 12.5 | 24.2 | 38.4 | 44.2 | 41.4 | 47.2 | 47.8 | 40.4 | 35.2 | 39.9 | 31.7 | Home mortgages |
| 40 | 1.3 | 1.4 | 1.2 | 1.4 | 1.4 | 1.4 | 1.4 | 1.4 | 1.4 | 1.4 | 1.4 | 1.4 | Other mortgages |
| 41 | 9.4 | 5.0 | 9.2 | 16.0 | 20.1 | 24.0 | 20.0 | 21.0 | 15.5 | 8.8 | 14.0 | 14.1 | Installment consumer credit |
| 42 | 1.0 | 1.1 | 2.0 | 3.1 | 2.8 | 1.6 | 4.6 | 1.3 | 3.8 | −0.6 | 3.2 | 1.7 | Other consumer credit |
| 43 | 1.0 | 0.9 | 1.8 | 2.8 | 1.8 | 4.5 | −2.8 | 5.6 | −0.2 | 4.9 | −8.1 | 5.4 | Bank loans n.e.c. |
| 44 | 3.0 | 2.6 | 1.4 | 1.3 | 2.5 | 1.5 | 1.7 | 3.5 | 3.3 | 1.7 | 3.3 | 3.4 | Other loans |
| 45 | −3.4 | −1.8 | 2.6 | 4.7 | −4.6 | −3.9 | −5.4 | −4.1 | −4.9 | 0.1 | 0.1 | −4.4 | Security credit |
| 46 | 0.5 | 0.5 | 0.3 | 0.6 | 0.6 | 0.6 | 0.6 | 0.6 | 0.6 | 0.6 | 0.6 | 0.6 | Trade debt |
| 47 | 0.4 | 0.4 | 0.3 | 0.5 | 0.4 | 0.4 | 0.4 | 0.4 | 0.4 | 0.4 | 0.4 | 0.4 | Miscellaneous |
| 48 | 3.5 | 0.2 | −0.5 | −8.3 | −6.0 | 3.8 | −18.0 | −4.0 | −5.8 | −8.2 | −12.0 | −11.8 | Discrepancy |

Memoranda

| | | 1 | 2 | 3 | 4 | 5 | 6 | 7 | 8 | 9 | 10 | 11 | 12 |
|---|---|---|---|---|---|---|---|---|---|---|---|---|---|
| | Net physical investment: | | | | | | | | | | | | |
| | (A) Residential construction | | | | | | | | | | | | |
| 49 | Expenditures | 22.0 | 19.6 | 26.9 | 34.3 | 37.5 | 37.3 | 37.9 | 38.0 | 37.0 | 32.8 | 30.6 | 33.2 |
| 50 | – Capital consumption | 8.7 | 9.0 | 9.3 | 10.0 | 10.4 | 10.2 | 10.5 | 10.3 | 10.4 | 10.5 | 10.8 | 10.6 |
| 51 | – Home mortgages | 16.1 | 12.5 | 24.2 | 38.4 | 44.2 | 41.4 | 47.2 | 47.8 | 40.4 | 35.2 | 39.9 | 31.7 |
| 52 | = Excess net investment | -2.8 | -1.9 | -6.6 | -14.1 | -17.0 | -14.4 | -19.9 | -20.1 | -13.7 | -12.8 | -20.1 | -9.2 |
| | (B) Consumer durables | | | | | | | | | | | | |
| 53 | Expenditures | 90.8 | 91.3 | 103.9 | 118.4 | 130.3 | 132.4 | 132.1 | 132.4 | 124.3 | 123.9 | 129.5 | 136.0 |
| 54 | – Capital consumption | 74.6 | 80.7 | 87.5 | 94.1 | 103.3 | 100.3 | 103.5 | 104.9 | 104.4 | 104.3 | 104.5 | 104.3 |
| 55 | = Net investment | 16.2 | 10.6 | 16.5 | 24.4 | 27.1 | 32.1 | 28.6 | 27.5 | 20.0 | 19.6 | 25.0 | 31.7 |
| 56 | – Consumer credit | 10.4 | 6.0 | 11.2 | 19.2 | 22.9 | 25.6 | 24.6 | 22.3 | 19.2 | 8.2 | 17.2 | 15.8 |
| 57 | = Excess net investment | 5.9 | 4.5 | 5.2 | 5.2 | 4.1 | 6.5 | 4.0 | 5.2 | 0.8 | 11.4 | 7.8 | 15.9 |
| | (C) Nonprofit plant and equipment | | | | | | | | | | | | |
| 58 | Expenditures | 5.1 | 5.3 | 5.6 | 6.0 | 6.3 | 6.3 | 6.5 | 6.3 | 6.1 | 6.5 | 6.4 | 6.2 |
| 59 | – Capital consumption | 1.6 | 1.7 | 1.9 | 2.0 | 2.1 | 2.1 | 2.1 | 2.1 | 2.2 | 2.2 | 2.3 | 2.3 |
| 60 | – Nonprofit mortgages | 1.3 | 1.4 | 1.2 | 1.4 | 1.4 | 1.4 | 1.4 | 1.4 | 1.4 | 1.4 | 1.4 | 1.4 |
| 61 | = Excess net investment | 2.2 | 2.2 | 2.5 | 2.6 | 2.7 | 2.8 | 2.9 | 2.7 | 2.6 | 2.9 | 2.7 | 2.5 |
| | Percent ratios: | | | | | | | | | | | | |
| 62 | Effective tax rate | 15.5 | 14.4 | 13.6 | 15.1 | 14.3 | 14.2 | 14.2 | 14.4 | 14.5 | 14.6 | 14.8 | 15.0 |
| 63 | Saving rate, NIA basis | 6.0 | 8.1 | 8.1 | 6.6 | 8.2 | 7.5 | 7.8 | 8.0 | 9.5 | 8.9 | 7.4 | 6.5 |
| | Percent of disposable income adjusted (2): | | | | | | | | | | | | |
| 64 | Gross saving | 23.1 | 23.9 | 24.5 | 24.0 | 25.1 | 25.3 | 25.3 | 24.8 | 24.9 | 24.1 | 23.9 | 22.5 |
| 65 | Capital expenditures | 18.3 | 16.6 | 18.0 | 19.5 | 19.0 | 19.9 | 19.4 | 19.1 | 17.6 | 17.0 | 16.8 | 17.5 |
| 66 | Acquisition of financial assets | 8.8 | 10.6 | 12.3 | 14.0 | 14.3 | 13.0 | 15.3 | 14.5 | 14.2 | 13.4 | 13.8 | 11.6 |
| 67 | Net increase in liabilities | 4.5 | 3.2 | 5.7 | 8.5 | 7.6 | 8.1 | 7.5 | 8.4 | 6.3 | 5.5 | 5.5 | 5.4 |
| 68 | Credit market borrowing | 4.9 | 3.3 | 5.3 | 7.7 | 7.9 | 8.4 | 7.9 | 8.7 | 6.8 | 5.3 | 5.4 | 5.7 |
| 69 | (2) Disposable income adjusted (NIA disposable income + government insurance credits + capital gains dividend) | 644.0 | 701.4 | 756.4 | 815.0 | 916.2 | 882.5 | 907.5 | 925.6 | 949.3 | 961.3 | 988.9 | 1,002.8 |

[a] Excludes corporate equities

Table 5

Sector statements of saving and investment: Total and noncorporate business (billions of dollars)

| | 1969 | 1970 | 1971 | 1972 | 1973 | 1973 I | 1973 II | 1973 III | 1973 IV | 1974 I | 1974 II | 1974 III | |
|---|---|---|---|---|---|---|---|---|---|---|---|---|---|
| Nonfinancial business (total) | | | | | | | | | | | | | |
| 1 | 139.5 | 128.2 | 137.5 | 155.2 | 183.9 | 177.3 | 180.7 | 186.9 | 190.6 | 181.6 | 176.0 | 179.4 | Income before taxes |
| 2 | 80.4 | 80.3 | 90.6 | 104.1 | 112.6 | 110.2 | 111.4 | 113.2 | 115.8 | 113.9 | 109.4 | 104.1 | Gross saving |
| 3 | 74.4 | 73.6 | 80.4 | 89.3 | 98.8 | 94.5 | 97.2 | 97.9 | 105.9 | 100.8 | 95.1 | 89.4 | Gross investment |
| 4 | 108.9 | 108.0 | 117.1 | 134.3 | 160.5 | 150.1 | 155.3 | 159.8 | 177.0 | 163.7 | 169.9 | 161.0 | Capital expenditures |
| 5 | 101.1 | 103.5 | 110.8 | 125.7 | 145.2 | 140.1 | 144.6 | 148.0 | 148.0 | 146.8 | 156.4 | 155.2 | Fixed investment |
| 6 | 90.5 | 92.0 | 95.0 | 106.4 | 125.7 | 119.2 | 124.1 | 127.9 | 131.5 | 131.7 | 138.5 | 142.1 | Business plant and equipment |
| 7 | 0.1 | 0.9 | 3.0 | 2.1 | -0.6 | 1.1 | 0.8 | -0.7 | -3.5 | -2.1 | 3.0 | 0.1 | Nonfarm home construction[a] |
| 8 | 10.4 | 10.6 | 12.8 | 17.3 | 20.0 | 19.7 | 19.7 | 20.7 | 20.1 | 17.2 | 15.0 | 13.1 | Multifamily residential |
| 9 | 7.8 | 4.5 | 6.3 | 8.5 | 15.4 | 10.0 | 10.7 | 11.8 | 28.9 | 16.9 | 13.5 | 5.8 | Change in inventories |
| 10 | -34.4 | -34.5 | -36.7 | -45.0 | -61.7 | -55.6 | -58.1 | -61.9 | -71.1 | -62.9 | -74.8 | -71.6 | Net financial investment |
| 11 | 30.2 | 14.8 | 25.3 | 33.8 | 43.9 | 49.5 | 53.3 | 40.7 | 32.1 | 59.6 | 64.5 | 70.3 | Financial uses of funds (net) |
| 12 | 64.7 | 49.2 | 62.0 | 78.7 | 105.5 | 105.1 | 111.4 | 102.5 | 103.2 | 122.5 | 139.3 | 141.9 | Financial sources of funds (net) |
| 13 | 3.4 | 5.7 | 11.4 | 10.9 | 7.4 | 7.0 | 8.7 | 5.1 | 8.9 | 6.2 | 5.0 | 5.4 | Corporate share issues |
| 14 | 46.0 | 42.3 | 48.2 | 59.6 | 77.6 | 85.8 | 80.5 | 79.3 | 64.9 | 82.5 | 103.3 | 96.1 | Credit market instruments |
| 15 | 12.0 | 19.8 | 18.8 | 12.2 | 9.2 | 7.9 | 9.7 | 10.5 | 8.5 | 17.1 | 19.0 | 19.3 | Corporate bonds |
| 16 | -0.4 | 0.3 | 1.9 | 1.2 | -0.9 | 0.5 | 0.3 | -0.9 | -3.4 | -2.2 | 1.8 | -0.6 | Home mortgages |
| 17 | 10.8 | 11.6 | 19.5 | 26.2 | 28.4 | 26.3 | 32.2 | 31.0 | 24.2 | 22.9 | 27.2 | 21.1 | Other mortgages |
| 18 | 14.5 | 5.8 | 5.9 | 16.1 | 34.0 | 55.0 | 28.8 | 30.4 | 21.8 | 30.6 | 42.4 | 28.0 | Bank loans n.e.c. |
| 19 | 9.2 | 4.9 | 1.9 | 3.3 | 5.1 | -5.2 | 7.3 | 6.2 | 12.0 | 12.5 | 11.5 | 26.8 | Other loans |
| 20 | 21.2 | 8.6 | 5.3 | 15.4 | 20.1 | 12.6 | 26.0 | 15.7 | 25.9 | 30.4 | 28.6 | 26.3 | Trade debt |
| 21 | -5.9 | -7.3 | -2.9 | -7.1 | 0.4 | -0.3 | -3.8 | 2.4 | 3.4 | 3.4 | 2.4 | 14.1 | Other liabilities |
| 22 | 6.0 | 6.7 | 10.2 | 14.8 | 13.8 | 15.7 | 14.3 | 15.3 | 10.0 | 13.1 | 14.3 | 14.7 | Discrepancy |
| Farm business | | | | | | | | | | | | | |
| 1 | 16.7 | 16.9 | 17.2 | 21.0 | 38.5 | 32.1 | 35.6 | 41.5 | 44.9 | 39.1 | 29.1 | 28.3 | Net income |
| 2 | * | -0.1 | * | 0.1 | 0.3 | 0.2 | 0.3 | 0.3 | 0.4 | 0.4 | 0.4 | 0.4 | Net saving |
| 3 | 6.6 | 6.4 | 7.0 | 7.5 | 8.4 | 8.0 | 8.5 | 8.5 | 8.8 | 9.0 | 9.3 | 9.5 | Capital consumption |

| # | | 1 | 2 | 3 | 4 | 5 | 6 | 7 | 8 | 9 | 10 | 11 | 12 |
|---|---|---|---|---|---|---|---|---|---|---|---|---|---|
| 4 | Corporate | 0.3 | 0.4 | 0.5 | 0.6 | 0.6 | 0.6 | 0.6 | 0.6 | 0.6 | 0.7 | 0.7 | 0.7 |
| 5 | Noncorporate | 6.2 | 6.0 | 6.5 | 6.9 | 7.8 | 7.4 | 7.8 | 7.8 | 8.1 | 8.4 | 8.6 | 8.8 |
| 6 | Current surplus = gross saving | 6.5 | 6.3 | 6.9 | 7.6 | 8.7 | 8.2 | 8.7 | 8.8 | 9.2 | 9.4 | 9.7 | 9.8 |
| 7 | Gross investment | 6.5 | 6.3 | 6.9 | 7.6 | 8.7 | 8.2 | 8.7 | 8.8 | 9.2 | 9.4 | 9.7 | 9.8 |
| 8 | Capital expenditures | 6.6 | 7.0 | 8.4 | 8.4 | 13.9 | 12.3 | 12.7 | 14.7 | 16.0 | 15.3 | 15.9 | 15.9 |
| 9 | Plant and equipment | 5.9 | 6.3 | 6.4 | 7.1 | 9.5 | 8.3 | 9.3 | 9.7 | 10.5 | 10.9 | 12.0 | 12.4 |
| 10 | Residential construction | 0.6 | 0.5 | 0.6 | 0.6 | 0.5 | 0.5 | 0.4 | 0.5 | 0.6 | 0.7 | 0.8 | 0.8 |
| 11 | Change in inventories | 0.1 | 0.2 | 1.4 | 0.7 | 4.0 | 3.5 | 3.0 | 4.4 | 4.9 | 3.8 | 3.1 | 2.7 |
| 12 | Net financial investment | -0.1 | -0.7 | -1.4 | -0.8 | -5.2 | -4.1 | -3.9 | -5.9 | -6.8 | -5.9 | -6.3 | -6.0 |
| 13 | Net increase in financial assets | 0.5 | 0.6 | 0.7 | 0.9 | 0.7 | 0.7 | 0.7 | 0.7 | 0.7 | 0.7 | 0.9 | 0.9 |
| 14 | Demand deposits and currency | 0.1 | 0.1 | 0.1 | 0.3 | — | 0.1 | * | -0.1 | * | 0.1 | * | 0.1 |
| 15 | Miscellaneous assets | 0.4 | 0.5 | 0.6 | 0.7 | 0.7 | 0.7 | 0.8 | 0.8 | 0.7 | 0.6 | 0.9 | 0.8 |
| 16 | Insurance receivables | 0.4 | 0.4 | 0.5 | 0.6 | 0.6 | 0.6 | 0.6 | 0.5 | 0.6 | 0.6 | 0.6 | 0.6 |
| 17 | Equity in sponsored agencies[b] | 0.1 | 0.1 | 0.1 | 0.1 | 0.2 | 0.1 | 0.2 | 0.2 | 0.1 | 0.1 | 0.4 | 0.2 |
| 18 | Net increase in liabilities | 0.6 | 1.4 | 2.1 | 1.7 | 5.9 | 4.9 | 4.7 | 6.6 | 7.5 | 6.6 | 7.2 | 6.9 |
| 19 | Credit market instruments | 3.2 | 3.2 | 4.1 | 4.9 | 8.6 | 7.4 | 7.7 | 9.6 | 9.8 | 6.3 | 8.5 | 8.7 |
| 20 | Mortgages | 1.9 | 1.8 | 2.0 | 2.6 | 4.4 | 3.9 | 4.4 | 4.7 | 4.5 | 3.8 | 4.8 | 4.4 |
| 21 | Bank loans n.e.c. | 0.6 | 0.8 | 1.3 | 1.8 | 3.0 | 2.7 | 2.2 | 3.1 | 4.0 | 1.8 | 1.2 | 1.8 |
| 22 | Other lonas | 0.6 | 0.6 | 0.7 | 0.5 | 1.2 | 0.8 | 1.0 | 1.7 | 1.3 | 0.7 | 2.6 | 2.4 |
| 23 | U.S. government | * | -0.1 | * | * | 0.1 | 0.1 | * | * | 0.4 | -0.2 | * | * |
| 24 | FICB | 0.6 | 0.7 | 0.7 | 0.4 | 1.1 | 0.7 | 1.0 | 1.7 | 0.9 | 0.9 | 2.6 | 2.4 |
| 25 | Trade debt | 0.7 | 0.9 | 1.1 | 1.5 | 1.5 | 1.6 | 1.3 | 1.2 | 1.7 | 2.2 | 1.3 | 1.6 |
| 26 | Proprietor net investment | -3.2 | -2.8 | -3.1 | -4.6 | -4.2 | -4.2 | -4.3 | -4.2 | -4.0 | -1.9 | -2.6 | -3.4 |

Nonfarm noncorporate business

| # | | 1 | 2 | 3 | 4 | 5 | 6 | 7 | 8 | 9 | 10 | 11 | 12 |
|---|---|---|---|---|---|---|---|---|---|---|---|---|---|
| 1 | Net income | 60.0 | 60.3 | 62.2 | 65.3 | 67.7 | 67.5 | 67.0 | 67.9 | 68.6 | 69.4 | 70.6 | 72.5 |
| 2 | Capital consumption | 13.1 | 14.6 | 15.7 | 17.7 | 19.3 | 18.3 | 19.2 | 19.6 | 20.3 | 20.6 | 21.2 | 21.5 |
| 3 | Current surplus = gross saving | 13.2 | 14.6 | 15.7 | 17.7 | 19.3 | 18.3 | 19.2 | 19.6 | 20.3 | 20.6 | 21.2 | 21.5 |
| 4 | Gross investment | 13.2 | 14.6 | 15.7 | 17.7 | 19.3 | 18.3 | 19.2 | 19.6 | 20.3 | 20.6 | 21.2 | 21.5 |
| 5 | Capital expenditures | 18.6 | 16.9 | 21.6 | 23.4 | 25.1 | 25.0 | 24.9 | 24.7 | 25.8 | 19.6 | 22.6 | 21.7 |
| 6 | Fixed capital | 17.6 | 18.3 | 21.7 | 25.3 | 26.6 | 27.2 | 27.3 | 26.8 | 25.0 | 23.9 | 24.6 | 21.7 |
| 7 | Plant and equipment | 10.6 | 10.6 | 11.5 | 12.2 | 12.9 | 13.0 | 13.0 | 12.9 | 12.8 | 12.8 | 12.9 | 12.9 |

333

Table 5 (cont'd)

| | 1969 | 1970 | 1971 | 1972 | 1973 | 1973 | | | | 1974 | | |
|---|---|---|---|---|---|---|---|---|---|---|---|---|
| | | | | | | I | II | III | IV | I | II | III |
| Nonfarm noncorporate business (cont'd) | | | | | | | | | | | | |
| 8 Home construction[a] | −0.3 | 0.2 | 1.2 | 0.8 | −0.5 | 0.3 | 0.2 | −0.6 | −2.1 | −1.4 | 1.1 | −0.4 |
| 9 Multifamily residential | 7.3 | 7.5 | 9.1 | 12.3 | 14.2 | 13.9 | 14.1 | 14.5 | 14.3 | 12.4 | 10.6 | 9.2 |
| 10 Change in inventories | 1.0 | −1.4 | −0.1 | −1.9 | −1.5 | −2.2 | −2.5 | −2.1 | 0.8 | −4.2 | −2.0 | — |
| 11 Net financial investment | −5.4 | −2.4 | −5.9 | −5.6 | −5.8 | −6.7 | −5.7 | −5.1 | −5.4 | 1.0 | −1.5 | −0.3 |
| 12 Net acquisition of financial assets | 1.3 | 1.3 | 1.5 | 2.1 | 2.3 | 1.6 | 2.3 | 2.2 | 2.9 | 0.7 | 2.5 | 3.1 |
| 13 Demand deposits and currency | — | — | — | — | — | — | — | — | — | — | — | — |
| 14 Consumer credit | 0.6 | 0.6 | 0.7 | 1.1 | 1.3 | 0.6 | 1.3 | 1.2 | 1.9 | −0.3 | 1.4 | 2.1 |
| 15 Miscellaneous assets | 0.7 | 0.7 | 0.8 | 1.0 | 1.0 | 1.0 | 1.0 | 1.0 | 1.0 | 1.0 | 1.1 | 1.0 |
| 16 Insurance receivables | 0.7 | 0.7 | 0.8 | 1.0 | 1.0 | 1.0 | 1.0 | 1.0 | 1.0 | 1.0 | 1.0 | 1.0 |
| 17 Equity in sponsored agencies[b] | * | * | * | * | * | * | * | * | * | * | 0.1 | * |
| 18 Net increase in liabilities | 6.7 | 3.7 | 7.4 | 7.7 | 8.0 | 8.3 | 8.0 | 7.3 | 8.3 | −0.4 | 3.9 | 3.3 |
| 19 Credit market instruments | 7.4 | 5.3 | 8.7 | 10.4 | 9.3 | 11.5 | 10.8 | 8.8 | 6.0 | 4.4 | 10.2 | 8.3 |
| 20 Mortgages | 3.8 | 4.9 | 8.0 | 9.2 | 7.1 | 7.8 | 9.7 | 7.8 | 3.0 | 5.1 | 8.3 | 6.8 |
| 21 Home mortgages | −0.2 | 0.2 | 1.0 | 0.6 | −0.4 | 0.3 | 0.2 | −0.5 | −1.7 | −1.1 | 0.9 | −0.3 |
| 22 Multifamily | 3.6 | 4.3 | 6.2 | 7.3 | 5.9 | 6.2 | 7.9 | 6.6 | 3.2 | 5.0 | 6.1 | 6.4 |
| 23 Commercial | 0.4 | 0.4 | 0.9 | 1.3 | 1.6 | 1.4 | 1.7 | 1.7 | 1.5 | 1.2 | 1.4 | 0.7 |
| 24 Bank loans n.e.c. | 2.1 | −0.6 | 0.2 | 0.7 | 0.4 | 0.6 | * | −0.5 | 1.5 | −2.1 | 0.4 | −0.4 |
| 25 Other loans | 1.5 | 1.0 | 0.5 | 0.4 | 1.8 | 3.1 | 1.1 | 1.5 | 1.6 | 1.3 | 1.5 | 1.8 |
| 26 Trade debt (net) | −0.5 | 0.2 | 0.3 | 0.2 | −1.0 | −0.3 | −1.1 | −1.6 | −1.0 | −0.1 | −1.4 | −0.7 |
| 27 Proprietor net investment | −0.2 | −1.8 | −1.6 | −2.8 | −0.3 | −2.9 | −1.7 | 0.2 | 3.4 | −4.7 | −4.8 | −4.3 |

[a]Change in work in process
[b]Shares in FICBs, Banks for Cooperatives, and Land Banks

# Table 6

Sector statements of saving and investment: Corporate business (billions of dollars)

| | 1969 | 1970 | 1971 | 1972 | 1973 | 1973 I | II | III | IV | 1974 I | II | III | |
|---|---|---|---|---|---|---|---|---|---|---|---|---|---|
| 1 | 67.9 | 55.7 | 63.1 | 76.0 | 95.2 | 94.2 | 98.1 | 94.9 | 93.5 | 104.1 | 114.1 | 137.1 | Profits before tax |
| 2 | 33.6 | 27.5 | 29.7 | 33.3 | 40.5 | 40.3 | 41.9 | 40.3 | 39.6 | 43.5 | 47.6 | 57.0 | − Profits tax accruals |
| 3 | 20.7 | 20.0 | 20.2 | 22.1 | 23.6 | 22.3 | 22.9 | 23.9 | 25.4 | 27.3 | 32.4 | 32.8 | − Net dividends paid |
| 4 | 13.6 | 8.3 | 13.3 | 20.7 | 31.0 | 31.6 | 33.3 | 30.7 | 28.5 | 33.3 | 34.2 | 47.3 | = Undistributed profits |
| 5 | 2.5 | 2.3 | 2.0 | 2.1 | 3.7 | 2.7 | 3.0 | 3.8 | 5.2 | 11.5 | 10.6 | 10.7 | + Foreign branch profits |
| 6 | −5.1 | −4.8 | −4.9 | −7.0 | −17.6 | −16.5 | −20.0 | −17.5 | −16.3 | −31.0 | −37.9 | −58.5 | + Investment valuation adjustment |
| 7 | 49.8 | 53.6 | 57.7 | 63.0 | 67.5 | 65.8 | 67.2 | 67.8 | 69.0 | 70.1 | 71.6 | 73.3 | + Capital consumption allowance |
| 8 | 60.7 | 59.4 | 68.0 | 78.7 | 84.6 | 83.7 | 83.6 | 84.8 | 86.3 | 83.8 | 78.5 | 72.8 | = Gross internal funds |
| 9 | 54.7 | 52.7 | 57.8 | 64.0 | 70.8 | 68.0 | 69.3 | 69.5 | 76.3 | 70.7 | 64.3 | 58.1 | Gross investment |
| 10 | 83.7 | 84.0 | 87.2 | 102.5 | 121.5 | 112.7 | 117.7 | 120.4 | 135.2 | 128.8 | 131.4 | 123.4 | Capital expenditures |
| 11 | 76.9 | 78.4 | 82.1 | 92.8 | 108.6 | 104.1 | 107.6 | 110.9 | 112.0 | 111.4 | 119.0 | 120.3 | Fixed investment |
| 12 | 74.0 | 75.1 | 77.1 | 87.1 | 103.3 | 97.9 | 101.9 | 105.3 | 108.2 | 108.0 | 113.5 | 116.8 | Plant and equipment |
| 13 | −0.3 | 0.2 | 1.2 | 0.8 | −0.5 | 0.3 | 0.2 | −0.6 | −2.1 | −1.4 | 1.1 | −0.4 | Home construction |
| 14 | 3.2 | 3.1 | 3.8 | 4.9 | 5.8 | 5.8 | 5.5 | 6.2 | 5.9 | 4.8 | 4.4 | 3.9 | Multifamily residential |
| 15 | 6.7 | 5.7 | 5.1 | 9.7 | 12.9 | 8.7 | 10.1 | 9.5 | 23.2 | 17.4 | 12.4 | 3.1 | Change in inventories |
| 16 | −28.9 | −31.3 | −29.4 | −38.5 | −50.7 | −44.8 | −48.4 | −50.9 | −58.8 | −58.0 | −67.1 | −65.3 | Net financial investment |
| 17 | 28.4 | 12.9 | 23.1 | 30.8 | 40.9 | 47.1 | 50.2 | 37.7 | 28.5 | 58.3 | 61.0 | 66.3 | Financial uses of funds (net) |
| 18 | 2.3 | −0.4 | 10.6 | 4.0 | 6.9 | 19.1 | 13.7 | 11.1 | −16.0 | 15.2 | 13.4 | 27.9 | Liquid assets |
| 19 | 2.6 | 0.9 | 0.5 | −0.1 | −0.3 | −1.2 | 2.7 | 0.8 | −3.3 | 1.7 | −1.1 | 0.2 | Demand deposits and currency |
| 20 | −2.4 | 1.7 | 3.6 | 3.1 | 1.4 | 14.3 | 0.2 | 3.6 | −12.7 | 4.4 | 10.8 | 9.1 | Time deposits |
| 21 | −2.3 | 0.5 | 2.2 | −2.4 | −1.8 | * | −1.2 | −3.4 | −2.6 | −1.7 | 2.6 | 8.3 | U.S. government securities |
| 22 | −1.0 | −0.6 | 1.0 | 1.0 | −0.1 | 1.0 | 2.5 | −1.5 | −2.5 | 2.1 | * | 0.1 | State and local obligations |
| 23 | 4.0 | 0.5 | 2.4 | 0.8 | 5.2 | −0.2 | 12.2 | 5.0 | 4.1 | 0.8 | 7.8 | 6.5 | Commercial paper |
| 24 | 1.4 | −3.4 | 0.8 | 1.6 | 2.6 | 5.3 | −2.7 | 6.6 | 1.0 | 7.8 | −6.7 | 3.7 | Security RP's |
| 25 | 0.3 | 0.7 | 0.6 | 1.6 | 2.0 | 0.9 | 3.5 | 0.7 | 2.9 | 0.1 | 2.9 | 1.1 | Consumer credit |
| 26 | 22.7 | 8.4 | 5.7 | 20.0 | 24.1 | 14.7 | 26.1 | 22.5 | 33.1 | 38.0 | 38.4 | 30.6 | Trade credit |
| 27 | 3.0 | 4.2 | 6.2 | 5.2 | 7.9 | 12.4 | 7.0 | 3.4 | 8.6 | 4.9 | 6.4 | 6.8 | Miscellaneous assets |
| 28 | 2.2 | 3.6 | 3.8 | 1.5 | 3.6 | 5.3 | 2.3 | 1.7 | 5.4 | 1.7 | 5.6 | 5.2 | Foreign direct investment[a] |

Table 6 (cont'd)

| | 1969 | 1970 | 1971 | 1972 | 1973 | 1973 | | | | 1974 | | |
|---|---|---|---|---|---|---|---|---|---|---|---|---|
| | | | | | | I | II | III | IV | I | II | III |
| 29 Foreign currencies | -0.4 | -0.4 | 1.4 | 1.8 | 2.6 | 5.4 | 3.1 | 0.1 | 1.6 | 1.6 | -0.8 | — |
| 30 Insurance receivables | 1.1 | 0.9 | 1.0 | 1.9 | 1.6 | 1.7 | 1.6 | 1.6 | 1.6 | 1.6 | 1.6 | 1.6 |
| 31 Equity in sponsored agencies | 0.1 | 0.1 | * | * | * | * | * | * | * | * | * | * |
| 32 Financial sources of funds (net) | 57.4 | 44.2 | 52.5 | 69.3 | 91.6 | 91.9 | 98.7 | 88.6 | 87.3 | 116.3 | 128.2 | 131.6 |
| 33 Net funds raised in markets | 38.9 | 39.5 | 46.8 | 55.3 | 67.2 | 73.9 | 70.7 | 66.1 | 57.9 | 78.0 | 89.7 | 84.6 |
| 34 Net new share issues | 3.4 | 5.7 | 11.4 | 10.9 | 7.4 | 7.0 | 8.7 | 5.1 | 8.9 | 6.2 | 5.0 | 5.4 |
| 35 Debt instruments | 35.5 | 33.8 | 35.4 | 44.4 | 59.7 | 66.9 | 62.0 | 60.9 | 49.1 | 71.8 | 84.7 | 79.1 |
| 36 Tax-exempt bonds | — | — | 0.1 | 0.5 | 1.8 | 1.3 | 2.1 | 2.0 | 1.8 | 1.6 | 1.5 | 1.4 |
| 37 Corporate bonds[a] | 12.0 | 19.8 | 18.8 | 12.2 | 9.2 | 7.9 | 9.7 | 10.5 | 8.5 | 17.1 | 19.0 | 19.3 |
| 38 Mortgages | 4.6 | 5.2 | 11.4 | 15.6 | 16.1 | 15.1 | 18.4 | 17.7 | 13.3 | 11.8 | 15.8 | 9.2 |
| 39 Home mortgages | -0.2 | 0.2 | 1.0 | 0.6 | -0.4 | 0.3 | 0.2 | -0.5 | -1.7 | -1.1 | 0.9 | -0.3 |
| 40 Multifamily | 1.2 | 1.5 | 2.6 | 3.0 | 2.5 | 2.3 | 3.2 | 3.1 | 1.4 | 2.1 | 2.7 | 2.8 |
| 41 Commercial | 3.7 | 3.6 | 7.9 | 12.0 | 14.1 | 12.5 | 15.1 | 15.0 | 13.7 | 10.8 | 12.3 | 6.7 |
| 42 Bank loans n.e.c. | 11.8 | 5.6 | 4.4 | 13.5 | 30.6 | 51.7 | 26.6 | 27.8 | 16.3 | 30.9 | 40.9 | 26.6 |
| 43 Open market paper | 2.7 | 2.6 | -1.5 | -0.5 | -0.3 | -11.3 | 3.6 | 0.4 | 6.1 | 6.8 | 6.7 | 13.1 |
| 44 Finance company loans | 4.3 | 0.4 | 1.9 | 2.8 | 2.0 | 1.5 | 1.3 | 2.4 | 2.7 | 4.0 | 0.5 | 9.4 |
| 45 U.S. government loans | 0.1 | 0.3 | 0.2 | 0.2 | 0.3 | 0.6 | 0.2 | 0.1 | 0.4 | -0.3 | 0.2 | 0.1 |
| 46 Profit tax liability | -3.3 | -3.7 | 2.0 | -0.1 | 2.3 | 5.3 | -0.2 | 2.9 | 1.2 | 4.9 | 3.7 | 14.8 |
| 47 Trade debt | 21.0 | 7.4 | 3.8 | 13.7 | 19.6 | 11.3 | 25.9 | 16.0 | 25.3 | 28.3 | 28.7 | 25.4 |
| 48 Miscellaneous liabilities | 0.8 | 1.0 | -0.1 | 0.4 | 2.5 | 1.4 | 2.4 | 3.5 | 2.8 | 5.1 | 6.1 | 6.9 |
| 49 Discrepancy | 6.0 | 6.7 | 10.2 | 14.8 | 13.8 | 15.7 | 14.3 | 15.3 | 10.0 | 13.1 | 14.3 | 14.7 |
| 50 Memo: net trade credit | 1.8 | 0.9 | 1.9 | 6.3 | 4.5 | 3.4 | 0.2 | 6.4 | 7.8 | 9.7 | 9.6 | 5.2 |
| 51 Profits tax payments | 36.4 | 30.3 | 27.8 | 33.7 | 38.1 | 36.2 | 41.2 | 37.2 | 37.8 | 39.9 | 43.1 | 41.9 |
| Percent ratios: | | | | | | | | | | | | |
| 52 Effective tax rate | 49.5 | 49.4 | 47.0 | 43.8 | 42.6 | 42.8 | 42.7 | 42.5 | 42.3 | 41.8 | 41.7 | 41.6 |
| 53 Capital outlays/internal funds | 137.8 | 141.4 | 128.3 | 130.1 | 143.6 | 134.7 | 140.9 | 142.0 | 156.6 | 153.6 | 167.3 | 169.5 |
| 54 Credit market borrowing/capital expenditure | 42.4 | 40.2 | 40.6 | 43.3 | 49.2 | 59.3 | 52.7 | 50.6 | 36.3 | 55.8 | 64.5 | 64.1 |

[a] Foreign investment excludes amounts financed by bond issues abroad, and bond issues outside the U.S. are excluded from financial sources of funds above

Table 7

Sector statements of savings and investment: Governments (billions of dollars)

State and local governments (general funds)

| | | 1969 | 1970 | 1971 | 1972 | 1973 | 1973 I | 1973 II | 1973 III | 1973 IV | 1974 I | 1974 II | 1974 III |
|---|---|---|---|---|---|---|---|---|---|---|---|---|---|
| 1 | Total receipts (NIA basis) | 119.7 | 135.0 | 152.2 | 177.2 | 193.5 | 190.2 | 192.0 | 194.6 | 197.3 | 200.8 | 205.6 | 210.9 |
| 2 | Tax receipts | 92.1 | 102.3 | 114.0 | 129.2 | 141.3 | 137.8 | 140.3 | 142.8 | 144.2 | 145.5 | 149.7 | 155.7 |
| 3 | Social insurance receipts | 7.3 | 8.3 | 9.2 | 10.6 | 11.7 | 11.3 | 11.6 | 11.9 | 12.1 | 12.4 | 12.7 | 13.0 |
| 4 | Grants-in-aid received | 20.3 | 24.4 | 29.0 | 37.4 | 40.5 | 41.1 | 40.1 | 39.8 | 41.0 | 42.9 | 43.2 | 42.2 |
| 5 | Total expenditures (NIA basis) | 119.0 | 133.2 | 148.8 | 164.9 | 184.4 | 177.0 | 181.7 | 186.1 | 192.7 | 197.4 | 203.3 | 208.3 |
| 6 | Purchase of goods and services | 111.2 | 123.3 | 136.6 | 150.8 | 169.8 | 162.6 | 167.1 | 171.6 | 177.9 | 184.8 | 190.1 | 194.8 |
| 7 | Net interest and transfers | 7.8 | 9.9 | 12.2 | 14.1 | 14.6 | 14.4 | 14.5 | 14.5 | 14.8 | 12.6 | 13.2 | 13.5 |
| 8 | Net surplus (NIA basis) | 0.7 | 1.8 | 3.4 | 12.3 | 9.2 | 13.2 | 10.4 | 8.4 | 4.6 | 3.4 | 2.2 | 2.7 |
| 9 | − Retirement credit to households | 5.5 | 6.3 | 6.3 | 7.9 | 9.4 | 9.8 | 9.9 | 9.7 | 8.2 | 8.4 | 11.7 | 11.7 |
| 10 | = Gross saving | −4.8 | −4.5 | −2.9 | 4.5 | −0.3 | 3.4 | 0.5 | −1.3 | −3.6 | −5.0 | −9.4 | −9.0 |
| 11 | Net financial investment | −9.3 | −4.3 | −12.1 | −2.7 | −5.4 | −4.0 | −6.0 | −1.7 | −9.9 | −4.1 | −10.7 | −9.0 |
| 12 | Net acquisition of financial assets | 1.9 | 7.6 | 6.4 | 12.2 | 7.9 | 7.0 | 4.7 | 14.8 | 5.2 | 11.3 | 7.6 | 3.5 |
| 13 | Total deposits and currency | −4.5 | 7.2 | 8.2 | 8.3 | 6.9 | 9.4 | 7.3 | 10.4 | 0.4 | 4.2 | 16.4 | 9.0 |
| 14 | Demand deposits and currency | 1.4 | −2.9 | 1.0 | 1.5 | −0.3 | −0.3 | 0.7 | −0.6 | −1.1 | 0.4 | 4.6 | 4.7 |
| 15 | Time deposits | −5.9 | 10.0 | 7.2 | 6.8 | 7.2 | 9.7 | 6.6 | 11.0 | 1.6 | 3.8 | 11.8 | 4.4 |
| 16 | Credit market instruments | 6.4 | 0.3 | −2.0 | 3.6 | 0.4 | −3.1 | −3.2 | 3.8 | 4.2 | 6.5 | −9.4 | −6.2 |
| 17 | U.S. government securities | 6.4 | 0.2 | −1.8 | 3.4 | 0.2 | −3.5 | −3.8 | 4.1 | 4.1 | 6.4 | −9.6 | −6.7 |
| 18 | Direct | 3.1 | 0.9 | −1.3 | 4.0 | 1.2 | 1.1 | −1.7 | 3.0 | 2.3 | 4.5 | −10.1 | −4.7 |
| 19 | U.S. government agency securities | 3.4 | −0.8 | −0.5 | −0.6 | −1.0 | −4.6 | −2.2 | 1.1 | 1.8 | 1.9 | 0.5 | −2.0 |
| 20 | State and local obligations | 0.1 | 0.2 | −0.3 | 0.2 | 0.2 | 0.5 | 0.6 | −0.2 | 0.1 | 0.2 | 0.2 | 0.6 |
| 21 | Home mortgages | −0.1 | * | * | * | * | — | — | * | * | * | — | — |
| 22 | Taxes receivable | * | 0.1 | 0.3 | 0.3 | 0.6 | 0.6 | 0.6 | 0.6 | 0.6 | 0.6 | 0.6 | 0.6 |
| 23 | Net increase in liabilities | 11.2 | 11.8 | 18.5 | 14.9 | 13.3 | 11.0 | 10.7 | 16.5 | 15.1 | 15.4 | 18.3 | 12.5 |
| 24 | Credit market borrowing | 10.7 | 11.3 | 17.8 | 14.2 | 12.3 | 10.0 | 9.6 | 15.4 | 14.1 | 14.5 | 17.4 | 11.5 |
| 25 | State and local obligations | 9.9 | 11.2 | 17.5 | 13.8 | 11.9 | 9.3 | 10.5 | 13.6 | 14.2 | 14.2 | 18.2 | 10.9 |
| 26 | Short-term | 2.8 | 2.3 | 2.5 | −0.7 | −0.2 | −1.2 | −1.8 | 0.7 | 1.4 | −0.4 | 3.3 | 4.5 |
| 27 | Other | 7.2 | 8.9 | 15.0 | 14.5 | 12.2 | 10.6 | 12.4 | 12.9 | 12.8 | 14.6 | 14.9 | 6.4 |

337

Table 7 (cont'd)

### State and local governments (general funds) (cont'd)

| | 1969 | 1970 | 1971 | 1972 | 1973 | 1973 I | 1973 II | 1973 III | 1973 IV | 1974 I | 1974 II | 1974 III | |
|---|---|---|---|---|---|---|---|---|---|---|---|---|---|
| 28 | 0.7 | 0.1 | 0.4 | 0.3 | 0.3 | 0.7 | -1.0 | 1.7 | -0.1 | 0.3 | -0.8 | 0.6 | U.S. government loans |
| 29 | 0.5 | 0.5 | 0.7 | 0.7 | 1.1 | 1.0 | 1.1 | 1.2 | 1.1 | 1.0 | 0.9 | 1.0 | Trade debt |
| 30 | 4.5 | -0.2 | 9.1 | 7.1 | 5.1 | 7.3 | 6.5 | 0.4 | 6.3 | -0.9 | 1.2 | * | Discrepancy Employee retirement funds are in insurance sector |

### U.S. government

| | 1969 | 1970 | 1971 | 1972 | 1973 | 1973 I | 1973 II | 1973 III | 1973 IV | 1974 I | 1974 II | 1974 III | |
|---|---|---|---|---|---|---|---|---|---|---|---|---|---|
| 1 | 197.3 | 192.0 | 198.5 | 227.2 | 258.5 | 249.1 | 255.0 | 261.8 | 268.3 | 279.4 | 290.3 | 307.2 | Total receipts (NIA basis) |
| 2 | 94.8 | 92.2 | 89.9 | 108.2 | 114.1 | 107.9 | 110.3 | 116.7 | 121.6 | 124.1 | 129.4 | 134.8 | Personal taxes |
| 3 | 36.6 | 31.0 | 33.4 | 36.6 | 43.7 | 42.8 | 44.7 | 43.8 | 43.5 | 47.2 | 50.9 | 60.0 | Corporate profits tax accruals |
| 4 | 19.0 | 19.3 | 20.4 | 20.0 | 21.2 | 20.9 | 21.4 | 21.0 | 21.3 | 21.5 | 21.9 | 22.5 | Indirect taxes |
| 5 | 46.9 | 49.5 | 54.6 | 62.5 | 79.5 | 77.4 | 78.6 | 80.2 | 81.8 | 86.7 | 88.1 | 89.9 | Social insurance receipts |
| 6 | 189.2 | 203.9 | 220.3 | 244.7 | 264.1 | 260.2 | 262.4 | 263.4 | 270.6 | 281.0 | 291.6 | 301.9 | Total expenditures (NIA basis) |
| 7 | 98.8 | 96.2 | 97.6 | 104.9 | 106.6 | 106.4 | 106.2 | 105.3 | 108.4 | 111.5 | 114.3 | 116.4 | Goods and services |
| 8 | 77.3 | 93.2 | 109.0 | 126.4 | 141.3 | 139.1 | 140.3 | 141.4 | 144.5 | 151.6 | 158.6 | 166.6 | Transfers, etc. |
| 9 | 13.1 | 14.6 | 13.6 | 13.5 | 16.3 | 14.8 | 15.9 | 16.8 | 17.6 | 17.9 | 18.7 | 18.9 | Net interest |
| 10 | 8.1 | -11.9 | -21.9 | -17.5 | -5.6 | -11.1 | -7.4 | -1.7 | -2.3 | -1.5 | -1.3 | 5.3 | Net surplus (NIA basis) |
| 11 | 1.6 | 2.5 | 2.9 | 3.2 | 2.1 | 1.9 | 4.2 | 1.1 | 1.3 | 1.6 | 9.9 | -0.6 | - Insurance credits to households |
| 12 | 6.5 | -14.4 | -24.8 | -20.7 | -7.8 | -13.1 | -11.6 | -2.7 | -3.6 | -3.1 | -11.1 | 5.9 | = Gross saving |
| 13 | 6.1 | -15.2 | -24.9 | -21.1 | -7.7 | -15.8 | -11.5 | -1.3 | -2.2 | -2.6 | -7.5 | 8.5 | Net financial investment |
| 14 | 3.7 | 0.7 | 4.2 | -0.1 | 4.3 | 20.7 | -5.0 | -8.2 | 9.9 | 8.0 | 5.2 | 23.5 | Net acquisition of financial assets |
| 15 | 1.4 | -2.0 | -2.2 | -0.3 | * | -0.1 | * | — | 0.1 | 0.9 | 1.1 | 3.4 | Gold, SDR's, official foreign exchange |
| 16 | 1.1 | 2.5 | 3.3 | -1.0 | -1.8 | 11.0 | -4.7 | -17.8 | 4.1 | -0.5 | -0.7 | * | Demand deposits and currency |
| 17 | -0.2 | 0.3 | 0.1 | 0.1 | -0.2 | 0.7 | -0.2 | -0.6 | -0.6 | 0.6 | -0.6 | 0.3 | Time deposits |
| 18 | 2.9 | 2.8 | 3.2 | 2.6 | 3.0 | 4.0 | -2.2 | 7.8 | 2.2 | 2.2 | 1.7 | 4.3 | Credit market instruments |
| 19 | -1.3 | -0.1 | * | * | * | * | * | * | * | * | * | * | Sponsored agency issues |
| 20 | 0.1 | -0.1 | -0.3 | -0.6 | -1.2 | -1.7 | -3.3 | 0.8 | -0.5 | — | 0.2 | 0.7 | Home mortgages |
| 21 | 0.6 | 0.5 | 0.4 | 0.4 | 0.6 | 0.5 | 0.2 | 2.1 | -0.3 | -0.6 | 0.6 | 1.8 | Other mortgages |
| 22 | 3.5 | 2.6 | 3.2 | 2.9 | 3.6 | 5.3 | 1.0 | 4.9 | 3.1 | 2.8 | 0.9 | 1.9 | Other loans |
| 23 | -2.6 | -2.3 | 1.4 | -0.8 | 2.2 | 4.2 | 0.3 | 2.8 | 1.3 | 3.3 | 4.3 | 14.9 | Taxes receivable |

Flow of funds — household/nonfinancial sector liabilities (continued) and Federally sponsored credit agencies.

| Line | Item | | | | | | | | | | | | |
|---|---|---|---|---|---|---|---|---|---|---|---|---|---|
| 24 | Trade credit | 0.9 | −0.8 | −1.7 | −0.8 | 0.3 | 0.4 | 0.4 | 1.3 | −0.4 | −0.3 | 0.9 | 0.4 |
| 25 | Miscellaneous | 0.1 | 0.3 | 0.1 | 0.1 | 1.0 | 0.4 | 0.4 | 0.4 | −0.1 | 3.1 | −1.4 | 0.2 |
| 26 | Net increase in liabilities | −2.5 | 15.9 | 29.1 | 21.0 | 12.0 | 36.4 | 6.5 | −6.9 | 12.1 | 10.5 | 12.8 | 15.0 |
| 27 | Treasury currency and SDR certificates | 0.3 | 0.6 | 0.5 | 0.5 | 0.4 | 0.4 | 0.8 | 0.3 | 0.3 | 0.3 | 0.4 | 0.4 |
| 28 | Credit market instruments | −3.6 | 12.8 | 25.5 | 17.3 | 20.3 | 32.8 | 2.9 | −7.1 | 10.3 | 8.7 | 2.1 | 15.1 |
| 29 | Savings bonds | −0.4 | 0.3 | 2.4 | 3.3 | 2.7 | 3.7 | 3.4 | 2.0 | 1.7 | 3.3 | 3.0 | 2.7 |
| 30 | Direct excluding savings bonds | −0.9 | 12.6 | 23.6 | 10.6 | 5.0 | 26.4 | −0.2 | −11.7 | 5.7 | 3.7 | −1.7 | 13.9 |
| 31 | Agency issues and mortgages | −2.4 | −0.1 | −0.5 | 3.4 | 2.0 | 2.6 | −0.2 | 2.6 | 2.9 | 1.7 | 0.8 | −1.5 |
| 32 | Life and retirement reserves | 1.6 | 2.5 | 2.9 | 3.2 | 2.1 | 1.9 | 4.2 | 1.1 | 1.3 | 1.6 | 9.9 | −0.6 |
| 33 | Trade debt | −0.3 | −0.6 | −0.7 | −0.1 | 0.1 | −0.6 | −0.1 | 0.1 | 1.0 | −1.3 | 2.1 | 0.3 |
| 34 | Miscellaneous | −0.4 | 0.6 | 0.6 | 0.4 | 0.2 | 1.7 | −0.6 | −0.9 | 0.5 | 0.3 | 0.8 | 0.5 |
| 35 | Discrepancy | 0.4 | 0.8 | 0.1 | 0.4 | −0.1 | 2.7 | −0.1 | −1.5 | −1.4 | −0.6 | −3.6 | −2.5 |
| 36 | Memo: corporate tax receipts (net) | 39.2 | 33.4 | 32.0 | 37.3 | 41.6 | 38.6 | 44.4 | 41.0 | 42.2 | 43.9 | 46.6 | 45.1 |

**Federally sponsored credit agencies**

| Line | Item | | | | | | | | | | | | |
|---|---|---|---|---|---|---|---|---|---|---|---|---|---|
| 1 | Current surplus | 0.1 | 0.1 | 0.1 | 0.1 | 0.2 | 0.2 | 0.2 | 0.3 | 0.3 | 0.3 | 0.3 | 0.3 |
| 2 | Net increase in assets | 9.2 | 10.8 | 3.4 | 6.6 | 22.0 | 13.3 | 24.3 | 29.5 | 21.0 | 12.3 | 28.6 | 26.4 |
| 3 | Demand deposits and currency | * | * | 0.1 | * | 0.1 | 0.2 | −0.2 | −0.1 | 0.4 | −0.1 | 0.3 | 0.4 |
| 4 | Credit market instruments | 8.9 | 10.0 | 3.2 | 7.0 | 20.3 | 13.3 | 23.3 | 27.8 | 16.6 | 13.0 | 27.6 | 25.3 |
| 5 | U.S. government securities | −0.4 | 1.9 | −1.2 | −0.4 | 1.3 | −2.6 | 1.2 | 3.9 | 2.8 | −5.5 | −0.6 | −4.7 |
| 6 | Residential mortgages[a] | 3.9 | 5.4 | 5.6 | 5.5 | 8.4 | 6.2 | 8.3 | 9.8 | 9.3 | 10.7 | 12.9 | 13.7 |
| 7 | Farm mortgages | 0.6 | 0.5 | 0.7 | 1.2 | 2.0 | 1.9 | 1.9 | 2.0 | 2.1 | 2.2 | 2.7 | 2.5 |
| 8 | Other loans | 4.8 | 2.3 | −2.0 | 0.8 | 8.5 | 8.0 | 11.8 | 12.1 | 2.4 | 5.8 | 12.4 | 13.9 |
| 9 | To coops (BC) | 0.2 | 0.3 | * | 0.3 | 0.3 | 1.9 | * | 0.1 | −0.9 | 1.6 | −0.5 | 1.7 |
| 10 | To farmers (FICB) | 0.6 | 0.7 | 0.7 | 0.4 | 1.1 | 0.7 | 1.0 | 1.7 | 0.9 | 0.9 | 2.6 | 2.4 |
| 11 | To S & L's (FHLB) | 4.0 | 1.3 | −2.7 | * | 7.2 | 5.4 | 10.7 | 10.2 | 2.4 | 3.3 | 10.4 | 9.8 |
| 12 | Miscellaneous assets | 0.3 | 0.8 | 0.2 | −0.4 | 1.7 | −0.1 | 1.1 | 1.8 | 3.9 | −0.6 | 1.1 | 0.9 |
| 13 | Net increase in liabilities | 9.1 | 10.8 | 3.3 | 6.5 | 21.8 | 13.1 | 24.0 | 29.2 | 20.7 | 12.1 | 28.1 | 25.8 |
| 14 | Credit market instruments | 8.8 | 8.2 | 3.8 | 6.2 | 19.6 | 12.6 | 22.1 | 26.7 | 17.0 | 9.3 | 24.3 | 21.2 |
| 15 | Sponsored agency issues[a] | 9.1 | 8.2 | 3.8 | 6.2 | 19.6 | 12.6 | 22.1 | 26.7 | 17.0 | 9.3 | 24.3 | 21.2 |
| 16 | U.S. government loans | −0.3 | — | — | — | — | — | — | — | — | — | — | — |
| 17 | Miscellaneous liabilities | 0.4 | 2.5 | −0.5 | 0.3 | 2.2 | 0.5 | 1.9 | 2.6 | 3.7 | 2.8 | 3.9 | 4.5 |
| 18 | Discrepancy | 0.1 | 0.1 | * | −0.1 | * | −0.1 | −0.1 | * | * | * | −0.2 | −0.3 |

[a] All GNMA-guaranteed securities backed by mortgage pools are included in agency securities. The mortgage pools are included in residential mortgages

Table 8

Sector statements of saving and investment: Banking system (billions of dollars)

| | 1969 | 1970 | 1971 | 1972 | 1973 | 1973 I | II | III | IV | 1974 I | II | III | |
|---|---|---|---|---|---|---|---|---|---|---|---|---|---|
| **Monetary authorities** | | | | | | | | | | | | | |
| 1 | * | * | -0.1 | 0.1 | 0.1 | 0.1 | 0.1 | 0.1 | 0.2 | 0.2 | 0.2 | 0.2 | Current surplus |
| 2 | 4.2 | 5.3 | 8.3 | 2.2 | 7.8 | 14.0 | 4.0 | 18.0 | -4.5 | 3.6 | 20.8 | 17.0 | Net acquisition of financial assets |
| 3 | -0.1 | -1.4 | -0.8 | -0.4 | -0.2 | -0.8 | -0.1 | 0.1 | — | * | 0.4 | 0.6 | Gold and foreign exchange |
| 4 | 0.1 | 0.7 | 0.5 | 0.7 | 0.4 | 0.4 | 0.4 | 0.3 | 0.5 | 0.2 | 0.6 | 0.4 | Treasury currency SDR certificates |
| 5 | * | 0.8 | 0.1 | -0.4 | -0.9 | -1.1 | -1.1 | 3.0 | -4.3 | 2.9 | -0.5 | -0.5 | Federal Reserve float |
| 6 | * | 0.2 | -0.3 | 1.9 | -0.7 | -1.9 | 1.6 | 9.0 | -11.6 | 1.5 | 7.3 | 5.8 | Federal Reserve loans to domestic banks |
| 7 | 4.2 | 5.0 | 8.9 | 0.3 | 9.2 | 17.2 | 3.1 | 5.7 | 10.9 | -1.0 | 13.1 | 10.6 | Credit market instruments |
| 8 | 4.2 | 5.0 | 8.7 | 0.4 | 9.3 | 17.1 | 3.4 | 5.8 | 10.8 | -1.2 | 12.4 | 9.9 | U.S. government securities |
| 9 | * | * | 0.2 | -0.2 | * | 0.2 | -0.3 | * | * | 0.2 | 0.7 | 0.7 | Acceptances |
| 10 | — | — | — | — | — | — | — | — | — | — | — | — | Bank loans n.e.c. |
| 11 | 4.1 | 5.3 | 8.4 | 2.1 | 7.7 | 13.9 | 3.8 | 17.9 | -4.7 | 3.5 | 20.7 | 16.8 | Net increase in liabilities |
| 12 | 0.2 | 2.1 | 3.6 | -2.1 | 1.4 | 1.6 | -2.6 | 22.5 | -15.8 | 1.6 | 12.8 | 6.0 | Member bank reserves |
| 13 | 0.1 | -0.3 | 0.5 | 1.1 | 2.0 | 0.4 | -2.4 | 4.4 | 5.7 | -4.8 | -2.5 | 4.2 | Vault cash of commercial banks |
| 14 | 3.3 | 3.1 | 4.4 | 3.2 | 3.4 | 10.3 | 9.0 | -10.1 | 4.3 | 7.7 | 9.9 | 6.4 | Demand deposits and currency |
| 15 | 0.5 | -0.4 | 0.9 | -1.1 | -0.5 | 7.0 | 0.7 | -11.4 | 1.7 | -1.2 | 1.2 | 2.2 | Due to U.S. government |
| 16 | -0.1 | * | 0.1 | -0.1 | -0.1 | 0.3 | * | 0.3 | -0.8 | 0.5 | 0.1 | 1.0 | Due to rest of the world |
| 17 | 2.8 | 3.5 | 3.4 | 4.4 | 3.9 | 3.0 | 8.3 | 1.0 | 3.4 | 8.4 | 8.6 | 3.1 | Currency outside banks |
| 18 | * | * | * | * | 0.1 | 0.2 | * | 0.2 | 0.1 | 0.1 | 0.2 | 0.2 | Taxes payable |
| 19 | 0.5 | 0.4 | -0.2 | -0.1 | 0.8 | 1.3 | -0.3 | 1.0 | 1.0 | -1.2 | 0.4 | * | Miscellaneous liabilities |
| **Commercial banking[a]** | | | | | | | | | | | | | |
| 1 | 3.7 | 3.3 | 2.9 | 3.5 | 4.4 | 4.2 | 4.4 | 4.4 | 4.7 | 4.7 | 4.7 | 5.6 | Current surplus |
| 2 | 1.9 | 2.1 | 2.3 | 2.7 | 3.0 | 2.9 | 2.9 | 3.1 | 3.2 | 4.4 | 3.1 | 3.2 | Plant and equipment |
| 3 | 22.0 | 45.2 | 58.5 | 78.3 | 100.2 | 128.5 | 99.3 | 101.1 | 72.0 | 75.5 | 162.1 | 50.7 | Net acquisition of financial assets |
| 4 | * | 0.1 | 0.1 | 0.2 | 0.3 | * | * | 0.6 | 0.5 | -0.5 | -0.5 | -0.2 | Demand deposits and currency |
| 5 | 17.2 | 36.6 | 51.4 | 75.4 | 83.3 | 94.5 | 84.9 | 78.5 | 75.1 | 65.2 | 107.1 | 45.5 | Total bank credit |
| 6 | 18.2 | 35.1 | 50.6 | 70.5 | 86.6 | 101.2 | 86.1 | 83.7 | 75.3 | 70.4 | 103.2 | 48.6 | Credit market instruments |

| # | Item | | | | | | | | | | | | |
|---|------|---|---|---|---|---|---|---|---|---|---|---|---|
| 7 | U.S. government securities | -10.0 | 10.4 | 6.9 | 6.5 | -1.3 | -14.1 | 5.9 | 1.7 | 1.4 | 8.8 | -4.4 | -1.7 |
| 8 | Direct | -9.7 | 6.9 | 3.1 | 2.4 | -8.8 | -15.7 | -3.8 | -9.0 | -6.9 | 4.2 | -10.0 | -4.5 |
| 9 | Agency issues | -0.3 | 3.5 | 3.8 | 4.1 | 7.6 | 1.6 | 9.6 | 10.7 | 8.3 | 4.6 | 5.5 | 2.9 |
| 10 | Other securities and mortgages | 5.6 | 13.9 | 23.8 | 25.7 | 25.9 | 21.8 | 24.8 | 25.0 | 32.1 | 20.3 | 23.5 | 3.4 |
| 11 | State and local obligations | 0.2 | 10.7 | 12.6 | 7.2 | 5.7 | 2.6 | 4.5 | 3.5 | 12.2 | 5.8 | 6.9 | -6.4 |
| 12 | Corporate bonds | -0.1 | 0.8 | 1.3 | 1.7 | 0.5 | -0.3 | -0.4 | 1.2 | 1.3 | 1.3 | 1.2 | 1.2 |
| 13 | Home mortgages | 3.0 | 0.9 | 5.7 | 9.0 | 11.0 | 10.5 | 11.4 | 11.4 | 10.6 | 7.7 | 8.9 | 4.3 |
| 14 | Other mortgages | 2.4 | 1.6 | 4.2 | 7.8 | 8.8 | 8.9 | 9.3 | 8.9 | 7.9 | 5.5 | 6.6 | 4.2 |
| 15 | Other credit excluding security | 22.7 | 10.7 | 19.8 | 38.4 | 62.0 | 93.5 | 55.5 | 57.0 | 41.8 | 41.4 | 84.1 | 46.9 |
| 16 | Consumer credit | 4.7 | 2.9 | 6.7 | 10.1 | 10.6 | 13.2 | 11.0 | 10.8 | 7.5 | 4.2 | 5.4 | 5.2 |
| 17 | Bank loans n.e.c. | 17.6 | 5.8 | 12.4 | 28.5 | 52.1 | 82.1 | 44.6 | 47.0 | 34.8 | 36.8 | 77.1 | 40.9 |
| 18 | Open market paper | 0.5 | 2.0 | 0.8 | -0.2 | -0.8 | -1.7 | -0.2 | -0.7 | -0.4 | 0.4 | 1.6 | 0.8 |
| 19 | Corporate equities | * | 0.1 | * | 0.1 | 0.1 | 0.2 | — | — | — | — | — | — |
| 20 | Security credit | -1.1 | 1.4 | 0.8 | 4.8 | -3.4 | -7.0 | -1.2 | -5.2 | -0.2 | -5.3 | 3.9 | -3.1 |
| 21 | Vault cash and member bank reserves | 0.3 | 1.8 | 4.1 | -1.0 | 3.5 | 2.1 | -5.0 | 26.8 | -10.1 | -3.2 | 10.2 | 10.2 |
| 22 | Other interbank claims | 1.6 | 1.7 | 1.7 | 1.4 | 6.0 | 16.5 | 11.6 | -12.2 | 8.1 | 6.1 | 25.9 | -8.7 |
| 23 | Miscellaneous assets | 2.8 | 5.0 | 1.2 | 2.3 | 7.2 | 15.5 | 7.7 | 7.4 | -1.6 | 7.9 | 19.3 | 4.0 |
| 24 | Net increase in liabilities | 19.8 | 43.6 | 56.8 | 76.3 | 97.3 | 126.5 | 95.7 | 98.4 | 68.7 | 73.1 | 157.8 | 46.1 |
| 25 | Demand deposits (net) | 4.9 | 11.2 | 13.0 | 16.3 | 12.6 | 13.7 | 5.8 | 3.3 | 27.5 | -0.7 | -1.1 | 0.5 |
| 26 | U.S. government | * | 2.9 | 2.2 | 0.7 | -1.0 | 6.1 | -6.8 | -6.4 | 3.1 | 0.8 | -4.4 | -0.9 |
| 27 | Other | 4.9 | 8.3 | 10.8 | 15.6 | 13.6 | 7.6 | 12.6 | 9.8 | 24.4 | -1.5 | 3.3 | 1.4 |
| 28 | Time deposits | -9.5 | 38.0 | 41.4 | 42.3 | 50.9 | 70.0 | 52.1 | 55.0 | 26.6 | 44.4 | 87.3 | 41.7 |
| 29 | Large negotiable CD's | -12.5 | 15.2 | 8.7 | 9.8 | 20.0 | 43.4 | 17.0 | 34.7 | -15.1 | 15.8 | 47.9 | 35.9 |
| 30 | Other at commercial banks | 2.9 | 22.4 | 32.4 | 33.0 | 30.3 | 25.7 | 34.8 | 19.7 | 41.0 | 28.5 | 39.3 | 5.2 |
| 31 | At foreign banking agencies | 0.2 | 0.4 | 0.3 | -0.5 | 0.6 | 0.9 | 0.4 | 0.5 | 0.6 | 0.1 | 0.1 | 0.6 |
| 32 | Corporate equities | * | 0.1 | 0.6 | 1.2 | 1.2 | 2.0 | 1.8 | 2.8 | -1.8 | 1.0 | 1.0 | 1.0 |
| 33 | Credit market debt | 5.8 | -5.0 | 3.2 | 4.4 | 10.6 | 21.3 | 4.3 | 12.7 | 4.3 | 4.0 | 12.8 | 8.2 |
| 34 | Federal Reserve float | * | 0.8 | 0.1 | -0.4 | -0.9 | -1.1 | -1.1 | 3.0 | -4.3 | 2.9 | -0.5 | -0.5 |
| 35 | Borrowing at Federal Reserve Banks | * | 0.2 | -0.3 | 1.9 | -0.7 | -1.9 | 1.6 | 9.0 | -11.6 | 1.5 | 7.3 | 5.8 |
| 36 | Other interbank claims | 1.6 | 1.7 | 1.7 | 1.4 | 6.0 | 16.5 | 11.6 | -12.2 | 8.1 | 6.1 | 25.9 | -8.7 |
| 37 | Taxes payable | 0.1 | 0.3 | * | -0.2 | 0.1 | 0.2 | 0.2 | * | * | 0.1 | 0.2 | 0.2 |

# Table 8 (cont'd)

| | 1969 | 1970 | 1971 | 1972 | 1973 | 1973 I | II | III | IV | 1974 I | II | III | |
|---|---|---|---|---|---|---|---|---|---|---|---|---|---|
| Commercial banking[a] (cont'd) | | | | | | | | | | | | | |
| 38 | 16.9 | -3.7 | -2.7 | 9.3 | 17.5 | 5.6 | 19.4 | 24.9 | 19.9 | 13.8 | 25.0 | -2.2 | Miscellaneous liabilities |
| 39 | 7.9 | -6.9 | -4.1 | 0.9 | 1.1 | -1.1 | 2.8 | 1.8 | 0.7 | 10.7 | 0.6 | -1.8 | Liabilities to foreign affiliates |
| 40 | 8.9 | 3.2 | 1.3 | 8.4 | 16.4 | 6.8 | 16.7 | 23.0 | 19.2 | 3.0 | 24.4 | -0.4 | Other |
| 41 | -0.3 | -0.4 | -1.1 | -1.1 | -1.6 | -0.7 | -2.1 | -1.5 | -1.9 | -2.1 | -2.6 | -2.2 | Discrepancy |

[a]Consists of chartered commercial banks, their domestic affiliates, Edge Act corporations, agencies of foreign banks, and banks in U.S. possessions. Edge Act corporations and agencies of foreign banks appear together in these tables as "foreign banking agencies."

# Table 9

Subsector statements for component groups in commercial banking (billions of dollars)

| | 1969 | 1970 | 1971 | 1972 | 1973 | 1973 I | II | III | IV | 1974 I | II | III | |
|---|---|---|---|---|---|---|---|---|---|---|---|---|---|
| Commercial banks | | | | | | | | | | | | | |
| 1 | 3.7 | 3.3 | 2.9 | 3.5 | 4.4 | 4.2 | 4.4 | 4.4 | 4.7 | 4.7 | 4.7 | 5.6 | Current surplus |
| 2 | 1.9 | 2.1 | 2.3 | 2.7 | 3.0 | 2.9 | 2.9 | 3.1 | 3.2 | 4.4 | 3.1 | 3.2 | Plant and equipment |
| 3 | 13.6 | 38.0 | 56.6 | 77.3 | 88.6 | 107.0 | 83.8 | 102.0 | 61.6 | 68.9 | 117.3 | 55.4 | Net acquisition of financial assets |
| 4 | 11.6 | 34.7 | 51.1 | 73.5 | 77.9 | 88.1 | 82.3 | 71.4 | 70.0 | 61.5 | 96.4 | 39.8 | Total bank credit |
| 5 | 12.7 | 33.3 | 50.3 | 68.8 | 80.9 | 93.7 | 82.8 | 75.6 | 71.4 | 65.6 | 92.5 | 42.8 | Credit market instruments |
| 6 | -10.1 | 10.5 | 7.0 | 6.0 | -1.3 | -13.8 | 6.3 | 1.4 | 1.0 | 9.0 | -4.4 | -1.4 | U.S. government securities |
| 7 | -9.8 | 7.0 | 3.2 | 2.1 | -8.8 | -15.2 | -3.3 | -9.4 | -7.2 | 4.8 | -9.9 | -4.3 | Direct |
| 8 | -0.3 | 3.5 | 3.8 | 3.9 | 7.5 | 1.4 | 9.6 | 10.7 | 8.2 | 4.2 | 5.5 | 2.9 | Agency issues |
| 9 | 5.3 | 13.6 | 23.9 | 25.3 | 25.7 | 21.8 | 24.8 | 24.4 | 31.6 | 19.5 | 22.9 | 2.8 | Other securities and mortgages |
| 10 | 0.2 | 10.5 | 12.8 | 7.1 | 5.6 | 2.6 | 4.5 | 3.2 | 12.1 | 5.4 | 6.4 | -6.8 | State and local obligations |
| 11 | -0.1 | 0.8 | 1.3 | 1.4 | 0.4 | -0.3 | -0.4 | 1.2 | 1.2 | 1.2 | 1.2 | 1.2 | Corporate bonds |
| 12 | 3.0 | 0.7 | 5.6 | 9.0 | 11.0 | 10.7 | 11.6 | 11.2 | 10.4 | 7.8 | 9.0 | 4.3 | Home mortgages |
| 13 | 2.3 | 1.6 | 4.2 | 7.8 | 8.7 | 8.8 | 9.1 | 8.9 | 7.9 | 5.2 | 6.3 | 4.0 | Other mortgages |

| No. | Item | | | | | | | | | | | | |
|---|---|---|---|---|---|---|---|---|---|---|---|---|---|
| 14 | Other credit excluding security | 41.5 | 74.0 | 37.0 | 38.8 | 49.8 | 51.7 | 85.7 | 56.5 | 37.6 | 19.4 | 9.1 | 17.5 |
| 15 | Consumer credit | 5.2 | 5.4 | 4.2 | 7.5 | 10.8 | 11.0 | 13.2 | 10.6 | 10.1 | 6.7 | 2.9 | 4.7 |
| 16 | Bank loans n.e.c. | 35.4 | 67.0 | 32.4 | 31.8 | 39.8 | 40.8 | 74.3 | 46.7 | 27.7 | 11.9 | 4.2 | 12.3 |
| 17 | Open market paper | 0.8 | 1.6 | 0.4 | -0.4 | -0.7 | -0.2 | -1.7 | -0.8 | -0.2 | 0.8 | 2.0 | 0.5 |
| 18 | Security credit | -3.0 | 4.0 | -4.0 | -1.4 | -4.3 | -0.6 | -5.6 | -3.0 | 4.7 | 0.8 | 1.4 | -1.1 |
| 19 | Interbank claims | 10.7 | 19.3 | -1.0 | -8.6 | 22.5 | * | 9.2 | 5.8 | 1.5 | 4.0 | 2.0 | 0.4 |
| 20 | Vault cash and member bank reserves | 10.2 | 10.2 | -3.2 | -10.1 | 26.8 | -5.0 | 2.1 | 3.5 | -1.0 | 4.1 | 1.8 | 0.3 |
| 21 | Deposits at foreign banking agencies | 0.4 | 9.0 | 2.2 | 1.5 | -4.3 | 5.0 | 7.1 | 2.3 | 2.5 | -0.1 | 0.2 | 0.1 |
| 22 | Miscellaneous assets | 5.0 | 1.6 | 8.3 | 0.2 | 8.1 | 1.5 | 9.7 | 4.9 | 2.3 | 1.5 | 1.3 | 1.6 |
| 23 | Net increase in liabilities | 50.8 | 113.0 | 66.5 | 58.3 | 99.3 | 80.2 | 104.9 | 85.7 | 75.3 | 54.9 | 36.3 | 11.5 |
| 24 | Demand deposits (net) | 8.7 | -13.3 | -8.0 | 28.5 | 5.3 | 3.4 | 14.7 | 13.0 | 20.1 | 13.0 | 4.6 | 4.6 |
| 25 | U.S. government | -0.9 | -4.4 | 0.8 | 3.1 | -6.4 | -6.8 | 6.1 | -1.0 | 0.7 | 2.2 | 2.9 | * |
| 26 | Other | 9.6 | -8.8 | -8.9 | 25.5 | 11.7 | 10.2 | 8.6 | 14.0 | 19.4 | 10.7 | 1.7 | 4.6 |
| 27 | Time deposits | 41.1 | 87.2 | 44.3 | 25.9 | 54.5 | 51.8 | 69.2 | 50.3 | 42.8 | 41.1 | 37.6 | -9.7 |
| 28 | Large negotiable CD's | 35.9 | 47.9 | 15.8 | -15.1 | 34.7 | 17.0 | 43.4 | 20.0 | 9.8 | 8.7 | 15.2 | -12.5 |
| 29 | Other | 5.2 | 39.3 | 28.5 | 41.0 | 19.7 | 34.8 | 25.7 | 30.3 | 33.0 | 32.4 | 22.4 | 2.9 |
| 30 | Corporate equities | 1.0 | 1.0 | 1.0 | -1.8 | 2.8 | 1.8 | 2.0 | 1.2 | 1.2 | 0.6 | 0.1 | * |
| 31 | Corporate bonds | 3.2 | 0.4 | 0.3 | 0.8 | -0.1 | -0.4 | -0.3 | * | 1.1 | 0.9 | 0.1 | -0.2 |
| 32 | Security R.P.'s | 4.4 | -6.0 | 8.5 | 0.1 | 7.1 | -4.3 | 10.3 | 3.3 | 1.7 | 1.1 | -3.3 | 1.6 |
| 33 | Profit tax liabilities | 0.2 | 0.2 | 0.1 | * | * | 0.2 | 0.2 | 0.1 | -0.2 | * | 0.3 | 0.1 |
| 34 | Interbank liabilities | -3.8 | 23.6 | 8.3 | -9.3 | 4.1 | 7.1 | 6.4 | 2.1 | 0.5 | 1.6 | 2.5 | 1.6 |
| 35 | Federal Reserve float | -0.5 | -0.5 | 2.9 | -4.3 | 3.0 | -1.1 | -1.1 | -0.9 | -0.4 | 0.1 | 0.8 | * |
| 36 | Borrowing at Federal Reserve banks | 5.8 | 7.3 | 1.5 | -11.6 | 9.0 | 1.6 | -1.9 | -0.7 | 1.9 | -0.3 | 0.2 | 0.8 |
| 37 | Demand deposits of foreign bank agencies | -9.7 | 22.4 | -1.4 | 5.7 | -6.3 | 6.5 | 4.3 | 2.6 | -1.2 | 1.3 | 1.2 | — |
| 38 | Time deposits of foreign bank agencies | 0.1 | 0.4 | * | 0.1 | 0.2 | -0.1 | 0.3 | 0.1 | -0.3 | * | 0.1 | 0.6 |
| 39 | Loans from affiliates | * | -0.4 | -0.4 | -0.1 | -2.3 | -1.4 | 2.1 | -0.4 | -0.4 | 0.3 | 0.1 | 0.1 |
| 40 | Loans from foreign bank agencies | 0.5 | -5.6 | 5.6 | 0.8 | 0.5 | 1.6 | 2.6 | 1.4 | 0.2 | 0.1 | 0.1 | |
| 41 | Miscellaneous liabilities | -4.0 | 19.8 | 12.0 | 14.1 | 25.7 | 20.6 | 2.3 | 15.7 | 8.1 | -3.2 | -5.6 | 13.5 |
| 42 | Liabilities to foreign branches | -1.8 | 1.7 | 4.8 | 0.1 | 0.8 | 1.6 | -1.1 | 0.4 | 0.5 | -4.8 | -7.2 | 6.8 |
| 43 | Other | -2.2 | 18.1 | 7.2 | 14.0 | 24.9 | 19.1 | 3.4 | 15.3 | 7.7 | 1.5 | 1.5 | 6.7 |
| 44 | Discrepancy | -2.2 | -2.6 | -2.1 | -1.9 | -1.5 | -2.1 | -0.7 | -1.6 | -1.1 | -1.1 | -0.4 | -0.3 |

Table 9 (cont'd)

| | | 1969 | 1970 | 1971 | 1972 | 1973 | 1973 I | 1973 II | 1973 III | 1973 IV | 1974 I | 1974 II | 1974 III |
|---|---|---|---|---|---|---|---|---|---|---|---|---|---|
| **Domestic affiliates of commercial banks** | | | | | | | | | | | | | |
| 1 | Net acquisition of financial assets | 4.5 | -0.9 | 0.2 | -0.6 | 1.3 | 4.4 | 0.1 | 2.1 | -1.4 | 2.0 | 1.5 | -0.6 |
| 2 | Bank loans n.e.c. | 3.9 | -1.0 | -0.1 | -0.2 | 1.7 | 2.3 | 1.4 | 4.5 | -1.3 | 2.4 | 1.9 | -0.6 |
| 3 | Loans to affiliate banks | 0.6 | 0.1 | 0.3 | -0.4 | -0.4 | 2.1 | -1.4 | -2.3 | -0.1 | -0.4 | -0.4 | * |
| 4 | Net increase in liabilities | 4.5 | -0.9 | 0.2 | -0.6 | 1.3 | 4.4 | 0.1 | 2.1 | -1.4 | 2.0 | 1.5 | -0.6 |
| 5 | Commercial paper issues | 4.2 | -1.9 | -0.4 | 0.7 | 2.2 | 3.3 | 3.3 | 3.8 | -1.4 | 4.7 | 3.6 | -0.6 |
| 6 | Miscellaneous liabilities | 0.3 | 1.0 | 0.6 | -1.3 | -1.0 | 1.1 | -3.2 | -1.7 | * | -2.6 | -2.1 | * |
| **Edge Act corporations and agencies of foreign banks** | | | | | | | | | | | | | |
| 1 | Net acquisition of financial assets | 2.7 | 7.7 | 1.2 | 1.2 | 9.9 | 17.0 | 15.9 | -4.3 | 10.8 | 4.7 | 43.5 | -4.4 |
| 2 | Credit market instruments | 1.3 | 2.7 | 0.1 | 1.7 | 3.9 | 5.6 | 2.2 | 3.0 | 4.7 | 2.4 | 8.3 | 6.0 |
| 3 | U.S. government securities | * | -0.1 | -0.2 | 0.3 | 0.1 | 0.1 | -0.1 | 0.1 | 0.2 | 0.3 | 0.1 | -0.2 |
| 4 | State and local obligations | * | 0.2 | -0.2 | * | * | — | * | 0.1 | * | 0.1 | 0.1 | 0.1 |
| 5 | Corporate bonds | — | * | — | 0.3 | * | * | * | 0.1 | 0.2 | 0.1 | * | * |
| 6 | Bank loans n.e.c. | 1.3 | 2.6 | 0.5 | 1.1 | 3.7 | 5.5 | 2.3 | 2.7 | 4.4 | 1.9 | 8.2 | 6.1 |
| 7 | Open market paper | — | — | — | — | — | — | — | — | — | — | — | — |
| 8 | Corporate equities | * | 0.1 | * | 0.1 | 0.1 | 0.2 | — | — | — | — | — | -0.1 |
| 9 | Security credit | — | — | — | 0.1 | -0.4 | -1.3 | -0.6 | -0.9 | 1.1 | -1.2 | * | — |
| 10 | Demand deposits at commercial banks | 0.8 | 1.2 | 1.3 | -1.2 | 2.6 | 4.3 | 6.5 | -6.3 | 5.7 | -1.4 | 22.4 | -9.7 |
| 11 | Time deposits at commercial banks | — | 0.1 | * | 0.3 | 0.1 | 0.3 | -0.1 | 0.2 | 0.1 | * | 0.4 | 0.1 |
| 12 | Loans to banks | 0.1 | 0.1 | 0.1 | 0.2 | 1.4 | 2.6 | 1.6 | 0.5 | 0.8 | 5.6 | -5.6 | 0.5 |
| 13 | Miscellaneous assets | 0.3 | 3.5 | -0.4 | * | 2.3 | 5.2 | 6.4 | -0.9 | -1.7 | -0.7 | 18.0 | -1.2 |
| 14 | Net increase in liabilities | 2.7 | 7.7 | 1.2 | 1.2 | 9.9 | 17.0 | 15.9 | -4.3 | 10.8 | 4.7 | 43.5 | -4.4 |
| 15 | Demand deposits in money stock | 0.3 | 6.6 | * | -3.7 | -0.4 | -1.0 | 2.3 | -1.9 | -1.0 | 7.3 | 12.1 | -8.2 |
| 16 | Time deposits | 0.2 | 0.4 | 0.3 | -0.5 | 0.6 | 0.9 | 0.4 | 0.5 | 0.6 | 0.1 | 0.1 | 0.6 |
| 17 | Deposits of banks | 0.1 | 0.2 | -0.1 | 2.5 | 2.3 | 7.1 | 5.0 | -4.3 | 1.5 | 2.2 | 9.0 | 0.4 |
| 18 | Loans from banks | 0.2 | 0.1 | 1.6 | 0.8 | 5.1 | 7.9 | 5.7 | 1.9 | 4.8 | -9.4 | 14.7 | 1.2 |
| 19 | Miscellaneous liabilities | 1.9 | 0.4 | -0.6 | 2.0 | 2.3 | 2.1 | 2.5 | -0.4 | 4.9 | 4.5 | 7.5 | 1.4 |
| 20 | Due to foreign affiliates | 1.2 | 0.2 | 0.7 | 0.4 | 0.7 | * | 1.2 | 1.0 | 0.6 | 5.9 | -1.1 | * |
| 21 | Other | 0.8 | 0.2 | -1.3 | 1.6 | 1.5 | 2.0 | 1.3 | -1.5 | 4.3 | -1.4 | 8.5 | 1.4 |

## Banks in U.S. possessions

| | 1969 | 1970 | 1971 | 1972 | 1973 | 1973 I | 1973 II | 1973 III | 1973 IV | 1974 I | 1974 II | 1974 III |
|---|---|---|---|---|---|---|---|---|---|---|---|---|
| 1 Net acquisition of financial assets | 1.1 | 0.5 | 0.5 | 0.5 | 0.5 | 0.2 | -0.5 | 1.2 | 1.0 | -0.2 | -0.2 | 0.3 |
| 2 Demand deposits and currency | * | 0.1 | 0.1 | 0.2 | 0.3 | * | * | 0.6 | 0.5 | -0.5 | -0.5 | -0.2 |
| 3 Credit market instruments | 0.2 | 0.1 | 0.3 | 0.3 | 0.1 | -0.3 | -0.3 | 0.5 | 0.5 | 0.1 | 0.5 | 0.4 |
| 4 U.S. government securities | * | * | 0.2 | 0.2 | -0.1 | -0.3 | -0.3 | 0.5 | 0.2 | -0.5 | -0.1 | -0.1 |
| 5 State and local obligations | * | * | * | 0.1 | 0.1 | * | * | 0.1 | 0.1 | 0.4 | 0.4 | 0.3 |
| 6 Corporate bonds | * | | * | * | * | * | * | — | — | * | — | — |
| 7 Home mortgages | * | 0.1 | 0.1 | * | * | -0.2 | -0.2 | 0.2 | 0.2 | -0.1 | -0.1 | * |
| 8 Commercial mortgages | 0.1 | * | * | * | 0.1 | 0.2 | 0.1 | * | * | 0.3 | 0.3 | 0.2 |
| 9 Miscellaneous assets | 0.9 | 0.3 | 0.1 | * | 0.1 | 0.5 | -0.2 | 0.1 | -0.1 | 0.2 | -0.2 | 0.2 |
| 10 Net increase in deposit liabilities | 1.1 | 0.5 | 0.5 | 0.5 | 0.5 | 0.2 | -0.5 | 1.2 | 1.0 | -0.2 | -0.2 | 0.3 |

## Table 10

### Sector statements of saving and investment: Nonbank financial institutions (billions of dollars)

Private nonbank financial institutions (total)

| | 1969 | 1970 | 1971 | 1972 | 1973 | 1973 I | 1973 II | 1973 III | 1973 IV | 1974 I | 1974 II | 1974 III |
|---|---|---|---|---|---|---|---|---|---|---|---|---|
| 1 Current surplus | -0.1 | 1.7 | 4.4 | 5.0 | 5.7 | 5.6 | 5.3 | 5.7 | 6.2 | 5.9 | 5.2 | 5.2 |
| 2 Physical investment | 1.2 | 1.2 | 1.8 | 2.1 | 2.0 | 2.5 | 2.6 | 1.8 | 1.1 | 3.0 | 1.7 | 1.0 |
| 3 Net acquisition of financial assets | 46.4 | 55.2 | 84.9 | 107.5 | 87.7 | 103.3 | 97.2 | 76.1 | 74.1 | 80.5 | 85.1 | 73.0 |
| 4 Demand deposits and currency | -0.4 | 1.0 | 1.1 | 1.6 | 2.0 | 0.6 | 3.4 | 3.1 | 0.9 | -0.7 | 1.2 | -0.1 |
| 5 Time deposits (MSB) | -0.1 | 0.2 | 0.2 | 0.2 | 0.1 | 0.2 | 0.3 | — | — | — | — | — |
| 6 S & L shares (credit union) | -0.1 | 0.1 | 0.1 | 0.2 | * | 0.6 | 1.4 | -2.0 | -0.1 | 2.1 | 0.9 | -2.4 |
| 7 Corporate shares | 12.2 | 11.3 | 19.3 | 15.9 | 13.4 | 12.4 | 13.5 | 7.0 | 20.6 | 9.0 | 8.1 | 5.6 |
| 8 Credit market instruments | 37.1 | 39.8 | 60.1 | 82.8 | 72.2 | 91.4 | 79.1 | 66.9 | 51.5 | 64.6 | 71.2 | 69.5 |
| 9 U.S. government securities | -2.2 | 3.8 | 2.6 | 7.1 | 0.9 | 6.6 | -0.4 | -5.1 | 2.6 | * | -1.2 | 3.1 |
| 10 State and local obligations | 1.0 | 1.8 | 4.4 | 5.1 | 3.6 | 2.8 | 2.3 | 5.0 | 4.2 | 2.1 | 4.9 | 4.5 |
| 11 Corporate and foreign bonds | 7.4 | 11.6 | 13.9 | 13.2 | 10.9 | 11.2 | 14.1 | 12.2 | 6.0 | 15.9 | 20.1 | 17.9 |
| 12 Home mortgages | 8.6 | 7.6 | 17.8 | 30.7 | 26.5 | 33.4 | 33.1 | 24.9 | 14.5 | 18.0 | 22.1 | 12.0 |

Table 10 (cont'd)

Private nonbank financial institutions (total) (cont'd)

| | 1969 | 1970 | 1971 | 1972 | 1973 | 1973 I | 1973 II | 1973 III | 1973 IV | 1974 I | 1974 II | 1974 III | |
|---|---|---|---|---|---|---|---|---|---|---|---|---|---|
| 13 | 7.6 | 10.1 | 14.6 | 16.8 | 15.4 | 14.6 | 18.4 | 15.5 | 13.0 | 14.0 | 14.1 | 10.0 | Other mortgages |
| 14 | 4.8 | 1.8 | 3.3 | 6.4 | 9.0 | 10.9 | 8.8 | 9.5 | 6.9 | 4.2 | 7.4 | 7.4 | Consumer credit |
| 15 | 9.9 | 3.1 | 3.5 | 3.5 | 5.9 | 11.8 | 2.8 | 4.9 | 4.2 | 10.5 | 3.7 | 14.7 | Other loans |
| 16 | -3.5 | -1.3 | 2.5 | 3.9 | -4.6 | -4.5 | -6.5 | -2.9 | -4.4 | 1.2 | -1.3 | -1.4 | Security credit |
| 17 | 0.4 | 0.5 | 0.3 | 1.2 | 0.7 | 0.8 | 0.7 | 0.6 | 0.6 | 0.6 | 0.6 | 0.5 | Trade credit |
| 18 | 0.8 | 3.6 | 1.4 | 1.7 | 3.9 | 1.7 | 5.4 | 3.5 | 4.9 | 3.8 | 4.5 | 1.2 | Miscellaneous assets |
| 19 | 49.2 | 55.0 | 82.2 | 103.5 | 82.3 | 97.7 | 92.5 | 72.0 | 66.9 | 78.5 | 80.6 | 68.1 | Net increase in liabilities |
| 20 | 7.9 | 17.0 | 40.6 | 46.1 | 28.1 | 44.2 | 33.7 | 7.8 | 26.8 | 39.7 | 16.4 | 5.3 | Time and savings accounts |
| 21 | 19.7 | 21.8 | 24.8 | 27.1 | 29.5 | 29.9 | 28.1 | 31.7 | 28.4 | 25.6 | 36.9 | 35.0 | Insurance and pension reserves |
| 22 | 6.1 | 4.5 | 2.7 | 1.3 | -0.4 | 0.1 | 0.6 | 2.2 | -4.4 | 0.5 | -1.5 | 2.8 | Corporate equities[a] |
| 23 | 13.0 | 4.7 | 6.2 | 15.9 | 21.0 | 20.7 | 26.8 | 26.2 | 10.2 | 11.3 | 20.9 | 17.8 | Credit market instruments |
| 24 | 1.7 | 3.0 | 4.2 | 5.8 | 2.3 | 2.5 | 4.1 | 1.2 | 1.5 | 1.8 | 1.5 | 1.8 | Corporate bonds |
| 25 | * | 0.6 | 2.0 | 1.2 | -1.5 | 1.1 | -0.3 | -2.3 | -4.6 | * | * | -2.8 | Mortgage loans in process |
| 26 | 0.2 | 0.1 | 0.1 | 0.5 | 0.3 | 0.5 | 0.6 | * | 0.2 | 0.3 | * | — | Other mortgages |
| 27 | 2.1 | -0.6 | 1.4 | 5.9 | 8.4 | 9.9 | 9.0 | 10.7 | 4.1 | 4.5 | 15.2 | 4.4 | Bank loans n.e.c. |
| 28 | 8.9 | 1.5 | -1.5 | 2.5 | 11.5 | 6.7 | 13.5 | 16.6 | 9.1 | 4.8 | 4.2 | 14.4 | Other loans |
| 29 | 4.9 | 0.2 | -1.2 | 2.5 | 4.3 | 1.3 | 2.7 | 6.4 | 6.7 | 1.5 | -6.2 | 4.7 | Open market paper |
| 30 | 4.0 | 1.3 | -2.7 | * | 7.2 | 5.4 | 10.7 | 10.2 | 2.4 | 3.3 | 10.4 | 9.8 | FHLB loans |
| 31 | -3.0 | 1.0 | 1.1 | 4.1 | -3.4 | -8.2 | -3.2 | -3.4 | 1.1 | -4.8 | 1.5 | * | Security credit |
| 32 | 0.1 | 0.2 | -0.1 | 0.2 | 0.1 | 0.3 | * | 0.1 | 0.1 | 0.1 | * | * | Taxes payable |
| 33 | 5.4 | 5.8 | 7.0 | 8.8 | 7.4 | 10.9 | 6.6 | 7.4 | 4.8 | 6.1 | 6.4 | 7.3 | Miscellaneous liabilities |
| 34 | 1.5 | 0.3 | * | -1.0 | -1.7 | -2.6 | -1.9 | -0.2 | -2.0 | 0.9 | -1.1 | -0.7 | Discrepancy |

Savings and loan associations

| | 1969 | 1970 | 1971 | 1972 | 1973 | 1973 I | 1973 II | 1973 III | 1973 IV | 1974 I | 1974 II | 1974 III | |
|---|---|---|---|---|---|---|---|---|---|---|---|---|---|
| 1 | 1.0 | 1.0 | 1.2 | 1.5 | 1.8 | 1.7 | 1.8 | 1.8 | 1.8 | 1.8 | 1.7 | 1.7 | Current surplus |
| 2 | 9.3 | 14.1 | 29.8 | 37.1 | 29.2 | 43.0 | 35.5 | 19.3 | 19.1 | 33.9 | 26.4 | 15.4 | Net acquisition of financial assets |
| 3 | -0.2 | 0.3 | 0.5 | 0.6 | 0.6 | -0.4 | 0.7 | 0.8 | 1.2 | -0.5 | 0.8 | 0.8 | Demand deposits and currency |

| Line | | | | | | | | | | | | | |
|---|---|--:|--:|--:|--:|--:|--:|--:|--:|--:|--:|--:|--:|
| 4 | Credit market instruments | 9.9 | 11.6 | 29.2 | 36.4 | 27.1 | 43.1 | 32.7 | 16.9 | 15.8 | 30.2 | 23.8 | 12.5 |
| 5 | U.S. government securities | 0.3 | 1.2 | 5.2 | 4.3 | * | 7.1 | -1.8 | -6.7 | 1.4 | 7.6 | -1.3 | -1.8 |
| 6 | Home mortgages | 7.7 | 7.2 | 17.3 | 24.8 | 22.0 | 29.0 | 28.5 | 18.6 | 11.9 | 17.3 | 19.9 | 10.7 |
| 7 | Other mortgages | 1.8 | 3.0 | 6.6 | 7.2 | 4.9 | 6.9 | 5.7 | 4.8 | 2.3 | 5.2 | 4.9 | 3.3 |
| 8 | Consumer credit | 0.2 | 0.3 | 0.1 | 0.2 | 0.2 | 0.2 | 0.2 | 0.2 | 0.2 | 0.1 | 0.3 | 0.2 |
| 9 | Miscellaneous assets | -0.4 | 2.2 | 0.1 | 0.1 | 1.5 | 0.2 | 2.1 | 1.6 | 2.1 | 4.2 | 1.7 | 2.1 |
| 10 | Net increase in liabilities | 8.4 | 13.3 | 29.0 | 35.5 | 27.4 | 40.8 | 33.4 | 17.4 | 17.8 | 32.3 | 24.6 | 14.4 |
| 11 | Savings shares | 3.9 | 10.9 | 27.8 | 32.6 | 20.5 | 30.7 | 22.9 | 6.6 | 21.8 | 27.3 | 11.1 | 4.0 |
| 12 | Credit market instruments | 4.1 | 1.8 | -0.1 | 2.0 | 6.0 | 6.5 | 10.3 | 10.1 | -3.1 | 3.6 | 13.6 | 10.2 |
| 13 | Mortgage loans in process | * | 0.6 | 2.0 | 1.2 | -1.5 | 1.1 | -0.3 | -2.3 | -4.6 | * | * | -2.8 |
| 14 | Bank loans n.e.c. | 0.1 | -0.1 | 0.7 | 0.7 | 0.3 | 0.1 | -0.1 | 2.2 | -0.9 | 0.3 | 3.2 | 3.2 |
| 15 | FHLB advances | 4.0 | 1.3 | -2.7 | * | 7.2 | 5.4 | 10.7 | 10.2 | 2.4 | 3.3 | 10.4 | 9.8 |
| 16 | Taxes payable | * | * | 0.1 | * | * | 0.2 | * | * | * | * | * | 0.1 |
| 17 | Miscellaneous liabilities | 0.4 | 0.6 | 1.2 | 0.9 | 0.9 | 3.4 | 0.3 | 0.7 | -0.9 | 1.4 | -0.1 | 0.1 |
| 18 | Discrepancy | 0.1 | 0.2 | 0.3 | -0.2 | -0.1 | -0.4 | -0.2 | -0.1 | 0.5 | 0.2 | -0.1 | 0.7 |

Mutual savings banks

| Line | | | | | | | | | | | | | |
|---|---|--:|--:|--:|--:|--:|--:|--:|--:|--:|--:|--:|--:|
| 1 | Current surplus | 0.3 | 0.2 | 0.4 | 0.4 | 0.6 | 0.5 | 0.6 | 0.6 | 0.6 | 0.6 | 0.6 | 0.6 |
| 2 | Net acquisition of financial assets | 3.1 | 4.7 | 10.4 | 11.0 | 6.0 | 11.3 | 8.1 | 1.3 | 3.1 | 8.9 | 1.5 | 0.6 |
| 3 | Demand deposits and currency | * | 0.1 | * | 0.1 | 0.2 | -0.1 | 0.5 | -0.7 | 1.0 | -0.8 | 0.1 | -0.8 |
| 4 | Time deposits | -0.1 | 0.2 | 0.2 | 0.2 | 0.1 | 0.2 | 0.3 | — | — | — | — | — |
| 5 | Corporate shares | 0.2 | 0.3 | 0.5 | 0.6 | 0.4 | 0.7 | 0.4 | -0.3 | 0.5 | 0.8 | -0.1 | 0.1 |
| 6 | Credit market instruments | 2.9 | 3.8 | 9.6 | 9.8 | 5.0 | 11.1 | 5.6 | 2.8 | 0.6 | 10.2 | 2.1 | 0.9 |
| 7 | U.S. government securities | -0.5 | 0.3 | 0.9 | 1.4 | -0.5 | 0.2 | 0.2 | -1.4 | -0.9 | -0.1 | | -0.3 |
| 8 | State and local obligations | * | * | 0.2 | 0.5 | * | 0.6 | * | -0.3 | -0.1 | 0.1 | -0.2 | * |
| 9 | Corporate bonds | 0.3 | 1.2 | 3.9 | 2.1 | -1.1 | 0.9 | -1.4 | -2.1 | -1.8 | 3.5 | 1.3 | -0.7 |
| 10 | Home mortgages | 1.4 | 0.9 | 1.3 | 3.0 | 2.6 | 3.5 | 1.9 | 2.9 | 2.0 | 0.9 | 1.0 | 0.7 |
| 11 | Other mortgages | 1.3 | 0.9 | 2.7 | 2.6 | 3.1 | 2.0 | 4.9 | 2.7 | 2.8 | 2.0 | 2.2 | 1.4 |
| 12 | Consumer credit | 0.1 | 0.1 | 0.1 | 0.3 | 0.2 | 1.1 | -0.3 | 0.1 | * | 0.3 | * | 0.3 |
| 13 | Commercial paper | 0.1 | 0.2 | 0.2 | -0.2 | -0.1 | -2.2 | 2.0 | 0.4 | -0.5 | 2.9 | -2.9 | -1.1 |
| 14 | Security RP's | 0.2 | 0.1 | 0.2 | 0.1 | 0.7 | 5.0 | -1.7 | 0.5 | -1.0 | 0.7 | 0.7 | 0.7 |
| 15 | Miscellaneous assets | * | 0.3 | 0.2 | 0.4 | 0.3 | -0.7 | 1.3 | -0.4 | 1.0 | -1.3 | -0.5 | 0.4 |

Table 10 (cont'd)

### Mutual savings banks (cont'd)

| | 1969 | 1970 | 1971 | 1972 | 1973 | 1973 I | 1973 II | 1973 III | 1973 IV | 1974 I | 1974 II | 1974 III | |
|---|---|---|---|---|---|---|---|---|---|---|---|---|---|
| 16 | 2.6 | 4.4 | 9.9 | 10.2 | 4.7 | 9.5 | 6.5 | 0.2 | 2.7 | 8.8 | 1.5 | * | Savings deposits |
| 17 | 0.2 | 0.1 | 0.1 | 0.2 | 0.6 | 0.6 | 0.7 | 1.4 | -0.3 | -0.5 | -0.4 | 0.2 | Miscellaneous liabilities |
| 18 | * | 0.1 | * | -0.2 | -0.1 | -0.7 | -0.3 | 0.9 | -0.2 | * | 0.1 | 0.1 | Discrepancy |

### Credit unions

| | 1969 | 1970 | 1971 | 1972 | 1973 | 1973 I | 1973 II | 1973 III | 1973 IV | 1974 I | 1974 II | 1974 III | |
|---|---|---|---|---|---|---|---|---|---|---|---|---|---|
| 1 | 1.4 | 1.7 | 2.9 | 3.4 | 2.9 | 4.0 | 4.3 | 1.0 | 2.3 | 3.6 | 3.8 | 1.2 | Net acquisition of financial assets |
| 2 | * | 0.2 | 0.1 | 0.1 | * | * | — | * | * | * | * | -0.2 | Demand deposits and currency |
| 3 | -0.1 | 0.1 | 0.1 | 0.2 | * | 0.6 | 1.4 | -2.0 | -0.1 | 2.1 | 0.9 | -2.4 | Savings and loan shares |
| 4 | 1.6 | 1.5 | 2.6 | 3.1 | 2.9 | 3.4 | 2.8 | 3.0 | 2.5 | 1.5 | 2.9 | 3.8 | Credit market instruments |
| 5 | -0.2 | 0.4 | 0.8 | 0.8 | 0.2 | 0.4 | 0.2 | 0.1 | 0.2 | 0.2 | 0.2 | -0.4 | U.S. government securities |
| 6 | * | 0.1 | * | 0.2 | — | * | * | * | * | | — | * | Home mortgages |
| 7 | 1.7 | 1.0 | 1.8 | 2.1 | 2.7 | 2.9 | 2.6 | 2.9 | 2.3 | 1.3 | 2.7 | 4.2 | Consumer credit |
| 8 | 1.4 | 1.7 | 2.9 | 3.4 | 2.9 | 4.0 | 4.3 | 1.0 | 2.3 | 3.6 | 3.8 | 1.2 | Credit union shares |

a includes investment company shares

Table 11

Sector statements of saving and investment: Insurance and pension funds (billions of dollars)

### Life insurance companies

| | 1969 | 1970 | 1971 | 1972 | 1973 | 1973 I | 1973 II | 1973 III | 1973 IV | 1974 I | 1974 II | 1974 III | |
|---|---|---|---|---|---|---|---|---|---|---|---|---|---|
| 1 | 0.9 | 0.8 | 1.0 | 1.6 | 1.8 | 1.7 | 1.7 | 1.8 | 1.8 | 1.9 | 1.9 | 2.0 | Current surplus |
| 2 | 0.8 | 1.0 | 1.4 | 1.0 | 1.3 | 1.4 | 1.3 | 1.4 | 1.0 | 1.7 | 1.0 | 1.0 | Physical investment |
| 3 | 9.2 | 9.9 | 12.7 | 15.0 | 16.6 | 16.9 | 15.9 | 15.5 | 18.1 | 11.5 | 19.8 | 17.8 | Net acquisition of financial assets |
| 4 | * | 0.1 | * | 0.2 | 0.1 | -0.2 | 1.0 | * | -0.4 | * | -1.3 | -0.1 | Demand deposits and currency |

| # | | 1 | 2 | 3 | 4 | 5 | 6 | 7 | 8 | 9 | 10 | 11 | 12 |
|---|---|---|---|---|---|---|---|---|---|---|---|---|---|
| 5 | Corporate shares | 1.7 | 2.0 | 3.6 | 3.5 | 3.6 | 3.5 | 4.6 | 3.1 | 3.1 | 1.5 | 1.1 | 0.9 |
| 6 | Credit market instruments | 6.7 | 7.0 | 8.1 | 10.3 | 12.1 | 12.7 | 9.5 | 11.6 | 14.4 | 9.1 | 19.1 | 16.2 |
| 7 | U.S. government securities | -0.3 | 0.1 | -0.2 | 0.3 | 0.1 | 0.1 | 0.4 | -0.2 | * | -0.9 | 0.4 | * |
| 8 | State and local obligations | * | 0.1 | 0.1 | * | * | -0.1 | 0.2 | 0.2 | -0.1 | 0.3 | 0.2 | 0.1 |
| 9 | Corporate bonds | 1.5 | 1.5 | 5.5 | 7.0 | 5.9 | 3.9 | 7.8 | 6.7 | 5.0 | 3.5 | 9.1 | 6.5 |
| 10 | Home mortgages | -1.1 | -1.3 | -2.1 | -2.1 | -0.5 | -1.1 | -1.3 | 0.4 | 0.1 | -0.7 | 0.1 | 1.2 |
| 11 | Other mortgages | 3.1 | 3.6 | 3.2 | 4.0 | 4.3 | 2.9 | 3.7 | 4.6 | 6.2 | 4.7 | 6.2 | 4.3 |
| 12 | Open market paper | 0.9 | 0.8 | 0.6 | 0.2 | * | 5.8 | -2.8 | -3.4 | 0.4 | 0.9 | 0.1 | 0.8 |
| 13 | Policy loans | 2.5 | 2.2 | 1.0 | 0.9 | 2.2 | 1.1 | 1.6 | 3.4 | 2.8 | 1.4 | 3.1 | 3.3 |
| 14 | Miscellaneous assets | 0.9 | 0.8 | 0.9 | 1.0 | 0.9 | 0.9 | 0.9 | 0.9 | 0.9 | 0.9 | 0.9 | 0.9 |
| 15 | Net increase in liabilities | 9.3 | 10.2 | 13.3 | 15.3 | 15.1 | 15.7 | 14.8 | 14.7 | 15.4 | 11.7 | 18.2 | 16.1 |
| 16 | Life insurance reserves | 4.9 | 5.1 | 6.1 | 6.5 | 7.2 | 7.0 | 7.3 | 7.4 | 7.2 | 7.1 | 7.4 | 7.2 |
| 17 | Pension fund reserves | 2.9 | 3.3 | 5.2 | 6.0 | 5.2 | 4.9 | 5.1 | 5.2 | 5.4 | 3.1 | 7.7 | 5.7 |
| 18 | Taxes payable | 0.1 | 0.1 | -0.1 | * | * | 0.1 | * | * | * | * | * | * |
| 19 | Miscellaneous liabilities | 1.4 | 1.7 | 2.1 | 2.9 | 2.7 | 3.7 | 2.4 | 2.1 | 2.8 | 1.5 | 3.1 | 3.2 |
| 20 | Discrepancy | 0.2 | 0.1 | 0.3 | 1.0 | -1.0 | -1.0 | -0.7 | -0.5 | -1.8 | 0.3 | -0.6 | -0.7 |

Private pension funds

| # | | 1 | 2 | 3 | 4 | 5 | 6 | 7 | 8 | 9 | 10 | 11 | 12 |
|---|---|---|---|---|---|---|---|---|---|---|---|---|---|
| 1 | Net acquisition of financial assets | 6.3 | 7.1 | 7.3 | 6.8 | 7.7 | 8.2 | 5.8 | 9.4 | 7.6 | 7.1 | 10.0 | 10.3 |
| 2 | Demand deposits and currency | * | 0.2 | -0.2 | 0.2 | 0.4 | 0.8 | 0.7 | 1.7 | -1.5 | 1.1 | 0.8 | 0.6 |
| 3 | Corporate shares | 5.4 | 4.6 | 8.9 | 7.1 | 5.3 | 5.0 | 4.4 | 2.9 | 8.8 | 3.1 | 1.7 | 1.6 |
| 4 | Credit market instruments | 0.6 | 2.4 | -1.6 | -0.5 | 2.0 | 2.3 | 0.9 | 4.1 | 0.5 | 2.6 | 5.2 | 7.9 |
| 5 | U.S. government securities | -0.2 | 0.2 | -0.3 | 1.0 | 0.6 | 0.7 | 0.4 | 0.7 | 0.8 | -0.4 | 0.7 | 0.8 |
| 6 | Corporate bonds | 0.6 | 2.1 | -0.7 | -0.8 | 1.6 | 2.1 | 0.9 | 3.5 | -0.1 | 3.0 | 4.7 | 7.2 |
| 7 | Home mortgages | 0.1 | 0.1 | -0.6 | -0.7 | -0.3 | -0.5 | -0.4 | -0.1 | -0.2 | * | -0.1 | -0.1 |
| 8 | Miscellaneous assets | 0.3 | * | 0.1 | 0.1 | 0.1 | 0.1 | -0.3 | 0.6 | -0.2 | 0.3 | 2.2 | 0.2 |

State and local government employee retirement funds

| # | | 1 | 2 | 3 | 4 | 5 | 6 | 7 | 8 | 9 | 10 | 11 | 12 |
|---|---|---|---|---|---|---|---|---|---|---|---|---|---|
| 1 | Net acquisition of financial assets | 5.5 | 6.3 | 6.3 | 7.9 | 9.4 | 9.8 | 9.9 | 9.7 | 8.2 | 8.4 | 11.7 | 11.7 |
| 2 | Demand deposits and currency | -0.1 | 0.1 | 0.1 | 0.1 | 0.2 | -0.6 | 0.5 | 0.5 | 0.3 | -0.5 | 0.6 | -0.5 |
| 3 | Corporate shares | 1.8 | 2.1 | 3.2 | 3.5 | 3.9 | 5.0 | 3.6 | 3.0 | 4.1 | 4.4 | 3.2 | 3.2 |
| 4 | Credit market instruments | 3.8 | 4.0 | 3.0 | 4.3 | 5.3 | 5.4 | 5.8 | 6.2 | 3.9 | 4.4 | 7.8 | 9.0 |
| 5 | U.S. government securities | -0.3 | -0.3 | -1.6 | -0.6 | 0.1 | 0.1 | -0.2 | -0.1 | 0.7 | -1.1 | 1.4 | 1.1 |
| 6 | Direct | -0.5 | -0.3 | -1.2 | -0.5 | -0.1 | * | -0.5 | -0.4 | 0.3 | -0.2 | 0.9 | 0.9 |

349

Table 11 (cont'd)

State and local government employee retirement funds (cont'd)

| | 1969 | 1970 | 1971 | 1972 | 1973 | 1973 I | II | III | IV | 1974 I | II | III | |
|---|---|---|---|---|---|---|---|---|---|---|---|---|---|
| 7 | 0.2 | * | -0.3 | -0.1 | 0.2 | * | 0.3 | 0.2 | 0.5 | -0.9 | 0.5 | 0.2 | Agency issues |
| 8 | -0.1 | -0.3 | 0.1 | -0.1 | -0.6 | -1.5 | -0.5 | 0.1 | -0.5 | -0.1 | -0.1 | -0.5 | State and local obligations |
| 9 | 3.6 | 3.8 | 4.2 | 5.3 | 5.9 | 7.2 | 6.1 | 6.6 | 3.9 | 5.5 | 6.4 | 8.2 | Corporate bonds |
| 10 | 0.6 | 0.8 | 0.3 | -0.3 | -0.1 | -0.2 | 0.5 | -0.4 | -0.2 | 0.1 | 0.1 | 0.2 | Mortgages |

Other insurance companies

| | 1969 | 1970 | 1971 | 1972 | 1973 | 1973 I | II | III | IV | 1974 I | II | III | |
|---|---|---|---|---|---|---|---|---|---|---|---|---|---|
| 1 | -0.1 | 0.8 | 1.8 | 2.0 | 1.9 | 2.1 | 1.9 | 1.8 | 1.7 | 1.7 | 1.5 | 1.5 | Current surplus |
| 2 | 2.9 | 5.5 | 6.6 | 7.9 | 5.6 | 5.7 | 5.8 | 5.6 | 5.4 | 6.0 | 5.8 | 5.8 | Net acquisition of financial assets |
| 3 | * | 0.1 | 0.1 | * | * | -0.9 | * | 0.4 | 0.4 | -0.2 | 0.2 | 0.3 | Demand deposits and currency |
| 4 | 1.0 | 1.0 | 2.5 | 3.0 | 2.2 | 3.3 | 1.4 | 1.7 | 2.2 | 2.0 | 1.1 | 0.9 | Corporate shares |
| 5 | 1.6 | 3.9 | 3.8 | 3.7 | 2.8 | 2.4 | 3.6 | 2.9 | 2.3 | 3.6 | 4.0 | 4.1 | Credit market instruments |
| 6 | -0.5 | 0.1 | -0.4 | -0.4 | -0.1 | -0.5 | -0.1 | 0.2 | 0.1 | * | -0.5 | * | U.S. government securities |
| 7 | 1.2 | 1.5 | 3.9 | 4.8 | 3.9 | 5.1 | 2.2 | 4.8 | 3.3 | 4.0 | 5.1 | 4.8 | State and local obligations |
| 8 | 0.8 | 2.3 | 0.3 | -0.7 | -1.0 | -2.1 | 1.5 | -2.1 | -1.2 | -0.3 | -0.6 | -0.7 | Corporate bonds |
| 9 | * | * | * | * | * | -0.1 | — | * | * | * | * | * | Commercial mortgages |
| 10 | 0.4 | 0.5 | 0.3 | 1.2 | 0.7 | 0.8 | 0.7 | 0.6 | 0.6 | 0.6 | 0.6 | 0.5 | Trade credit |
| 11 | 3.9 | 3.9 | 4.1 | 5.4 | 3.7 | 3.6 | 3.7 | 3.7 | 3.7 | 4.3 | 4.2 | 4.3 | Net increase in liabilities |
| 12 | 0.5 | 0.4 | 0.6 | 0.5 | 0.5 | 0.4 | 0.4 | 0.5 | 0.5 | 0.4 | 0.4 | 0.4 | Corporate equities |
| 13 | 0.1 | 0.1 | -0.1 | 0.1 | * | * | * | * | * | * | * | * | Taxes payable |
| 14 | 3.3 | 3.4 | 3.6 | 4.8 | 3.2 | 3.1 | 3.2 | 3.2 | 3.2 | 3.8 | 3.8 | 3.9 | Policy payables |
| 15 | 0.9 | -0.8 | -0.8 | -0.4 | -0.1 | * | -0.2 | * | * | * | * | * | Discrepancy |

Table 12

Sector statements of saving and investment: Finance not elsewhere classified (billions of dollars)

| | 1969 | 1970 | 1971 | 1972 | 1973 | 1973 I | 1973 II | 1973 III | 1973 IV | 1974 I | 1974 II | 1974 III | |
|---|---|---|---|---|---|---|---|---|---|---|---|---|---|
| 1 | −2.2 | −1.1 | * | −0.5 | −0.3 | −0.4 | −0.7 | −0.3 | 0.3 | −0.2 | −0.6 | −0.6 | Current surplus of group |

Finance companies

| | 1969 | 1970 | 1971 | 1972 | 1973 | 1973 I | 1973 II | 1973 III | 1973 IV | 1974 I | 1974 II | 1974 III | |
|---|---|---|---|---|---|---|---|---|---|---|---|---|---|
| 1 | 8.1 | 0.9 | 4.4 | 11.0 | 10.4 | 9.9 | 11.6 | 11.1 | 8.8 | 4.3 | 6.2 | 10.3 | Net acquisition of financial assets |
| 2 | 0.1 | 0.2 | 0.3 | 0.3 | 0.2 | 0.3 | 0.2 | 0.2 | 0.2 | 0.2 | 0.2 | 0.2 | Demand deposits and currency |
| 3 | 0.3 | 0.1 | 1.1 | 4.1 | 1.4 | 1.1 | 2.9 | 1.7 | −0.3 | −0.2 | 0.9 | −0.7 | Home mortgages |
| 4 | 2.8 | 0.5 | 1.3 | 3.8 | 5.9 | 6.8 | 6.2 | 6.3 | 4.3 | 2.5 | 4.4 | 2.8 | Consumer credit |
| 5 | 5.0 | 0.1 | 1.8 | 2.8 | 2.9 | 1.8 | 2.2 | 2.9 | 4.5 | 1.8 | 0.7 | 8.0 | Other loans (to business) |
| 6 | 8.3 | 1.6 | 4.2 | 9.3 | 9.4 | 9.0 | 10.6 | 10.1 | 7.9 | 4.1 | 5.2 | 9.1 | Net increase in liabilities |
| 7 | 1.6 | 2.5 | 3.8 | 5.4 | 1.8 | 1.9 | 3.4 | 1.0 | 0.8 | 1.2 | 1.4 | 1.8 | Corporate bonds |
| 8 | 1.9 | −1.1 | * | 3.8 | 4.1 | 5.2 | 4.6 | 5.9 | 0.6 | −1.0 | 2.7 | 0.7 | Bank loans n.e.c. |
| 9 | 4.9 | 0.2 | 0.4 | * | 3.5 | 1.8 | 2.7 | 3.2 | 6.5 | 3.9 | 1.0 | 6.7 | Open market paper |
| 10 | * | * | * | * | 0.1 | 0.1 | * | 0.1 | 0.1 | 0.1 | 0.1 | 0.1 | Taxes payable |

Real estate investment trusts

| | 1969 | 1970 | 1971 | 1972 | 1973 | 1973 I | 1973 II | 1973 III | 1973 IV | 1974 I | 1974 II | 1974 III | |
|---|---|---|---|---|---|---|---|---|---|---|---|---|---|
| 1 | 0.3 | 0.2 | 0.4 | 1.1 | 0.7 | 1.2 | 1.3 | 0.3 | 0.1 | 1.4 | 0.7 | * | Physical investment |
| 2 | 0.1 | 0.1 | 0.1 | 0.4 | 0.2 | 0.4 | 0.4 | 0.1 | * | 0.4 | 0.2 | * | Multifamily structures |
| 3 | 0.2 | 0.2 | 0.3 | 0.8 | 0.5 | 0.8 | 0.9 | 0.2 | 0.1 | 0.9 | 0.5 | * | Nonresidential structures |
| 4 | 1.0 | 2.4 | 2.6 | 5.0 | 5.6 | 5.7 | 6.4 | 6.2 | 4.0 | 2.4 | 1.2 | −1.4 | Net acquisition of financial assets |
| 5 | 0.1 | 0.5 | 0.7 | 1.4 | 1.3 | 1.3 | 1.4 | 1.4 | 1.0 | 0.7 | 0.3 | 0.2 | Home mortgages |
| 6 | 0.3 | 0.6 | 0.7 | 1.2 | 0.7 | 0.5 | 1.3 | 1.4 | −0.3 | 0.7 | 0.4 | 0.3 | Multifamily mortgages |
| 7 | 0.4 | 1.0 | 1.1 | 2.3 | 2.5 | 2.8 | 2.4 | 2.5 | 2.3 | 1.3 | 0.4 | 0.4 | Commercial mortgages |
| 8 | 0.1 | 0.3 | * | 0.2 | 1.1 | 1.2 | 1.4 | 0.8 | 1.1 | −0.4 | 0.1 | −2.4 | Miscellaneous assets |
| 9 | 1.3 | 2.7 | 3.0 | 6.1 | 6.3 | 6.9 | 7.7 | 6.5 | 4.2 | 3.7 | 1.9 | −1.4 | Net increase in liabilities |
| 10 | 0.8 | 1.4 | 0.9 | 1.5 | 0.7 | 1.8 | 1.9 | 0.5 | −1.2 | 0.1 | −0.3 | 0.1 | Corporate equities |
| 11 | 0.5 | 1.3 | 2.1 | 4.6 | 5.6 | 5.1 | 5.8 | 6.0 | 5.4 | 3.6 | 2.2 | −1.5 | Credit market instruments |
| 12 | 0.2 | 0.1 | 0.1 | 0.5 | 0.3 | 0.5 | 0.6 | * | 0.2 | 0.3 | * | — | Mortgages |
| 13 | 0.1 | * | * | 0.2 | 0.1 | 0.2 | 0.2 | * | 0.1 | 0.1 | * | — | Multifamily residential |
| 14 | 0.2 | 0.1 | 0.1 | 0.3 | 0.2 | 0.3 | 0.4 | * | 0.1 | 0.2 | * | — | Commercial |
| 15 | 0.1 | 0.5 | 0.4 | 0.4 | 0.6 | 0.6 | 0.7 | 0.2 | 0.7 | 0.5 | * | — | Corporate bonds |

## Table 12 (cont'd)

|  | 1969 | 1970 | 1971 | 1972 | 1973 | 1973 I | 1973 II | 1973 III | 1973 IV | 1974 I | 1974 II | 1974 III |  |
|---|---|---|---|---|---|---|---|---|---|---|---|---|---|
| **Real estate investment trusts (cont'd)** | | | | | | | | | | | | | |
| 16 | 0.2 | 0.6 | 0.7 | 1.3 | 4.0 | 4.6 | 4.5 | 2.5 | 4.3 | 5.2 | 9.3 | 0.5 | Bank loans n.e.c. |
| 17 | — | — | 0.8 | 2.5 | 0.7 | -0.6 | 0.1 | 3.2 | 0.2 | -2.4 | -7.2 | -2.0 | Open market paper |
| 18 | — | — | — | — | — | — | — | — | — | — | — | — | Miscellaneous liabilities |
| **Open-end investment companies** | | | | | | | | | | | | | |
| 1 | -2.2 | -0.9 | -0.6 | -1.1 | -0.6 | -0.9 | -1.0 | -0.6 | * | -0.4 | -0.7 | -0.6 | Current surplus |
| 2 | 2.6 | 1.7 | 0.6 | -1.8 | -2.2 | -3.0 | -2.8 | 0.6 | -3.6 | -0.4 | -2.2 | 1.7 | Net acquisition of financial assets |
| 3 | -0.1 | * | 0.1 | * | 0.3 | 1.6 | -0.3 | 0.3 | -0.4 | -0.1 | -0.3 | -0.5 | Demand deposits and currency |
| 4 | 1.7 | 1.2 | 0.4 | -1.8 | -2.3 | -5.2 | -2.3 | -2.2 | 0.4 | -2.7 | -0.3 | 0.3 | Corporate shares |
| 5 | 0.9 | 0.5 | * | * | -0.2 | 0.6 | -0.2 | 2.5 | -3.6 | 2.5 | -1.6 | 1.9 | Credit market instruments |
| 6 | -0.5 | 0.2 | -0.3 | 0.1 | 0.5 | 1.2 | 0.3 | 0.5 | -0.1 | -1.2 | -1.5 | * | U.S. government securities |
| 7 | 0.2 | 0.7 | 0.6 | 0.2 | -0.9 | -0.8 | -2.1 | 0.9 | -1.4 | 0.8 | -2.1 | -1.0 | Corporate bonds |
| 8 | 1.2 | -0.4 | -0.3 | -0.3 | 0.2 | 0.2 | 1.6 | 1.2 | -2.1 | 2.9 | 1.9 | 2.9 | Open market paper |
| 9 | 4.8 | 2.6 | 1.1 | -0.7 | -1.6 | -2.1 | -1.8 | 1.2 | -3.7 | * | -1.6 | 2.3 | Net share issues |
| **Security brokers and dealers** | | | | | | | | | | | | | |
| 1 | -3.1 | 0.8 | 1.4 | 4.3 | -3.5 | -8.2 | -3.3 | -3.5 | 0.9 | -5.1 | 1.0 | -0.6 | Net acquisition of financial assets |
| 2 | -0.1 | -0.3 | * | * | * | — | * | * | * | * | * | * | Demand deposits and currency |
| 3 | 0.4 | 0.1 | 0.2 | 0.1 | 0.4 | 0.1 | 1.3 | -1.3 | 1.6 | * | 1.4 | -1.4 | Corporate shares |
| 4 | 0.1 | 2.3 | -1.3 | 0.2 | 0.6 | -3.8 | 1.9 | 0.6 | 3.7 | -6.3 | 0.8 | 2.2 | Credit market instruments |
| 5 | * | 1.7 | -1.6 | 0.2 | * | -2.6 | 0.3 | 1.8 | 0.5 | -4.1 | -0.6 | 3.6 | U.S. government securities |
| 6 | -0.2 | 0.6 | 0.1 | -0.1 | 0.2 | -1.3 | 0.4 | 0.1 | 1.6 | -2.2 | * | 0.1 | State and local obligations |
| 7 | 0.4 | 0.1 | 0.2 | 0.1 | 0.4 | 0.1 | 1.3 | -1.3 | 1.5 | * | 1.4 | -1.4 | Corporate bonds |
| 8 | -3.5 | -1.3 | 2.5 | 3.9 | -4.6 | -4.5 | -6.5 | -2.9 | -4.4 | 1.2 | -1.3 | -1.4 | Security credit |
| 9 | -3.1 | 1.0 | 1.1 | 4.1 | -3.5 | -8.2 | -3.2 | -3.4 | 1.0 | -4.9 | 1.4 | -0.2 | Net increase in liabilities |
| 10 | -3.0 | 1.0 | 1.1 | 4.1 | -3.4 | -8.2 | -3.2 | -3.4 | 1.1 | -4.8 | 1.5 | * | Security credit |
| 11 | -1.0 | 1.9 | 0.7 | 3.9 | -3.2 | -7.3 | -1.9 | -4.0 | 0.4 | -4.3 | 2.5 | -0.2 | From banks |
| 12 | -2.0 | -1.0 | 0.5 | 0.2 | -0.2 | -0.9 | -1.3 | 0.6 | 0.6 | -0.6 | -1.0 | 0.1 | Customer credit balances |
| 13 | -0.1 | — | * | * | * | * | * | 0.6 | * | -0.1 | -0.1 | -0.1 | Taxes payable |

Table 13

Sector statements of saving and investment: Rest of the world (billions of dollars)

| | 1969 | 1970 | 1971 | 1972 | 1973 | 1973 I | 1973 II | 1973 III | 1973 IV | 1974 I | 1974 II | 1974 III |
|---|---|---|---|---|---|---|---|---|---|---|---|---|
| 1 Net U.S. exports | 1.9 | 3.6 | -0.2 | -6.0 | 3.9 | -0.8 | 0.5 | 6.7 | 9.3 | 11.3 | -1.5 | -4.1 |
| 2 U.S. exports | 55.5 | 62.9 | 65.5 | 72.4 | 100.4 | 88.8 | 95.4 | 103.7 | 113.6 | 131.2 | 138.5 | 143.9 |
| 3 U.S. imports | 53.6 | 59.3 | 65.6 | 78.4 | 96.4 | 89.5 | 94.9 | 96.9 | 104.3 | 119.9 | 140.0 | 148.0 |
| 4 Transfer receipts from U.S. | 2.9 | 3.2 | 3.6 | 3.8 | 3.9 | 3.0 | 4.2 | 3.6 | 4.7 | 3.7 | 3.7 | 3.3 |
| 5 Current account balance (U.S. balance, sign reversed) | 1.0 | -0.4 | 3.8 | 9.8 | -0.1 | 3.8 | 3.7 | -3.1 | -4.7 | -7.6 | 5.2 | 7.5 |
| 6 Net financial investment | 3.4 | 0.8 | 13.6 | 11.6 | 2.1 | 22.2 | 1.0 | -6.0 | -8.7 | -9.9 | 0.8 | 2.5 |
| 7 Net acquisition of financial assets | 10.3 | 5.9 | 22.7 | 19.7 | 17.4 | 46.7 | 9.6 | 5.8 | 7.6 | 29.5 | 39.2 | 26.3 |
| 8 Gold and SDR's[a] | -1.0 | 0.8 | 1.3 | 0.6 | * | — | * | — | — | — | -0.1 | -0.5 |
| 9 U.S. demand deposits and currency | 0.3 | 0.2 | 0.3 | 1.5 | 2.5 | -1.1 | 1.7 | 2.9 | 6.6 | 1.6 | 2.1 | 3.2 |
| 10 U.S. time deposits | 1.1 | -1.7 | 0.5 | 2.7 | 2.9 | 5.0 | 3.2 | * | 3.4 | -1.3 | 6.8 | 12.7 |
| 11 U.S. corporate shares | 1.6 | 0.7 | 0.8 | 2.3 | 2.8 | 5.1 | 0.5 | 3.5 | 1.9 | 1.5 | * | 0.4 |
| 12 Credit market instruments | -0.3 | 10.3 | 26.4 | 8.4 | 0.7 | 30.3 | -7.0 | -14.0 | -6.3 | -0.4 | 19.4 | 1.3 |
| 13 U.S. government securities | -1.8 | 9.1 | 26.3 | 8.4 | 0.3 | 29.8 | -7.7 | -14.5 | -6.2 | -3.1 | 15.0 | -7.3 |
| 14 U.S. corporate bonds[b] | 0.5 | 0.7 | 0.3 | 0.1 | 0.1 | 0.2 | 0.3 | 0.5 | -0.7 | 1.1 | 1.3 | 2.8 |
| 15 Acceptances | 1.0 | 0.5 | -0.2 | -0.1 | 0.3 | 0.2 | 0.3 | -0.1 | 0.7 | 1.6 | 3.1 | 5.9 |
| 16 Security credit | -0.2 | -0.1 | * | 0.1 | * | -0.2 | | -0.1 | 0.2 | 0.2 | -0.1 | * |
| 17 Trade credit | 0.8 | 1.4 | 0.1 | 0.8 | 1.0 | 0.6 | -0.1 | 2.3 | 1.2 | 1.1 | 0.6 | 0.7 |
| 18 Miscellaneous assets | 8.0 | -5.6 | -6.8 | 3.4 | 7.6 | 7.1 | 11.3 | 11.3 | 0.6 | 26.7 | 10.4 | 8.3 |
| 19 U.S. bank liabilities to foreign affiliates | 7.9 | -6.9 | -4.1 | 0.9 | 1.1 | -1.1 | 2.8 | 1.8 | 0.7 | 10.7 | 0.6 | -1.8 |
| 20 Direct investment in U.S. | 0.8 | 1.0 | -0.1 | 0.4 | 2.5 | 1.4 | 2.4 | 3.5 | 2.8 | 5.1 | 6.1 | 6.9 |
| 21 Other | -0.8 | 0.3 | -2.6 | 2.1 | 4.0 | 6.9 | 6.2 | 5.9 | -3.0 | 10.9 | 3.8 | 3.1 |
| 22 Net increase in liabilities | 6.9 | 5.1 | 9.1 | 8.2 | 15.3 | 24.6 | 8.6 | 11.8 | 16.3 | 39.4 | 38.4 | 23.8 |
| 23 U.S. foreign exchange + net IMF position | 0.3 | -2.5 | -1.7 | -0.2 | -0.2 | -0.9 | * | 0.1 | 0.1 | 0.8 | 1.3 | 3.5 |
| 24 Foreign corporate shares | 0.5 | 0.1 | * | -0.4 | -0.2 | -0.7 | -0.2 | * | * | 0.1 | -0.5 | * |
| 25 Credit market instruments | 3.2 | 2.7 | 4.6 | 4.7 | 7.7 | 9.1 | 7.7 | 4.2 | 9.9 | 14.0 | 25.6 | 13.3 |

## Table 13 (cont'd)

| | 1969 | 1970 | 1971 | 1972 | 1973 | 1973 I | II | III | IV | 1974 I | II | III | |
|---|---|---|---|---|---|---|---|---|---|---|---|---|---|
| 26 | 1.0 | 0.9 | 0.9 | 1.0 | 1.0 | 0.5 | 0.7 | 0.8 | 2.0 | 2.5 | 1.9 | 2.5 | Corporate bonds |
| 27 | -0.2 | -0.3 | 1.6 | 2.9 | 2.8 | 4.7 | 3.9 | -1.6 | 4.2 | 6.1 | 12.8 | 1.9 | Bank loans n.e.c. |
| 28 | 2.4 | 2.1 | 2.1 | 0.8 | 3.9 | 3.9 | 3.2 | 5.0 | 3.7 | 5.3 | 10.9 | 9.0 | Other loans |
| 29 | -0.2 | * | * | 0.1 | -0.2 | -0.2 | -0.5 | * | -0.1 | * | 0.1 | 0.1 | Security debt |
| 30 | 0.8 | 1.0 | 0.5 | 0.5 | 1.9 | 0.6 | 0.7 | 2.2 | 4.0 | 6.7 | 1.3 | 1.9 | Trade debt |
| 31 | 2.4 | 4.0 | 5.6 | 3.5 | 6.3 | 16.6 | 0.9 | 5.4 | 2.3 | 17.8 | 10.5 | 5.0 | Miscellaneous liabilities |
| 32 | 0.2 | 0.2 | 0.3 | 0.3 | 0.3 | 0.3 | 0.3 | * | 0.8 | 0.5 | 0.9 | 0.3 | U.S. government equity in IBRD, etc. |
| 33 | -0.5 | 0.5 | 1.4 | 3.6 | 4.8 | 11.6 | 1.6 | -0.3 | 6.2 | 9.5 | -3.0 | -0.5 | Foreign currency held in U.S. |
| 34 | 2.2 | 3.6 | 3.8 | 1.5 | 3.6 | 5.3 | 2.3 | 1.7 | 5.4 | 1.7 | 5.6 | 5.2 | U.S. direct investment abroad[b] |
| 35 | 0.4 | -0.4 | 0.3 | -1.9 | -2.5 | -0.6 | -3.4 | 4.0 | -10.0 | 6.2 | 7.0 | * | Other |
| 36 | -2.3 | -1.2 | -9.8 | -1.8 | -2.2 | -18.3 | 2.8 | 2.9 | 4.0 | 2.2 | 4.4 | 5.0 | Discrepancy |

[a] Consists only of net purchases from United States. Excludes acquisitions from other sources
[b] Net of U.S. security issues in foreign markets to finance U.S. investment abroad

## Table 14

### Gold, official foreign exchange, treasury currency, and insurance reserves (billions of dollars)

| | 1969 | 1970 | 1971 | 1972 | 1973 | 1973 I | II | III | IV | 1974 I | II | III | |
|---|---|---|---|---|---|---|---|---|---|---|---|---|---|
| | | | | | | | | | | | | | Gold and official foreign exchange holdings[a] |
| 1 | 1.3 | -3.3 | -3.1 | -0.7 | -0.2 | -0.9 | -0.1 | 0.1 | 0.1 | 0.8 | 1.4 | 4.0 | Total U.S. reserves |
| 2 | 1.0 | -0.8 | -1.3 | -0.6 | * | — | * | — | — | — | 0.1 | 0.5 | U.S. gold stock and SDR's |
| 3 | 1.0 | -1.2 | -0.7 | * | * | — | * | — | — | — | 0.1 | 0.5 | U.S. government external stabilization fund |
| 4 | — | 0.4 | -0.6 | -0.5 | — | — | — | — | — | — | — | — | Monetary authorities[b] |
| 5 | 0.3 | -2.5 | -1.7 | -0.2 | -0.2 | -0.9 | * | 0.1 | 0.1 | 0.8 | 1.3 | 3.5 | U.S. foreign exchange position |

Table (time-series columns read left→right):

| # | Description | | | | | | | | | | | | |
|---|---|---|---|---|---|---|---|---|---|---|---|---|---|
| 6 | Official foreign currency holdings | -0.7 | -2.2 | -0.4 | * | -0.2 | -0.9 | — | — | — | * | 0.3 | 0.6 |
| 7 | Treasury | -0.7 | -0.4 | -0.1 | -0.2 | * | -0.2 | — | — | — | * | * | — |
| 8 | Monetary authorities | -0.1 | -1.7 | -0.2 | 0.2 | -0.2 | -0.8 | — | — | — | * | 0.3 | 0.6 |
| 9 | Net IMF position | 1.0 | -0.4 | -1.4 | -0.1 | * | 0.1 | * | 0.1 | 0.1 | 0.8 | 1.0 | 2.9 |
| 10 | U.S. government assets | 1.0 | -0.4 | -1.3 | -0.1 | * | 0.1 | * | — | 0.1 | 0.9 | 1.0 | 2.9 |
| 11 | Monetary authorities | * | * | * | * | * | * | -0.1 | 0.1 | — | * | * | * |

### Treasury currency and SDR certificates

| # | Description | | | | | | | | | | | | |
|---|---|---|---|---|---|---|---|---|---|---|---|---|---|
| 1 | Total U.S. government liability | 0.3 | 0.6 | 0.5 | 0.5 | 0.4 | 0.4 | 0.8 | 0.3 | 0.3 | 0.3 | 0.4 | 0.4 |
| 2 | Monetary authorities asset | 0.1 | 0.7 | 0.5 | 0.7 | 0.4 | 0.4 | 0.4 | 0.3 | 0.5 | 0.2 | 0.6 | 0.4 |
| 3 | Unallocated assets | 0.2 | -0.1 | -0.2 | -0.2 | * | -0.1 | 0.3 | — | -0.2 | 0.1 | -0.2 | * |

### Insurance and pension fund reserves

| # | Description | | | | | | | | | | | | |
|---|---|---|---|---|---|---|---|---|---|---|---|---|---|
| 1 | Life insurance reserves: Net change in liabilities | 5.0 | 5.2 | 6.2 | 6.6 | 7.3 | 7.1 | 7.4 | 7.4 | 7.2 | 7.1 | 7.5 | 7.3 |
| 2 | U.S. government | 0.1 | 0.1 | 0.1 | 0.1 | 0.1 | 0.1 | 0.1 | 0.1 | 0.1 | 0.1 | 0.1 | 0.1 |
| 3 | Life insurance companies | 4.9 | 5.1 | 6.1 | 6.5 | 7.2 | 7.0 | 7.3 | 7.4 | 7.2 | 7.1 | 7.4 | 7.2 |
| 4 | Net change in assets (households) | 5.0 | 5.2 | 6.2 | 6.6 | 7.3 | 7.1 | 7.4 | 7.4 | 7.2 | 7.1 | 7.5 | 7.3 |
| 5 | Pension fund reserves: Net change in liabilities | 16.3 | 19.1 | 21.6 | 23.8 | 24.4 | 24.8 | 24.9 | 25.3 | 22.5 | 20.1 | 39.2 | 27.1 |
| 6 | U.S. government | 1.5 | 2.4 | 2.8 | 3.2 | 2.1 | 1.9 | 4.1 | 1.0 | 1.2 | 1.5 | 9.8 | -0.6 |
| 7 | Insurance sector | 14.8 | 16.7 | 18.7 | 20.6 | 22.3 | 22.9 | 20.8 | 24.3 | 21.2 | 18.5 | 29.4 | 27.7 |
| 8 | Life insurance companies | 2.9 | 3.3 | 5.2 | 6.0 | 5.2 | 4.9 | 5.1 | 5.2 | 5.4 | 3.1 | 7.7 | 5.7 |
| 9 | Private pension funds | 6.3 | 7.1 | 7.3 | 6.8 | 7.7 | 8.2 | 5.8 | 9.4 | 7.6 | 7.1 | 10.0 | 10.3 |
|  | State and local government, retirement funds | | | | | | | | | | | | |
| 10 | Net change in assets (households) | 5.5 | 6.3 | 6.3 | 7.9 | 9.4 | 9.8 | 9.9 | 9.7 | 8.2 | 8.4 | 11.7 | 11.7 |
| 11 | Net change in assets (households) | 16.3 | 19.1 | 21.6 | 23.8 | 24.4 | 24.8 | 24.9 | 25.3 | 22.5 | 20.1 | 39.2 | 27.1 |

### Interbank claims

| # | Description | | | | | | | | | | | | |
|---|---|---|---|---|---|---|---|---|---|---|---|---|---|
| 1 | Net change in liabilities | 2.0 | 4.5 | 5.6 | 2.0 | 7.9 | 15.6 | 7.1 | 26.6 | -17.9 | 7.3 | 42.9 | 6.9 |
| 2 | Monetary authorities: member bank reserves | 0.2 | 2.1 | 3.6 | -2.1 | 1.4 | 1.6 | -2.6 | 22.5 | -15.8 | 1.6 | 12.8 | 6.0 |
| 3 | Vault cash | 0.1 | -0.3 | 0.5 | 1.1 | 2.0 | 0.4 | -2.4 | 4.4 | 5.7 | -4.8 | -2.5 | 4.2 |

Table 14 (cont'd)

Interbank claims (cont'd)

| | | | | | | | | 1973 | | | 1974 | | |
|---|---|---|---|---|---|---|---|---|---|---|---|---|---|
| | 1969 | 1970 | 1971 | 1972 | 1973 | I | II | III | IV | I | II | III | |
| 4 | 1.6 | 2.7 | 1.5 | 3.0 | 4.4 | 13.6 | 12.1 | -0.2 | -7.8 | 10.5 | 32.7 | -3.4 | Commercial banking (total) |
| 5 | 1.6 | 2.5 | 1.6 | 0.5 | 2.1 | 6.4 | 7.1 | 4.1 | -9.3 | 8.3 | 23.6 | -3.8 | Commercial banks |
| 6 | * | 1.0 | -0.2 | 1.6 | -1.6 | -2.9 | 0.5 | 11.9 | -15.9 | 4.4 | 6.8 | 5.3 | To monetary authorities |
| 7 | 0.6 | 0.1 | 0.3 | -0.4 | -0.4 | 2.1 | -1.4 | -2.3 | -0.1 | -0.4 | -0.4 | * | Loans from affiliates |
| 8 | 0.1 | 0.1 | 0.1 | 0.2 | 1.4 | 2.6 | 1.6 | 0.5 | 0.8 | 5.6 | -5.6 | 0.5 | Loans from foreign bank agencies |
| 9 | 0.8 | 1.2 | 1.3 | -1.2 | 2.6 | 4.3 | 6.5 | -6.3 | 5.7 | -1.4 | 22.4 | -9.7 | Demand deposits of foreign bank agencies |
| 10 | — | 0.1 | * | 0.3 | 0.1 | 0.3 | -0.1 | 0.2 | 0.1 | * | 0.4 | 0.1 | Time deposits of foreign bank agencies |
| 11 | 0.1 | 0.2 | -0.1 | 2.5 | 2.3 | 7.1 | 5.0 | -4.3 | 1.5 | 2.2 | 9.0 | 0.4 | Foreign banking agencies (deposits of banks) |
| 12 | 2.0 | 4.5 | 5.6 | 2.0 | 7.9 | 15.6 | 7.1 | 26.6 | -17.9 | 7.3 | 42.9 | 6.9 | Net change in assets |
| 13 | * | 1.0 | -0.2 | 1.6 | -1.6 | -2.9 | 0.5 | 11.9 | -15.9 | 4.4 | 6.8 | 5.3 | Monetary authorities |
| 14 | * | 0.8 | 0.1 | -0.4 | -0.9 | -1.1 | -1.1 | 3.0 | -4.3 | 2.9 | -0.5 | -0.5 | Federal Reserve float |
| 15 | * | 0.2 | -0.3 | 1.9 | -0.7 | -1.9 | 1.6 | 9.0 | -11.6 | 1.5 | 7.3 | 5.8 | Laons to member banks |
| 16 | 2.0 | 3.5 | 5.8 | 0.4 | 9.5 | 18.6 | 6.6 | 14.7 | -2.0 | 2.9 | 36.1 | 1.5 | Commercial banking (total) |
| 17 | 0.4 | 2.0 | 4.0 | 1.5 | 5.8 | 9.2 | * | 22.5 | -8.6 | -1.0 | 19.3 | 10.7 | Commercial banks |
| 18 | 0.2 | 2.1 | 3.6 | -2.1 | 1.4 | 1.6 | -2.6 | 22.5 | -15.8 | 1.6 | 12.8 | 6.0 | Member bank reserves |
| 19 | 0.1 | -0.3 | 0.5 | 1.1 | 2.0 | 0.4 | -2.4 | 4.4 | 5.7 | -4.8 | -2.5 | 4.2 | Vault cash |
| 20 | 0.1 | 0.2 | -0.1 | 2.5 | 2.3 | 7.1 | 5.0 | -4.3 | 1.5 | 2.2 | 9.0 | 0.4 | Deposits at foreign bank agencies |
| 21 | 0.6 | 0.1 | 0.3 | -0.4 | -0.4 | 2.1 | -1.4 | -2.3 | -0.1 | -0.4 | -0.4 | * | Bank affiliates (loans to affiliate banks) |
| 22 | 1.0 | 1.4 | 1.5 | -0.7 | 4.1 | 7.2 | 8.0 | -5.5 | 6.6 | 4.3 | 17.2 | -9.2 | Foreign banking agencies |
| 23 | 0.8 | 1.2 | 1.3 | -1.2 | 2.6 | 4.3 | 6.5 | -6.3 | 5.7 | -1.4 | 22.4 | -9.7 | Demand deposits at banks |
| 24 | — | 0.1 | * | 0.3 | 0.1 | 0.3 | -0.1 | 0.2 | 0.1 | * | 0.4 | 0.1 | Time deposits at banks |
| 25 | 0.1 | 0.1 | 0.1 | 0.2 | 1.4 | 2.6 | 1.6 | 0.5 | 0.8 | 5.6 | -5.6 | 0.5 | Loans to banks |

[a]Lines 1 and 2 exclude initial allocation of SDR's of $867 million in January 1970, $717 million in January 1971, and $710 million in January 1972. Transactions in SDR's are in line 2. Also excluded from the table are revaluations of foreign currency holdings, gold, SDR's, and IMF position. These allocations and revaluations are included in tables on outstandings
[b]Treasury gold stock

Table 15

Money stock and time and savings accounts (billions of dollars)

| | | | | | | | 1973 | | | | 1974 | |
|---|---|---|---|---|---|---|---|---|---|---|---|---|
| | 1969 | 1970 | 1971 | 1972 | 1973 | I | II | III | IV | I | II | III |

**Demand deposits and currency**

| | | 1969 | 1970 | 1971 | 1972 | 1973 | I | II | III | IV | I | II | III |
|---|---|---|---|---|---|---|---|---|---|---|---|---|---|
| 1 | Net change in assets | 8.2 | 14.3 | 17.4 | 19.6 | 16.0 | 24.0 | 14.8 | -6.8 | 31.8 | 7.0 | 8.7 | 6.9 |
| 2 | Money stock | 7.6 | 11.8 | 14.3 | 20.0 | 17.5 | 10.9 | 20.9 | 11.0 | 27.0 | 7.4 | 12.0 | 5.6 |
| 3 | Domestic sectors | 7.4 | 11.6 | 14.0 | 18.4 | 15.0 | 12.0 | 19.2 | 8.1 | 20.5 | 5.8 | 9.9 | 2.3 |
| 4 | Households | 1.5 | 11.2 | 11.0 | 11.8 | 13.1 | 10.5 | 10.3 | 5.5 | 26.0 | 4.1 | 0.9 | -4.7 |
| 5 | Nonfinancial business | 2.7 | 1.1 | 0.6 | 0.2 | -0.3 | -1.2 | 2.6 | 0.8 | -3.3 | 1.8 | -1.1 | 0.3 |
| 6 | State and local governments | 1.4 | -2.9 | 1.0 | 1.5 | -0.3 | -0.3 | 0.7 | -0.6 | -1.1 | 0.4 | 4.6 | 4.7 |
| 7 | Financial sectors | -0.3 | 1.0 | 1.3 | 1.7 | 2.4 | 0.8 | 3.3 | 3.6 | 1.9 | -1.3 | 0.5 | * |
| 8 | Mail float | 2.1 | 1.2 | 0.1 | 3.2 | 0.1 | 2.2 | 2.3 | -1.1 | -3.0 | 0.8 | 4.9 | 2.1 |
| 9 | Rest of the world | 0.3 | 0.2 | 0.3 | 1.5 | 2.5 | -1.1 | 1.7 | 2.9 | 6.6 | 1.6 | 2.1 | 3.2 |
| 10 | U.S. government deposits | 0.6 | 2.5 | 3.1 | -0.4 | -1.5 | 13.1 | -6.1 | -17.8 | 4.8 | -0.4 | -3.2 | 1.3 |
| 11 | Net change in banking system liabilities | 8.2 | 14.3 | 17.4 | 19.6 | 16.0 | 24.0 | 14.8 | -6.8 | 31.8 | 7.0 | 8.7 | 6.9 |
| 12 | Monetary authorities | 3.3 | 3.1 | 4.4 | 3.2 | 3.4 | 10.3 | 9.0 | -10.1 | 4.3 | 7.7 | 9.9 | 6.4 |
| 13 | U.S. government cash and deposits | 0.5 | -0.4 | 0.9 | -1.1 | -0.5 | 7.0 | 0.7 | -11.4 | 1.7 | -1.2 | 1.2 | 2.2 |
| 14 | Foreign deposits | -0.1 | * | 0.1 | -0.1 | -0.1 | 0.3 | * | 0.3 | -0.8 | 0.5 | 0.1 | 1.0 |
| 15 | Currency | 2.8 | 3.5 | 3.4 | 4.4 | 3.9 | 3.0 | 8.3 | 1.0 | 3.4 | 8.4 | 8.6 | 3.1 |
| 16 | Commercial banking | 4.9 | 11.2 | 13.0 | 16.3 | 12.6 | 13.7 | 5.8 | 3.3 | 27.5 | -0.7 | -1.1 | 0.5 |
| 17 | U.S. government deposits | * | 2.9 | 2.2 | 0.7 | -1.0 | 6.1 | -6.8 | -6.4 | 3.1 | 0.8 | -4.4 | -0.9 |
| 18 | Foreign deposits | 0.4 | 0.2 | 0.2 | 1.6 | 2.6 | -1.4 | 1.7 | 2.6 | 7.4 | 1.1 | 2.0 | 2.2 |
| 19 | Private domestic | 4.5 | 8.1 | 10.6 | 14.0 | 11.0 | 9.0 | 10.8 | 7.1 | 17.1 | -2.7 | 1.3 | -0.8 |

**Time deposits and savings accounts**

| | | 1969 | 1970 | 1971 | 1972 | 1973 | I | II | III | IV | I | II | III |
|---|---|---|---|---|---|---|---|---|---|---|---|---|---|
| 1 | Net change (total) | -1.5 | 54.9 | 81.9 | 88.5 | 79.1 | 114.2 | 85.8 | 62.8 | 53.4 | 84.1 | 103.7 | 47.0 |
| 2 | Commercial banking liability | -9.5 | 38.0 | 41.4 | 42.3 | 50.9 | 70.0 | 52.1 | 55.0 | 26.6 | 44.4 | 87.3 | 41.7 |
| 3 | Large negotiable CD's | -12.5 | 15.2 | 8.7 | 9.8 | 20.0 | 43.4 | 17.0 | 34.7 | -15.1 | 15.8 | 47.9 | 35.9 |
| 4 | Other at commercial banks | 2.9 | 22.4 | 32.4 | 33.0 | 30.3 | 25.7 | 34.8 | 19.7 | 41.0 | 28.5 | 39.3 | 5.2 |
| 5 | At foreign banking agencies | 0.2 | 0.4 | 0.3 | -0.5 | 0.6 | 0.9 | 0.4 | 0.5 | 0.6 | 0.1 | 0.1 | 0.6 |

**Table 15 (cont'd)**

Time deposits and savings accounts (cont'd)

| | 1969 | 1970 | 1971 | 1972 | 1973 | 1973 I | II | III | IV | 1974 I | II | III | |
|---|---|---|---|---|---|---|---|---|---|---|---|---|---|
| | | | | | | | | | | | | | Acquired by: |
| 6 | -2.0 | 27.5 | 29.8 | 29.5 | 39.5 | 40.2 | 42.0 | 41.0 | 34.9 | 36.9 | 58.4 | 15.3 | Households |
| 7 | -2.4 | 1.7 | 3.6 | 3.1 | 1.4 | 14.3 | 0.2 | 3.6 | -12.7 | 4.4 | 10.8 | 9.1 | Corporate business |
| 8 | -5.9 | 10.0 | 7.2 | 6.8 | 7.2 | 9.7 | 6.6 | 11.0 | 1.6 | 3.8 | 11.8 | 4.4 | State and local governments |
| 9 | -0.2 | 0.3 | 0.1 | 0.1 | -0.2 | 0.7 | -0.2 | -0.6 | -0.6 | 0.6 | -0.6 | 0.3 | U.S. government |
| 10 | -0.1 | 0.2 | 0.2 | 0.2 | 0.1 | 0.2 | 0.3 | — | — | — | — | — | Mutual savings banks |
| 11 | 1.1 | -1.7 | 0.5 | 2.7 | 2.9 | 5.0 | 3.2 | * | 3.4 | -1.3 | 6.8 | 12.7 | Foreign |
| 12 | 7.9 | 17.0 | 40.6 | 46.1 | 28.1 | 44.2 | 33.7 | 7.8 | 26.8 | 39.7 | 16.4 | 5.3 | At savings institutions |
| 13 | 2.6 | 4.4 | 9.9 | 10.2 | 4.7 | 9.5 | 6.5 | 0.2 | 2.7 | 8.8 | 1.5 | * | Mutual savings banks |
| 14 | 1.4 | 1.7 | 2.9 | 3.4 | 2.9 | 4.0 | 4.3 | 1.0 | 2.3 | 3.6 | 3.8 | 1.2 | Credit unions |
| 15 | 3.9 | 10.9 | 27.8 | 32.6 | 20.5 | 30.7 | 22.9 | 6.6 | 21.8 | 27.3 | 11.1 | 4.0 | Savings and loan associations |
| 16 | 4.0 | 10.8 | 27.7 | 32.3 | 20.5 | 30.1 | 21.5 | 8.6 | 21.9 | 25.1 | 10.2 | 6.4 | Held by households |
| 17 | -0.1 | 0.1 | 0.1 | 0.2 | * | 0.6 | 1.4 | -2.0 | -0.1 | 2.1 | 0.9 | -2.4 | Held by credit unions |
| 18 | 6.0 | 44.4 | 70.3 | 75.4 | 67.7 | 83.8 | 74.2 | 50.8 | 61.9 | 74.4 | 73.9 | 22.9 | Memo: total of households time and savings accounts |

**Table 16**

Relation of Flow of Funds money stock data to daily average series (billions of dollars)

I. Total money stock

| | 1969 | 1970 | 1971 | 1972 | 1973 | 1973 I | II | III | IV | 1974 I | II | III | |
|---|---|---|---|---|---|---|---|---|---|---|---|---|---|
| | | | | | | | | | | | | | Net changes, S.A. quarterly rate: |
| 1 | 30.5 | 11.8 | 14.3 | 20.0 | 17.5 | 10.9 | 20.9 | 11.0 | 27.0 | 7.4 | 12.0 | 5.6 | Flow of Funds demand deposits and currency |
| 2 | 28.7 | 12.5 | 13.9 | 20.5 | 15.7 | 9.6 | 29.9 | -0.3 | 23.8 | 15.2 | 17.7 | 5.1 | Daily average (DAMS) |
| 3 | 1.8 | -0.8 | 0.4 | -0.5 | 1.7 | 1.3 | -9.0 | 11.4 | 3.2 | -7.8 | -5.7 | 0.5 | Total difference |

| Line | | | | | | | | | | | | | Description |
|---|---|---|---|---|---|---|---|---|---|---|---|---|---|
| 4 | 0.4 | -0.8 | 0.4 | -0.6 | 1.7 | 0.3 | -2.3 | 2.8 | 0.8 | -2.0 | -1.4 | 0.1 | Total difference at quarterly rate |
| 5 | -0.6 | 0.3 | -0.4 | -2.5 | -0.9 | 4.0 | -0.4 | 1.5 | -5.9 | 6.5 | -1.1 | -1.8 | From data differences |
| 6 | 1.1 | -1.3 | 0.3 | 1.4 | 2.3 | -9.5 | 3.6 | -5.6 | 13.8 | -13.6 | 5.3 | -5.5 | From timing differences |
| 7 | * | 0.3 | 0.4 | 0.6 | 0.3 | 5.8 | -5.4 | 6.9 | -7.0 | 5.2 | -5.6 | 7.4 | From seasonals |

## II. Demand deposits

| Line | | | | | | | | | | | | | Description |
|---|---|---|---|---|---|---|---|---|---|---|---|---|---|
| | | | | | | | | | | | | | Net change, S.A. quarterly rate: |
| 1 | 4.8 | 8.3 | 10.9 | 15.5 | 13.5 | 2.0 | 3.1 | 2.5 | 5.9 | -0.3 | 0.9 | 0.6 | Flow of Funds |
| 2 | 4.6 | 9.5 | 10.4 | 16.2 | 11.0 | 1.3 | 6.1 | -0.9 | 4.4 | 2.2 | 3.0 | 0.1 | DAMS |
| 3 | 0.2 | -1.2 | 0.5 | -0.6 | 2.6 | 0.6 | -3.0 | 3.4 | 1.5 | -2.4 | -2.1 | 0.5 | Difference |
| 4 | 0.2 | -1.5 | 0.1 | -1.2 | 2.2 | -4.6 | 1.5 | -2.1 | 7.4 | -7.0 | 2.5 | -5.4 | Difference in unadjusted |
| 5 | -0.6 | 0.3 | -0.4 | -2.5 | -0.9 | 4.0 | -0.4 | 1.5 | -5.9 | 6.5 | -1.1 | -1.8 | Data difference |
| 6 | 0.9 | -1.8 | 0.5 | 1.4 | 3.1 | -8.6 | 2.0 | -3.6 | 13.3 | -13.5 | 3.6 | -3.6 | Timing difference |
| 7 | * | 0.3 | 0.3 | 0.5 | 0.4 | 5.3 | -4.5 | 5.5 | -5.9 | 4.5 | -4.6 | 5.9 | Difference in seasonals |
| 8 | * | 0.3 | 0.3 | 0.5 | 0.4 | -1.8 | -0.5 | 1.4 | 1.3 | -2.2 | -0.4 | 1.6 | Flows vs. levels |
| 9 | — | — | — | — | — | 6.2 | -2.4 | 3.9 | -7.7 | 5.8 | -2.1 | 3.9 | One-day vs. daily average |
| 10 | * | * | * | * | * | 0.9 | -1.6 | 0.2 | 0.6 | 1.0 | -2.1 | 0.4 | Seasonal balance adjustment |

## III. Currency

| Line | | | | | | | | | | | | | Description |
|---|---|---|---|---|---|---|---|---|---|---|---|---|---|
| | | | | | | | | | | | | | Net change, S.A. quarterly rate: |
| 1 | 2.8 | 3.5 | 3.4 | 4.4 | 3.9 | 0.8 | 2.1 | 0.3 | 0.9 | 2.1 | 2.1 | 0.8 | Flow of Funds |
| 2 | 2.6 | 3.0 | 3.5 | 4.3 | 4.8 | 1.1 | 1.4 | 0.8 | 1.5 | 1.6 | 1.5 | 1.1 | DAMS |
| 3 | 0.2 | 0.5 | -0.1 | 0.1 | -0.8 | -0.3 | 0.7 | -0.6 | -0.7 | 0.5 | 0.7 | -0.4 | Difference |
| 4 | 0.2 | 0.5 | -0.2 | * | -0.8 | -0.9 | 1.6 | -2.0 | 0.5 | -0.2 | 1.6 | -1.9 | Timing difference |
| 5 | * | * | * | 0.1 | * | 0.6 | -0.9 | 1.5 | -1.1 | 0.7 | -1.0 | 1.5 | Difference in seasonals |
| 6 | * | * | * | 0.1 | * | -0.2 | 0.1 | 0.1 | -0.1 | -0.2 | 0.2 | 0.1 | Flows vs. levels |
| 7 | — | — | — | — | — | 0.7 | -1.0 | 1.3 | -1.1 | 0.8 | -1.0 | 1.4 | One-day vs. daily average |
| 8 | * | * | * | * | * | 0.1 | -0.1 | * | * | 0.1 | -0.1 | * | Seasonal balance adjustment |

Money-Stock Relationship

| Part | Line | |
|---|---|---|
| I | 1 | Line 1 of Table 15 |
| | 2 | Daily averages in this table are increments in month averages from last month of preceding quarter to last month of this quarter. |
| | 3 | 1 - 2. |
| | 4 | 5 + 6 + 7 |

## Table 16 (cont'd)

| Part | Line | |
|---|---|---|
| II | 5 | See Part II, line 5 |
| | 6 | Part II, line 6 + Part III, line 4 |
| | 7 | Part II, line 7 + Part III, line 5. "Seasonal" here means dollar excess of seasonally adjusted flow over unadjusted flow. |
| II | 1 | Lines 14 + 18 + 19 of Table 15 at quarterly rates |
| | 5 | Differences between money-stock concept of demand deposits derived from last preceding all-bank total (either last Wednesday of quarter or Call Report) and figure for that one day, e.g. March 29, 1972, derived from data going into daily-average statistics. Quarterly increments in this difference. |
| | 6 | Difference between figure for period derived from daily-average data and average for last month of quarter. Quarterly increments in this difference. |
| | 7 | 8 + 9 + 10 − 11 |
| | 8 | Difference in adjustment method: seasonal in daily-average series (month average) adjusted as flows less seasonal in published daily-average series |
| | 9 | Seasonal in Flow of Funds demand deposit (based on net change from last day of one quarter to last day of next) less seasonal in daily average adjusted as flows |
| | 10 | Adjustment to seasonal needed as part of the balancing of all seasonally adjusted sources and uses of funds in the Flow of Funds matrix |
| III | 4 | No statistical difference between the two series. In unadjusted data, only difference is between one-day figure for end of quarter and three-week average. |
| | 5–9 | Correspond to lines 7 through 11 in Part II. |

## Table 17

### U.S. government securities market summary (billions of dollars)

| | 1969 | 1970 | 1971 | 1972 | 1973 | 1973 | | | | 1974 | | |
|---|---|---|---|---|---|---|---|---|---|---|---|---|
| | | | | | | I | II | III | IV | I | II | III |
| 1  Total net issues | 5.5 | 21.1 | 29.4 | 23.6 | 29.4 | 45.4 | 25.2 | 19.7 | 27.3 | 17.9 | 26.4 | 36.5 |
| 2  Treasury issues | -1.3 | 12.9 | 26.0 | 13.9 | 7.7 | 30.1 | 3.1 | -9.7 | 7.4 | 7.0 | 1.3 | 16.6 |
| 3  Household savings bonds | -0.4 | 0.3 | 2.4 | 3.3 | 2.7 | 3.7 | 3.4 | 2.0 | 1.7 | 3.3 | 3.0 | 2.7 |
| 4  Treasury excluding savings bonds | -0.9 | 12.6 | 23.6 | 10.6 | 5.0 | 26.4 | -0.2 | -11.7 | 5.7 | 3.7 | -1.7 | 13.9 |
| 5  Other | 6.8 | 8.2 | 3.4 | 9.7 | 21.6 | 15.3 | 22.0 | 29.4 | 19.9 | 11.0 | 25.1 | 19.9 |
| 6  Budget agency issues | -0.4 | 0.3 | 0.6 | 2.0 | 0.7 | 0.4 | -0.7 | 1.3 | 1.9 | 1.4 | 1.0 | -1.1 |
| 7  Loan participations[a] | -1.9 | -0.3 | -1.1 | 1.5 | 1.3 | 2.3 | 0.5 | 1.4 | 1.0 | 0.3 | -0.1 | -0.2 |
| 8  Sponsored agency issues[b] | 9.1 | 8.2 | 3.8 | 6.2 | 19.6 | 12.6 | 22.1 | 26.7 | 17.0 | 9.3 | 24.3 | 21.2 |
| 9  Net acquisitions, by sector | 5.5 | 21.1 | 29.4 | 23.6 | 29.4 | 45.4 | 25.2 | 19.7 | 27.3 | 17.9 | 26.4 | 36.5 |
| 10  U.S. government (agency sector) | -1.3 | -0.1 | * | * | * | * | * | * | * | -5.5 | * | * |
| 11  Sponsored credit agencies | -0.4 | 1.9 | -1.2 | -0.4 | 1.3 | -2.6 | 1.2 | 3.9 | 2.8 |  | -0.6 | -4.7 |

| # | | C1 | C2 | C3 | C4 | C5 | C6 | C7 | C8 | C9 | C10 | C11 | C12 |
|---|---|---|---|---|---|---|---|---|---|---|---|---|---|
| 12 | Treasury marketable | -4.7 | -0.6 | -5.5 | 2.8 | 3.9 | 1.3 | -2.5 | 1.4 | -0.3 | -1.1 | 2.0 | -0.7 |
| 13 | FHLB special issue | — | — | — | — | — | * | -0.1 | * | -0.1 | -0.1 | -0.2 | 0.3 |
| 14 | Federal Reserve system | 9.9 | 12.4 | -1.2 | 10.8 | 5.8 | 3.4 | 17.1 | 9.3 | 0.4 | 8.7 | 5.0 | 4.2 |
| 15 | Foreign | -7.3 | 15.0 | -3.1 | -6.2 | -14.5 | -7.7 | 29.8 | 0.3 | 8.4 | 26.3 | 9.1 | -1.8 |
| 16 | Short-term marketable | -0.4 | 17.1 | 1.0 | 5.5 | -12.7 | -7.6 | -8.1 | -5.7 | 1.3 | 13.9 | 7.8 | -2.2 |
| 17 | Other | -6.9 | -2.1 | -4.1 | -11.8 | -1.8 | -0.1 | 37.9 | 6.1 | 7.2 | 12.4 | 1.3 | 0.4 |
| 18 | Total private domestic | 38.7 | -0.4 | 27.7 | 19.9 | 24.4 | 28.3 | 1.1 | 18.4 | 15.2 | -4.4 | 5.2 | 4.8 |
| 19 | Private domestic nonfinancial | 37.4 | 5.3 | 19.0 | 15.8 | 27.8 | 22.8 | 8.6 | 18.8 | 1.6 | -14.0 | -9.0 | 17.0 |
| 20 | Savings bonds (households) | 2.7 | 3.0 | 3.3 | 1.7 | 2.0 | 3.4 | 3.7 | 2.7 | 3.3 | 2.4 | 0.3 | -0.4 |
| 21 | Treasury excluding savings bonds | 21.4 | -13.7 | 15.1 | 6.0 | 6.7 | 8.8 | -2.8 | 4.7 | -1.7 | -11.0 | -11.4 | 10.7 |
| 22 | Agency issues | 13.3 | 16.0 | 0.6 | 8.1 | 19.2 | 10.6 | 7.7 | 11.4 | 0.1 | -5.4 | 2.1 | 6.7 |
| | Private domestic nonfinancial, by sector | | | | | | | | | | | | |
| 23 | Households | 35.8 | 12.3 | 14.3 | 14.4 | 27.1 | 27.8 | 12.1 | 20.4 | 0.6 | -14.4 | -9.7 | 12.8 |
| 24 | Savings bonds | 2.7 | 3.0 | 3.3 | 1.7 | 2.0 | 3.4 | 3.7 | 2.7 | 3.3 | 2.4 | 0.3 | -0.4 |
| 25 | Treasury excluding savings bonds | 17.4 | -5.9 | 12.5 | 6.6 | 8.9 | 13.1 | -2.5 | 6.5 | -2.6 | -11.8 | -12.7 | 10.5 |
| 26 | Agency issues | 15.7 | 15.2 | -1.4 | 6.1 | 16.2 | 11.4 | 10.8 | 11.1 | -0.1 | -5.0 | 2.8 | 2.8 |
| 27 | Corporate business | 8.3 | 2.6 | -1.7 | -2.6 | -3.4 | -1.2 | * | -1.8 | -2.4 | 2.2 | 0.5 | -2.3 |
| 28 | Treasury issues | 8.7 | 2.3 | -1.8 | -2.8 | -5.2 | -2.6 | -1.4 | -3.0 | -3.2 | 2.1 | 0.4 | -2.8 |
| 29 | Agency issues | -0.4 | 0.3 | 0.1 | 0.2 | 1.8 | 1.4 | 1.5 | 1.2 | 0.7 | 0.1 | 0.1 | 0.5 |
| 30 | State and local governments | -6.7 | -9.6 | 6.4 | 4.1 | 4.1 | -3.8 | -3.5 | 0.2 | 3.4 | -1.8 | 0.2 | 6.4 |
| 31 | Treasury issues | -4.7 | -10.1 | 4.5 | 2.3 | 3.0 | -1.7 | 1.1 | 1.2 | 4.0 | -1.3 | 0.9 | 3.1 |
| 32 | Agency issues | -2.0 | 0.5 | 1.9 | 1.8 | 1.1 | -2.2 | -4.6 | -1.0 | -0.6 | -0.5 | -0.8 | 3.4 |
| 33 | Commercial banking | -1.7 | -4.4 | 8.8 | 1.4 | 1.7 | 5.9 | -14.1 | -1.3 | 6.5 | 6.9 | 10.4 | -10.0 |
| 34 | Treasury issues | -4.5 | -10.0 | 4.2 | -6.9 | -9.0 | -3.8 | -15.7 | -8.8 | 2.4 | 3.1 | 6.9 | -9.7 |
| 35 | Agency issues | 2.9 | 5.5 | 4.6 | 8.3 | 10.7 | 9.6 | 1.6 | 7.6 | 4.1 | 3.8 | 3.5 | -0.3 |
| 36 | Private nonbank finance | 3.1 | -1.2 | * | 2.6 | -5.1 | -0.4 | 6.6 | 0.9 | 7.1 | 2.6 | 3.8 | -2.2 |
| 37 | Treasury issues | 3.7 | -0.9 | -5.1 | 0.4 | -3.8 | -1.8 | 0.8 | -1.1 | 2.3 | -1.7 | 1.1 | -3.9 |
| 38 | Agency issues | -0.6 | -0.3 | 5.1 | 2.2 | -1.3 | 1.4 | 5.9 | 2.0 | 4.8 | 4.3 | 2.7 | 1.7 |
| | Private nonbank financial, by sector | | | | | | | | | | | | |
| 39 | Savings and loan associations | 3.1 | -1.2 | * | 2.6 | -5.1 | -0.4 | 6.6 | 0.9 | 7.1 | 2.6 | 3.8 | -2.2 |
| 40 | | -1.8 | -1.3 | 7.6 | 1.4 | -6.7 | -1.8 | 7.1 | * | 4.3 | 5.2 | 1.2 | 0.3 |

Table 17 (cont'd)

| | 1969 | 1970 | 1971 | 1972 | 1973 | 1973 | | | | 1974 | | |
|---|---|---|---|---|---|---|---|---|---|---|---|---|
| | | | | | | I | II | III | IV | I | II | III |
| 41 Treasury issues | -1.0 | -0.4 | 1.4 | 0.9 | -1.0 | 3.2 | -1.6 | -5.2 | -0.4 | 3.1 | 1.0 | -0.6 |
| 42 Agency issues | 1.3 | 1.5 | 3.9 | 3.4 | 1.0 | 3.9 | -0.2 | -1.5 | 1.8 | 4.5 | -2.3 | -1.2 |
| 43 Mutual savings banks | -0.5 | 0.3 | 0.9 | 1.4 | -0.5 | 0.2 | 0.2 | -1.4 | -0.9 | -0.1 | * | -0.3 |
| 44 Treasury issues | -0.6 | -0.2 | 0.1 | 0.3 | -0.6 | -0.5 | -0.6 | -0.9 | -0.2 | -1.0 | -0.7 | 0.4 |
| 45 Agency issues | 0.1 | 0.5 | 0.8 | 1.1 | 0.1 | 0.7 | 0.8 | -0.5 | -0.7 | 0.9 | 0.7 | -0.7 |
| 46 Credit unions | -0.2 | 0.4 | 0.8 | 0.8 | 0.2 | 0.4 | 0.2 | 0.1 | 0.2 | 0.2 | 0.2 | -0.4 |
| 47 Treasury issues | -0.1 | 0.3 | 0.3 | 0.4 | 0.2 | 0.3 | 0.2 | 0.2 | 0.2 | 0.2 | 0.2 | -0.1 |
| 48 Agency issues | -0.1 | 0.1 | 0.5 | 0.4 | * | 0.1 | * | -0.1 | * | * | * | -0.3 |
| 49 Life insurance | -0.3 | 0.1 | -0.2 | 0.3 | 0.1 | 0.1 | 0.4 | -0.2 | * | -0.9 | 0.4 | * |
| 50 Treasury issues | -0.3 | -0.1 | -0.2 | 0.3 | -0.2 | -0.1 | -0.1 | -0.5 | * | -1.0 | 0.1 | -0.2 |
| 51 Agency issues | * | 0.1 | 0.1 | * | 0.2 | 0.2 | 0.5 | 0.2 | * | 0.2 | 0.2 | 0.2 |
| 52 Private pension funds | -0.2 | 0.2 | -0.3 | 1.0 | 0.6 | 0.7 | 0.4 | 0.7 | 0.8 | -0.4 | 0.7 | 0.8 |
| 53 Treasury issues | -0.4 | -0.1 | * | 0.9 | 0.1 | -0.4 | 0.3 | 0.5 | 0.1 | -0.8 | 0.2 | * |
| 54 Agency issues | 0.2 | 0.3 | -0.3 | 0.1 | 0.5 | 1.1 | 0.1 | 0.3 | 0.6 | 0.4 | 0.4 | 0.8 |
| 55 State and local government, retirement funds | -0.3 | -0.3 | -1.6 | -0.6 | 0.1 | 0.1 | -0.2 | -0.1 | 0.7 | -1.1 | 1.4 | 1.1 |
| 56 Treasury issues | -0.5 | -0.3 | -1.2 | -0.5 | -0.1 | * | -0.5 | -0.4 | 0.3 | -0.2 | 0.9 | 0.9 |
| 57 Agency issues | 0.2 | * | -0.3 | -0.1 | 0.2 | * | 0.3 | 0.2 | 0.5 | -0.9 | 0.5 | 0.2 |
| 58 Other insurance companies | -0.5 | 0.1 | -0.4 | -0.4 | -0.1 | -0.5 | -0.1 | 0.2 | 0.1 | * | -0.5 | * |
| 59 Treasury issues | -0.5 | -0.1 | -0.2 | -0.3 | -0.1 | -0.4 | * | 0.1 | 0.1 | * | -0.6 | -0.4 |
| 60 Agency issues | * | 0.1 | -0.2 | -0.1 | * | -0.1 | -0.1 | 0.1 | * | * | 0.1 | 0.3 |
| 61 Investment companies (Treasury) | -0.5 | 0.2 | -0.3 | 0.1 | 0.5 | 1.2 | 0.3 | 0.5 | -0.1 | -1.2 | -1.5 | * |
| 62 Security brokers and dealers (Treasury) | * | 1.7 | -1.6 | 0.2 | * | -2.6 | 0.3 | 1.8 | 0.5 | -4.1 | -0.6 | 3.6 |

a Where not shown separately, loan participations are included with agency issues

b These issues are outside the budget and outside the U.S. government sector in Flow of Funds Accounts. They are included in credit market debt of financial institutions. Sponsored agency issues include GNMA-guaranteed securities backed by mortgage pools

Table 18

Private securities and mortgages (billions of dollars)

| | 1969 | 1970 | 1971 | 1972 | 1973 | 1973 I | II | III | IV | 1974 I | II | III | |
|---|---|---|---|---|---|---|---|---|---|---|---|---|---|
| **State and local government securities** | | | | | | | | | | | | | |
| 1 | 9.9 | 11.2 | 17.6 | 14.4 | 13.7 | 10.6 | 12.7 | 15.6 | 16.0 | 15.8 | 19.7 | 12.3 | Net change in liabilities |
| 2 | 9.9 | 11.2 | 17.5 | 13.8 | 11.9 | 9.3 | 10.5 | 13.6 | 14.2 | 14.2 | 18.2 | 10.9 | State and local governments |
| 3 | 2.8 | 2.3 | 2.5 | -0.7 | -0.2 | -1.2 | -1.8 | 0.7 | 1.4 | -0.4 | 3.3 | 4.5 | Short-term |
| 4 | 7.2 | 8.9 | 15.0 | 14.5 | 12.2 | 10.6 | 12.4 | 12.9 | 12.8 | 14.6 | 14.9 | 6.4 | Other |
| 5 | — | — | 0.1 | 0.5 | 1.8 | 1.3 | 2.1 | 2.0 | 1.8 | 1.6 | 1.5 | 1.4 | Corporate business (pollution control) |
| 6 | 9.9 | 11.2 | 17.6 | 14.4 | 13.7 | 10.6 | 12.7 | 15.6 | 16.0 | 15.8 | 19.7 | 12.3 | Net change in assets |
| 7 | 9.6 | -0.8 | -0.2 | 1.0 | 4.3 | 3.7 | 2.8 | 8.9 | 2.0 | 5.6 | 7.7 | 13.5 | Households |
| 8 | -1.0 | -0.6 | 1.0 | 1.0 | -0.1 | 1.0 | 2.5 | -1.5 | -2.5 | 2.1 | * | 0.1 | Corporate business |
| 9 | 0.1 | 0.2 | -0.3 | 0.2 | 0.2 | 0.5 | 0.6 | -0.2 | 0.1 | 0.2 | 0.2 | 0.6 | State and local government, general funds |
| 10 | 0.2 | 10.7 | 12.6 | 7.2 | 5.7 | 2.6 | 4.5 | 3.5 | 12.2 | 5.8 | 6.9 | -6.4 | Commercial banking |
| 11 | * | * | 0.2 | 0.5 | * | 0.6 | * | -0.3 | -0.1 | 0.1 | -0.2 | * | Mutual savings banks |
| 12 | * | 0.1 | 0.1 | * | * | -0.1 | 0.2 | 0.2 | -0.1 | 0.3 | 0.2 | 0.1 | Life insurance companies |
| 13 | -0.1 | -0.3 | 0.1 | -0.1 | -0.6 | -1.5 | -0.5 | 0.1 | -0.5 | -0.1 | -0.1 | -0.5 | State and local government, retirement funds |
| 14 | 1.2 | 1.5 | 3.9 | 4.8 | 3.9 | 5.1 | 2.2 | 4.8 | 3.3 | 4.0 | 5.1 | 4.8 | Other insurance companies |
| 15 | -0.2 | 0.6 | 0.1 | -0.1 | 0.2 | -1.3 | 0.4 | 0.1 | 1.6 | -2.2 | * | 0.1 | Brokers and dealers |
| **Corporate and foreign bonds** | | | | | | | | | | | | | |
| 1 | 14.5 | 23.8 | 24.8 | 20.2 | 12.5 | 10.7 | 14.1 | 12.5 | 12.7 | 21.7 | 22.8 | 26.7 | Net issues |
| 2 | 12.0 | 19.8 | 18.8 | 12.2 | 9.2 | 7.9 | 9.7 | 10.5 | 8.5 | 17.1 | 19.0 | 19.3 | Corporate business |
| 3 | -0.2 | 0.1 | 0.9 | 1.1 | * | -0.3 | -0.4 | -0.1 | 0.8 | 0.3 | 0.4 | 3.2 | Commercial banks |
| 4 | 1.6 | 2.5 | 3.8 | 5.4 | 1.8 | 1.9 | 3.4 | 1.0 | 0.8 | 1.2 | 1.4 | 1.8 | Finance companies |
| 5 | 0.1 | 0.5 | 0.4 | 0.4 | 0.6 | 0.6 | 0.7 | 0.2 | 0.7 | 0.5 | * | — | REITs |
| 6 | 1.0 | 0.9 | 0.9 | 1.0 | 1.0 | 0.5 | 0.7 | 0.8 | 2.0 | 2.5 | 1.9 | 2.5 | Rest of the world |
| 7 | 14.5 | 23.8 | 24.8 | 20.2 | 12.5 | 10.7 | 14.1 | 12.5 | 12.7 | 21.7 | 22.8 | 26.7 | Net purchases |
| 8 | 6.6 | 10.7 | 9.3 | 5.2 | 1.1 | -0.5 | * | -1.4 | 6.1 | 3.4 | 0.3 | 4.9 | Households |
| 9 | -0.1 | 0.8 | 1.3 | 1.7 | 0.5 | -0.3 | -0.4 | 1.2 | 1.3 | 1.3 | 1.2 | 1.2 | Commercial banking |
| 10 | 0.3 | 1.2 | 3.9 | 2.1 | -1.1 | 0.9 | -1.4 | -2.1 | -1.8 | 3.5 | 1.3 | -0.7 | Mutual savings banks |

363

Table 18 (cont'd)

| | 1969 | 1970 | 1971 | 1972 | 1973 | 1973 I | 1973 II | 1973 III | 1973 IV | 1974 I | 1974 II | 1974 III | |
|---|---|---|---|---|---|---|---|---|---|---|---|---|---|
| **Corporate and foreign bonds (cont'd)** | | | | | | | | | | | | | |
| 11 | 6.5 | 9.6 | 9.3 | 10.8 | 12.4 | 11.0 | 16.3 | 14.7 | 7.7 | 11.6 | 19.6 | 21.1 | Insurance |
| 12 | 1.5 | 1.5 | 5.5 | 7.0 | 5.9 | 3.9 | 7.8 | 6.7 | 5.0 | 3.5 | 9.1 | 6.5 | Life insurance companies |
| 13 | 0.6 | 2.1 | -0.7 | -0.8 | 1.6 | 2.1 | 0.9 | 3.5 | -0.1 | 3.0 | 4.7 | 7.2 | Private pension funds |
| 14 | 3.6 | 3.8 | 4.2 | 5.3 | 5.9 | 7.2 | 6.1 | 6.6 | 3.9 | 5.5 | 6.4 | 8.2 | State and local government, retirement funds |
| 15 | 0.8 | 2.3 | 0.3 | -0.7 | -1.0 | -2.1 | 1.5 | -2.1 | -1.2 | -0.3 | -0.6 | -0.7 | Other insurance companies |
| 16 | 0.2 | 0.7 | 0.6 | 0.2 | -0.9 | -0.8 | -2.1 | 0.9 | -1.4 | 0.8 | -2.1 | -1.0 | Open-end investment companies |
| 17 | 0.4 | 0.1 | 0.2 | 0.1 | 0.4 | 0.1 | 1.3 | -1.3 | 1.5 | * | 1.4 | -1.4 | Brokers and dealers |
| 18 | 0.5 | 0.7 | 0.3 | 0.1 | 0.1 | 0.2 | 0.3 | 0.5 | -0.7 | 1.1 | 1.3 | 2.8 | Rest of the world |
| **Corporate equities** | | | | | | | | | | | | | |
| 1 | 10.0 | 10.4 | 14.8 | 12.9 | 8.0 | 8.4 | 10.9 | 10.1 | 2.7 | 7.8 | 4.0 | 9.2 | Net issues |
| 2 | 4.8 | 2.6 | 1.1 | -0.7 | -1.6 | -2.1 | -1.8 | 1.2 | -3.7 | * | -1.6 | 2.3 | Open-end investment companies |
| 3 | 5.2 | 7.7 | 13.6 | 13.6 | 9.6 | 10.5 | 12.7 | 8.9 | 6.3 | 7.8 | 5.6 | 6.9 | Other sectors |
| 4 | 3.4 | 5.7 | 11.4 | 10.9 | 7.4 | 7.0 | 8.7 | 5.1 | 8.9 | 6.2 | 5.0 | 5.4 | Corporate business |
| 5 | * | 0.1 | 0.6 | 1.2 | 1.2 | 2.0 | 1.8 | 2.8 | -1.8 | 1.0 | 1.0 | 1.0 | Commercial banks |
| 6 | 0.5 | 0.4 | 0.6 | 0.5 | 0.5 | 0.4 | 0.4 | 0.5 | 0.5 | 0.4 | 0.4 | 0.4 | Other insurance companies |
| 7 | 0.8 | 1.4 | 0.9 | 1.5 | 0.7 | 1.8 | 1.9 | 0.5 | -1.2 | 0.1 | -0.3 | 0.1 | REITs |
| 8 | 0.5 | 0.1 | * | -0.4 | -0.2 | -0.7 | -0.2 | * | * | 0.1 | -0.5 | * | Rest of the world |
| 9 | 10.0 | 10.4 | 14.8 | 12.9 | 8.0 | 8.4 | 10.9 | 10.1 | 2.7 | 7.8 | 4.0 | 9.2 | Net purchases |
| 10 | -3.8 | -1.7 | -5.3 | -5.4 | -8.2 | -9.3 | -3.1 | -0.3 | -19.9 | -2.7 | -4.1 | 3.2 | Households |
| 11 | * | 0.1 | | 0.1 | 0.1 | 0.2 | — | — | — | — | — | — | Commercial banking |
| 12 | 0.2 | 0.3 | 0.5 | 0.6 | 0.4 | 0.7 | 0.4 | -0.3 | 0.5 | 0.8 | -0.1 | 0.1 | Mutual savings banks |
| 13 | 9.9 | 9.7 | 18.2 | 17.0 | 14.9 | 16.8 | 14.0 | 10.8 | 18.2 | 11.0 | 7.1 | 6.6 | Insurance |
| 14 | 1.7 | 2.0 | 3.6 | 3.5 | 3.6 | 3.5 | 4.6 | 3.1 | 3.1 | 1.5 | 1.1 | 0.9 | Life insurance companies |
| 15 | 5.4 | 4.6 | 8.9 | 7.1 | 5.3 | 5.0 | 4.4 | 2.9 | 8.8 | 3.1 | 1.7 | 1.6 | Private pension funds |
| 16 | 1.8 | 2.1 | 3.2 | 3.5 | 3.9 | 5.0 | 3.6 | 3.0 | 4.1 | 4.4 | 3.2 | 3.2 | State and local government, retirement funds |
| 17 | 1.0 | 1.0 | 2.5 | 3.0 | 2.2 | 3.3 | 1.4 | 1.7 | 2.2 | 2.0 | 1.1 | 0.9 | Other insurance companies |
| 18 | 1.7 | 1.2 | 0.4 | -1.8 | -2.3 | -5.2 | -2.3 | -2.2 | 0.4 | -2.7 | -0.3 | 0.3 | Open-end investment companies |
| 19 | 0.4 | 0.1 | 0.2 | 0.1 | 0.4 | 0.1 | 1.3 | -1.3 | 1.6 | * | 1.4 | -1.4 | Brokers and dealers |
| 20 | 1.6 | 0.7 | 0.8 | 2.3 | 2.8 | 5.1 | 0.5 | 3.5 | 1.9 | 1.5 | * | 0.4 | Rest of the world |

## Total mortgages

| | | | | | | | | | | | | | |
|---|---|---|---|---|---|---|---|---|---|---|---|---|---|
| 1 | Net change in mortgages borrowed by: | 50.6 | 70.1 | 57.6 | 58.1 | 77.0 | 81.4 | 71.2 | 71.9 | 68.8 | 48.9 | 26.4 | 27.8 |
| 2 | U.S. government | -0.2 | -0.1 | * | * | -0.1 | -0.1 | -0.1 | -0.1 | -0.1 | -0.1 | -0.1 | -0.1 |
| 3 | Savings and loan associations | -2.8 | * | * | -4.6 | -2.3 | -0.3 | 1.1 | -1.5 | 1.2 | 2.0 | 0.6 | * |
| 4 | REITs | — | * | 0.3 | 0.2 | * | 0.6 | 0.5 | 0.3 | 0.5 | 0.1 | 0.1 | 0.2 |
| 5 | Private nonfinancial sectors | 53.5 | 70.2 | 57.3 | 62.6 | 79.3 | 81.2 | 69.6 | 73.2 | 67.3 | 46.9 | 25.7 | 27.7 |
| 6 | Households | 31.7 | 39.9 | 35.2 | 40.4 | 47.8 | 47.2 | 41.4 | 44.2 | 38.4 | 24.2 | 12.5 | 16.1 |
| 7 | Nonprofit institutions | 1.4 | 1.4 | 1.4 | 1.4 | 1.4 | 1.4 | 1.4 | 1.4 | 1.4 | 1.2 | 1.4 | 1.3 |
| 8 | Business | 20.5 | 28.9 | 20.7 | 20.9 | 30.1 | 32.6 | 26.8 | 27.6 | 27.4 | 21.5 | 11.9 | 10.3 |
| 9 | Farms | 4.4 | 4.8 | 3.8 | 4.5 | 4.7 | 4.4 | 3.9 | 4.4 | 2.6 | 2.0 | 1.8 | 1.9 |
| 10 | Nonfarm noncorporate | 6.8 | 8.3 | 5.1 | 3.0 | 7.8 | 9.7 | 7.8 | 7.1 | 9.2 | 8.0 | 4.9 | 3.8 |
| 11 | Corporate | 9.2 | 15.8 | 11.8 | 13.3 | 17.7 | 18.4 | 15.1 | 16.1 | 15.6 | 11.4 | 5.2 | 4.6 |
| 12 | Funds advanced by: | 50.6 | 70.1 | 57.6 | 58.1 | 77.0 | 81.4 | 71.2 | 71.9 | 68.8 | 48.9 | 26.4 | 27.8 |
| 13 | Households | 1.4 | 1.9 | 0.3 | 1.4 | 1.6 | 1.9 | -3.0 | 0.5 | -1.8 | 0.2 | 0.1 | 1.1 |
| 14 | U.S. government | 2.5 | 0.8 | -0.6 | -0.9 | 2.9 | -3.1 | -1.2 | -0.6 | -0.2 | * | 0.3 | 0.7 |
| 15 | State and local government, general funds | — | — | * | * | * | — | — | * | * | * | * | -0.1 |
| 16 | Sponsored credit agencies[a, b] | 16.1 | 15.8 | 12.7 | 11.4 | 11.8 | 10.3 | 7.9 | 10.4 | 6.7 | 6.3 | 5.8 | 4.5 |
| 17 | Private financial institutions | 30.5 | 51.7 | 45.1 | 46.2 | 60.8 | 72.2 | 67.4 | 61.6 | 64.2 | 42.3 | 20.1 | 21.6 |
| 18 | Commercial banking | 8.5 | 15.5 | 13.2 | 18.6 | 20.3 | 20.7 | 19.4 | 19.8 | 16.8 | 9.9 | 2.5 | 5.4 |
| 19 | Savings institutions | 16.2 | 28.0 | 25.4 | 19.0 | 29.0 | 41.1 | 41.4 | 32.6 | 37.7 | 28.0 | 12.1 | 12.2 |
| 20 | S & L associations[a] | 14.1 | 24.8 | 22.5 | 14.2 | 23.4 | 34.2 | 35.9 | 26.9 | 31.9 | 23.9 | 10.2 | 9.5 |
| 21 | Mutual savings banks | 2.1 | 3.2 | 2.9 | 4.8 | 5.6 | 6.9 | 5.5 | 5.7 | 5.6 | 4.0 | 1.8 | 2.7 |
| 22 | Credit unions | | | | * | * | * | * | — | 0.2 | * | 0.1 | * |
| 23 | Insurance | 5.6 | 6.3 | 4.1 | 5.9 | 4.4 | 2.5 | 1.0 | 3.4 | 0.8 | 0.8 | 3.3 | 2.8 |
| 24 | Life companies | 5.5 | 6.2 | 3.9 | 6.3 | 5.0 | 2.4 | 1.8 | 3.9 | 1.8 | 1.1 | 2.3 | 2.1 |
| 25 | Private pension funds | -0.1 | -0.1 | * | -0.2 | -0.1 | -0.4 | -0.5 | -0.3 | -0.7 | -0.6 | 0.1 | 0.1 |
| 26 | State and local government, retirement funds | 0.2 | 0.1 | 0.1 | -0.2 | -0.4 | 0.5 | -0.2 | -0.1 | -0.3 | 0.3 | 0.8 | 0.6 |
| 27 | Other insurance companies | * | * | * | * | * | — | -0.1 | * | * | * | * | * |
| 28 | Finance companies | -0.7 | 0.9 | -0.2 | -0.3 | 1.7 | 2.9 | 1.1 | 1.4 | 4.1 | 1.1 | 0.1 | 0.3 |
| 29 | REITs | 0.9 | 1.1 | 2.7 | 3.0 | 5.3 | 5.1 | 4.6 | 4.5 | 4.9 | 2.5 | 2.1 | 0.9 |
| 30 | | 9.8 | 10.4 | 3.3 | 2.4 | 10.2 | 10.7 | 5.4 | 7.2 | * | -2.7 | 1.3 | 4.0 |

[a] Memo: FHLB loans to S & L associations (included in "other loans" category)
[b] Includes mortgage pools backing GNMA-guaranteed pass-through securities

## Table 19

### Mortgage markets by type of mortgage (billions of dollars)

| | 1969 | 1970 | 1971 | 1972 | 1973 | 1973 I | 1973 II | 1973 III | 1973 IV | 1974 I | 1974 II | 1974 III |
|---|---|---|---|---|---|---|---|---|---|---|---|---|
| **Home mortgages** | | | | | | | | | | | | |
| 1 Net borrowing | 15.6 | 13.4 | 28.0 | 40.7 | 41.7 | 43.0 | 47.1 | 44.5 | 32.4 | 33.0 | 41.5 | 28.1 |
| 2 Households | 16.1 | 12.5 | 24.2 | 38.4 | 44.2 | 41.4 | 47.2 | 47.8 | 40.4 | 35.2 | 39.9 | 31.7 |
| 3 Nonfarm noncorporate business | -0.2 | 0.2 | 1.0 | 0.6 | -0.4 | 0.3 | 0.2 | -0.5 | -1.7 | -1.1 | 0.9 | -0.3 |
| 4 Corporate business | -0.2 | 0.2 | 1.0 | 0.6 | -0.4 | 0.3 | 0.2 | -0.5 | -1.7 | -1.1 | 0.9 | -0.3 |
| 5 U.S. government | -0.1 | -0.1 | -0.1 | -0.1 | -0.1 | -0.1 | -0.1 | -0.1 | * | * | -0.1 | -0.2 |
| 6 Savings and loan associations | * | 0.6 | 2.0 | 1.2 | -1.5 | 1.1 | -0.3 | -2.3 | -4.6 | * | * | -2.8 |
| 7 Net change in assets | 15.6 | 13.4 | 28.0 | 40.7 | 41.7 | 43.0 | 47.1 | 44.5 | 32.4 | 33.0 | 41.5 | 28.1 |
| 8 Households | 0.1 | * | * | -2.6 | -0.9 | -4.0 | -0.1 | -0.1 | 0.5 | -0.7 | -0.2 | -0.1 |
| 9 U.S. government | 0.1 | -0.1 | -0.3 | -0.6 | -1.2 | -1.7 | -3.3 | 0.8 | -0.5 | — | 0.2 | 0.7 |
| 10 State and local governments | -0.1 | | | | * | | — | * | * | * | * | * |
| 11 Sponsored credit agencies[a] | 3.9 | 5.1 | 4.8 | 4.3 | 6.4 | 4.8 | 6.0 | 7.5 | 7.2 | 8.0 | 10.6 | 11.2 |
| 12 Commercial banking | 3.0 | 0.9 | 5.7 | 9.0 | 11.0 | 10.5 | 11.4 | 11.4 | 10.6 | 7.7 | 8.9 | 4.3 |
| 13 Savings institutions | 9.1 | 8.2 | 18.7 | 27.9 | 24.6 | 32.5 | 30.4 | 21.5 | 13.9 | 18.2 | 20.9 | 11.4 |
| 14 Savings and loan associations | 7.7 | 7.2 | 17.3 | 24.8 | 22.0 | 29.0 | 28.5 | 18.6 | 11.9 | 17.3 | 19.9 | 10.7 |
| 15 Mutual savings banks | 1.4 | 0.9 | 1.3 | 3.0 | 2.6 | 3.5 | 1.9 | 2.9 | 2.0 | 0.9 | 1.0 | 0.7 |
| 16 Credit unions | * | 0.1 | * | 0.2 | — | * | * | * | * | — | — | * |
| 17 Insurance | -0.9 | -1.2 | -2.7 | -2.8 | -0.8 | -1.6 | -1.6 | 0.3 | -0.1 | -0.7 | * | 1.1 |
| 18 Life insurance companies | -1.1 | -1.3 | -2.1 | -2.1 | -0.5 | -1.1 | -1.3 | 0.4 | 0.1 | -0.7 | 0.1 | 1.2 |
| 19 Private pension funds | 0.1 | 0.1 | -0.6 | -0.7 | -0.3 | -0.5 | -0.4 | -0.1 | -0.2 | — | -0.1 | -0.1 |
| 20 Finance companies | 0.3 | 0.1 | 1.1 | 4.1 | 1.4 | 1.1 | 2.9 | 1.7 | -0.3 | -0.2 | 0.9 | -0.7 |
| 21 REITs | 0.1 | 0.5 | 0.7 | 1.4 | 1.3 | 1.3 | 1.4 | 1.4 | 1.0 | 0.7 | 0.3 | 0.2 |
| **Multifamily residential mortgages** | | | | | | | | | | | | |
| 1 Net borrowing | 4.8 | 5.9 | 8.8 | 10.4 | 8.5 | 8.6 | 11.2 | 9.7 | 4.6 | 7.2 | 8.7 | 9.2 |
| 2 Nonfarm noncorporate business | 3.6 | 4.3 | 6.2 | 7.3 | 5.9 | 6.2 | 7.9 | 6.6 | 3.2 | 5.0 | 6.1 | 6.4 |
| 3 Corporate business | 1.2 | 1.5 | 2.6 | 3.0 | 2.5 | 2.3 | 3.2 | 3.1 | 1.4 | 2.1 | 2.7 | 2.8 |
| 4 REITs | 0.1 | * | * | 0.2 | 0.1 | 0.2 | 0.2 | * | 0.1 | 0.1 | 0.3 | — |

| | Row | | | | | | | | | | | | |
|---|---|---|---|---|---|---|---|---|---|---|---|---|---|
| Net change in assets | 5 | 4.8 | 5.9 | 8.8 | 10.4 | 8.5 | 8.6 | 11.2 | 9.7 | 4.6 | 7.2 | 8.7 | 9.2 |
| Households | 6 | -0.5 | -0.8 | -0.1 | 1.2 | 0.1 | 0.1 | 0.1 | 0.1 | * | 0.1 | 0.7 | 1.2 |
| U.S. government | 7 | 0.7 | 0.5 | 0.4 | 0.3 | 0.4 | 0.5 | 0.1 | 1.9 | -0.8 | -0.8 | 0.4 | 1.5 |
| Sponsored credit agencies[a] | 8 | * | 0.3 | 0.8 | 1.2 | 2.0 | 1.2 | 2.4 | 2.3 | 2.1 | 2.5 | 2.5 | 2.4 |
| Commercial banks | 9 | 0.5 | 0.1 | 0.7 | 1.8 | 1.2 | 1.3 | 1.4 | 1.1 | 0.7 | 1.0 | 1.0 | 0.7 |
| Savings institutions | 10 | 1.7 | 2.4 | 5.3 | 4.5 | 3.1 | 3.7 | 4.5 | 2.6 | 1.8 | 2.4 | 2.2 | 1.6 |
| Savings and loan associations | 11 | 1.2 | 2.1 | 3.5 | 3.4 | 1.8 | 3.0 | 1.6 | 1.9 | 0.7 | 1.7 | 1.8 | 1.1 |
| Mutual savings banks | 12 | 0.5 | 0.4 | 1.8 | 1.1 | 1.4 | 0.6 | 3.0 | 0.7 | 1.1 | 0.7 | 0.4 | 0.5 |
| Life insurance companies | 13 | 1.4 | 1.9 | 0.7 | 0.5 | 1.1 | 1.7 | 0.9 | 0.7 | 1.3 | 1.2 | 1.5 | 1.3 |
| State and local government, retirement funds | 14 | 0.6 | 0.8 | 0.3 | -0.3 | -0.1 | -0.2 | 0.5 | -0.4 | -0.2 | 0.1 | 0.1 | 0.2 |
| REITs | 15 | 0.3 | 0.6 | 0.7 | 1.2 | 0.7 | 0.5 | 1.3 | 1.4 | -0.3 | 0.7 | 0.4 | 0.3 |

## Commercial mortgages

| | Row | | | | | | | | | | | | |
|---|---|---|---|---|---|---|---|---|---|---|---|---|---|
| Net borrowing | 1 | 5.5 | 5.4 | 10.1 | 15.1 | 17.3 | 15.6 | 18.6 | 18.1 | 16.7 | 13.6 | 15.1 | 8.8 |
| Households | 2 | 1.3 | 1.4 | 1.2 | 1.4 | 1.4 | 1.4 | 1.4 | 1.4 | 1.5 | 1.4 | 1.4 | 1.4 |
| Nonfarm noncorporate business | 3 | 0.4 | 0.4 | 0.9 | 1.3 | 1.6 | 1.4 | 1.7 | 1.7 | 1.5 | 1.2 | 1.4 | 0.7 |
| Corporate business | 4 | 3.7 | 3.6 | 7.9 | 12.0 | 14.1 | 12.5 | 15.1 | 15.0 | 13.7 | 10.8 | 12.3 | 6.7 |
| REITs | 5 | 0.2 | 0.1 | 0.1 | 0.3 | 0.2 | 0.3 | 0.4 | * | 0.1 | 0.2 | * | — |
| Net change in assets | 6 | 5.5 | 5.4 | 10.1 | 15.1 | 17.3 | 15.6 | 18.6 | 18.1 | 16.7 | 13.6 | 15.1 | 8.8 |
| Households | 7 | 0.3 | -0.2 | -0.6 | -1.2 | 0.1 | — | 0.4 | — | * | * | 0.5 | -0.6 |
| U.S. government | 8 | * | * | * | * | — | — | — | — | — | — | — | — |
| Commercial banking | 9 | 1.6 | 1.2 | 3.0 | 5.4 | 6.9 | 6.8 | 7.1 | 7.2 | 6.7 | 4.3 | 5.1 | 3.0 |
| Savings institutions | 10 | 1.4 | 1.5 | 4.1 | 5.2 | 4.9 | 5.2 | 6.1 | 4.9 | 3.3 | 4.8 | 4.8 | 3.2 |
| Savings and loan associations | 11 | 0.6 | 1.0 | 3.1 | 3.7 | 3.1 | 3.8 | 4.1 | 3.0 | 1.6 | 3.5 | 3.1 | 2.3 |
| Mutual savings banks | 12 | 0.8 | 0.6 | 1.0 | 1.5 | 1.7 | 1.3 | 2.0 | 2.0 | 1.7 | 1.4 | 1.7 | 1.0 |
| Life insurance companies | 13 | 1.8 | 1.8 | 2.5 | 3.4 | 2.9 | 1.0 | 2.6 | 3.5 | 4.4 | 3.1 | 4.3 | 2.8 |
| Other insurance companies | 14 | * | * | * | * | * | -0.1 | — | * | * | * | * | * |
| REITs | 15 | 0.4 | 1.0 | 1.1 | 2.3 | 2.5 | 2.8 | 2.4 | 2.5 | 2.3 | 1.3 | 0.4 | 0.4 |

## Farm mortgages

| | Row | | | | | | | | | | | | |
|---|---|---|---|---|---|---|---|---|---|---|---|---|---|
| Net borrowing | 1 | 1.9 | 1.8 | 2.0 | 2.6 | 4.4 | 3.9 | 4.4 | 4.7 | 4.5 | 3.8 | 4.8 | 4.4 |
| Net change in assets | 2 | 1.9 | 1.8 | 2.0 | 2.6 | 4.4 | 3.9 | 4.4 | 4.7 | 4.5 | 3.8 | 4.8 | 4.4 |

Table 19 (cont'd)

## Farm mortgages (cont'd)

| | 1969 | 1970 | 1971 | 1972 | 1973 | 1973 I | II | III | IV | 1974 I | II | III | |
|---|---|---|---|---|---|---|---|---|---|---|---|---|---|
| 3 | 1.2 | 1.1 | 0.9 | 0.7 | 1.3 | 1.0 | 1.6 | 1.5 | 1.0 | 0.9 | 1.0 | 1.0 | Households |
| 4 | * | * | * | * | 0.2 | * | 0.1 | 0.2 | 0.5 | 0.2 | 0.2 | 0.2 | U.S. government |
| 5 | 0.6 | 0.5 | 0.7 | 1.2 | 2.0 | 1.9 | 1.9 | 2.0 | 2.1 | 2.2 | 2.7 | 2.5 | Sponsored credit agencies |
| 6 | 0.3 | 0.3 | 0.6 | 0.6 | 0.7 | 0.8 | 0.8 | 0.6 | 0.5 | 0.2 | 0.5 | 0.5 | Commercial banks |
| 7 | * | * | -0.1 | * | * | * | * | — | * | * | 0.1 | — | Mutual savings banks |
| 8 | * | -0.1 | * | 0.1 | 0.3 | 0.2 | 0.1 | 0.4 | 0.5 | 0.3 | 0.4 | 0.3 | Life insurance companies |

ᵃIncludes mortgage pools backing GNMA-guaranteed securities

Table 20

## Consumer credit and bank loans not elsewhere classified (billions of dollars)

### Consumer credit

| | 1969 | 1970 | 1971 | 1972 | 1973 | 1973 I | II | III | IV | 1974 I | II | III | |
|---|---|---|---|---|---|---|---|---|---|---|---|---|---|
| 1 | 10.4 | 6.0 | 11.2 | 19.2 | 22.9 | 25.6 | 24.6 | 22.3 | 19.2 | 8.2 | 17.2 | 15.8 | Net change in liabilities (households) |
| 2 | 9.4 | 5.0 | 9.2 | 16.0 | 20.1 | 24.0 | 20.0 | 21.0 | 15.5 | 8.8 | 14.0 | 14.1 | Installment credit |
| 3 | 1.0 | 1.1 | 2.0 | 3.1 | 2.8 | 1.6 | 4.6 | 1.3 | 3.8 | -0.6 | 3.2 | 1.7 | Noninstallment credit |
| 4 | 10.4 | 6.0 | 11.2 | 19.2 | 22.9 | 25.6 | 24.6 | 22.3 | 19.2 | 8.2 | 17.2 | 15.8 | Net change in assets |
| 5 | 9.4 | 5.0 | 9.2 | 16.0 | 20.1 | 24.0 | 20.0 | 21.0 | 15.5 | 8.8 | 14.0 | 14.1 | Installment credit |
| 6 | 0.1 | 0.1 | * | 0.2 | 0.2 | 0.2 | 0.2 | 0.2 | 0.2 | * | 0.2 | 0.2 | Nonfarm noncorporate business |
| 7 | * | 0.1 | 0.1 | 1.0 | 1.2 | 1.2 | 1.4 | 1.0 | 1.3 | 0.5 | 1.1 | 0.7 | Corporate business |
| 8 | 4.5 | 3.0 | 5.8 | 8.5 | 9.7 | 12.0 | 9.6 | 10.2 | 7.0 | 4.2 | 5.3 | 5.6 | Commercial banking |
| 9 | 0.2 | 0.3 | 0.1 | 0.1 | 0.2 | 0.1 | 0.2 | 0.2 | 0.2 | 0.1 | 0.3 | 0.2 | Savings and loan associations |
| 10 | 0.1 | 0.1 | 0.1 | 0.2 | 0.2 | 0.9 | -0.3 | 0.1 | * | 0.3 | * | 0.3 | Mutual savings banks |
| 11 | 1.7 | 1.0 | 1.8 | 2.1 | 2.7 | 2.9 | 2.6 | 2.9 | 2.3 | 1.3 | 2.7 | 4.2 | Credit unions |
| 12 | 2.8 | 0.5 | 1.3 | 3.8 | 5.9 | 6.8 | 6.2 | 6.3 | 4.3 | 2.5 | 4.4 | 2.8 | Finance companies |

Bank loans not elsewhere classified, Flow of Funds basis

| No. | Item | | | | | | | | | | | | |
|---|---|---|---|---|---|---|---|---|---|---|---|---|---|
| 13 | Noninstallment credit | 1.0 | 1.1 | 2.0 | 3.1 | 2.8 | 1.6 | 4.6 | 1.3 | 3.8 | -0.6 | 3.2 | 1.7 |
| 14 | Nonfarm noncorporate business | 0.5 | 0.5 | 0.7 | 0.9 | 1.0 | 0.5 | 1.0 | 1.0 | 1.7 | -0.4 | 1.3 | 1.8 |
| 15 | Corporate business | 0.3 | 0.6 | 0.4 | 0.6 | 0.8 | -0.3 | 2.1 | -0.3 | 1.6 | -0.3 | 1.8 | 0.4 |
| 16 | Commercial banking | 0.2 | -0.1 | 0.8 | 1.5 | 0.9 | 1.2 | 1.4 | 0.6 | 0.4 | * | 0.1 | -0.4 |
| 17 | Savings and loan associations | * | * | * | 0.1 | * | * | 0.1 | * | * | * | * | * |
| 18 | Mutual savings banks | * | * | * | 0.1 | * | 0.2 | -0.1 | * | * | 0.1 | * | * |
| 1 | Total loans at commercial banks, Flow of Funds basis | 21.6 | 12.9 | 30.0 | 59.0 | 73.2 | 99.5 | 71.8 | 65.6 | 55.8 | 45.9 | 93.2 | 46.8 |
| | − Loans elsewhere classified: | | | | | | | | | | | | |
| 2 | Mortgages | 5.2 | 2.4 | 9.8 | 16.8 | 19.6 | 19.5 | 20.7 | 20.1 | 18.3 | 12.9 | 15.2 | 8.3 |
| 3 | Consumer credit | 4.7 | 2.9 | 6.7 | 10.1 | 10.6 | 13.2 | 11.0 | 10.8 | 7.5 | 4.2 | 5.4 | 5.2 |
| 4 | Security credit | -1.1 | 1.4 | 0.8 | 4.7 | -3.0 | -5.6 | -0.6 | -4.3 | -1.4 | -4.0 | 4.0 | -3.0 |
| 5 | Open market paper | 0.5 | 2.0 | 0.8 | -0.2 | -0.8 | -1.7 | -0.2 | -0.7 | -0.4 | 0.4 | 1.6 | 0.8 |
| 6 | Hypothecated deposits | — | — | — | — | — | — | — | — | — | — | — | — |
| 7 | = Bank loans n.e.c. at commercial banks | 12.3 | 4.2 | 11.9 | 27.7 | 46.7 | 74.3 | 40.8 | 39.8 | 31.8 | 32.4 | 67.0 | 35.4 |
| | + Bank loans n.e.c. at other banking subsectors: | | | | | | | | | | | | |
| 8 | Domestic affiliates | 3.9 | -1.0 | -0.1 | -0.2 | 1.7 | 2.3 | 1.4 | 4.5 | -1.3 | 2.4 | 1.9 | -0.6 |
| 9 | Foreign banking agencies | 1.3 | 2.6 | 0.5 | 1.1 | 3.7 | 5.5 | 2.3 | 2.7 | 4.4 | 1.9 | 8.2 | 6.1 |
| 10 | = Banking sector total bank loans n.e.c. | 17.6 | 5.8 | 12.4 | 28.5 | 52.1 | 82.1 | 44.6 | 47.0 | 34.8 | 36.8 | 77.1 | 40.9 |
| 11 | + Loans by Federal Reserve banks | — | — | — | — | — | — | — | — | — | — | — | — |
| 12 | = Total bank loans n.e.c. | 17.6 | 5.8 | 12.4 | 28.5 | 52.1 | 82.1 | 44.6 | 47.0 | 34.8 | 36.8 | 77.1 | 40.9 |
| | Net change in liabilities | | | | | | | | | | | | |
| 13 | Nonfinancial sectors | 17.6 | 5.8 | 12.4 | 28.5 | 52.1 | 82.1 | 44.6 | 47.0 | 34.8 | 36.8 | 77.1 | 40.9 |
| 14 | Households | 15.3 | 6.4 | 9.3 | 21.8 | 38.6 | 64.3 | 29.9 | 34.4 | 25.9 | 41.7 | 47.1 | 35.2 |
| 15 | Farm business | 1.0 | 0.9 | 1.8 | 2.8 | 1.8 | 4.5 | -2.8 | 5.6 | -0.2 | 4.9 | -8.1 | 5.4 |
| 16 | Nonfarm noncorporate business | 0.6 | 0.8 | 1.3 | 1.8 | 3.0 | 2.7 | 2.2 | 3.1 | 4.0 | 1.8 | 1.2 | 1.8 |
| 17 | Corporate business | 2.1 | -0.6 | 0.2 | 0.7 | 0.4 | 0.6 | * | -0.5 | 1.5 | -2.1 | 0.4 | -0.4 |
| 18 | Nonfarm noncorporate business | 11.8 | 5.6 | 4.4 | 13.5 | 30.6 | 51.7 | 26.6 | 27.8 | 16.3 | 30.9 | 40.9 | 26.6 |
| 19 | Rest of the world | -0.2 | -0.3 | 1.6 | 2.9 | 2.8 | 4.7 | 3.9 | -1.6 | 4.2 | 6.1 | 12.8 | 1.9 |
| 20 | Financial sectors | 2.3 | -0.5 | 3.0 | 6.8 | 13.5 | 17.8 | 14.7 | 12.6 | 8.9 | -4.9 | 30.0 | 5.7 |
| 21 | Savings and loan associations | 0.1 | -0.1 | 0.7 | 0.7 | 0.3 | 0.1 | -0.1 | 2.2 | -0.9 | 0.3 | 3.2 | 3.2 |
| 22 | Finance companies | 1.9 | -1.1 | * | 3.8 | 4.1 | 5.2 | 4.6 | 5.9 | 0.6 | -1.0 | 2.7 | 0.7 |
| 23 | REITs | 0.2 | 0.6 | 0.7 | 1.3 | 4.0 | 4.6 | 4.5 | 2.5 | 4.3 | 5.2 | 9.3 | 0.5 |
| 24 | Foreign banking agencies | 0.2 | 0.1 | 1.6 | 0.8 | 5.1 | 7.9 | 5.7 | 1.9 | 4.8 | -9.4 | 14.7 | 1.2 |

## Table 21

### Open market paper and other loans (billions of dollars)

#### Other loans (sector totals)

| | | 1969 | 1970 | 1971 | 1972 | 1973 | 1973 I | 1973 II | 1973 III | 1973 IV | 1974 I | 1974 II | 1974 III |
|---|---|---|---|---|---|---|---|---|---|---|---|---|---|
| 1 | Net increase in liabilities | 29.8 | 6.0 | 4.9 | 10.7 | 28.8 | 21.1 | 23.6 | 43.9 | 26.7 | 37.8 | 26.7 | 58.1 |
| 2 | Nonfinancial sectors | 15.4 | 9.7 | 5.7 | 5.8 | 11.8 | 0.9 | 11.2 | 16.4 | 18.9 | 19.8 | 24.9 | 39.8 |
| 3 | Households | 3.0 | 2.6 | 1.4 | 1.3 | 2.5 | 1.5 | 1.7 | 3.5 | 3.3 | 1.7 | 3.3 | 3.4 |
| 4 | Farm business | 0.6 | 0.6 | 0.7 | 0.5 | 1.2 | 0.8 | 1.0 | 1.7 | 1.3 | 0.7 | 2.6 | 2.4 |
| 5 | Nonfarm noncorporate business | 1.5 | 1.0 | 0.5 | 0.4 | 1.8 | 3.1 | 1.1 | 1.5 | 1.6 | 1.3 | 1.5 | 1.8 |
| 6 | Corporate business | 7.1 | 3.2 | 0.7 | 2.5 | 2.0 | -9.2 | 5.1 | 3.0 | 9.2 | 10.5 | 7.4 | 22.6 |
| 7 | Sate and local governments | 0.7 | 0.1 | 0.4 | 0.3 | 0.3 | 0.7 | -1.0 | 1.7 | -0.1 | 0.3 | -0.8 | 0.6 |
| 8 | Rest of the world | 2.4 | 2.1 | 2.1 | 0.8 | 3.9 | 3.9 | 3.2 | 5.0 | 3.7 | 5.3 | 10.9 | 9.0 |
| 9 | Financial sectors | 14.5 | -3.6 | -0.8 | 5.0 | 17.0 | 20.3 | 12.4 | 27.5 | 7.8 | 17.9 | 1.8 | 18.3 |
| 10 | Sponsored credit agencies | -0.3 | — | — | — | — | — | -1.0 | 10.9 | -1.3 | — | — | — |
| 11 | Commercial banking | 5.8 | -5.1 | 0.7 | 2.4 | 5.5 | 13.6 | 10.7 | 10.2 | 2.4 | 13.2 | -2.4 | 3.8 |
| 12 | Savings and loan associations | 4.0 | 1.3 | -2.7 | * | 7.2 | 5.4 | 2.7 | 3.2 | 6.5 | 3.3 | 10.4 | 9.8 |
| 13 | Finance companies | 4.9 | 0.2 | 0.4 | * | 3.5 | 1.8 | 0.1 | 3.2 | 0.2 | 3.9 | 1.0 | 6.7 |
| 14 | REITs | — | — | 0.8 | 2.5 | 0.7 | -0.6 | | | | -2.4 | -7.2 | -2.0 |
| 15 | Net increase in assets | 29.8 | 6.0 | 4.9 | 10.7 | 28.8 | 21.1 | 23.6 | 43.9 | 26.7 | 37.8 | 26.7 | 58.1 |
| 16 | Households | 4.8 | -1.5 | -3.9 | 1.5 | 3.5 | -7.7 | -1.3 | 11.2 | 11.6 | 7.8 | 3.1 | 10.0 |
| 17 | Corporate business | 5.4 | -2.9 | 3.3 | 3.4 | 7.8 | 5.1 | 9.5 | 11.6 | 5.1 | 8.7 | 1.1 | 10.2 |
| 18 | U.S. government | 3.5 | 2.6 | 3.2 | 2.9 | 3.6 | 5.3 | 1.0 | 4.9 | 3.1 | 2.8 | 0.9 | 1.9 |
| 19 | Sponsored credit agencies | 4.8 | 2.3 | -2.0 | 0.8 | 8.5 | 8.0 | 11.8 | 12.1 | 2.4 | 5.8 | 12.4 | 13.9 |
| 20 | Monetary authorities | * | * | 0.2 | -0.2 | * | 0.2 | -0.3 | * | * | 0.2 | 0.7 | 0.7 |
| 21 | Commercial banking | 0.5 | 2.0 | 0.8 | -0.2 | -0.8 | -1.7 | -0.2 | -0.7 | -0.4 | 0.4 | 1.6 | 0.8 |
| 22 | Mutual savings banks | 0.3 | 0.3 | 0.5 | -0.1 | 0.6 | 2.9 | 0.3 | 0.8 | -1.4 | 3.6 | -2.2 | -0.4 |
| 23 | Life insurance companies | 3.4 | 3.0 | 1.6 | 1.1 | 2.2 | 7.0 | -1.2 | * | 3.2 | 2.2 | 3.3 | 4.1 |
| 24 | Finance n.e.c. | 6.2 | -0.3 | 1.4 | 2.5 | 3.1 | 2.0 | 3.8 | 4.1 | 2.4 | 4.7 | 2.7 | 11.0 |
| 25 | Rest of the world | 1.0 | 0.5 | -0.2 | -0.1 | 0.3 | 0.2 | 0.3 | -0.1 | 0.7 | 1.6 | 3.1 | 5.9 |

#### Open market paper

| | | 1969 | 1970 | 1971 | 1972 | 1973 | 1973 I | 1973 II | 1973 III | 1973 IV | 1974 I | 1974 II | 1974 III |
|---|---|---|---|---|---|---|---|---|---|---|---|---|---|
| 1 | Net issues, by type and sector | 14.1 | -1.2 | 0.9 | 3.3 | 11.6 | 4.9 | 7.0 | 20.6 | 14.0 | 26.1 | 9.5 | 31.0 |

| # | | | | | | | | | | | | | |
|---|---|---|---|---|---|---|---|---|---|---|---|---|---|
| 2 | 5.2 | -0.4 | 7.1 | -0.2 | 8.2 | 5.3 | 8.5 | 5.5 | 1.8 | 0.3 | -0.4 | 6.8 | Directly placed paper |
| 3 | 0.3 | 3.1 | 3.9 | -1.2 | 3.1 | 2.6 | 3.0 | 1.9 | 0.2 | -0.5 | -1.1 | 3.0 | Bank affiliates |
| 4 | 6.1 | -0.1 | 0.9 | 5.1 | 3.0 | 2.4 | 5.9 | 4.1 | 0.4 | 0.5 | 0.7 | 3.8 | Finance companies |
| 5 | -1.3 | -3.4 | 2.2 | -4.0 | 2.1 | 0.2 | -0.4 | -0.5 | 1.2 | 0.3 | — | — | REITs |
| 6 | 10.7 | 3.6 | 4.2 | 12.0 | 2.2 | 4.3 | -15.0 | 0.9 | 0.8 | -1.3 | 0.9 | 4.6 | Dealer-placed paper |
| 7 | 11.8 | 5.6 | 5.1 | 6.5 | 0.3 | 3.5 | -11.0 | -0.2 | -0.6 | -1.7 | 2.2 | 2.3 | Corporate business |
| 8 | -0.9 | 0.5 | 0.8 | -0.2 | 0.7 | 0.7 | 0.3 | 0.4 | 0.4 | 0.1 | -0.8 | 1.2 | Bank affiliates |
| 9 | 0.5 | 1.1 | 2.9 | 1.4 | 0.2 | 0.2 | -4.0 | -0.6 | -0.4 | -0.1 | -0.5 | 1.1 | Finance companies |
| 10 | -0.7 | -3.7 | -4.6 | 4.2 | 1.1 | -0.2 | -0.2 | 1.2 | 1.3 | 0.5 | — | — | REITs |
| 11 | 10.7 | 12.4 | 6.3 | 2.1 | 3.1 | 1.8 | 1.0 | 2.0 | -1.0 | 0.8 | 1.6 | 1.0 | Bankers' acceptances |
| 12 | 2.6 | 2.2 | 3.4 | -0.8 | 0.4 | 0.1 | -0.6 | -0.2 | 0.1 | 0.5 | 0.8 | 0.7 | Nonfinancial business |
| 13 | 1.3 | 1.1 | 1.7 | -0.4 | 0.2 | 0.1 | -0.3 | -0.1 | * | 0.3 | 0.4 | 0.4 | Noncorporate |
| 14 | 1.3 | 1.1 | 1.7 | -0.4 | 0.2 | 0.1 | -0.3 | -0.1 | * | 0.3 | 0.4 | 0.4 | Corporate |
| 15 | 8.0 | 10.2 | 2.9 | 2.9 | 2.7 | 1.7 | 1.6 | 2.2 | -1.0 | 0.3 | 0.8 | 0.3 | Rest of the world |
| 16 | 4.4 | -6.0 | 8.5 | 0.1 | 7.1 | -4.3 | 10.3 | 3.3 | 1.7 | 1.1 | -3.3 | 1.6 | Nonbank credit to banks In security RP's |
| 17 | 31.0 | 9.5 | 26.1 | 14.0 | 20.6 | 7.0 | 4.9 | 11.6 | 3.3 | 0.9 | -1.2 | 14.1 | Net purchases, by sector |
| 18 | 10.0 | 3.1 | 7.8 | 11.6 | 11.2 | -1.3 | -7.7 | 3.5 | 1.5 | -3.9 | -1.5 | 4.8 | Households |
| 19 | 10.2 | 1.1 | 8.7 | 5.1 | 11.6 | 9.5 | 5.1 | 7.8 | 2.4 | 3.3 | -2.9 | 5.4 | Corporate business |
| 20 | 6.5 | 7.8 | 0.8 | 4.1 | 5.0 | 12.2 | -0.2 | 5.2 | 0.8 | 2.4 | 0.5 | 4.0 | Commercial paper |
| 21 | 3.7 | -6.7 | 7.8 | 1.0 | 6.6 | -2.7 | 5.3 | 2.6 | 1.6 | 0.8 | -3.4 | 1.4 | Security RP's |
| 22 | 0.7 | 0.7 | 0.2 | * | * | -0.3 | 0.2 | * | -0.2 | 0.2 | * | * | Monetary authorities |
| 23 | 0.8 | 1.6 | 0.4 | -0.4 | -0.7 | -0.2 | -1.7 | -0.8 | -0.2 | 0.8 | 2.0 | 0.5 | Commercial banking |
| 24 | -0.4 | -2.2 | 3.6 | -1.4 | 0.8 | 0.3 | 2.9 | 0.6 | -0.1 | 0.5 | 0.3 | 0.3 | Mutual savings banks |
| 25 | -1.1 | -2.9 | 2.9 | -0.5 | 0.4 | 2.0 | -2.2 | -0.1 | -0.2 | 0.2 | 0.2 | 0.1 | Commercial paper |
| 26 | 0.7 | 0.7 | 0.7 | -1.0 | 0.5 | -1.7 | 5.0 | 0.7 | 0.1 | 0.2 | 0.1 | 0.2 | Security RP's |
| 27 | 0.8 | 0.1 | 0.9 | 0.4 | -3.4 | -2.8 | 5.8 | * | 0.2 | 0.6 | 0.8 | 0.9 | Life insurance companies |
| 28 | 2.9 | 1.9 | 2.9 | -2.1 | 1.2 | 1.6 | 0.2 | 0.2 | -0.3 | -0.3 | -0.4 | 1.2 | Investment companies |
| 29 | 5.9 | 3.1 | 1.6 | 0.7 | -0.1 | 0.3 | 0.2 | 0.3 | -0.1 | -0.2 | 0.5 | 1.0 | Rest of the world |

Table 21 (cont'd)

| | 1969 | 1970 | 1971 | 1972 | 1973 | 1973 I | 1973 II | 1973 III | 1973 IV | 1974 I | 1974 II | 1974 III |
|---|---|---|---|---|---|---|---|---|---|---|---|---|
| **Other types** | | | | | | | | | | | | |
| 1 Finance company loans to business | 5.0 | 0.1 | 1.8 | 2.8 | 2.9 | 1.8 | 2.2 | 2.9 | 4.5 | 1.8 | 0.7 | 8.0 |
| Liability of | | | | | | | | | | | | |
| 2 Noncorporate business | 0.6 | -0.3 | -0.1 | * | 0.9 | 0.3 | 0.9 | 0.5 | 1.8 | -2.2 | 0.3 | -1.3 |
| 3 Corporate business | 4.3 | 0.4 | 1.9 | 2.8 | 2.0 | 1.5 | 1.3 | 2.4 | 2.7 | 4.0 | 0.5 | 9.4 |
| 4 U.S. government loans | 3.4 | 2.5 | 3.2 | 2.9 | 3.5 | 5.2 | 1.0 | 4.9 | 3.0 | 2.8 | 0.9 | 1.9 |
| Liability of | | | | | | | | | | | | |
| 5 Households | 0.4 | 0.3 | 0.4 | 0.4 | 0.3 | 0.3 | 0.1 | 0.1 | 0.5 | 0.4 | 0.1 | 0.1 |
| 6 Farm business | * | -0.1 | * | * | 0.1 | 0.1 | * | * | 0.4 | -0.2 | * | * |
| 7 Nonfarm noncorporate business | 0.3 | 0.6 | 0.4 | 0.1 | 0.8 | 1.2 | 0.2 | 0.7 | 1.1 | 0.2 | 0.7 | 0.2 |
| 8 Corporate business | 0.1 | 0.3 | 0.2 | 0.2 | 0.3 | 0.6 | 0.2 | 0.1 | 0.4 | -0.3 | 0.2 | 0.1 |
| 9 State and local governments | 0.7 | 0.1 | 0.4 | 0.3 | 0.3 | 0.7 | -1.0 | 1.7 | -0.1 | 0.3 | -0.8 | 0.6 |
| 10 Sponsored credit agencies | -0.3 | — | — | — | — | — | — | — | — | — | — | — |
| 11 Rest of the world | 2.1 | 1.3 | 1.8 | 1.8 | 1.7 | 2.3 | 1.5 | 2.2 | 0.7 | 2.5 | 0.7 | 0.9 |
| 12 Sponsored credit agency loans | 4.8 | 2.3 | -2.0 | 0.8 | 8.5 | 8.0 | 11.8 | 12.1 | 2.4 | 5.8 | 12.4 | 13.9 |
| Liability of | | | | | | | | | | | | |
| 13 Farm business (FICB) | 0.6 | 0.7 | 0.7 | 0.4 | 1.1 | 0.7 | 1.0 | 1.7 | 0.9 | 0.9 | 2.6 | 2.4 |
| 14 Nonfarm noncorporate business (BC) | 0.2 | 0.3 | * | 0.3 | 0.3 | 1.9 | * | 0.1 | -0.9 | 1.6 | -0.5 | 1.7 |
| 15 S & L associations (FHLB) | 4.0 | 1.3 | -2.7 | * | 7.2 | 5.4 | 10.7 | 10.2 | 2.4 | 3.3 | 10.4 | 9.8 |
| 16 Policy loans (household liability) | 2.6 | 2.3 | 1.0 | 0.9 | 2.2 | 1.2 | 1.6 | 3.4 | 2.8 | 1.4 | 3.1 | 3.3 |
| Asset of | | | | | | | | | | | | |
| 17 U.S. government | 0.1 | 0.1 | * | * | * | * | * | * | * | * | * | * |
| 18 Life insurance companies | 2.5 | 2.2 | 1.0 | 0.9 | 2.2 | 1.1 | 1.6 | 3.4 | 2.8 | 1.4 | 3.1 | 3.3 |
| 19 Hypothecated deposits (household liability) | — | — | — | — | — | — | — | — | — | — | — | — |
| Asset of commercial banks | | | | | | | | | | | | |

Table 22

Security credit, trade credit, and taxes payable (billions of dollars)

| | | 1969 | 1970 | 1971 | 1972 | 1973 | 1973 I | 1973 II | 1973 III | 1973 IV | 1974 I | 1974 II | 1974 III |
|---|---|---|---|---|---|---|---|---|---|---|---|---|---|
| **Security credit** | | | | | | | | | | | | | |
| 1 | Net change in liabilities | -6.7 | -0.8 | 3.8 | 8.9 | -8.2 | -12.4 | -9.0 | -7.4 | -4.0 | -4.7 | 1.6 | -4.4 |
| 2 | Households | -3.4 | -1.8 | 2.6 | 4.7 | -4.6 | -3.9 | -5.4 | -4.1 | -4.9 | 0.1 | 0.1 | -4.4 |
| 3 | Foreign | -0.2 | * | * | 0.1 | -0.2 | -0.2 | -0.5 | * | -0.1 | * | 0.1 | 0.1 |
| 4 | Brokers and dealers | -3.0 | 1.0 | 1.1 | 4.1 | -3.4 | -8.2 | -3.2 | -3.4 | 1.1 | -4.8 | 1.5 | * |
| 5 | From commercial banks | -1.0 | 1.9 | 0.7 | 3.8 | -2.8 | -6.0 | -1.3 | -3.1 | -0.7 | -3.0 | 2.5 | -0.1 |
| 6 | From foreign banking agencies | — | — | — | 0.1 | -0.4 | -1.3 | -0.6 | -0.9 | 1.1 | -1.2 | * | -0.1 |
| 7 | Customer credit balances | -2.0 | -1.0 | 0.5 | 0.2 | -0.2 | -0.9 | -1.3 | 0.6 | 0.6 | -0.6 | -1.0 | 0.1 |
| 8 | Net change in assets | -6.7 | -0.8 | 3.8 | 8.9 | -8.2 | -12.4 | -9.0 | -7.4 | -4.0 | -4.7 | 1.6 | -4.4 |
| 9 | Households | -1.8 | -0.9 | 0.5 | 0.1 | -0.2 | -0.7 | -1.3 | 0.7 | 0.5 | -0.8 | -0.9 | 0.1 |
| 10 | Commercial banking | -1.1 | 1.4 | 0.8 | 4.8 | -3.4 | -7.0 | -1.2 | -5.2 | -0.2 | -5.3 | 3.9 | -3.1 |
| 11 | Brokers and dealers | -3.5 | -1.3 | 2.5 | 3.9 | -4.6 | -4.5 | -6.5 | -2.9 | -4.4 | 1.2 | -1.3 | -1.4 |
| 12 | Foreign | -0.2 | -0.1 | * | 0.1 | * | -0.2 | * | -0.1 | 0.2 | 0.2 | -0.1 | * |
| **Trade credit** | | | | | | | | | | | | | |
| 1 | Net change in liabilities | 22.7 | 10.0 | 6.1 | 17.0 | 23.7 | 14.2 | 28.4 | 19.8 | 32.6 | 37.3 | 33.5 | 30.1 |
| 2 | Households | 0.5 | 0.5 | 0.3 | 0.6 | 0.6 | 0.6 | 0.6 | 0.6 | 0.6 | 0.6 | 0.6 | 0.6 |
| 3 | Farm business | 0.7 | 0.9 | 1.1 | 1.5 | 1.5 | 1.6 | 1.3 | 1.2 | 1.7 | 2.2 | 1.3 | 1.6 |
| 4 | Nonfarm noncorporate business (payables less receivables) | -0.5 | 0.2 | 0.3 | 0.2 | -1.0 | -0.3 | -1.1 | -1.6 | -1.0 | -0.1 | -1.4 | -0.7 |
| 5 | Corporate business | 21.0 | 7.4 | 3.8 | 13.7 | 19.6 | 11.3 | 25.9 | 16.0 | 25.3 | 28.3 | 28.7 | 25.4 |
| 6 | State and local governments | 0.5 | 0.5 | 0.7 | 0.7 | 1.1 | 1.0 | 1.1 | 1.2 | 1.1 | 1.0 | 0.9 | 1.0 |
| 7 | U.S. government | -0.3 | -0.6 | -0.7 | -0.1 | 0.1 | -0.6 | -0.1 | 0.1 | 1.0 | -1.3 | 2.1 | 0.3 |
| 8 | Foreign | 0.8 | 1.0 | 0.5 | 0.5 | 1.9 | 0.6 | 0.7 | 2.2 | 4.0 | 6.7 | 1.3 | 1.9 |
| 9 | Net change in assets | 24.8 | 9.4 | 4.4 | 21.2 | 26.0 | 16.5 | 27.9 | 24.9 | 34.6 | 40.5 | 40.5 | 32.3 |
| 10 | Corporate business | 22.7 | 8.4 | 5.7 | 20.0 | 24.1 | 14.7 | 26.1 | 22.5 | 33.1 | 38.0 | 38.4 | 30.6 |
| 11 | U.S. government | 0.9 | -0.8 | -1.7 | -0.8 | 0.3 | 0.4 | 1.3 | -0.4 | -0.3 | 0.8 | 0.9 | 0.4 |

Table 22 (cont'd)

| | 1969 | 1970 | 1971 | 1972 | 1973 | 1973 | | | | 1974 | | |
|---|---|---|---|---|---|---|---|---|---|---|---|---|
| | | | | | | I | II | III | IV | I | II | III |
| **Trade credit (cont'd)** | | | | | | | | | | | | |
| 12 Other insurance companies | 0.4 | 0.5 | 0.3 | 1.2 | 0.7 | 0.8 | 0.7 | 0.6 | 0.6 | 0.6 | 0.6 | 0.5 |
| 13 Foreign | 0.8 | 1.4 | 0.1 | 0.8 | 1.0 | 0.6 | -0.1 | 2.3 | 1.2 | 1.1 | 0.6 | 0.7 |
| 14 Discrepancy | -2.1 | 0.5 | 1.7 | -4.1 | -2.3 | -2.3 | 0.5 | -5.2 | -2.0 | -3.2 | -6.9 | -2.2 |
| **Profit taxes payable** | | | | | | | | | | | | |
| 1 Net change in taxes payable | -3.1 | -3.1 | 1.8 | -0.1 | 2.7 | 6.0 | * | 3.2 | 1.4 | 5.2 | 4.1 | 15.2 |
| 2 Corporate business | -3.3 | -3.7 | 2.0 | -0.1 | 2.3 | 5.3 | -0.2 | 2.9 | 1.2 | 4.9 | 3.7 | 14.8 |
| 3 Monetary authorities | * | * | * | * | 0.1 | 0.2 | * | 0.2 | 0.1 | 0.1 | 0.2 | 0.2 |
| 4 Commercial banks | 0.1 | 0.3 | * | -0.2 | 0.1 | 0.2 | 0.2 | * | * | 0.1 | 0.2 | 0.2 |
| 5 Savings and loan associations | * | * | 0.1 | * | * | 0.2 | * | * | * | * | * | 0.1 |
| 6 Life insurance companies | 0.1 | 0.1 | -0.1 | * | * | 0.1 | * | * | * | * | * | * |
| 7 Other insurance companies | 0.1 | 0.1 | -0.1 | 0.1 | * | * | * | * | * | * | * | * |
| 8 Finance companies | * | * | * | * | 0.1 | 0.1 | * | 0.1 | 0.1 | 0.1 | 0.1 | 0.1 |
| 9 Brokers and dealers | -0.1 | — | * | * | * | * | * | * | * | -0.1 | -0.1 | -0.1 |
| 10 Net change in taxes receivable | -2.6 | -2.2 | 1.7 | -0.5 | 2.8 | 4.9 | 0.9 | 3.4 | 1.9 | 3.9 | 4.9 | 15.5 |
| 11 State and local governments | * | 0.1 | 0.3 | 0.3 | 0.6 | 0.6 | 0.6 | 0.6 | 0.6 | 0.6 | 0.6 | 0.6 |
| 12 U.S. government | -2.6 | -2.3 | 1.4 | -0.8 | 2.2 | 4.2 | 0.3 | 2.8 | 1.3 | 3.3 | 4.3 | 14.9 |
| 13 Discrepancy | -0.5 | -0.9 | 0.1 | 0.4 | -0.1 | 1.2 | -0.9 | -0.2 | -0.5 | 1.3 | -0.8 | -0.4 |
| **Proprietors' equity in noncorporate business** | | | | | | | | | | | | |
| 1 Total household investment | -3.5 | -4.7 | -4.7 | -7.4 | -4.4 | -7.1 | -6.0 | -4.1 | -0.6 | -6.6 | -7.4 | -7.6 |
| 2 Farm business | -3.2 | -2.8 | -3.1 | -4.6 | -4.2 | -4.3 | -4.3 | -4.2 | -4.0 | -1.9 | -2.6 | -3.4 |
| 3 Nonfarm noncorporate business | -0.2 | -1.8 | -1.6 | -2.8 | -0.3 | -2.9 | -1.7 | 0.2 | 3.4 | -4.7 | -4.8 | -4.3 |

Table 23

Miscellaneous financial claims (billions of dollars)

| | | 1969 | 1970 | 1971 | 1972 | 1973 | 1973 I | 1973 II | 1973 III | 1973 IV | 1974 I | 1974 II | 1974 III |
|---|---|---|---|---|---|---|---|---|---|---|---|---|---|
| 1 | Net change in liabilities | 26.3 | 11.0 | 10.2 | 22.7 | 36.7 | 38.8 | 30.0 | 43.7 | 34.2 | 46.1 | 50.9 | 21.8 |
| 2 | Households | 0.4 | 0.4 | 0.3 | 0.5 | 0.4 | 0.4 | 0.4 | 0.4 | 0.4 | 0.4 | 0.4 | 0.4 |
| 3 | Corporate business | 0.1 | 1.0 | -0.1 | 0.4 | 2.5 | 1.4 | 2.4 | 3.5 | 2.8 | 5.1 | 6.1 | 6.9 |
| 4 | U.S. government | -0.4 | 0.5 | 0.8 | * | -0.4 | 2.0 | -1.3 | -1.3 | -0.9 | 1.2 | -1.7 | -0.2 |
| 5 | Total finance | 23.1 | 5.0 | 3.6 | 18.3 | 27.8 | 18.3 | 27.6 | 35.8 | 29.5 | 21.5 | 35.6 | 9.7 |
| 6 | Sponsored credit agencies | 0.4 | 2.5 | -0.5 | 0.3 | 2.2 | 0.5 | 1.9 | 2.6 | 3.7 | 2.8 | 3.9 | 4.5 |
| 7 | Monetary authorities | 0.5 | 0.4 | -0.2 | -0.1 | 0.8 | 1.3 | -0.3 | 1.0 | 1.0 | -1.2 | 0.4 | * |
| 8 | Commercial banking | 16.9 | -3.7 | -2.7 | 9.3 | 17.5 | 5.6 | 19.4 | 24.9 | 19.9 | 13.8 | 25.0 | -2.2 |
| 9 | Savings and loan associations | 0.4 | 0.6 | 1.2 | 0.9 | 0.9 | 3.4 | 0.3 | 0.7 | -0.9 | 1.4 | -0.1 | 0.1 |
| 10 | Mutual savings banks | 0.2 | 0.1 | 0.1 | 0.2 | 0.6 | 0.6 | 0.7 | 1.4 | -0.3 | -0.5 | -0.4 | 0.2 |
| 11 | Life insurance companies | 1.4 | 1.7 | 2.1 | 2.9 | 2.7 | 3.7 | 2.4 | 2.1 | 2.8 | 1.5 | 3.1 | 3.2 |
| 12 | Nonlife insurance companies | 3.3 | 3.4 | 3.6 | 4.8 | 3.2 | 3.1 | 3.2 | 3.2 | 3.2 | 3.8 | 3.8 | 3.9 |
| 13 | REITs | — | — | — | — | — | — | — | — | — | — | — | — |
| 14 | Rest of the world | 2.4 | 4.0 | 5.6 | 3.5 | 6.3 | 16.6 | 0.9 | 5.4 | 2.3 | 17.8 | 10.5 | 5.0 |
| 15 | Net change in assets | 18.2 | 12.1 | 6.0 | 16.6 | 32.4 | 39.9 | 36.2 | 30.6 | 22.7 | 47.2 | 44.6 | 25.3 |
| 16 | Households | 2.1 | 2.6 | 2.3 | 2.7 | 1.5 | 1.3 | 1.5 | 1.6 | 1.6 | 2.2 | 2.2 | 2.3 |
| 17 | Farm business | 0.4 | 0.5 | 0.6 | 0.7 | 0.7 | 0.7 | 0.8 | 0.8 | 0.7 | 0.6 | 0.9 | 0.8 |
| 18 | Nonfarm noncorporate business | 0.7 | 0.7 | 0.8 | 1.0 | 1.0 | 1.0 | 1.0 | 1.0 | 1.0 | 1.0 | 1.1 | 1.0 |
| 19 | Corporate business | 3.0 | 4.2 | 6.2 | 5.2 | 7.9 | 12.4 | 7.0 | 3.4 | 8.6 | 4.9 | 6.4 | 6.8 |
| 20 | U.S. government | 0.1 | 0.3 | 0.1 | 0.1 | 1.0 | 0.4 | 0.4 | -0.1 | 3.1 | 0.7 | -1.4 | 0.2 |
| 21 | Total finance | 3.9 | 9.5 | 2.8 | 3.6 | 12.8 | 17.0 | 14.2 | 12.7 | 7.2 | 11.1 | 25.0 | 6.0 |
| 22 | Sponsored credit agencies | 0.3 | 0.8 | 0.2 | -0.4 | 1.7 | -0.1 | 1.1 | 1.8 | 3.9 | -0.6 | 1.1 | 0.9 |
| 23 | Commercial banking | 2.8 | 5.0 | 1.2 | 2.3 | 7.2 | 15.5 | 7.7 | 7.4 | -1.6 | 7.9 | 19.3 | 4.0 |
| 24 | Savings and loan associations | -0.4 | 2.2 | 0.1 | 0.1 | 1.5 | 0.2 | 2.1 | 1.6 | 2.1 | 4.2 | 1.7 | 2.1 |
| 25 | Mutual savings banks | * | 0.3 | 0.2 | 0.4 | 0.3 | -0.7 | 1.3 | -0.4 | 1.0 | -1.3 | -0.5 | 0.4 |
| 26 | Life insurance companies | 0.9 | 0.8 | 0.9 | 1.0 | 0.9 | 0.9 | 0.9 | 0.9 | 0.9 | 0.9 | 0.9 | 0.9 |

Table 23 (cont'd)

| | 1969 | 1970 | 1971 | 1972 | 1973 | I | II | III | IV | I | II | III |
|---|---|---|---|---|---|---|---|---|---|---|---|---|
| | | | | | | | 1973 | | | | 1974 | |
| 27 Private pension funds | 0.3 | * | 0.1 | 0.1 | 0.1 | 0.1 | -0.3 | 0.6 | -0.2 | 0.3 | 2.2 | 0.2 |
| 28 REITs | 0.1 | 0.3 | * | 0.2 | 1.1 | 1.2 | 1.4 | 0.8 | 1.1 | -0.4 | 0.1 | -2.4 |
| 29 Rest of the world | 8.0 | -5.6 | -6.8 | 3.4 | 7.6 | 7.1 | 11.3 | 11.3 | 0.6 | 26.7 | 10.4 | 8.3 |
| 30 Unallocated, net | 8.1 | -1.1 | 4.3 | 6.1 | 4.3 | -1.2 | -6.2 | 13.1 | 11.6 | -1.2 | 6.4 | -3.4 |

Foreign claims

| | 1969 | 1970 | 1971 | 1972 | 1973 | I | II | III | IV | I | II | III |
|---|---|---|---|---|---|---|---|---|---|---|---|---|
| 31 Commercial bank liability to foreign affiliates Asset—rest of the world | 7.9 | -6.9 | -4.1 | 0.9 | 1.1 | -1.1 | 2.8 | 1.8 | 0.7 | 10.7 | 0.6 | -1.8 |
| 32 Liabilities—commercial banks | 6.8 | -7.2 | -4.8 | 0.5 | 0.4 | -1.1 | 1.6 | 0.8 | 0.1 | 4.8 | 1.7 | -1.8 |
| 33 Foreign banking agencies | 1.2 | 0.2 | 0.7 | 0.4 | 0.7 | * | 1.2 | 1.0 | 0.6 | 5.9 | -1.1 | * |
| 34 Direct foreign investment by U.S. corporations Liabilities—rest of the world | 2.2 | 3.6 | 3.8 | 1.5 | 3.6 | 5.3 | 2.3 | 1.7 | 5.4 | 1.7 | 5.6 | 5.2 |
| 35 Direct foreign investment in United States Liabilities—corporate business | 0.8 | 1.0 | -0.1 | 0.4 | 2.5 | 1.4 | 2.4 | 3.5 | 2.8 | 5.1 | 6.1 | 6.9 |
| 36 U.S. government equity in IBRD, etc. Liabilities—rest of the world | 0.2 | 0.2 | 0.3 | 0.3 | 0.3 | 0.3 | 0.3 | * | 0.8 | 0.5 | 0.9 | 0.3 |
| 37 Foreign currency, except official Liabilities—rest of the world | -0.5 | 0.5 | 1.4 | 3.6 | 4.8 | 11.6 | 1.6 | -0.3 | 6.2 | 9.5 | -3.0 | -0.5 |
| 38 Asset—corporate business | -0.4 | -0.4 | 1.4 | 1.8 | 2.6 | 5.4 | 3.1 | 0.1 | 1.6 | 1.6 | -0.8 | — |
| 39 U.S. government | -0.1 | * | -0.2 | -0.2 | 0.6 | 0.1 | 0.1 | -0.1 | 2.3 | 0.3 | -2.4 | -0.2 |
| 40 Commercial banks | * | 0.1 | 0.2 | 0.2 | 0.2 | 4.6 | -4.6 | -0.2 | 0.9 | 7.5 | -6.2 | 0.1 |
| 41 Foreign banking agencies | * | 0.8 | * | 1.7 | 1.4 | 1.5 | 3.0 | -0.1 | 1.4 | 0.1 | 6.4 | -0.5 |

U.S. government claims

| | 1969 | 1970 | 1971 | 1972 | 1973 | I | II | III | IV | I | II | III |
|---|---|---|---|---|---|---|---|---|---|---|---|---|
| 42 Postal savings deposits (liabilities—U.S. government) Asset—households | — | — | — | — | — | — | — | — | — | — | — | — |

| # | Description | | | | | | | | | | | | |
|---|---|---|---|---|---|---|---|---|---|---|---|---|---|
| 43 | Deposits at FHLB (asset—S & L associations) / Liabilities—sponsored credit agencies | -0.3 | 1.3 | -0.5 | -0.2 | 0.2 | -1.3 | 1.1 | 0.4 | 0.6 | 0.8 | 1.1 | 1.5 |
| | **Equity in U.S. government credit agencies** | | | | | | | | | | | | |
| 44 | U.S. government | 0.2 | 0.3 | 0.1 | 0.3 | 0.6 | 0.7 | 0.6 | 0.6 | 0.3 | 0.6 | 1.0 | 0.8 |
| 45 | Private | — | — | — | — | — | — | — | — | — | — | — | — |
| 46 | Farm business (FICB and FLB) | 0.1 | 0.1 | 0.1 | 0.1 | 0.2 | 0.1 | 0.2 | 0.2 | 0.1 | 0.1 | 0.4 | 0.2 |
| 47 | Nonfarm noncorporate (BC) | * | 0.1 | * | * | * | * | * | * | * | * | 0.1 | * |
| 48 | Corporate business (FNMA) | 0.1 | 0.1 | * | * | * | * | * | * | * | * | * | * |
| 49 | S & L associations (FHLB) | 0.1 | 0.1 | * | 0.1 | 0.4 | 0.6 | 0.3 | 0.4 | 0.2 | 0.5 | 0.5 | 0.6 |
| | **Life insurance claims** | | | | | | | | | | | | |
| | Deferred and unpaid premiums (asset—life insurance) | | | | | | | | | | | | |
| 1 | Liabilities—households | 0.4 | 0.4 | 0.3 | 0.5 | 0.4 | 0.4 | 0.4 | 0.4 | 0.4 | 0.4 | 0.4 | 0.4 |
| | Life company reserves (Assets—households) | | | | | | | | | | | | |
| 2 | Liabilities—life insurance companies | 1.0 | 1.2 | 1.1 | 1.3 | 1.4 | 1.4 | 1.4 | 1.5 | 1.5 | 1.5 | 1.5 | 1.5 |
| 3 | Accident and health | 0.4 | 0.6 | 0.4 | 0.5 | 0.6 | 0.5 | 0.6 | 0.6 | 0.6 | 0.6 | 0.6 | 0.6 |
| 4 | Policy dividend accumulation | 0.6 | 0.6 | 0.6 | 0.8 | 0.9 | 0.9 | 0.9 | 0.9 | 0.9 | 0.9 | 0.9 | 0.9 |
| | **Nonlife insurance claims** | | | | | | | | | | | | |
| 5 | Liabilities—other insurance | 3.3 | 3.4 | 3.6 | 4.8 | 3.2 | 3.1 | 3.2 | 3.2 | 3.2 | 3.8 | 3.8 | 3.9 |
| 6 | Asset—households | 1.2 | 1.4 | 1.2 | 1.4 | 0.1 | -0.1 | 0.1 | 0.1 | 0.1 | 0.7 | 0.7 | 0.8 |
| 7 | Farm business | 0.4 | 0.4 | 0.5 | 0.6 | 0.6 | 0.6 | 0.6 | 0.5 | 0.6 | 0.6 | 0.6 | 0.6 |
| 8 | Nonfarm noncorporate business | 0.7 | 0.7 | 0.8 | 1.0 | 1.0 | 1.0 | 1.0 | 1.0 | 1.0 | 1.0 | 1.0 | 1.0 |
| 9 | Corporate business | 1.1 | 0.9 | 1.0 | 1.9 | 1.6 | 1.7 | 1.6 | 1.6 | 1.6 | 1.6 | 1.6 | 1.6 |
| | **Unallocated assets and liabilities** | | | | | | | | | | | | |
| 10 | Net total (liabilities less assets) | 8.1 | -1.1 | 4.3 | 6.1 | 4.3 | -1.2 | -6.2 | 13.1 | 11.6 | -1.2 | 6.4 | -3.4 |
| 11 | Net change in liabilities | 11.0 | 6.0 | 4.5 | 9.4 | 18.5 | 16.9 | 13.9 | 30.9 | 12.3 | 11.4 | 33.0 | 3.6 |
| 12 | U.S. government | -0.3 | -0.6 | * | * | — | — | — | — | — | — | — | — |
| 13 | U.S. government, without levels | -0.1 | 1.2 | 0.8 | * | -0.4 | 2.0 | -1.3 | -1.3 | -0.9 | 1.2 | -1.7 | -0.2 |
| 14 | Sponsored credit agencies | 0.5 | 0.9 | -0.1 | 0.3 | 1.4 | 1.1 | 0.2 | 1.6 | 2.8 | 1.4 | 1.8 | 2.2 |
| 15 | Monetary authorities | 0.5 | 0.4 | -0.2 | -0.1 | 0.8 | 1.3 | -0.3 | 1.0 | 1.0 | -1.2 | 0.4 | * |

Table 23 (cont'd)

## Unallocated assets and liabilities (cont'd)

| | | 1969 | 1970 | 1971 | 1972 | 1973 | 1973 I | 1973 II | 1973 III | 1973 IV | 1974 I | 1974 II | 1974 III |
|---|---|---|---|---|---|---|---|---|---|---|---|---|---|
| 16 | Commercial banking | 5.9 | 4.0 | 1.9 | 6.8 | 5.0 | 4.5 | 11.2 | -4.6 | 9.1 | 1.8 | 15.6 | 5.9 |
| 17 | Commercial banks | 3.7 | 2.4 | 2.1 | 6.1 | 4.0 | 1.2 | 13.6 | -2.7 | 3.9 | 5.9 | 9.4 | 4.1 |
| 18 | Bank affiliates | 0.3 | 1.0 | 0.6 | -1.3 | -1.0 | 1.1 | -3.2 | -1.7 | * | -2.6 | -2.1 | * |
| 19 | Foreign banking agencies | 0.8 | 0.2 | -1.3 | 1.6 | 1.5 | 2.0 | 1.3 | -1.5 | 4.3 | -1.4 | 8.5 | 1.4 |
| 20 | Banks in U.S. possessions | 1.1 | 0.5 | 0.5 | 0.5 | 0.5 | 0.2 | -0.5 | 1.2 | 1.0 | -0.2 | -0.2 | 0.3 |
| 21 | Floats in commercial bank statements | 3.1 | -0.8 | -0.6 | 1.5 | 11.4 | 2.3 | 5.5 | 27.6 | 10.1 | 1.3 | 8.7 | -6.3 |
| 22 | On interbank deposits | -0.5 | -0.1 | -1.1 | 2.3 | 1.4 | -9.4 | -1.3 | 6.3 | 9.9 | -1.7 | 1.3 | -10.0 |
| 23 | On interbank loans | 3.5 | -1.0 | 1.0 | -0.1 | 10.3 | 11.6 | 6.7 | 22.0 | 1.0 | 2.5 | 5.4 | 6.4 |
| 24 | Less: on member bank reserves | * | -0.2 | 0.5 | 0.7 | 0.3 | -0.1 | -0.1 | 0.7 | 0.8 | -0.5 | -2.0 | 2.7 |
| 25 | Savings and loan associations | 0.4 | 0.6 | 1.2 | 0.9 | 0.9 | 3.4 | 0.3 | 0.7 | -0.9 | 1.4 | -0.1 | 0.1 |
| 26 | Mutual savings banks | 0.2 | 0.1 | 0.1 | 0.2 | 0.6 | 0.6 | 0.7 | 1.4 | -0.3 | -0.5 | -0.4 | 0.2 |
| 27 | Life insurance | 0.5 | 0.5 | 1.1 | 1.6 | 1.3 | 2.3 | 1.0 | 0.6 | 1.3 | * | 1.6 | 1.6 |
| 28 | REITs | — | — | — | — | — | — | — | — | — | — | — | — |
| 29 | Rest of the world | 0.4 | -0.4 | 0.3 | -1.9 | -2.5 | -0.6 | -3.4 | 4.0 | -10.0 | 6.2 | 7.0 | * |
| 30 | Net change in assets | 2.9 | 7.1 | 0.3 | 3.3 | 14.2 | 18.1 | 20.1 | 17.8 | 0.7 | 12.6 | 26.6 | 7.0 |
| 31 | Sponsored credit agencies | 0.3 | 0.8 | 0.2 | -0.4 | 1.7 | -0.1 | 1.1 | 1.8 | 3.9 | -0.6 | 1.1 | 0.9 |
| 32 | Commercial banks | 1.6 | 1.2 | 1.3 | 2.0 | 4.7 | 5.2 | 6.1 | 8.4 | -0.8 | 0.8 | 7.8 | 4.8 |
| 33 | Foreign banking agencies | 0.3 | 2.7 | -0.3 | -1.7 | 0.8 | 3.7 | 3.4 | -0.8 | -3.0 | -0.8 | 11.5 | -0.7 |
| 34 | Banks in U.S. possessions | 0.9 | 0.3 | 0.1 | * | 0.1 | 0.5 | -0.2 | 0.1 | -0.1 | 0.2 | -0.2 | 0.2 |
| 35 | Savings and loan associations | -0.2 | 0.8 | 0.6 | 0.2 | 0.9 | 1.0 | 0.7 | 0.8 | 1.3 | 2.9 | 0.2 | * |
| 36 | Mutual savings banks | * | 0.3 | 0.2 | 0.4 | 0.3 | -0.7 | 1.3 | -0.4 | 1.0 | -1.3 | -0.5 | 0.4 |
| 37 | Life insurance | 0.5 | 0.4 | 0.6 | 0.5 | 0.5 | 0.5 | 0.5 | 0.5 | 0.5 | 0.5 | 0.5 | 0.5 |
| 38 | Private pension funds | 0.3 | * | 0.1 | 0.1 | 0.1 | 0.1 | -0.3 | 0.6 | -0.2 | 0.3 | 2.2 | 0.2 |
| 39 | REITs | 0.1 | 0.3 | * | 0.2 | 1.1 | 1.2 | 1.4 | 0.8 | 1.1 | -0.4 | 0.1 | -2.4 |
| 40 | Rest of the world | -0.8 | 0.3 | -2.6 | 2.1 | 4.0 | 6.9 | 6.2 | 5.9 | -3.0 | 10.9 | 3.8 | 3.1 |

Table 24

Total financial assets and liabilities (billions of dollars)

Total funds raised and advanced in credit markets

|  |  | 1969 | 1970 | 1971 | 1972 | 1973 | 1973 I | 1973 II | 1973 III | 1973 IV | 1974 I | 1974 II | 1974 III |
|---|---|---|---|---|---|---|---|---|---|---|---|---|---|
|  | Total funds raised in credit markets by: |  |  |  |  |  |  |  |  |  |  |  |  |
| 1 | Nonfinancial sectors | 125.5 | 110.8 | 163.9 | 198.3 | 239.4 | 275.0 | 237.0 | 248.0 | 197.4 | 203.5 | 264.0 | 250.2 |
| 2 | U.S. government | 91.8 | 98.2 | 147.4 | 169.4 | 187.4 | 218.5 | 181.4 | 177.4 | 172.2 | 177.3 | 206.5 | 199.1 |
| 3 | Foreign | -3.6 | 12.8 | 25.5 | 17.3 | 9.7 | 32.8 | 2.9 | -7.1 | 10.3 | 8.7 | 2.1 | 15.1 |
| 4 | Private domestic | 3.7 | 2.7 | 4.6 | 4.3 | 7.5 | 8.4 | 7.5 | 4.2 | 10.0 | 14.1 | 25.1 | 13.3 |
| 5 | Households | 91.8 | 82.7 | 117.3 | 147.8 | 170.1 | 177.3 | 170.9 | 180.3 | 152.0 | 154.6 | 179.3 | 170.7 |
| 6 | Farm business | 31.7 | 23.4 | 39.8 | 63.1 | 72.8 | 74.5 | 72.1 | 80.5 | 64.1 | 51.4 | 53.6 | 57.6 |
| 7 | Nonfarm noncorporate business | 3.2 | 3.2 | 4.1 | 4.9 | 8.6 | 7.4 | 7.7 | 9.6 | 9.8 | 6.3 | 8.5 | 8.7 |
| 8 | Corporate business | 7.4 | 5.3 | 8.7 | 10.4 | 9.3 | 11.5 | 10.8 | 8.8 | 6.0 | 4.4 | 10.2 | 8.3 |
| 9 | State and local governments | 39.9 | 39.5 | 46.8 | 55.3 | 67.2 | 73.9 | 70.7 | 66.1 | 57.9 | 78.0 | 89.7 | 84.6 |
| 10 |  | 10.7 | 11.3 | 17.8 | 14.2 | 12.3 | 10.0 | 9.6 | 15.4 | 14.1 | 14.5 | 17.4 | 11.5 |
| 11 | Financial sectors | 33.7 | 12.6 | 16.5 | 28.9 | 52.0 | 56.6 | 55.6 | 70.6 | 25.2 | 26.1 | 57.5 | 51.1 |
| 12 | Sponsored credit agencies | 8.8 | 8.2 | 3.8 | 6.2 | 19.6 | 12.6 | 22.1 | 26.7 | 17.0 | 9.3 | 24.3 | 21.2 |
| 13 | Commercial banks | 1.4 | -3.1 | 2.5 | 4.0 | 4.5 | 12.1 | -2.9 | 9.8 | -0.9 | 9.8 | -4.6 | 8.6 |
| 14 | Bank affiliates | 4.2 | -1.9 | -0.4 | 0.7 | 2.2 | 3.3 | 3.3 | 3.8 | -1.4 | 4.7 | 3.6 | -0.6 |
| 15 | Foreign banking agencies | 0.2 | 0.1 | 1.6 | 0.8 | 5.1 | 7.9 | 5.7 | 1.9 | 4.8 | -9.4 | 14.7 | 1.2 |
| 16 | Savings and loan associations | 4.1 | 1.8 | -0.1 | 2.0 | 6.0 | 6.5 | 10.3 | 10.1 | -3.1 | 3.6 | 13.6 | 10.2 |
| 17 | Other insurance companies | 0.5 | 0.4 | 0.6 | 0.5 | 0.5 | 0.4 | 0.4 | 0.5 | 0.5 | 0.4 | 0.4 | 0.4 |
| 18 | Finance companies | 8.3 | 1.6 | 4.2 | 9.3 | 9.4 | 9.0 | 10.6 | 10.1 | 7.9 | 4.1 | 5.2 | 9.1 |
| 19 | REITs | 1.3 | 2.7 | 3.0 | 6.1 | 6.3 | 6.9 | 7.7 | 6.5 | 4.2 | 3.7 | 1.9 | -1.4 |
| 20 | Open-end investment companies | 4.8 | 2.6 | 1.1 | -0.7 | -1.6 | -2.1 | -1.8 | 1.2 | -3.7 | * | -1.6 | 2.3 |
|  | Total funds advanced in credit markets by: |  |  |  |  |  |  |  |  |  |  |  |  |
| 21 | Private domestic nonfinancial sectors | 125.5 | 110.8 | 163.9 | 198.3 | 239.4 | 275.0 | 237.0 | 248.0 | 197.4 | 203.5 | 264.0 | 250.2 |
| 22 | Households | 40.7 | -4.3 | -8.6 | 8.3 | 31.1 | -0.2 | 40.5 | 59.7 | 24.5 | 44.1 | 19.8 | 84.5 |
| 23 | Nonfarm noncorporate business | 31.2 | -2.9 | -14.3 | 1.1 | 21.5 | -4.7 | 28.2 | 47.2 | 15.6 | 28.7 | 21.2 | 68.8 |
| 24 | Corporate business | 0.6 | 0.6 | 0.7 | 1.1 | 1.3 | 0.6 | 1.3 | 1.2 | 1.9 | -0.3 | 1.4 | 2.1 |
| 25 | State and local governments | 2.5 | -2.3 | 7.0 | 2.6 | 7.9 | 7.0 | 14.2 | 7.5 | 2.8 | 9.2 | 6.6 | 19.7 |
| 26 |  | 6.4 | 0.3 | -2.0 | 3.6 | 0.4 | -3.1 | -3.2 | 3.8 | 4.2 | 6.5 | -9.4 | -6.2 |
| 27 | U.S. government | 2.9 | 2.8 | 3.2 | 2.6 | 3.0 | 4.0 | -2.2 | 7.8 | 2.2 | 2.2 | 1.7 | 4.3 |

Table 24 (cont'd)

| | 1969 | 1970 | 1971 | 1972 | 1973 | 1973 I | 1973 II | 1973 III | 1973 IV | 1974 I | 1974 II | 1974 III | |
|---|---|---|---|---|---|---|---|---|---|---|---|---|---|
| | | | | | | | | | | | | | |

**Total funds raised and advanced in credit markets (cont'd)**

| # | 1969 | 1970 | 1971 | 1972 | 1973 | I | II | III | IV | I | II | III | |
|---|---|---|---|---|---|---|---|---|---|---|---|---|---|
| 28 | 80.7 | 101.3 | 142.0 | 176.7 | 201.8 | 235.9 | 205.2 | 191.0 | 175.0 | 156.1 | 223.1 | 159.6 | Financial institutions |
| 29 | 8.9 | 10.0 | 3.2 | 7.0 | 20.3 | 13.3 | 23.3 | 27.8 | 16.6 | 13.0 | 27.6 | 25.3 | Sponsored credit agencies |
| 30 | 4.2 | 5.0 | 8.9 | 0.3 | 9.2 | 17.2 | 3.1 | 5.7 | 10.9 | -1.0 | 13.1 | 10.6 | Federal Reserve system |
| 31 | 18.3 | 35.2 | 50.6 | 70.7 | 86.7 | 101.5 | 86.1 | 83.7 | 75.3 | 70.4 | 103.2 | 48.6 | Commercial banking |
| 32 | 12.7 | 33.3 | 50.3 | 68.8 | 80.9 | 93.7 | 82.8 | 75.6 | 71.4 | 65.6 | 92.5 | 42.8 | Commercial banks |
| 33 | 3.9 | -1.0 | -0.1 | -0.2 | 1.7 | 2.3 | 1.4 | 4.5 | -1.3 | 2.4 | 1.9 | -0.6 | Bank affiliates |
| 34 | 1.4 | 2.8 | 0.1 | 1.8 | 4.0 | 5.9 | 2.2 | 3.0 | 4.7 | 2.4 | 8.3 | 6.0 | Foreign banking agencies |
| 35 | 0.2 | 0.1 | 0.3 | 0.3 | 0.1 | -0.3 | -0.3 | 0.5 | 0.5 | 0.1 | 0.5 | 0.4 | Banks in U.S. possessions |
| 36 | 49.3 | 51.1 | 79.4 | 98.7 | 85.6 | 103.9 | 92.6 | 73.8 | 72.2 | 73.6 | 79.2 | 75.1 | Private nonbank finance |
| 37 | 9.9 | 11.6 | 29.2 | 36.4 | 27.1 | 43.1 | 32.7 | 16.9 | 15.8 | 30.2 | 23.8 | 12.5 | Savings and loan associations |
| 38 | 3.2 | 4.1 | 10.0 | 10.4 | 5.4 | 11.8 | 6.1 | 2.5 | 1.1 | 11.0 | 1.9 | 1.0 | Mutual savings banks |
| 39 | 1.6 | 1.5 | 2.6 | 3.1 | 2.9 | 3.4 | 2.8 | 3.0 | 2.5 | 1.5 | 2.9 | 3.8 | Credit unions |
| 40 | 8.4 | 9.0 | 11.8 | 13.8 | 15.6 | 16.1 | 14.0 | 14.7 | 17.6 | 10.6 | 20.2 | 17.1 | Life insurance companies |
| 41 | 6.0 | 6.9 | 7.4 | 6.5 | 7.2 | 7.3 | 5.3 | 7.1 | 9.3 | 5.7 | 7.0 | 9.5 | Private pension funds |
| 42 | 5.6 | 6.1 | 6.2 | 7.8 | 9.2 | 10.4 | 9.4 | 9.2 | 7.9 | 8.8 | 11.0 | 12.2 | State and local government, retirement fund |
| 43 | 2.6 | 4.9 | 6.2 | 6.6 | 5.0 | 5.7 | 5.1 | 4.6 | 4.5 | 5.6 | 5.0 | 5.0 | Other insurance companies |
| 44 | 8.0 | 0.7 | 4.1 | 10.8 | 10.1 | 9.7 | 11.4 | 10.9 | 8.6 | 4.1 | 6.0 | 10.1 | Finance companies |
| 45 | 0.9 | 2.1 | 2.5 | 4.9 | 4.5 | 4.6 | 5.1 | 5.3 | 3.0 | 2.7 | 1.1 | 0.9 | REITs |
| 46 | 2.6 | 1.7 | 0.4 | -1.8 | -2.5 | -4.6 | -2.5 | 0.3 | -3.3 | -0.2 | -2.0 | 2.2 | Open-end investment companies |
| 47 | 0.5 | 2.4 | -1.2 | 0.3 | 1.0 | -3.7 | 3.3 | -0.7 | 5.2 | -6.3 | 2.2 | 0.8 | Security brokers and dealers |
| 48 | 1.3 | 11.0 | 27.3 | 10.7 | 3.5 | 35.3 | -6.5 | -10.5 | -4.3 | 1.1 | 19.4 | 1.8 | Rest of the world |

**Total claims and their relation to total financial assets**

| # | 1969 | 1970 | 1971 | 1972 | 1973 | I | II | III | IV | I | II | III | |
|---|---|---|---|---|---|---|---|---|---|---|---|---|---|
| 1 | 125.5 | 110.8 | 163.9 | 198.3 | 239.4 | 275.0 | 237.0 | 248.0 | 197.4 | 203.5 | 264.0 | 250.2 | Total funds raised (from preceding table) |
| | | | | | | | | | | | | | Other liabilities: |
| 2 | 0.3 | -2.5 | -1.7 | -0.2 | -0.2 | -0.9 | * | 0.1 | 0.1 | 0.8 | 1.3 | 3.5 | Official foreign exchange |
| 3 | 0.3 | 0.6 | 0.5 | 0.5 | 0.4 | 0.4 | 0.8 | 0.3 | 0.3 | 0.3 | 0.4 | 0.4 | Treasury currency and SDR certificates |

| # | | A | B | C | D | E | F | G | H | I | J | K | L |
|---|---|---|---|---|---|---|---|---|---|---|---|---|---|
| 4 | Deposits at financial institutions | 6.7 | 69.2 | 99.3 | 108.0 | 95.0 | 138.3 | 100.6 | 56.0 | 85.2 | 91.1 | 112.4 | 53.9 |
| 5 | Banking system | −1.3 | 52.2 | 58.8 | 61.9 | 66.9 | 94.1 | 66.9 | 48.2 | 58.4 | 51.4 | 96.0 | 48.7 |
| 6 | Demand deposits and currency | 8.2 | 14.3 | 17.4 | 19.6 | 16.0 | 24.0 | 14.8 | −6.8 | 31.8 | 7.0 | 8.7 | 6.9 |
| 7 | Time and savings deposits | −9.5 | 38.0 | 41.4 | 42.3 | 50.9 | 70.0 | 52.1 | 55.0 | 26.6 | 44.4 | 87.3 | 41.7 |
| 8 | Savings institutions | 7.9 | 17.0 | 40.6 | 46.1 | 28.1 | 44.2 | 33.7 | 7.8 | 26.8 | 39.7 | 16.4 | 5.3 |
| 9 | Insurance and pension reserves | 21.3 | 24.3 | 27.7 | 30.3 | 31.6 | 31.8 | 32.2 | 32.7 | 29.7 | 27.2 | 46.7 | 34.4 |
| 10 | Security credit | −6.7 | −0.8 | 3.8 | 8.9 | −8.2 | −12.4 | −9.0 | −7.4 | −4.0 | −4.7 | 1.6 | −4.4 |
| 11 | Trade debt | 22.7 | 10.0 | 6.1 | 17.0 | 23.7 | 14.2 | 28.4 | 19.8 | 32.6 | 37.3 | 33.5 | 30.1 |
| 12 | Profit taxes payable | −3.1 | −3.1 | 1.8 | −0.1 | 2.7 | 6.0 | * | 3.2 | 1.4 | 5.2 | 4.1 | 15.2 |
| 13 | Noncorporate proprietors' equity | −3.5 | −4.7 | −4.7 | −7.4 | −4.4 | −7.1 | −6.0 | −4.1 | −0.6 | −6.6 | −7.4 | −7.6 |
| 14 | Miscellaneous | 26.3 | 11.0 | 10.2 | 22.7 | 36.7 | 38.8 | 30.0 | 43.7 | 34.2 | 46.1 | 50.9 | 21.8 |
| 15 | Interbank claims | 2.0 | 4.5 | 5.6 | 2.0 | 7.9 | 15.6 | 7.1 | 26.6 | −17.9 | 7.3 | 42.9 | 6.9 |
| 16 | Total liabilities above | 191.7 | 219.2 | 312.5 | 380.1 | 424.6 | 499.8 | 421.1 | 418.9 | 358.4 | 407.6 | 550.6 | 404.3 |
| | − Floats not included in assets | | | | | | | | | | | | |
| 17 | Demand deposits—U.S. government | −0.6 | 0.1 | −0.2 | 0.6 | 0.3 | 2.1 | −1.4 | * | 0.7 | 0.2 | −2.5 | 1.4 |
| 18 | Demand deposits—other | 2.1 | 1.2 | 0.1 | 3.2 | 0.1 | 2.2 | 2.3 | −1.1 | −3.0 | 0.8 | 4.9 | 2.1 |
| 19 | Trade credit | −2.1 | 0.5 | 1.7 | −4.1 | −2.3 | −2.3 | 0.5 | −5.2 | −2.0 | −3.2 | −6.9 | −2.2 |
| | − Liabilities not allocated as assets | | | | | | | | | | | | |
| 20 | Treasury currency | 0.2 | −0.1 | * | −0.2 | * | −0.1 | 0.3 | — | −0.2 | 0.1 | −0.2 | * |
| 21 | Taxes payable | −0.5 | −0.9 | 0.1 | 0.4 | −0.1 | 1.2 | −0.9 | −0.2 | −0.5 | 1.3 | −0.8 | −0.4 |
| 22 | Miscellaneous | 8.1 | −1.1 | 4.3 | 6.1 | 4.3 | −1.2 | −6.2 | 13.1 | 11.6 | −1.2 | 6.4 | −3.4 |
| 23 | Totals allocated to sectors as assets | 184.6 | 219.5 | 306.5 | 374.2 | 422.1 | 498.0 | 426.5 | 412.2 | 351.9 | 409.6 | 549.8 | 406.9 |

a Includes corporate equities

Table 25

Amount and composition of individuals' saving[a] (billions of dollars)

| | 1969 | 1970 | 1971 | 1972 | 1973 | 1973 | | | | 1974 | | |
|---|---|---|---|---|---|---|---|---|---|---|---|---|
| | | | | | | I | II | III | IV | I | II | III |
| 1 Increase in financial assets | 62.1 | 80.6 | 99.7 | 124.4 | 138.2 | 124.3 | 148.1 | 141.4 | 138.8 | 137.1 | 147.5 | 127.8 |
| 2 Demand deposits and currency | 1.6 | 11.3 | 11.1 | 12.1 | 13.1 | 10.6 | 10.3 | 5.4 | 26.0 | 4.1 | 0.9 | -4.6 |
| 3 Savings accounts | 6.0 | 44.4 | 70.3 | 75.4 | 67.7 | 83.8 | 74.2 | 50.8 | 61.9 | 74.4 | 73.9 | 22.9 |
| 4 Securities | 30.0 | -3.0 | -14.5 | 2.9 | 21.0 | -1.8 | 26.2 | 45.6 | 14.2 | 28.4 | 19.3 | 67.4 |
| 5 U.S. savings bonds | -0.4 | 0.3 | 2.4 | 3.3 | 2.7 | 3.7 | 3.4 | 2.0 | 1.7 | 3.3 | 3.0 | 2.7 |
| 6 Other U.S. treasury securities | 10.5 | -12.7 | -11.8 | -2.6 | 6.5 | -2.5 | 13.1 | 8.9 | 6.6 | 12.5 | -5.9 | 17.4 |
| 7 U.S. government agency securities | 2.8 | 2.8 | -5.0 | -0.1 | 11.1 | 10.8 | 11.4 | 16.2 | 6.1 | -1.4 | 15.2 | 15.7 |
| 8 State and local obligations | 9.6 | -0.8 | -0.2 | 1.0 | 4.3 | 3.7 | 2.8 | 8.9 | 2.0 | 5.6 | 7.7 | 13.5 |
| 9 Corporate and foreign bonds | 6.6 | 10.7 | 9.3 | 5.2 | 1.1 | -0.5 | * | -1.4 | 6.1 | 3.4 | 0.3 | 4.9 |
| 10 Commercial paper | 4.8 | -1.5 | -3.9 | 1.5 | 3.5 | -7.7 | -1.3 | 11.2 | 11.6 | 7.8 | 3.1 | 10.0 |
| 11 Investment company shares | 4.8 | 2.6 | 1.1 | -0.7 | -1.6 | -2.1 | -1.8 | 1.2 | -3.7 | * | -1.6 | 2.3 |
| 12 Other corporate equities | -8.6 | -4.4 | -6.5 | -4.7 | -6.6 | -7.2 | -1.3 | -1.5 | -16.3 | -2.7 | -2.5 | 0.9 |
| 13 Private life insurance reserves | 4.9 | 5.1 | 6.1 | 6.5 | 7.2 | 7.0 | 7.3 | 7.4 | 7.2 | 7.1 | 7.4 | 7.2 |
| 14 Private insured pension reserves | 2.9 | 3.3 | 5.2 | 6.0 | 5.2 | 4.9 | 5.1 | 5.2 | 5.4 | 3.1 | 7.7 | 5.7 |
| 15 Private noninsured pension reserves | 6.3 | 7.1 | 7.3 | 6.8 | 7.7 | 8.2 | 5.8 | 9.4 | 7.6 | 7.1 | 10.0 | 10.3 |
| 16 Government insurance and pension reserves | 7.1 | 8.8 | 9.2 | 11.1 | 11.5 | 11.8 | 14.1 | 10.8 | 9.6 | 10.0 | 21.5 | 11.1 |
| 17 Miscellaneous financial assets | 3.1 | 3.6 | 5.1 | 3.7 | 4.8 | -0.1 | 5.2 | 6.9 | 7.0 | 3.0 | 6.6 | 7.7 |
| 18 Gross investment in tangible assets | 143.0 | 140.2 | 166.4 | 190.6 | 213.1 | 213.2 | 214.0 | 216.0 | 209.3 | 198.2 | 205.1 | 212.9 |
| 19 Nonfarm homes | 22.0 | 19.6 | 26.9 | 34.3 | 37.5 | 37.3 | 37.9 | 38.0 | 37.0 | 32.8 | 30.6 | 33.2 |
| 20 Noncorporate business plant and equipment | 29.2 | 30.4 | 34.3 | 39.0 | 42.8 | 42.3 | 43.4 | 43.3 | 42.2 | 41.9 | 43.8 | 41.1 |
| 21 Consumer durables | 90.8 | 91.3 | 103.9 | 118.4 | 130.3 | 132.4 | 132.1 | 132.4 | 124.3 | 123.9 | 129.5 | 136.0 |
| 22 Inventories | 1.1 | -1.1 | 1.3 | -1.2 | 2.5 | 1.3 | 0.6 | 2.3 | 5.7 | -0.5 | 1.1 | 2.7 |
| 23 Capital consumption allowances | 104.5 | 112.4 | 121.3 | 131.3 | 143.5 | 138.9 | 143.7 | 145.4 | 146.1 | 146.6 | 148.0 | 148.1 |
| 24 Nonfarm homes | 8.7 | 9.0 | 9.3 | 10.0 | 10.4 | 10.2 | 10.5 | 10.3 | 10.4 | 10.5 | 10.8 | 10.6 |
| 25 Noncorporate business plant and equipment | 21.3 | 22.6 | 24.5 | 27.2 | 29.9 | 28.4 | 29.7 | 30.2 | 31.3 | 31.9 | 32.7 | 33.2 |
| 26 Consumer durables | 74.6 | 80.7 | 87.5 | 94.1 | 103.3 | 100.3 | 103.5 | 104.9 | 104.4 | 104.3 | 104.5 | 104.3 |

| # | | 1 | 2 | 3 | 4 | 5 | 6 | 7 | 8 | 9 | 10 | 11 | 12 |
|---|---|---|---|---|---|---|---|---|---|---|---|---|---|
| 27 | Net investment in tangible assets | 64.8 | 57.0 | 51.6 | 63.2 | 70.7 | 70.2 | 74.3 | 69.6 | 59.3 | 45.1 | 27.8 | 38.5 |
| 28 | Nonfarm homes | 22.5 | 19.9 | 22.4 | 26.6 | 27.7 | 27.4 | 27.0 | 27.2 | 24.3 | 17.6 | 10.6 | 13.3 |
| 29 | Noncorporate business plant and equipment | 7.9 | 11.1 | 10.0 | 10.9 | 13.1 | 13.7 | 13.9 | 12.9 | 11.8 | 9.8 | 7.7 | 7.9 |
| 30 | Consumer durables | 31.7 | 25.0 | 19.6 | 20.0 | 27.5 | 28.6 | 32.1 | 27.1 | 24.4 | 16.5 | 10.6 | 16.2 |
| 31 | Inventories | 2.7 | 1.1 | -0.5 | 5.7 | 2.3 | 0.6 | 1.3 | 2.5 | -1.2 | 1.3 | -1.1 | 1.1 |
| 32 | Increase in debt | 72.1 | 73.2 | 65.4 | 76.6 | 95.4 | 86.4 | 91.9 | 87.6 | 85.8 | 57.3 | 32.2 | 40.0 |
| 33 | Mortgage debt on nonfarm homes | 31.7 | 39.9 | 35.2 | 40.4 | 47.8 | 47.2 | 41.4 | 44.2 | 38.4 | 24.2 | 12.5 | 16.1 |
| 34 | Noncorporate business mortgage debt | 12.6 | 14.4 | 10.3 | 8.9 | 13.9 | 15.5 | 13.1 | 12.9 | 13.2 | 11.2 | 8.0 | 7.0 |
| 35 | Consumer credit | 15.8 | 17.2 | 8.2 | 19.2 | 22.3 | 24.6 | 25.6 | 22.9 | 19.2 | 11.2 | 6.0 | 10.4 |
| 36 | Security credit | -4.4 | 0.1 | 0.1 | -4.9 | -4.1 | -5.4 | -3.9 | -4.6 | 4.7 | 2.6 | -1.8 | -3.4 |
| 37 | Policy loans | 3.3 | 3.1 | 1.4 | 2.8 | 3.4 | 1.6 | 1.2 | 2.2 | 0.9 | 1.0 | 2.3 | 2.6 |
| 38 | Other debt | 13.0 | -1.6 | 10.2 | 10.3 | 12.1 | 2.9 | 14.5 | 10.0 | 9.4 | 7.1 | 5.1 | 7.3 |
| 39 | Individuals' saving (1 + 27 − 32) | 120.5 | 131.3 | 123.3 | 125.4 | 116.7 | 131.9 | 106.8 | 120.2 | 97.9 | 87.4 | 76.2 | 60.6 |
| 40 | − Government insurance and pension reserves | 11.1 | 21.5 | 10.0 | 9.6 | 10.8 | 14.1 | 11.8 | 11.5 | 11.1 | 9.2 | 8.8 | 7.1 |
| 41 | − Net investment in consumer durables | 31.7 | 25.0 | 19.6 | 20.0 | 27.5 | 28.6 | 32.1 | 27.1 | 24.4 | 16.5 | 10.6 | 16.2 |
| 42 | − Capital gains dividends from investment companies | 0.9 | 0.9 | 0.7 | 0.3 | 1.0 | 1.3 | 1.2 | 0.9 | 1.4 | 0.8 | 0.9 | 2.5 |
| 43 | − Net saving by farm corporations | 0.4 | 0.4 | 0.4 | 0.4 | 0.3 | 0.3 | 0.2 | 0.3 | 0.1 | * | -0.1 | * |
| 44 | = Personal saving, F/F basis | 76.4 | 83.5 | 92.7 | 95.1 | 77.2 | 87.6 | 61.5 | 80.3 | 60.9 | 61.0 | 56.1 | 34.8 |
| 45 | Personal saving, NIA basis | 64.6 | 71.5 | 84.4 | 89.3 | 73.2 | 69.6 | 65.3 | 74.3 | 52.6 | 60.5 | 56.2 | 38.2 |
| 46 | Difference | 11.8 | 12.0 | 8.2 | 5.8 | 4.0 | 18.0 | -3.8 | 6.0 | 8.3 | 0.5 | -0.1 | -3.4 |

a Combined statement for households, farm, and nonfarm noncorporate business

# Table 26

## Discrepancies: Summary for sectors and transactions (billions of dollars)

| | 1969 | 1970 | 1971 | 1972 | 1973 | 1973 I | 1973 II | 1973 III | 1973 IV | 1974 I | 1974 II | 1974 III |
|---|---|---|---|---|---|---|---|---|---|---|---|---|
| **Sector discrepancies** | | | | | | | | | | | | |
| 1 Total, all sectors | 13.2 | 6.1 | 8.0 | 10.1 | 7.4 | 7.7 | 1.3 | 11.5 | 9.1 | 4.3 | 0.5 | 2.1 |
| 2 Households | 3.5 | 0.2 | -0.5 | -8.3 | -6.0 | 3.8 | -18.0 | -4.0 | -5.8 | -8.2 | -12.0 | -11.8 |
| 3 Corporate business | 6.0 | 6.7 | 10.2 | 14.8 | 13.8 | 15.7 | 14.3 | 15.3 | 10.0 | 13.1 | 14.3 | 14.7 |
| 4 State and local governments | 4.5 | -0.2 | 9.1 | 7.1 | 5.1 | 7.3 | 6.5 | 0.4 | 6.3 | -0.9 | 1.2 | * |
| 5 U.S. government | 0.4 | 0.8 | 0.1 | 0.4 | -0.1 | 2.7 | -0.1 | -1.5 | -1.4 | -0.6 | -3.6 | -2.5 |
| 6 Foreign | -2.3 | -1.2 | -9.8 | -1.8 | -2.2 | -18.3 | 2.8 | 2.9 | 4.0 | 2.2 | 4.4 | 5.0 |
| 7 Financial sectors | 1.3 | -0.1 | -1.1 | -2.2 | -3.3 | -3.4 | -4.1 | -1.7 | -3.9 | -1.3 | -3.9 | -3.2 |
| 8 Sponsored agencies | 0.1 | 0.1 | * | -0.1 | * | -0.1 | -0.1 | * | * | * | -0.2 | -0.3 |
| 9 Monetary authorities | — | — | — | — | — | — | — | — | — | * | — | * |
| 10 Commercial banks | -0.3 | -0.4 | -1.1 | -1.1 | -1.6 | -0.7 | -2.1 | -1.5 | -1.9 | -2.1 | -2.6 | -2.2 |
| 11 Private nonbank finance | 1.5 | 0.3 | * | -1.0 | -1.7 | -2.6 | -1.9 | -0.2 | -2.0 | 0.9 | -1.1 | -0.7 |
| 12 Savings and loan associations | 0.1 | 0.2 | 0.3 | -0.2 | -0.1 | -0.4 | -0.2 | -0.1 | 0.5 | 0.2 | -0.1 | 0.7 |
| 13 Mutual savings banks | * | 0.1 | * | -0.2 | -0.1 | -0.7 | -0.3 | 0.9 | -0.2 | * | 0.1 | 0.1 |
| 14 Life insurance | 0.2 | 0.1 | 0.3 | 1.0 | -1.0 | -1.0 | -0.7 | -0.5 | -1.8 | 0.3 | -0.6 | -0.7 |
| 15 Other insurance | 0.9 | -0.8 | -0.8 | -0.4 | -0.1 | * | -0.2 | * | * | * | * | * |
| 16 Finance n.e.c. | 0.3 | 0.7 | 0.1 | -1.2 | -0.5 | -0.5 | -0.5 | -0.4 | -0.5 | 0.3 | -0.5 | -0.7 |
| **Transaction discrepancies** | | | | | | | | | | | | |
| 1 Total, all types | 13.2 | 6.1 | 8.0 | 10.1 | 7.4 | 7.7 | 1.3 | 11.5 | 9.1 | 4.3 | 0.5 | 2.1 |
| 2 Treasury currency | 0.2 | -0.1 | * | -0.2 | * | -0.1 | 0.3 | — | -0.2 | 0.1 | -0.2 | * |
| 3 Demand deposit mail floats U.S. government | -0.6 | 0.1 | -0.2 | 0.6 | 0.3 | 2.1 | -1.4 | * | 0.7 | 0.2 | -2.5 | 1.4 |
| 4 Other | 2.1 | 1.2 | 0.1 | 3.2 | 0.1 | 2.2 | 2.3 | -1.1 | -3.0 | 0.8 | 4.9 | 2.1 |
| 5 Trade credit | -2.1 | 0.5 | 1.7 | -4.1 | -2.3 | -2.3 | 0.5 | -5.2 | -2.0 | -3.2 | -6.9 | -2.2 |
| 6 Taxes payable | -0.5 | -0.9 | 0.1 | 0.4 | -0.1 | 1.2 | -0.9 | -0.2 | -0.5 | 1.3 | -0.8 | -0.4 |
| 7 Miscellaneous | 8.1 | -1.1 | 4.3 | 6.1 | 4.3 | -1.2 | -6.2 | 13.1 | 11.6 | -1.2 | 6.4 | -3.4 |
| 8 Nonfinancial | 6.1 | 6.4 | 2.0 | 4.1 | 5.0 | 5.9 | 6.7 | 4.9 | 2.6 | 6.3 | -0.3 | 4.6 |

| | | | | | | | | | | | | |
|---|---|---|---|---|---|---|---|---|---|---|---|---|
| Nonfinancial components: | | | | | | | | | | | | |
| 9 NIA discrepancy (negative) | -6.1 | -6.4 | -2.3 | -3.8 | -5.0 | -5.9 | -6.5 | -4.9 | -2.6 | -6.3 | 0.3 | -4.6 |
| 10 Farm discrepancy (negative) | — | * | * | * | * | * | * | — | — | — | — | — |
| 11 Nonfarm noncorporate discrepancy (negative) | * | * | * | * | * | — | — | — | — | — | — | — |
| 12 Trade debt (positive) | * | * | * | * | * | — | — | — | — | — | — | — |
| 13 Total nonfinancial discrepancy | 6.1 | 6.4 | 2.0 | 4.1 | 5.0 | 5.9 | 6.7 | 4.9 | 2.6 | 6.3 | -0.3 | 4.6 |

# Index